Value Added Tax 2019

Value Added Tax 2019/20

Andrew Needham BA CTA, VAT Specialists Limited

Based upon the original work by A St John Price FCA

Series General Editor: Mark McLaughlin CTA (Fellow) ATT (Fellow) TEP

Bloomsbury Professional

LONDON · DUBLIN · EDINBURGH · NEW YORK · NEW DELHI · SYDNEY

Bloomsbury Professional
Bloomsbury Publishing Plc
41–43 Boltro Road, Haywards Heath, RH16 1BJ, UK

**BLOOMSBURY and the Diana logo are trademarks of
Bloomsbury Publishing Plc**

© Bloomsbury Professional Ltd 2019
Reprinted 2019

British Library Cataloguing-in-Publication Data

A catalogue record for this book is available from the British Library.

ISBN: 978-1-52650-994-9

Typeset by Evolution Design & Digital Ltd (Kent)
Printed and bound by CPI Group (UK) Ltd, Croydon, CR0 4YY

To find out more about our authors and books visit www.bloomsburyprofessional.
com. Here you will find extracts, author information, details of forthcoming events
and the option to sign up for our newsletters

Preface

There have been a number of minor changes to the legislation this year but for the most part it has been a quiet year due mainly to the Brexit uncertainty keeping HMRC policy units occupied at the expense of normal evolution of the tax. No doubt once things have been decided there could be quite far reaching developments in the tax. HMRC are increasingly aggressive in their attitude to taxpayers and businesses have to be careful to avoid making errors in order to avoid the increasingly draconian penalties.

I do deal with VAT planning—but of the straightforward kind, most of which involves using the VAT-efficient way of handling a transaction as opposed to the one which will cost you more and these are highlighted in the text as planning points. I also highlight numerous pitfalls.

The issues I continue not to cover in this book are the complicated and expensive VAT-avoidance schemes and the anti-avoidance law introduced to stop them. For these, you will need the latest expensive advice, not this book!

Andrew Needham

May 2019

Contents

Contents

Contents

Contents

Contents

Contents

Contents

Table of examples

Table of statutes

Table of statutory instruments and other guidance

[All references are to paragraph number]

Table of cases

B

D

E

Table of cases

I

J

K

N

O

U

Z

DECISIONS OF THE EUROPEAN COURT OF JUSTICE ARE LISTED BELOW NUMERICALLY.

These decisions are also included in the preceding alphabetical list.

Abbreviations and references

Throughout this book, legal references are to the *Value Added Tax Act 1994*, unless otherwise stated.

The Act is divided into sections, sometimes abbreviated as 's', and schedules abbreviated as 'Sch', within which there are Groups and/or paragraphs.

'SI 20xx/xxxx' refers to a Statutory Instrument, followed by the year of issue and number. Statutory Instruments are either Treasury Orders divided into articles abbreviated as 'art' or a single SI called The VAT Regulations made by HMRC. References to this are abbreviated as 'reg'.

In case references LON, MAN, EDN and BEL refer respectively to the London, Manchester, Edinburgh and Belfast Tribunal Centres.

The 6th Directive means the European Community 6th VAT Directive—explained in Chapter 2, *Where to find the law.* It has been replaced by a new EC VAT Directive 2006/112/EC, with effect from 1 January 2007: see **2.2**.

CA = Court of Appeal

Ch D = Chancery Division of the High Court. An appeal from a tribunal decision did normally go to the Ch D, although a procedure used occasionally permits reference direct to the CA. From 2009 an appeal from the First-tier Tribunal proceeds to the Upper Tribunal and the High Court no longer hears VAT appeals.

CJEC = the Court of Justice of the European Communities

CJEU = the Court of Justice of the European Union

CMLR = Common Market Law Reports

FA = Finance Act

FTT = First-tier Tribunal

HC = High Court

HL = House of Lords

HMRC = Her Majesty's Revenue & Customs

LVO = Local VAT Office

NAS = National Advice Service

PBR = Pre-Budget Report

STC = Simons Tax Cases

SWTI = Simon's Weekly Tax Intelligence

VATTR = Value Added Tax Tribunals Reports published by The Stationery Office

CONTACTING HMRC

The days when you could ring up your local VAT office with a query are gone! Now, one normally only deals with the Local VAT Office (LVO) on points arising out of a visit. One can contact HMRC by telephone, by letter or by e-mail and the systems are different.

Website

On www.gov.uk/government/organisations/hm-revenue-customs, click *VAT*. Make the result your 'favourite' link to the VAT home page. For Notices scroll down to *VAT Notices* and for Business Briefs, Manuals, forms, information sheets, etc scroll down to *Forms and Reference Material*.

Chapter 2, *Where to find the law,* comments on how law changes and the significance of VAT Notices and VAT Notes. Chapter 19 *How does a business keep up to date on changes in VAT?* explains how to find out about Tribunal and court cases and how to use the HMRC website to find Notices, Business Briefs, Information Sheets etc.

Telephone enquiries

The National Advice Service number is 0300 200 3700 Monday–Friday 8 am–6 pm. This is a call centre operation so a call could be routed to, for instance, Cardiff and another to Glasgow a few minutes later. Ask for a call reference, so that you can follow up the enquiry later and so that you have a record of it if HMRC subsequently dispute what you think you were told.

E-mail enquiries

You can no longer e-mail a query direct to HMRC. You are now required to contact them online via the *VAT general enquiry form* at https://online. hmrc.gov.uk/shortforms/form/VATGenEnq?dept-name=&sub-dept-name=&location=47

Postal enquiries

On HMRC home page (www.gov.uk/government/organisations/hm-revenue-customs) scroll down to Contact HMRC, and click on the contact form for HMRC enquiries and then on VAT. The written enquiries address for long questions or those with an attachment is: HM Revenue and Customs – VAT Written Enquiries Team, Portcullis House, 21 India Street, Glasgow, G2 4PZ.

Registration

Most VAT registration is now done online. However, certain registrations may be done by post. Postal VAT registration applications are now handled by Wolverhampton. To find the address on the website, go to the HMRC home page as above and click *VAT* then *VAT Registration* and then *How to register* and see *When you can't register online.*

Voluntary disclosures

A voluntary disclosure or error correction as they are now called must be sent to one of eight regional *Error Correction Teams*. Details are in Notice 700/45 (Updated July 2017). See earlier under *Website* for how to find the notice, at the end of which is the update.

MEMBERSHIP OF THE EU

Currently the membership of the EU is 28 countries. The UK is currently scheduled to leave the EU on 31 October 2019.

Austria	Italy, bar communes of Livigno and Campione d'Italia and the Italian part of Lake Lugano
Belgium	Latvia
Republic of Bulgaria	Lithuania
Cyprus (But the EU acquis is suspended where the Government of the Republic of Cyprus has no effective control)	Luxembourg
Croatia	Malta
Czech Republic	The Netherlands
Denmark, except the Faroe Islands and Greenland	Poland

Estonia	Portugal, including the Azores and Madeira
Finland	Romania
France, including Monaco	Slovakia
Germany, except Busingen and the Island of Heligoland	Slovenia
Greece	Spain, including the Balearic Islands but excluding Ceuta and Melilla
Hungary	Sweden
The Republic of Ireland	United Kingdom, including the Isle of Man

Not in the VAT territory of the EU:

Åland Islands (Finland)	Mount Athos, also known as Agion Oros (Greece)
Andorra	Overseas departments of France (Guadeloupe, Martinique, Reunion, St Pierre and Miquelon, and French Guiana)
Canary Islands (Spain)	Republic of San Marino
Channel Islands and Gibraltar	Vatican City

Introduction

This is designed to be a guide to VAT—in plain English! I have tried to achieve clear explanations not just in saying what, but also by explaining why and by providing examples. Thus, this book offers the reader an in-depth understanding of all the key parts of VAT and of what really matters to someone running a business. I have divided the subject into three sections:

- those parts of the system which a business will meet sooner or later;

- other parts such as the rules on property and the export of goods and services, which are important for the many businesses they affect, though that might not be for all;

- specialist topics, such as the *Retail Schemes*, which concern only certain businesses.

There are many books on VAT. They tend to be solid textbooks rather than readable guides, because of the amount of detail they try to cover. This one is different. I do not attempt to cover everything. Instead, I concentrate on what everyone needs to know, on explaining the principles in plain English, and on highlighting numerous pitfalls and planning points. Throughout, I quote tribunal and court decisions, which are often important keys to understanding the law. If you understand the contents of this book, you will know more than most people do about VAT! You can then go on to study the particular complexities which affect your business or your clients.

VAT is an enormous subject because it affects every kind of business. No one person can be familiar with every aspect of it—even within HM Revenue and Customs (HMRC). When, after long years of experience, some of us think we are getting quite close to that ideal, they change the law! Even more disconcerting are the court decisions, which, from time to time, force us all to rethink some aspect of the tax which we thought we had understood!

So, a warning: in trying to cover what matters but to keep it concise, I am bound to have oversimplified here and there, or I may have omitted a detail which could be relevant to your problem.

Before taking action on the basis of what you read in this book:

- Always check whether the law, on which it is based, has changed.

- Think carefully about the facts of your case. Do they match the law and/ or the situation described?

- If the sum at risk matters to you or you are in any doubt, take specialist advice.

Chapter 1

How VAT works—an outline of the system

SIGNPOSTS

- VAT is an indirect tax charged on goods and services that sticks with the final consumer. It is based on European law and is administered by HM Revenue & Customs (HMRC) (see **1.1–1.3**).

- Businesses charge VAT on their taxable supplies (output tax) and reclaim VAT on their taxable purchases (input tax); they then pay or reclaim the difference between the two to HMRC (see **1.4–1.7**).

- The standard rate of VAT is currently 20% but there is also a lower rate of 5% and a zero rate. Some goods or services are also exempt from VAT (see **1.8**).

- Although there is no VAT charged on either zero-rated or exempt supplies the key difference between the two is that VAT can be reclaimed on purchases relating to zero-rated supplies but cannot be reclaimed on purchases relating to exempt supplies (see **1.9**).

- A business is liable to register for VAT if it makes 'taxable supplies' in the 'course or furtherance of business' and its turnover exceeds the VAT registration threshold. It can register voluntarily below the threshold (see **1.14–1.16**).

INTRODUCTION

1.1   This chapter outlines the subject of value added tax (VAT), explaining how the tax works, and basic issues like the difference between an input and an output, and between zero-rating and exemption.

VALUE ADDED TAX IS AN INDIRECT TAX

1.2   VAT is an 'indirect' tax, and income and corporation tax are 'direct' taxes. VAT is a tax on consumption, and is charged and reclaimed by businesses

1

in the transaction chain. The tax eventually 'sticks' with private individuals and companies that cannot recover their VAT, normally at the end of the chain.

In the UK, *Her Majesty's Revenue & Customs* (HMRC) administers VAT.

THE EUROPEAN BASIS FOR VAT

1.3   The current VAT system originated with the European Union (EU), and is contained in the former *6th VAT Directive* (now *Directive 2006/112/ EC*: see **2.2**) which is applicable to all Member States of the EU. VAT systems have proved popular with governments, as they are relatively cheap and easy to administer. Consequently, it has spread throughout the world with countries as far apart as Mexico, Russia and New Zealand adopting it.

Following the UK's decision to leave the EU it is unlikely that the UK system will continue to converge with that in the remaining EU Member States.

INPUTS AND OUTPUTS

1.4   *Inputs* are the goods or materials a business buys, or the expenses it incurs; *input tax* is the VAT incurred on them. Similarly, outputs are sales and certain other transactions upon which the business has to charge output tax.

THE THEORY OF VAT

1.5   VAT is charged by the supplier and recovered by the customer at each stage of the commercial chain, until one reaches the final consumer. In the example below, a manufacturer buys in materials costing £2.00 and has overheads of 70p on which he incurs input tax of 14p (Note: all examples show VAT at the current standard rate of 20% from 4 January 2011). When he sells on to the wholesaler B Ltd at £5.20, he charges output tax of £1.04, deducts the input tax he has paid totalling 54p, and pays the balance of 50p to HMRC on his next return.

B Ltd, in turn, incurs overheads, sells on to the retailer C & Co, and pays 18p to HMRC. Finally, C & Co sell to Mrs D, the consumer, at £10 (£10.00) on which the output tax is £2.00. The net sum due to HMRC is 60p.

If I draw a line after the sale by C & Co to Mrs D, the final consumer, and start again, I have the final price of £10 charged by C. Deducting the cost of the goods and the total of the three sums of overheads gives a 'value added' down the chain of £6.40. 20% of this is £1.28. This tallies with the output tax of £2.00 less input tax on materials of 40p and on expenses of 32p and also agrees with the total of the three payments to HMRC.

Incidentally, the profit margins of the three businesses look large in the example because they are before deducting costs, like salaries and business rates, which do not carry VAT.

Example 1.1—Calculating VAT in the supply chain

Note. The VAT is rounded to the nearest penny

	Net	20% VAT	Payable to HMRC
Manufactured by A & Co from materials costing	£2.00		
+ VAT on materials		40p	
Standard rated expenses of A & Co	70p	14p	
Sold to wholesaler B Ltd	£5.20	£1.04	50p
Standard rated expenses of B Ltd	40p	8p	
Sold to retailer C & Co	£6.50	£1.30	18p
Standard rated expenses of C & Co	50p	10p	
Sold to Mrs D (final consumer)	£10.00	£2.00	60p
Final price charged by C	£10.00	£2.00	
Less:			
goods	£2.00	40p	
expenses	£1.60	32p	
Total 'Value Added'	£6.40		
Total payable to HMRC		£1.28	£1.28

IT DOES NOT MATTER WHAT THE BUSINESS SELLS

1.6   The tax works in the same way no matter whether the business is a manufacturer, a wholesaler, or a retailer, whether it supplies goods or services, or whether it is acting as an agent. VAT is charged down the chain of transactions until reaching someone who is not registered for VAT. Thus, VAT covers every single commercial transaction, although not everything is standard-rated.

VAT IS SUFFERED BY THE CONSUMER

1.7   A 'consumer' for VAT purposes is not just a citizen buying in a private capacity. It also includes any organisation not registered for VAT, either because it does not make any taxable supplies, or because its sales are below the registration limit. It also includes the non-business side of an organisation, like a charity, whose main activity is outside the scope of VAT, but which is registered because it is also in business: for instance, it might have a charity shop making taxable supplies.

RATES OF VAT

1.8   The standard rate of VAT has been 20% from 4 January 2011. There is also a reduced rate of 5%. This is growing in importance, and now covers various supplies such as fuel for domestic heating, women's sanitary protection, and certain work in converting or renovating residential accommodation.

There is also a zero rate. Zero-rated sales are taxable at a nil rate of tax, although these still count as taxable supplies.

These three rates of VAT will not rise during the duration of this Parliament as the government has introduced a 'tax lock' to prevent these rates from rising.

The business does not have to charge any output tax on zero-rated sales, but can recover all the related input tax.

At the time of writing, such goods as food, books and newspapers, and children's clothing are zero-rated. However, as already mentioned, the UK is the exception amongst the EU Member States in zero-rating so extensively but this is likely to remain the case since the decision to leave the EU.

Incidentally, other EU Member States tend to refer to what we call zero-rated as *exemption with recovery*.

THE DIFFERENCE BETWEEN EXEMPTION AND ZERO-RATING

1.9   The difference between zero-rating and exemption is important because of its impact on input tax recovery. Exemption is not a rate of tax. Thus, although the good news for the business making exempt sales is that it charges no output tax to its customers, the bad news is that it cannot recover the input tax it incurs in making those exempt sales.

Examples of exempt transactions are insurance premiums, interest on loans, sales of shares on the Stock Exchange, and healthcare.

In contrast to zero-rating, which is a derogation from the normal EU rules, the exemption rules are, in theory, the same throughout the EU. It is, therefore, much less likely that these rules will change substantially in the UK, although they are amended on points of detail from time to time.

OUTSIDE THE SCOPE OF VAT

1.10   This fifth category covers transactions which, although business, do not fall within the scope of UK VAT. There are two main kinds:

- sales, mostly of services, for which the place of supply is treated as being outside the UK, are outside the scope of UK VAT. Input tax incurred in the UK may or may not be recoverable. The rules are complex and are explained in Chapter 23, *Exports and Imports of Services*;

- sundry transactions which, for a variety of reasons, are not subject to VAT. Because these are business transactions, input tax related to them is nevertheless recoverable. Examples include:

  (i)   a government subsidy paid to a manufacturer towards the cost of building a factory in a high unemployment area;

  (ii) transactions between companies within the same VAT group. See Chapter 4, *VAT Groups*;

  (iii) goods located outside the UK at the time of their supply.

NON-BUSINESS

1.11   The sixth category is 'non-business'. If a transaction is non-business, any related input tax is not recoverable. To put it another way, if a business receives some money in the course of a non-business activity, the corollary of not charging output tax is that it has no right to recover any input tax.

Once a business is in business, it is unusual for it to receive money in the course of something which is not a business activity, as explained later. Any such non-business transactions that go through its accounts are likely to be expenses rather than income, examples being:

- local authority business rates. These are a local tax, not payment to the local authority for services which it provides;

- staff wages and salaries. Staff do provide services to the business but they do so as employees, not as independent contractors in business.

However, non-business activities can be an important part of the VAT accounting of some organisations. That is to say, they are in business for a part of what they do, but they also have a non-business side. Examples are:

- charities, which raise money via business activities such as charity shops, but whose main activity is charitable, and not subject to VAT;

- museums to which entry is free, but which charge for special exhibitions;

- churches where entry to the main body of the church is free, but which charge for access to certain parts or have shops selling books, souvenirs etc.

In such cases, the organisation has to be careful to distinguish between VAT related to its business side, which it can recover, and that related to the non-business one, which it cannot.

VAT CATCHES ALL MANNER OF TRANSACTIONS

1.12   VAT is an all-embracing tax. It catches for instance:

- sales of goods;

- sales of services—whether manual repair work or professional charges such as those of accountants and lawyers;

- charges between associated businesses, often called 'management charges';

- leasing or renting goods;

- royalties from copyright and similar rights;

- certain sales of land and buildings;

- sales in the canteen, or of old equipment, to staff etc;

- recharging staff salaries to a third party.

It is irrelevant whether the transaction is part of the profit-earning sales of the business, or simply something which is incidental to it, such as sales in the canteen. If the business charges somebody money, or accepts payment in kind for it, the transaction is probably within the scope of VAT.

As a rule of thumb, all supplies are standard-rated unless legislation specifically exempts, zero-rates, or reduced-rates them.

WHAT IS A 'SUPPLY'?

1.13   The word 'supply' is used in VAT as an alternative to 'output'. It covers much more than the ordinary sales of the business, as you can see from the above examples.

SO WHAT IS IT THAT MAKES A BUSINESS LIABLE TO REGISTER?

1.14   The law on this is in the *Value Added Tax Act 1994* (*VATA 1994*), *s 4*. A person must register if he makes:

- taxable supplies;

- as a taxable person;

- in the course or furtherance of any business carried on by him.

Taxable supplies means positive or zero-rated supplies but not exempt ones.

6

Taxable person also includes someone who should have registered but has not informed HMRC yet, as well as businesses already registered for VAT.

The phrase *in the course or furtherance of any business carried on by him* is deliberately wide and vague because it is intended to be all-embracing. If a business charges somebody money for something, the chances are that it is done in the course or furtherance either of an existing business, or of some new one.

However, an individual can make a sale which is not a part of his business. For instance, a shopkeeper can sell a piece of his household furniture. Although furniture is standard-rated, the sale would not be made as part of the retail business—unless, perhaps, he was unwise enough to put it in the shop window.

Section 94 of the *VATA 1994* says that the word *business* includes *any trade, profession or vocation*. See Chapter 28, *What is a business?* for more comment on what is or is not a business activity.

WHO MUST REGISTER?

1.15   A business can only have one VAT registration for all the business activities it engages in.

In contrast, a partnership must register separately if the partners are different. Thus, a mother and father might be in partnership in one business, the father and their son in another, and the mother and their son in a third. There could be three separate VAT registrations, each family member being a partner in two of them.

An ordinary partnership is not the same as a Limited Liability Partnership (LLP), although there is only one main difference for VAT purposes. The *Limited Liability Partnerships Act 2000*, which took effect from 6 April 2001, enables LLPs to register with the Registrar of Companies as corporate bodies. This means that, if the partners in an LLP control a limited company, the LLP can be grouped with it. See Chapter 4, *VAT Groups* for information about grouping.

A limited company must register for VAT on its own unless it is part of a VAT group. If companies are under common control, they can be grouped together for VAT purposes in one VAT registration, with one member of the group acting as the representative member. See Chapter 4 on *VAT Groups*.

Other kinds of organisations such as clubs, societies and charities are also potentially liable to register. It does not matter who they are or what they do. Even a temporary committee set up to organise an event can be caught.

No matter how worthy their objectives, they must register if they make 'taxable supplies in the course or furtherance of a business' to a value exceeding the registration limit.

See Chapter 3, *When to register and deregister for VAT* for more on registration.

PROFIT IS IRRELEVANT

1.16 VAT is a tax upon transactions, not on profits or losses. An organisation does not escape liability to register merely because it is not out to make a profit. If in doubt whether there is a business activity for VAT purposes, take specialist advice. There are penalties for failing to register promptly, which could make getting it wrong very expensive!

SOME INPUT TAX IS NOT RECOVERABLE

1.17 Not all input tax can be recovered. Obviously, a person cannot reclaim tax on private expenses. VAT on these is not classed as input tax in the first place, let alone recoverable input tax. When he incurs living costs, he is a consumer, even if he has a VAT registration.

VAT is also irrecoverable on a number of specific business expenses, of which the main ones are motor cars, with limited exceptions, and entertaining.

THE VAT FRACTION

1.18 The VAT fraction calculates the amount of tax in a tax inclusive sum.

It is currently $\dfrac{20}{120}$ or $\dfrac{\text{VAT rate}}{100 + \text{the VAT rate}}$

This can be simplified to 1/6

Thus, the tax at 20% included in £3,000 is £3,000 × 1/6th = £500.

Chapter 2

Where to find the law

SIGNPOSTS

- The law is currently contained, in order of precedence, in European Directives, UK Statutes (*VAT Act 1994*), Statutory Instruments and Public Notices that have the force of law. The law is updated by the Finance Act and Statutory Instruments (see **2.1–2.6**).

- Most Public Notices are only HMRC's interpretation of the law and have often proved to be inaccurate. It is important to have current editions of Public Notices as they are updated regularly (see **2.7** and **2.11**).

- Tribunal and Court decisions interpret and define the law and set a precedent that can bind HMRC (see **2.9**).

2.1   It is important to know what is law and what is not, if only because HMRC officers sometimes quote a VAT Public Notice as if it is the law, when in fact, it is merely departmental guidance. Therefore, you need to have some idea of what the law consists of in order to distinguish between a ruling from HMRC for which there is direct legal authority, and one which is merely based on their interpretation of the law.

Also included is some comment about the VAT Public Notices published by HMRC, as well as VAT Notes and Court decisions which are not law, but which often play an important role in the 'system'. VAT law consists of:

- various *VAT Directives* of the European Economic Community. The new *Directive 2006/112/EC* is the main one, which recasts the old *6th VAT Directive*: see **2.2**;

- the *Value Added Tax Act 1994*;

- certain statutory instruments;

- certain VAT Public Notices, or sections of Public Notices published by HMRC which have the force of law.

THE EC VAT DIRECTIVES

2.2   The starting point for VAT law is the old *6th VAT Directive* of the European Economic Community, which took effect from 1 January 1978. VAT has existed in the UK since 1973, and in other Member States for longer still. The purpose of the *6th VAT Directive* was, therefore, to eliminate many of the variations between the different national systems, and thus increase harmonisation.

On 28 November 2006, the EU Council of Ministers adopted a revised (re-cast) EC VAT Directive (*Directive 2006/112/EC*) to replace both the *First* and the *Sixth EC VAT Directives*. Its provisions came into force on 1 January 2007, but do not change current EC and UK VAT law. See *Business Brief 22/06*.

Much of the former *6th VAT Directive* (and now the new Directive) is mandatory upon the Member States because Article 189 of the Treaty of Rome, which, in 1957, established the European Economic Community, empowers the Council and the Commission to issue directives. It says that 'a directive shall be binding, as to the result to be achieved, upon each Member State to which it is addressed, but shall leave to the national authorities the choice of form and methods'. This will remain the case until the UK leaves the EU.

The Court of Justice of the European Communities (ECJ) has stated that 'the freedom left to the Member States by Article 189 as to the choice of forms and methods of implementation of directives does not affect their obligation to choose the most appropriate forms and methods to ensure the effectiveness of the directives'.

Various cases before the ECJ established that Member States had to implement the *6th VAT Directive* accurately. This will now apply to the new Directive. Should a State fail to embody a provision of the Directive in its national law, the Directive has direct effect. That is to say, an individual in that State can rely upon the Directive in the absence of the appropriate provision in the national legislation, or where national legislation incorrectly interprets or implements the Directive.

That's not just a piece of legal theory. Such a situation has occurred in the UK. In the case of *Yoga for Health Foundation v Customs and Excise Comrs* ([1984] STC 630), it was argued in the Tribunal that the taxpayer was entitled to exemption for its residential courses in yoga because they qualified as welfare services for which there was an exemption in the Directive. The Tribunal did not accept this but, on appeal in October 1984, the High Court reversed the decision in favour of the taxpayer. This case showed that there was a gap in UK law, which was only filled when the exemption for welfare services was added to what is now *VATA 1994, Sch 9, Group 7*. In the interim, indeed since 1 January 1978 when the *6th VAT Directive* came into force, one could rely upon the latter.

Not all the provisions of the Directive are mandatory. In some cases, the Directive says that Member States *may* rather than *must* do something, and thus gives them discretion. They also have a certain amount of freedom in the way in which they implement the Directive, though subject to the comment of the ECJ quoted above that the form and method of implementation must be appropriate to ensure the effectiveness of the Directive.

Mostly, UK law does implement the Directive. However, if you have an argument with HMRC on a particular point, it could be worth checking the Directive to see whether or not UK law accords with it.

THE VALUE ADDED TAX ACT 1994

2.3   The main UK legislation is the *Value Added Tax Act 1994*, otherwise known as *VATA 1994*.

However, the Act is by no means the end of the matter. It contains most of the main principles of VAT law, but it omits many key details. Nowadays, much law on many subjects is made by Statutory Instrument (SI).

STATUTORY INSTRUMENTS

2.4   A Statutory Instrument is effectively law made by administrative decree. It does have to be laid before Parliament, but it does not go through all the lengthy procedures required for an Act. SIs provide a means of simplifying and speeding up the process of government by allowing Ministers and their departments to sort out the detailed rules once the principles of a law have been decided.

In VAT there are two kinds of SI, *Treasury Orders* and *HMRC Regulations*.

As the names suggest, Treasury Orders are made by the Treasury, whereas HMRC Regulations are made by HMRC.

For example, when the registration limit alters, the change is made by Treasury Order. Alterations to the rate of VAT applicable to a supply are also often made by SI.

Treasury Orders also restrict the recovery of input tax. *Section 25(7)* gives the Treasury a general power to make an order disallowing the recovery of input tax on such kinds of expense as it may decide. Examples of disallowances under the *Input Tax Order (SI 1992/3222)* are tax on entertainment and on motor cars where there is any private use.

Similarly, various provisions of the *VATA 1994* give the Commissioners of HMRC power to make Regulations that give details of the way in which VAT works, such as the precise information required on a tax invoice.

The rules made by HMRC are mainly to be found in a single SI called the *VAT Regulations (SI 1995/2518)*.

Thus, some SIs are law in their own right, such as the *Input Tax Order* and the *VAT Regulations*. Others merely amend the existing law, for example, when the registration limit is raised.

HOW VAT LAW CHANGES

2.5

Focus

- The Finance Act updates the VAT Act annually.

- Statutory Instruments update the law regularly.

In practice, every Finance Act amends the VAT Act in some respect, so that over the years, it has become more complex and unwieldy. Therefore, you need an updated version of *VATA 1994* after every Budget. Unfortunately, that's far from being the end of it. A Finance Act can contain new law in its own right as well as amendments to the existing law. For example, for nine years, the main rules were in *VATA 1983* but those on penalties were in *FA 1985*. At the time of writing, there has been no substantial new law in a Finance Act for some years, merely amendments to the existing VAT Act. However, the UK does not have a system of putting all changes in taxation legislation into a single Act. As a result, Consolidating Acts were needed in 1983, and again in 1994, to bring all the law together.

Meanwhile, the law also changes regularly with amending SIs. SIs do not just amend the VAT Act. They are also used to change those SIs which are law in their own right, such as the *Input Tax Order*.

There have been as many as 49 SIs in a single year. A more normal number is around 16–18, so you can see why, taking the Finance Act changes into account, it can be said that VAT law changes on average twice a month.

VAT NOTICES PUBLISHED BY HMRC

2.6

Focus

HMRC publish many Public Notices, make sure you have a current edition or access them on HMRC's website and remember that most are only HMRC's opinion and can be wrong.

HMRC publish numerous notices and leaflets on VAT. Most of these are no more than interpretation and guidance. Take care with statements such as 'you must do so and so' or 'such and such a product is standard-rated'. Most of the time, HMRC are right. Nevertheless, Tribunal (First-tier and Upper Tribunal) and Court of Appeal decisions regularly show that they have got it wrong on a particular point, so never take what a Notice says for granted, unless there is a statement in the Notice that the text in question 'has the force of law' (see **2.8** below). HMRC, from time to time, publish a new version of a Notice without mentioning in it that they have lost a case on a particular point it covers, so that the interpretation contained in it may not accurately reflect the current legal position. Their excuse for this is that they have appealed against the decision and are maintaining their view in the meantime. See later in this chapter for more on Court decisions.

Even though most of the Notices are no more than interpretation and guidance, they can still be valuable as an explanation of that interpretation on which you can normally rely. If, for example, HMRC say in a Notice that something is zero-rated, they will stand by this until they announce a change of mind, provided of course that the product in question is exactly the same. On a few occasions, HMRC have been accused of reneging on something said in a Notice, but the circumstances have been of limited significance. Generally, you can rely on a Notice provided that your version is up to date for any changes in the law.

THE PITFALL IN OUT-OF-DATE NOTICES

2.7   The HMRC National Advice Service can provide paper Notices on request and if you require this, either do so in writing or make a note, signed and dated, of your telephone conversation. It is also advisable to ask whether the current version of the Notice is up to date. It can take a year or more before an up-to-date version is published following a change in the law. You can also download all Public Notices and Leaflets from the HMRC website which is now the method recommended by HMRC.

HMRC officers routinely quote the Notices to traders, and use the dates of them as an indication of when a trader is supposed to have been told about points contained in them. On a number of occasions, it has been demonstrated that a taxpayer, who had been assessed, could not have known about a change of policy at the date from which tax had been assessed because the new Notice had not been published. Most traders, and all too many HMRC officers, assume that the date quoted in a Notice is when it was available.

SOME NOTICES HAVE THE FORCE OF LAW

2.8   Certain Public Notices have the force of law because they are what is called tertiary legislation, ie HMRC publish them under powers given to them by SI to make further regulations. Thus, *VATA 1994* gives HMRC power to make Regulations providing for the Retail Schemes. They have done so in an SI called the *VAT Regulations (SI 1995/2518)*. However, the relevant regulations say relatively little but give HMRC power to make further detailed rules in the form of the *Retail Schemes Notice* which have the force of law.

The reason for this is that the rules concerning the calculations which a scheme user must make, and the records which must be kept, have to be not only enforceable in law, but also have to be explained to every scheme user. So, for Schemes such as those for Retailers, Tour Operators, Cash Accounting, Annual Accounting and Payments on Account, the relevant Notice has the force of law, at least to the extent that it describes the records to be kept and the calculations to be made.

COURT DECISIONS

2.9   Any VAT registered business can appeal to the Taxation Chamber of the Tribunal Service against a ruling or assessment made by HMRC. Normally, appeals will be heard by the First-tier Tribunal, but complex case can go straight to the Upper Tribunal. Either side can then appeal that decision to the Upper Tribunal (if heard in the First-tier) and from there, to the Court of Appeal and to the Supreme Court. In Scotland, appeals go from the Tribunal to the Court of Session and then to the Supreme Court. At any point in this process, the case may be referred to the ECJ, which is the ultimate arbiter. The structure of the Tribunal service changed on 1 April 2009, and further changes were made in 2010—see Chapter 40, *Taking an Appeal to the Tribunal* for details.

Tribunal decisions are published in batches several times a month. Many are either unimportant, or concern points of interest only to specialists. Most of the more interesting ones are reported in the professional press.

Court of Appeal decisions are far fewer, but do, of course, tend to be much more important. Court decisions do not either make or change VAT law, however, they do create precedents which are binding on HMRC, and often result in a change in the law, or a new interpretation of the legislation.

When the taxpayer wins, it is common for businesses in the same sector to find that they have overpaid VAT. Anyone who takes VAT seriously needs to keep an eye on the reports of cases going through the Tribunal Service and, on appeal, through the Court of Appeal. This is an important planning point because, if one pays too much VAT, one can only reclaim it from HMRC for a period of four years. (see Chapter 39, *Assessment and VAT Penalties* for details)

If someone wins a Tribunal case on a point which affects a business sector, it is vital to submit a claim into HMRC as early as possible.

Do not wait for the appeal to go through the Courts, as the process can take several years. If a point is referred to the ECJ, it is likely to add at least another two years to the process. If, in the meantime, you have not protected the right to reclaim overpaid VAT by submitting a claim to HMRC, they will only make a repayment for a maximum of four years and you may lose out. See **5.31**.

VAT NOTES

2.10   VAT Notes is a mini-newsletter from HMRC which is issued four times a year. With the introduction of online filing of VAT returns most businesses can only access VAT Notes via the HMRC website.

It is advisable to obtain VAT Notes as soon as it is available, because you could find that it gives details of changes which are important to your clients and which may affect the completion of the VAT return. As some of these changes are brought in at short notice, the sooner you know of anything which affects your clients, the better. VAT Notes is published on the HMRC website (www. hmrc.gov.uk).

If HMRC change their minds on a point of interpretation of VAT law, the only way they can be sure of informing all traders is via VAT Notes, so it is advisable to keep up to date. A further point is that the main publicity for any changes to VAT Notices and leaflets, which have legal effect, is also in VAT Notes. Since the taxpayer would be deemed to have been notified of that change when he received his copy, the latter might effectively alter the law covered by the Notice, though of course, technically, it is the amendment slip to the Notice which does so from the date it is issued, never mind when the taxpayer gets to know about it.

That's less worrying than it may sound, because it only concerns those Notices which have legal effect. As explained above, most of them are only advice and guidance.

IT IS NOT SO JUST BECAUSE HMRC SAY IT IS!

2.11   Laymen tend to think that, because an officer of HMRC says something it must be correct. Being human, however, HMRC regularly make mistakes. This book has numerous references to cases which they have lost. Of course, HMRC get it right most of the time but, do not assume they are correct, and if you have doubts, check the relevant legislation. It is not unknown for an officer to misinterpret not only the legislation, but also HMRC Public Notices and their own Internal Guidance (which can be viewed on the HMRC website).

Chapter 3

When to register and deregister for VAT

SIGNPOSTS

- You need to register for VAT when your turnover exceeds the registration limit, currently £85,000 p.a. in the previous rolling 12-month period, or if you expect to exceed the limit in the next 30 days. You include your zero-rated sales but not exempt sales in your taxable turnover. You also include the previous 12 months' turnover of any business that you buy. You can also register voluntarily under this limit (see **3.2–3.21** and **3.28–3.29**).

- Be careful when choosing a registration date: too early and you could have to account for too much VAT and too late and you could receive a penalty (see **3.23–3.27**).

- Certain input VAT incurred pre-registration can be recovered (see **3.30**).

- Splitting a business into separate legal entities to avoid VAT registration may not work as HMRC have the power to direct them to be treated as one (see **3.33–3.38**).

- When your turnover falls below £83,000 you can de-register from VAT but VAT may be due on assets on hand (see **3.40–3.45**).

3.1 This chapter is about when and how a business has to register for VAT. It highlights a number of pitfalls in the registration process, and how to simplify that process. It is also of use to advisers considering the effects of deregistering a business that has slipped below the deregistration limits.

HMRC's Online Services now include a new way for businesses to register for VAT and also to notify them of variations in registration details.

Together these changes mean that businesses can now do the following online:

- Register for VAT.

- Attach necessary documents, for example when applying for group registration (forms VAT 50 and VAT 51), or notifying of an option to tax (form VAT 1614A).

- Make changes to the principal place of business and contact details. *Note*: agents cannot change the principal place of business or bank details on behalf of their client.

- Deregister for VAT.

- Apply for Annual Accounting or the Flat Rate Scheme.

- View and print the VAT certificate. *Note*: agents will only be able to do this if they have been authorised to act on behalf of their client for VAT using the online agent authorisation service.

- Be automatically enrolled for VAT Online, so that returns can be submitted online.

Note: if an agent submits a VAT registration online on behalf of a client, the client and agent will not be automatically enrolled to use the VAT Online service and will need to do this separately. This is to protect online security.

Businesses can set up a 'delegate' to help them register for VAT and they will be able to review or amend the application before it is submitted. The delegate could be a friend, colleague or an accountant (or other professional adviser).

When completing an application, the business does not need to enter all the information at once. It can be saved and the application completed at a later date.

WHO MUST REGISTER?

3.2   See **1.15** for the explanation of who must register.

THE REGISTRATION LIMIT

3.3   From 1 April 2017, the registration limit is £85k a year, but it is increased in each Budget so check the current figure. The law is in *VATA 1994, Schs 1, 2* and *3*.

A business *has* to register for VAT if:

(a)   its taxable outputs, which include zero-rated sales (but not exempt, non-business, or outside the scope supplies), have exceeded the registration limit in the previous 12 calendar months—unless it can satisfy HMRC that its taxable supplies in the following 12 months will not exceed a figure £2K under the registration limit (ie £83k currently); or

(b)   there are reasonable grounds for thinking that its taxable outputs in the next 30 days will exceed the limit; or

(c)   it takes over 'as a going concern' a business to which (a) or (b) applies. See **3.8** below.

A business should check its turnover at the end of each calendar month. On reaching the registration limit, a trader can only avoid registration if it can persuade HMRC that its sales will drop to at least £2k below the registration threshold in the next year. A business can also avoid registration if it can convince HMRC that it has only exceeded the VAT registration limit as a result of a one-off transaction or short-term 'blip' in turnover, and that its turnover will again fall below the de-registration threshold after the said transaction or blip has ended. HMRC refer to this as an application for 'exception from registration'. If a business makes only, or mostly, zero-rated supplies, it can apply for 'exemption from registration' if it does not wish to register for VAT. However, it will not be able to recover any of the VAT on its purchases. In the case of *Mark Mills-Henning v Revenue & Customs Commissioners* [2012] UKFTT 444 (TC) the business exceeded the VAT registration threshold following a sudden, short, period of increased sales. He did not notice this at the time but his accountant picked it up when preparing the annual accounts. The accountant noticed that the turnover had fallen again and that as such he was again below the VAT registration threshold so need not register for VAT under *VATA 1994, Sch 1, para 1(3)* which allowed exemption from registration based on anticipated future turnover being below the limit.

To benefit from the exemption he should have notified HMRC when he exceeded the VAT registration threshold and supplied details of his predicted turnover so that HMRC could decide if *para 1(3)* applied. Unfortunately his accountant made the decision himself without reference to HMRC, so when the actual registration was processed HMRC could not take into account the predicted fall in future turnover as they had not received the information at the correct time.

As a result the Tribunal agreed with HMRC that the registration was due from the date Mr Mills-Henning exceeded the registration threshold.

This is an important reminder to monitor your turnover and if you think that your increased turnover is only a 'blip' you must give HMRC all the facts in a timely manner so they can decide if exemption from registration applies.

Note: The sale of a 'capital asset', such as office equipment, a van, or building does not count towards the limit. But the sale, lease, or licence of a building, on which the option to tax has been exercised by the business or is a 'new' commercial building and automatically standard rated (less than three years old), does.

THE PAST TURNOVER MEASURE

3.4   In its first year of trading, a business should add up its sales cumulatively month by month. If after, for example, eight months, the taxable turnover exceeds the registration limit, it must tell HMRC within 30 days, and it will be registered from the end of the month following that in which it exceeded the limit.

For example, if the turnover exceeds the registration threshold in January, the trader will have to inform HMRC before the end of February, and it will be registered from 1 March, so it effectively gets one month free. There are penalties for late registration, see Chapter 39, *Assessment and VAT Penalties*.

Once a business has traded for 12 months without exceeding the limit, it should add a month and drop off the earliest one each time, so that it has a 'rolling' 12 months of turnover. Thus, if it has traded for the full calendar year 2013 without exceeding the limit, it must review the position at the end of January 2013, adding in that month and dropping off January 2012.

If an existing business, which is not registered, is taken over, see also **3.8** below.

FUTURE TURNOVER METHOD

3.5   A business must register if it expects its taxable outputs in the next 30 days to exceed the VAT registration limit and the future turnover method is designed to catch large 'one-off' transactions such as a property deal. If the transaction is standard-rated, the business must tell HMRC once the completion date is less than 31 days away. The business will be registered from the start of the 30-day period in order to catch the transaction.

IDENTIFYING ALL THE TAXABLE SALES OF A BUSINESS

3.6   Sales, which count towards the limit include:

- zero-rated sales—but not exempt ones, which are not 'taxable';

- subsidiary activities in the same ownership—a farmer with holiday cottages or a campsite;

- a 'hobby' carried on in such a way, and on such scale by a sole trader as to constitute a business—such as, a plumber, who also performs as an entertainer in clubs. All business activities carried out by the sole trader have to be taken into account when measuring the taxable turnover.

HAS A BUSINESS GOT THE VALUES RIGHT?

3.7   To get the registration date right, a business must measure its turnover correctly. One pitfall is income, such as royalties or holiday lettings, which comes net of commission via an agent. It is the gross values which count for VAT registration, not what is actually received.

Under the *Second-hand Goods Scheme*, the value of the supply and thus the turnover for registration purposes is the selling price, even though you only account for VAT on the profit margin when registered.

In contrast, turnover under the *Tour Operators' Margin Scheme* is only the margin, which is subject to VAT, not the price charged to the customer. For a disaster related to this pitfall, see **3.26** below.

In the case of *Bromley Emergency Training and Development Ltd v Revenue & Customs Comrs* [2012] UKFTT 30 the company appealed against the decision that it was registrable with effect from 1 September 2008 and contended that the correct date was 1 November 2008.

The appellant provided training courses of one or two days in emergency medicine to post-graduate doctors. The issue concerned the treatment of pre-payments received for courses in determining when the appellant exceeded the registration threshold.

The appellant submitted that on recognised accounting principles the payments could not be recognised as income until the courses relating to the payments were delivered.

HMRC submitted that the time of supply provision of the *VATA 1994, s 6* applied when a person is liable to register under *Sch 1* and that the receipt of deposits counts towards the taxable turnover when considering the liability to register for VAT. The Tribunal agreed with HMRC and the appeal was dismissed. Deposits, therefore, have to be included in turnover when calculating registration requirement.

BUYING AN EXISTING BUSINESS

3.8   If a business takes over an existing business under the *Transfer of a Going Concern* rules explained in Chapter 38, *Buying or Selling a Business*, it must register immediately if the vendor is a taxable person (*Sch 1, para 1(2) (a)*). *'Taxable person'* includes someone liable to register, but who has not done so. In *Shu yin Chau* (LON/1343 No 1726), a purchaser, who had been given accounts by the vendor showing sales for the last three years above the registration limit, was held liable for VAT from the date of the takeover, not when her own sales subsequently exceeded the limit.

If a business does not have to register immediately, it must count the sales of the vendor when working out its liability to register from that date on the rolling 12-month basis (*s 49*).

REGISTRATION DUE TO ACQUISITIONS OF GOODS OR THE REVERSE CHARGE

3.9   An unregistered business, which buys goods from other EU Member States to a value above the registration limit in the *calendar year to 31 December,* must register for VAT. This would be an unusual situation, since buying that quantity of goods would normally mean that a business was making taxable supplies in the UK and liable to register in the usual way. However, a business, which only made exempt supplies and which bought the goods to use in its business rather than for resale, might not be registered. This rule prevents such a business benefiting by buying goods in another Member State at a lower rate of VAT than that in the UK.

Unlike the normal registration limit, that for acquisitions restarts on 1 January each year and ignores sales in the preceding year.

Similarly, if an unregistered business spends more than the registration limit on services from outside the UK, which are subject to the reverse charge— explained in Chapter 23, *Exports and Imports of Services*—it must register. In that case, the normal VAT registration limit rules do apply, the value of the reverse charge merely being added to any existing taxable supplies.

REGISTRATION DUE TO DISTANCE SELLING IN THE UK

3.10   A business in another EU State, which sells goods by mail order to private customers in the UK, must register here if the value of its sales in the UK exceeds £70,000 a year. See **20.22** for more details. As with acquisitions of goods, the registration limit is for the calendar year to 31 December and restarts on 1 January each year.

REGISTRATION DUE TO ELECTRONIC SUPPLIES VIA THE INTERNET

3.11   Under the EC *VAT E-commerce Directive 2002/38/EEC* in effect from 1 July 2003, a business based outside the EU, which electronically supplies services to private customers, has to register in the EU. The services in question include those relating to websites, computer software, including maintenance of it, pictures, text and information, music and distance teaching. See Chapter 23, *Exports and Imports of Services* for more details.

The business can choose the Member State in which to register. It will then charge each customer at the VAT rate applicable in the State of that customer.

It must notify electronically the Member State of its choice with its name and address, electronic addresses, including websites and its national tax number if it has one, together with a statement that it is not already registered within the EU.

It must then submit electronically a VAT return for each calendar quarter within 20 days of the end thereof showing the total of its supplies in each Member State, the VAT rate and the VAT due thereon. The return must be in euros, unless a Member State, which has not adopted the euro, requires it in its

21

national currency—as does the UK. The exchange rate used shall be that of the last day of the reporting period, as published by the European Central Bank. Payment shall be in euros or in the currency of the Member State.

If the non-EU business incurs any VAT within the EU in relation to its electronic sales, it can reclaim it under the *13th VAT Directive* from the Member State in which it incurs it. See Chapter 27, *Recovery of Foreign VAT*.

The detailed rules are in *Schs 3A* and *3B* including such points as the submission of returns and the correction of errors.

REGISTRATION OF OVERSEAS BUSINESSES TRADING ON THE INTERNET

3.12　　UK small businesses have been increasingly disadvantaged by overseas businesses selling into the UK through online market places such as Amazon and eBay and not registering for UK VAT. This means that UK businesses are effectively being undercut by 20%.

In the 2016 Budget HMRC introduced a new measure aimed at tackling this loophole and forcing overseas businesses to register for UK VAT and create a level playing field for UK businesses. There are two aspects to the measure. The first part makes changes to the existing rules which allow HMRC to direct an overseas business to appoint a VAT representative with joint and several liability. The changes make this a more effective power and also give HMRC greater flexibility in respect of seeking a security. The second part is the introduction of a new provision which will enable HMRC to hold an online marketplace jointly and severally liable for the unpaid VAT of an overseas business that sells goods in the UK via that online marketplace. Neither of these changes will apply automatically to any businesses and HMRC will use them on the highest risk cases to tackle non-compliance.

This measure was further extended in late 2017. It will:

- enable HMRC to hold online marketplaces jointly and severally liable for any future unpaid VAT of a UK business arising from sales of goods in the UK via that online marketplace;

- enable HMRC to hold online marketplaces jointly and severally liable for any unpaid VAT of a non-UK business arising from sales of goods in the UK via that online marketplace where that marketplace knew or should have known that the non-UK business should be registered for VAT in the UK; and

- require online marketplaces to display a valid VAT number for all their sellers using their platform, when they are provided with one. They will also be required to ensure that VAT numbers displayed on their website are valid. This ensures that fictitious and hijacked VAT numbers are not displayed. These requirements will be supported by a penalty.

The legislation only applies to those businesses who are not compliant with their VAT obligations and HMRC will only issue notices to online marketplaces where it is satisfied that a business is non-compliant.

The objective of this measure is to give HMRC strengthened operational powers to tackle the non-compliance from some overseas businesses that avoid paying UK VAT on sales of goods made to UK consumers via online marketplaces. It is directed at getting overseas businesses that are or should be VAT registered in the UK paying VAT due either directly or through a VAT representative.

In conjunction with this HMRC has introduced the *Fulfilment House Due Diligence Scheme* for businesses that store goods in the UK for sellers established outside the EU and explains when and how they should apply for registration for the Fulfilment House Due Diligence Scheme. It also explains that business that do not register on time will be subject to penalties.

Businesses will be able to apply online from 1 April 2018. Businesses trading as a fulfilment business before 1 April 2018 will need to apply on or before 30 June 2018. Businesses that start trading on or after 1 April 2018 need to apply on or before 30 September 2018.

PLANNING POINT – OVERSEAS REGISTRATIONS

3.13   An overseas business that has to register for VAT in the UK can either:

- deal directly with HMRC or appoint an accountant;

- appoint a VAT representative; or

- appoint a VAT agent.

Deal directly with HMRC

3.14   An overseas business that has to register for VAT in the UK can decide to deal directly with HMRC or appoint an accountant to deal with its day-to-day VAT affairs.

If a business decides to deal with all its relevant VAT obligations (including registration, returns and record keeping) personally it can register for VAT as a 'non-established taxable person' through the Aberdeen VAT Office. If a business decides to do this it can still appoint an accountant to deal with its day to day affairs in the same way as a UK established business.

The accountant can submit VAT returns and other online returns on behalf of an overseas client by using the 'VAT for Agents' online service to set up an authorisation; alternatively it can complete a paper authorisation form 64-8, and send it to HMRC.

However, the overseas business is still legally responsible for registering for VAT, submitting accurate VAT and other returns and paying VAT on time.

VAT representatives

3.15   The overseas business may appoint a VAT representative who will be jointly and severally liable for any VAT debts. In practice, very few businesses are prepared to provide the services of a VAT representative because of the joint and several liability issue. In effect, any money due from the overseas business can be recovered from the VAT representative if the principle is unable to pay its debts to HMRC.

If the overseas business registers for VAT online then it will be provided with the opportunity to appoint a tax representative as part of that process.

Alternatively both the overseas business and the representative can complete form VAT 1TR (which can be downloaded from the HMRC website) to inform HMRC of the appointment of a VAT representative.

VAT agent

3.16   A VAT agent is responsible for maintaining the VAT records and accounting for UK VAT on behalf of its overseas client but it is not jointly and severally liable for any VAT debts incurred by the overseas business. This is, therefore, a much more attractive alternative to being a VAT representative.

If the overseas business registers for VAT online then it will be provided with the opportunity to appoint an agent as part of that process. Alternatively, it should send a letter of authorisation to HMRC.

REGISTRATION OF TRUSTS

3.17   Many trusts do not have to register because they only have exempt investment income. However, a trust can have taxable income such as rents from commercial property, which are standard-rated if opted to tax—as explained in Chapter 26, *Property*—or, for example, royalties from books written by the deceased author, who created the trust.

HMRC normally register the trustees in the name of the trust because it is they who are making the supplies. Trusts can be registered under *s 46*, as an unincorporated association or under *s 45* as a partnership where there is joint ownership of land. However, in the case of a bare trust—where the trustees merely hold the assets on behalf of the beneficiary—it can be the latter who is making the supplies. Give HMRC the full facts when suggesting in whose name the registration should be.

IF IN DOUBT, TAKE ADVICE

3.18   If a business is not registered but might be liable to do so, take professional advice on the basis of all the facts. There are penalties for late registration so it could be expensive to delay!

WHEN A BUSINESS HAS TO TELL HMRC

3.19   A business has to tell HMRC:

- within 30 days of the end of the relevant month (past sales); or
- by the end of the 30-day period (expected sales).

DATE OF REGISTRATION

Past sales

3.20   At the end of the month after that when annual limit was exceeded.

Example 3.1—When to register for VAT

Limit exceeded in the 12 months to 31 January.

The 30-day notification period runs to 2 March.

But registration will be from 1 March.

Future turnover

3.21   At the beginning of the 30-day period during which the business expected to exceed the registration limit.

BE CAREFUL WITH YOUR APPLICATION FORM

3.22   Think about the answers to questions on the form. Trouble sometimes arises because of careless completion. For example, 'any old figure' is entered for, say, expected future sales, or the date of the first expected taxable supply is unrealistic. This can cause awkward questions later.

CHOOSING THE VAT REGISTRATION PERIOD

3.23   Assuming a business has registered on time, and that the returns will be quarterly, not monthly, the first one is normally for three, four or five months—depending upon when HMRC process the application, and which quarterly return date they choose. If a business wants its return date to coincide with its annual accounts, request it in a letter with the application.

If the registration was late, the first return will start from the date on which the business should have registered.

If the business is seasonal, a possible planning point is to ask for a return date at the end of the period in which the business has its maximum input tax. Thus, a retailer with a main sales period in November–December may find a quarter ending 31 October favourable, if much of the stock has been bought by then. The substantial input tax incurred on that stock will be recovered as soon as possible whilst the peak output tax on sales in the period November–January will not be due until 28 February.

THE RIGHT DATE IS IMPORTANT

3.24   A business has to state the date on which it is liable to register. The application goes to a special processing centre, which does not check that date—it does not have the information to do so anyway. HMRC only check the date when they visit the business, which could be years later. If they then find that the business failed to register early enough, they will backdate the registration, which could prove very expensive.

This catches out people who fail to check their sales properly and do not realise they have gone over the limit:

- when HMRC find out, the registration is backdated to the correct date, which could be years earlier;

- it is then no good pointing out that the sales have since reduced below the registration limit again.

CONSIDER THE SAD STORY OF MR BRUCE

3.25   *PS Bruce* (LON/93/2930 No 12484) began trading in tyres in his spare time in April 1990. By October it was evident that, in the coming year, his sales would exceed the limit.

His registration application dated 29 October showed:

- the date of the first supply as 11 April 1990;

- his sales in the 12 months from then as £25,000—the limit then being £25,400;

- the date of 11 April as that of both compulsory and voluntary registration.

26

An officer, who queried this, clearly failed to explain the difference between the date of starting trading and that of liability to register. She later said that Bruce had agreed registration from 11 April. He thought the date of registration was 7 November, that of the large LVO rubber stamp.

The assessment for £1,516 VAT not accounted for from 11 April to 7 November was dated 15 October 1993, *three years* later.

Granted, the problem resulted from Bruce's inability to understand the basic rules or failure to read the paperwork properly, but what's new? In theory, Bruce's accountant could have spotted the problem when doing the accounts, but did he or she even think to check the registration date?

REGISTERING TOO EARLY IS ALSO A MISTAKE!

3.26   If a business miscalculates its sales and registers too early, it cannot subsequently demand retrospective deregistration. *N Goodrich t/a UYE Tours* (LON/01/584 No 17707) should have used the *Tour Operators' Margin Scheme*. He thought he had to register because his sales exceeded the limit whereas, as noted earlier at **3.7**, it is the profit margin which counts under that Scheme.

Although HMRC repaid the VAT on the difference between his profit margin and his sales values, that left a substantial sum of VAT on the profit margin. As that margin had been below the limit, he never needed to register. However, having done so, his registration was, in effect, voluntary as explained below. It could not be cancelled retrospectively in order to get back the VAT paid unnecessarily.

THE PENALTY FOR LATE REGISTRATION

3.27   The penalty for late registration is now covered by the standard legal framework covering all taxes. Prior to 1 April 2010 the law was in *s 67*. Late registration incurred a penalty of up to 15% of the net tax due from the date a business should have registered, to that on which it eventually notified HMRC, or they found out. See Chapter 39, *Assessment and VAT Penalties*.

A BUSINESS CAN REGISTER VOLUNTARILY

3.28   If the sales of a business are below the limit, or it has not yet made any, it can apply to register voluntarily, thus enabling it to reclaim the input tax incurred.

Voluntary registration is not intended to allow a business to recover input tax without ever making any taxable supplies. Taxable supplies, remember, include zero-rated ones, so that it does not necessarily mean that the output tax must exceed the input tax. A business is entitled to registration at the start of a project, even if it may be several years before it produces taxable outputs, provided that it can show that it has genuinely started a business. See Chapter 28, *What is a business?*

If all the outputs of a business are exempt, it cannot register for VAT. This is because it does not make any taxable supplies.

Why would a business want to register voluntarily?

3.29　A business does not want to register for VAT if it sells mostly to the public, and charging VAT means that it either must increase its retail prices or reduce its profits.

A business does want to register for VAT if it sells to other registered businesses, which are fully taxable. They can recover the VAT which is charged to them. The costs of the business are reduced by the input tax, which it can recover.

If a business sells to businesses which have exempt outputs, such as finance or insurance brokers, undertakers, schools or hospitals, which cannot recover all their VAT, they may prefer that their suppliers are not to be registered for VAT. However, they have to pay VAT on most of their transactions with other businesses anyway, and being VAT registered may give it an increased credibility, which will make it easier to sell to them.

If a business is incurring VAT now, it should act now! The rules explained below give a business only limited rights to recover input tax retrospectively, so think about the date. A business can only ask for a retrospective voluntary registration at the time of its application for registration. Once a business is registered, any application to backdate, so as to recover VAT incurred earlier, will be refused.

Perhaps the biggest reason for registering immediately is where a business is about to start spending money on a property, or incurs other large expenditure in the setting up of the business. In *Oriental Delicacy Ltd* (EDN/04/147 No 19129), the Tribunal confirmed that VAT could not be recovered on invoices from the builder dated more than six months before the registration date. Perhaps it was less than the VAT not payable on the takings in the first five months prior to registration. In such a situation, you cannot score both ways so plan it one way or the other!

VAT THAT CAN BE RECOVERED UPON REGISTRATION

3.30　When a business registers, it is entitled to recover VAT under the *VAT Regulations (SI 1995/2518), reg 111* on:

- assets used in the business and goods for resale held at the date of registration which were bought within four years previously, and on which VAT was incurred; and

- services received for the purpose of the ongoing business within six months prior to the date of registration.

Input tax on services cannot be recovered if they have been supplied on, or if they have been used on goods that have been supplied prior to registration, for example, the repair of a machine that is sold prior to registration.

A business should claim this VAT on its first return, although it can still be claimed up to four years after the due date for the first return. Keep lists of both the goods and services together with the invoices.

The only extension of the above rules is a concession concerning VAT incurred prior to opting to tax a property. See the comments on the option to tax in Chapter 26, *Property*.

In the Tribunal case of *Denise Jerzynek* (MAN/03/0452 No 18767), one of my own clients, VAT paid on rent in the six months prior to registration was held to be recoverable because *reg 111(2)(d)* only disallows input tax on services incurred more than six months prior to registration. HMRC had contended that their new policy, that input tax on services consumed prior to registration could not be claimed, was correct, even though this was contrary to the relevant legislation, the Public Notice and their own Internal Guidance. This is a classic example of questioning a decision by HMRC which clearly has no legal basis. My only surprise is that it ever progressed to Tribunal.

In a mirror image of the above case, *Sam Smith t/a Heliops UK v Revenue & Customs* [2015] UKFTT 24 (TC) appealed against a decision by HMRC to disallow input tax on helicopter training incurred more than six months before VAT registration. The appellant argued that it was the purchase of a capital assets but the Tribunal agreed with HMRC that it was a service and therefore input tax could not be reclaimed on it as the costs had been incurred more than six months before VAT registration.

Where a taxpayer de-registers due to reduced turnover they may have to declare output tax on goods on hand at de-registration on which they have claimed input tax, under *VATA 1994, Sch 4, para 8*. This is a deemed self-supply when a person ceases to be VAT registered, to ensure that their future consumption of the assets (as a non-taxable person) is properly taxed.

If the business turnover increases again after de-registration the business may once again become a taxable person and have to register for VAT. If this occurs, and to the extent that the goods are still held and will be used in the new VAT registration, VAT on the deemed supply at de-registration can be considered when establishing an input tax claim under *reg 111*.

As there will be no VAT invoice to support any such claim, HMRC now considers that its discretion to allow alternative evidence as set out in the *VAT Regulations 1995, reg 29(2)* can be applied to claims under the *VAT Regulations 1995, reg 111*. HMRC has therefore revised its policy in this area and accepts that where proof that payment of VAT on the deemed supply was made to HMRC on de-registration, this will be accepted as alternative evidence in support of an input tax claim.

See also **28.15** for comment on VAT incurred before the organisation realised it was in business.

CLUBS AND ASSOCIATIONS—DO THE ACCOUNTS TELL THE TRUTH?

3.31   Show the gross turnover figures in the accounts of clubs and associations in an extra schedule or note if necessary. Such accounts often show net sums after charging expenses against income for specific activities. Examples are:

- bar—gross profit only shown;

- publications, seminars and exhibitions—costs netted against income.

This means that it is impossible to tell what the taxable outputs are. Possible consequences include:

- liability to register not realised;

- it is impossible to compare turnover per accounts with figures declared on VAT returns;

- gross profit shortages are concealed.

THE ROLE OF A PROFESSIONAL ACCOUNTANT

3.32   VAT registration is the one aspect of VAT on which a professional accountant is likely to have an immediate duty of care towards the client. Failure to advise could commence from the initial contact with the client. So, if a new client is not VAT-registered, I suggest that the adviser should ask what the current levels of turnover are, and point out the penalty for getting it wrong if there seems any likelihood of the registration limit being exceeded. This advice should be put in writing because it is all too easy for clients to forget what they are told and subsequently to claim that they were not properly advised, especially if the advice is given at the time of starting up the business.

The letter should also say that it is then up to the client to provide his accountant with prompt information if they are to advise further on whether there is a liability to register. However, when the annual accounts are prepared, the registration position should be checked. This means reviewing not just the turnover shown in the accounts, but the figures on a rolling 12-month basis throughout the year.

Failure to realise that a business has become liable to register at some time during the year, even though the annual accounts show the turnover as being below the registration limit, is a pitfall which has caught out many small businesses and their professional advisers.

When an adviser does find that a client is liable to register, and advises, accordingly, they should follow up the matter before they receive the next set of records from which to prepare the accounts.

In many late registration cases, accountants have been shown up as being perilously close to negligent in not confirming with clients that action has been taken to register. Some accountants may not see it as their duty to 'nanny' the client to this extent. However, many small businesses have had to pay substantial penalties because neither they nor their accountants have dealt efficiently with registration. Sometimes, the registration form is said to have been sent off, but no action is taken to chase it up when HMRC fail to react. Sometimes the client thinks the accountant has dealt with the registration and vice versa.

The above may seem like overkill but real money is involved, in some cases sufficient to bankrupt new businesses. Chasing up need not involve partner time. Why not give the receptionist the interest and the responsibility?

DIVIDING A BUSINESS TO ESCAPE REGISTRATION

3.33 It is difficult to divide a business into two parts so as to avoid registration for one or both (a practice that HMRC refers to as 'disaggregation'). Under *Sch 1, para 2,* HMRC can direct that two or more businesses be combined for VAT purposes if, as a result, they catch one or more for registration.

HMRC need only be 'satisfied' that the activities in question are all part of the same business. Worse still, the Tribunal can only allow an appeal against such a direction if it considers that HMRC 'could not reasonably have been satisfied that there were grounds for making the direction' (*s 84(7)*). It is tricky to show that HMRC could not reasonably have been satisfied about something. It has been done, but the chances are that, if a business has divided itself to avoid registration, it will be obvious and, therefore, reasonable for HMRC to issue a direction. (For examples, see the High Court cases of *Chamberlain* [1989] STC 505 and *Osman* [1989] STC 596.)

A directive cannot be retrospective. Separation is, therefore, effective until HMRC spot the situation. If none of the businesses concerned are registered, and HMRC therefore do not visit them, VAT may be avoided for some years, even if a direction is eventually imposed.

If you try to separate two businesses in order to keep one or both out of VAT registration, do it properly with written agreements, separate records etc. HMRC do not need to use their powers to direct that they be treated as a single business if they can show that they were never in fact separate. The problem is to demonstrate that as a matter of substance and reality:

- the so-called separate businesses are sufficiently at arm's length from each other; and

- they have normal commercial relationships with each other.

These criteria were approved in *Burrell* ([1997] STC 1413), in which the High Court supported the Tribunal's decision that Mr Burrell was not in partnership with his father in an aerobics business separately from a health club.

In *RE & RL Newton (t/a RE Newton)* (LON/2000/84 No 17222), two partnerships of a carpenter with his father, which was VAT registered, and an unregistered one with his mother, were held to be genuinely separate businesses, despite the latter having been formed specifically to do work for customers who could not recover VAT. The Tribunal noted the following factors for and against.

For separation

3.34

- there was a written partnership agreement;

- the unregistered partnership was formed to do private work, which would otherwise have been lost to unregistered competitors and which was therefore not available to the registered partnership;

- separate invoices;

- separate records, bank accounts, annual accounts and HMRC returns;

- the only vehicle used by both partnerships was Mr Newton's car which was not in the accounts of either;

- the small value of supplies by the unregistered partnership meant this was not a case where separation kept both businesses out of registration;

- the Tribunal was satisfied that the unregistered partnership was properly formed and existed independently;

- if a contract was about to be lost because of the addition of VAT, the customer was told of the unregistered partnership so its customers knew that it would do the work.

Against separation

3.35

- all advertising was done by the registered partnership—though the spend was small and most work was obtained by personal recommendation;

- some confusion in the accounting over the allocation of suppliers' invoices—though little or no input tax incorrectly claimed;

- most expenditure charged to the registered partnership—though the use by the unregistered one was small and it might not have been worthwhile to separate it;

- the parents on occasion worked for both partnerships—though the work by the mother for the registered partnership could equally have been done in her capacity as a mother and, as a matter of substance and reality, relationships between a son and his parents would not be expected to be wholly at arm's length or commercial.

Neutral factors

3.36

- only the registered partnership had a public liability insurance policy; but it was not needed by the unregistered partnership, presumably because the work was done in the customers' houses;

- there was only one set of tools—but the son owned these.

As can be seen from the list, decisions on whether or not businesses are separate are often based on fine points of detail, and on the relative balance between the factors each way. HMRC have often won in the numerous other cases on this subject over the years, but by no means always. Many arguments have concerned whether catering in a public house, often run by the publican's wife, was separate from the publican's sales of alcohol. Normally, it is difficult to show that it is, if only because the two businesses go together naturally, and because of the close relationship between the owners. Thus, in *AE Fraser and ME Fraser* (LON/99/0453 No 16761), a restaurant run by the wife was found to be a part of the public house business which she and her husband ran. The restaurant made no contribution towards the premises costs and each activity supported the other. In contrast, a cafe run by a husband and wife in partnership was held to be separate from a fish and chip business run by the husband from the same premises (*BR Parker and JG Parker (t/a Sea Breeze Cafe)* (LON/98/1284 No 16350)).

Then, in *G & M Treta (t/a The Golden Fry)* (1/2 EDN/99/119 No 16690), a nephew, who took over a fish and chip shop for eight weeks whilst the owners, his employers, were on holiday, was held to be in business for that period on his own account. In *AC James and GC James* (LON/00/29 No 16988), a high-quality dry-cleaning business run by a father was held to be separate from the normal high-volume one run by his son from the same premises.

In *D Townsend and M Townsend* (LON/00/349-50 No 17081), a husband and wife were found to be running separate businesses consisting of the wife's shop selling pottery painted by herself and local artists and the sale of handmade pieces made by her husband through the shop and elsewhere. This was despite the informality of accounting. The types of pottery were different and the couple had no involvement in each other's businesses.

On the bare facts above, some of these cases seem unlikely victories, but they show the vital importance of clarifying the full facts and of producing evidence in support of them. Remember that once HMRC are aware of the situation, they can consider directing that the businesses be treated as one for VAT purposes—as they may well have done in the above cases after having lost the argument about whether they were separate—and that such a direction is much more difficult to defeat because of the limited powers of the Tribunal to overturn it.

In the case of *A D and J Forster v Revenue & Customs Comrs* ([2011] UKFTT 469 (TC) the appellants appealed against a decision of HMRC to make a direction under *VATA 1994, Sch 1, para 1A* (disaggregation) that two businesses should be jointly registered for VAT.

Mr Forster and Mrs Forster are husband and wife, and live at the farmhouse at Parsonage Farm. Their son lives at a house in the village. The two businesses are: (i) Mrs Forster's sole proprietorship which trades as a bed and breakfast from the farmhouse; and (ii) a farming partnership in which all three appellants are partners.

The Tribunal determined unanimously that HMRC could not have been reasonably satisfied that there was an artificial separation of the farming and B&B businesses, having regard to the extent to which Mrs Forster and the farming partnership were closely bound to each other by financial, economic and organisational links.

In reaching this decision the Tribunal noted that HMRC did not take into consideration the fact that the B&B business had been started by Mrs Forster in 1975, when her parents-in-law were the main partners in the farm. The B&B business had been started by Mrs Forster independently of the farming business for entirely legitimate and understandable reasons.

Mrs Forster runs the business herself separately from the farm, with her own bank account and books of account. She meets the direct costs of the business herself. If for any reason she is not available (for example because of illness or holidays), the business closes.

The Tribunal also noted that the B&B business is carried on from the farmhouse, which is no longer used by the farming partnership for its farming business, and the partnership recharges Mr Forster for the private use of the farmhouse by Mr and Mrs Forster (including the B&B) through the partnership books.

The Tribunal therefore concluded that the B&B business is not closely bound to the farming business by financial, economic or organisational links.

The Tribunal noted that the inspector did not seek to inspect the farmhouse premises where the B&B business was conducted.

As a result the Tribunal was satisfied that HMRC could not reasonably have concluded that it was appropriate to make a direction. The appeal was allowed.

Self-employed stylists in hairdressing salons—a planning point

3.37   A salon owner charging self-employed stylists for the use of their respective chairs and facilities is still making a taxable supply as HMRC has clarified the position in the 2012 Budget so that all chair rentals are standard-rated from 1 October 2012 rather than exempt licences to occupy. See the comment on licences to occupy in **11.7**.

A more important planning point is that, if the takings in a hairdressing salon belong to the stylists rather than to the salon owner, there is a considerable VAT saving, assuming that the individual stylists are not VAT registered. Various Tribunal decisions have gone either way; when the owner lost, it was often because the paperwork was not done properly.

However, the High Court decision in *Kieran Mullin Ltd* ([2003] STC 274) suggests that it should be possible in most cases for a simple rent-a-chair contract to establish that the salon supplies facilities to the stylists, and that the stylists sell to the customers. The HC held that, as there was a proper contract, substantiated by receipts issued by KML to the stylists for payments for the facilities, the position was consistent with it being the stylists who supplied the hairdressing to the customers. The fact that they had no control over prices and hours of work, and there was no appointment system ensuring customers were allocated on a rota basis, did not alter the contractual position. It did not mean that the stylists were supplying hairdressing services to KML rather than to the customers.

OUTPUT TAX MAY BE DUE ON ASSETS PUT INTO A PARTNERSHIP

3.38   When someone already VAT registered joins an existing partnership—or gets together with other people to form a new one—there can be VAT problems!

In *KapHag Renditefonds* (C-442/01), the ECJ held that no supply occurred when an incoming partner made a capital contribution in cash. However, HMRC claim in *Business Brief 21/04* that:

- if the incoming partner—or the people joining to form a partnership—contribute goods or pass on services on which they have already recovered input tax under their existing VAT registrations, they must pay output tax. As the goods or services have been handed over for no consideration, the rules explained in **6.1** apply concerning gifts of goods or services;

- however, no VAT is due if what is handed over amounts to a business or a part of one and therefore qualifies as the *Transfer of a Going Concern* (TOGC). See Chapter 38, *Buying or Selling a Business*; and

- moreover, if it is land or a computer covered by the *Capital Goods Scheme*, handing over the asset will either count as a disposal winding up the existing Scheme or, if the transfer is part of a TOGC, the existing Scheme will have to be carried on by the receiving partnership under the rules explained in Chapter 25.

To enable the receiving partnership to recover input tax, the person providing the goods or services issues a document:

- like an ordinary invoice, ie showing full details and the amount of VAT accounted for as output tax;

- but overwritten: *'Certificate for tax on partnership contribution. No payment is necessary for these goods/services. Output tax has been accounted for on the supply'*.

Thus, although there is no supply between the parties, the new partnership can recover as input tax what has had to be paid as output tax.

HMRC say the same rules apply when a partner leaves a partnership taking a share of the assets. If input tax was recovered by the partnership on those assets, and they do not qualify as a TOGC, output tax is due.

A TRAP RE PARTNERS: SECTION 45(2)

3.39   A departing partner has an ongoing liability for VAT:

- on future trading if HMRC are not informed of the change;

- on past trading until the VAT return is submitted and tax paid;

- on any errors subsequently discovered in past returns.

That this problem is for real was confirmed by the High Court in *Jamieson* ([2002] STC 1418). This confirmed the liability of Mrs Jamieson for VAT due on trading in a public house for periods after she had left a partnership with her husband. So, if you leave a partnership, see that the VAT returns are up to date before you go and make sure that HMRC are informed of the change!

On the other hand, in *TAZ Hussein and M Asim (t/a Pressing Dry Cleaners)* ([2003] V & DR 439), a former partner, now trading as a sole trader, was found not liable to register and account for VAT on the sales he made up to the date on which he verbally informed HMRC of the dissolution of the partnership. Of course, he will have had a liability as a partner for those sales, which were treated as made by the partnership.

DEREGISTRATION—HOW TO ESCAPE THE SYSTEM

3.40   The law is in *Sch 1, paras 3* and *4*, and *Sch 4, paras 8* and *9*. See also Notice 700/11 *Cancelling your registration.*

A business *must* deregister if it stops making taxable supplies—or it stops intending to if it has registered voluntarily. Ceasing to make taxable supplies means that you have no right to recover any input tax.

A business can ask to deregister:

- if its outputs in the last 12 months have been below the de-registration limit;

- if it can persuade HMRC that its taxable turnover in the next 12 months will be below the deregistration limit. At the time of writing, the latter is £2,000 below the registration limit at £83,000 p.a.;

- if its taxable turnover is above the registration limit, but it will be due repayments because they are zero-rated. However, if the situation is clear-cut, the net repayment will probably justify the cost of filling in the VAT return.

THE TRANSFER OF A BUSINESS AS A 'GOING CONCERN'

3.41   If a business sells or gives away its business, or it transfers it to another owner, such as a limited company, the transaction may be outside the scope of VAT as the 'transfer of a going concern'. See Chapter 38, *Buying or Selling a Business.*

DO NOT DELAY THE APPLICATION

3.42   If a business wants to deregister, my advice would be to do so promptly. Deregistration will only be backdated if a business has ceased to be entitled to registration because, for instance, it has sold its business. If a business is deregistering voluntarily because its sales are below the registration limit, HMRC will refuse to backdate it.

- HMRC can only consider an application to deregister once it is made to them. That, of course, cannot be done until they are aware of your liability to register in the first place;

- so, even if a business immediately requests deregistration on the grounds that its sales are below the registration limit, this will be a voluntary exit from the system, and cannot be retrospective.

Be aware of changes in the nature of the business

3.43   These sad stories show the need for thought if the nature of a business alters.

Mr H Zemmel (LON/77/298 No 498) was a wholesaler, who became a taxi driver. Because he failed to request deregistration, he had to pay VAT on his taxi takings despite their being well below the registration limit.

In *WA Renton* (EDN/79/12 No 870), a coal merchant inherited a boarding house. Although the Tribunal accepted that he had handed over his coal business to his daughter, albeit without telling HMRC, he remained liable for output tax on the boarding house sales because he had not deregistered.

Until an existing registration of a business is cancelled, VAT is due on its sales no matter how small they are.

VAT due on deregistration

3.44   A business has to account for VAT on assets held at the date of deregistration if the tax exceeds £1,000 (*Sch 4, para 8*).

The assets in question include:

- stock;

- plant and machinery, office equipment and furniture;

- commercial vehicles—and on any car on which the business recovered VAT because, for instance, it was being used as a taxi;

- land and property if the business recovered VAT on it when it was acquired, and the property is either less than three years old, or the vendor has opted to tax it.

VAT is not due on anything on which a business did not recover input tax when it bought it—with the exception of goods acquired as part of a business bought as a going concern, and bought-in services, which includes construction services. See Chapter 38, *Buying or Selling a Business*.

When a business deregisters, it has to account for VAT on any stocks and assets it has not sold off, if the tax exceeds £1K (*Sch 4, para 8*). The value on which the VAT is calculated, is stated in Notice 700/11 (July 2005) to be what a business would expect to pay for them:

- in their present condition; or

- for similar property or goods—presumably if the same is not available; or

- the price the goods would cost to produce. I assume HMRC mean in their present condition and if nothing similar is available when it deregisters. Surely, if such an item has any value at all, it must be as an antique or collectors item!

The assets in question include:

- stock;

- plant and machinery, office equipment and furniture;

- commercial vehicles—and any car on which a trader recovered VAT because, for instance, if it was being used as a taxi;

- land or property covered by the *Capital Goods Scheme*: see Chapter 25, *The Capital Goods Scheme*. A supply is held to occur if a trader deregisters within the ten-year adjustment period.

- land or property not covered by the *Capital Goods Scheme* on which a business recovered input tax, and in which an interest would be taxable. That means where it is a freehold commercial building less than three years old or the business has opted to tax it. A business does not owe output tax merely because it recovered input tax charged by the vendor when they bought it. A business would not have needed to opt to tax it if it were able to attribute the input tax to taxable supplies made from the business occupying the property.

Note: although no output tax is due at deregistration where there is land and property on hand upon which no input tax was recovered, but the assets have subsequently been used to make standard-rated supplies (ie an option to tax was taken, or the property was used as holiday accommodation), it should be remembered that any future sale of the property in the following 20 years will be standard-rated and constitute turnover for VAT registration purposes.

VAT is not due on assets, other than property, on which a trader did not recover input tax when they bought them—unless they did so as part of a business bought as a going concern. See Chapter 38, *Buying or Selling a Business.*

However, there is a problem with VAT on deregistration for partly exempt businesses.

- In the example of a flying club, if it had been unable to recover any VAT on its gliders because they were only used for exempt purposes, it would not need to account for any VAT on them at the time of deregistration. However, it had included them as non-attributable ('residual') assets, because there was both taxable and exempt use of them, so it had to account for VAT on them based on the full market value at the time of deregistration even though it only had partial VAT recovery on the purchase.

This is clearly not very fair on partly exempt businesses, but unfortunately, the rules as they stand on this are quite clear.

BUT A BUSINESS CAN RECLAIM CERTAIN VAT AFTER DEREGISTERING

3.45 There are two situations in which a business can recover VAT after having deregistered. Ask the *NAS* (see *Contacting HMRC*, page lxvii) for form 427 on which to make a claim.

- A business can claim VAT incurred earlier on either goods or services which they did not claim on the correct VAT return, either because they did not have the purchase invoice, or because of a mistake.

- But VAT incurred after deregistration is only recoverable on services, not on goods (*reg 111(5)*). The services must also relate to pre-deregistration trading.

The three-year time limit applies in both situations.

VAT INCURRED AFTER SALES CEASE

3.46 In a Danish case, *I/S Fini H* (C-32/03), the ECJ held that, although there were no sales, VAT could be recovered by Fini on rent, heat, light, and telephone costs incurred on premises in which its restaurant had closed down. This was still input tax related to the previous business, despite continuing for five years, because Fini could not get rid of the lease.

Fini had remained VAT registered but the Danish tax authorities demanded repayment arguing that it was no longer in business. The ECJ held that *Art 4(1)–(3)* of the *EC 6th VAT Directive* allowed recovery of VAT on rent due because the lease contained a non-termination clause. The partnership was still regarded as a taxable person, there being a direct and immediate link between the payments made and the commercial activity and in the absence of any fraudulent or abusive intent.

IS A COMPANY BEING DISSOLVED OR STRUCK OFF THE REGISTER?

3.47 Once a company has been dissolved, HMRC will not be able to repay any VAT—so don't liquidate a company if there is a repayment return still outstanding.

Chapter 4

VAT groups

SIGNPOSTS

- Two or more corporate bodies under common control can form a VAT group registration. The VAT group has a representative member and a single VAT return covering all members of the VAT group. Transactions between group members are ignored for VAT purposes. Forming a VAT group can allow tax planning opportunities and increase input tax recovery (see **4.1–4.6**).

- There are some disadvantages to VAT grouping, including joint and several liability for members of the VAT group, a single partial exemption de minimis limit covering the group as a whole and a single limit for Payments on Account (see **4.7–4.10**).

4.1   This chapter explains how two or more limited companies can form a VAT group, which has a single VAT return covering all the companies in the group.

Currently only 'bodies corporate' can be grouped for VAT purposes. This normally means limited companies although, for instance, universities are corporate bodies, and can therefore be grouped with their trading subsidiaries. Limited liability partnerships also qualify. The law is in *ss 43* and *43A–C*. Notice 700/2 *Group and divisional registration* refers.

However, legislation will be introduced in Finance Bill 2018–19 amending *VATA 1994, s 43A* to allow a non-corporate entity (eg partnership or individual) to join a VAT group with its body corporate subsidiaries if it controls all of the members in a VAT group.

Under the new amendment, the non-corporate entity must demonstrate that it controls all of its body corporate subsidiaries. The test at *s 43AZA* will apply assuming the non-corporate entity would pass the test if it was a corporate body.

Secondary legislation in the *VAT (Groups: Eligibility) Order 2004* will be amended to prevent a misuse of the new VAT grouping eligibility criteria.

The main advantage of VAT grouping is to avoid creating output tax on, say, management charges between associated companies, where the recipient company cannot recover input tax because it is partially exempt. Thus, associated companies in the financial and insurance sectors are usually grouped together.

EFFECT OF GROUPING

4.2   One company acts as the 'representative member' of the group. All inputs and outputs are treated as being those of the representative member. Transactions between companies in the same VAT group are ignored for VAT purposes.

KEY POINTS

4.3

Focus

- Companies and limited liability partnerships only; not ordinary partnerships. A sole trader can only have one registration anyway.

- At the option of the trader the business can apply to group—or to degroup, or should it wish, to alter the membership of the group. HMRC can refuse or can remove a company from a group, but these powers are normally only used if they think the business is trying to save VAT with an artificial avoidance scheme.

- The companies must be under common control. 'Control' usually means over 50% of the votes of the share capital. Normally, that means a majority of the shares.

- Control can be held by another limited company, not necessarily a member of the VAT group, or by an individual or two or more individuals carrying on a business in partnership. The controlling person can be anywhere in the world.

- Alternative criteria are that a company is empowered by statute to control the other company's activities or that it is the holding company under *Companies Act 2006, s 1159 and Sch 6*, ie it has a right to appoint a majority of the directors.

Do not confuse the concept of VAT grouping with that under different rules for corporation tax or under the *Companies Act*.

EFFECT ON INPUT TAX RECOVERY

4.4   Input tax recovery is determined in accordance with the use by the group, as a whole, of the goods and services received by each individual member.

For example, if group member A buys in computer equipment and leases it to group member B, who uses the equipment to make exempt supplies to third parties outside the group, the input tax on the original purchase will be attributable to exempt supplies and restricted, subject to the normal partial exemption *de minimis* limits. See Chapter 24, *Partial Exemption.*

Input tax incurred by all the group members can be deducted to the extent that it is attributable to supplies made to persons outside the group which carry the right to deduct input tax.

VAT grouping can decrease the amount of input tax that is irrecoverable by certain members of the VAT group, for example:

● if company A makes a management charge to company B, whose outputs are mostly exempt, and they are not in a VAT group, VAT on the management charge would be largely if not entirely attributable to the exempt outputs of B, and irrecoverable;

● if they are in a VAT group, A does not have to add VAT to its charge;

● however, some of A's input tax may be disallowed because it relates to the exempt business of B, which A is supporting through the services it provides.

The extent of any disallowance of input tax to A will depend upon the precise circumstances, and upon the partial exemption method adopted.

A VAT group can reclaim input tax on VAT invoices which are addressed to the wrong VAT group member, provided the company which received the supply is in the VAT group. This saves trying to obtain a fresh VAT invoice from the supplier.

If the wrong member of a VAT group issues a VAT invoice in respect of a supply made by another member of the VAT group, the invoice needs no amendment because the supply is treated as being made by the representative member.

HOLDING COMPANIES

4.5   The position of holding companies with regard to VAT has been examined by the courts on a number of occasions. The consistent problem has been to determine to what extent a holding company, which may make no taxable supplies in its own capacity, can be properly considered to be carrying on a business.

4.5 *VAT groups*

The holding of investments in the form of shares in other companies for the purpose of receiving dividends or participating in the management of those other companies is no different in principle to the role of private investors whose activities are not considered to amount to a 'business'.

This interpretation of the status of holding companies was upheld in the European Court of Justice case of *Polysar Investments* (C-60/90). The Court held that:

> 'the mere acquisition of a holding in a company, and the dividends which flow from such a holding, did not amount to the exploitation of property for the purpose of obtaining income and was therefore not an economic activity.'

In its simplest sense, a holding company describes a company with shareholdings in one or more subsidiaries. The structure and purpose of holding companies can, however, be diverse, ranging from companies with minimal activities where shares are held in subsidiaries and dividends received, but no part is played in management of the investment, to businesses fully integrated with trading subsidiaries and where the holding company is actively concerned with the supervision and management of the subsidiaries.

The basic functions of a holding company are the:

- acquisition of shares in subsidiaries;
- receipt of dividends arising from the shareholdings;
- defence of itself and its subsidiaries from takeovers; and
- disposal of shares in subsidiaries.

These activities alone do not create 'taxable' supplies for VAT purposes and registration for VAT is not permissible if these are the only activities of the holding company.

To be registered for VAT, the holding company must make or intend to make taxable supplies. These may consist, wholly or partly, of supplies of management services to one or more of the holding company's subsidiaries.

A holding company that makes no taxable supplies can, however, join a VAT group registration comprising some or all of its subsidiary companies provided those companies make taxable supplies outside the group. The key point is that the holding company is part of a VAT Group, some of whose members make supplies outside the group.

HMRC generally accept that a UK holding company of an active trading group is concerned in managing the group and so is a taxable person.

Holding companies having only non-business activities cannot register for VAT in their own capacity and are therefore unable to recover the VAT they incur.

For partly exempt holding companies, input tax on overheads is treated as residual input tax.

This administrative concession is permitted in order to reduce burdens on businesses and to ensure that holding companies based in the UK receive similar treatment to that applied elsewhere in the EU.

The EU Commission challenged the UK's inclusion of holding companies in VAT groups, but lost the case in the ECJ. This decision confirms that the UK's treatment of holding companies is correct and they can be included in a VAT group with other trading companies.

ENTERTAINMENT

4.6   A minor advantage of grouping is no disallowance for entertaining when executives of companies within the VAT group visit each other. The normal disallowance does apply for visits to an associated company which is not VAT grouped.

DISADVANTAGES OF GROUPING

4.7   Every company within a VAT group is responsible for the entire VAT debt of the group. This could disadvantage minority shareholders in a grouped company since, if part of the group becomes insolvent, the rest must pay its VAT liability.

An administrative disadvantage is that, to get the group VAT return to HMRC on time, the other companies in the group must submit their figures to the representative member earlier than if they sent them in direct. Some groups ask for the figures as early as the middle of the month. This imposes an unnecessary demand for speed and thus an additional strain on the accounting resources of the subsidiaries. It also means that the cut-off for recovery of input tax on invoices received from suppliers is at least a week earlier than it need be, with an obvious cash flow disadvantage.

Businesses should consider collecting the figures by e-mail. Then they can be collated on a spreadsheet electronically, which is both faster and avoids transposition and arithmetical errors. This would mean that they need only be received one day before the return is due to be dispatched to HMRC, plus whatever safety margin is deemed sensible to allow for any unexpected problems.

In addition, the partial exemption *de minimis* limits apply to the group as a whole rather than the total for all the members of the group, so it is possible that otherwise recoverable exempt input tax may be lost.

EFFECTS OF JOINT AND SEVERAL LIABILITY FOR VAT GROUP MEMBERS

4.8   The liability for the VAT debt of the group, mentioned above, can take time to materialise and is a potential loss for any member, past or present, of that group. See **38.3** for the pitfall in buying a company out of a VAT group. Notice 700/2 *Group and divisional registration* refers.

In *J & W Waste Management Ltd/J & W Plant and Tool Hire Ltd* (LON/02/ 239 No 18069), VAT owed by the group's representative member, a company put into liquidation nine months earlier, was claimed from two other group members. HMRC argued that only the Liquidator had the right of appeal. The Tribunal rejected the idea that entry into a VAT group implied giving up that right, though it directed the Appellants to confirm whether or not the Liquidator intended to appeal.

GROUP PAYMENT AND REPAYMENT COMPANIES SEPARATELY

4.9   A company claiming repayments is best not grouped with one making payments because a repayment can be claimed on a monthly return as soon after the end of the month as the return is ready. That could get the business a repayment up to two months earlier than they could otherwise offset it against the payment due quarterly.

PAYMENTS ON ACCOUNT SCHEME

4.10   A possible reason for not grouping is that, if the total payable by the VAT group exceeds £2m a year, the *Payments on Account Scheme* will apply, and result in a cash flow disadvantage. See Chapter 5, *The VAT Return*.

A SEPARATE COMPANY FOR EXPORTS?

4.11   If a business puts its export sales through an export company, the latter can recover on a monthly return the tax charged to it by your other companies perhaps two months before they pay it. This provides a 'one–off' gain in working capital.

This scheme is only suitable for very big companies. To justify the cost of running the export company, the interest saving must be substantial. Even £1m @ 10% for two months is only £16,667 a year.

Moreover, in *Business Brief 12/05,* HMRC have threatened to align the VAT periods of separate companies where the only reason for the different dates is the cash flow advantage.

THE ANTI-AVOIDANCE RULES

4.12   The law on grouping gives HMRC extensive powers to refuse to allow a company to be grouped, or to compulsorily degroup it. These resulted from *Thorn Materials Supply* ((1998) STC 725) which concerned an attempt to use the grouping rules legally, but artificially to reclaim several £ millions of input tax. With Thorn having won in the tribunal, the law was changed to introduce some serious potential complications. However, these will not affect a business unless they attempt blatant VAT avoidance. One of the problems with artificial tax planning is that, no matter how clever it is, if the end result seems not to 'smell right', the judges can often find a way of deciding against it!

From 1 August 2004, the *Value Added Tax (Groups: eligibility) Order (SI 2004/1931)* modified *s 43A* to prevent avoidance schemes involving companies in a VAT group, which are in reality controlled by third parties. Such schemes had been used by groups with exempt outputs to obtain purchases without VAT from suppliers.

DATE OF LEAVING A VAT GROUP

4.13   In *Barclays Bank plc* ([2001] STC 1558), the Court of Appeal held that, when a member of the group ceases to be eligible because, for instance, ownership of the company has changed, the date of its departure from the group is that specified in a notice issued by HMRC, not that of the change of control.

In theory, this could lead to serious problems over the submission of VAT returns for the group, which must include the figures for the business now sold during the period between the change of control and the date of leaving the group. The liability for any outstanding VAT could also be an issue. Whether that is so in practice remains to be seen. *Business Brief 30/02* sets out HMRC's policy.

PROPERTY TRANSACTIONS

4.14   If a VAT group member opts to tax some land that option applies to all other current or future members of the VAT group in relation to that land, even if they leave the group (*VATA 1994, Sch 10, paras 2(1)* and *3(7)*).

See Chapter 38, *Buying or Selling a Business* for the position when a tenanted property is bought into or sold out of a VAT group.

A capital goods scheme adjustment may be required when a company joins or leaves a VAT group. A capital goods scheme 'interval' ends when a company joins or leaves a VAT group during the adjustment period. A new interval then starts and ends 12 months later. When a company joins a group, the representative member is responsible for making adjustments arising after the event. A corporate body leaving a VAT group is responsible for later adjustments.

EU COMMISSION'S PROPOSALS FOR HARMONISING VAT GROUPING

4.15 The European Commission has adopted a Communication setting out its position on VAT grouping schemes. The Communication includes guidelines which are aimed at ensuring a correct, coherent and uniform application of the VAT grouping option.

Lászl ó Kovács, Commissioner responsible for Taxation and Customs Union said:

'The practice has shown that the VAT grouping scheme, although being a simplification measure for operators, could lead to tax evasion. For that reason the Commission proposes clear guidelines on how to apply in practice this scheme'.

The Communication sets out the Commission's view on how the provisions of *Art 11* of the *VAT Directive* should be translated into practical arrangements whilst respecting the basic principles of the Community VAT system and ensuring that the effects of using the option scheme remain restricted to the Member State applying it. The Communication includes the following aspects:

- Only taxable persons may join a VAT group. Additionally, a taxable person should only be able to join one VAT group at a time.

- The group is itself a taxable person subject to the same rights and obligations as any other taxable person and all the provisions of the *VAT Directive* as well as the rulings by the European Court of Justice apply to it.

- The group, as a single taxable person, should be identified for VAT purposes by a single number.

- Only companies or fixed establishments physically present in the Member State that has introduced the VAT grouping scheme may be members of a VAT group. A VAT grouping scheme should be open to all sectors of economic activity in the Member State which introduces such a scheme.

- The financial, economic and organisational links must exist simultaneously.

- The VAT group's right to deduct input VAT shall be determined on the basis of the transactions of the group as a whole with third parties.

- One of the most important consequences of forming a VAT group is the 'disappearance' from a VAT perspective of transactions between the members of the group, ie transactions for consideration between the individual members of the group. These transactions are considered non-existent for VAT purposes.

- It is of utmost importance that Member States take all necessary measures to prevent tax evasion or avoidance, as well as abusive practices, through the use of their national VAT grouping schemes. No unjustified advantage or unjustified harm should arise from the implementation of the VAT grouping option.

There are now 16 Member States which have introduced VAT grouping schemes into their national legislation. It has become evident that there are wide differences between the VAT grouping schemes implemented by Member States.

One of the potential changes that could affect the UK would be to extend VAT grouping to partnerships and sole proprietors. For example, an individual with a sole proprietor business, the main shareholder of a limited company and the controlling partner in a partnership could conceivably form a VAT group with the three legal entities. This could be a useful change for many smaller businesses with inter-company charges. It is unlikely that these changes will be implemented before the UK leaves the EU but they may, however, still affect the UK rules at some point.

Chapter 5

The VAT return

SIGNPOSTS

- VAT returns are due quarterly but businesses receiving regular repayments of VAT can apply for monthly returns and should be received by HMRC with payments, usually one month after the end of the VAT quarter. All businesses have to submit electronic returns and payments, with a few exceptions for religious or computer access reasons. Most businesses are now required to submit their VAT returns through Making Tax Digital (see **5.3–5.18**).

- There are penalties for late VAT returns and payments but you can avoid a penalty if you have a 'reasonable excuse' (see **5.19–5.26**).

- If you discover an error you can adjust it on your VAT return within certain monetary and time limits (see **5.34–5.36**).

5.1　　This chapter is designed to give a basic guide to the completion of the VAT return.

HMRC has introduced a new reporting system called 'Making Tax Digital' (MTD) which will see the abolition of the traditional VAT return for most businesses from 1 April 2019, with the remaining businesses being liable from 1 October 2019.

This means that those affected will have to provide summary tax data to HMRC quarterly, using digital tools – the summary tax data will be automatically generated for the business from its electronic records. For VAT registered businesses these quarterly updates will effectively replace the VAT return. HMRC has agreed that it will accept submission using spreadsheets but they should meet certain criteria to be acceptable to them. The result of the introduction of MTD is that in future all businesses will be required to keep their records electronically.

There are certain limited exemptions from MTD if HMRC is satisfied that:

- the business is run entirely by practising members of a religious society whose beliefs are incompatible with the requirements of the regulations (for example, those religious beliefs prevent them from using computers);

- it is not reasonably practicable to use digital tools to keep the business records or submit returns, for reasons of age, disability, remoteness of location or for any other reason; or

- the business is subject to an insolvency procedure.

Functional compatible software is a software program or set of compatible software programs that must be able to:

- record and preserve electronic records in an electronic form;

- provide to HMRC information and returns from the electronic records in an electronic form and by using the API platform; and

- receive information from HMRC.

HMRC has produced a list of functionally compatible software that can be accessed on its website.

As VAT already requires quarterly returns, no business will need to provide information to HMRC more regularly during this initial phase than they do now.

The intention is that VAT reporting may be synchronised with the new quarterly reporting requirements for income tax and corporation tax if the business is VAT-registered.

BASIC ACCOUNTING FOR VAT

5.2   VAT is accounted for on a VAT return.

Box 1—enter the output tax charged to customers.

Box 2—is for any tax due on 'acquisitions'—goods which have been acquired from a supplier in another EU Member State. There being no frontier controls within the EU, VAT is not collected when the goods enter the UK. You declare it as acquisition VAT. In most cases, no VAT is actually paid because the same sum is recoverable as part of the input tax in box 4.

Acquisition VAT is only a cost if it is not recoverable because it relates to an exempt transaction. For more details, see Chapter 21, *Imports and Acquisitions of Goods*.

Box 3—is the total of boxes 1 and 2.

Box 4—enter the input tax being reclaimed on the goods or services that have been bought. This includes tax on any capital expenditure, such as buildings or equipment, not just that on running expenses—though there are some limits to what can be reclaimed.

Box 5—put the net difference, normally the sum payable by the business, but which could also be a repayment due to the business.

Boxes 6 and 7 are for the statistics. These are the outputs for the quarter in box 6, including any which are zero-rated or exempt and the inputs in box 7. Both figures are net of VAT. The inputs figure includes most of the business's costs but not wages or salaries and certain other items. There are instructions on what to include or leave out in VAT Notice 700/12.

Boxes 8 and 9 record, if applicable, sales of goods to, and purchases of goods from, other Member States of the EU. These boxes are for sales and purchases of *goods* only. The wording does mention 'associated services', but this means only insurance and freight related to the goods.

HOW OFTEN IS THE RETURN DUE?

5.3   Most businesses have to submit quarterly returns. The quarters are staggered so that some finish at the end of March, some at the end of April, and some at the end of May. However, a business can ask to have the return date which suits it. A business can even have dates which coincide with its accounting periods, if it works in 12- or 13-week periods, rather than in calendar quarters. These are available on application, and are known as 'non-standard accounting periods'.

If a business regularly reclaims tax from HMRC, it can have a monthly return in order to get the money back quicker.

The EU Commission has proposed a single VAT return for all EU Member States with a proposed introduction date of 1 January 2017. This will provide greater consistency across the EU. However, the current proposal would require all businesses with a turnover exceeding €2 million (£1.7 million) to submit monthly VAT returns.

WHEN IS THE RETURN DUE WITH HMRC?

5.4   The return and payment are due with HMRC seven days after the last day of the month following the end of the period to which it relates (*reg 25(1)*). If HMRC have agreed non-standard accounting periods to coincide with, for instance, 13-week accounting periods, the return is due a month and seven days after the end of the period.

ELECTRONIC PAYMENTS

5.5   HMRC offer businesses an extra seven days if they pay electronically after the due date for the VAT return. However, if the seven-day extension ends at a weekend or on a bank holiday, payment must be in HMRC's account at the Bank of England by the previous working day. There are systems which allow one to give instructions in advance for same-day payment. Note also that the extension does not apply to the very big businesses, which pay under the Payments on Account Scheme.

Businesses can pay their VAT Returns by direct debit. HMRC recommend that businesses pay by direct debit because payments are collected automatically from their bank account on the third bank working day after the extra seven calendar days following the standard due date.

A business cannot use the online VAT direct debit payment facility if it:

- makes payments on account and submits quarterly returns; or

- uses the Annual Accounting Scheme, except to make a balancing payment—but it can set up manual direct debit payments.

ELECTRONIC VAT RETURN

5.6   From 1 April 2012 all businesses have to submit their VAT returns electronically unless they have a religious objection to using electronic means. The advantages of electronic submission are:

- the business gets an additional seven days—calendar days, not working days—in which to submit the figures online. For example, if the 30 September, is a Sunday, the due date for an electronic return will be Monday 8 October;

- businesses also have to pay electronically! If the business chooses to pay by direct debit (DD), they only have to authorise it for future returns. From then on, the sum declared will be collected automatically;

- further good news is that the DD will not be claimed by HMRC until three working days after the return was due; thus it will only hit the bank account of a business at least 10 days after the month end—much later than a payment by BACS or CHAPS would be taken from it. For a return due electronically on 7 July, the DD was collected on 12 July, with the 9 and 10 July being a weekend. For the return due 8 August, a Monday, the DD date was 10 August;

- businesses can also submit the figures as soon as they have the information ready, but HMRC will still not claim the DD until the due date;

- so, if a sole proprietor or businessman is going on holiday, will be away from the office, or will be just in a busy period over the due date, they can get the VAT return done and submitted earlier without having to worry about paying any sooner. That also applies in bigger businesses, where a member of staff approves the figures and the senior person responsible for approving them is not always available.

According to HMRC, the vast majority of businesses have found it easy to make the transition from paper filing to online filing. However, very small numbers of businesses have contacted HMRC to explain their difficulties in filing VAT returns online. In such circumstances, HMRC has advised businesses of other options to help them to meet their legal obligations. Such options include using public libraries, using computers owned by friends and family, using the services of an accountant or, if none of these options are appropriate, using a filing by telephone service.

However, following appeals against the requirement to file online, the First-tier Tribunal (in the case of *L H Bishop Electrical Co Ltd. A F Sheldon t/a Aztec Distributors*) ruled that the failure of the VAT Regulations 1995 to take account of a person's ability to comply on account of:

- age;

- disability;

- computer illiteracy (linked to age); or

- remoteness of location

was a breach of the European Convention on Human Rights.

HMRC has amended the VAT Regulations so that businesses that satisfy them that they meet certain criteria will not be required to file their VAT returns using an electronic return system. Those criteria will be that it is not reasonably practicable for them to use either the current method of electronic filing or telephone filing on account of:

- age;

- disability;

- remoteness of location; or

- any other reason.

HMRC has introduced a number of features to make the telephone filing service more accessible. These include introducing the option for authorised telephone filers to call to file their return, rather than make an appointment for HMRC to call them, to make the service available outside normal working hours and to introduce a dedicated line to ensure that calls are dealt with by telephone filing experts and are answered promptly.

Businesses that disagree with the requirement that they file their VAT returns online now have a right of appeal against this.

Following the introduction of MTD, the HMRC portal will be closed to businesses required to use MTD so they will only be able to submit their VAT returns via MTD.

To register to make electronic returns

5.7   For how to register for online returns go to: http://www.hmrc.gov.uk/vat/vat-online/submit.htm

Before a business can use VAT online services, it will need to register with HMRC's online services. During the registration process it will be able to enrol for various services, including VAT Online, which can be used to file a VAT return online.

To enrol for VAT online, a business will need the following five pieces of information:

1.   VAT registration number;

2.   the postcode of the principal place of business;

3.   the effective date of registration for VAT;

4.   the final month of the last VAT return submitted; and

5.   the *'Box 5'* figure from the last VAT return submitted.

A business will be able to find the first three pieces of information on the VAT4 (Certificate of Registration) and the fourth and fifth on the last VAT return submitted. If you cannot find your VAT4 then you can request a copy from the VAT helpline.

If a business has recently registered for VAT and has not yet submitted a return it will need to select N/A for the 'final month of last VAT return submitted' and enter 0 (zero) for the *'Box 5'* figure on last VAT return submitted.

A copy of any VAT returns submitted online since 23 November 2009 will be automatically saved on the business's VAT online services account. It will store the details for a period of 15 months after submission.

Once a business has submitted its return to HMRC it will get an on-screen unique submission receipt reference number. It's a good idea to save or print a copy of this on-screen confirmation, as the business will only receive an email confirmation of receipt if it has registered its email address for VAT messages. When you have successfully submitted the return you can save the PDF document to your PC and print a copy for your records, this will include the submission number, date and time. It also tells you what date the payment is due electronically.

If a business would prefer to use a commercial software package to submit its VAT return it can do so providing it is enrolled for the VAT online services.

Using a commercial product is a quick and easy way of submitting VAT returns online—the business can submit its return almost instantly because the information is sent directly from the accounting software. So there's less chance of making mistakes like typing in a figure incorrectly or putting the wrong figure in the wrong box. Once a business has checked its return on screen, all it takes is the click of a button to send it to HMRC.

Businesses that already have a PAYE ID

5.8   If a business already has an ID and password for PAYE return purposes, they can log in straightaway the Username box is where they put their ID which is a mix of letters and numbers. Note, however, that they can only use an existing ID for one VAT registration. If they have two or more businesses each with their own VAT registration, they will have to create separate IDs for the second one onwards.

To obtain an ID—or a second one

5.9   To obtain an ID, or a second one if a business has already used its PAYE ID for one of its VAT registrations, click on *Obtain a Government Gateway Account*.

That takes users to *Sign up for an Online Account*, which asks for:

- Your full name—personal, not that of the business. Users will find they do not need either the name or the address of the business. If moving the cursor does not work, click tab on the computer to move from box to box, not the return key.

- Your e-mail address—which presumably can be that of the business.

- A password, which is created as a mix of letters and numbers. If the business already has a password for an existing ID, they can use the same one. It is the ID which has to be different for each VAT registration.

- Then click *Next* at the foot of the page—the return key may not work.

Next, the business ticks the box to confirm that they have read and accepted the *terms and conditions*—which can be seen by clicking on that phrase.

When the business clicks *Submit*, a welcome page appears with the name and the new ID—a 12-unit mix of letters and numbers. The business should print off that page or make a note of the ID just in case they do not receive a confirmation of the ID in due course. The business then enters that ID as the username and the password, which they have just created. That takes the business to the *Welcome to Online Services* page.

There, the business has to confirm the e-mail address already given as the one to which general messages concerning their online services will be sent or provide another one.

On the next page fill in:

- the VAT registration number;

- postcode—of the business address;

- date of registration—to be found on the VAT registration certificate;

- the month of the last return of the business; ie if it was for the quarter to 31 March, select March;

- the amount of VAT payable or repayable shown in box 5 on that return.

The system checks the details that have been provided. If accepted, press Submit again. The business will receive a confirmation letter in a few days. It does not need its activation PIN—also a mix of 12 letters and numbers—which should arrive by post in 7–10 days. That is only needed to enable the business to access *Change to VAT Registration* service.

See below concerning setting up payment by direct debit and how to fill in a return.

Activating an ID

5.10   Once the business has its PIN, it activates the service ID on the Government Gateway website—www.gateway.gov.uk:

- click the *Enter the Government Gateway* button on this page;

- enter in the boxes the ID and password. The ID is not case sensitive but check for the letter I and the number 1—easy to confuse;

- login produces the *Services list* page—which alerts users to an e-mail message. Clicking on that produces the e-mail box with a *welcome* message, which warns that businesses need to read the e-mail reply;

- delete that and, on return to the e-mail page, click *Services* to get back to the Services list;

- there, on the line, which records the registration for VAT returns, click *Activate*;

- on *Activate services* enter in the box the PIN—make sure it is the temporary PIN, not the permanent ID. Again, watch for the letter I and the number 1; also, take care with the letter O and the number 0. Then click *Activate service*. In case of error, the business has two more chances. Failing them means restarting the process of getting the ID and then waiting for the PIN by post;

- the *Service Activation Confirmation* page confirms that the VAT return service has been activated. Businesses are offered *Access to and how to use the New VAT Returns service* or *Services list*. Use the former, which takes businesses to a small box showing part of the HMRC homepage;

- scroll down the box of the HMRC VAT homepage and click the VAT online link, which can be seen on the left-hand side. This takes businesses to the online services login page. Fill in the username (ID) and password boxes and click *Next*;

- the *Additional information* page already contains the individual applicant's name and e-mail address. It asks for the applicant's title, a telephone number, either office or mobile, and, as security information, the applicant's first and second schools, a memorable place and memorable name of 6–15 letters, plus a memorable date. For the date, applicants have to click in the boxes of day and month and then choose them; type in the year. The Help page says that the security information is only needed for contact by telephone or for use of certain unstated services, but not for submitting a VAT return, and that businesses will only have to supply individual letters, not the complete item:

- print this page as a record of the security data—using your browser;

- clicking *Next* then takes businesses to *My services* page. On that, click *Submit returns*, which then suggests businesses set up the DD facility. At the bottom of the page, *Continue* takes businesses to *Set up Direct Debit.*

Setting up payment by direct debit

5.11   When a business submits its first return, it can set up the DD facility. The business needs to do this at least five days before the return is due electronically—see below for the potential problem under *Potential problems*. At the bottom of the page, *Continue* takes you to *Set up Direct Debit*:

- this page explains the advantages; note the business must arrange the DD before submitting a return to be paid that way. It then gives the business a form to fill in with the bank account details—only the first 18 letters of the account can be entered;

- having clicked *Continue*, there is a *Confirmation* page. Once confirmed, an *Acknowledgement* page is shown. Print it using the web browser;

- if the business wishes to fill in the return, click on *Return to online services*. That takes you to *Submit a VAT return*—which is dealt with as below under *Filling in the return.*

Filing returns under MTD

5.12   MTD was introduced for VAT registered businesses from 1 April 2019. The following businesses had MTD deferred until 1 October 2019:

- VAT groups;

- VAT divisions;

- Non-resident traders;

- Trusts;

- Businesses on annual accounting;

- Unincorporated charities; and

- Businesses on payments on account.

The six-month deferral will also apply to public sector entities required to provide additional information on their VAT return, such as government departments and NHS Trusts, local authorities and public corporations. In addition, businesses with a turnover of less than the VAT registration threshold of £85,000 per annum need not participate in MTD but can do so voluntarily.

Businesses will submit their VAT return via MTD compatible software, the method of submission will depend on the software used. There will be no need to separately complete a VAT return online. Businesses not required to participate in MTD will still use the system detailed below

Filling in the return

5.13

- To login from scratch, go to the HMRC VAT homepage and click *Businesses & corporations*. Click *VAT online services* on the left-hand side for the login page;

- at *My Services*, which welcomes the business by name, the traders VAT number and Submit return are shown. The latter takes the business to a page of details. Click on *Next* at the foot to go to the terms and conditions. To get to the return click *Accept* the terms and then click *Next*;

- on the return page, take care with the figures—cover the '0.00' with the mouse in order to substitute the entry and include the dot to indicate the pence. The statistics also need a '.00'—unlike the paper return where it is filled in;

- click *Next* to go to the *Confirm* page. On confirmation, an *Acknowledgement* page is shown; print it. It shows when the bank account will be direct debited together with the due date for the return, the date it was submitted, and the figures. You can also print and save a PDF copy of the VAT return for your records showing all the information.

Potential problems

5.14   Allow time to set up the direct debit.

HMRC warn in their FAQs about DDs that it takes five working days to set one up, so you might have to use another electronic method.

Potential payment problems

5.15   HMRC have no flexibility within the system to allow payment by a different method if, on a particular occasion, a business does not have the money in the right account to meet the DD.

However, if the business recognises the problem in time it should consider whether it can make a payment from another account using the BACS system— as explained previously under *Cheque payments compared with electronic payments*.

The security risk

5.16   There is a security issue. Anyone with access to the username and password of a business could complete the return electronically; moreover, that could be done before the period has even ended. Of course, it is more likely that this would be done by mistake than on purpose with the wrong figures— but those wrong figures could include a repayment claim. Large unusual claims are checked first by HMRC but not necessarily the smaller figures. So, I recommend that businesses restrict access to their username and password.

Submission of returns electronically by agents

5.17   An agent, such as a professional adviser, can submit a return on behalf of a business. First, the business must obtain an ID in the usual way and the agent must do so as an agent by clicking on the relevant page on the *Government Gateway*. Then, the business adds to the business ID the agent's identification, which allows the agent to submit the return.

That of course creates a control problem. Both need to consider what checking and confirmation of the figures can be done by the business.

EVIDENCE OF ELECTRONIC PAYMENT

5.18   With electronic payment, a business has no record of payment. Often, a bank's system does not allow the business to print a note of the instruction and it is questionable whether any file note, even dated and signed, will have the same credibility for an electronic entry as it would for a physical posting of a letter. The only way a business could create a record would be to go back online the following day and print a copy of the statement. Whilst that would establish when the money was sent, it would be no help if, for some reason, the paying bank's computer system failed to implement an instruction.

WHAT IF THE RETURN IS LATE?

5.19   If a business submits a late return the default surcharge system applies. See Chapter 39, *Assessment and VAT Penalties*. The default surcharge is a draconian penalty to be avoided at all costs.

A default surcharge can be avoided if it can be shown that the business has a 'reasonable excuse'. HMRC's general approach is to apply the 'reasonable conscientious businessman' test of Medd J in *Comm of HM Customs & Excise v Appropriate Technology Ltd* (LON/90/1350 No 5696).

5.20   From 24 November 2008, HMRC introduced a Business Payment Support Service.

The service, announced in the Pre-Budget Report (PBR), gives businesses the opportunity to pay VAT through payment timetables which they can afford. The service is designed to assist all businesses that will be unable to pay their tax that is about to fall due, and in the majority of cases, HMRC will be able to make a decision in around ten minutes. Interestingly, where an approach is made to HMRC prior to the due date having expired, and they grant time to pay, HMRC will not normally count this as a default for surcharge purposes, and no penalty will be imposed.

In most cases, HMRC should be able to give you a decision in about ten minutes. For larger payment debts and those that are more complicated, they may need to have a longer, more detailed discussion with you, and may need to call you back before finalising payment arrangements.

HMRC ask that the following information be to hand:

- your tax reference number;

- details of the tax that you are or will have trouble paying; and

- basic details of your business's income and outgoings.

Business Payment Support Service can be contacted on 0845 302 1435 and are open Monday–Friday 8.00 am to 8.00 pm, Saturday and Sunday 8.00 am–4.00 pm.

Indications are that the Business Payment Support Service is now being run down, with fewer enquiries and a greater reluctance by HMRC to agree time to pay. It is likely that it will be phased out in the near future.

Please note: The Support Line is intended for new enquiries only.

Reasonable excuses

5.21   With regard to default surcharges, HMRC might consider that a reasonable excuse is established due to:

1   computer breakdown. The Tribunal looks at how severe the problem was to the preparation or submission of the return, as well as the availability of personnel to resolve the problem, including, where relevant, the preparation of a return by alternative means. Generally, HMRC expect to see evidence of an engineer being called to try and solve the problem, and a copy of his report;

2   illness or compassionate reasons. If the business shows that the person who is usually responsible for preparing the return was either seriously ill, or recovering from such an illness, then there could be a reasonable excuse. However, this argument would not work for a large organisation where there should be more than one person who is able to complete the return;

3   loss of key personnel;

4   unexpected cash crisis; or

5   loss of records (Notice 700/50/2004, para 4). Allegedly, many businesses have suffered a fire or burglary only days before a VAT officer arrives to check their records. A genuine fire, flood or burglary can create a 'reasonable excuse' if the records for the current VAT period were lost. In such circumstances, however, there would again need to be evidence of the problem (insurance claim for a fire, photographic evidence of fire damage, or a police or newspaper report). However, if records are unavailable, a taxpayer may be able to estimate the figures to be declared on the VAT return.

Example 5.1—Reasonable excuse for late return

Troubles Ltd submitted four successive VAT returns late for different reasons.

1   The first return was late because the book-keeper took a holiday and was out of the country in the last week of the month when the return was due.

> There is almost certainly no reasonable excuse because the book-keeper is expected: (a) to complete the return before going on holiday; or (b) to arrange for the company's accountants to prepare the return.

2   The second return was late because on last 29 October the company's computer crashed and an engineer had to remove the computer for four days. Thus, the VAT return for the period to last 30 September was not submitted and paid until last 2 November.

> The computer crash is probably a reasonable excuse if there is evidence of the crash, and HMRC were satisfied that the crash was genuine.

3   As regards the return for the period to last 31 December, the book-keeper over-drank at the office party, and posted the return in a red dustbin instead of a red post box. The error was only realised when the default surcharge notice arrived in February.

> The posting of the VAT return in the dustbin is not a reasonable excuse because the company cannot rely on another person to perform a task.

4   In March, an important customer, accounting for 4% of the company's total turnover, did not pay his account on time. The amount unpaid equalled 50% of the VAT bill for the last March quarter.

> These were the facts in *Design and Stereos* [2004] BVC 4017, where the Tribunal decided that non-payment by a customer who only accounted for 4% of a company's turnover could not be classed as an unexpected cash crisis that would justify the reasonable excuse claim.

Statute-barred excuses

5.22   The scope of the reasonable excuse defence is restricted by *VATA 1994, s 71(1)* as follows:

(a)   an insufficiency of funds to pay any VAT due is not a reasonable excuse; and

(b)   where reliance is placed on any other person to perform any task, neither the fact of that reliance nor any dilatoriness or inaccuracy on the part of the person relied upon is a reasonable excuse.

Nevertheless, consider the underlying cause of the trader's actions which triggered the penalty. Sometimes the underlying cause is a reasonable excuse.

Insufficiency of funds

5.23   An insufficiency of funds to pay any VAT due is not a reasonable excuse (*VATA 1994, s 71(1)(a)*). Arguably, this is inequitable, since an honest tradesman may be unable to pay VAT declared on the return because of the default by one of his large customers. For instance, a small business might have made a large supply during one accounting period to a business which goes into liquidation without paying the VAT. The business is responsible for the VAT shown on the VAT invoice as payable, for making payment to HMRC at the end of its prescribed accounting period (although later relief may be available for the bad debt). It may not have the money because of the default of its customer, and yet it may not only suffer the loss of the money, but also be liable to a surcharge. In one case, the late paying debtor was HMRC, but nevertheless the surcharge was imposed.

Reason for insufficiency of funds

5.24   Although 'insufficiency of funds' is barred by statute (*VATA 1994, s 71(1)(a)*) from amounting to 'reasonable excuse', the reason for such insufficiency may be a defence.

If a cash shortage derived from the sudden non-payment by a normally reliable customer, then a reasonable excuse could apply. However, it must be proved that this customer's business represented a major part of the claimant's trading. Thus, a company with an annual turnover of £5m could not successfully argue that it had a reasonable excuse for paying its VAT liability after the due date, merely because one customer failed to pay a £1,000 invoice.

In *C & E Comrs v Salevon Ltd* (1989) 4 BVC 199, the purchaser of a company discovered, after the purchase, that the capital of the company was less than was shown in the books due to dishonesty on the part of the former company secretary. There was a direct tax and VAT back liability, which the purchaser agreed with the revenue authorities should be paid off by instalments. As a result of this liability and later bad debts, the usual VAT payments were in arrears, and a surcharge assessment was issued. On appeal, the Tribunal decided that the real cause of the defaults was the dishonesty of the previous company secretary, which resulted in the company having less capital than the purchaser realised. This was the 'cause' of the insufficiency of funds, and it was a 'cause' which amounted to reasonable excuse for the default. The Tribunal emphasised that an insufficiency of funds caused by normal trading hazards, such as over-optimism or the taking of undue risks, would not amount to reasonable excuse. This decision was upheld by the Queen's Bench Division.

The Court of Appeal held in *C & E Comrs v Steptoe* [1992] BVC 142 that a taxpayer's late VAT payment could be excused because the single customer, on whom he was reliant for 95% of his business, consistently paid its bills late.

That case established the need to look beyond the immediate cause of the late payment (in *Steptoe* insufficiency of funds—an excuse disallowed by statute) to the underlying cause. In *Steptoe*, that underlying cause was the late payment by the single customer. Clifton has shown that the same principle can work for the taxpayer where an important element of the underlying cause is late payment by a number of customers.

No reasonable excuse

5.25   Defences that have been found not to constitute a reasonable excuse include:

- ignorance of the law;

- oversight or misunderstanding within a business;

- error;

- preoccupation with work;

- inexperience of business affairs;

- no intent to escape payment of tax.

HMRC views on reasonable excuse following the introduction of electronic filing

5.26   HMRC will allow late returns without imposing a penalty (default surcharge) if **their** software breaks down and the business cannot submit its return on time. However, if a business has a problem with its software or its service provider breaks down, it could still be liable to a penalty for late submission of its return. I have asked HMRC if businesses could submit a paper return if their computer systems have broken down, to ensure that the returns arrive on time and, therefore, avoiding a penalty for late returns. Helpfully, I have been told that electronic filing is mandatory, so they will not accept paper or faxed returns after the initial 12-month 'light touch' period, and any that are submitted that way will be ignored and a default surcharge will arise—nice!

It seems likely that there will be a lot of reasonable excuse cases before the VAT Tribunals following these changes, as businesses try and show that late returns were as a result of unforeseen computer breakdowns, and outside their control. I would expect the Tribunals to take a reasonable view in these cases, particularly if a business has tried to submit a paper return and HMRC has refused it!

WHAT IF HMRC DELAY A REPAYMENT?

5.27   If HMRC are slow to repay a business, it may be entitled to a *Repayment Supplement*. To qualify for this, the return must be on time and accurate to within £250 or, if higher, 5% of the repayment claim. If HMRC then fail to repay the business:

- within 30 days of the date on which they receive it;

- or, if later, within 30 days of that on which it was due;

- as extended by any time taken by the business to answer reasonable inquiries, which HMRC may make or in bringing the past returns up to date or by HMRC in correcting any errors in the return,

the business is entitled to a repayment supplement of 5%, with a minimum of £50 (*s 79* and *VAT Regulations, regs 198, 199*). The supplement is free of income or corporation tax.

In the case of *Our Communications Ltd v Revenue & Customs Commissioners* [2012] UKFTT 604 (TC) the appellant submitted a voluntary disclosure for underclaimed input tax and HMRC was dilatory in making the repayment. The appellant asked for repayment supplement, but HMRC refused saying that it was only due on the late repayment of claims submitted on VAT returns, The appellant appealed this decision and, finding for the appellant, the Tribunal Judge said:

> 'It seems strange to us that the government should, as a matter of policy, encourage the efficient payment of a VAT credit claimed in a return but not one claimed as allowed or directed by HMRC but otherwise than in a return. In our view, the efficient processing and payment of claims for VAT credits is as desirable in the case of claims made in returns as it is in the case of late claims.'

IS INTEREST PAYABLE AS WELL?

5.28   Interest payable under *s 78* is not due on any sum increased by a repayment supplement due under *s 79*. However, *s 78* only applies if *s 84(8)* does not. See **18.10** for more about that.

THE REPAYMENT SUPPLEMENT VERSUS INTEREST

5.29   When only *s 78* has applied, HMRC have sometimes paid interest rather than a repayment supplement. Yet, the latter will usually be a larger sum. If they do that, a business should quote the case of *Leisure Two Partnership* (LON/99/373 No 16876) where HMRC refused to repay a claim, which they subsequently accepted was correct. The Tribunal rejected their argument that, having denied the claim, they had dealt with the return so that, when their mistake was recognised, only interest was due. The repayment supplement was due although the interest already paid had to be offset. However, interest was not payable as well as the repayment supplement.

In the *Leisure Two Partnership case*, the repayment supplement was higher than the interest. A repayment supplement will usually be, but not necessarily, higher than interest. Granted, if the argument about a repayment claim went to a Tribunal hearing, the delay could easily exceed a year; in which case an interest rate of 5% or more would mean that the gross sum would be higher than a repayment supplement. However, income or corporation tax is payable on interest received from HMRC but not on a repayment supplement so the latter might still be a better deal.

See Chapter 39, *Assessment and VAT Penalties,* for the rules on interest payable to HMRC under *s 74* and by HMRC under *s 79.*

WHY MIGHT A REPAYMENT BE DUE?

5.30   The most likely reason for receiving regular repayments is that a business sells zero-rated goods or services. Because they're taxable, the business can reclaim all the associated input tax. If a business has few standard-rated outputs, the input tax that is reclaimed may be more than the output tax due.

A trader who normally makes payments may have an exceptional repayment if he incurs a large amount of input tax on, say, a standard-rated building or a large machine. If this happens, the business should write to its local VAT office (LVO) warning them and explaining why there will be a repayment as soon as it is aware of the situation. If the computer rejects the return for further enquiry because of the exceptional repayment, the LVO will probably deal with it quicker if they have already had an explanation.

Some traders also occasionally receive repayments because their businesses are seasonal. Thus, an ice-cream vendor at the seaside will have most of his sales in the summer with perhaps not enough to cover his expenses subject to VAT during the winter. A fireworks manufacturer will have large sales each autumn out of all proportion to those during the rest of the year. Either might receive a repayment in the quarter with the lowest sales.

SUBMITTING THE VAT RETURN

5.31   It is all too easy to make mistakes when filling in a return, such as transposing the figures for input tax and output tax so that the sum in the Net Tax box becomes a repayment instead of a payment. This may sound unbelievably careless or silly, but it does happen because we all make careless mistakes from time to time. The trick, of course, is to spot them before they do any harm.

If a business underpays the VAT due as a result of such a mistake, it will be charged interest and may also be liable to a penalty. If possible, a completed VAT return should be reviewed by a third party.

Commonsense precautions include checking:

- figures correctly taken from backup schedules?

- figures in correct boxes?

- arithmetic correct?

- tax due or repayable makes sense? How does it compare with the last return or with the same period for last year?

- retail scheme box entered if applicable?

- copy of return kept for VAT returns file?

- payment instruction correct?

All the above points are mistakes which other people have made!

BACK-UP SCHEDULES

5.32   The VAT return should be supported by proper back-up schedules, which show:

- the source of all the figures, such as purchase day book, cash book, petty cash book or salaries summary sheet. If the figures are taken from the VAT account in the nominal ledger.

- journal entries required, such as for scale charge on private petrol, VAT included in deductions from salaries or recovery of tax on expense claims;

- any special checks or information routinely required.

Examples of the latter are:

- any income or payments by standing order picked up from bank statements;

- agents' statements of sales made, rents collected etc, which may include VAT;

- hire-purchase agreements entered into, which may be for sums including VAT;

- royalties statements, which can include both output VAT on income and input VAT on any commissions.

SPOTTING ERRORS

5.33   *Plastic Developments Ltd* (MAN/00/914 No 17416) incurred VAT on imported goods, which it paid to its handling agents. The invoice from the agents asking for the VAT of £6,345 was not of course the document required to recover that sum as import VAT. The document needed for that was form C 79, which arrived in due course. Meanwhile, the bookkeeper had recorded the total payment to the agents as carriage and packaging. The VAT was, therefore, treated as a cost, not recoverable tax. Presumably, the C 79 was simply filed, it not occurring to anyone to check the import VAT recovery.

The mistake was only discovered after the then three-year (now four-year) time limit, explained below, had elapsed. The Tribunal confirmed HMRC's refusal of the repayment claim.

The first line of defence against such mistakes is for the person who signs the return to review the figures to see whether they make sense in the light of what has gone on during the period.

Of course, whether the omission of a sum of either input tax or output tax was obvious would depend on its amount in relation to the size of the business. However, comparison of the figures with previous returns may be a useful check.

DISCLOSING ERRORS OF EITHER OVERPAID OR UNDERPAID VAT

5.34   Errors cannot be corrected on your VAT return unless the net value of errors you find in a period is under £10,000 or 1% of turnover as declared on the VAT return for the period in which the errors are found, subject to an upper limit of £50,000 (*VAT Regulations (SI 1995/2518), reg 34(3)*). Correcting on the current return means that the business escapes interest as well as any penalty.

Net errors totalling in excess of £10,000 or 1% of turnover as declared on the VAT return for the period in which the errors are found, subject to an upper limit of £50,000 must be disclosed separately. HMRC provide *Form 652* but a business can write a letter provided that details of the periods involved are given. By making a voluntary disclosure, the business pays interest but avoids paying a penalty—explained at **39.26**.

See page lxviii at the start of the book for details on where to write to.

In order to keep track of the value of errors on previous returns, period by period, a business needs to be able to identify the journal entries correcting them or, where the tax is on purchase or sales invoices recorded late, to identify those invoices.

Instant disclosure is not essential. If a business normally discloses at the end of each period, it will still be regarded as voluntary even if a visit has meanwhile uncovered the problem. However, I suggest a business records each error as it is found as proof of an intention to disclose.

A business will, of course, have to keep the disclosure figures separate from those recorded on its VAT return because any payment must be made separately and a repayment claim is an outstanding claim on HMRC, which they may or may not agree to pay.

THE FOUR-YEAR CAP

5.35   As explained in Chapter 39, *Assessments and VAT Penalties*, HMRC can only assess to correct errors retrospectively for four years. Similarly, *s 80(4)* says a business can only claim back VAT for four years after it has been overpaid. That means that, as soon as a business becomes aware of an overpayment it should submit a claim to HMRC for the past four years in order to prevent any of the claim being time barred.

See page lxviii at the start of the book for details on where to write to.

Even if a claim for overpaid output tax is within the four-year time limit explained below, HMRC may be able to refuse to repay it under the unjust enrichment rules: see **18.9**.

WHAT IF A BUSINESS DISCOVERS ERRORS MADE OVER FOUR YEARS AGO?

5.36   The four-year cap explained above works both ways. Although a business cannot correct an overpayment made more than four years ago, you do not have to tell HMRC of any underpayments over four years ago either. Thus, if a mistake continues for several years, the four-year cap limits the payment or repayment.

The four-year time limit starts as follows:

under *s 77(1)*:

● assessment by HMRC for underpaid VAT—the end of the VAT period covered by the return on which the error occurred;

under *s 80(4ZA)*:

● reclaim of output tax declared on a VAT return—end of the period covered by the return;

● overstatement of output tax on a voluntary disclosure—end of the period in which the disclosure was made;

● assessment overstated for output tax based on a voluntary disclosure—end of the period in which the disclosure was made;

● overpayments to HMRC due to mistakes other than overstating output tax or understating input tax—the date on which the payment was made—an example being a duplicate payment.

under *reg 29(1A)*:

- reclaim of input tax not recovered—the date on which the return covering the tax point of the input invoice was due.

As a concession, HMRC will allow recovery of input tax on an invoice received from a trader, who did not originally charge it and has now registered more than four years after the supply. A business must have paid the VAT to the trader and the latter must have paid it to HMRC, whether by assessment or on the initial VAT return.

For more on claims of input tax made within the four-year limit, see **13.4**.

Notice 700/45 (March 2002 with three updates) *How to correct VAT errors and make adjustments or claims* contains HMRC's views.

Quintain Estates Development plc (LON/03/994 No 18877) was held to have submitted its claim in time despite it having gone astray and Quintain not having followed it up for 11 months. The key was the evidence that it had dispatched the claim, not whether it had been received.

Warning—do not abuse the four-year time limit by not disclosing an error, once found, in the hope that HMRC will not discover it in time. To do so converts an innocent error into a dishonest one and raises the time limit to 20 years, as explained at **39.3**.

Another error is to correct a mistake exceeding £10,000 or 1% of turnover as declared on the VAT return for the period in which the errors are found, subject to an upper limit of £50,000 on your return without telling HMRC. A separate Voluntary Disclosure is required.

HAVE A PERMANENT VAT FILE?

5.37   Supporting notes on a permanent file should make it possible for anyone to understand the entries required, and where the information comes from. Many an error has resulted from someone having to take over the VAT return because key staff are on holiday, are sick, have left etc. If the previous schedules are handwritten, probably with little or no explanation, mistakes are likely.

VAT GROUPS

5.38   The representative member of a VAT group should receive at least some supporting information with the internal returns for each member company. Whether it should receive full schedules is a policy decision but, unless some details are obtained, the person signing the return has no way of assessing whether the figures are likely to be right. See Chapter 4 re VAT grouping.

THE PAYMENTS ON ACCOUNT SCHEME

5.39   The *Payments on Account Scheme* is a means of collecting VAT earlier from the very largest businesses.

If the VAT payable by a company or a VAT group exceeds £2 million a year, it is required to make monthly payments of estimated amounts. It then prepares the return for each quarter in the usual way, deducts the two payments on account already made, and pays or reclaims the balance.

The law is in *VAT Regulations (SI 1995/2518), regs 44–48* made under the *Payments on Account Order (SI 1993/2001)*, as amended, which was itself made under *s 28*.

HMRC notify the business of the monthly payments on account, which they calculate by dividing the annual liability during the previous reference year by 24. The sums can be altered if the annual liability varies by more than 20%.

Both the estimated and the quarterly balancing amounts have to be paid by the last working day of the month in which they are due and no extension for electronic payment is allowed. See Notice 700/60 *Payments on account*.

Chapter 6

So what must VAT be charged on?

SIGNPOSTS
<ul><li>Money a business receives will normally be subject to standard rated VAT unless it is lower or zero-rated, exempt or outside the scope of VAT (see **6.1–6.6**).</li><li>There are special rules for monies received in certain circumstances (see **6.7–6.18**).</li><li>VAT can be due on certain business gifts and special rules apply to loans of goods, the free supply of services and goods put to private use (see **6.19–6.30**).</li></ul>

6.1   In Chapter 1, *How VAT Works*, I explained that VAT is chargeable on most sales at the standard rate, but that some are reduced-rated, some are zero-rated, some are exempt, and some are outside the scope of VAT. Reduced-rating, zero-rating, and exemption are explained in more detail in their respective chapters, and international 'outside the scope' sales in that on *Exports and Imports of Services*.

Here I discuss when VAT is due on sundry other transactions, which are not 'sales' in the sense of what the business earns its living from. The chapter covers:

- why output tax is usually due on sundry receipts—and some exceptions;
- expenses recharged;
- gifts of goods and services;
- loans of business assets.

'MONEY IN' MEANS VAT PAYABLE

6.2   As stated in the introductory chapter *How VAT Works*, VAT is due on:

- taxable supplies;
- made by a taxable person in the course or furtherance of any business.

6.3 *So what must VAT be charged on?*

Once someone is in business, anything they do is likely to be either:

- in the course of that business; or

- in the course of an activity amounting to another business, which is covered by the same VAT registration.

So, if a business charges for doing something, it has to add VAT, unless the supply happens to be zero-rated, exempt or outside the scope. Of course, once a business accounting system is set up to account for VAT, charging it on invoices or, if the business is a retailer, on its takings, is relatively simple.

However, a business of any size may have various sources of cash coming in for which a sales ledger invoice has not been issued, and which are therefore treated as cash book receipts. Such income often gets omitted from VAT returns. Sometimes this is because it never occurs to people that VAT might be due.

IF IN DOUBT, TRY THE 'WHAT IF?' QUESTION

6.3   People tend to look for excuses as to why VAT is not due on money received. For instance, they see canteen sales as being part of being 'staff welfare', and assume that that in some way makes them outside the scope of VAT. The 'what if' routine is a useful defence mechanism against incorrect assumptions. 'What if' canteen takings were indeed outside the scope of VAT? It would create a distortion of competition between the canteen and the café in the street. The canteen is probably already subsidised; if it did not pay VAT on the prices charged, that would distort the position further. Often, stopping to ask 'what if?' suggests that the first reason or excuse for not accounting for VAT is unlikely to be correct.

If a business receives payment for something, output tax is usually due. If a business starts from the principle that tax is payable unless it can find a good reason why not, it will be less likely to make errors.

SALES LEDGER RECEIPTS

6.4   VAT is not normally due when payment is received against a sales ledger balance. VAT was accounted for in the period in which the tax invoice was issued. There are two exceptions:

- if bad debt relief has already been claimed, VAT is due on any sum subsequently received from the customer. See Chapter 16, *Bad Debt Relief*;

- if it is a small business using the *Cash Accounting Scheme*; see Chapter 34.

STANDARD RATING APPLIES IF THE FUTURE SUPPLY CANNOT BE IDENTIFIED

6.5   A payment upfront, which can be used to pay for future supplies, may well be standard-rated despite the expectation that many of the supplies will be zero-rated or exempt.

In *The Highland Council* (EDN/05/16 No 19542) a card giving access to various facilities, including exempt education, was held to be a standard-rated right of access. The nature of the supplies was not identifiable at the time of issue of the card. It was for the cardholder to choose.

Similarly, in *McDonald Resorts Ltd* (EDN/04/36 No 19599), 'points rights' were standard-rated because the buyer would choose in due course where and when the timeshare interest in holiday accommodation would be taken up. It could be in the UK or elsewhere, and could also be in a hotel rather than a holiday unit.

The problem is that a business must be able to identify the nature of the supply at the time a payment is received.

This should not be confused with the sale of a face value voucher, which can be redeemed at a future date and on which VAT is due at the time of redemption. See **8.25** *et seq.*

INCOME ON WHICH VAT IS NOT DUE

6.6   There are a few special cases which are outside the scope of VAT.

A *dividend* is outside the scope because it is not payment for any supply by the shareholder. It is merely a share of the profit earned by the company.

A *Government grant*, such as a payment towards the cost of building a factory in a high unemployment area, is outside the scope, if nothing is done in return for it.

However, the definition of the consideration for a supply under *Art 11A(1)(a)* of the *EC 6th VAT Directive* (now *Directive 2006/112/EC, Art 73*) includes a subsidy. The latter can be a part of the value of the supply if:

- the price of the goods or service is fixed at the time of the event triggering the subsidy;

- the right to receive it depends on the recipient making a supply to a third party.

In *Keeping Newcastle Warm* (C-353/00 ([2002] STC 943)) the ECJ held that payments of £10 by the *Energy Action Grants Agency* to an organisation which advised householders how to improve energy efficiency, were part of the consideration received by that organisation for the work it did for the householders.

That case illustrates the difference between a global subsidy to cover general operating costs, and one paid to facilitate a specific service to a third party. Public subsidies are granted to further the public interest rather than to procure goods or services for the State, so any supply must be to a third party.

In the case of *Hope in the Community v Revenue & Customs Commissioners* [2012] UKFTT 498 (TC) (which the taxpayer lost) the Tribunal set down a number of useful pointers in deciding if 'grant' income is really a grant or payment for a supply of goods or services.

Indicators that a payment is not for a supply:

- income is described as a 'grant';

- the giving organisation is known as an organisation which gives grants and is treating the payment as a grant within its own audited accounts;

- the grantor is a local, central or European government body giving the money through an established grant scheme;

- the grant was acquired through a grant application process, rather than through a competitive tender;

- the direct beneficiaries of the project are other than the grantor. (The grantor will invariably have an interest in seeing a benefit accrue to the beneficiaries, but this does not create a direct benefit to the grantor.);

- the grant payments are not treated as trading income or expenditure in the accounts of either party;

- funding is drawn down as a reimbursement of expenditure incurred, rather than as payment for services.

Factors which are generally not conclusive in either direction:

- the conditions of funding are complicated and detailed;

- the grantee is obliged to provide reports and information to the grantor in relation to the funded project;

- during the course of the project the grantee may carry out work which would be taxable in another context;

- a service level agreement is in place.

Indicators that the income is likely to be taxable:

- the arrangement between the parties is subject to a commercial contract for the provision of goods and services;

- the contractor is treating the transactions as trading expenditure in its accounts;

- the contractor is not an organisation which normally gives grants or runs grant schemes;

- the contract was entered into following a competitive tendering process;

- the contractor is clearly the direct beneficiary of the work to be carried out.

Compensation is usually outside the scope of VAT, being compensation for a loss suffered by the recipient, not payment for a supply by that person.

Examples are:

- a business's offices are damaged by fire. The money received under its insurance policy is compensation paid towards the loss in putting right the damage. The insurer pays the costs net of VAT unless that VAT is not reclaimable by the business because it is partly or wholly exempt;

- another business infringes copyright. A sum received in settlement of the claim for damages is not payment for any supply made by the business.

Do not assume that compensation for the termination of a contract is outside the scope of VAT. Although HMRC have often accepted that it is, there is a potential pitfall, and *Themis FTSE Fledgling Index Trust plc* (LON/2000/501 No 17039) has now highlighted the problem. HMRC argued that compensation for the right to terminate a contract early was a taxable supply of services. They lost the case because this particular contract had been repudiated first. Once the other party had accepted this, the only right surrendered by that party in return for the compensation was the right to pursue a claim in the courts. This was not a variation of the contract, or a surrender of rights under it.

Although this decision does not fully clarify the position, it seems likely that, if instead of one side simply repudiating a contract, the two parties negotiated terms upon which it could be terminated, HMRC would argue that there was a standard-rated surrender of rights.

Goods on which input tax recovery is blocked, such as a second-hand car, are exempt when sold (*Sch 9, Group 14*).

Charges to staff for the use of cars are outside the scope of VAT, assuming that input tax was not recovered on the purchase price of the car.

FEES RECEIVED BY A BUSINESS FOR THE SERVICES OF A PARTNER OR OWNER

6.7 Partnerships often require that fees received by their partners for outside appointments are paid into the business. HMRC are likely to argue that such fees are payment for a standard-rated supply of the services of the individual if the appointment results from and involves the use of the professional expertise exercised in the business. This is inconvenient if the body in question cannot recover that VAT. See leaflet 700/34 *Staff* for HMRC's views.

However, in *Birketts* (LON/1999/1007 No 17515), a Tribunal held that fees from non-executive directorships of Health Service Trusts, held by partners in a firm of solicitors, were not subject to VAT because the individuals had been appointed on the grounds of their personal merit, occupational skills, and standing in the community as distinct from professional expertise. Therefore, they had not been accepted in the course or furtherance of their profession as solicitors. In contrast, a directorship of a Building Society was held to be partnership income because the partner was expected to provide the experience of a property solicitor, and to keep the Board up to date on conveyancing practice. Since the fees from the Building Society were paid into the partnership as compensation for the time spent on the appointment, and were treated as income of the practice, they were received in the course or furtherance of the partnership business and were subject to VAT.

For a partnership, the way round this problem is to allow the individual partner to receive the income personally. That is not of course possible for a sole trader, since business income remains business even if paid into a private account.

COMPANIES WHOSE DIRECTORS HOLD OTHER DIRECTORSHIPS

6.8   If fees to a director of company A are paid to company B, rather than received by the director personally, Notice 700/34 *Staff* says that they are payment for a supply, except where B has a legal or contractual right to appoint the director—for example, to a subsidiary or a company in which it holds an investment. See also **24.55**.

PART-TIME JUDICIAL APPOINTMENTS

6.9   The *Birketts* decision, mentioned at **6.7**, also notes that HMRC accept that part-time judicial appointments, such as a chairman of the Insolvency Practitioners Tribunal or a member of a First-tier Tax Tribunal are outside the scope of VAT.

EXAMPLES OF SUNDRY INCOME

6.10   Cases where a tax invoice may not have been issued are sales:

- to staff, such as surplus or substandard goods;
- of scrap;
- in the canteen or from vending machines;
- of assets, such as machinery or commercial vehicles;
- of management services.

Transfers in the accounting records of a business, known in accounting jargon as 'journal entries', are especially dangerous because they are outside the main VAT accounting system. It is all too easy for the person making the journal entry to ignore the VAT.

Management charges to associated businesses are often made provisionally in draft accounts. Whilst the mere inclusion of a figure in draft accounts does not create a tax point, the formal approval of the accounts by the directors does, because the sum then becomes a debt due to the maker of the charge.

Moreover, if any sums have already been received on account, either in cash or by offset against amounts owing to the associated business, tax points for those amounts may have been created earlier.

In the ECJ judgment in *Astra Zeneca* (Case C-40/09), the Court found that the provision of vouchers to staff amounted to a supply of services affected for consideration. As a consequence, whilst Astra Zeneca was able to recover VAT incurred on acquiring the vouchers, output tax was due on the consideration received from its employees.

Although this case was concerned with the supply of vouchers to employees, the principles considered by the Court are of general application and will apply to other supplies of goods and services to employees.

Following earlier decisions by the UK courts, HMRC policy was to make a distinction between the VAT treatment of supplies of goods and services to employees by a deduction from salary, and those provided under a salary sacrifice arrangement.

Deduction from salary occurs where an amount is deducted from an employee's pay in return for a supply of goods or services by the employer. Output tax has always been and continues to be due on the amount deducted from salary. Input tax is recoverable in accordance with the normal rules.

For VAT purposes 'salary sacrifice' has a very narrow and specific meaning. It describes an arrangement such as where an employee opts to receive services and forgoes part of their salary in return. The employee enters into a new employment contract or has their existing contract amended to reflect the new arrangement which they are tied into.

In relation to such schemes HMRC have, to date, accepted that the reduction in the salary did not constitute consideration for the benefits received and output tax was not due. Employers were able to recover the related VAT as input tax, subject to the normal rules.

As far as arrangements involving deductions from salaries are concerned, the ECJ judgment supports HMRC's existing policy that these are consideration for a supply for VAT purposes.

However, HMRC considers that the rationale used by the ECJ goes wider than deductions from salary, and as a consequence of this there is no longer a distinction between deductions from salary and a salary sacrifice. Therefore, the amount of salary foregone is consideration for supplies of the benefits whether provided under a salary sacrifice or by a deduction from salary.

Businesses providing benefits under arrangements, which qualify as salary sacrifice schemes for VAT purposes, must account for output VAT on these supplies, where they are subject to VAT. In order to allow businesses time to make the necessary adjustments, HMRC did not require output tax to be accounted for on taxable benefits provided under salary sacrifice schemes until 1 January 2012.

COSTS RECHARGED ARE STANDARD-RATED

6.11   A business must standard-rate charges made to recover its costs. A business cannot resell its own expenses—they are a component part of the price at which the goods or services are supplied. Thus, if a consultant charges a client for the cost of a rail ticket, it is standard-rated. The zero-rated rail travel is supplied by the rail company to the consultant. The latter in turn sells consultancy services, not rail travel. The re-charge is merely justifying a part of the fees for consultancy in relation to the cost which the consultant has incurred.

SALARIES RECHARGED ARE STANDARD-RATED

6.12   Similarly, salaries recharged by an employer to another UK business are standard-rated as a supply of the services of the employee to the other business. This is so even if there is no profit element. If the other business is outside the UK, the supply is probably outside the scope under the place of supply rules.

The exception is where the salary is being collected from the business with which the employee has a contract of employment. This only happens when a business administers the payroll of another, and reclaims from the other the salaries which it has paid out on its behalf.

If the second organisation cannot recover VAT, consider the 'payroll concession' in para 3.3 of Notice 700/34/05 *Supplies of staff*. HMRC say:

Paymaster services commonly arise in two situations:

- where employees are jointly employed by two or more companies and one company undertakes to pay all salaries, National Insurance and pension contributions, which are then recovered from the other employers; or

- where each of a number of associated companies employs its own staff, but one (paymaster) company pays all salaries, National Insurance and pension contributions on behalf of the others; each associate then pays its share of the costs to the paymaster.

Recovery of monies paid out by the paymaster in either of these situations is not subject to VAT as it is a disbursement (see Notice 700: *The VAT Guide*). If a charge is made for the paymaster's services to the other companies, over and above the reimbursement of the costs paid out on their behalf, the paymaster must account for VAT on this charge. However, such supplies are disregarded where they are made between companies within the same VAT group registration.

That fits in with *Central Council of Physical Recreation* (LON/00/1354 No 17803). The Tribunal held that there was no supply of staff when CCPR, in its capacity as trustee of the British Sports Trust and out of funds held for the latter, paid for the salaries of people whose contracts of employment were with CCPR.

There is another concession available in Notice 700/34/05, whereby secondments of staff (for no profit) can also be made free of VAT. Section 4 of the Notice reads as follows:

B. Secondment of staff by businesses other than employment businesses

1.   The arrangements described in paragraph 2 below apply from 1 April 1997.

2.   The secondment by an employer (other than an employment business within the meaning of the Employment Agencies Act 1973) of a member of its staff (the employee) to another business which:

(a)   exercises exclusive control over the allocation and performance of the employee's duties during the period of secondment;

(b)   is responsible for paying the employee's remuneration directly to the employee; and/or

(c)   discharges the employer's obligations to pay to any third party PAYE, NICs, pension contributions and similar payments relating to the employee,

then, to the extent that any such payments as are mentioned in paragraphs (b) and (c) above form the consideration or part of the consideration for the secondment of the employee to the other business, they shall be disregarded in determining the value of seconding the employee.

3.   For the purposes of paragraph 2 above, an employer shall not be treated as seconding an employee to another business, if the placing of the employee with that other business is done with a view to the employer's (or any other person associated with him) deriving any financial gain from:

6.13   *So what must VAT be charged on?*

> (a)   the placing of the employee with the other business, or
>
> (b)   any other arrangements or understandings (whether or not contractually binding and whether or not for any consideration) between the employer (or any other person associated with him) and the other business (or any person associated with it) with which the employee is placed.

SALARIES CHARGED BY EMPLOYMENT AGENCIES

6.13   Up to 1 April 2009, an employment agency need not have charged VAT on the salary and associated costs if it fulfilled certain criteria.

From 1 April 2009 VAT became due on the full hire amount, and is an increased cost for those that cannot recover some or all the VAT they incur (eg businesses operating in the welfare or childcare sectors, and charities at large). It should be noted, however, that the payroll concession and secondment concessions mentioned in **6.12** above continue to be available.

However, following the First-tier Tribunal (FTT) decision in the case of *Reed Employment Limited v Revenue and Customs Commissioners* (LON/2004/0130) it was held that, in providing temporary staff to its clients, Reed was supplying introductory services rather than making supplies of staff. Accordingly, the company was only liable to account for VAT on the commission element of its charge and not on the overall amount paid by the client, which included the wages paid to the temporary staff and associated National Insurance contributions.

HMRC takes the view that, as a judgment of the FTT, it is only binding on the parties to the appeal. HMRC does not regard Reed as having any wider impact. This view was supported in the case of *Adecco UK Limited v Commissioners of HMRC* (TC04743), which on identical circumstances ruled that VAT was due on the full payment received.

HMRC's view of the correct VAT treatment for employment bureaus remains that set out in VAT Information Note 03/09. In essence a bureau acting as an agent only has to account for VAT on its commission whereas a bureau acting as a principal has to account for VAT on the full amount charged to clients including the temporary staffs' wages and employers' National Insurance contributions.

SERVICE CHARGES IN RESTAURANTS

6.14   Restaurant owners are liable for VAT on service charges unless they are voluntary, and given to the staff.

DISBURSEMENTS

6.15 A disbursement, for VAT purposes, is a sum of money which is paid on behalf of someone else for a supply which they receive. A disbursement is outside the scope of VAT. However, what a solicitor calls a 'disbursement' is often not a disbursement for VAT purposes.

In Notice 700 (April 2002) *The VAT Guide*, para 25, HMRC say that, to qualify as a disbursement for VAT, a payment must meet *all* the following conditions. It must be:

(a)   for goods or services received and used by the client, not by the adviser, and which are clearly additional to those supplied by them;

(b)   shown separately on the adviser's invoice as the exact sum paid out;

(c)   paid as the agent on behalf of the customer;

(d)   a sum for which the customer was responsible for paying the third party;

(e)   authorised by the customer to be paid on his or her behalf;

(f)   for a supply which the customer knew would be provided by a third party.

The key criteria are (a) and (b). Conditions (c) and (f) are automatic if (d) and (e) are met. The danger is that the agent may have no evidence of any such responsibility or authorisation.

A potential problem is the difference between a fee paid by a solicitor for a personal search of, say, the Land Registry, and a fee for a postal search. HMRC see the former as a supply of access used by the solicitor in order to provide advice to the client; in contrast, they say a document by post is obtained on behalf of the client, and normally used by the latter for his or her own purposes, such as to obtain a loan.

If a business recharges something as a disbursement, then normally:

● no VAT can be recovered on the item by the client;

● no VAT can be separately charged by the business—any VAT has to be included in a 'global' sum;

● the client, if registered, can only recover VAT on the disbursement if it passed on the original invoice, which must be in the client's name.

A disbursement should be shown as a separate entry on a VAT invoice. For clarity, it is best to subtotal the sum subject to VAT, add the VAT, and then add the disbursement.

Example 6.1—VAT on disbursements

	£
Fees for advice	1,000.00
VAT @ 20%	£200
Disbursement paid out on client's behalf	100.00
Invoice total	£1,300

Treating an item as a disbursement only conveys a VAT advantage if the client is unregistered, and there was no VAT on the expense in the first place. Stamp duty is an example.

It makes no difference if the cost is standard-rated, ie hotel accommodation. Since the agent cannot recover the VAT on the expense, because it was a supply to the client, the agent must recharge it to the client gross. Thus, if the VAT rate is 20%, the cost to an unregistered client is still the gross, £120, not £100 .

In *Cromford Hill Motor Sales* (MAN/97/1095 No 16152), road fund licences shown separately on invoices for second-hand cars were held to be disbursements.

However, that was not so when *Autolease (UK) Ltd* (MAN/04/695 No 19136), having obtained inquiries on the Internet from potential clients, sold to them nearly new demonstrator cars, which it had found on their behalf. When it bought the cars from dealers, they were already licensed; it was, therefore, unable to show that it had obtained each licence on behalf of the customer, and was held to sell the car with the licence for an all-in price.

Moreover, in *Clowance Owners Club Ltd* (LON/2002/0565 No 18787), costs of rates, water, insurance, loan interest and charitable donations were those of the club, not disbursements on behalf of individual timeshare owners. Only on TV licences did VAT not have to be charged to them.

The MOT test fees problems

6.16 MOT test fees paid to a test centre by a car repair workshop frequently cause problems. Historically, HMRC has maintained that the 'outside the scope' status of the fee can be maintained if the sum paid out is shown separately on the sales invoice. Any further sum charged was viewed by HMRC as a standard-rated fee for arranging the test. However, the test centre probably has no relationship with the customer, and the paperwork of small businesses is not usually designed with the care needed to establish points (d) and (e) above.

All too often the workshop receives a discount from the test centre, but charges the full fee without VAT on its invoice. HMRC then say that the payment to the test centre was not a disbursement, and have won various Tribunal cases on the point.

However, in the case of *Duncan (t/a G Duncan Motor Services) v Revenue and Customs Comrs* V&DR 114 the appellant was a garage not authorised to provide MOT tests, so took his customers' cars to two garages that were. He charged £44 on his invoices and paid £35 to the two garages, (the figures were not disclosed to the customers). HMRC argued the appellant provided a single supply of arranging an MOT and moving the vehicle to and from the testing garage. HMRC stated that, in accordance with their guidance in Notice 700, the £35 could only be treated as a disbursement if the MOT test element and the delivery and collection element were separately identified on the invoice to the customer.

The chairman said the HMRC assessment was not in 'best judgment' and that the true value of the appellant's supply was the retained £9. He rejected HMRC's argument, because it failed to recognise the reality that an MOT test was not a supply or service that the appellant could lawfully provide. Also, Notice 700 did not have force of law, and failed to recognise the legal monopoly position of authorised MOT testing stations. This view has subsequently been supported by other Tribunals.

In another recent Tribunal case, *Lower and Another* (VTD 20,567) the Appellant concerned was again unable to carry out MOTs itself. Therefore, in order to not lose trade, the garage uses an approved centre. As in the 'Duncan' case, the MOT centre gave the Appellant a discount for the referred business.

The Tribunal chairman set out the 'normal VAT' position as part of his decision, and how this all hinged on the garage acting as agent for the MOT provider. Effectively, the MOT centre provided a discount, say £8, on the normal maximum statutory MOT charge of £44. The garage, acting as agent, passed on the £36 to the customer, and charged £8 for its (taxable) services.

The 'common trap', as the Tribunal chairman referred to it, was where the garage contracted as principal or failed to treat the disbursement element correctly. Then VAT became due on the full £44 charged to customers, resulting in a VAT cost for the garage. In this case, the scenario was identical to the one above, except that it was the MOT centre that paid the garage to pick up and deliver the cars.

The Tribunal allowed the appeal, finding that there was an agency relationship between the garage and the car owner, and dismissed HMRC's argument that there was only a single supply rather than two separate ones. The chairman went into great detail, and at times, great criticism of HMRC, even going to the trouble of providing a template notice for similar garages to display prominently in their garage reception areas!

POSTAGE CHARGED BY MAILING HOUSES

6.17   When a mailing house bulk mails brochures, HMRC only accept that the postage is an outside the scope disbursement on behalf of the client if the exact sum is charged. This means that, if the mailing house receives a bulk mail discount, it must pass that on to the client, if necessary by apportioning between clients any overall rebate.

In Notice 700/24 (April 2003) *Postage and Delivery Charges*, HMRC also require that:

- the client receives the postal services—which of course occurs when its material is posted on its behalf and is responsible for paying;

- the mailing house is authorised to act as the agent of the client in making that payment;

- the postage disbursed is shown separately on the mailing house's invoice;

- the client either produces the mailing list or is given access to it prior to dispatch;

- the mailing house's responsibility for the mail ceases on acceptance by Royal Mail.

WHAT IF THE TAX INVOICE IS IN THE AGENT'S NAME?

6.18   If an agent incurs an expense on behalf of a principal, but the invoice is addressed to the agent, not to the principal, HMRC do not object to the agent recovering the input tax, provided that he, in turn, issues a tax invoice to his principal, and accounts for the corresponding output tax. This has the same effect as if the item had been treated as a disbursement, but ensures that a principal, who is registered for VAT, receives a tax invoice in his name, which supports the recovery of tax.

GIVING GOODS AWAY CAN BE A VAT COST TO A BUSINESS—BUSINESS GIFT RULES

6.19   If a business gives goods away which cost it more than £50 plus VAT, whether bought in, or produced in-house, output tax is due on the cost price when the goods are given away. In practice, HMRC usually accept that a business can disallow the input tax when they buy the goods, which may be more convenient than having to pay output tax when each gift is given away.

Gifts of goods are caught if:

- the cost of the gift to the business exceeds £50 net of VAT; or

- if you make more than one gift to the same person:

  — *up to 30 September 2003*, VAT was due on the cost of each gift over £15;

  — *from 1 October 2003*, if a business makes more than one gift to the same person: VAT is only due then if the cost of that gift, plus those in the previous year, exceeds £50. Thus, if the total cost of the gifts to someone within any 12-month period goes over £50, you account for VAT on that cost. A new 12-month period then starts with the value at nil (*Sch 4, para 5*).

However, there is a relief for samples which are not covered by the business gift rules following the ECJ case of *EMI* (C-581/08) on 30 September 2010. From 19 July 2011, the date of Royal Assent of the Finance Bill 2011, any sample of a product that is given away free by a business will not create a VAT charge. This will apply even if a number of samples are given to the same person. Note that the £50 limit only applies to business gifts. If a business cannot justify the gift as being for business purposes, it is taxable whatever its cost.

Will the recipient of the gift use it for business purposes?

6.20   If the gift will be used by the recipient for business purposes, the supplier of the gift can increase its value by providing an invoice giving full details of it, and showing the amount of output tax which has been accounted on its cost. The invoice must be overwritten:

'Tax Certificate

No payment is necessary for these goods. Output tax has been accounted for on the supply.'

Example 6.2—— What is a business gift?

- a desk diary embossed with a company logo, cost £25, is not caught;

- but a leather-bound version costing £60 is—regardless that it advertises the business.

Many people find it difficult to believe the impact of the gifts rules until it is spelt out for them. Even then, they often do not at first believe that they affect such routine commercial transactions as:

- long-service awards;

- Christmas gifts;

- display equipment given by a manufacturer to a retailer;

- prizes or incentive awards for salesmen;

- equipment given by a manufacturer to a local school or university.

This is a draconian rule, which is intended to prevent avoidance. Without it, an employer might be able to buy in goods selected by staff and give them to the latter free of VAT. The price of preventing such artificial schemes is that the rule catches numerous ordinary commercial situations. However, with careful forethought, one can sometimes avoid the rule in such cases.

DON'T GIVE IT, LEND IT!

6.21 Display equipment given to a retailer by a manufacturer is caught by the gifts rule. The business may think it absurd that a manufacturer must account for output tax on a merchandiser, such as a unit designed to display cosmetics or confectionery on the retailer's counter. The provision of such units to customers is fundamental to the business of many manufacturers and there is no element of VAT avoidance in doing this. However, HMRC have said they would assess for output tax in such cases under the gifts rule.

It is common practice to avoid this pitfall by sticking a label on the back of the units stating that they are the property of the manufacturer and must be returned upon request. In this way, ownership has been retained so the item is not a gift. As explained below, there is a rule which catches the loan of a business asset for a non-business purpose. However, this is unlikely to apply in such a situation because the manufacturer could argue that the unit was lent for the purposes of its business—furthering sales of the products displayed.

CAN A BUSINESS SELL IT RATHER THAN GIVE IT AWAY?

6.22 Businesses often give used equipment away to local institutions, such as schools. Such transactions are also caught under the gifts rule, although VAT will be due on the current value of the item, not on the original cost.

The most common example must be of computer equipment. In the case of an individual machine, the current market value may well be so low that the output tax is trivial. However, it would be more material if a number of machines were being given. The tax could be significant if a manufacturer gave away a piece of sophisticated production equipment. Suppose a business needs to re-equip in order to remain competitive. The old machine, though no longer state-of-the-art, may be fine for training students in modern production techniques, and thus, very useful to the engineering department of a local college or university, which produces potential recruits for the business. For example if the machine originally cost £100,000 four years ago and could now be sold for £20,000;

the willingness of the business to give it away—partly out of self-interest and partly because of the benefit to the local community—will cost it £4000 in output VAT.

To avoid this pitfall:

- the business could donate, say, £120 or £1,200 to the local institution; and

- the institution could buy the equipment for £100 or £1,000 plus VAT.

Yes, the price is artificial and, yes, there is an artificial prices rule, which I explain in Chapter 8, *The Value of Supply Rules*. However, it only catches transactions between 'connected persons' and the local institution and the manufacturer will not be so related. However, selling the item for £1 would be asking for trouble. If a business waves such a red rag at its local VAT officer, he or she is likely to argue the matter, which can cause unnecessary aggravation to the business even if it is successful. Give HMRC a little output tax on a more substantial sum, and the officer may well decide not to challenge the transaction.

BEWARE OF 'ENTIRELY FREE GIFTS'

6.23   Beware of gifts which are not true gifts. 'Entirely free gifts' are usually no such thing because something has to be done in order to get them. That means that there is 'non-monetary consideration' received in return. See Chapter 8, *The Value of Supply Rules* for how that can increase the output tax due and sometimes makes it due on low-value goods, despite the transaction not being caught under the gifts rules explained earlier.

A BUSINESS CANNOT RECOVER VAT ON GIFTS GIVEN AWAY BY A MARKETING AGENT

6.24   The gifts rules prevent recovery of input tax on charges by a marketing agent for gifts handed out to customers. *Baxi Group Ltd* (MAN/04/341 No 19431) argued that the gifts were part of the marketing services provided to it by its agent—which handed out items in exchange for points earned by Baxi customers. The Tribunal found that the goods—and the gifts of services—were provided to Baxi and handed out on its behalf.

FREE SUPPLIES OF SERVICES

6.25   The gifts rules apply only to gifts of goods. There is no VAT due if a business provides services free. Thus, no output tax is due on the services provided free of charge when:

- an accountant prepares accounts for a local charity;

- a plumber installs a bathroom for his brother—but, if the plumber takes goods, such as piping, from stock on which he has recovered input tax, the gifts rules apply to those goods;

- a lawyer does work for a potential client at no charge.

In such situations, remember that there must be nothing done in return. If there is any non-monetary consideration in the form of services or goods received in exchange, VAT is due on the market value of the supply, as explained in Chapter 8, *The Value of Supply Rules.*

A LOAN OF GOODS IS A SUPPLY OF SERVICES

6.26 If a business lends an asset for a non-business purpose, that is a supply of services, which is taxed on the cost of making the item available. (*Sch 4, para 5(4)* and *Sch 6, para 6 (7)(b)*).

For example, a business owns a yacht for business reasons; perhaps a business builds yachts, makes equipment for yachts, or charters them out. However, when the yacht is not in use for business purposes, ie a director, partner, or their family use it, the business is liable for output tax on the cost of making the yacht available for private use.

The rule applies primarily to such assets as yachts and aeroplanes although, in theory, it catches such minor cases as the loan of a digger by a builder to his brother for the weekend.

Output tax is due on the basis of the total cost of running the yacht, including depreciation, divided by the number of days during the year on which it is in use. The High Court has rejected an argument that the cost was based on a 365-day year because, of course, if that were the right calculation, anyone owning their own business could reduce considerably the expense of owning something like a yacht by putting it through the business and only paying VAT for the days on which they used it.

SERVICES BOUGHT IN ARE TAXED IF PUT TO PRIVATE USE

6.27 If a business buys in a service for business purposes, which it then puts partly to private use, it is liable for output tax under the *Supply of Services Order (SI 1993/1507)* as amended. The value for this purpose is that part of the value of the supply which fairly and reasonably represents the cost to the business of providing the services.

Most cases caught are likely to be of non-business use of a part of a service. If none of it is used for business, there will often be no right to recover input tax on it in the first place.

In *Telecential Communications Ltd* (LON/97/321 No 15361), the telephone and cable TV services it sold were held not to be provided for business purposes when supplied free to staff.

Obviously, there are only a limited number of cases in which a service bought in, as opposed to created from the business' own resources, is of interest to staff. In such a situation, the business may be able to avoid the pitfall if it can justify the provision to others without charge on business grounds, such as requiring quality control reports.

Legal and tax advice may be a more common problem than Telecential-type situations. As explained in Chapter 13, *What Can a Business Recover Input Tax on?*, it is usually very difficult to justify the reclaiming of input tax on legal expenses incurred in defending the owners or senior management of a business. However, supposing that defending an employee can be justified for business reasons, as in the *P & O* case explained in that chapter, HMRC might be able to demand output tax on the grounds that, despite the business justification for input tax recovery, there must be some non-business use for the private purposes of the person concerned.

The same applies if advice on tax and/or completion of the tax return for an employee is included in a tax adviser's invoice.

Work on property

6.28   If a business recovers input tax in full on work on property, but the use subsequently changes to partly or fully non-business, it creates a supply as described above.

See **13.39** for the rules requiring apportionment of the input tax when partial non-business use is expected from the outset.

Example 6.3— VAT on private property

When the rule came in, HMRC quoted the example of someone who enlarges their house to provide an office, and told them off! For example, enlarging an office will certainly have been justified by 12–15 years' business use, but the value of the building work will not have depreciated; indeed, it may have enhanced that of the house. However, the subsequent value of the work to a private owner is probably not the same as a fair and reasonable cost to the business, if the latter has used it for business over an extended period.

Suppose a company pays for an extension to its owner's house, but has to leave three years later because of the expansion of its business. What will be the cost to the company? Given only three years' business use, there will be a written-down value of the expenditure in the balance sheet.

Arguably, there is no cost of provision of the services for private use at that stage. The extension, which represents those services, is merely having to be abandoned, its value to the company having been reduced to nil. However, HMRC are likely to argue that the 'full cost of providing the service' is at least that reduction—the sum written off from the balance sheet.

MOBILE TELEPHONES

6.29   If a business allows staff to claim for calls on their mobile telephones, some of which are private, it may have to account for output tax on the latter. See **13.54** and **13.55**.

GAS AND ELECTRICITY

6.30   The 2014 Budget introduced a reverse charge for wholesale supplies of gas and electricity which means the customer is liable to account for the VAT rather than the supplier. It does not apply to domestic supplies or to businesses not registered or liable to be registered for VAT.

This is an anti-fraud measure which removes the opportunity for fraudsters to charge VAT and then go missing before paying it over to the Exchequer.

There will be further informal consultations with the industry to determine an operative date, taking account of the time businesses will need to make the necessary IT changes and other preparations for the orderly introduction of the reverse charge.

Chapter 7

Time of supply—when VAT must be paid

SIGNPOSTS

- Basic tax point rules—tax points created by the earlier of the issue of an invoice, the receipt of payment or the supply of goods or services (see **7.1–7.5**).

- There are different rules for 'continuous supplies of services' rather than a 'long job' (see **7.6–7.7**).

- There are special rules relating to the issue of pro forma invoices, supplies subject to an annual tax point and hire purchase (see **7.8–7.13**).

- Special tax point rules for the change of VAT rate (see **7.15**).

7.1   The time of supply or tax point rules are a fundamental part of the VAT system. They fix the time, and, therefore, the VAT return on which a business must account for output tax, and on which it is entitled to recover input tax.

The tax point rules are not difficult, but they do need to be understood properly. If a business gets its tax point wrong, it will not affect the total VAT that is eventually payable or recoverable, but it could cost the business interest payable to HMRC, and, possibly, a penalty if the business recovered too early or paid late. Of course, if the business makes a mistake the other way round by, for instance, claiming input tax late, it then has a cash-flow disadvantage.

The law is in *s 6*, and for continuous supplies of services, in *VAT Regulations (SI 1995/2518), regs 90, 90A* and *90B*.

THE KEY RULES

7.2

Focus

The basic tax point is the date the goods or services are supplied or 'made available' to the customer. This is overridden by the actual tax point, or time of supply, which is the earliest of the following dates:

- the issue of a tax invoice, if within 14 days of the basic tax point (to the extent of the sum invoiced); or

- a payment is received (tax value is the sum received, which is treated as including VAT).

THE ISSUE OF A TAX INVOICE CREATES A TAX POINT

7.3   Issuing a tax invoice in advance of making a supply creates a liability to pay the output tax shown on it, regardless of whether the business is ever paid by the customer or, indeed, whether it ever supplies any goods or services. The reason is that the customer can reclaim the input tax shown on the invoice, subject to the bad debt relief rules.

Having issued a tax invoice, a business may be able to reduce the value of it with a credit note. However, it must account for output tax in the VAT period in which the invoice was issued.

Bad debt relief will become available six months after the due date for payment, if the customer does not pay.

See Chapters 15, *Credit Notes* and 16, *Bad Debt Relief* for more details.

THE SUPPLY OF THE GOODS OR SERVICES CREATES A TAX POINT

7.4   For goods, the tax point is usually created by physical delivery. However, that is not necessarily so. It can be varied by the terms of the contract.

Suppose a customer wants, say, 1,000 units of a product, and the supplier needs to produce the order in a single production run, and has no room to store the goods. The supplier might agree with the customer that the latter will take delivery, but that ownership of the goods will only pass once they are used by the customer, or according to an agreed schedule. The date ownership passes will be the tax point, not the date of delivery (*VAT Regulations, reg 88(1)*).

94

An example might be new signs for a chain of retail shops, to be installed over a period of several months. An alternative situation would be a customer wanting, say, 10,000 components for his own product, which he expects to produce at the rate of 2,000 per month. However, the supplier again needs to produce them in a single run in order to keep the price down. They agree that the customer will pay for them, but that they shall remain in the supplier's warehouse until the customer calls them off. This time the tax point occurs when ownership passes upon payment, even though physical possession remains with the supplier, and delivery will be over an extended period.

With services, being intangible, the tax point is usually when the invoice is issued because this is done either under the terms of a prior agreement, or because the customer or client agrees that the supply has been completed. However, see the comment on continuous supplies of services at **7.6**.

The tax point for expenses repaid to staff is the date that person paid the bill, not the date of reimbursement by the business (*The Little Bradley Farm Partnership* (LON/02/773 No 18420)).

IF A BUSINESS HAS BEEN PAID, SOME VAT IS DUE

7.5   Money received in advance of doing the work creates a tax point. Some businesses routinely take deposits from customers. Examples include double glazing or fitted kitchen suppliers, and holiday accommodation.

Even if such a deposit is returnable, it creates a tax point when it is received because it is always intended that it shall be offset against the price of the transaction in due course. Examples are:

- a double glazing company must account for output tax on the value of a deposit received on the VAT return covering that period, even though it may not supply the goods for some months;

- a seaside landlady may have to register for VAT in January because of deposits received for holidays to be taken during the summer, even though they are returnable.

The only circumstances in which a deposit does not create a tax point are where it is always intended that the full amount shall be returned to the customer. There are not many such cases, but one example is the deposit for a hotel safe key. The hotel charges a rate per day for use of the hotel safe. The deposit taken in addition is returned when the key is handed back. Should the key be lost, the hotel retains the deposit as compensation for the loss incurred as a result of having to cut the safe open. The same principle applies to hire companies that take a deposit that is returnable when the goods are returned in good condition.

There are no exceptions to the above principles. *Section 6(2)(c)* of the *VAT Act 1994*, concerning sales on approval, etc does not apply. The tax point being created by the payment received is not covered by the rule in *s 6(4)* on payment received (Court of Session in *Robertsons Electrical Ltd* (EDN/04/18 No 18765)). The *Robertsons* decision is agreed to apply to *Grattan plc* (MAN/05/175 No 19515). Grattan lost its argument that the tax point was the end of the 14-day period in which goods sold by mail order could be returned.

The Tribunal held that *s 6(2)(c)* applies because *Distance Selling Regulations, reg 10* gives the customer an unqualified right to return goods sold by mail order or on the Internet. Although the delivery tax point is said to occur, once it is certain that the supply has taken place—after seven working days in the case of distance selling—the goods were invoiced at or shortly after the date of dispatch; thus *Robertsons* treated the tax point as the earlier of the date of the tax invoice, or the seventh working day after dispatch.

Following judgments of the CJEU, HMRC have reviewed their policy on the VAT treatment of payments for unfulfilled supplies. An unfulfilled supply is where a customer does not use a service or collect goods that they have paid for.

HMRC's current policy lets businesses treat many payments for services and part-payments for goods as outside the scope of VAT where the customer does not:

- use the service; or

- collect the goods.

CJEU decisions given after this policy started make it clear that this treatment must be amended.

When a full or part payment is made on account for a taxable supply, a chargeable event occurs and VAT becomes due on the amount paid.

If the supply does not take place, the VAT must not be reduced, unless the payment is refunded. This is because when a customer makes or commits to make a payment, it is for a supply. It cannot be reclassified as a payment to compensate the supplier for a loss once it is known the customer will not use the goods or services.

THE EXCEPTION FOR CONTINUOUS SERVICES

7.6   For services which qualify as 'continuous supplies of services', *SI 1995/2518, reg 90* says that performance does not create a tax point.

Focus

The latter only occurs at the earlier of the two following events:

- a tax invoice is issued; or

- payment is received.

So, if a business issues a request for payment rather than a tax invoice, it does not create a tax point, and no VAT is due until it is paid. Then, of course, a tax invoice must be issued.

That is a very useful cash-flow planning point for anyone who makes continuous supplies of services. Note that this only applies for services, not goods.

See the example of a request for payment below; note that this does not show either a VAT number or the amount of VAT. Local VAT Officers sometimes accept that a request for payment may show the VAT number provided that it does not state the amount of VAT. Alternatively, the officer may allow it to show the amount of VAT provided that there is no VAT number.

I suggest that to show either may lead an inexperienced member of the customer's staff to reclaim VAT to which the customer is not entitled at that stage. Indeed, I have often seen documents, which look so like tax invoices that they might have been designed to encourage mistakes by the customer! So, take care with the layout.

An Example of a request for payment

Knock-em-Out Accounting Associates
Taxation House
53 Old Road
London

Request for Payment

Mr and Mrs Client
Greasy Joes
2021 High Road
London

Date: 21 September 2004

Request Note No: 543

Professional services up to 30 September 2004
including VAT   £1,175.00

VAT is not recoverable against this document. We will send you a VAT invoice on receipt of your payment

A LONG JOB IS NOT 'CONTINUOUS'

7.7   A service is not 'continuous' merely because it is provided over a long period. There must be an ongoing relationship. Examples include:

- the services of professional accountants normally count as continuous supplies of services, because audit or tax advice is given throughout the year;

- those of a lawyer or a consultant mostly do not because, by definition, he or she is usually engaged for a specific one-off task

Of course, if a one-off job continues for a long time, there is no performance tax point until it is completed. Therefore, one can use a request for payment rather than a tax invoice to ask for money on account as one goes along. Once a payment has been received, an invoice for that amount can be issued.

Example 7.1—Poor cash-flow planning

If a business maintains equipment under annual contracts payable in advance, and it does not understand the VAT rules, it may miss an opportunity for cash-flow planning. For example, a provider of computer maintenance to small businesses may wish to send out requests for contract renewals some months before the end of the contract, and it is important to make sure the paper work is correct so as not to create a tax point before it is necessary. If they send out an invoice in June for a renewal date at 31 October, output tax would become due in the period when the invoice was issued. If payment was not received until November, the supplier would be at a cash-flow disadvantage. However, an invitation to renew the contract in the form of a request for payment would have reminded the customer to renew the contract just as well, and without creating a tax point. Another example of creating a VAT liability before a business needs to is issuing a tax invoice for standard-rated rent, rather than issuing a rent demand.

In contrast, a provider of continuous supplies of services does not have to invoice up to date if it becomes apparent that the customer has ceased paying. The law is in *VAT Regulations (SI 1995/2518), regs 90, 90A, 90B*. Similar continuous supply rules apply to royalties, services of barristers and advocates and to the construction industry (*regs 91–93*).

PRO FORMA INVOICES

7.8   Pro forma invoices are similar to requests for payment, but are usually used for goods. For instance, a manufacturer who does not wish to give credit to a retailer, can issue a pro forma invoice listing the goods ordered, prices, values etc, the total, of which, the retailer must pay before the goods are delivered.

A pro forma invoice does not create a tax point. However, it should be clearly marked as such, and should state that it is 'Not a tax invoice' to prevent customers from inadvertently deducting input tax on it. Once payment has been received, a tax point is created and an invoice should be issued.

THE ANNUAL TAX POINT RULE

7.9   From 1 October 2003, the annual tax point rule in *reg 94B* prevents the avoidance of VAT on continuous supplies to an associated business, which cannot recover its VAT. If a business does not receive payment or issue a tax invoice, the rule creates a tax point every 12 months.

Focus

It applies when a positive-rated (not zero-rated or exempt) supply of:

- a continuous supply of services; or

- water, gas, electricity or any other form of power, heat, refrigeration or ventilation; or

- rights over or licences to occupy land such as car parking, holiday accommodation, timber and sporting rights—but not rent which is opted to tax,

is made to:

- a connected person or a group undertaking,

- unless that person or undertaking can recover all the VAT it incurs on that supply.

A group undertaking means one required to be covered by group accounts, or which is specifically exempted from that requirement.

If the records of a group undertaking are not available at the offices of the business, HMRC will normally accept a letter confirming that it can recover any VAT charged to it.

DATE OF THE TAX POINT

7.10   The tax point is 12 months from the start of the supplies, or, for those already being made on 1 October 2003, 30 September 2004 and annually thereafter. However, if a date within 12 months would suit, a business should inform HMRC. Subsequent annual tax points are then 12 months forward.

However, if within six months after the annual tax point date, a business receives payment or issues a tax invoice, that date is substituted for the annual one unless the business notifies HMRC that it does not want it to. Thus, if the business expects to receive payment or to issue a tax invoice in the next six months, it can ignore the annual date. If neither event occurs within the six months, the tax point reverts to the annual date.

HMRC say that, if a business has genuine commercial reasons for doing so, it can request to vary the six-month period. Presumably, they mean a business can ask them to extend it.

LEASING OF ASSETS VIA A CHAIN

7.11   The annual tax point rule still applies even if a business leases or hires assets, such as equipment, to a connected person or a group undertaking via an unconnected person.

WATCH THOSE TAX POINTS!

7.12   Getting the tax points right requires more than just knowing the basic rules explained above. A business should ask itself how the business it is dealing with works, and consider when tax points occur as a result of work being done, invoices issued, or money coming in. It should also check the procedures for accounting for the tax generated.

Beware of exceptional transactions. Exceptional outputs can cause trouble by the very fact that they are exceptional, and are thus not necessarily automatically picked up by the accounting system. This can affect inputs as well as outputs, and as such, there could be a risk of not recovering input tax through an oversight.

HIRE-PURCHASE

7.13   Hire-purchase transactions can cause trouble for businesses. Is there a tax invoice, or does the hire agreement effectively serve as one? There is output tax to account for, and input tax to recover, when the agreement starts.

A business should not make the mistake of assuming that a tax invoice will be issued to it when it pays the initial deposit, or signs the hire-purchase documents. This can occur several weeks before the transaction is processed by the finance company—which must itself first obtain title to the goods from the supplier so that it can sell them on under the agreement. When the business eventually gets the tax invoice, it may therefore be dated in a VAT period subsequent to that in which the documents were signed or the deposit paid. If the business has already recovered the VAT, it may be liable to an assessment for recovering it too early

TAX POINT PROBLEMS FOR RETAILERS

7.14   For example, a retailer's takings are recorded weekly, and the dates do not match the calendar quarters. Agreeing special return dates to match 12- or 13-weekly periods only sorts out the takings problem up to a point. How are the weekly takings arrived at? When are the retail tills cashed up? If this is at, say, 4pm instead of at the close of business on the Saturday night, has this been agreed with HMRC? Theoretically, output tax is due in that period for the money taken between cashing up and closing time. HMRC have been known to raise the point, and might demand that an estimate be made.

What about the purchases? Are they accounted for to the same dates? If the goods are imported from outside the EU, what about the import VAT records? They must be on the same basis, not in calendar months.

CHANGE OF VAT RATE

7.15   Following recent changes of rate I thought it would be useful to cover the basic rules.

For any sales of standard-rated goods or services that take place on or after a rate change a business should charge VAT at the new rate. For cash businesses they will need to be aware of the new VAT fraction which will be:

The rate of VAT + 100

For a business making standard-rated sales, it depends how it normally accounts for VAT.

A retail business making mainly cash sales to customers that are not registered for VAT (eg a shop, restaurant, takeaway, or hairdresser) should use the new rate for all takings that they receive on or after the change of rate, except where the customer pays for something they took away (or were delivered) before the date the rate changed (eg where customers have an account).

In this case, the sale took place before the rate change, and the business must use the old rate of VAT.

A business that sells mainly to other VAT-registered businesses, and has to issue VAT invoices, should use the new rate for all VAT invoices issued on or after the date of the rate change, except where:

- a business provides goods or services more than 14 days before the issue of the VAT invoice; or

- payment was received before the rate change.

In these cases, the sale took place before the rate change and the business must therefore use the old rate.

For continuous supplies of services, such as ongoing construction work, businesses should account for the VAT due whenever they issue a VAT invoice or receive payment, whichever is the earlier.

If a business receives a payment or issued an invoice before the rate change for goods that will be provided (or services delivered) after the rate change, the business has a choice. It can choose to account for VAT at the new rate on the amounts already received or invoiced. It does not need to tell HMRC if it does this. In these circumstances, any payments received or invoices issued after the rate change will always be subject to the new rate of VAT. But businesses do need to issue a credit note to their customers if they have already issued a VAT invoice showing the old rate of VAT.

As a result of the change in the VAT rate from 4 January 2011 anti-forestalling legislation was introduced to prevent tax avoidance. The legislation applies to standard-rated goods and services. It prevents forestalling by introducing a supplementary charge to VAT on the supply of goods or services where the customer cannot recover all the VAT on the supply, and one or more of the following conditions are met:

- the supplier and customer are connected parties;

- the value of the supply (and any related supplies made under the same scheme) exceeds £100,000. But this does not apply if the prepayment or issuing an advance VAT invoice is normal commercial practice;

- the supplier or someone connected to the supplier funds a prepayment for the goods or services; or

- an advance VAT invoice is issued where payment is not due in full within six months (except hire purchase invoices issued in accordance with normal commercial practice).

The supplementary charge to VAT was due on 4 January 2011 and must be accounted for on the supplier's VAT return covering that date.

The general rule is that a business can claim back the VAT it has been charged by its supplier in the normal way. Businesses will still be receiving invoices after the rate change showing the old rate—that will be expected—as these will be invoices relating to purchases made before the rate change. In these cases, businesses can claim back VAT at the old rate.

For VAT return periods that cover both before and after the rate change, businesses will need to add together the VAT on sales charged at the old rate and the VAT on sales charged at the new rate, to work out the total VAT on sales to be included in Box 1 of the VAT return. Flat Rate Scheme percentages will change to reflect the new rate of VAT.

MONEY RECEIVED WITHOUT THE KNOWLEDGE OF A BUSINESS

7.16   Is money received at locations outside the immediate control of a business?

If so, the accounting routine needs to be adequate to pick up this income at the end of the VAT period.

Examples:

- takings from vending machines and telephones at a shopping mall. The tax point is when the machines are emptied and the money banked, not when the cash is credited on the bank statement, perhaps after the end of the VAT period;

- income, such as royalties or standard-rated rents, which is received by an agent on behalf of the business, but not forwarded immediately. Perhaps the agent even retains some of it to fund expenditure. A business needs to ensure that it gets prompt statements of account from the agent.

INCOME CONFIRMED BY BANK STATEMENTS

7.17   Are the bank statements of a business received only monthly? If so, is the statement made up to a date shortly after the end of the VAT period, rather than just before?

With the increasing use of direct payment into or out of bank accounts, it would be easy to miss standing orders received or paid and other items, if the statement is not available for the full period covered by the return. Getting the statement early in the next month gives a business the time to pick up these items.

Property transactions are an example already mentioned. If the sale or the rent is standard rated, who has issued the tax invoice, and where has it got to? It could be with a solicitor, or in a file outside the accounts department.

If an agent is collecting the rent using the tax point rules correctly (ie with a rent demand rather than a tax invoice), that agent will be responsible for issuing tax invoices for rent, on which the opted to tax has been exercised, when it is received. The business will need to ensure that it is notified of it in time to account for the tax on the correct VAT return.

WHAT IF A BUSINESS IS ASKED TO RE-INVOICE SOMEONE ELSE?

7.18   If a customer requests that an original invoice be cancelled and re-invoiced to another business, do not destroy the first document. Many computer systems do not allow the issue of a new invoice using the same invoice number.

A business should issue a credit note to the first business that cross-refers to the second invoice. Then the other business can be invoiced.

However, a business should be careful what is shown on that invoice. If a business considers that the supply was actually to the first business, say so together with wording such as '*goods delivered to ABC Ltd. Invoiced at their request to XYZ Ltd*'. ABC Ltd may have good reasons for wanting the invoice addressed to XYZ Ltd, but it is for the latter to satisfy HMRC that it is entitled to recover the VAT—for instance because the goods were passed on to it. However, businesses sometimes think that VAT which is not recoverable by one company because it is related to exempt outputs, will become recoverable if the invoice is addressed to another company which is fully taxable, and can request re-invoicing for this reason.

Chapter 8

The value of supply rules

SIGNPOSTS

- The value of the supply is normally the 'consideration' received (see **8.1–8.2**).

- There are special rules relating to discounts (see **8.3–8.4**).

- There are anti-avoidance rules for connected parties selling at below cost where the recipient cannot recover all of their VAT (see **8.7**).

- The consideration received includes not only cash but also any other goods or services supplied, barter transactions and money off coupons (see **8.10–8.15**).

- There are special rules relating to trade-in and part exchange situations (see **8.21–8.22**).

- There are detailed valuation rules relating to commissions, vouchers and rebates (see **8.23–8.35**).

8.1   The value of supply rules are another fundamental part of VAT law. Whilst most of the time a business simply charges VAT on the value of its sales, there are a few exceptions to this. It could be very expensive to get it wrong.

This chapter deals with such topics as discounts, barter transactions (when part or all of the payment you receive is in goods or services rather than cash), and when a 'gift' is not a gift because the recipient has to do something in return; ie provides 'non-monetary consideration' for it.

Then, the last part of the chapter covers some of the more sophisticated cases, which concern, for example, discounts given in the form of vouchers.

For additional guidance on some marketing methods, see Notice 700/7 *Business promotion schemes*. For details of the linked supplies concession concerning minor items at different rates of VAT, see **12.4**.

SPECIAL OFFERS

8.2   Normally, VAT is due on the price charged if that is the only consideration received. However, see later re barter transactions and non-monetary consideration.

A business can offer 'Buy one get one free' (BOGOF), '13 for the price of 12' or 'buy a sofa and get a free footstool,' and HMRC accept the deal as for an all-in price. The only complication is if it has to be apportioned because the goods are at different rates of VAT.

However, a business must be careful the way it presents and invoices a special offer to a customer. *Boodle & Dunthorne Ltd* ([2004] SWTI 1000) occasionally gave an extra item to the purchaser of an expensive piece of jewellery; thus, an item, which had cost £1k, might be given to the buyer of a piece priced at £10k. Boodle claimed that it would only be done in order to clinch a deal; however, the only evidence of the circumstances was the invoices for 5 out of 12 transactions, on all of which the extra item was stated as being 'with compliments'.

The Tribunal held these to be gifts with output tax due on the cost of them under the business gifts rules, not items sold with the main ones for an all-in price.

A retailer who offers to 'pay the VAT' on a sale is offering a discount. To calculate the tax due, apply the VAT fraction to the sum that the customer pays.

PROMPT PAYMENT DISCOUNTS (SCH 6, PARA 4)

8.3

Focus

The rules relating to prompt payment discounts (PPD) were changed in the 2014 Budget. The changes are being phased in in two tranches, the first from 1 May 2014 and the final changes on 1 April 2015. Up to 1 April 2015, the rules were that if a business offered its customers a discount for paying promptly, the VAT was charged on the optional lower price, ie the price net of the discount. It is irrelevant whether or not the customer takes that discount.

For example, a business offers a 2.5% cash discount for payment within 30 days:

On an invoice for:	£100.00
The calculation of VAT is 17.5% of £97.50	£17.06
Invoice total	£117.06

This rule was mandatory, not optional, and is a point sometimes overlooked by computer programmers when setting up new systems. Whilst it makes no difference to fully taxable businesses, it offers small savings to those that cannot recover the VAT.

Historically, prompt payment discounts have mainly been offered on business to business (B2B) supplies and recipients have generally been entitled to recover any VAT charged.

HMRC has found that prompt payment discounts are increasingly being offered to final consumers (B2C) or businesses that are not registered for VAT, who cannot recover the VAT they are charged. In particular, HMRC has identified several instances of suppliers of B2C services offering prompt payment discounts in the telecommunication and broadcasting sectors. Under the existing interpretation this results in a tax loss to HMRC where prompt payment discounts are not taken up.

HMRC says that the change announced in the Budget will 'protect the revenue' by putting it beyond doubt that UK VAT legislation on prompt payment discounts is aligned with EU VAT legislation and ensuring VAT is accounted for on the full consideration actually paid.

This measure came into force for supplies of telecommunication and broadcasting services 'where there is no obligation to provide a VAT invoice' made on and after 1 May 2014, that is to customers who are not VAT registered. For all other supplies the measure will have effect for supplies made on and after 1 April 2015, including all B2B supplies. If HMRC find other areas of VAT avoidance, targeted legislation will be brought forward to combat this prior to 1 April 2015 if considered necessary.

Clearly HMRC has identified a tax loss and the potential for future increasing losses, but there is a problem for businesses in the administrative difficulties in accounting for the changes.

Currently a business issues an invoice showing the VAT on the discounted amount and if the discount is not taken up there is no need to do anything and simply account for the VAT on the discounted amount.

HMRC says that from 1 April 2015 suppliers should issue a VAT invoice recording the VAT on the full price. If offering a PPD, suppliers must also show the rate of the discount offered. As the supplier will not know if the discount has been taken up until they are paid the supplier will need to decide which of the two procedures they will adopt to adjust their accounts in order to record a reduction in payment if a discount is taken-up.

Suppliers may either issue and retain a credit note to show the reduction in the payment received or, if they do not wish to issue a credit note, the invoice must contain the following information (in addition to the normal invoicing requirements):

- the terms of the PPD (PPD terms must include, but need not be limited to, the time by which the discounted price must be made); and

- a statement that the customer can only recover as input tax the VAT paid to the supplier.

Additionally HMRC say that it might be helpful for invoices to show:

- the discounted price;

- the VAT on the discounted price; and

- the total amount due if the PPD is taken up.

If a business has adopted the second option, the supplier will need to show proof of the receipt of the discounted price (eg a bank statement), the supplier can account for VAT on the amount actually received.

If the customer does not pay when the invoice is first issued, they must record the full price and VAT in their records shown on the invoice. If they subsequently decide to take up the PPD then if they have received an invoice setting out the PPD terms which states no credit note will be issued they may adjust the VAT in their records when payment is made. They should retain a document that shows the date and amount of payment (eg a bank statement) in addition to the invoice to evidence the reduction in consideration. Otherwise they will need to record any credit note received.

TURNOVER DISCOUNTS AND VOLUME REBATES

8.4   Prompt payment discounts should not be confused with turnover discounts or volume rebates. These are only earned after the event, being based on the value of purchases by the customer over a stated period of time. The price to the customer is then reduced by a credit note. It is up to the supplier and the customer to agree whether VAT should be added to the value of the credit. Naturally, a customer, who was unable to recover the original VAT, will want it to be included on the credit note.

HMRC issued *Revenue & Customs Brief 08/07* which gave useful guidance on manufacturers' 'cash back' discounts.

The term 'cash back' refers to a payment usually made by a manufacturer directly (or via a recovery agency) to the customer of a wholesaler or retailer. Similar payments can also be made under manufacturers' discount schemes (often referred to as 'volume bonuses'). Cash back payments like these occur outside the direct supply chain, and credit notes should not be used in relation to them.

HMRC say they are aware some businesses are treating cash backs incorrectly, and so are clarifying the issues to stop further confusion. HMRC say the VAT treatment of payments of this nature was laid down in two ECJ cases: *Elida*

Gibbs v Customs and Excise (C-317/94) [1997] QB 499 and *Commission of the European Communities v Germany* (C-427/98). Current HMRC policy is set out at Section 7.5 in VAT Notice 700/7, which states that manufacturers are entitled to reduce the output tax on their sales in respect of the 'cash backs', provided they charged and accounted for VAT on the original supply.

HMRC advise that if a business is VAT registered and receives a cash back relating to a taxable supply, this reduces the taxable value of its purchase, and it must reduce its input tax in the proportion in which it claimed it.

From 1 March 2007 businesses providing cash backs are entitled to reduce their output tax provided that they charged and accounted for VAT on their original supply. However, any cash back payments from a manufacturer to a customer that do not affect the wholesaler, do not require the wholesaler to make any VAT adjustments.

HMRC state that where cash backs are paid between businesses in different EU Member States, no VAT adjustments should be made.

In practice, this means that:

- where a UK manufacturer pays a cash back to a recipient in another Member State, the manufacturer cannot reduce his output tax; and

- where a UK recipient receives a cash back from a manufacturer in another Member State, no input tax deduction is required by the recipient.

HMRC close by stating that where the VAT liability of the goods changes in the supply chain (eg where a charity buys zero-rated goods from the wholesaler which were standard-rated for VAT when supplied by the manufacturer), manufacturers cannot reduce their output tax in relation to the cash back paid to the charity. Where the cash back relates to goods that were supplied VAT-free to a business receiving the cash back, no adjustments should be made.

See also **8.23**.

NO VAT ON FREE MEALS TO STAFF

8.5   If an employer makes provision in the course of catering of food or beverages to his employees, VAT is only due on the price he charges (*Sch 9, para 10*); so if the employer subsidises the canteen VAT is only due on the amount charged not the open market value. Thus, no VAT is due on free canteen meals. Any related input tax is reclaimable in full as it is a legitimate business expense.

ACCOMMODATION FOR STAFF IN HOTELS AND PUBS

8.6   The above rule for meals also applies to accommodation for employees in a hotel, inn, boarding house, or similar establishment. Although it is not clear from the wording in *para 10*, the relief is clearly meant to apply to accommodation for staff working there. For comments on bought-in accommodation, see **13.15** and **13.19**.

ANTI-AVOIDANCE RULES TO STOP ARTIFICIAL PRICING

8.7   The legislation is contained in *Sch 6, para 1,* and stops businesses reducing their non-recoverable input tax by, for instance, forming a management services company, which incurs all costs and recharges them to the main business at a lower price. HMRC can act retrospectively, and go back for four years by directing the substitution of market value for the price charged if a supply is:

● at an artificial price; and

● between connected persons; and

● the purchaser cannot recover its input VAT—being unregistered or partially exempt.

In *Oughtred & Harrison Ltd* (MAN/87/160 No 3174), the Tribunal confirmed the direction in a case where charges for use of a computer by an insurance broker had been at below cost.

PRIVATE USE OF A CAR FROM A MOTOR TRADER'S STOCK

8.8   Having recovered all the input tax on a new car held in stock, a manufacturer or trader must account for output tax on its private use if it is provided free of charge to a director or employee. HMRC have agreed with the *Society of Motor Manufacturers and Traders Ltd* a simplified method of calculating the VAT due. Details are published in an *Administrative Agreement* available from HMRC, which quotes lump sums payable depending upon the value of the car.

A similar agreement with the *Retail Motor Industry Federation* quotes figures for motor dealers who make demonstrator cars available for private use.

HMRC say that the agreed rates result in about £120–£140 per year per employee being payable. To prevent dealers avoiding this by an artificial charge to the employee, *Sch 6, para 1A* has been added by *FA 2004*. From 1 January 2005, HMRC can issue a direction substituting market value.

THE PARTY PLAN RULES

8.9   Businesses, which sell under the party plan system, often do so through unregistered representatives or demonstrators. If the latter buy and resell the goods, rather than take a commission as agents, the profit margin escapes VAT.

Schedule 6, para 2 gives the Commissioners power to prevent this by issuing a direction to the business to pay tax on market value rather than on the sale price, which it invoices to the representatives. In theory, this stops them competing unfairly with retail shops. The effect is that, to earn the same profit margin, they have to charge the same price as the shop.

That's the theory. In practice, prices of goods sold direct under the party plan system are not necessarily lower than those in ordinary shops. The system involves substantial selling costs and there may be little difference. Moreover, party plan directions catch businesses selling surplus stocks of, for instance, cosmetics to women in factories and offices who resell to their workmates. They also catch school photographers who sell to the schools, who resell to the parents.

Neither of these businesses competes directly with ordinary retailers, since the surplus stocks have already failed to sell through normal outlets, whilst the school photographers provide a different service to that of the high street photographer.

Any party plan direction that HMRC issues cannot be retrospective. However, that will be of little consolation. There is unlikely to be anything a business can do to challenge HMRC, because the subject has been well aired in the courts. In *Direct Cosmetics Ltd* ([1985] STC 479; [1988] STC 540), the client's case was referred to the ECJ twice, and confirmed HMRC's right to issue directions. More recently, *H Tempest Ltd* ([1993] VATTR 482 No 11210) has thoroughly ventilated the subject in relation to school photographs, also without success.

BARTER TRANSACTIONS—THE GROSS VALUES COUNT!

8.10

Focus

If a business trades goods or services in part payment for purchases, they must account for VAT on the gross values. VAT is a tax on transactions, not on the net money paid as reduced by something taken in part exchange.

If two businesses regularly buy and sell from each other, VAT is due on each transaction, not the net sum payable at the end of the month. This is important because either business may not be able to recover the VAT it incurs. If one could net off transactions against each other for VAT purposes, it would be easy to subvert the system!

The law is in *s 19* as explained shortly. The money paid is not the full measure of the deal.

Example 8.1— VAT on barter transactions

If you buy a new car for £10,000, and sell a commercial vehicle, such as a van, in part exchange for £4,000, you pay VAT on the £10,000, not on the net £6,000. The correct arithmetic is as follows:

	£	£
New motor car		10,000
Add VAT @ 20%		2,000
		£12,000
Less trade allowance on used van	4,000	
Add VAT	800	
		4,800
Net payment		£7,200

The net payment of £7,200 is the same as would have been arrived at by charging VAT on the value of the car less the trade-in allowance. However, the consequences of doing it the correct way are different.

Firstly, input tax on the new car of £2,000 is probably not recoverable. Secondly, the business must account for output tax of £800 on the van. The motor dealer accounts for £1,200, being his output tax less the input tax charged to him on the van. He recovers this input tax because he is buying a used commercial vehicle on which he will charge output tax when he sells it.

Thus, VAT is charged on the gross value of the deal, not the net cash paid.

Note: The sale of a second-hand car is exempt if you did not recover VAT when you bought it for use in your business.

'CONSIDERATION' MEANS MORE THAN JUST PAYMENTS RECEIVED

8.11   If the terms of a deal require your customer to do something in addition to paying money, there is 'non-monetary consideration'. In that case, VAT is due on the full value of the deal, not just on the money element.

> **Focus**
>
> This affects a variety of situations such as:
>
> - part exchange deals like the vehicle one explained above;
> - discount offers—special prices in certain situations;
> - 'gifts' which are not gifts because something has to be done in return.

8.12   The rule on non-monetary consideration is in *s 19(3)*. It states:

'If the supply is for a consideration not consisting or not wholly consisting of money, its value shall be taken to be such amount in money as, with the addition of the VAT chargeable, is equivalent to the consideration.'

It means that, if part of the price paid is not in money, VAT is due on the full value of the transaction. Thus, if a business swaps goods or services for other goods or services, they have to pay VAT on that full value.

HOW DOES A BUSINESS VALUE NON-MONETARY CONSIDERATION?

8.13   Usually, the value applicable is market value and, since that is a term readily understood in comparison with cost, it is used in this book. However, it is not necessarily the correct figure, which could be some other value that the two parties have attributed to the transaction.

For instance, in *Empire Stores Ltd* (LON/89/887 No 8859), gifts were offered to new mail-order customers which were not included in the catalogue, and, for which, there was no retail price. The Tribunal noted that the ECJ had stated in *Naturally Yours Cosmetics* ([1988] STC 879), a case quoted later, that a supply for non-monetary consideration is only taxable on its open market value if the parties have not themselves attributed a value to it. The taxable amount is, thus, to be ascertained subjectively. Since the recipient could only guess at the value, whereas Empire knew the cost, the latter was the value of the supply.

That view was confirmed in *Ping (Europe) Ltd* (MAN/99/74 No 17001: [2001] STC 1144: [2002] EWCA Civ 1115, [2002] STC 1186)—explained later at **8.22**. An exchanged golf club was held to be worth the subjective value to the supplier, not the objective difference between the sum paid and the normal retail price. Moreover, that objective difference was based on a hypothetical market, which could have existed had some customers preferred to sell their clubs together with the right to exchange rather than exercise it. The case concerned the actual exchanges by Ping, not hypothetical transactions.

The cases commented on below show that the subjective value depends upon the facts of each case. However, the judge in *Ping* referred to the sound taxation principle that no one should be accountable to tax on more than the value to him (that is the subjective value), of what he had received.

In *Bertelsmann AG* ([2001] STC 1153), the ECJ ruled that the value of goods given in return for introducing customers included the cost of delivery to the recipient.

In the case of *Loyalty Management UK Ltd v Revenue and Customs Comrs* ([2007] EWCA Civ 965), the appellant operated the Nectar loyalty scheme, under which there is a tripartite agreement between retailers, redeemers, and customers. Retailers would issue points to customers on a qualifying purchase and would pay the appellant a specified sum for each point, in addition to an annual fee for the marketing of the scheme. When sufficient points had been collected, they could be used to discount the price of reward goods or services. When the customer obtained the reward goods/services, the appellant would pay the redeemer an agreed value for these.

HMRC contended that when the appellant made a payment to suppliers in respect of points redeemed, the payment represented third party consideration by it in respect of the supplies of goods made to customers. The appellant, however, considered the payments to be consideration for a supply of redemption services offered by the supplier, which was taxable, and in connection with which, they were entitled to recover input tax.

The Court of Appeal overturned the High Court judgment, finding that the payments made by the appellant were indeed for redemption services and did not constitute third party consideration. HMRC have appealed the decision to the House of Lords, which has, in turn, referred the matter to the ECJ (C-53/09).

In the High Court case (which had found in favour of HMRC), Mr Justice Lindsay stated that this case differed from *Redrow,* in that the appellant had no discretion over what goods or services the end customer chose to redeem his points against. This distinction meant that *Redrow* had no judicial precedent to the appellant. However, the CA rejected this conclusion. It held that there was nothing in the *Redrow* case that suggested that its findings were restricted to instances where the end customer has no choice in what he would receive, and thus, it was applicable to the appellant.

The CA agreed with the Tribunal's approach, meaning that, for the transaction between the supplier and the customer, there was no sale at the list price. The customer, when redeeming points, had no obligation to pay the supplier. The supply of goods or services to the customer arose from the contractual arrangements which existed between the appellant and the supplier. Accordingly, the proper analysis of the transaction, under which the supplier provides goods or services to a customer in return for points, is that the supplier is providing a service to the appellant in assisting it to discharge its obligations to customers that they can acquire rewards in return for points. The CA further stated that he did not feel it necessary to refer questions to the ECJ, as the decisions in *Redrow* and *Plantiflor* were sufficient in interpreting the EC Legislation.

This is a positive decision for the taxpayer and other businesses with third party loyalty schemes. This CA judgment has extended the *Redrow* principle to situations where the end consumer has a choice about the goods or services he obtains. Businesses operating similar tripartite loyalty schemes should not have their input tax recovery restricted, and should now be considering the submission of repayment claims if applicable.

Consideration is sometimes difficult to spot. It can seem to the layman a tenuous concept—in English law it can be a peppercorn. The European view of consideration is somewhat different, as demonstrated in the *Boots* case explained below.

MONEY-OFF COUPONS

8.14   *Boots The Chemists* ([1990] STC 387) sold certain products with which purchasers got a 'money-off' coupon giving them a reduction in price if they then bought another product. The UK courts decided that there was non-monetary consideration in the form of the coupon. The customer only got the reduced price from the second product as a result of having bought the first one.

However, the ECJ ruled that the coupons were merely acknowledgement of the commitment to give the consumer a reduction on the second purchase. They had no value in themselves, so the value for VAT purposes of the second transaction was merely the money received.

See later in this chapter for more on this subject in the comment on the cases concerning vouchers.

SOME EXAMPLES OF NON-MONETARY CONSIDERATION

8.15   In *Naturally Yours Cosmetics* ([1988] STC 879), a company selling at private parties allowed the independent dealers, through whom it sold, to buy items of cosmetics at below the normal price. The dealers gave the cosmetics to party hostesses as rewards for recruiting hostesses for future parties. The ECJ held that, in addition to the money paid, there was further non-monetary consideration provided—the finding of more hostesses—so VAT was due on the full retail price.

Pippa Dee Parties Ltd ([1981] STC 495) sold clothes using the party plan system. A hostess could have a commission in cash of £4.57 per £100 of clothes sold at the party in her house; alternatively, she could choose £11.67

worth of clothes at catalogue value. Pippa Dee argued that it was only liable for output tax on the cash commission earned. Naturally, HMRC demanded it on the catalogue value.

The Divisional Court held that market value applied, as the hostess only obtained the right to the clothes by holding the party, which was non-monetary consideration. Output tax was therefore due on the catalogue value, not on the cash commission foregone.

Another case concerning this point is *Rosgill Group Ltd* ([1997] STC 811).

THE PROMOTIONAL GIFTS PROBLEM

8.16 As explained in Chapter 6, *So what must VAT be charged on?*, a business has to pay output VAT on the cost of goods which are given away, if the cost exceeds £50. If the business receives non-monetary consideration in return, they do not qualify as gifts. The result is:

- output tax is due whatever the value;

- and it is calculated on the market value of the gifts, not on their cost.

Thus, the non-monetary consideration rule catches some transactions which would not be caught under the gift rules, being below the £50 limit.

In *GUS Merchandise Corpn Ltd* ([1981] STC 569), a set of baking tins was held to be a reward to prospective mail order agents who:

- applied to become an agent with a view to obtaining future orders (consideration does not have to be instantaneous: 'give me the baking set now and I'll try and get you more orders'); and

- obtained an initial £10 order.

Both these actions were held to constitute consideration, and GUS were, thus, caught for output tax on the baking set. Had the gifts rules applied, they would have escaped due to the cost being under the limit.

AWARDS AND REWARDS

8.17 In Notice 700/7 (March 2002) *Business promotion schemes*, para 3.3, HMRC accept that a prize to a salesman for reaching a sales target or being the champion salesman, is not for non-monetary consideration, and is, therefore, a gift. This reasoning seems odd, since the goods are in return for achieving the sales target, or for selling more than anyone else. However, the point will usually not matter, since the goods will have been bought in at market value anyway.

HMRC also accept that a reward to a customer for buying more than a stated quantity is a gift.

SOME MORE COMPLICATED POINTS

8.18   So far, this chapter has dealt with the main points, which everyone needs to understand. From here on, it deals with some of the more sophisticated arguments, which have occurred concerning the value of supply of transactions, many of which are complicated and concern special situations.

INTEREST-FREE CREDIT

8.19   'Interest-free credit' is often offered by retailers. Granted, the customer only pays the normal price, despite doing so in instalments, but credit is not interest-free from a finance house. The finance company charges the retailer interest.

So, supposing that the retail value of the goods is	£1,000
and the finance house charges interest of	£100
so the retailer receives net	£900

Is the value of the sale by the retailer for VAT purposes £900 or £1,000?

The leading case on this is *Primback Ltd* (LON/92/1142 No 10460; CA [1996] STC 757; ECJ C-34/99; [2001] STC 803). The Tribunal held that the value of the goods was that invoiced to the customer. The deduction by the finance house was for interest. The Divisional Court agreed, but the Court of Appeal said the VAT was only due on the sum actually received by Primback via the finance house. The House of Lords then referred the matter to the ECJ, which held that the value of the sale was that agreed between Primback and its customer. The Court found it important that price did not vary whether the customer paid up front or by instalments through the finance house, and that the customer was unaware of the charge made by the finance house to Primback. Although Primback might allow a discount for immediate payment, it did not offer this; the customer had to ask for and negotiate it, and it would, therefore, not necessarily be the same amount as the commission charged by the finance house. The Court saw that commission as an expense of Primback incurred in order to increase its sales and to avoid having to accept payment by instalments.

The planning point there seems to be to sell the goods to the finance house at a reduced price, and for it to then sell them on to the customer at the retail value. Thus, in *A & D Stevenson (Trading) Ltd* (LON/97/696 No 17979), HMRC's arguments based on *Primback* were rejected, and a conditional sale agreement was held to involve a sale by the dealer to the finance company, the value of the supply being the sum the dealer got, ie it was net of the interest charged, not the full sale price agreed with the customer.

GOODS RETURNED OR REPOSSESSED UNDER HIRE-PURCHASE AGREEMENTS

8.20 The *Cars Order (SI 2006/874)* was amended so that, for finance agreements entered into from 13 April 2006, and, under which, a car was delivered on or after 1 September 2006, the disposal of it, if repossessed, is standard rated if the output tax on the original supply is adjusted.

Similarly, the *Special Provisions Order (SI 1995/1268)* was amended for finance agreements entered into from 13 April 2006 under which works of art, antiques and collector's items and second-hand goods were supplied on or after 1 September 2006.

These changes alter the advantageous situation gained in *General Motors Acceptance Corpn (UK) plc* (LON/01/242 No 17990: [2004] STC 577). It was held that the original value of supply under a hire-purchase agreement was reduced if the hirer exercised a right to return a car instead of making the outstanding payments. The reduced value was the sum paid plus the outstanding payments. It did not include the proceeds of the car, when sold by the hire-purchase company. That sale was outside the scope of VAT just as was the sale of a car repossessed because of a customer default (*Art 4(1)(a)* of *The Cars Order (SI 1992/3122)*).

The four-year limit did not apply to the reduction in value where the supply was over four years ago. *Article 11(C)(1)* of the *EC 6th VAT Directive* (see now *Directive 2006/112/EC, Art 90*), in allowing a Member State to impose conditions, did not permit it to limit that right.

This is a complicated case, and this is just a summary. See *VAT Information Sheet 06/2003* for more details. Having lost in the High Court, HMRC have accepted the decision—which applies to any goods, not just cars.

TRADE-IN VALUES OFFERED BY MOTOR DEALERS

8.21 When people part-exchange their cars, they like to feel that they are getting a good trade-in price for their existing vehicle. Motor dealers exploit this as part of their sales techniques, but often they either do not understand the VAT consequences, or they try to adjust the values subsequently. Consider the following example.

	£
Price of new car including VAT	15,000
Trade-in allowance for part exchange car	5,000
Net payment due	£10,000

If the dealer can only sell the part exchange car for £4,000, there will be a loss of £1,000 under the *Second-hand Goods Scheme*, which, under the rules explained in Chapter 31, cannot be offset against profits on other vehicles. Output tax will of course be due on the £15,000 paid for the new car.

If the dealer had reduced the price of the new car by a discount of £1,000 and shown the trade-in allowance as only £4,000, output tax on the new car would have been due on £14,000, not £15,000, and there would still be no output tax due under the *Second-hand Goods Scheme.* Many Tribunal cases have concerned attempts by dealers to alter the values in their records. The problem is, of course, that this is subsequent to the deal, and the customer is unaware of the change.

It is clear from the ECJ's decision in *Primback,* discussed above, that it saw the key to the answer as being the subjective value advertised and invoiced to the customer. In other words, if you tell the customer that the price is £x, you cannot argue that the VAT owed to HMRC should be based on £y. This supports the decisions in *North Anderson Cars Ltd* (EDN/97/93 No 15415; [1999] STC 902) and *Lex Service plc* (LON/98/287 No 16097; [2001] STC 697; [2001] EWCA Civ 1542; [2001] STC 1568: [2004] STC 73). In the *North Anderson* case, cars were sold under hire-purchase agreements to finance companies with trade-in values inflated, so as to create the necessary deposit required by the company. The Tribunal regarded these manual invoices as correctly stating the value of the supply, not the sales order forms and internal computer-generated sales invoices, which showed the realistic trade-in values as agreed with the customers.

In the *Lex* case, the value of supply of part-exchange cars was again held to be that agreed with the customers and shown in the documents, even in cases not financed under hire-purchase, rather than the lower sum repayable under a 30-day guarantee of satisfaction if the customer returned the car bought, and the trade-in car had already been sold.

Hartwell plc (LON/00/101 No 17065; [2002] STC 22; [2003] STC 396) solved the problem with *Purchase Plus Discount Notes* given to customers on top of the sum given for the trade-in vehicle. Those vouchers then formed part of the deposit required under the hire-purchase transaction for the replacement vehicle. This avoided inflating the price of the trade-in vehicle whilst assisting with the deposit required by the finance company. The Court of Appeal confirmed that the vouchers were not issued in return for any consideration, and were not part of the consideration for either vehicle. Thus, VAT was only due on the sum received from the finance company.

OTHER TRADE-IN SITUATIONS

8.22   In the case of *Alfred Bugeja* (LON/96/341 No 15586; [2000] STC 1) the Appellant sold videos at £20 each, which could then be exchanged for others for a further £10 a time. HMRC argued that the value of the later deals was £20, being the £10 cash plus the value at £10 of the video returned. The

Tribunal rejected that saying that, since Bugeja was obliged to accept the returned video, if it was in good condition, the value was £10 only. On appeal by HMRC, the High Court held that the consideration consisted partly of the £10 in cash, and partly of the second-hand video, since that could be resold. However, its value was the price at which Bugeja could buy in videos for stock. Finally, the Court of Appeal said that the second-hand video was worth £10 because that was the difference between the first time sale of £20 and the sum payable when a video was part-exchanged for another. Mr Bugeja would resell the part-exchange video for £10—or £20 on a first time sale.

In such a situation, the additional £1.49 payable on the part-exchange value would be a serious drain on profit. The solution appears to be to use *Global Accounting* under the *Second-hand Goods Scheme*. See Chapter 31.

If a retailer offers a trade-in allowance for, say, an old television set, which then has to be scrapped, HMRC normally accept that the allowance is in reality a discount off the price of the new set and the VAT is only due on cash received.

The case of *Ping (Europe) Ltd* (MAN/99/74 No 17001: [2001] STC 1144): [2002] STC 1186) concerned Ping Eye 2 irons declared not to conform to the rules of golf, and which players would therefore have to cease using. Ping offered to exchange them for a new conforming version at a special price of £22, which was just above cost. The normal wholesale price was £49.99 and the recommended retail price £72. HMRC of course argued that there was non-monetary consideration—the old club—and that the value of this was the price reduction from wholesale.

Ping received nothing for the surrendered clubs from the manufacturer, to which it returned them. The Tribunal noted that each surrendered club represented a burden on Ping, not an advantage to it. It would be surprising and unfair if Ping had to pay VAT on £49.99 for each new club supplied when it had only received £22. The difference between the latter and the wholesale price was likely to be a secret kept from a retail customer. If that reduction was unknown to the latter, it could not form the subjective value of the old club. The subjective value of it to Ping was nil so VAT was due on the £22. This was confirmed on appeal. The value in question of the returned club was that to Ping, not that to the owner returning it.

MORE ON DISCOUNTS, REBATES AND COMMISSIONS

8.23   A retrospective discount, such as a volume rebate, reduces the taxable value of the sales of a business, as noted earlier in this chapter. Sometimes, a commission can count as a discount too.

Directive 2006/112/EC, Art 79 (see also *Art 87*) (previously *Art 11(A)(3)* of the *EC 6th VAT Directive*) says:

'The taxable amount shall not include:

    (a)   price reductions by way of discount for early payment;

    (b)   price discounts and rebates granted to the customer and obtained by him at the time of the supply.'

Thus, if, as part of the marketing of a business, it offered price reductions, the question is whether they are:

- discounts or rebates, which reduce your taxable sales; or

- rewards to the recipient for doing something in return, which do not reduce the value of your taxable supplies.

An example of a rebate situation is *Co-operative Retail Services Ltd* (MAN/89/843 No 7527). Customers, who deposited at least £50, became members of the Co-op. They were entitled to a shareholder Visa card and to a 'dividend' of 5% on all non-food purchases, which was credited annually into the share account. HMRC argued that this was a distribution of profit. The Tribunal found that it was a contractual obligation to the members rather than a share of net profit, and that it could, therefore, be treated as a rebate on taxable sales. The use of the word 'dividend' was irrelevant because this had a double meaning in the co-operative movement.

It did not matter that the customer had to be a member in order to qualify, and to have a minimum balance in their share account. Many companies offered benefits to shareholders. Once they had purchased goods, they were entitled to the 5%, subject only to retaining that balance. It was, in that sense, accounted for at the time of supply, and it did not matter that it was only credited annually. The Tribunal held that a discount must mean something different to a rebate, and that the latter was the relevant word here.

Littlewoods Organisation plc (MAN/98/99 No 16318; [2000] STC 588; [2001] EWCA Civ 1542; [2001] STC 1568) offered discounts to mail-order agents. The agent earned a commission of 10% when she paid for goods bought either for herself or for a customer, and an additional 2.5% if she used the commission to buy additional goods rather than offset it against the outstanding balance on her account or take it in cash. HMRC accepted that the commission was a reduction in the price of goods if it was taken in cash. They also accepted that 10% was a discount if additional goods were bought—so that the transactions were treated the same. However, they argued that the extra 2.5% was payment for the service of generating sales to customers.

The Tribunal found the 2.5% to be an extra discount. The Divisional Court disagreed, saying that it was a further payment for finding the customers but the Court of Appeal overruled that. There was no direct link between the 2.5% and the sales to customers. It was only credited to the agent as the payments were received, and was indeed an extra discount on the price of the further goods.

In the case of *Everest Ltd v Revenue & Customs* [2010] UKFTT 621 (TC) the Appellant supplied home improvement products and services to members of the general public. Everest is a well-known supplier and fitter of double-glazing and other related home improvement products and services, such as replacement windows, doors and conservatories.

A customer can choose to pay for Everest's supply by paying a deposit and then taking out a loan with Clydesdale Financial Services Ltd ('Clydesdale'), subject to receiving credit approval.

In Everest's experience, the order value is higher if funded by credit than if paid in cash by the customer. In addition, if the customer opens a loan account with Clydesdale, Everest receives commission from Clydesdale. Clydesdale can recover any commission paid to Everest if the customer settles the loan account within four months of the advance date. Clydesdale also pays Everest the full net cash price of the home improvement supplied to the customer, ie the full price minus the deposit paid by the customer.

Everest's promotional literature makes reference to various discounts and promotions offered. One such promotional offer was a 'cash back' of 10%: Everest told its potential customers that if they open a loan account and keep it open for at least 180 days after the loan is taken out, they will pay the customer 10% of the amount of the loan. This is described by Everest as a 'cash back' offer.

Everest's practice was to adjust its VAT account to reduce its VAT liability if it paid 10% of the loan amount to the customer, as it treated the amount paid to the customer as a reduction in the customer's consideration for its supply.

It is agreed that the above arrangements give rise to three distinct supplies:

- First, there is a home improvement supply from Everest to the customer. The consideration for this supply is the payment by the customer.

- Secondly, there is the exempt supply of credit by Clydesdale to the customer. The consideration for this supply is the payment of interest from the customer to Clydesdale.

- Thirdly, there is the supply of introduction services from Everest to Clydesdale, ie the introduction of Everest's customer by them to Clydesdale. The consideration for this supply is the payment of commission from Clydesdale to Everest.

HMRC wrote to Everest in April 2006 and informed them that they considered that the 'cash back' offer was an inducement for the customer to enter into a loan agreement with a third party. HMRC therefore stated that Everest was not entitled to reduce the value of its supply by the value of the payments made to customers under the 'cash back' scheme.

Having considered all of the facts the Tribunal found in favour of Everest and agreed that the 'cash back' was a discount and the VAT due on the transaction had been properly reduced.

THE TIME OF SUPPLY OF A DISCOUNT

8.24 In *Freemans plc* (Case C-86/99: [2001] STC 960), the ECJ held on 29 May 2001 that a discount could only be deducted from the value of a supply at the time at which it was used by the recipient. Freemans credited a sum to the account of an agent each time a payment was received. The agent could then either draw it in cash or use it to buy other goods. The time of supply of the original sale was when the products were adopted by the agent, and at that time, the amount payable by the agents was the full catalogue price. The 10% credits only occurred later as and when instalments of purchase price were paid, and the value of supply of Freeman's sales was only reduced when the agent used those credits.

BOOK TOKENS, GIFT VOUCHERS AND TELEPHONE CARDS

8.25 Face value vouchers, such as book tokens, gift vouchers and telephone cards, issued on or before 8 April 2003, were only taxable at the time of issue to the extent that the price paid exceeded the face value, ie on any commission or service charge (*Sch 5, para 6*). VAT was due on the goods or services supplied when the voucher was redeemed.

That was the case for vouchers issued since then, but, to prevent certain avoidance schemes, the rules have been changed to repeal *para 6* and substitute *Sch 10A* as explained below.

However, in order to simplify the treatment of vouchers, new rules have been introduced for vouchers issued after 1 January 2019. The rules outlined below apply to any vouchers issued before 1 January 2019.

Retailer and credit vouchers

8.26 A retailer voucher is one issued by a trader, who will either redeem it for goods or services, or will reimburse another trader who does so. A gift voucher is an example.

A credit voucher is one issued by an organisation, such as a trade association, which will not redeem it, but will reimburse the trader, who does.

In both cases, the initial issue price of the voucher is outside the scope of VAT—unless the trader redeeming it fails to account for the VAT due on the goods or services supplied against it. Any subsequent sales of retailer vouchers by other traders are subject to VAT as explained below at **8.30**. That does not apply to credit vouchers.

In the case of *Leisure Pass Group Ltd* (VTD 20,910), the Appellant sells the 'London Pass', which is a pass enabling holders to get entry to a number of attractions in London without further payment. It charges customers for the pass, and then pays the owner of the relevant attractions at an agreed rate if a pass holder uses the pass to gain entry. Some of the attractions included in the pass were exempt cultural bodies.

At Tribunal, HMRC argued that the pass was not a voucher, and that VAT was due on the sale of the pass. LPG argued that the pass was a face value credit voucher, with the result being that no VAT should be charged on its issue. Instead, VAT was due on the redemption of the pass by the attractions (assuming the attraction is not exempt). The case turned on whether the pass represented a right to receive goods or services to the value of an amount stated on it or recorded in it, as per *para 1* of *Sch 10A* to *VATA 1994*.

This argument was first run unsuccessfully in Tribunal in 2007 (appealed unsuccessfully to the High Court in 2008) with a version of the pass which had no stated value or monetary limit. The Appellant had argued that it had recorded in it the value of all the attractions put together, as this was the maximum value available to the holder. This argument was dismissed on the basis that this was a meaningless value, and that, effectively, there was no monetary limit to the pass, as the only limit was a temporal one, namely the duration of the validity of the pass (anything from one to six days depending on the price paid).

The terms of the pass were then amended so that it had a monetary limit of £70 per day. A chip in the pass calculates the value of the holder's daily entries and blocks entry once this limit is reached. The new Tribunal agreed that following this change, the pass fell within the definition of a face value voucher.

HMRC argued that it would be contrary to the basic principles of VAT if the Appellant's profits were not taxed, but the Tribunal dismissed this argument. It said it is a commercial reality that issuers and intermediaries buying and selling credit vouchers will almost invariably do so at a profit having agreed discounts on the face value of the vouchers. Without this, there would be no point in them making the supplies. As the legislation provides for certain vouchers to be bought and sold by intermediaries without attracting VAT, the legislators must have envisaged that the intermediaries' profits in this case should not bear any VAT.

Electronic and top up vouchers

8.27 Electronic vouchers are treated in the same way as paper ones. That covers, for instance, top up cards, which do not bear a face value, the sums being recorded electronically. See *Business Brief 29/03* for more comments on telephone cards, including that, when bought from outside the UK, they are taxed under the reverse charge rules—explained in Chapter 23, *Exports and Imports of Services*.

Postage stamps

8.28   Postage stamps remain outside the scope of VAT as before. The eventual supply of postal services by the Post Office is of course exempt.

Other kinds of face value voucher

8.29   Other kinds of face value voucher not covered above are taxed when sold at the rate applicable to the goods or services against which they will be redeemed. If different rates are involved, an apportionment must be made on a just and reasonable basis.

Sales to and by intermediaries

8.30   A retailer can still reduce its own output tax by selling retailer vouchers at a discount to an associated company. The rules are as follows:

- the retailer does not account for the VAT included in that discounted price until it redeems the vouchers;

- however, the intermediary can recover that tax as input VAT, but needs a tax invoice;

- to sort this situation, HMRC suggest in *VAT Information Sheet 03/2003* that the retailer issues a VAT invoice and states on it, as justification for not immediately paying the VAT shown on it: '*The issuer of the voucher will account for output tax under the face value voucher provisions introduced in Sch 10A VAT Act 1994*'. The invoice should also show the percentage split at different rates of VAT, if applicable, and if known at the time of sale; see below;

- when the intermediary then sells the vouchers on, it must charge VAT. If it can show that the vouchers will be redeemed against non-standard rated supplies, the intermediary can use a percentage split to calculate the VAT due, based on information from the redeemer. The split can be on an average basis, such as retail scheme percentages. If the information is not available at the time of the sale, the adjustment can be retrospective.

These rules stop avoidance schemes based on *Argos Distributors Ltd* (MAN/ 94/307 No 13025: ECJ C-288/94: [1996] STC 1359). Argos sold vouchers at a discount from face value to other organisations which typically used them as incentives for staff or customers. The ECJ said that, when the voucher was redeemed by Argos, it only had to account for VAT on the sum it had received.

This meant that a voucher could be sold at a discount to an associated company, which could resell it outside the scope at a profit. The profit thus escaped VAT. Taxing the sales by intermediaries prevents that.

However, in the case of *HMRC v Associated Newspapers Limited* [2015] UKUT 641 (TCC) the Upper Tribunal found that the provision of free vouchers redeemable at high street retailers as part of a business promotion scheme was not a supply of services and no output tax was therefore due on them. It also found that Associated Newspapers Limited ('ANL') was entitled to recover the input tax on the purchase of the vouchers. From Royal Assent of the *Finance Act 2012* (17 July 2012) single purpose face value vouchers will be taxed when they are issued. This will affect all single purpose vouchers, whether credit, retailer or other types of voucher.

A single purpose face value voucher is one that carries the right to receive only one type of goods or services which are all subject to a single rate of VAT. For example, where a prepaid telephone card can only be redeemed for telecommunication services it will be a single purpose voucher.

As the announced changes remove single purpose vouchers from *Sch 10A*, the special rules for face value vouchers will no longer apply.

Instead, where a single purpose voucher is sold both initially and by retailers or distributors, it is treated as a supply of the goods or services for which it can be redeemed. This will apply whether the voucher is issued by the person from whom it can be redeemed or by a third party.

Vouchers supplied with other goods or services

8.31   If a business includes a voucher with goods or services at a price which is the same as, or not significantly different to, the normal one, the voucher is treated as supplied for no consideration. This prevents one reducing a taxable supply by the value of a voucher in circumstances such as:

- a hotel issues vouchers to customers when they pay their bills—knowing that few will return and redeem them;

- a retailer offers a voucher with sales above a certain value but with restrictions which limit the number of customers able to redeem it;

- a mobile phone includes a telephone card but the customer cannot reduce the price by rejecting the card.

In *Hartwell plc* (LON/00/101 No 17065; [2002] STC 22; [2003] STC 396), the Court of Appeal held that no part of the sale value of a car could be attributed to MOT vouchers included with it, the sale price not having been split on the invoice.

In *Tesco plc* ([2002] EWHC 2131 (Ch); [2002] STC 1332; CA [2003] STC 1561), the High Court held that Clubcard points were the offer of a discount on future purchases, so the reduction in the sales value was of the redemption goods, not that of the sale against which they were issued. The CA then held that, in any case, it was the points, which were obtained on the initial purchase, not the vouchers. Since the vouchers were only issued once sufficient points had been earned by the customer, they could not be a discount on the initial purchase.

New rules relating to vouchers from 1 January 2019

8.31A   These changes introduce legislation providing for the VAT treatment of vouchers issued on or after 1 January 2019. It affects only vouchers for which a payment has been made and which will be used to buy something. The measure does not apply to vouchers issued before 1 January 2019, for which existing rules will continue to apply.

Vouchers in this context are gift cards and gift tokens, with examples including simple book tokens, gift vouchers, and electronic vouchers purchased from specialist businesses. The changes do not apply to discount vouchers or money-off tokens.

Under current UK VAT legislation, the customer is deemed to be receiving two supplies:

(1)   a voucher; and

(2)   an underlying supply of goods or services.

The measure makes it clear that for VAT purposes there will no longer be a separate supply of a voucher. Instead the rules will be simplified so that there is only the supply of the underlying goods or services, which will be provided in exchange for the voucher at a later date.

The new rules will introduce some new concepts and changes in the chain of buying and selling certain types of voucher but, from the consumer's perspective, there should not be any noticeable change. A £50 voucher will still buy £50 worth of identifiable goods or services from one or more identifiable supplier.

The effect of the new rules is that many more vouchers will become 'Single Purpose vouchers', meaning that the issuer will have to account for VAT at an earlier date than under the old rules and will no longer obtain the benefit of non-redemption ('breakage') of vouchers. The value on which VAT is to be accounted will also be different and intermediaries selling certain vouchers will no longer make a supply of the voucher.

From 2019, a voucher will be regarded as a Single Purpose voucher where the place of supply of the ultimate goods or services is known at the time the voucher is issued and where the voucher can only be used for goods/services at a single rate of VAT. VAT will be due on such a voucher when it is issued and not when the goods or services are actually provided, so VAT will still be due even if it is never used. Any subsequent sale of a single purpose voucher will be treated as a supply of the underlying goods or service and VAT accounted for as appropriate.

Under the current VAT rules, a voucher that can be used for different goods or services is not a single purpose voucher, even if the underlying supplies are liable to VAT at the same rate, so VAT is only due when it is redeemed. This change of definition will, therefore, affect businesses that issue vouchers covering different goods or services that are liable to VAT at the same rate. To determine whether they will be affected by this change, businesses should review which goods or services can be purchased with the voucher and if the voucher can be used in a number of countries.

As at present, a voucher that is not classified as a single purpose voucher will be classified as a 'multi-purpose voucher' for VAT purposes and VAT will only be payable by the issuer when the goods or services are actually provided. However, there are other changes that will affect the sale of such a voucher. The VAT will no longer be due on the price that the voucher was sold for (as was decided in the 1996 ECJ judgment in *Argos*). Instead, VAT will be due on the price paid by the last person who purchased the voucher or, if that price is not known, on the face value of the voucher. Although an issuer of a multi-purpose voucher will account for VAT at the same time as they do now, from 2019 the VAT may be due on a higher price.

The new rules will also affect intermediaries selling multi-purpose vouchers in their own name, as the sale of such a voucher by an intermediary will no longer be treated as a supply for VAT purposes. This means that the intermediary will no longer be able to issue a VAT invoice for such a sale and will not be able to recover input tax in relation to the supply of the voucher. Intermediaries may therefore need to re-visit their business model and act as an agent for the sale of such vouchers instead of selling them in their own name. If they only act as an agent their turnover would then fall.

Discount vouchers

8.32   A voucher, which offers a discount, is not a face value voucher and is taxable when sold, as was held in *F & I Services Ltd* (LON/98/869 No 15958: [2000] STC 364). The books of vouchers, which offered discounts on various goods and services, did not give the right to them, merely to a reduction from the normal price.

Cash-back coupons

8.33   A manufacturer, that offers consumers refunds against cash-back coupons printed on the packaging of its products, can deduct their value from its taxable sales.

In *Elida Gibbs Ltd v C & E Comrs* ((C-317/94) [1996] STC 1387), the goods had, of course, first been sold to the wholesaler or retailer at the normal price.

HMRC objected to the reduction because the repayment was to a third party, the retail customer. The ECJ said a basic VAT principle was to tax only the final consumer on the price paid by that consumer. Gibbs should be taxed on the sum received net of the repayment. Otherwise, HMRC would collect tax on more than the consumer paid.

THE VALUE OF A VOUCHER WHEN REDEEMED

8.34 Following *Elida Gibbs*, *Yorkshire Co-operatives Ltd* (MAN/97/ 207 No 15821: C-398/99: [2003] STC 234) argued that the value of a sale for which it accepted a price reduction voucher was just the cash element, and that the subsequent refund of the value of the voucher by the manufacturer was a rebate or discount. The ECJ rejected that, holding that the value of the supply to the consumer included sums paid by the third party, the manufacturer.

Focus

The value of the taxable supply is not reduced by a discount given by another party.

The ECJ ruled on 19/6/03, in *First Choice Holidays plc* ((C-149/01) [2003] STC 934), that a tour operator must account for VAT on the full price paid to it by travel agents. It could not reduce the value of its supply by discounts allowed to customers, and funded by the travel agents out of their commissions.

GOODS GIVEN IN RETURN FOR ACCUMULATED STAMPS OR POINTS

8.35 If a business give its customers stamps or points, which they can redeem in due course against 'free gifts', output tax is due on those gifts if their cost exceeds the limit explained in the comment on the gifts rules earlier in this chapter.

Kuwait Petroleum (GB) Ltd (LON/95/2338 Nos 14,668 & 16,582: ECJ C-48/97; [1999] STC 488) failed with an argument that the gifts were included in the price charged for its fuel, and that, therefore, no further output tax was due. The petrol station sold the fuel to the motorist on the basis that he would receive 'sails' in relation to the volume of fuel bought. The sails were tokens with a minute cash value. Under the rules of the promotion, Kuwait promised to redeem the sails against redemption goods as chosen. Only when the motorist handed in sails at the garage, did Kuwait become liable to do that. The Tribunal found that the sails were, in this sense, obtained 'free of charge'. In buying the petrol, the motorist was not making a part payment towards possibly acquiring the redemption goods. On referral to the ECJ, the latter supported the Tribunal's view that:

- there was no agreement between the customer and the petrol station that part of the price paid for the fuel was for the sails or for the redemption goods;

- the latter were supplied otherwise than for a consideration and were therefore taxable under the gifts rules.

In the case of *Total UK Ltd v Revenue and Customs Comrs* ([2007] EWCA Civ 987), the taxpayer entered into a sales promotions scheme whereby it provided customers with £5 gift vouchers for buying fuel at their filling stations. The vouchers could be redeemed at certain national retailers (eg Boots), and were earned by collecting 'points' for each litre of fuel purchased. Total sought to reduce the output tax due on the supply of the fuel by the value of the voucher which it purchased from the retailers.

The Tribunal had earlier decided (VTD 19,502) that the taxable turnover could not be so reduced. However, the High Court had later allowed Total's appeal against the Tribunal decision, finding that the issue of the gift voucher was part of the supply chain involving the supply of fuel and that the principle of neutrality required the reduction for which the appellant contended. Accordingly, the Tribunal's decision was incorrect.

By a 3–0 majority, the Court of Appeal overturned the High Court's decision, and ruled in favour of HMRC that the consideration for the supply of fuel could be reduced by the value of the vouchers purchased by Total. Total had asked the Court to refer the matter to the ECJ, but this was declined by the Court.

DEDUCTIONS BY CREDIT PROVIDERS FROM PAYMENTS TO RETAILERS

8.36 When a retailer submits credit card slips to a credit card company, the latter deducts a discount from its payment to the retailer. However, this is not a reduction in the latter's taxable sales. *Diners Club Ltd* (CA [1989] STC 407) established that it is payment for the financial service of extending credit to and collecting payment from the cardholder.

Similarly, in *Kingfisher plc* (LON/09/990 No 16332 affd [2000] STC 992), discounts deducted from the value of Provident vouchers paid to retailers were payment for the exempt service of dealing in money, not a reduction in the taxable supply made by Kingfisher.

Chapter 9

So what is reduced-rated?

SIGNPOSTS

- A reduced rate of 5% applies to a number of items included in *Sch 7A* to the *VAT Act 1994* details of which are covered in this chapter (see **9.1–9.14**)

9.1   The reduced rate rules are in *Sch A1*. From 1 November 2001, they were moved to a new *Sch 7A*. They have been expanded in recent years although the coverage is still limited. If any of the more important zero-ratings, such as for food, books or children's clothing, were to be abandoned, it would probably be the 5% reduced rate which would then apply rather than the standard rate.

THE CONTENTS OF SCHEDULE 7A

9.2

Focus

Group 1 Domestic fuel and power

Group 2 Installation of energy-saving materials

Group 3 Grant funded installation of heating equipment or security goods or connection of gas supply

Group 4 Women's sanitary products

Group 5 Children's car seats

Group 6 Residential conversions

Group 7 Residential renovations and alterations

Group 8 Contraceptive products

Group 9 Welfare advice or information

Group 10 Installation of mobility aids for the elderly—from 1 April 2007

Group 11 Smoking cessation products—from 1 April 2007

Group 12 Caravans—from 6 April 2013

Group 13 Small cabled suspended transport systems—from 1 April 2013

At the time of writing, the reduced rate is 5%.

Several of the above Groups are of limited general interest. For comment on *Groups 6 and 7* concerning the conversion, renovation or alterations of certain buildings, see Chapter 26, *Property*. Below are some brief comments on the remainder.

DOMESTIC FUEL AND POWER—SCH 7A GROUP 1

9.3 *Group 1* covers coal, gas, fuel oil, electricity etc when sold for:

- domestic use; or

- use by a charity for non-business purposes (removed from 1 August 2013).

Domestic use means in a dwelling, for a relevant residential purpose, for self-catering holiday accommodation and for a caravan or houseboat.

Relevant residential purpose is defined in *Note 7(1)*, which is the same as *Note (4)* to *Sch 8, Group 5*. See Chapter 26 on *Property*.

There are various de minimis quantities such as, for fuel oil, up to 2,300 litres, for which the supply is always deemed to be for domestic use. Alternatively, if at least 60% of the supply qualifies, the entire sum can be reduced rated. Otherwise, it must be apportioned.

INSTALLATION OF ENERGY-SAVING MATERIALS— SCH 7A GROUP 2

9.4 *Group 2* covers both supplying the materials and installing them in residential accommodation. Up to 1 August 2013 it also applied to a building intended for use solely for a relevant residential purpose.

Energy-saving materials (ESM) does not just mean insulation and draught stripping. It includes central heating and hot water system controls, solar panels, wind and water turbines, ground source heat pumps and, from 7/4/05, air source heat pumps and micro combined heat and power units.

From 1 January 2006, boilers designed to be fuelled solely by wood, straw or similar vegetable matter were added.

The scope of the reduced rate is very tightly drawn, and is only applicable to the supply and installation (as a single supply) of certain specified materials whose primary purpose is energy saving.

The installation of materials whose energy-saving potential is only secondary to their primary purpose does not qualify for the reduced rate. For example, the supply and installation of a condensing boiler is not included in this relief, as its primary purpose is to provide heat.

In *Revenue and Customs Brief 9 (2018): VAT – damp proofing products*, HMRC clarified its policy on the VAT liability of damp proofing products like paints, creams and gels from 1 September 2018. These products are not eligible for reduced rating as energy-saving materials and are therefore subject to standard rated VAT from 1 September 2018.

This group should not be confused with *Group 3* under which, for instance, a central heating system must be grant funded.

Residential accommodation means dwellings, including caravans permanently lived in and houseboats, together with buildings used for a relevant residential purpose. The latter is as defined in *Group 1*. That is to say it is the same definition as in *Sch 8, Group 5* re constructing buildings—as is also the definition of *relevant charitable purpose*. See Chapter 26 on *Property*.

Beware of the distinction between the supply and installation of the materials in an existing building, and work which creates something new. In *BECO Products Ltd/BAG Building Contractors* (MAN/01/4 No 18638), the construction of extensions to houses using *Wallform* polystyrene building blocks was held to be standard-rated because the nature of the contract was construction work. To qualify for the reduced rate as insulating materials, the blocks had to be supplied separately.

In the case of *Pinevale Limited v Revenue & Customs* [2014] UKUT 0202 (TCC), the Upper Tribunal found for HMRC on the issue of whether roof panels manufactured and installed in conservatories qualified as energy-saving materials.

The roof panels were used to form the roof of a conservatory, either replacing or constituting the entire roof, or replacing parts of an existing roof. Their purpose was to achieve much higher levels of insulation than would be the case with a conventional conservatory roof, including a double glazed roof.

Pinevale argued that the panels were 'insulation for roofs' because they provided insulation by forming a barrier to reduce or stop heat loss or, in summer, heat gain. HMRC's case was that the panels are not 'insulation for roofs', but were the roof itself. So, if an entire existing roof is replaced, the panels constitute the new roof, not just insulation for a roof. Likewise, the replacement of individual panels with Pinevale's panels was the supply of new roof panels, not the supply of insulation for a roof.

The Upper Tribunal agreed with HMRC and their appeal was therefore allowed.

However in the case of *Wetheralds Construction Ltd v HMRC* [2016] UKFTT 827 (TC) a Solid Roof System was applied to the exterior of the roof which was covered by heat reflective plastic tiles which give the impression of a tiled roof. The Tribunal decided that what the appellant provided to its customers was a system to make a conservatory far more useable and liveable in for a much longer time in the year and from the evidence that was presented a customer wanted a fully insulated conservatory and not a replacement roof.

The Tribunal decided that since the entire supply by the appellant of the Solid Roof System was a single supply, and it was a single supply of insulation for roofs, it followed that the entire supply fell to be reduced-rated, so the Tribunal found in favour of the appellant. On 21 June 2012, the EC published a Reasoned Opinion which is the first public step in the process of taking infringement action against the UK in respect of its reduced rate for ESM (whether installed in residential accommodation or in buildings intended for use solely for a relevant charitable purpose). HMRC's view is that the reduced rate for the installation of ESM in residential accommodation is consistent with the VAT Directive and it will be defending this. However, from 1 August 2013 the reduced rate for ESM installed in a building intended for use solely for a relevant charitable purpose has been withdrawn subject to certain transitional rules.

On 4 June 2015, the European Court of Justice (CJEU) published its decision (C161/14) *European Commission v United Kingdom* and found against the UK and Ireland. The result of this is that the UK will now have to change the law and remove the 5% reduced rate of VAT from the installation of most energy-saving materials. Among the items affected will be microcombi boilers, insulation and solar panels.

This case was brought by the EU Commission who viewed the UK and Ireland's approach as overly generous. The CJEU agreed with the EU Commission and ruled that the reduced rate on both installation services and the energy saving materials themselves should be removed if the sales are not part of either 'the provision, construction, renovation and alteration of housing, as part of a social policy' or the 'renovation and repairing of private dwellings'.

In addition to this, even if the sales are part of the renovation and repair of private dwellings, the reduced rating should not apply if those sales include materials that account for a significant part of the value of the services supplied, which would certainly adversely affect the installation of solar panels.

The UK had defended the application of the 5% VAT rate, stating that its application of the reduced VAT rate was for 'social policy' purposes and linked to the UK's Green Deal to improve the energy efficiency of buildings.

In December 2015 HMRC released a policy paper detailing the proposed legislative changes and will effect supplies made after 1 August 2016. The measure amends the reduced rate of 5% VAT on the installation of certain energy saving materials retaining as much of the relief as permissible under EU law following a judgement of the CJEU. The changes:

- retain the remainder of the relief in full (subject to the second bullet point below):

  — for all existing customers except where the cost of the goods installed is greater than the labour cost of installing those goods. In that situation, the labour only will be subject to the reduced rate and the goods installed will be subject to the standard rate (VAT at 20%);

  — the goods installed will still be subject to the reduced rate irrespective of whether its cost is greater than the labour cost if the customer is over 60 years of age, on certain benefits, is a building used solely for a relevant residential purpose or a relevant housing associations;

- withdraw the reduced rate from the installation of solar panels, wind turbines and water turbines.

See VAT Notice 708/6 for details.

CERTAIN GRANT FUNDED WORK—SCH 7A GROUP 3

9.5   *Group 3* covers a range of supplies but only when they are grant-funded, and to people aged 60 or over or who are in receipt of certain benefits.

If you think that a supply might be covered, read the rules carefully.

The *VAT (Reduced Rate) Order 1998 (SI 1998/1375)* introduced a reduced rate of 5% VAT for the grant-funded installation—in the homes of less well-off people (those on certain specific benefits)—of the following energy-saving materials:

- insulation for walls, floors, ceilings, roofs, lofts, water tanks, pipes and other plumbing fittings;

- draught stripping for windows and doors;

- central heating system controls; and

- hot water system controls.

This relief applied to supplies made on and after 1 July 1998. The effect of the Order was to add new provisions to the then Reduced Rate Schedule, *Sch A1* to the *VAT Act 1994*. This was done to make the grant-funding go further, allowing more vulnerable households to benefit.

The relief covered all the supplies made under the Government's Home Energy Efficiency Scheme (HEES), to the extent that the installation was paid for by grant-funding.

GRANT-FUNDED INSTALLATION OF 'HEATING SYSTEMS MEASURES' AND 'QUALIFYING SECURITY GOODS'

9.6   In order to reflect the 2000 extension of the HEES, the relief was extended to the grant-funded installations of the following 'heating system measures':

- gas room heaters with thermostatic control;

- electric storage heaters;

- closed solid fuel fire cassettes;

- electric dual immersion water heaters with foam-insulated water tanks;

- gas-fired boilers;

- oil-fired boilers; and

- radiators.

Also, under a Home Office scheme linked to the HEES, the grant-funded installation of the following 'qualifying security goods' was included in the relief:

- locks and bolts for windows;

- locks, bolts and security chain for doors;

- spy holes; and

- smoke alarms.

See VAT Notice 708/6 for details.

WOMEN'S SANITARY PRODUCTS—SCH 7A GROUP 4

9.7   *Group 4* covers tampons, panty liners, and sanitary belts, but not incontinence products, protective briefs, or any other form of clothing.

CHILDREN'S CAR SEATS—SCH 7A GROUP 5

9.8   *Group 5* includes seats designed for use also with a framework as a pushchair, together with booster seats and cushions. From 1 July 2009, the reduced rate also applies to children's car seat bases.

RESIDENTIAL CONVERSIONS—SCH 7A GROUP 6

9.9   See below.

RESIDENTIAL RENOVATIONS AND ALTERATIONS— SCH 7A GROUP 7

9.10   *Groups 6* and *7* deal with conversions of buildings into living accommodation of various kinds, and with the renovation or alteration of living accommodation which has been empty for at least two years. The time limit had been three years prior to 1 January 2008, but was reduced in *Revenue & Customs Brief 74/07*. For full coverage of the rules, see Chapter 26 on *Property*.

CONTRACEPTIVE PRODUCTS—SCH 7A GROUP 8

9.11   *Group 8* covers supplies of contraceptive products including emergency contraception—unless they are zero-rated on prescription, or they qualify for exemption under *item 4 Group 7 Sch 9*, ie part of exempt care in a hospital. It does not include any product designed to monitor fertility or used for natural family planning.

WELFARE ADVICE OR INFORMATION—SCH 7A GROUP 9

9.12   *Group 9* relates to welfare advice, or information supplied by a charity or by a state-regulated private welfare institution or agency.

It means advice or information directly related to the physical or mental welfare of elderly, sick, distressed or disabled persons, or the care or protection of children and young persons.

It does not affect the exemption under *Group 6 Sch 9* of any supply by an eligible body. Nor does it cover goods unless they are supplied wholly or almost wholly for the purpose of conveying the advice or information.

It further does not cover supplies provided solely to benefit a particular individual or according to his personal circumstances.

INSTALLATION OF MOBILITY AIDS FOR THE ELDERLY—SCH 7A GROUP 10

9.13   Since 1 July 2007 a 5% reduced rate has been applicable to certain housing alterations for persons over 60 years of age. The reduced rate applies to the services of installation of mobility aids and the mobility aids themselves for use in domestic properties.

SMOKING CESSATION PRODUCTS—SCH 7A GROUP 11

9.14   'Over the counter' sales of smoking cessation products, such as chewing gum and patches, became subject to the 5% reduced rate with effect from 1 July 2007. This was initially for a period of one year, but in Budget 2008, it was extended indefinitely by the *Value Added Tax (Reduced) (Smoking Cessation Products) Order 2008 (SI 2008/1410)*.

CARAVANS—SCH 7A GROUP 12

9.15   These changes apply to supplies of affected caravans that are made on or after 6 April 2013. The sale of a caravan will be reduced-rated if it is longer than 7m or wider than 2.55m, and is not manufactured to BS 3632:2005.

Caravans that are less than 7m or wider than 2.55m are standard-rated and those that are manufactured to BS 3632:2005 are zero-rated.

SMALL CABLE-SUSPENDED TRANSPORT SYSTEMS— SCH 7A GROUP 13

9.16   From 1 April 2013 there is a reduced VAT rate of 5% for the transport of passengers by small cable-suspended transport systems, in place of the standard rate which had applied. Most cable-suspended transport systems carry fare-paying passengers from one point to another, but do not benefit from the same VAT reliefs as most other forms of public transport. As far as possible under EU law, this measure seeks to bring the VAT treatment of such systems more in line with other forms of public transport, most of which are zero-rated for VAT.

Chapter 10

So what is zero-rated?

SIGNPOSTS

• Most of the zero-ratings that businesses will come across regularly are contained in *Sch 8* to the *VAT Act 1994* and the various groups. The rate of VAT applicable applies to the goods or services being supplied and their place of supply (see **10.1–10.9**).

• Detailed analysis of what is covered in the groups is given in the rest of the chapter (see **10.10–10.47**).

• The VAT liability of foodstuffs and the exceptions for catering and the sales of hot takeaway food have caused much litigation and summarises the current position (see **10.10–10.17**).

• Printed matter—what items come within the zero-rating and what do not with case precedence (see **10.19–10.26**).

THE LAW

10.1   The law on zero-rating is mostly contained in *Sch 8*, although that for commodity transactions is in *s 34* and the *The Value Added Tax (Terminal Markets) Order 1973 (SI 1973/173)* (the '*Terminal Markets Order*').

THE TERMINAL MARKETS ORDER

10.2   The *Terminal Markets Order* zero-rates transactions on a large number of terminal markets, such as those for metals, rubber, oil, bullion, foods such as cocoa, coffee and sugar, futures markets, such as those for meat, grain and potatoes together with the London Securities and Derivatives Exchange. Notice 701/9/02 *Derivatives and Terminal Markets* refers.

The zero-rating is limited to transactions involving a member of the market involved, and is subject to various rules such as that, if one of the parties is not a member of the market, it must not lead to delivery of the goods.

If a business or adviser comes across commodity transactions on one of the markets, do not take the zero-rating for granted. I have seen several situations in which it did not apply, so check the detailed rules.

THE ZERO-RATING IN SCH 8

10.3 This chapter is obviously of most interest to readers who are involved with businesses selling zero-rated goods or services, and contains a detailed overview of zero-rating. This chapter and that on exemption are, therefore, a good start in understanding what are often highly technical issues.

However, always check whether, since this edition was published, there have been further developments.

This chapter, and the next one on exemption, are best read in conjunction with a copy of the law. If readers do not have one of the updating services available, try Notice 701/39 *VAT liability law*.

THE CONTENTS OF SCH 8

10.4

Focus

Group 1 Food

Group 2 Sewerage services and water

Group 3 Books

Group 4 Talking books for the blind and handicapped, etc

Group 5 Construction of buildings, etc

Group 6 Protected buildings

Group 7 International services

Group 8 Transport

Group 9 Caravans and houseboats

Group 10 Gold

Group 11 Bank notes

Group 12 Drugs, medicines, aids for the handicapped, etc

Group 13 Imports, exports, etc

Group 14 This has been deleted

Group 15 Charities

Group 16 Clothing and footwear

Group 17 Emissions Allowances

THE FOLLOWING GROUPS ARE NOT COVERED IN THIS CHAPTER

10.5   Sch 8 Group 5—Construction of buildings etc

See Chapter 26, *Property* for coverage of this Group.

Sch 8 Group 6—Protected buildings—withdrawn from October 2012

See Chapter 26, *Property* for coverage of this Group.

Sch 8 Group 7—International services

See Chapter 23, *Exports and Imports of Services* for coverage of this Group.

DO NOT ASK IF IT IS STANDARD-RATED!

10.6

Focus

The question 'Is it standard-rated?' is a natural one to ask, but it approaches the issue from the wrong direction. The law does not contain any list of transactions which are standard-rated. There is a list of what is reduced rated, what is zero-rated, and another of what is exempt, in *Schs 7A, 8* and *9* to the *VAT Act 1994* respectively. Everything else is standard-rated.

WHAT ABOUT OUTSIDE THE SCOPE?

10.7   There is also the possibility that the supplies a business makes or receives is outside the scope of VAT because it is not payment for any supply. There is no list of such transactions in the law, but, for most businesses, they are unimportant. They tend to be expenses such as wages and local authority rates. See Chapter 6, *So what must VAT be charged on?* for comment on dividends, government grants, and compensation.

'Outside the scope' is a term also used to describe transactions where the place of supply is not the UK under the rules for exports of goods or services. See those chapters for more details.

Once readers understand that a sale which is not reduced-rated, zero-rated, exempt, or outside the scope of VAT, must be standard-rated, it follows that the questions are:

- Is it reduced-rated under *Sch 7A*?

- Is it zero-rated under *Sch 8*?

- Is it exempt under *Sch 9*?

- Is it perhaps outside the scope?

No? Then it must be standard-rated!

This is, of course, assuming that the sale is one made in the course or furtherance of business. If readers have any doubts about whether the transaction could be treated as non-business, see Chapters 6, *So what must VAT be charged on?* and 28, *What is a business?*

WHAT SUPPLY IS BEING MADE?

10.8   The question 'What is being supplied?' is often a valuable aid to clear thinking. Usually, the rate of VAT depends on what's supplied:

- not who supplies it;

- nor who the customer is;

- nor what the customer thinks he's getting;

- nor the nature of the supplier's costs.

There are exceptions, but if a customer thinks a supply ought to be zero-rated, ask which part of *Sch 8* the customer thinks applies. All too often, customers haven't a clue what the law says, and many such claims are based on a lack of understanding.

There are some zero-ratings which depend on who the customer is, but they are limited to specific circumstances. The most likely ones are the rules on Aids for the Handicapped in *Sch 8 Group 12,* and on Charities in *Sch 8 Group 15.* In both cases, the customer is required to provide a certificate.

CHECK WHAT THE LAW SAYS

10.9   Popular perceptions about what the law covers are often inaccurate. It is vital to look up the law to check precisely what it says in relation to the transactions being considered. Numerous Tribunal decisions over the years have contained stories of people getting into trouble because they have failed to do that.

FOOD—SCH 8 GROUP 1

10.10   It is a popular fallacy that all food is zero-rated. Of course, most food is, but *Sch 8 Group 1* contains numerous exceptions. Some of these are well known, such as ice cream and potato crisps. Others are not at all what one would expect, such as orange juice and mineral water.

It may assist readers in understanding this section if they have a copy of the relevant legislation available to read in conjunction.

The zero-rating for food is set out in four parts:

- *the general items*, which are zero-rated;
- *some exceptions* which are standard-rated, for instance, catering and beverages;
- *exceptions to the exceptions* which put back into zero-rating, for instance, such drinks as milk, tea and coffee;
- *notes*. When reading the law, always check the notes. Often, what appears to be zero-rated or an exemption in the items can be either removed from the relief or qualified for the relief by the notes.

The law begins by saying that the following are zero-rated:

- human food;
- animal feed;
- seeds or the means of propagating plants which produce either of these;
- live animals of a kind generally used as, yielding or producing human food.

Catering

10.11   The exception for catering is right at the start of *Group 1*. It includes (*note (3)*):

- food sold for consumption on the premises on which it is supplied;
- 'hot' takeaway food. In other words, 'cold' takeaway food is zero-rated.

Unfortunately, it is not that simple because, to qualify as 'takeaway', the food must be removed from the premises on which it is sold. That does not just mean the café or snack bar; 'premises' includes any area to which access is restricted, such as a racecourse or an amusement park, even though not owned by the food outlet trading from it.

However, in *J Bishop and P Elcocks* (LON/01/690 No 17620), the premises were held to be the Portakabin from which the food was sold, not the entire Royal Naval Air Station, Culdrose, in which it was sited under a licence from the Secretary of State for Defence.

Similarly, in *Compass Contract Services UK Ltd* [2006] BVC 569, the Court of Appeal upheld the earlier decision of the VAT Tribunal that sales of cold food from take-away counters within the BBC TV Centre were not supplies of catering; nor did the Centre qualify as the premises on which they were supplied. See that case for a review of many of the earlier ones.

In *Made to Order Ltd* (VTD 20,959), the Appellant appealed against a ruling by HMRC that cold food sold by the Appellant should be standard-rated.

The disputed supplies were the 'made to order' cold sandwiches sold from Subway kiosks in three different food courts. The Appellant argued that the seating areas next to the kiosks were not 'premises' from which the food was supplied, because the kiosks shared those seating areas with other food outlets in the food court, and had no control over them. The Appellant further argued that the supplies of cold food were not supplied 'for consumption on the premises on which they were supplied', and that because they were not otherwise 'in the course of catering', and were clearly supplies of food for human consumption, they had to be zero-rated.

In reaching its decision, the Tribunal held that 'the facts of this case indicate perfectly clearly that the kiosks are not in any common sense terms the same premises as the places where the food is consumed. No food could be consumed in the kiosks, and in respect of none of the three outlets does the lease even purport to give any rights of occupation or even use over the seated areas to the appellant.' The supplies of cold food from the three kiosks were correctly zero-rated because they did not fall under the term 'catering.' The Appellant's appeal was therefore allowed.

Changes in the *Finance Act 2012* have effectively reversed this decision so that 'premises' includes all areas that are set aside for the consumption of food even if those areas are shared with other retailers.

Examples of areas affected by this change include: tables and chairs on the pavement outside a café, food courts in shopping centres, other similar shared eating premises such as in motorway service stations, airports, railway stations, etc.

Examples of areas not affected by this change include: benches in a shopping centre for resting, airport departure seating, etc.

There have also been many cases on what is or is not 'catering' when food is supplied ready for consumption. If a sandwich bar makes up platters containing a finger buffet complete with napkins and paper plates, so that all the host or hostess has to do is to remove the cling film, the supply is likely to be a supply of standard-rated catering even though the food is cold.

However, the point is a fine one and in *Safeway Stores plc* (LON/94/2963 No 14067: [1997] STC 163), 'party trays' packed on disposable foil trays in a display box for 12-20 people were held not to be catering. Similarly, in *Remo Bardetti and Anna Bardetti (t/a Obertelli Quality Sandwiches)* (LON/99/0561 No 16758), sandwiches on platters delivered to offices were held not to be catering. There was little difference between them and bags of sandwiches. There was no accompanying service, the supply was not for any party or event and it included no crockery, cutlery or other items.

In *Happy Place Ltd (t/a The Munch Box)* (LON/00/1218 No 17654), the platters did include paper plates and napkins but, on the basis of the *Safeway* case, the factors pointing towards catering were outweighed by those against it, including the impression that the food tended to be bought for office meetings over lunch.

In *A Leach (t/a Carlton Catering)* (LON/01/46 No 17767), food delivered to a school hot, as required by the *Food and Hygiene Regulations*, was held not to be a supply of catering. The school reheated and plated the food.

The fact that standard-rating for catering includes food sold for consumption on the premises and hot takeaway food means that those two inclusions are merely examples of what is standard-rated. They do not limit the definition; thus if a supply qualifies as catering by its nature, it is standard-rated even if the customer collects the food. Whilst much catering is in relation to events, such as a party, an individual meal cooked for a single person could also be caught.

There have also been cases on what is or is not hot food, ie food heated for consumption whilst hot. A pie may be hot when sold because it has just been cooked. The sale is not necessarily standard-rated just because the cooking was deliberately timed for a meal time. Thus, in *John Pimblett & Sons Ltd* ([1988] STC 358, CA), hot pies, baked on the premises in time to be sold at lunchtime, were held to be zero-rated. The baking created a pleasant smell and atmosphere and the objective was to provide freshly baked pies. Pimblett neither kept them hot nor reheated them. Some customers bought pies to eat at once; others did not.

In *Lewis's Group Ltd* (MAN/89/389 No 4931), chickens cooked on the premises and then kept warm for food safety reasons were also held to be zero-rated. Lewis's did not heat the chickens so their customers could eat them hot, or warm, or at any particular temperature. If the customer wanted hot chicken and timed the purchase accordingly, that was a consequence, not the purpose of the cooking.

Again, in *Great American Bagel Factory Ltd* (LON/00/659 No 17018), toasted bagels were held not to be standard-rated hot food because they were heated to give a crisp inner texture, not for consumption when warm. They cooled rapidly, yet were often taken back to customers' offices and they remained crisp when cool.

However, in *Domino's Pizza Group Ltd* (LON/02/139 & 310 No 18866), freshly baked pizzas were held to be standard-rated because they were deliberately kept as hot as possible and delivered as soon as possible; the marketing emphasised that they were delivered 'piping hot'.

In the Tribunal decision in *Ainsleys of Leeds (VTD 19,694)*, they found that the sale of 'ciabatta melts' was zero-rated even though the ciabatta melts were sold still warm (for optimum freshness and to provide a tasty aroma in the shops).

There has been a long running battle between HMRC and the Subway chain of franchised food restaurants centring on the VAT liability of toasted sandwiches ('Subs'), with HMRC saying that it is standard-rated hot toasted food and Subway arguing that it is zero-rated cold food sold at the ambient air temperature.

The Tribunal decided that:

- toasted Subs met the definition of hot food in *Sch 8 Group 1 note 3(b)* of the *VAT Act 1994*, and supplies of toasted Subs were standard rated for VAT purposes;

- meatball marinara met the definition of hot food in *Sch 8 Group 1 note 3(b)* of the *VAT Act 1994*, and supplies of meatball marinara were standard rated for VAT purposes.

The Tribunal, therefore, dismissed the Appeal.

In a joint case brought before the ECJ on appeal from the German tax authorities (*Finanzamt Burgdorf v Manfred Bog* (C-497/09), *CinemaxX Entertainment GmbH & Co KG v Finanzamt Hamburg-Barmbek-Uhlenhorst* (C-499/09), *Lothar Lohmeyer v Finanzamt Minden* (C-501/09) and *Fleischerei Nier GmbH & Co KG v Finanzamt Detmold* (C-502/09)), a number of German taxpayers argued that supplies of hot food for immediate consumption were supplies of goods rather than services and as such were subject to a lower rate of VAT in Germany.

The taxpayers ran hot food stalls, cinema food kiosks, etc and argued that as the food stuffs sold required minimum preparation they were a supply of goods at the lower rate of VAT rather than services subject to standard rated VAT.

The ECJ found that as there was very little preparation involved in the sale of sausages, burgers, etc they could be treated as supplies of goods rather than services and so found for the taxpayers. The ECJ judgment considers that 'foodstuffs' includes cooked and prepared food ready for immediate consumption but that such foodstuffs will only become restaurant or catering services when there is sufficient additional provision of other service elements (such as tables, chairs, cutlery and crockery and waitressing). It was held that the sale of hot food from Mr Manfred Bog's market stall was not catering and, as such, he was correct in using the reduced rate.

HMRC published *Revenue & Customs Brief 19/11* stating that they did not believe the decision had 'application in the UK'. 'Both supplies of food and supplies made in the course of catering in the UK are treated as supplies of goods.'

In the case of *Deliverance Ltd v Revenue and Customs Commissioners* ([2011] UKUT 58 (TCC)) the taxpayer was a catering company which supplied a wide range of freshly prepared food for delivery to customers. All food was cooked to order and delivered to the customer by motorcycle within 45 minutes of ordering. Some items were cooked and delivered to customers above the ambient air temperature when they left their premises. HMRC had ruled that such goods were supplied hot and thus were subject to VAT at the standard rate. The First-tier Tax Tribunal agreed with HMRC.

However, Deliverance Ltd appealed to the Upper Tribunal, which overturned the original decision of the First-tier Tribunal and in so doing could have created a potential opportunity for some businesses. This case relates to whether certain takeaway food items, mainly linked to Indian and Chinese dishes, could qualify as zero-rated because they are 'freshly baked' rather than standard-rated because they are 'hot'.

The products concerned were:

- aromatic crispy duck pancakes;
- spring rolls with dip, falafels with dip;
- sesame prawn toast;
- onion bhajis;
- naan;
- pittam garlic; and
- peshwari breads.

Deliverance Ltd was able to demonstrate that their purpose in keeping and delivering the food whilst still hot was to show that the food was freshly cooked and to comply with food safety regulations. The food was kept hot on a heated shelf for up to 15 minutes then put into a padded bag in a lined box on a motorcycle for delivery to the customer.

They were packaged together with other items which were intended to be consumed hot because that was the convenient way to transport them, and still being hot when delivered showed that they were freshly cooked. In addition, food safety regulations required that food which had been heated must either be kept above a certain temperature or blast-chilled to below a certain temperature, and blast-chilling was not appropriate for these items. Their contention that the items of food in question had *not* 'been heated for the purposes of enabling it to be consumed at a temperature above the ambient air temperature' was accepted by the Tribunal.

Following this extensive litigation the 2012 Budget introduced a tightening of the legislation regarding the definition of 'hot' and premises that extended the scope of the standard-rating.

This change clarifies the definition of 'hot takeaway food'. Zero-rating will still apply to freshly backed/cooked products allowed to cool naturally but standard rating will be extended to apply to all foods kept warm, reheated or held out for sale hot. It also clarifies the definition of 'premises' to confirm that: (i) all food sold for consumption on the premises on which it is supplied; and (ii) all food sold for consumption in areas adjacent to those premises or in areas shared with other retailers is subject to VAT at the standard rate.

Examples of products affected by the change include: rotisserie chicken products, pies, pasties, toasted sandwiches, etc but not when allowed to cool naturally.

See Notice 709/2 *Catering and takeaway food* for HMRC's views.

Human food

10.12 The law says '*Food of a kind used for human consumption.*' There are, however, numerous exceptions from the zero-rating. Examples of the detailed distinctions are:

A yoghurt is zero-rated—but not if it is frozen.

There is a difference between chocolate cake and chocolate biscuits!

- ie food is zero-rated;

- but not confectionery;

- except cakes or biscuits, which are therefore zero-rated;

- but biscuits wholly or partly covered with chocolate are standard-rated.

Most drinks are standard-rated—including breakfast orange juice and bottled water. But milk, tea, cocoa and coffee are zero-rated.

Peanuts in shell are zero-rated. Taken out, they are zero-rated until you put salt on them; cover them in chocolate or yoghurt and they are standard-rated; roast them and they are also standard-rated—unless they are still in their shell!

Excepted items

10.13

- ice cream, ice lollies, frozen yoghurt, water ices and similar together with mixes and powders for making them;

- confectionery, not including cakes or biscuits other than biscuits wholly or partly covered with chocolate or similar;

- alcohol;

- other drinks (including fruit juices and bottled waters) and syrups concentrates etc used to produce them;

- when packed for human consumption without further preparation, potato crisps and the like, savoury food products obtained by swelling cereals or cereal products and salted or roasted nuts other than nuts in shell;

- pet foods—see **10.15**;

- goods for the domestic production of beer, cider, perry or wine;

- sports nutrition drinks, whether or not they are consumed for nutritional purposes (Budget 2012).

Exceptions to the exceptions—items overriding them

10.14

- frozen yoghurt not suitable for immediate consumption;

- drained cherries;

- candied peels;

- tea, maté, herbal teas and similar products/preparations/extracts thereof;

- cocoa, coffee, chicory, other roasted coffee substitutes/preparations/extracts thereof;

- milk and preparations and extracts thereof;

- preparations and extracts of meat, yeast or egg.

A well-known Tribunal case is that on Jaffa cakes *(United Biscuits (UK) Ltd* (LON/91/160 No 6344)). HMRC argued that Jaffa cakes were biscuits. Since they are partly covered in chocolate, that would make them standard-rated. The Tribunal noted that, when a cake goes stale, it goes hard whereas a biscuit goes soft. Apparently Jaffa cakes go rock hard—so they are zero-rated!

As mentioned earlier, the *Notes* to a group qualify what the items say. Here, two of them clarify in saying that *food* includes *drink* and *animal* includes a *bird* or a *fish*. *Note (5)* says that 'confectionery' includes *chocolates, sweets and biscuits; drained, glacé or crystallised fruits; and any item of sweetened prepared food which is normally eaten with the fingers.*

HMRC argued that last phrase standard-rated fruit and cereal bars produced by *Organix Brands plc* (LON/04/204 No 19134) because they were sweetened. The Tribunal rejected that noting that the two juice concentrates were required to flavour the products, to combine with the other ingredients so that they would stick together to create bars and to give them the necessary moisture content to remain as bars.

In *SiS (Science in Sport) Ltd* (MAN/00/69 No 17116), Go-Bars were also held not to be prepared sweetened food because the swapping of grape juice for the apple juice in the apple content reduced the sugar content, not increased it. In contrast, *Torq Ltd* (LON/05/205 No 19389), accepted that its sports nutrition bars were sweetened. Accepting that lost its case because the bars were held not to be cakes. Torq argued that they were flapjacks. The Tribunal rejected that—and questioned whether HMRC were right in seeing traditional flapjacks as cake-like!

Excepted item 4, which standard-rates non-alcoholic 'beverages', ie drinks, was held in *Grove Fresh Ltd* (LON/2004/2306 No 19,241) to cover litre cartons of vegetable juices. They would normally be drunk from glasses and were not soups, nor meal replacement drinks for slimmers.

The standard-rating in *excepted item 5* for various products made from the potato, such as potato crisps and savoury food products obtained by the swelling of cereals or cereal products, produces a curious result. *Hula Hoops*, corn hoops made from maize, are zero-rated whereas an otherwise identical one made of potato is standard-rated (*United Biscuits (UK) Ltd* (MAN/01/60 No 17391))! The phrase *obtained by the swelling* was interpreted as meaning on purpose as part of the manufacturing process. Though *Hula Hoops* swelled by about 1/3, this was incidental, not a part of the process. However, *Hula Hoops* and *Shake 2 flava*, are, apparently, of potato.

Procter and Gamble appealed to the VAT Tribunal on the grounds that a 'Pringle' was not similar to a crisp and that it was not wholly or mainly made from a potato product. The Tribunal did not accept this argument, and found in favour of HMRC.

Procter & Gamble appealed to the High Court, which found in their favour on the basis that the regular Pringles were not wholly or mainly made from potato. However, HMRC appealed to the Court of Appeal, which has now upheld the original Tribunal decision (CH/2007/APP/0432).

In *United Biscuits (UK) Ltd* (MAN/03/823 No 18947), they lost the argument that, because the packet included a sachet of further flavouring, that created the *further preparation*, the need for which keeps goods zero-rated which are otherwise caught by *excepted item 5*. The Tribunal held that adding the sachet was a matter of choice, not necessary preparation!

In *Procter and Gamble UK* (LON/2002/0896 No 18381), a 'dipping chip' was held to be zero-rated because:

- it was not similar to the products mentioned in *excepted item 5*;

- being marketed for consumption with a dip, it was not *packaged for human consumption without further preparation*; and

- it was not made *1/4 from potato flour*, this being only 38% of the dry content including the cooking oil.

No doubt, that was why *United Biscuits (UK) Ltd* (MAN/04/285 No 19319) tried again with *McCoy's Dips*. Yet, although the 95g tub of the dip was agreed as zero-rated, the 100g of crisps were held to be standard-rated. This Tribunal disagreed with that in *Proctor and Gamble*. Dipping a crisp into a pot was eating, not preparation!

Over the years, there have been a number of cases on the difference between dietary products which count as food and those which do not. For instance, HMRC accept that meal replacement products for slimmers are zero-rated, unless caught as confectionery. However, appetite suppressants in pill or powder form are not.

In *SIS (Science in Sport) Ltd* (MAN/98/844 No 16555), a powder, which was mixed with water in order to take it, was argued by HMRC to be a drink and thus caught by *excepted item 4*. The Tribunal held that the product taken in liquid form was zero-rated as a 'dietary integrator' which happened to be made up as a drink for sports persons. It was not a sports drink, which would be caught as a beverage. The Tribunal considered that HMRC's policy was flawed in failing to distinguish between 'sports drinks' that were in reality drinks, and 'dietary integrators' made as drinks.

In *Kalron Foods v Revenue and Customs Comrs* [2007] EWHC 695 (Ch), HMRC successfully argued that 'smoothies' made from whole fruit or vegetables were standard-rated beverages, rather than items of liquefied food. Contrast this with the decision by HMRC later in 2007 to agree out of court with Premier Foods that its 'extra-thick' fruit smoothies qualified for zero-rating. It is assumed HMRC backed down due to the significant amount of yoghurt in the items, as this means they can be treated as 'preparations of milk' under the list of items 'overriding the exceptions'.

In *Rivella (UK) Ltd* (LON/99/562 No 16382), Rivella, a drink comprising 35% lactoserum, an extract of milk was held to be covered by *overriding item 6* (overriding the exceptions) as milk. Its ingredients and the manufacturing process were decisive factors, supported by the marketing process, which linked in the minds of consumers the principal source of the product as extracts of milk. This was despite it being a clear fizzy liquid, herb flavoured and with no resemblance to milk.

In contrast, linseed oil was held to be a supplement, not a food, in *Durwin Banks* (LON/2004/1030 No 18904).

For HMRC's Views, see Notice 701/14 *Food*.

Animal feed

10.15 Zero-rating for animal feed is restricted by *excepted item 6*, which standard-rates *pet foods, canned, packaged or prepared; packaged foods (not being pet foods) for birds other than poultry or game; and biscuits and meal for cats and dogs.* This then creates the interesting distinction between food for dogs kept as pets and that for working dogs such as sheepdogs and greyhounds.

See Notice 701/15 *Food for animals* for HMRC's views. For instance, they accept zero-rating for food specifically packaged for working dogs provided that it is not sold as equally suitable for all breeds, sizes and ages of dogs.

In *Bambers Frozen Meats Ltd* (MAN//01/0629 No 17626), a product, described on the packaging as a biscuit and which was produced in rough bone shaped lumps, was held not to be a biscuit. The description was a mistake, which should be corrected! The texture was rougher and flakier than that of biscuits. It also contained the nutrients normally absent from dog biscuits and it swelled in the digestive system rather than merely disintegrate in contact with gastric juices, as did biscuits. The product was a cereal, not meal, because it was 73.5% wheat. It therefore qualified for zero-rating, being sold for working dogs.

Seeds and plants

10.16 The coverage of this is obvious much of the time, but be careful. Shrubs and trees are generally standard-rated, but a walnut tree producing edible nuts is zero-rated, as are fruit trees generally. Notice 701/38 *Seeds and plants* provides extensive guidance.

Live animals

10.17 The fourth category of zero-rating for *Live Animals of a kind generally used as yielding or producing human food* covers farm animals generally. It also includes rabbits and ostriches!

It does not include a horse, even a carthorse, because the latter does not yield as a cow yields milk or produce like a hen produces eggs. Although it may assist in the production of a crop by tilling the land, that is too far removed from the sense in which the word 'producing' is used.

Even if it were possible to show that horsemeat was occasionally eaten in the UK, that would not enable zero-rating because such consumption would not meet the *generally used as* test. This means that a business must be able to show that the event in question happens regularly and all over the UK. That is not the same as saying that it happens everywhere and all the time but it must be common.

SEWERAGE SERVICES AND WATER—SCH 8 GROUP 2

10.18   This group is largely self-explanatory, but it does not cover:

- water supplied to organisations carrying on a 'relevant industrial activity'. That means one of those described in divisions 1–5 of the Standard Industrial Classification;

- distilled water, de-ionised water and water of similar purity;

- the bottled water excepted from the zero-rating in *Group 1* for food;

- hot water—this stops avoidance schemes based on outsourcing the heating of water and then claiming zero-rating for it.

Notice 701/16 *Sewerage and water* refers.

BOOKS—SCH 8 GROUP 3

10.19   The law on the zero-rating for books, newspapers, etc is as delightfully brief as that for food is lengthy. Unfortunately, this brevity has not provided the simplicity necessary to avoid disputes, and there have been just as many Tribunal cases concerning *Group 3* as there have on *Group 1*.

Arguments have mostly concerned the nature of:

- a book;

- a booklet, brochure, pamphlet or leaflet;

- a newspaper, journal or periodical.

The key test

10.20

Focus

The key test is often whether the item in question qualifies as reading matter designed to be held in the hand. Thus, a poster does not qualify, even though it may contain a substantial amount of text, because it is not a brochure, pamphlet, or leaflet, and is designed to be displayed on a wall. Nor does something like a score card qualify because, essentially, it is designed to be filled in.

Brochures and application forms

10.21   To cope with the case of something like a brochure with an application form, HMRC have a rule that it can be zero-rated provided that the space occupied by the application form is no more than 25% of the total. The entire page is counted if there is nothing else on the page, not just the spaces to be completed. That is not law, merely an administrative ruling, but it might be difficult to persuade a Tribunal that any item with less than 75% text qualified as a brochure, pamphlet, or leaflet.

The 25% ruling assumes that the form for completion is intended to be detached. If the entire item is intended to be returned, HMRC say it is standard-rated.

Other items

10.22   Notice 701/10 *Printed and similar matter* lists HMRC's views on numerous other items. Again, these rulings are not law, merely interpretation, but they are mostly common sense.

So ...

10.23   If something is essentially reading matter, it is likely to be zero-rated. If its nature is more akin to stationery, it is probably standard-rated. Letter headings, diaries, calendars, and greeting cards are all standard-rated items. If tempted to argue that a particular item, such as a calendar, has extensive wording, remember that the test in law is whether it is a book, booklet, brochure, pamphlet, leaflet, newspaper, etc. The reading matter test is merely a guide.

The above is a distillation of points from the numerous cases on what is covered by *Group 3*. The precise nature and purpose of the item are usually the key to whether something is or is not, for instance, a leaflet.

In *GNP Booth Ltd* (EDN/01/129 No 17555), the Tribunal commented that the purpose is the key when deciding if an item qualifies as a leaflet. Items the size of a visiting card are too small, but the weight of the paper is unimportant.

'Model' books for children

10.24   A book, which a child can dismantle to create a model, can qualify for zero-rating. A binder containing seven laminated sheets, which were removed to make a model house but of which six could be replaced in the binder, was held to be a book in *The Book People Ltd* (LON/02/1053 No 18240).

Books in electronic form

10.25   A book in electronic form is standard-rated, unless it is covered by the special relief for talking books for the blind—see *Group 4* below.

The European Court of Justice (CJEU) has decided that e-books cannot be subject to a reduced rate of VAT ((C479/13) *European Commission v French Republic*). Since 1 January 2012, France has applied a reduced VAT rate of 5.5% to the supply of electronic books, and Luxembourg has used a 'super-reduced' rate of 3%. The full rate of VAT is 20% in France and 17% in Luxembourg, but books, in physical or electronic form, are taxed at the lower rates. The European Commission commenced infraction proceedings and referred the matter to the ECJ.

Both France and Luxembourg, with the support of Belgium, had argued that electronic books are covered by *Annex III* of the *Principle VAT Directive*, which allows reduced VAT on certain goods, including paper books and was arguably designed to cope with technical progress and changes to the meaning of 'book', which included books in an electronic format.

However, the CJEU agreed with the European Commission's argument that as the Annex referred to the 'supply of books ... on all physical means of support', it is only applicable to 'the supply of a book found in a physical medium'. As the electronic format was not a means of physical support it was not covered by the Annex.

Quite how this fits in with the earlier ECJ decision in *K Oy* (C219/13) judgment on e-books, which accepted that in some cases a reduced rate could apply, is something of a contradiction and will cause some uncertainty for those challenging the liability of e-books.

In this case the ECJ decided to proceed straight to a judgment without an initial opinion from the Advocate General, who might have explored these questions in more depth and given a more balanced decision. However, following the France and Luxembourg decision it would appear that in order to apply a reduced rate to all e-books EU legislation must be amended to make an explicit reference to such a rate and the Commission is currently trying to amend the legislation accordingly.

It must be hoped that the eventual outcome of these cases is not that it is accepted that both e-books and printed books serve the same needs and should both be standard rated.

Quite how this case impacts on attempts to argue that e-book sales in the UK should be zero-rated remains to be seen. The UK zero-rate is based on a different EU legal provision so there may not be an automatic read across. However, if e-books must be standard rated electronic services in France and Luxembourg then it is hard to see how they can be zero-rated in the UK.

In the case of *News Corp UK & Ireland Limited v HMRC* [2018] UKFTT 129 (TC), the appellant was the representative member of a VAT group and appealed against decisions of HMRC that digital versions of *The Times*, *The Sunday Times*, *The Sun* and *The Sun on Sunday* could not be zero-rated under

VATA 1994, Sch 8, Group 3, Item 2 and were therefore standard rated for VAT purposes.

The appellant argued that there was essentially no difference in the journalistic content or news teams for the newsprint and digital editions. The appellant submitted that *VATA 1994, Sch 8, Group 3, Item 2* should be interpreted purposively. The purpose of the provision was to promote literacy, the dissemination of information and democratic accountability.

There was, however, a further principle of statutory interpretation which formed an important part of the appellant's case. This principle was that legislation once enacted had to be kept up-to-date with, inter alia, technological advances so that, in other words, a statutory provision is 'always speaking'. This was important in the present case because digital editions of newspapers did not exist in 1973.

The appellant submitted that it was necessary to identify the purpose of the relevant provision and then consider whether that new item, new technology or new state of affairs shared the same inherent characteristics as those supplies which were admitted to be covered by the wording.

HMRC submitted that all the items in *Group 3* of *Sch 8* to *VATA 1984* consisted of goods, not services. In other words, *Item 2* applied only to newsprint newspapers. The supply of the digital editions of the titles constituted a supply of services. *Group 3* of *Sch 8* did not apply to the supply of services. Treating these digital editions as zero rated 'newspapers' was contrary to the applicable UK legislation and would be an impermissible extension of zero rating contrary to the derogation requirements of *Art 110* of the *PVD*. The newsprint and digital editions were not comparable and, even if they were, the principle of fiscal neutrality was not breached.

It was common ground that the digital editions of the titles when supplied to readers constituted a supply of services. The Tribunal considered that this point was fatal to the appellant's argument because *VATA 1994, Sch 8, Group 3, Item 2* deals only with supplies of goods, ie 'newspapers, journals and periodicals' in physical form and therefore the appeal had to be dismissed.

The latest position is that as of October 2018 agreement was reached by Finance Ministers and agreed to by the European Council that changes to EU laws and directives will be made to allow reduced or zero-rating on e-books and online newspapers. Only specific goods listed within Annex III of the EU VAT Directive may benefit from reduced rates. E-books and similar digital products had not been created at the time of the drawing-up of Annex III, and so were excluded. The right to reduce VAT rates on such products comes after many failed ECJ attempts to change the interpretation of the VAT Directive. Malta has become the first EU Member State to implement the change with a 5% VAT rate on both paper and e-books and periodicals.

Printed material supplied with other goods or services

10.26   Where printed material is supplied with a package of goods or services, HMRC have often accepted that part of the supply is zero-rated. Examples include:

- a subscription, which includes a magazine;

- a book and a CD-ROM sold together.

It is no longer safe to assume that the printed material is a separate zero-rated supply merely because it has a physical existence, and would be zero-rated if sold on its own. See Chapter 12 for comment on the numerous cases on whether there is one supply or two. If there is only one supply, the question is which one is dominant and therefore decides the rate of VAT applicable.

However, two Tribunal decisions in 2004/05 held that packs of materials should be partly zero-rated, no one item being dominant. *Eddie Stobart Group Ltd* (MAN/04/32 No 18873) had a fan club for which the subscription was a mixed supply. The main benefits were a spotter guide (accepted as zero-rated), access to the membership area of a website (accepted as standard-rated) and a fleet list for filling in details vehicle by vehicle of when seen and where they were seen—held to be standard-rated because its main function was to record spotting details—what fun!

Charterhall Marketing Ltd (EDN/04/127 No 19050) produced and posted sales letters and accompanying leaflets to potential customers. The letters were to named individuals and were standard-rated; the leaflets were a separate zero-rated supply.

Following the *Telewest Communications plc* (LON/01/0679 No 17986; [2004] STC 517; [2005] STC 481) case HMRC have amended *Sch 8 Group 3* of the *VAT Act 1994* relating to printed matter so that there will be no zero-rated supply where there is a contract with a customer with two separate, but connected businesses, for the supply of zero-rated printed matter and a separate supply of a service. HMRC claim that this clause prevents tax avoidance schemes designed to obtain a tax treatment that would apply if separate supplies were being made, when in substance the business is making a single supply. In particular they take the view that such arrangements aim to attribute a value for tax purposes to something for which no charge is being made commercially. European and domestic judgments have stated in clear terms that supplies that comprise a single service from an economic point of view should not be artificially split.

This change would apply in the following example: a training course is provided by Company A but a connected Company B provides the manuals which are ancillary to the training service.

In Revenue & Customs Brief 10/15 – 'VAT – direct marketing services using printed matter' – HMRC has identified that a number of suppliers of printed matter combined with other services have been treating the supply as one of zero-rated delivered goods. In HMRC's view, these supplies should properly be characterised as a supply of standard-rated direct marketing services.

This brief explains HMRC's approach to supplies of direct marketing that have been wrongly treated as zero-rated supplies of delivered goods.

It sets out those circumstances where HMRC will not take action to assess for past errors. HMRC have agreed with trade representatives a transitional period, which ends on 31 July 2015, for certain cases where businesses have treated supplies of direct marketing incorrectly for VAT purposes.

It also describes the settlement terms available to businesses whose supplies do not come within the scope of the transitional arrangements.

TALKING BOOKS FOR THE BLIND AND HANDICAPPED AND WIRELESS SETS FOR THE BLIND—SCH 8 GROUP 4

10.27 This covers:

- supplies to charities for the blind of specialist audio tape and specialised equipment for recording or reproduction of speech;

- supplies to any charity of radio receivers and cassette recorders/players.

TRANSPORT—SCH 8 GROUP 8

10.28 This group covers a large number of services connected with ships and aircraft and with the transporting of people or goods in them.

Examples are:

- sale of or repair or maintenance of ships except those below 15 tons and aircraft below 8,000 kg prior to 1 September 2010 when the zero-rating requirement changed to aircraft by airlines operating for reward chiefly on international routes or where the ship or aircraft are designed or adapted for recreation or pleasure;

- various parts and equipment of a kind ordinarily installed or incorporated in and to be so fitted into a qualifying ship or aircraft—including lifejackets, life rafts, smoke hoods and similar safety equipment;

- to a charity providing rescue or assistance at sea, the supply, repair or maintenance of lifeboats and associated equipment, such as tractors or winches, together with slipways solely for launching them and, from 1 August 2006, fuel for use in them;

- transport of people in vehicles, ships or aircraft taking 10 or more passengers, or by the Post Office or on a scheduled flight;

- transport of people to or from a place outside the UK;

- transport of goods to or from a place outside the EU;

- various services, such as pilotage, agency work, handling and storage connected with the import or export of goods.

Some of these zero-ratings cover only specific services in limited circumstances so, if a business comes across them, check both the law and HMRC's interpretation of it.

For instance, 'fun' transport within such tourist attractions as a coal mine or a safari park, when supplied by the person who charges admission, and recreational trips in aircraft, are generally standard-rated.

In VAT Information Sheet 15/07, HMRC took the opportunity to clarify its existing policy for the zero-rating of certain services supplied in relation to qualifying ships and aircraft.

A case concerning handling goods under items 6 and 11

10.29   In *EB Central Services Ltd* ([2007] EWHC 201), the High Court ruled that the provision of left luggage facilities to travellers on the 'landside' part of airports was a zero-rated supply of handling or storage.

In the earlier Tribunal case, the Tribunal held that *item 6* did not apply because it referred to goods carried in a ship or aircraft, which must be interpreted in the light of *Art 15(9)* of the *EC 6th VAT Directive* (now *Directive 2006/112/ EC, Art 148(g)*); the latter referred to supplies to meet the direct needs of the aircraft or of their cargoes so *item 6* must be construed in this context as akin to cargo, ie as having a commercial requirement.

Since *item 11* merely refers to the handling or storage of goods at, or their transport to or from, a place at which they are to be exported to or have been imported from a place outside the Member States, and thus does not mention the carriage in a ship or aircraft, the Tribunal gave goods a less restricted meaning there than in *item 6*.

Of course, the question of where the luggage was going to or coming from complicated the matter. EB's claim that 76% of the luggage was moving in or out of the EU, based on a two-week survey, was accepted by the Tribunal as the basis for zero-rating, it not having been challenged by HMRC.

In such a situation, it would be wise to obtain further evidence from time to time. Even if HMRC did not demand a regular survey, they would certainly require updated information sooner or later.

Relevant Notices are 744A *Passenger transport* and 744B *Freight transport and associated services.*

Some more about boats, aircraft and transport on them

10.30   *Directive 2006/112/EC, Art 146(1)(b)* (previously *Art 15(2)* of the *EC 6th VAT Directive*) standard-rates goods for the equipping, fuelling, and provisioning of pleasure boats and private aircraft, or any other means of transport, for private use. Private use includes by organisations, such as state, regional and local government authorities and bodies governed by public law, except in circumstances in which they are operating business activities.

Although the standard-rating of ships *designed or adapted for recreation or pleasure* does not catch use as a home, you cannot zero-rate a yacht just because the customer intends to live on it. What matters is design for commercial use rather than for recreation or pleasure—though see below re *Cirdan* concerning use as opposed to design. *Group 9* re houseboats covers static boats.

Several cases have concerned transport on aircraft, trains and yachts and whether other supplies are made as well. See Chapter 12, *Is there one supply or two?*, *Re British Airways*—a meal included with a ticket is not a separate supply, and *Sea Containers Services Ltd*—catering on a luxury train is.

In *Cirdan Sailing Trust* (LON/2003/0912 No 18865), the charter, with crews, of four sailing vessels of varying designs to organisations, which took groups of young people on trips, was held to be the supply of transport.

None of the boats were designed or adapted for recreation or pleasure. Two were originally commercial; two had been and still were yachts. For all four, the present design or adaptation depended upon the current state of the boat, its function and its use by the end user.

Although the disadvantaged young people were encouraged to help run the boats, they were not crew. The sport and physical education was provided on board not by Cirdan, but by the chartering organisations. The use by the latter was to further the education and welfare of the people, not merely for recreation or pleasure.

However, transport in one of the vessels was standard-rated because it was only authorised to carry nine passengers. The High Court rejected Cirdan's appeal that its capacity was 14 on day trips because, mainly, its trips were longer, and the use of the nine berths reflected the principal purpose.

CARAVANS AND HOUSEBOATS—SCH 8 GROUP 9

10.31   This Group zero-rates:

- caravans over legal towing size (ie residential) up to 6 April 2013 when new regulations came into force that restrict the zero-rate to the sale of caravans that conform to British Standard BS 3632:2015 (or equivalent);

- houseboats without own means of propulsion,

but not the supply of accommodation in them. Nor does it cover removable contents such as furnishings or furniture unless the item qualifies as building materials when fitted in a house—explained in Chapter 26, *Property*. The argument for a single zero-rated supply was rejected by the European Court of Justice in *Talacre Beach Caravan Sales Ltd* (C-251/05), following a referral from the Court of Appeal—see Chapter 12, *Is there one supply or two?*

Thus, although the sale or renting of residential caravans or houseboats is zero-rated, short-term accommodation is not. This prevents a potential distortion of competition with hotel rooms or with other forms of holiday accommodation, both of which are standard-rated by exception from the exemption for licences to occupy land in *Sch 9 Group 1*.

In the case of *Colaingrove Ltd v Revenue & Customs* [2015] UKUT 2 (TCC) the Upper Tribunal found that the supply of a veranda sold separately with the caravan and bolted to it, and in some cases secured to the ground as well, was covered by the zero-rating for static caravans.

Notice 701/20 *Caravans and houseboats* refers.

GOLD—SCH 8 GROUP 10

10.32   This zero-rating is confined to transactions involving a Central Bank.

BANK NOTES—SCH 8 GROUP 11

10.33   This is for the benefit of those Scottish and Irish Banks, which have the right to issue their own banknotes.

DRUGS, MEDICINES, AIDS FOR THE HANDICAPPED ETC—SCH 8 GROUP 12

10.34   This group has numerous items including some which zero-rate aids for the disabled, whether supplied to the handicapped person direct or to a charity. It covers, for example:

- drugs and other goods when supplied on prescription by a chemist;
- goods designed or adapted for use in connection with medical or surgical treatment when supplied by order of a doctor;
- certain specialised equipment designed for use by handicapped people;
- certain work to facilitate use of a building by handicapped persons when supplied to:

    (i)   a *handicapped person* in his private residence; or

161

(ii)   a *charity* if the building qualifies—see comment in brackets.

The work is:

(a)   building a ramp or widening a doorway or passage (in any building when supplied to a charity);

(b)   creating or adapting a bathroom, washroom or lavatory (in residential accommodation or in a day centre where at least 20% of the users are handicapped; or a washroom or lavatory (not bathroom) in any building used principally by a charity for charitable purposes);

(c)   installing a lift (in a permanent or temporary residence or day centre for handicapped persons);

• alarm systems for the handicapped when supplied to the latter or to a charity for making available to handicapped people.

See Notice 701/7 *Reliefs for disabled people*. To explain the law in detail here would mean virtually printing it verbatim, since the 20 items in *Group 12* are carefully worded to cover limited circumstances only, and are supported by numerous detailed notes. If a business is involved in this sector it will need to study these rules in detail. To cover that detail here would take more space than their specialist nature justifies.

However, the Group does potentially zero-rate a wide range of goods, and many businesses have found themselves in the Tribunals in the process of trying to claim that zero-rating. The comments on some of these arguments below illustrate its restricted nature. Often, a complete understanding requires reading the full decision.

The design problem

10.35   Where the law requires the goods to be specifically designed for use by handicapped people, it means what it says! In *Donald Bell* (LON/83/147 No 1480), standard fittings installed in a special kitchen for a disabled person did not qualify. They were merely fixed at a lower height than normal, not specially designed. Compare that with *Softley Ltd (t/a Softley Kitchens)* (LON/96/1810 No 15034), in which the units, although made of standard components, had design features, such as special plinths, which made them unsuitable for use other than by handicapped persons.

In *Kirton Healthcare Group Ltd* (LON/00/498 No 17062), a chair was found to be designed for the chronically sick and disabled, but a second design only qualified when equipped with certain optional accessories.

In *Hulsta Furniture (UK) Ltd* (LON/98/936 No 16289), an electrically adjustable bed was held to be designed for people temporarily or permanently suffering from disabilities. In *Tempur Pedic (UK) Ltd* (LON/95/458 No 13744), a very high-density foam mattress and pillow was held to be equipment designed solely for use by the chronically sick.

In *Medivac Healthcare Ltd* (LON/99/1271 No 16829), bedding covers, a special vacuum cleaner, a dehumidifier, and other products were accepted as designed solely for the chronically sick and disabled on the basis of evidence that they were for use only by people seriously affected by allergy to house mites. An anti-allergen spray was also *equipment* or an *appliance*, the canister being essential to the use of the spray.

In *Bettine Symons* (LON/04/1141 No 19174), equipment that was standard in nature, but put together as a system to filter the air in the house of a sufferer from dystonia, was specifically designed for use by a handicapped person.

In *Royal Midland Counties Home for Disabled People* (MAN/00/24 No 17010), a generator, which provided emergency standby power for essential aids for severely handicapped people, was held not to be an accessory to relevant goods. The generator, when in use, was the sole means of providing power, not an optional extra. The decision contains a useful review of the meaning of *accessory*.

In *Arthritis Care* (LON/95/2611 No 13974), a specially constructed staircase, designed with extra fire protection so as to provide a rescue point at a hotel for arthritis sufferers for use by people unable to use the stairs, was not *equipment*. Even if it had been, it was not designed solely for use by handicapped persons.

In *Joulesave Emes Ltd* (MAN/99/462 No 17115), radiator and pipe covers were held to be designed solely for use by handicapped persons on the basis of the designer's intention, how they were marketed and sold, and to whom. It did not matter that they also provided protection to the able bodied.

In *Boys' and Girls' Welfare Society* (MAN/96/1041 No 15274) the design and installation of a hydrotherapy pool and its environmental control system (heating, water cleansing, humidity control, etc) at a residential home for handicapped children was held to qualify as *equipment and appliances*, being a separate element from the building in which it was housed. Although supplied by a sub-contractor to the main contractor, it was then supplied on as a separate element by the main contractor.

However, the installation of special low surface temperature radiators in the residential unit was altering the heating system, not adapting goods.

Moreover, in *Cheltenham Old People's Housing Society Ltd* (LON/2002/ 0651 No 18795), a heating system, designed not to burn a person in contact with it, was for use by the elderly generally, not specifically the handicapped. The system was not 'adapted' when all bar the boilers was replaced. That was a new system. Bathrooms were also not 'adapted' merely by changing of the radiators therein.

Meaning of 'chronically sick or disabled'

10.36 *Note (3)* defines *handicapped* as meaning '*chronically sick or disabled*'. Tribunals have interpreted this strictly. In *Benefoot UK Ltd* (LON/98/942 No 17022), a man able to do a route march with the aid of an 'orthotic' appliance in his boot was held not to qualify.

So, mental, visual or hearing disabilities need to be serious and long term—but dyslexia *might* be accepted by HMRC.

In *Foxer Industries* (LON/95/1452 Nos 13817 and 14469), single-seater golf buggies did not meet the design requirement. In the second decision, the Tribunal decided whether the work of adapting individual buggies to special requirements did on the basis of whether each customer qualified as handicapped, and on the nature of the modification.

The customer problem

10.37 The zero-ratings in *Group 12* mostly include in their requirements that the supply is to a handicapped person or to a charity. This creates problems where another body is paying for the work. Thus, in *Cross Electrical and Building Services Ltd* (MAN/99/1070 No 16954), the supply was held not to be to the tenant when a housing action trust ordered the work, and received and paid the invoice. Similarly, in *Mrs DM Brand as Trustee of Racket Sports for Children with Special Needs* (LON/95/2751 No 14080), the work of widening doorways, etc to facilitate access for handicapped people, was not supplied to the charity which funded the work, but to the tennis club owning the premises, which contracted with, and paid, the builder.

The premises problem

10.38 Some of the zero-ratings only apply if the goods are installed in a particular kind of building. For instance, *items 16-18* between them zero-rate, to a handicapped person, the installation of a lift in his or her house, or to a charity in its home or day centre for handicapped persons. In *Union of Students of the University of Warwick* (MAN/95/802 No 13821), the Union failed to get zero-rating for the installation of a lift at their premises. Although the lift was used mostly by handicapped students, and the Union's activities were charitable, the premises were a day centre for all students, not just handicapped ones.

In the VAT Tribunal case of *Friends of the Elderly v Revenue and Customs Comrs* (VTD 20,597), it was held that zero-rating for the installation of a lift in a care home could be extended to include the architect's services.

The appellant was a charity providing a permanent residence for the elderly, and had appealed against an HMRC decision that the architect's services relating to the installation of a new lift in a care home did not qualify for zero rating. HMRC argued that the words '*in the installation of a lift*' in *item 17* of *Group 12* of *Sch 8* of *VATA 1994* referred only to the physical act of installing the lift. However, the Tribunal was in agreement with the appellant's interpretation of the words in the legislation, that the installation of the lift is the end result and, hence, the zero rating includes all the services necessarily performed in achieving that end result. The Tribunal Chairman stated:

> '... this includes the architect's services, which are clearly necessary to the installation because without them the building that holds the lift could not have been designed or built.'

The case may lead to VAT refunds for charitable institutions which have received zero-rated installations of lifts. It may also apply to registered social landlords and other care home providers, where the contractor had not charged VAT on the installation of a lift due to the issuing of a 'certificate' by the recipient of the services.

Under *Sch 8, Group 6, item 2*, professional services received in connection with the installation of a lift are specifically excluded from zero rating when a building is constructed. However *item 17* of *Group 12* (which grants zero-rating on the installation of a lift) does not explicitly exclude such fees. It uses the phrase '*the services necessarily performed in the installation of a lift*', and the Tribunal found the architect's services in the appellant's case were '*necessarily performed*', and could, therefore, benefit from zero-rating.

As *item 2* of *Group 6* excludes the services of an '*architect, surveyor or any person acting as a consultant or in a supervisory capacity*', the decision would appear to open up these services as candidates for zero-rating too, when supplied for the installation of a zero-rated lift.

At the time of going to print, HMRC had not issued any formal response to the case.

IMPORTS, EXPORTS ETC—SCH 8 GROUP 13

10.39   This provides three specialist zero-ratings for:

- the sale of goods not yet cleared through Customs;

- supplies of goods or services in connection with international defence projects;

- the supply to an overseas customer of jigs, patterns, templates, dies, punches, and similar machine tools used in the UK solely to produce goods for export outside the EU.

The last of the above enables a manufacturer to zero-rate his charge for tooling required to produce the goods to the customer's specification, which are exported. He cannot zero-rate the tooling under the ordinary rules for the export of goods because it never leaves his factory.

CHARITIES—SCH 8 GROUP 15

10.40   This zero-rates a variety of supplies either by a charity, or to a charity, including:

- the sale by a charity, or its trading subsidiary, of goods donated to it;

- the donation of goods to a charity, or its trading subsidiary, for sale or export;

- the export of any goods by a charity;

- the supply of relevant goods, primarily medical equipment of various kinds and vehicles designed or adapted to carry handicapped persons, either to an eligible body or for donation to one. 'Eligible body' means hospitals, NHS bodies of various kinds and certain others. The zero-rating enables, for example, a local appeal committee to get a piece of medical equipment for donation to a local hospital free of VAT or that hospital to buy it direct using any charitable funds which it may happen to have. Many National Health institutions benefit from trust funds dating from before the NHS was formed;

- advertising supplied to a charity.

The above is only a synopsis of detailed rules which cover several pages of the law. As with the rules on aids for the handicapped in *Group 12*, a business will need to study the law in detail, if it is affected by them.

The following guidance has been issued by HMRC:

- Notice 701/1 *Charities*;

- Information Sheet 8/98 (June 1998) (plus correction) *Charities: Supply, repair and maintenance of relevant goods—including adapted motor vehicles*;

- Notice 701/6 plus supplement *Charity funded equipment for medical, veterinary uses etc*;

- Notice 701/58 *Zero-rating of charity advertising*.

Donated goods

10.41   Donated goods can be created out of a variety of goods and services. For example, the calendars sold via the BBC 'Hearts of Gold' programme in 1993 on behalf of SOS for children qualified, having been produced from goods and services supplied without charge. The relief does not zero-rate all sales of a charity shop. Bought-in goods are standard-rated.

A concession zero-rates the disposal of goods unsuitable for sale to the public because of poor quality (Notice 48 (March 2002) para 3.21).

In the Tribunal case of *Gablesfarm Dogs & Cats Home* (VTD 20,519), HMRC unsuccessfully argued that the sale of abandoned pets should be standard-rated because the animals were not truly donated goods. The appellant was a charity providing rescue and shelter for abandoned/unwanted cats and dogs. When animals were re-homed a charge was made to the new owner which was treated as zero rated under *Sch 8, Group 15, item 1* as sale of donated goods by a charity. HMRC considered that the zero rating should only apply to the sale of unwanted animals donated by their original owners, not those received from the local authority, police or general public as strays. They argued that only the original owner could transfer the ownership of the goods and make a donation, and the first argument before the Tribunal centred on whether ownership was a prerequisite of donation.

Gablesfarm were under contract with the local authority to kennel dogs brought by them for seven days, enabling the local authority to discharge their obligations under the *Environmental Protection Act 1990*. The local authority paid for administration, kennelling and vet's fees for seven days, after which their obligations ceased and the dogs became the property of Gablesfarm under the *Environmental Protection Act 1990*. HMRC's secondary argument was that the sale of dogs received from the local authority were excluded from zero rating for not meeting the conditions set out in *Note 1* of *Sch 8, Group 15*, specifically that the sale took place as a result of a prior arrangement in place before the goods were made available for sale. The Tribunal dismissed this view. The terms of the contract did not regulate what happened to the dogs after the expiry of the seven days, and the Tribunal was satisfied that the sales took place as a result of Gablesfarm's charitable objectives, not as a result of its contract with the city council. They considered *Note 1* to be an anti-avoidance measure, and the contract bore no hallmarks of avoidance and was not an arrangement within the meaning of *Note 1*.

On the issue of donation, the Tribunal considered that ownership was not an absolute concept in English law. The local authority warden has statutory power to give stray dogs to such a centre, which effects ownership by Gablesfarm, and members of the public acquire the right of possession of a stray unless the original owner demands its return, so can also transfer ownership. Furthermore Gablesfarm made no payment to people who brought in lost or abandoned animals, and HMRC guidance focuses on the point that goods given freely to a charity can be sold at the zero rate, rather than making any mention of the ownership of the goods. The social reason for the UK's zero rating legislation in this area is to help charities raise funds for their charitable objectives. The Tribunal concluded that HMRC's approach of distinguishing between the sales of animals directly given by their owners and those abandoned, produced an irrational result when set against the specific purpose of animal protection. The Tribunal concluded that the sales may be zero-rated, and the appeal was allowed in full.

HMRC subsequently acknowledged their acceptance of the Tribunal's decision in *Revenue & Customs Brief 14/08*, and invited claims for VAT refunds from any other animal charities that had standard-rated such sales.

Relevant goods

10.42 *Relevant goods* is defined in *Note (3)* and includes many of the items zero-rated as aids for the handicapped under *Group 12*. It includes:

- medical, scientific, computer, video, sterilising, laboratory or refrigeration equipment if it is:

    (i)   for use in medical research, training, diagnosis or treatment; or

    (ii)   parts and accessories for use in or with the above.

A careful study of the above wording shows that it is not enough for goods to be used in medical training. They must be medical in nature. This prevents equipment, such as an overhead projector, being zero-rated merely because of the use to which it is put.

However, HMRC used to argue that it was not enough for goods to be designed for medical training, and that they must also be of a kind used for diagnosis or treatment. On that basis, resuscitation training models would not qualify but an extra-statutory concession was announced on 8 July 1998, effective from March 1997. Further details were given in *Business Brief 10/99* dated 22 April 1999.

This 'concession' was probably unnecessary. In *Medical and Dental Staff Training Ltd* (LON/98/1442 No 17031), the Tribunal was persuaded that 'phantom heads' used in training dentists, were *medical equipment*. 'Phantom heads' are specialist equipment, which reproduce the physical characteristics and limitations of a human head. Witnesses gave evidence that the heads were used to some extent in postgraduate training on actual patient cases in which the equipment was used to plan and practise the dental treatment to be later carried out on the patient. Thus, there was an element of use for treatment which blurred the distinction between training and treatment.

In *Anglodent Co* (LON/2000/271 No 16891), a case concerning similar equipment, another Tribunal took an even firmer line, commenting that the words of the statute suggested that the words *for use in medical training* suggested that medical training equipment was intended to qualify as *medical equipment*. Whilst equipment with a variety of possible uses did not become medical merely because it was for use in medical training, the goods in question had a unique purpose at the time of supply and therefore qualified as medical.

See also under *Group 12* for notes on the numerous cases concerning aids for the handicapped, some of which also qualify as relevant goods.

In *Supplier Ltd* (No 18247—anonymous because of the sensitive nature of the supplies), specialist animal cages used in research were held to be laboratory equipment. Specialised animal bedding, nesting materials, liners and litter were accessories. Protective clothing, disinfectants, etc were found mostly not to qualify, being for general rather than specialised use.

In *Research Establishment* (LON/03/931 No 19095), also anonymous, an air ventilation system was held to be laboratory equipment because of the specialist nature of the equipment designed to sustain scientific research work.

Rescue equipment

10.43   *Note (3)(g)* says that *relevant goods* includes certain specialist equipment *solely for use for the purpose of rescue or first-aid services undertaken by a charitable institution providing such services*. In *Severnside Siren Trust Ltd* (LON/99/88 No 16640), a siren system for alerting the public to danger from toxic gasses etc resulting from industrial accidents was held to be for the purpose of rescue services and thus to be *relevant goods*.

Evidence to justify zero-rating

10.44   The supplier must obtain evidence that the supply is to a charity and is eligible for zero-rating. Where that zero-rating depends upon the specific circumstances of the customer, the latter must provide a certificate to the supplier. Check on the precise terms of the certificate—see examples in the notices listed earlier.

CLOTHING AND FOOTWEAR—SCH 8 GROUP 16

10.45   The zero-rating is for children's clothing and protective boots and helmets, including cycle helmets, both motor and pedal, to private purchasers (not when supplied to a business for use by its employees).

Children's clothing is not automatically zero-rated!

The law requires the clothing or footwear to be:

● designed for young children; and

● not suitable for older persons.

The issue of size

10.46   Although Notice 714 (January 2002) *Zero-rating young children's clothing and footwear* contains detailed guidance on, and sizes for, different items accepted as qualifying for zero rating, this is subject to the overall requirements of design and suitability. Mere size is insufficient, as a matter of law, despite the misleading suggestion otherwise in para 4.2 of the Notice!

The sizes are intended to provide a cut-off point on a child's 14th birthday. However, many small women can wear children's sizes, and many children need adult sizes. Since, as soon as a child understands the difference between children's clothing and that for adults, it wants to wear the adult version, HMRC have a control problem.

The result is an unsatisfactory situation in which retailers have a difficult problem differentiating between adult and children's clothing at the margin, and where there is some revenue leakage because women wear children's sizes. On the other hand, some 12-year-olds need adult sizes, and have to pay VAT.

If a business is involved in this sector, it should take the design requirement seriously!

In *Brays of Glastonbury* (CAR/78/95 No 650), moccasins were held to be standard-rated because there was no evident feature of design for young children. Evidence at the hearing included the point that 60% of UK women could wear shoes of size 5 or smaller despite the Notice stating that zero-rating was acceptable up to size 5½!

In *Smart Alex Ltd* (LON/01/1307 No 17832), the Tribunal said an XL size sweatshirt for an 11-year-old, to which a school logo and the pupil's name was added by the wholesaler to create a school uniform, was standard-rated. The evidence of the design intention was the size of the item, not the age of the user.

An item is not clothing just because it is worn! Wrist bands and ear muffs are an example (*Vidhani Brothers Ltd* (MAN/04/0296 No 18997)).

EMISSIONS ALLOWANCES—SCH 8 GROUP 17

10.47   An 'emissions allowance' means:

- a Community tradeable emissions allowance;

- a unit issued pursuant to the Kyoto Protocol; or

- any option relating to any such allowance or unit.

In response to the escalating threat of VAT fraud in connection with trading of emissions allowances (often called 'carbon credits'), the Government has introduced legislation to zero rate the supply of emissions allowances within the UK with effect from 31 July 2009. This is an interim measure that the Government expects to remain in force until an EU-wide solution is implemented. It follows similar action taken by France and the Netherlands. The UK has applied to the EU for a retrospective derogation to remove VAT from these products.

Chapter 11

So what is exempt?

SIGNPOSTS

- Supplies of land and property are exempt from VAT except for the freehold sale of new commercial buildings less than three years old which are standard rated, the sale or long lease of new residential property which is zero-rated and commercial property on which the option to tax has been exercised. Some further short-term rights are excluded from the exemption, for example parking facilities, shooting rights etc (see **11.3–11.14**).

- The exemption for insurance extends to insurance brokers and other intermediaries and some outsourced services (see **11.14–11.35**).

- The exemption for financial services covers banks and financial institutions, the sale of securities, the provision of credit and hire purchase and the services of financial intermediaries (see **11.38–11.66**).

- The exemption for education covers 'eligible bodies' which include state and private schools, universities and colleges, charities and other non-profit making bodies, private tuition provided by sole proprietors and partnerships (but not limited companies) and some vocational training (see **11.67–11.80**).

- Exemption applies to one-off charity fund raising events and supplies of associated goods but not to other goods and services supplied by a charity (see **11.114–11.115**).

11.1 This chapter provides in-depth coverage of much of the detail—referring to numerous court decisions. This chapter and that on zero-rating are, therefore, a good start in understanding what are often highly technical points.

However, always check whether, since this edition was published, there have been further developments. If a business wants to be sure of what the precise position is currently on either zero-rating or exemption, it must firstly check with the law and commentary in an updating service in case there has been a change in the law not yet reflected in the law pages, or a recent decision not yet reflected in the commentary.

- A business should check the law and/or comment in any regularly updated service to which it subscribes.

- *VAT Notes, Revenue & Customs Briefs,* and other sources of information published since this edition of this book should be checked. They are explained in Chapter 2, *Where to find the law?* and can be found on the HMRC website. See page lxvii under *Contacting HMRC* on how to find them.

THE CONTENTS OF SCH 9

11.2

Focus

Group 1 Land

Group 2 Insurance

Group 3 Postal services

Group 4 Betting, gaming and lotteries

Group 5 Finance

Group 6 Education

Group 7 Health

Group 8 Burial and cremation

Group 9 Trade unions, professionals and other interest bodies

Group 10 Sports, sports competitions and physical education

Group 11 Works of art, etc

Group 12 Fund-raising events by charities and other qualifying bodies

Group 13 Cultural services, etc

Group 14 Supplies of goods where input tax cannot be recovered

Group 15 Investment gold

Group 16 Cost sharing exemption

LAND—SCH 9 GROUP 1

11.3   The exemption for land is brief. It covers *the grant of any interest in, right over or any licence to occupy land* with a rider, which adapts that for Scottish land law.

'Grant' includes an assignment or surrender of a lease. It also covers a reverse surrender, ie a case where a tenant has to make a payment to a landlord in order to get out of obligations under an onerous lease (*Note (1)*).

Then come the words 'other than' at the start of a long list of exceptions in *Items 1(a)–(n)*. Being exceptions to the exemption, they are standard-rated. Thus, *Item 1(d)* standard-rates the supply of hotel accommodation.

Note: A business should be precise in its language over land transactions. For instance, people routinely refer to the 'sale' of a property when they mean either a sub-lease or an assignment at a premium. The VAT status can be different.

The exemption

11.4

Focus

Thus, subject to the exceptions, the exemption is for:

- any interest in land. This means a freehold or a lease, which must be in writing;

- a right over land. Rights of way and mineral rights are examples;

- any licence to occupy land. Licences do not have to be in writing, and they are often informal. A licence to occupy land can be for as short a period as an afternoon, and for as small an area as that occupied by a market stall.

What is an exempt freehold sale?

11.5   In *Virtue(t/a Lammermuir Game Services) v Revenue and Customs Comrs* ([2007] BVC 2618), the appellants were farmers in the Scottish Borders who had diversified their activities to include the sale of parts of their land to DIY housebuilders as serviced plots of land.

The activity involved employing contractors to undertake preparatory earthworks, and to construct a spine road and associated drainage and lighting (it was accepted that this was a zero-rated supply by the contractors to the appellant). The appellant also arranged for the utilities to lay water and electricity connections up to the boundaries of the individual plots (enabling the DIY housebuilder to arrange their own individual connections). The DIY housebuilders were obliged to construct the properties to meet general criteria within the overall planning permission obtained by the appellant, who made a single charge for each serviced plot. The dispute comes down to a single v multiple supply argument deriving from the provision of the pre-sale engineering works and services.

HMRC issued a ruling after a visit in 2006 that the engineering works were not a means of better enjoying the principal supply of the land, but were an aim in themselves to the purchaser. Furthermore, HMRC ruled that the engineering works were not supplied in the course of construction as a building, and were thus standard-rated, thereby necessitating an apportionment of the plot sale price. HMRC tried to argue that this analysis might give a better overall VAT position for the DIY housebuilder than the arguments of the appellant. The appellant's main argument was that, under CPP principles, there was a single exempt supply of land. The alternative argument was that, if there were multiple supplies, they were a mix of exempt land and zero-rated engineering works and services supplied in the course of construction of dwellings.

The Tribunal Chairman concluded that the engineering works and services are not an aim in themselves, and that it would be entirely artificial to make the split suggested by HMRC. As such, there was a single supply, correctly regarded as an exempt supply of land. Although that conclusion decided the case, the Chairman considered the alternative argument and concluded that, if there was a multiple supply, it was a mix of exempt supply of land and zero-rated engineering works and services supplied in the course of construction of dwellings. The Chairman observed that both these conclusions avoid any VAT cost, express or hidden, falling upon the DIY housebuilder (unlike the HMRC analysis). The appeal was accordingly allowed.

What is or is not a licence to occupy?

11.6   The precise definition of a licence to occupy was referred by the House of Lords to the ECJ in *Sinclair Collis Ltd* ([1999] STC 701: [2001] UKHL 30: [2001] STC 989: [2003] STC 898). This is an important case which helps to clarify the borderline between exempt licences to occupy land and standard-rated rights related to its use.

Sinclair Collis's (SC) agreement with each publican gave it the right to install its cigarette vending machine and to operate and maintain it in the premises for two years in a place decided on by the publican.

Directive 2006/112/EC, Art 135(1)(l) (previously *Art 13(B)(b)*, of the *EC 6th VAT Directive*) exempts the leasing or letting of immovable property, so that is the basis for interpreting any licence to occupy land. The ECJ held that the agreement with SC did not amount to a letting of immovable property. The publican could move the machine about, as necessary. SC had no right of possession of any specific area; moreover the public also had access to the machine. SC's right of access, limited to opening hours, was to the inside of the machine in order to service it.

The ECJ decision will not of course cover all possible licences. The House of Lords, which came to the same conclusion on a majority of 3:2 before referring the matter to the ECJ, commented that the mere right to occupy space is not exempt. Otherwise, that would cover permission to display a picture on the walls of a gallery. Thus, a key distinction made by both courts seems to be between the mere right to use a spot for a particular purpose and the right to exclusive occupation of a specific area. The right to place a public telephone in someone else's premises also seems likely not to qualify for exemption on the basis of *SC*.

In the case of *HMRC v Zombory-Moldovan (t/a Craft Carnival)* [2016] UKUT 433 (TCC), the Upper Tribunal found that that the provision of stalls/stands at craft fairs organised by the appellant were not exempt licences to occupy land. The Tribunal considered that the supplies by the appellant went much further than the passive granting of a licence to occupy land but there was an overarching supply of participating in an expertly-run antiques and collectors fair which was standard rated.

In the case of *Blue Chip Hotels Limited v HMRC* [2017] UKUT 204 (TCC) the Upper Tribunal held that the renting of room in a hotel used for civil wedding ceremonies was a standard rated supply of a bundle of services rather than an exempt supply of land.

Chairs to stylists in hairdressing salons

11.7   Another example is whether the right to use a chair in a hairdressing salon, granted to a self-employed stylist, is exempt. The nature of the supply has been the subject of numerous Tribunal decisions, and in an attempt to clarify the situation a set of guidelines was agreed between Customs (now HMRC) and the Hairdressers' Federation in 1992. The trend of decisions has been that this is a standard-rated supply of the right to carry on a hairdressing business in the salon including the use of the chair and access to other facilities, rather than an exempt licence to occupy. See, for example, *Mrs SV Cranmer* (LON/95/3120 No 17037).

From 1 October 2012 the legislation was clarified so that all chair rentals are now viewed as a standard-rated taxable supply.

However, in *Kieran Mullin Ltd* [2003] EWHC 4 (Ch), it was held that self-employed stylists who occupied space in and used the facilities of the taxpayer's hairdressing salon in return for a fee under 'rent a chair' agreements, were supplying their hairdressing services direct to customers. This was despite the fact that the contractual structure between the taxpayer and the stylists did not come within the National Hairdressers' Federation guidelines. As such, the salon was not required to account for VAT on the consideration received from customers.

KML had operated a number of salons which had a number of employed stylists and self-employed stylists. The dispute concerned only the self-employed stylists, and the issue was whether their services were supplied to the customer by KML or by the stylist. If the hairdressing services were supplied by KML, then KML would have to account for VAT on the income, whereas if the services were supplied by the self-employed stylists, who are not generally VAT registered, no VAT would be due. KML charged the self-employed stylists for renting a chair and other services on which VAT is accounted for.

Each self-employed stylist had entered into a 'rent a chair agreement' with KML. Customs argued that 'the self-employed stylists do not exercise control over their own actions' and 'as a consequence' KML was required 'to account for tax on the total value of the supplies to the public'. Factors considered important by Customs in reaching their decision included the appointment of locums, holiday arrangements, sick leave arrangements, etc. Customs also issued questionnaires to a number of self-employed stylists, raising further questions on prices, insurance, keys, etc.

In finding for KML, Mr Justice Park placed reliance on the 'Rent a Chair contract', saying '*I hope that questionnaires will not start to develop into regular substitutes for witness statements.*'

Leases

11.8   Rent under a lease is exempt unless you opt to tax it, as explained in Chapter 26, *Property*. Any references to an exempt supply below are subject to the option to tax, and if exercised, the supply becomes taxable at the standard rate.

A business should be aware of any additional terms of the lease, such as that either side shall pay a premium or for work to be done. Usually, such payments will have the same character as the rent because they are paid as part of the conditions under which the property is occupied. For example, HMRC used to argue that a premium was only exempt if paid by the tenant to the landlord. Then the ECJ held in *Lubbock Fine* ([1993] ECR 1–6665, [1994] STC 101) that a reverse premium, paid by a landlord to induce a tenant to take on a lease, was also exempt.

However, in *Cantor Fitzgerald International* ([2001] STC 1453) the ECJ held that the exemption applies to the grant of leases, not to transactions, which are merely based on them, or are ancillary to them. Therefore, when CFI was paid by the existing tenant to accept the assignment of a lease, it made a standard-rated supply to that existing tenant.

In *Mirror Group plc* ([2001] STC 1453), heard at the same time, the ECJ held that a reverse premium paid to MG by the landlord as an inducement to take up a lease was also not payment for an exempt supply. The Court also said that merely undertaking to become a tenant in such a case was not a supply of services to the landlord. However, the High Court noted that the Tribunal had held that there had been a supply, and refused to remit the case for a further hearing.

Thus, if a premium is charged by a landlord for granting a lease, or by a tenant for assigning one, the supply is exempt. So are payments for surrenders and reverse surrenders, as noted at the start of the comments on *Group 1*. This is because, in each of those cases, there is the supply of an interest in land. Neither CFI nor MG had any interest in the land in question at the time of the payments to them; each was acquiring it, not supplying it.

In *Business Brief 12/05*, HMRC accept that payment by a landlord to a tenant as an inducement to take a lease does not normally create a taxable supply by the tenant unless the latter does something in return outside normal lease terms—such as carrying out work on the building. HMRC also refer to acting as an anchor tenant although they admit that that is questionable—and do not explain what they think it means anyway!

HMRC do accept, in para 10.5, Notice 742 (March 2002) *Land and Property* that variations to existing leases, such as changing the permitted use, altering the length of the lease or the property covered by it are exempt. Nevertheless, the *CFI* and *MG* cases have shown that the scope of the exemption for interests in land is not as wide as was previously thought.

Thus, an important planning point is that, before entering into any agreement concerning property, the parties agree on the VAT status of the transaction. In the most simple situation of an ordinary lease with no premium, the one supplying the interest in land may wish to waive exemption for (opt to tax) the rent so as to make it standard-rated and the associated input tax recoverable. The VAT involved may be considerable if there has been expenditure on, for instance, refurbishing the building. However, a tenant, who is partly exempt or not even VAT registered will not wish to be charged VAT. Depending on the input tax involved, it may be better for the landlord to negotiate a higher rent with such a tenant rather than to opt to tax it.

As soon as the agreement becomes more complicated with payments other than rent, careful consideration should be given to whether they qualify for exemption. If they do not, the option to tax is irrelevant.

A planning point concerns any work needed on the property, which may seem obvious but which all too frequently seems not to be understood. If the rent is exempt, and the landlord therefore could not recover VAT incurred on the property, but the tenant can, the landlord should leave it to the tenant to do the work by issuing a tenant-repairing lease. The tenant will be able to recover the VAT if the property is to be used for the purposes of a taxable business.

However, the landlord should not write into the terms of the lease a requirement that the tenant shall do specific work, or they will be in danger of increasing the value of the exempt rent by the value of the work done by the tenant. The same applies if a rent-free period is part of the formal terms of the lease, as opposed to merely arising from the fact that the rent only starts from a date subsequent to occupation.

Similarly, a landlord cannot recover VAT incurred on work done to meet the requirements of the tenant merely by including a provision that the value of the work will be invoiced separately. The work will be supplied by the builder to the landlord, not to the tenant, and the onward supply can hardly be of building work. Thus, in *West Devon Borough Council* (LON/97/549 No 17107), a contribution from a tenant towards the cost of refurbishing the property was held to be a premium for the lease, not payment for the work.

Virtual assignments of leases

11.9 A 'virtual assignment' of a lease is created when a tenant agrees with the third party for the latter to take on responsibility for the rent in return for charging to the tenant a similar amount plus a margin for managing the property. It is done when the tenant cannot readily obtain permission from the landlord to assign the lease to the third party. In *Abbey National plc* (LON/03/0303 No 18666: [2005] EWHC 831; [2006] EWCA Civ 886), the CA restored the Tribunal's decision. The supply by the third party to Abbey National was standard-rated. A right of occupation was an essential and fundamental element of a transaction of leasing or letting of premises. Interpretation of the exemption for supplies of land under EU law must be consistent, and cannot, therefore, vary according to the law on property in each State, but exemption cannot apply without that right of occupation.

Property owned by the owners of a business

11.10 An associated point concerns the situation where a business occupies an office or factory owned by one or more of its directors, or by their pension fund. In such situations, directors tend to take it for granted that their company can recover any VAT incurred on expenditure on the property, regardless of the fact that it does not own it. Of course, many 'leasehold improvements' will have little or no ongoing value in an industrial context; that is to say, work in adapting the fabric or altering the layout of the building for the purposes of the business occupying it may be irrelevant to the next user.

However, suppose a property was substantially improved at the expense of the occupying company and then sold on for a substantial capital gain; VAT recovered by the company on the cost of the improvement work would represent a significant saving to a property owner not registered for VAT. If HMRC realised what had happened, they would obviously query it.

Neither the directors nor their pension fund are likely to be registered for VAT. The arrangements are probably informal, but common sense suggests a written agreement under which an initial rent is determined, and the business is made responsible for all expenditure on the property needed for that business. I suggest making a note of the normal commercial rent payable for such a property at the time, and the reduction due to the business assuming liability for repairs. However, do not build into the agreement a rent reduction or a rent-free period in return for a formal obligation of the business to carry out improvements.

Although, for arrangements not at arm's length, a formal lease and security of tenure may be unnecessary, it seems to me that something in writing is needed in order to confirm the basis for VAT recovery. Board minutes setting out the reasons for major expenditure as it occurs could also be useful evidence of why it was necessary for the purposes of the business.

Service charges for property

11.11

Focus

Normally service charges follow the liability of the main supply, so if the rent is exempt the service charge is normally exempt and if the rent is standard-rated the service charge is normally standard-rated.

A service charge made under a property lease is normally just rent under a different name because it is an additional sum due under the lease. Its status is, therefore, the same as the rent, and is exempt unless you make the rent standard-rated by opting to tax it—explained in Chapter 26, *Property*.

That does not cover service charges to freehold owners of dwellings, because there is no exempt rent. However, by concession, HMRC will allow such charges to be treated as exempt in order to prevent unfairness as between different owners. See Notice 742 *Land and property* for details.

An exception to the exemption was found in *Canary Wharf Ltd* (LON/95/ 2869 No 14513). Repairs and maintenance, servicing common areas and car parking were held to be separate standard-rated supplies rather than part of the rent, when supplied by a management company direct to the tenants. The decision was based on the wording of the lease, and the fact that the services supplied were more extensive than those necessary to ensure 'quiet enjoyment' of the property by the tenants.

A service charge covers heat and light if that is a part of the costs covered by the service charge; ie it is merely a lump sum included. However, if the fuel and power are separately metered, the charge is taxable—possibly at the reduced rate if at the de minimis quantities mentioned at **9.3**.

THE STANDARD-RATED EXCEPTIONS

11.12   *Items 1(a)–(n)* standard-rate the following supplies.

(a)   *Sale of the freehold*—(fee simple) in commercial and industrial buildings, whether still under construction or within three years of completion (*Notes (2) and (4)*). See Chapter 26, *Property*, for further comment.

(b)   *Supplies under developmental tenancies etc*—now of no practical effect.

(c)   *Sporting rights*—(shooting, fishing, etc) unless included in the freehold of the land in question. A lease, which includes sporting rights, must be apportioned (*Note (8)*).

(d)   *Hotel accommodation.*

(e)   *Self storage.*

This is wider than it sounds because it covers a bed in a hotel, inn, boarding house, or 'similar establishment,' together with any room provided in conjunction with the sleeping accommodation, or for the purpose of a supply of catering, such as at a wedding reception.

Similar establishment also includes furnished houses and flats which are used by or advertised as suitable for use by visitors or travellers, even if without board or facilities for preparing food (*Note (9)*).

Similar establishment has been held to cover a hostel for the homeless, even though, in order to obtain a place, the individual had to be on Social Security and the average stay was several weeks rather than the few nights more typical of a hotel (*Namecourt Ltd* [1984] VATTR 22, 1560). A Tribunal reached the same conclusion in *Westminster City Council* ([1989] VATTR 71 No 3367), concerning a hostel called Bruce House in which the accommodation was basic cubicles. So did that in *Look Ahead Housing and Care Ltd* (LON/00/1133 No 17613), a hostel providing accommodation mostly for homeless people.

However, in *International Student House* (LON/95/3142 No 14420), the Tribunal observed that the 'predominant characteristic' of a hotel, inn or boarding house was 'the offer of use of accommodation for gain'. ISH, a charity, whose objective was to further international understanding by providing accommodation to students from the UK and overseas, was not operating a *similar establishment*.

Then, in *Dinaro Ltd (t/a Fairway Lodge)* (LON/99/855 No 17148), a 42-room hostel for people with mental health problems and in need of care was held not to be one either. This was because of the selectivity in the choice of residents— people with mental health problems, the high degree of care and supervision, most of the residents being in receipt of the middle rate care component of the Disability Living Allowance and the emphasis on the residents being part of a 'family'.

11.13 *So what is exempt?*

The hire of premises including catering is standard-rated.

If you provide catering in a place, which is not a hotel, the entire charge is likely to be standard-rated even if you price the use of the venue separately from the food and drink. In *Leez Priory* (LON/02/181 No 18185), the venue charge for the use for weddings of a period house set in parkland was held to be part of a composite supply with the catering and other facilities offered, which included overnight accommodation for guests. Even if that was wrong, it was a similar establishment despite the sleeping accommodation only being on offer to guests attending a wedding.

From 1 October 2012 self-storage charges will all become standard-rated as these are to be added to the exceptions from exemption.

The use of a conference/function room can be exempt

11.13 HMRC accept that the use of a room for a conference or a function is exempt even if there is an inclusive charge to those attending for a meal and/or sleeping accommodation. In other words, the *8-hour rate*, which is per person for use of the room and a meal and the *24-hour rate*, which includes accommodation, cover separate supplies of space, food and accommodation. The use of the space is exempt—unless the business has opted to tax the building.

This view was announced in *Business Brief 1/06*, effective from 18 January 2006. Previously, HMRC had seen the *24-hour rate* as for a single standard-rated supply.

The 28-day rule for long-stay accommodation

11.14 See *Sch 6, para 9* for a special rule, which reduces to a minimum of 20% the value of the supply to an individual once a stay exceeds 28 days. This means that, from day 29 on, the value reduces to that of the facilities provided, such as cleaning and linen. The minimum value for the latter is 20%. VAT must also be charged on the value attributable to any meals provided. The balance of the charges, up to 80%, is outside the scope of VAT, not exempt.

In *The Afro Caribbean Housing Association Ltd* (LON/05/382 No 19450) the four-week rule was held to apply to accommodation similar to hotel rooms, which was provided to individual asylum seekers but invoiced to the British Refugee Council. The supply did not have to be to the individual. Following this case, HMRC announced in *Business Brief 15/06* that they now accepted that the accommodation does not have to be supplied to the occupant, and that where the room in question is being paid for by a local authority or charitable organisation, the reduced-value rule can be applied from the 29th day of occupation.

(e)   Holiday accommodation.

This includes any accommodation in a building, hut (such as a beach hut or chalet), caravan, houseboat, or tent, if the accommodation is advertised (or held out) as holiday accommodation, or suitable for holiday or leisure use (*Note (13)*).

It also includes houses, flats, chalets and the like:

- where the lease prevents the tenant living there throughout the year. Timeshares are an example;

- where living there throughout the year is similarly prevented by the terms of any covenant or planning permission. Seaside chalets are a possible example (*Note (11)* via *Sch 8, Group 5, Note (13)*).

However, if the building is more than three years old, neither the freehold, nor a premium for a tenancy, lease or licence in it, are caught. In other words, the sale of, say, a holiday flat is only standard-rated until it is more than three years old (*Note (12)*) unless the option to tax has been exercised. Moreover, the rule normally only affects places in which there is no right to live all the year round, since, if permanent occupation is possible, a place will not usually be marketed as holiday accommodation.

In *Loch Tay Highland Lodges Ltd* (EDN/01/101 No 18785), the sale of the freehold of holiday lodges by the constructor was held to be standard-rated; the planning permission stated the lodges should be used solely for holiday accommodation, not occupied as anyone's sole or main residence. The Tribunal felt that the earlier decision in *Livingstone Homes UK Ltd* (EDN99/88 No 16649) was wrong. It was incorrect that houses could be principal private residences, even though the terms of the planning consent were that they *shall be used as holiday dwelling houses only and for no other purpose and shall never in any way be sub-divided.*

In the case of *HMRC v Fortyseven Park Street Ltd (Tax)* [2018] UKUT 41 (TCC), the Upper Tribunal decided that the grant of fractional interests in a property in Mayfair were exempt from VAT. The appellant had a 60-year lease on a property which had formerly been an hotel. The appellant refurbished the property and created 49 self-contained apartments. The appellant then sold 617 fractional interests in the property in a similar manner to a time share property.

HMRC's case, put shortly, was that the membership agreement, properly understood, imposed obligations and responsibilities on the appellant of such a nature that its supply could not be regarded as a mere passive letting activity, but must be found to be active exploitation of the residences which add significant value to the supply and therefore standard rated.

The Upper Tribunal consider that, in the context of the supply made by the appellant, the FTT erred in law in focusing on the duration of the individual stays that could be made by a member by virtue of the Fractional Interest which the member acquired. The Tribunal considered that the FTT had failed to have proper regard to the nature of the supply made by the appellant. That supply was not of a series of individual short-term stays; it was a supply of a long-term right to occupy a reserved residence during the relevant periods. The Upper Tribunal therefore found that the supply was exempt from VAT.

(f)   Seasonal pitches for caravans and associated facilities at caravan parks.

This particular exclusion was closely examined in *Tallington Lakes Ltd* [2007] EWHC 1955 (Ch),where HMRC had sought to apply exclusion (f) on the basis that the taxpayer fell foul of the 'prevented by any covenant, statutory planning consent, or similar permission from occupying, by living in a caravan at all times throughout the period' definition of a 'seasonal pitch'.

In 2004, TLL had purchased a number of sites within a leisure complex area. Some of the sites accommodated touring caravans, but others consisted of concrete pitches rented long-term to owners of static caravans (which were anchored by metal straps and chains, had their towing bar and wheels removed, and were permanently connected to the electricity mains, gas supply and BT lines). The dispute concerned the latter 'static' pitches. TLL had initially charged VAT on the rentals, but then sought to make a voluntary disclosure for overpaid output tax which HMRC refused. The root of the dispute was that TLL had 'inherited' a range of planning permissions for the site, one of which was a planning licence issued in the 1980s by the district council for 12 sites, which included in respect of three of the sites the condition 'no caravan on the site shall be occupied between 31 January and 1 March in any year'. The rental agreements between TLL and the caravan owners repeated this restriction, although TLL later dropped it to reflect the reality that the restriction had never been enforced.

HMRC's main argument was that the term in the rental agreement, and the term in the planning licence condition, precluded exemption. HMRC also advanced various circumstantial evidence that the site was a seasonal holiday park as opposed to a residential park, including the annual duration of the rental agreements, the payment of non-domestic rates, and terminology used in a previous website. TLL argued that it did not operate a seasonal holiday park, and that the references to the February occupation prohibition in the planning licence should be disregarded, as they had never been enforced, and the period of time during which the Council could have taken action for non-compliance was long elapsed, such that, in practice there was a mutually accepted variation of the prohibition. TLL also argued that the prohibition only applied to certain sites.

The Tribunal Chairman disregarded HMRC's circumstantial evidence on the basis that it should focus only on the application of exclusion (f) to the occupation restrictions, opting instead for TLL's arguments on the planning prohibition. In addition to allowing the appeal, the Tribunal went on to criticise

HMRC for maintaining guidance in an extant edition of Notice 701/20 which they stated in evidence at the Tribunal no longer represented their position!

There was to be no happy ending for TLL, however, as HMRC appealed to the High Court, which allowed the appeal largely on the basis that the Tribunal Chairman had misunderstood the planning licence position!

(g) **Pitches for tents and camping facilities.**

(h) **Parking facilities for vehicles.**

Businesses should be aware of any right over land which includes the right to park on it—including a lock-up garage. The nature of the land is important, and the intention of the customer as to use is irrelevant. It is no good merely getting a statement from a tenant of a wish to park a sofa rather than a motor! To avoid standard-rating the rent of a lock-up garage, the tenancy agreement must expressly prohibit the parking of a vehicle (*Trinity Motor Factors* [1994] STC 504).

In *Internoms Ltd* (LON/98/1112 No 16257) a sub-lease of a piece of land for 120 years, for which planning permission for two cars had been granted, was held to be a standard-rated supply of the facility to park a vehicle, not an exempt interest in land. Then in *Venuebest* (MAN/00/942 No 17685: [2002] EWHC 2870 (Ch): [2003] STC 433), it was held that a lease of land used as a car park was a supply of parking rights in the absence of an express term to the contrary in the lease. The Tribunal had been wrong to say that the rent was exempt merely because the lease granted unfettered use of the land with no reference to parking.

In Notice 742 (March 2002) *Land and property*, HMRC say:

- a *freehold* interest in a car park is exempt, once it is over three years old— one on bare land presumably being seen as a civil engineering work;

- a *lease* for the purpose of car parking in various circumstances, including a car park to a car park operator, of a taxi rank and of storage for bicycles or touring caravans is standard rated;

- but that a lease of land, except for a garage, which says nothing about use for parking vehicles or of land on which a tenant will store its own property, such as the stock of a motor dealer, is exempt.

In the light of *Venuebest*, the last indent above seems doubtful if the land is laid out as a car park or planning permission has been granted for that purpose.

(i) **Deleted.**

(j) **Timber rights, ie the right to fell and remove trees.**

(k) **Housing or storage of aircraft or the mooring or storage of ships and boats.**

(ka) **The grant of facilities for the self storage of goods.**

(l) **Boxes, seats or other accommodation at sports grounds, theatres, concert halls or other places of entertainment.** This catches, for instance, a box at the Albert Hall or a season ticket at a football ground.

(m) **Facilities for playing sport or participating in physical recreation.**

Note (16) puts back into exemption a grant of sports facilities for more than 24 hours or a series of ten or more periods, no matter what the total time provided that:

- they are for the same activity at the same place;

- at intervals of at least a day but not more than 14 days;

- under a written agreement for single price;

- for exclusive use of the facilities;

- the customer is a school, club, association or organisation representing affiliated clubs or constituent associations.

There is no legal definition of 'club'. It can consist of an informal team formed just for a competition involving ten or more events.

For further comment on other rules concerning land, including those on the waiver of exemption or option to tax, see Chapter 26, *Property*.

(ma) **The grant of facilities for the supply of hairdressing services.**

(n) **Specific to Scotland**. Rights under Scottish land law to be granted an interest or right covered by the above paragraphs.

INSURANCE—SCH 9 GROUP 2

11.15 See Notice 701/36 *Insurance* (May 2002) for additional specialist comment on the nature of insurance. The comment here relates only to the exemption for UK insurance risks. For international transactions, see **24.8** and **24.11**. Chapters 23, *Exports and Imports of Services* and 24, *Partial Exemption* explain the rules under which a premium to an insured who belongs outside the EU, or one which is related to an export of goods outside the EU, together with commissions thereon, changes to outside the scope of VAT with recovery of the associated input tax.

Item 1: Insurance premiums

11.16 The insurance exemption covers insurance transactions and reinsurance transactions. The VAT law was simplified from 1 January 2005 removing the requirement to be authorised. However, if a business did not meet the requirements of the *Financial Services and Markets Act 2000 (FSMA 2000)*, it would be in trouble elsewhere! HMRC accept that the following are exempt insurance even though they are not seen as such for regulatory purposes under the *FSMA 2000*:

- funeral plans written under contracts of insurance;

- vehicle breakdown insurance;

- recharges under block insurance policies.

The policyholder acts as a principal, ie as the insurer, not as an intermediary, when charging for the insurance. Thus, the entire recharge is an exempt supply.

The term *block policy* does not include delegated authority arrangements under which a broker enters into contracts on behalf of the insurance company. There, the broker is acting as an intermediary, and his supply is the value of his commission.

RECHARGES UNDER BLOCK INSURANCE POLICIES

11.17

Focus

A block insurance policy allows the policyholder, acting in his name, to buy insurance for third parties on terms with the insurer and the third parties under which he then recharges the insurance to those parties. The policy may include cover for the policyholder's own liability to its customers or members.

Examples are:

- a removal company which provides insurance against the risk of damage during the move;

- insurance provided with car hire – although HMRC unsuccessfully challenged this in *Wheels Private Hire Ltd v HMRC* [2015] UKFTT 363 (TC);

- a sports organisation, which provides its members with cover against the risk of injury or liability to another person whilst taking part in an event.

PRODUCT GUARANTEES AND WARRANTIES

11.18   If a guarantee or a warranty is recognised as insurance by the *Financial Services Authority* (FSA), it is exempt, subject to the rules in *Note (3)* explained later at **11.26**. Those provided by manufacturers and retailers are not usually seen by the FSA as insurance, and HMRC regard them as standard rated. However, it is probably preferable to have a standard-rated warranty if you are the supplier of the goods. This is because an exempt supply incurs Insurance Premium Tax at 17.5%; a standard-rated supply at least lets you recover the associated input tax.

'RUN-OFF' SITUATIONS

11.19   If an insurer ceases to issue new policies, the business is in 'run-off' whilst it deals with claims under contracts already written. The treatment of any additional premium under those existing policies is the same as that of the original one.

If handling the 'run-off' is contracted out to a third party, a planning point arises over the contract. To qualify for exemption as an insurance related service, the third party must make a composite charge for all its services. If it separates that for administration, such as accountancy or the management of invested premiums, that part of the supply will be standard-rated.

An insurer with contracts in 'run-off', which is using a partial exemption method based on premium values, may need to discuss its calculations with HMRC if using the current output values would distort the position. For instance, HMRC might agree the use of the percentage recovery achieved in the last three years of active underwriting.

ENGINEERING INSURANCE AND INSPECTION

11.20   Engineering insurance covers such plant as boilers, cranes and lifts. The contract often requires the plant to be inspected and this may be covered by the premium. In para 4.5 of Notice 701/36 (May 2002), HMRC require insurers to decide whether they are making a separate supply of insurance and inspection or a composite one of either exempt insurance or standard-rated inspection. A key consideration will obviously be whether the premium is calculated and quoted in separate amounts.

Item 4: Insurance brokers

11.21   *Item 4* exempts the services as an *insurance intermediary* of a broker or insurance agent if they are related to a supply, actual or proposed, of insurance or reinsurance covered by *Item 1,* and provided when *acting* in an *intermediary capacity.*

What are the services of an insurance intermediary?

11.22

Focus

A service qualifies as that of an insurance intermediary if it is within any of the following (*Note (1)*):

- the bringing together, with a view to the insurance of risks, of persons seeking insurance and those who provide it;

- work preparatory to concluding insurance contracts;

- assistance in administering and performing such contracts including handling claims;

- collecting premiums.

Exclusion of market research and similar services

11.23   *Note (7)* excludes from the *Item 4* exemption:

- market research, product design, advertising, promotional or similar services;

- the collection, collation and provision of information for use in connection with market research, product design, advertising, promotional or similar activities.

To avoid being caught by the exclusion of advertising services, HMRC say that an organisation which, say, inserts a leaflet in a customer mailing, must:

- be paid per policy sold;

- endorse the product or the insurer;

- target its own customer base.

The last point seems of doubtful validity. It would appear to make no difference whether the person mailed is a customer, a supplier or a blind date!

What is acting in an intermediary capacity?

11.24   *Note (2)* says that a broker or agent is acting in an intermediary capacity wherever he is acting as an intermediary for one or both parties involving:

- an insurer; and

- an actual or prospective buyer of insurance.

11.25 *So what is exempt?*

The above wordings are an attempted simplification of the law intended to make it easier to follow. See the law itself for the actual wording.

Some cases on acting in an intermediary capacity

11.25 In *Teletech (UK) Ltd* (EDN/02/52 No 18080), the Tribunal rejected HMRC's argument that the services of a call centre cold calling to sell insurance by telephone were promotional. A successful call, which sold a policy, put the insurance company on risk so Teletech was an insurance agent supplying services related to insurance transactions. In *Business Brief 07/03,* HMRC accepted this.

In *SOC Private Capital Ltd* (LON/2000/0810 No 17747), the insurers in the Lloyd's market were held to be the underwriting Members, not the Syndicates. The Members' Agents were insurance agents, who supplied both insurance and reinsurance services and services related to insurance transactions. They were a part of the chain between the insured and the insurers and thus participated in insurance transactions. They were authorised to act on behalf of the underwriting Members, they introduced them to the Syndicates, entered on their behalf into commitments with the Managing Agents of those Syndicates and carried out work preparatory to the contracts of insurance.

However, setting up, training and maintaining a sales force of self-employed sales agents, who supplied their services direct to the insurance company was itself not an intermediary service (*Agentevent Ltd* (LON/00/1331 No 17764)). The *Insurance Intermediaries Directive 77/92*, to which it was permissible to refer in interpreting the *EC 6th VAT Directive*, appeared to regard an insurance broker or agent as having a direct relationship with the insured.

In *Morganash Ltd v Revenue and Customs Comrs* (MAN/2005/0749 No 19,777), where I myself represented the taxpayer, MorganAsh supplied outsourced services to the insurance industry. Its main activity was the collection of information from potential customers of insurance companies wishing to obtain life or health insurance.

Once this information had been obtained, MorganAsh normally passed it to the insurance company with a recommendation as to the suitability of the applicant for insurance cover. In some cases MorganAsh offered the services of processing the application and making the decision on behalf the insurance company whether to insure the applicant.

Although not a 'traditional' insurance broker or agent, MorganAsh argued that it was clearly an intermediary making supplies of 'related services', which also fall within the exemption. MorganAsh argued that *Note 1(b)*—the carrying out of work preparatory to the conclusion of contracts of insurance—precisely defines the work it carries out.

The Tribunal found in favour of MorganAsh, and HMRC accepted the decision in *Business Brief 06/07.*

However, in the case of *Risktop Consulting Limited v HM Revenue & Customs* [2015] UKFTT 469 (TC) in very similar circumstances the FTT found for HMRC. This was an appeal against a decision by HMRC that the appellant's 'Assist Service' and 'Support Service' were not exempt under Item 4, Group 2, Sch 9 of the VAT Act 1994 as insurance intermediaries.

In 2001 the appellant developed and introduced a product which involved it liaising directly with the insured to assist the Insured in satisfying the Risk Improvement Requirements by the deadlines. The subject of the appeal is the VAT status of fees paid by Insurers for two of the appellant's products:

(1)   *Support Service* – the provision of Questionnaire Surveys to the Insurers.

(2)   *Assist Service* – the assistance provided to the insured towards satisfying the Risk Improvement Requirements by the deadlines.

The appellant was not involved in any claims process – its work was at the front end when the cover was being taken on. The preparation of the questionnaire by the appellant would be done in conjunction with the insurer, to ensure it captured the information necessary for the insurer to evaluate the risk, but relied mainly on the appellant's expertise in identifying the areas to be addressed and designing the questionnaire.

The appellant argued that its services were a fundamental part of the insurance process, they were part of the appraisal and management of the risk which determined whether to accept the business, and on what terms and was therefore covered by the exemption for insurance intermediaries.

As recognised by HMRC in the Manual at VATINS5210, Item 4 was drafted wider than the Directive had been interpreted in *Arthur Andersen* but a taxpayer was entitled to rely on the wording of Item 4. In the VAT Tribunal case of *Morganash Ltd* (2006) V19777 the services comprised 'the completion of health questionnaires by persons submitting proposals for life assurance policies'.

However, the FTT considered that *Morganash* was not compatible with the test as explained (four years later) by Etherton LJ in *InsuranceWide*.

The Tribunal considered it unsatisfactory that, a decade after the *Andersen* decision, the UK domestic legislation had still not been amended in line with art 135. However, for current purposes none of that assisted the appellant. Although Item 4 may range wider than art 135, the Tribunal found that the appellant was not an insurance agent for Item 4 purposes and that was sufficient to dismiss the appeal.

In *Leadx Ltd* (VTD 20,904), the appellant was involved in the provision of an open market, where sales leads involving loans and insurance products could be bought from and sold to brokers who were willing to purchase them via an internet-based bidding system. The issue to hand was whether these activities were exempt, as argued by the appellant, or taxable, as ruled by HMRC.

The Tribunal considered whether the services constituted a supply involving the negotiation of credit, the arrangement of credit, or the arrangement of insurance as an intermediary. It concluded that the supply was simply the collection and sale of data, which was taxable. The decision includes a detailed analysis of the scope and meaning of the finance and insurance exemptions, especially the meaning of insurance broker/agent (a question which has arisen several times in recent cases). The Tribunal held that the appellant's activities were not carried out with the intention of securing a loan contract or insurance contract, so there was insufficient nexus with its activities and loans and insurance services for exemption to apply. The process was driven by what a broker would pay for a lead, not the needs of the consumer. The activities of the appellant were not essential for a loan or insurance contract to happen, and the appellant was paid for each lead transaction it brokered, whether or not a contract was concluded from that lead. The fact that the appellant had no relationship with insurer or insured was also a key factor in denying the insurance exemption.

This decision looks correct when you look at what the appellant actually did for its money, given that exemptions should be construed strictly, but the case does highlight once again the complexity of these areas.

In the case of *Insurancewide.com Services Ltd*, [2009] EWHC 999 (Ch); [2009] WLR(D) 156 the Court of Appeal confirmed the High Court Chancery Division decision in a joined case where both appellants provide online introductory services between people seeking insurance and a panel of insurers.

The preceding Tribunal cases had produced contradictory answers on similar facts (Trader Media won its appeal, but Insurancewide lost). The court asked itself two questions. The first question was whether a taxpayer who merely introduced parties to each other can be regarded as an insurance agent/broker. The second one was whether the appellants' activities comprised the exempt services of an insurance broker or agent acting as an insurance intermediary, as set out in UK law or if it was advertising. Answering both questions in the affirmative, the court ruled the taxpayer services were exempt.

See **11.28** below for more cases about what qualifies as exempt agency services.

Insurance commissions associated with taxable supplies

11.26 *Note (3)* says that if insurance is sold:

- in connection with a standard-rated supply of goods or services; and

- by the supplier thereof or a person connected with him who deals directly with the customer,

the insurance-related services, apart from the handling of claims, are standard-rated unless:

- the amount of the premium; and

- any other amount that the customer must pay, ie the commission,

are disclosed in writing to the customer. This stops car dealers, for example, reducing the output tax due on their profit margins by attributing artificially large sums to exempt warranties.

In *C R Smith Glaziers (Dunfermline) Ltd* ([2001] STC 770; [2003] UKHL 7; [2003] STC 419) the House of Lords overturned the ruling by the Court of Session and the Tribunal view that the above rule requires that the customer be told exactly how much is charged for an insurance service. A simple formula, such as 10% of the total price, was sufficient.

The Card Protection Plan case

11.27   *Card Protection Plan* (LON/90/282 No 5484; on appeal [1992] STC 797; affd [1994] STC 199, CA; revsd [2001] STC 174, HL; ECJ [1999] STC 270) is an important case:

- because it decided that a credit card registration service was a supply of exempt insurance;

- as a decision that there was a single supply rather than a multiple one at different rates of VAT. See Chapter 12, *Is there one supply or two?*

CPP claimed to provide 15 benefits as shown below:

1. **Confidential Registration of all Cards**—accurate computer records will be kept of all your valuable cards.

2. **£750 Insurance Cover**—against fraudulent use on any one claim, provided loss notification is received within 24 hours of discovery of loss.

3. **Unlimited Protection**—you have £750 cover up to the moment of your call to CPP. After that your protection against fraudulent use is unlimited.

4. **Immediate Loss Notification**—free 24-hour ACTIONLINE to receive your loss reports and act immediately to protect you. ACTIONLINE stickers provided for your phone, diary or wallet, so our vital ACTIONLINE number is always at hand.

5. **Replacement Cards**—can be ordered when losses are notified, thus minimising your inconvenience.

6. **Change of Address Service**—all card insurers can be notified before you move to ensure your cards don't get into the wrong hands.

7. **Lost Key Location**—key tags with your unique policy number and our FREEPOST address help ensure keys can quickly be returned to you in confidence, when found.

8. **Valuable Property & Document Protection**—register serial numbers of your property and details of policies, shares, passports, etc for your own security and to assist in notifying police or making insurance claims in the event of loss or theft. Through our insurance cover you can claim up to £25 on communications costs when assisting police or claiming against personal insurance in respect of items registered with CPP. Includes phone calls, correspondence, postage, etc but not travel costs.

9. **£500 Emergency Cash**—rushed anywhere in the world (upon approval) if you are stranded and have lost your cards. An interest-free advance repayment within 14 days.

10. **Lost Luggage Recovery**—with CPP stickers lost luggage and other personal property such as briefcase or handbag can be quickly identified and owners advised of its location. Our special insurance cover entitles you to claim up to £25 on communications costs incurred arranging recovery of keys or luggage protected by CPP tags and stickers. This includes phone calls, correspondence, postage, etc, but not travel costs.

11. **Emergency Medical Cover Worldwide**—in the event of illness or an accident abroad you need professional help, fast. We provide 24-hour emergency cover and one phone call secures medical advice and assistance in English and other languages, anywhere in the world. If necessary, at your expense, a full consultation, and even medical repatriation by air—with all necessary specialist personnel—can be arranged for you.

12. **Emergency Airline Ticket**—if your credit cards and cash are lost or stolen and you're stranded overseas, CPP's travel cover means arrangements can be made, upon approval, to issue an air ticket to get you home. Cost repayable within 14 days.

13. **Computer Update Services**—confidential printout of your card details for you to check, annually.

14. **Medical Emergency/Warning Card**—dual purpose—to warn that all your cards are protected, and also to provide medical information that can save vital seconds in an emergency. Carry with you at all times.

15. **Car Hire Discounts**—you can claim valuable discounts on car rental from Hertz, Avis and Europcar worldwide.

The case went to the House of Lords, via the ECJ, the decisions being:

Tribunal: standard-rated, there being no supply of insurance.

High Court: multiple supply of exempt insurance and standard-rated other services, which must be apportioned.

Court of Appeal: standard-rated card registration service to which the insurance elements were incidental.

ECJ: House of Lords must decide whether there were:

- two supplies—of insurance and a card registration service; or

- one principal supply to which the other was ancillary.

The House of Lords commented:

- the ECJ's judgment showed that at least some of the supply was insurance;

- whether there was a single supply with ancillary services or two separate supplies depended on whether the key features of the transaction were several distinct principal services or a single one;

- take an overall view; avoid over-zealous dissection and analysis.

The judgment then said:

- points 2, 3 and 8 were insurance. People joined the scheme to get insurance against loss due to misuse of credit cards;

- points 4, 9, 10, 11 and 12 were 'assistance' covered by class 18, point A of the annexe to the First Insurance Directive. That referred to *assistance for persons who get into difficulties while travelling, while away from home or while away from their permanent residence.* The Directive also said that the assistance could be in kind rather than in cash. That the emergency cash advance and air ticket had to be reimbursed did not prevent them being 'assistance';

- the up-to-date record of cards and ordering replacements were valuable in minimising the loss. The luggage tags and medical warning card were useful in assisting in the administration of the scheme. Those services, which were not insurance, were ancillary to the main objective of financial protection against loss and some were minor features. They were preconditions to the client making a claim for indemnity or assistance or for the furnishing of insurance cover;

- even if they could be seen as sufficiently coherent to be treated as a separate supply, it was ancillary to the insurance;

- to regard the insurance as ancillary or subsidiary to the registration of credit card numbers was unreal. The consequences for the client of being able to take protective action with CPP, with whom the cards were registered, were closely linked to the insurance service. One could not say that some elements of the transaction were economically dissociable from the others.

The outsourcing problem

11.28

- outsourcing ordinary administration services, such as running the computer department, has long been recognised as standard-rated;

- but it now appears that administering the principal activity of an insurance company is also standard-rated unless:

    (i)   that work involves direct contact with the insured; or

    (ii)   is a service of a kind normally provided by an insurance broker or agent.

The ECJ decision in *Arthur Andersen and Co Accountants CS* (C-472/03), a Dutch case, confirms that Andersen managed insurance applications and the resulting policies by:

- assessing the risks to be insured;

- deciding whether a medical examination was required;

- where it was not, deciding whether to accept the risk;

- managing and rescinding insurance policies;

- amending contracts in modifying premiums;

- collecting premiums and managing claims;

- setting and paying commission to insurance agents and maintaining contact with them;

- handling aspects relating to reinsurance;

- supplying information to insured parties, insurance agents and others such as the tax authorities.

The ECJ held that, although they contributed to the essence of the activities of an insurance company, the services were not ones typical of an insurance agent:

- the last three bullet points were clearly not activities of an agent;

- moreover, Andersen did not handle essential agency work such as the finding of prospects and their introduction to the insurer. It provided the insurer with the human and administrative resources it lacked and services fundamental to its insurance activities;

- thus what Andersen did was 'back office' activities of an insurance company rather than services of an insurance agent.

HMRC expect that the definition of the services of an insurance intermediary in item 4 will have to be changed. Following a public consultation, the Treasury will take a decision on what to do. Only then will it be clear how far Andersen will affect the UK treatment of outsourced services to an insurance company. The law and/or policy may be changed in due course. In the meantime, however, UK businesses can still take advantage of the wider exemption provided by existing UK legislation. See *Morganash Ltd v Revenue and Customs Comrs* (MAN/2005/0749 No 19,777).

In *Business Brief 23/05* it was stated that the decision on what to do would await the results of a review which the European Commission had announced. Assuming that the review is in-depth and with consultation with Member States, and given that the Treasury has promised sufficient notice in advance of the implementation, no change is likely before 1/1/09 at the earliest.

When that happens, it seems likely that *Century Life and C & V (Advice Line) Services*, described under the next heading, will cease to be followed, if only because the ECJ did not see as significant the definition of an insurance agent in what is now the *Mediation Directive*.

Outsourcing a mis-selling review is exempt

11.29   Until 1 April 2013 the UK took the view that mis-selling reviews were exempt from VAT. This was based on the requirement that the broker act in an intermediary capacity and may have gone beyond the terms of *Art 13(B)(a)* of the *EC 6th VAT Directive* (now *Directive 2006/112/EC, Art 135(1)(a)*). In *Century Life plc* ([2001] STC 38, CA), a decision accepted by HMRC, the Court of Appeal rejected HMRC's argument that an insurance agent or broker must act as such in making a supply; ie that the service must be of a kind normally provided by insurance brokers of agents. The nature of the services was already defined by the Directive as *insurance* and *reinsurance transactions, including related services*.

- it was sufficient that CFS, the provider of the services (a mis-selling review), was an insurance agent because of its other activities;

- the Court agreed that there must be a close nexus between the service and reinsurance transactions;

- however, a mis-selling review making sure that a policy complied with the regulations, concerned its nature, and was intimately related to it;

- that the policy had been sold made no difference, since compliance was a continuing obligation.

Similarly, in *C & V (Advice Line) Services Ltd* (LON/00/153 No 17310), operating a helpline and a service of screening claims and issuing claim forms, the claims then being handled by the insurer, was held to be provided in an intermediary capacity. The Tribunal based this on the definition of an insurance agent in the *Insurance Intermediaries Directive*.

Revenue & Customs Brief 33/12 announced a change in the UK VAT treatment of supplies to insurers of certain mis-selling review services and helpline services following enquiries received from the European Commission. From 1 April 2013 all mis-selling reviews and help-line services are treated as standard-rated.

Outsourcing insurance administration is probably standard-rated

11.30   The ECJ ruled in a Swedish case, *Skandia* ([2001] STC 754), that charges by an insurance company for running the business of its 100%-owned subsidiary would be standard-rated. This ruling was in response to a reference to it by the Swedish court, which was dealing with an appeal by Skandia against a preliminary opinion. The opinion concerned a proposal that the subsidiary would continue to write the business, but would become, in other respects, a shell with all the activity carried out by Skandia.

Difference between Skandia and Century Life

11.31

● *Skandia* would have no relationship with the insured;

● *Century Life* dealt direct with the insured on behalf of the insurance company.

Initial and annual management charges for personal pension schemes

11.32   In *Winterthur Life (UK) Ltd* (LON/1787 No 14935), personal pension schemes were held to embody contracts of insurance between Winterthur and the members of the schemes.

Administrative services incidental to implementing the contracts were part and parcel of the provision of insurance, and, therefore, qualified for exemption:

● despite being provided by two subsidiaries, which were not authorised insurers; and

● despite the member of each scheme controlling the investment policy.

If that were wrong, the two subsidiaries acted as agents for Winterthur in administering the schemes.

In a second Winterthur case, (LON/98/1339 No 17572), the outsourced administration of the self-invested part of a pension scheme was held to be exempt under *Group 2, Item 4* as the services of:

● an insurance agent performing services related to insurance; and

● acting as an insurance intermediary providing assistance in the administration and performance of insurance contracts.

Having accepted that the personal pension plan was a supply of insurance, the Tribunal refused to separate the self-invested part. It noted that *Art 2(1)(b) of* the *EC Insurance Intermediaries Directive 77/92*, which dealt with the rights of establishment of insurance agents and brokers, included in its definition of agents' activities the provision of such assistance. The outsourcing company was closely concerned with the administration of the part of the insurance transaction, which was the self-administered scheme. It acted as an intermediary in certain respects and had a direct relationship with scheme members.

For more cases on outsourcing, see **11.57** below.

Watch the wording of commission agreements

11.33   A payment made by an insurance company or a broker to a third party is not necessarily exempt just because it is concerned with the provision of insurance.

In *British Horse Society Ltd* (MAN/98/736 No 16204), a 'contingent discount', earned on the society's own policies and on those taken out by its members, was held not to reduce the premium but to be payment for the standard-rated exclusivity in advertising to BHS members and promoting the broker's services.

In Notice 701/36, para 8.3, HMRC accept that introductory services *can* qualify for exemption. However, the recipient of the commission has to do more than merely include advertising material in its mailouts.

Fees to the insured for advice are not exempt

11.34   Where a flat fee is charged to an insured instead of the usual commission to the insurer, its VAT status depends upon the service provided. It is as likely to be for consultancy services as it is for 'the services of an insurance intermediary'. Only the latter are exempt.

To charge a standard-rated fee rather than an exempt commission can be advantageous because of the increased input tax recovery.

Handling a claim is also exempt but not other services

11.35   Checking and processing of a claim is exempt *(Note 1(c))*. However, a service is not exempt merely because it is connected with insurance.

Note (8) excludes valuation or inspection services.

Note (9) excludes supplies by loss adjusters, average adjusters, motor assessors, surveyors or other experts except for:

● handling an insurance claim; and

● with written authority from the insurer to accept or reject it and to settle any amounts payable. This may be via a broker who has power to delegate such authority.

Note (10) excludes services provided to the policyholder and paid for by the insurer in settling a claim.

> **Example 11.1— What is claims handling?**
>
> The insured finds and pays a plumber. The plumber's services to the insurer do not qualify as handling a claim.

POSTAL SERVICES—SCH 9 GROUP 3

11.36 This only covers postal services by the Post Office. Although privatisation of the Post Office in the UK seems unlikely at the time of writing, postal services in the EU are increasingly open to competition. It is therefore probable that the Post Office's privileged position on carrying letters will be reduced, and that this exemption will then be restricted, or perhaps even withdrawn.

All other postal operators—both before and after full deregulation of the postal sector in the UK on 1 January 2006—are required to charge VAT at the standard rate on their services.

Following a legal challenge to the scope of the exemption as applied in the UK, the European Court of Justice, in the case of *TNT Post UK Ltd*, (Case C-357/07) has confirmed that Royal Mail, as the operator providing the public postal service, is the only postal body in the UK eligible to exempt postal services from VAT. However, it has also ruled that exemption applies to the public postal services (that is, Royal Mail) acting as such and does not apply to supplies made by Royal Mail for which the terms have been individually negotiated.

As a result, some postal services as supplied by Royal Mail—those which are individually negotiated or not subject to any price and regulatory control—which have been treated as exempt, will become liable to VAT. This includes, but is not limited to:

- all individually negotiated services;
- Parcelforce services;
- door-to-door (unaddressed mail); and
- mailroom services.

In the case of *Zipvit Ltd v Revenue & Customs* [2014] UKFTT 649 (TC), the appellant claimed overpaid input tax on postage it had paid that should have been subject to VAT as a result of the *TNT* decision, even though these supplies had wrongly been treated as exempt by Royal Mail.

HMRC agreed that the Royal Mail's 'Mailmedia' supplies should have been standard rated as a matter of EU law. It was agreed by the parties that Royal Mail treated the supplies of 'Mailmedia' to Zipvit as exempt. It did not account to HMRC for VAT on the supplies and it did not issue VAT invoices to Zipvit in respect of these supplies. There was absolutely nothing in the information provided by Royal Mail about their Mailmedia service that mentioned VAT.

The appellant's position was that Royal Mail's supplies of Mailmedia were standard rated as a matter of UK law and that it was therefore entitled to recover input tax from HMRC on the output tax which Royal Mail should have accounted to them.

HMRC's case was that the appellant had not really borne the burden of VAT at all. The supplies of Mailmedia services to Zipvit were treated as exempt so no VAT was added to the price. The ECJ has said in many cases that the purpose of the right to offset input tax was to remove the burden of VAT from taxable persons making taxable supplies, but if the appellant's appeal was upheld it would achieve recovery of VAT which it never paid and which was never in reality a burden on it.

The tribunal therefore found in favour of HMRC and dismissed the appeal. It was subsequently appealed to the Upper Tribunal, which upheld the decision.

Services which Royal Mail is obligated to provide under, or pursuant to, the terms of its licence—and which are therefore subject to price and regulatory control—will remain exempt from VAT (subject to there being no individual negotiation). This means:

- services covered by Royal Mail's Universal Service Obligation (including stamped mail);

- regulated services; and

- access to its network for private postal operators.

Legislative changes will have effect for supplies made on and after 31 January 2011(*Sch 9 Group 3* to be amended).

BETTING, GAMING AND LOTTERIES—SCH 9 GROUP 4

11.37   *Item 1* exempts 'the provision of any facilities for the placing of bets or the playing of any games of chance'. That covers income from video races for instance.

Item 2 exempts 'the granting of a right to take part in a lottery', which covers tickets for raffles, tombola, etc.

The exemption covers the gambling itself, not:

- admission to the premises in which it takes place;

- a membership subscription;

- gaming machines up to 1 February 2013 when the takings on dutiable machines became exempt from VAT and subject to Machine Games Duty (MGD).

Note (1) removes from the exemption charges for entry to premises where the gambling takes place and session or participation charges. In the 2009 Budget, *Note 1(b)* was removed so that from 27 April 2009, gaming and bingo participation fees are exempt from VAT. In *Rum Runner Casino Ltd* (MAN/80/33 No 1036), payments made by players to play games such as backgammon, poker, mahjong, and bridge, were held to be participation charges, even though they were distributed to the players as winnings.

In *Fakenham Conservative Association Bingo Club* (LON/73/164 No 76), a 'jackpot participation fee' paid for the right to take part in the cash jackpot was also held to be a participation charge, although a charge for the jackpot card was exempt.

The law prior to 1 September 2007 meant that charges made under the *Gaming Act 1968* or the *Betting, Gaming, Lotteries & Amusements (Northern Ireland) Order 1985*, to take part in a game of chance, were taxable at the standard rate. The effect of this was to tax participation fees for bingo and other gaming, with some exceptions for small-scale operations.

The *VAT (Betting, Gaming and Lotteries) Order 2007(SI 2007/2163)* came into effect on 1 September 2007, and broadly speaking, it will maintain the existing exemptions. However, for the first time, VAT will be chargeable on participation fees which are calculated on the basis of a percentage of the stakes risked in a game, and those charged for games against the house.

HMRC say that participation fees will continue to be exempt from VAT in relation to:

- remote gaming for the purpose of remote gaming duty;

- prize gaming under a permit or at any qualifying centre or fair;

- non-commercial gaming;

- equal chance gaming at a qualifying club or institute;

- gaming for small prizes at a bingo hall.

In *United Utilities* (MAN/01/146 No 17582; [2003] STC 223), an outsourced service of taking bets by telephone was held to be a standard-rated call centre and information technology service, not the exempt services of a bookmaker's agent.

Note (3), which defines a gaming machine, was changed from 6 December 2005 by the *VAT (Betting, Gaming and Lotteries) Order (SI 2005/3328)*. It is now a machine which is designed or adapted for use by individuals to gamble, whether or not it can also be used for other purposes. That does not cover a machine for use to bet on future real events or bingo where bingo duty is charged. Nor is it a gaming machine if it is designed or adapted for the playing of a real game of chance, which is subject to dutiable gaming. The change was intended to bring the definition in line with that in the *Gambling Act,* and to stop attempts to avoid VAT by reconfiguring machines to site the random number generator externally.

Business Brief 23/05 notified businesses that the definition contained in *s 23,* which could not be changed by an SI, would be amended in *FA 2006* retrospectively from 6 December 2005.

In the case of *Sportech & others v Revenue & Customs* [2014] UKUT 0398 (TCC), the Upper Tribunal decided that 'Spot the Ball' competitions were not a 'game of chance' but a 'game of skill' and so were a standard rated supply as they were not covered by the exemption.

One amusing case concerned target shooting at a fairground (*W & D Grantham* (MAN/70/102 No 853)) in which charges by a shooting gallery were held to be gambling. In order to win a prize, one had to remove the entire bullseye. It was a matter of chance whether one did so because putting all one's shots into the black was no guarantee of success. In fact only about 30 attempts out of 18,000 by the public in an average year succeeded. In tests, expert marksmen could not make winning scores regularly. The Tribunal found it to be a matter of chance whether one removed the bullseye entirely, however good a shot one was, and that the fees were therefore indeed exempt as the right to take part in a game of chance.

FINANCE—SCH 9 GROUP 5

11.38   The comment here relates only to the exemption for financial services to UK customers. For international transactions, see **24.8** and **24.11**. Chapters 23 and 24 explain the rules under which a financial service to a customer who belongs outside the EU or a service which is related to an export of goods outside the EU, together with commissions thereon, changes to outside the scope of VAT with recovery of the associated input tax.

This group exempts dealings in money, as set out later, except for:

- the supply of coins or banknotes as collectors pieces or investment articles (*Note (2)*). Examples include Maundy money and platinum nobles (*Art 15 EU Council Reg 1777/2005*). However, see *Group 15* for the exemption of investment gold and certain gold coins and Chapter 31, *The Second-hand Goods Scheme* under which VAT is due only on the profit margin for goods bought without input tax—normally from private individuals;

- the mere handling of money, such as sorting and counting it, moving it from one location to another or restocking cash machines. Such activities are similar to moving any kind of goods and do not amount to financial transactions.

Item 1: Dealings in money

11.39   *Item 1* exempts 'the issue, transfer or receipt of, or any dealing with, money, any security for money or any note or order for the payment of money'.

Dealings with money—The issue or cashing of travellers' cheques is an example of an exempt dealing with money.

Security for money—A 'security for money' in this context means something like a bond or indemnity given as security, not the kind of stock exchange security or secondary security covered by *Item 6*. Examples are fees for:

- bank guarantee given to HMRC as security for a trader meeting the liability for import VAT;

- performance bond guaranteeing the carrying out of, say, a construction contract;

- confirming house guarantee of payment by an importer to a foreign supplier.

Any note or order for the payment of money—A note or order for the payment of money includes:

- bills of exchange (local authority or commercial);

- instruments and paper negotiable for cash;

- trading paper coupons (from bearer bonds; ie the right to the dividend).

The value of the supply is the price paid both at issue and on any subsequent sale. Only at redemption is the transaction outside the scope.

In Notice 701/49 (August 2006) *Finance*, HMRC also accept as exempt under *Item 1*:

- the assignment of a debt;

- charges for accepting payment of bills on behalf of another business;

- foreign exchange transactions.

Item 1 does not cover work preparatory to the carrying out of an *Item 1* service (*Note (1A))*.

Cryptocurrencies—HMRC has published guidance (*Revenue & Customs Brief 09/14*) on the VAT implications of the new cryptocurrency Bitcoin. Bitcoin is the world's first decentralised currency, otherwise known as 'cryptocurrency'. The advent of cryptocurrencies such as Bitcoin is a new and developing area and HMRC says that determining their legal and regulatory status is ongoing.

As an EU tax, the VAT treatment for cryptocurrencies adopted by the UK must be consistent with any treatment that may eventually be implemented across the EU.

Given this, the evolutionary nature of these cryptocurrencies, and the legal and regulatory environments in which they currently operate, HMRC has decided to issue provisional guidance on the VAT treatment pending further developments. HMRC says that taxpayers can rely on the VAT treatment outlined below unless and until it announces any changes which will not apply retrospectively.

For VAT purposes Bitcoin and similar cryptocurrencies will be treated as follows:

- Income received from Bitcoin mining activities will generally be outside the scope of VAT on the basis that the activity does not constitute an economic activity for VAT purposes because there is an insufficient link between any services provided and any consideration received.

- Income received by miners for other activities, such as for the provision of services in connection with the verification of specific transactions for which specific charges are made, will be exempt from VAT as falling within the definition of 'transactions, including negotiation, concerning deposit and current accounts, payments, transfers, debts, cheques and other negotiable instruments.'

- When Bitcoin is exchanged for sterling or for foreign currencies, such as euros or dollars, no VAT will be due on the value of the Bitcoins themselves.

- Charges (in whatever form) made over and above the value of the Bitcoin for arranging or carrying out any transactions in Bitcoin will be exempt from VAT.

However, in all instances, VAT will be due in the normal way from suppliers of any goods or services sold in exchange for Bitcoin or other similar cryptocurrency. The value of the supply of goods or services on which VAT is due will be the sterling value of the cryptocurrency at the point the transaction takes place.

In the case of *Coinstar Ltd v HMRC* [2017] UKUT 256 (TCC), the appellant operated 'self service coin kiosks', of which it had almost 2,000 located in supermarkets. When a customer used the machine he would enter the coins he wished to exchange and would be provided with a voucher for use in the supermarket and would be charged a small commission. The appellant's primary case is that the service supplied by them was an exchange of money for another (more convenient and usable) form of money (the voucher) which involves a change in the legal and financial position of the parties. A supply of that service was an exempt supply. HMRC's position was that the appellant's customer was paying for his coins to be sorted and counted, to save the customer the time he would spend otherwise doing this task himself and taking the coins to the bank and was therefore standard rated. The Tribunal decided that this was an exempt supply of financial services.

Securitisation of credit card receivables—is it a supply?

11.40   Securitisation by a credit card company of the amounts payable by its cardholders is a means of financing its business. It passes over to another organisation the sums due by the cardholders and the finance thus obtained enables it to continue and to expand its business.

In *Capital One Bank (Europe) plc* (MAN/03/628 No 19,238) and *MBNA Europe Bank Ltd* (MAN/03/533 No 19,413), those companies claimed that they were selling their card balances to charitable trusts in Jersey. The importance of this was that financial services supplied to customers outside the EU change from exempt to outside the scope with recovery of input tax, as explained in Chapters 23 and 24. However, the Tribunal in *Capital One* held that the transfer of the card balances was the provision of security for a loan received, not a supply so that no input tax recovery could thereby be created. In *MBNA Europe*, the same arguments were put forward by the same teams before a different Tribunal, which came to the same conclusion.

These cases are important because, if the companies were able to bring into their partial exemption calculations substantial outputs, which were outside the scope with recovery, the input tax reclaimed would increase considerably.

See **11.50** et seq below for detailed comment on foreign exchange, debt factoring and outsourcing services.

Item 2: Loans and trade credit

11.41   *Item 2 exempts the making of any advance or the granting of any credit.*

Loans and bank overdrafts are thus exempt, the value of the supply being the interest paid. The interest is payment for the service of making the money available.

When goods are sold under a credit agreement, the interest charge is exempt if separate from the charge for the goods or services and it is disclosed to the purchaser *(Note (3))*. Any charge associated with the loan is also exempt. Thus, a commitment fee is exempt as part of the charge for the credit, albeit not called interest. So is a facility fee for an overdraft.

Item 2 also covers charges made by credit card companies (*Note (4)*):

- annually to cardholders;

- to retailers, made by deducting discounts from the sums paid to them; and

- interest on overdue balances charged to cardholders.

Penalties charged to holders of chargecards who fail to pay on time, are seen as outside the scope of VAT because there is no supply. The cardholder is not supposed to take extended credit.

Prior to 18 September 2004 HMRC's policy on deferred payment of an annual subscription to a health or membership club was to maintain that where the subscription was paid over 12 months and it charged an additional fee for this service, the additional fee was not consideration for credit and was therefore taxable. They now accept, however, that where a health or membership club offers annual membership and allows members to defer payment over the 12-month period, exemption will apply to any additional charge made for this service. This additional charge is regarded as exempt under *item 2*.

Item 2A: The management of credit by the person granting it

11.42   This item was added from 1 August 2003 and *Notes (2A)* and *(2B)* concerning the management of credit were deleted.

Item 3: Hire-purchase and credit sale agreements

11.43   *Item 3* exempts hire-purchase interest if a separate charge for the facility is disclosed to the purchaser of the goods.

Do not confuse the exempt interest charge with the standard-rated supply of the goods themselves. The supplier charges VAT on the goods to the finance company which charges it on when it resells them to the customer.

'Lease-purchase' agreements are also accepted by HMRC as being a supply of goods. Technically, lease-purchase is the hiring of goods for a fixed period at the end of which the hirer can buy them. The charges are based on the purchase price of the goods plus a finance charge.

Item 4: Option and documentation fees

11.44   *Item 4* exempts option fees, documentation fees and similar charges in hire-purchase, conditional sale or credit sale agreements, provided that they do not exceed £10 per agreement. That limit only applies if the charge relates to the goods, as opposed to the credit. See the two cases quoted below, which illustrate the pitfall/planning point involved.

> In a typical example of the pitfalls of not understanding one's own contractual terms, option fees exceeding £10, which *General Motors Acceptance Corpn (UK) plc* (LON/97/1471 No 16137) charged at the start of hire-purchase agreements, were held to be standard-rated, not ancillary to the charge for credit. They were for the right to purchase the car, which was exercised automatically if all instalments were paid.
>
> On the other hand, a £65 'administration fee', charged at the start of a hire-purchase agreement, was held to be part of the charge for the facility of instalment credit finance. It was included in the 'total charge for credit' shown in the agreement signed by the customer (*Wagon Finance Ltd* (LON/98/215 No 16288)). The Tribunal rejected HMRC's argument that it was, in part, related to the supply of the car.

Item 5: Commissions re transactions exempt under Items 1–4 and 6

11.45   *Item 5* exempts:

- 'intermediary services … by a person acting in an intermediary capacity'; and

- in relation to a transaction covered by *Items 1–4* and *6*.

'Intermediary services' and 'acting in an intermediary capacity' are defined by *Notes (5)* and *(5A)*.

Focus

Examples of exempt commissions are:

- hire-purchase commissions;

- the services of mortgage brokers and money brokers in arranging loans;

- building society commissions on investment and mortgage business.

Electronic dealing systems

11.46   Charges for carrying out transactions under an electronic dealing system, which allows subscribers to deal on it, are exempt as an intermediary service.

Booking charges paid by credit or debit card can be exempt

11.47

Focus

The default position for booking charges is that they are standard-rated. However, HMRC now accept that booking fees relating to payments made by credit and debit card can be exempt where the booking service includes the transmission of card information with the necessary security information and card issuers' authorisation codes.

This reflects the court decisions in *Bookit Ltd* ([2006] EWCA, Civ 550), and *Scottish Exhibition Centre Ltd* ([2006] Scot CS CSIH 42). After being refused leave to appeal to the House of Lords HMRC in the *Bookit* case, HMRC decided not to appeal the SEC case and issued *Business Brief 18/06* confirming the revised exempt treatment.

In the *Bookit* case, BL supplied cinema tickets by phone or Internet for an additional fee over and above the price of the ticket. Bookit contended this fee was for credit or debit card handling services, and was exempt as a transaction concerning payments or transfers. The Tribunal found the booking fee to be a taxable service, but the High Court disagreed and said it was an exempt card handling service. The Court of Appeal, in upholding the High Court judgment, found that the supply by Bookit was exempt because of the fact that it transmitted the card information with the necessary security information and the card issuers' authorisation codes to Girobank. This had the effect of transferring funds to Bookit's account with Girobank, which made exemption available.

The SEC case concerned the supply of tickets to events held in the Scottish Exhibition and Conference Centre in Glasgow. SEC acted as agent of the promoter in the selling of tickets and charged an additional fee to customers on tickets that were paid for by credit and debit card. SEC contended this fee was for card handling services and was VAT exempt. The Tribunal found in HMRC's favour, stating that SEC was providing a single taxable booking service, with the taxable card handling service representing an ancillary aspect enhancing the main service. The Court of Session, however, followed the Court of Appeal decision in *Bookit*, and overturned the Tribunal decision, finding that SEC was also carrying out an exempt card handling service.

The key thing to remember is that where transmission of the relevant card information is absent, exemption cannot be applied. HMRC say this will also be the case for charges levied on a cardholder for payment by credit and debit card in any other circumstances.

Advice is standard-rated

11.48

Focus

Do not confuse a standard-rate fee for investment advice with an exempt commission. A commission on a specific transaction is not the same as a fee for general advice.

Also standard-rated is advice from accountants, lawyers and merchant banks, which is connected with a sale or an issue of shares, but is not in itself an intermediary service. Examples of this are where the accountant is not the lead adviser in the share issue or sale, or the advice is given prior to taking the decision to sell.

Individual voluntary arrangements

11.49   In the case of *Paymex Ltd v Revenue & Customs Commisssioners* ([2011] UKFTT 350 (TC)) the appellant appealed against decisions of HMRC that supplies made in connection with consumer Individual Voluntary Arrangements (IVA) are taxable supplies for VAT purposes. The appellant claimed that the supplies are exempt within both the EU legislation, namely *Art 13B(d)(3)* of the *EC 6th Directive* and *Art 135(1)(d)* of the *Principal VAT Directive*, and the relevant domestic legislation (*VATA 1994, s 31* and *Sch 9, Group 5, item 5*).

The Tribunal concluded that the service supplied covered both the nominee and supervisory stages in the IVA process and constituted a single supply. The single supply is made up of a number of elements, of which part is negotiation of debts and part is transactions concerning payments, and not debt collection. Although there are other elements to the service, including advice on the suitability of an IVA, overall supervision of performance of the IPA and reporting to creditors and, up to 6 April 2010, the court, and those elements are themselves integral and key to the overall process, it is clear that all these aspects of the service are ancillary to the core elements of negotiation and payment handling, and that accordingly, viewed overall, the supply is exempt as falling within *Art 135(1)(d)* of the *Principal VAT Directive*.

HMRC have accepted this decision and have agreed that exemption will apply to IVAs, Partnership Voluntary Arrangements, Company Voluntary Arrangements and Trust Deeds in Scotland. This will impact on insolvency practitioners who will now be able to exempt these services, but they will need to consider the partial exemption impact on input tax recovery.

Item 5A: Underwriting fees re Items 1 and 6

11.50 *Item 5A* covers commissions and underwriting fees earned on transactions covered by *Items 1 and 6.*

A commission is only exempt if it is an *intermediary service* done in an *intermediary capacity.* Advertising and promotion are excluded by *Note (5),* which defines *intermediary services* as:

- bringing together seekers and providers of financial services;

- together with work preparatory to the conclusion of contracts,

but excludes:

- market research, product design, advertising, promotional or similar services or the collection, collation and provision of information in connection therewith.

Note (5A) defines acting in an *intermediary capacity* as:

- acting as an intermediary, or one of them, between providers and seekers of financial services.

Foreign exchange dealings create supplies

11.51 Although the exchange of one currency for another may not appear to involve a supply, it is a dealing in money. This may be good or bad news for a financial institution depending upon the extent to which its forex dealings are with counterparties outside the EU and thus outside the scope of VAT with recovery of input tax instead of exempt. See Chapter 23, *Exports and Imports of Services* for transactions which are outside the scope, with or without recovery.

In *First National Bank of Chicago,* the ECJ held that the consideration is *the net result of the supplier's transactions over a given period of time.* As that consideration is either exempt or outside the scope of VAT, it is not necessary to identify that net result for output tax purposes.

However, in *Willis Pension Trustees Ltd* (LON/04/1303 No 19183), it was held that no supply was made when forward foreign exchange transactions were left open until maturity resulting in a profit: that was not consideration. Nor was there any consideration when the transactions closed with a loss. The transactions were undertaken to protect the trustees against losses due to any fall in currencies in which foreign investments were held.

In *Revenue & Customs Brief 05/07,* HMRC say the circumstances in *Willis* were very specific, and care needs to be taken when trying to give it wider application. The ECJ's decision in *First National Bank of Chicago* remains the lead case on the VAT treatment of forex transactions.

The Brief outlines the practice of 'hedging' adopted by *Willis*, a practice used to reduce exposure to risk of loss resulting from currency fluctuations. HMRC say, however, that hedging is not itself a test for determining whether there is a supply for VAT purposes.

HMRC's view is that forex transactions are supplies for VAT purposes whenever a 'spread' position is adopted over a period of time for buying and selling currency (a spread position means a difference between a bid price and a sell price from which you expect to derive a profit). HMRC say that where there is uncertainty as to whether forex activities fall within the principle of adopting a spread position', where a business is able to set the selling price, it will also be able to determine the consideration due by setting a spread. As such, its activities are likely to be supplies for VAT purposes, and will be exempt under *VATA 1994, Sch 9, Group 5, Item 1*.

HMRC give the following examples of when forex transactions are unlikely to be supplies for VAT purposes:

- A business simply exchanging one currency for another to realise foreign earnings into sterling

- Acquiring currency to settle liabilities incurred outside the UK

- Entering into forex deals to limit its exposure to forex fluctuations for future obligations

HMRC caveat the three examples by adding that they should not form part of a wider economic activity being carried out for an identifiable consideration.

Intermediaries acting in relation to a forex transaction can exempt their services whether or not the underlying forex transaction is a supply for VAT purposes.

In terms of input tax recovery, HMRC say the normal rules apply. Businesses making supplies of finance cannot normally recover associated input tax unless the recipient is located outside the EU. However, input tax relating to forex transactions not seen as supplies for VAT purposes, can be treated as residual input tax.

Intermediaries can recover associated input tax where the recipient of their services is outside the EU, or the underlying forex transaction is a supply made outside the EU. However, where the underlying forex transaction is not a supply for VAT purposes, but the recipient is located in the UK or elsewhere in the EU, there is no right to input tax recovery.

HMRC say that businesses may wish to clarify their current partial exemption methods with them, as some may now need to be revised.

Effect on partial exemption methods

11.52   The value of forex transactions could be included in an apportionment calculation for partial exemption purposes using the standard method.

However, HMRC say that this will 'normally be unacceptable' because they believe it unlikely to result in a fair and reasonable attribution of input tax to those supplies which are outside the scope with recovery. Their preferred approach is to isolate the input tax incurred on forex costs and to apportion this as a separate calculation within the partial exemption method. A possible basis is the proportion of outside the scope with recovery transactions to total transactions. However, they will accept any method, which appears to achieve a fair and reasonable result.

Foreign exchange activity which merely supports other activities

11.53   As outlined at **11.51** above, large industrial companies can often undertake forex transactions to fix the sterling value of future trading income, and to ensure that currency is available to meet anticipated non-sterling liabilities. Banks also engage in foreign exchange trading purely to meet the needs of their customers, as opposed to trading speculatively for profit. Further to the provisions of *Revenue & Customs Brief 05/07*, HMRC may be prepared to allow recovery of input tax related to such activities on the basis of 'looking through' the immediate transactions to those, which the forex activity supports.

Debt factoring

11.54   A business can finance its sales by assigning the debts due from its customers to a Factor. The latter takes over responsibility for collecting the debts. The Factor may provide various services, such as advancing a proportion of the debts before they are collected and administering the client's sales ledger. *Recourse factoring* allows the Factor to reassign to the client any unpaid debts. *Invoice discounting* involves an advance to the client of a proportion of the debts. They are not assigned to the Factor, and the client remains responsible for collecting the debts.

The assignment of the debt by the client is exempt under *Item 1*. So is any reassignment back by the Factor. The interest or discount charged by the Factor is exempt under *Item 2*. Credit advice and sales ledger administration charges are standard-rated. So are fees for collecting debts not assigned to the Factor.

On 26/6/03, the ECJ held in *MKG-Kraftfahrzeuge-Factoring GmbH* (C-305/01) that debt factoring, for which the German company charged fees totalling 3% of the face value of the debts purchased, is, like debt collection, excluded from exemption under *Art 13B(d)(3)*. This seems to mean that factoring charges should be standard-rated, whether the basis is with or without recourse. HMRC have not made any comment on this to date.

213

The problems of outsourcing services

11.55   A prime reason for outsourcing services is to reduce costs. If you incur non-recoverable VAT on those outsourced services, much of the benefit will disappear.

When work is done in-house, the only VAT incurred is that on taxable expenses. The most important cost, salaries, are outside the scope of VAT.

HMRC have argued in various cases, explained in the following pages, that outsourced financial services are standard-rated. See also the comment on outsourcing under *Insurance—Sch 9 Group 2* at **11.28**.

LIFE ASSURANCE AND INVESTMENT ARE DIFFERENT TO INSURANCE

11.56   A commission on selling life assurance or an investment product is covered by the rules on finance, not insurance. For finance commissions, the key word in an intermediary situation is *negotiation*. *Directive 2006/112/EC, Art 135(1)(f)* (previously *Art 13(B)(d)(5)* of the *EC 6th VAT Directive*) exempts the *negotiation* of transactions in securities.

Compare that with the exemption for insurance commissions in *para (1)(a)* for *related services performed by insurance brokers and insurance agents*. The difference has been important in a number of outsourcing cases.

SOME OUTSOURCING CASES

The Sparekassernes case

11.57   If a service amounts to a dealing in money, it is exempt under *Item 1* provided that it is not merely preparatory. It must have the characteristics of a financial transaction. The *Sparekassernes Datacenter* case ([1997] STC 932) demonstrates how fine the nuances are between a standard-rated and an exempt service. Sparekassernes Datacenter, a Danish company, provided back-office services in maintaining customers' accounts such as:

- cheque clearance and processing;
- calculating interest and crediting or debiting it to accounts;
- standing order payments and foreign exchange transactions;
- administration of cash cards;
- customer enquiry handling and other services.

The ECJ held that it was not necessary for the supply to be to the final recipient of the exempt service, but the service, viewed as a whole, had to constitute a transaction listed in the *EC 6th VAT Directive*. It was not sufficient merely for a service to be needed in order to carry out an exempt financial transaction. A distinction must be drawn between exempt services and the provision of a facility, such as a computing system. It was for the national court to rule on the nature of the services provided, including the extent of Sparekassernes' liability to the banks. The Danish tax authorities are said to have agreed a 60:40 split between exempt and standard-rated.

In *FDR Ltd* (LON/95/2887 No 16040; CA [2000] STC 672), the Tribunal held that similar services for credit card issuers and merchant acquirers were mostly exempt. FDR did carry on various activities in providing its services to card issuers and merchant acquirers. However, there was a single or core supply to both issuers and acquirers of processing all their card transactions and settling their liabilities and claims under these transactions to meet the obligations of the issuers and acquirers. This included opening and maintaining accounts, authorising transactions, ascertaining the credits and debits, and statementing. These were either integral parts of the principal supply or necessary for its performance.

This was confirmed by the Court of Appeal. It held that:

- FDR made 'transfers', which were exempt under *Art 13B(d)(3)*;

- the Tribunal's analysis of the supplies made was correct. There was a single core supply;

- supply consisted of the movement of money between cardholder, merchant, issuer and acquirer.

HMRC's argument, that merely giving instructions for payment via BACS did not amount to a transfer of money, was rejected.

In *CSC Financial Services Ltd* (C-235/00; [2002] STC 57), formerly known as *Continuum (Europe) Ltd*, the ECJ ruled that transactions, in the context of *Art 13B(d)(1)*, means:

'Transactions liable to create, alter, or extinguish parties' rights and obligations in respect of securities.'

It commented that administrative services, which did not alter the legal or financial position of the parties, were not covered. Nor was the supply of financial information. The mere fact that a service was essential to completing an exempt transaction did not make that service exempt.

The ECJ said that *negotiation* means:

'The activity of an intermediary, who does not occupy the position of any party to a contract relating to a financial product and whose activity amounts to something other than the provision of contractual services typically undertaken by the parties to such contracts. Negotiation is a service rendered to and remunerated by a contractual party as a distinct act of mediation. It may consist, amongst other things, in pointing out suitable opportunities for the conclusion of such a contract, making contact with another party or negotiating, in the name of and on behalf of a client, the detail of the payments to be made by either side. The purpose of negotiation is therefore to do all that is necessary in order for two parties to enter into a contract, without the negotiator having any interest of his own in the terms of the contract.

On the other hand, it is not negotiation where one of the parties entrusts to a subcontractor some of the clerical formalities related to the contract, such as providing information to the other party and receiving and processing applications for subscription to the securities which form the subject matter of contract. In such a case, the subcontractor occupies the same position as the party selling the financial product and is not therefore an intermediary who does not occupy the position of one of the parties to the contract, within the meaning of the provision in question.'

Electronic Data Systems Ltd (LON/2000/91 No 17611: CA [2003] STC 688) ran a call centre at which applications for loans were recorded, validated under a credit scoring system and accepted or rejected; loans were paid out and repayments collected, early settlements dealt with, interest calculated, statements produced etc on behalf of Lloyds Bank. Lloyds merely advertised the loans and dealt with borrowers in arrears. EDS did everything else. The money was paid out and collected into accounts held by the Bank, which were cleared daily.

The Tribunal found EDS's services to be exempt as the granting of credit on behalf of the Bank. If that was wrong, they were exempt as being for *transactions, including negotiation, concerning deposits and current accounts, payments transfers and debts*. The Court of Appeal found them to be *transactions concerning payments, transfers*. It was sympathetic to the view that they were negotiation but would have referred to the ECJ on whether they were the *granting of credit*.

Cases on intermediary services

11.58   *BAA plc* (LON/00/867 No 17377; [2002] STC 327) concerned a credit card co-branded with Bank of Scotland. BAA offered it to its customers, checked application forms, and screened out applications not meeting the bank's requirements. It was paid a one-off introduction and processing fee, and an ongoing commission fee based on the bank's interest income.

Customs argued that BAA was providing credit management in the form of promotional and similar services, advertising, credit checking and decision taking. They said that credit management and credit negotiation were mutually exclusive, and any supply containing elements of credit management could not properly be described as *negotiation*.

BAA argued that *negotiation* had the wider dictionary meaning of acting as an intermediary. BAA was not involved with the management of credit. The decision on whether to issue a card was left to BOS and BAA did not do the credit checking.

The High Court and Court of Appeal agreed with BAA in the light of the comments of the ECJ in *CSC*. The *negotiation of credit* within *Art 13B(d) (1)* was not restricted to the brokering of an actual exempt transaction by an intermediary who had power to affect the transaction itself. BAA performed an *act of mediation*. Without its services, the individual contracts for the issue of the credit cards would not take place. Its activities were not mere clerical formalities carried out as a subcontractor of the bank. Its role was not passive. Nor did it merely carry out promotional or marketing activities for the bank.

In *Prudential Insurance Co Ltd* (LON/2002/983), charges by Boots Co plc in connection with the creation of a joint credit card, use of which generated Advantage Points, were held to be exempt as part of the negotiation of credit. This was a more complicated case, but the Tribunal saw no material difference between it and *BAA*.

In *Debt Management Associates Ltd* (MAN/01/0631 No 17880), the negotiation of extended payment terms for outstanding debts was held to be an exempt supply, even though no revised contract was created.

In *Lindum Resources Ltd* (MAN/93/784 No 12445), an application fee charged to a potential borrower by a broker was held to be exempt because it was the first stage in the exempt making of arrangements for a loan, even if a feasibility study showed the loan to be impractical.

The key point is the nature of the intended supply. The status of a fee cannot depend upon success in arranging a loan, as the rate of tax has to be known when the tax point is created by payment of the fee at the start of the broker's work.

The services of *Smarter Money Ltd* (EDN/05/86 No 19632) in providing information on prospective customers via several websites, such as details of prospective mortgage seekers to mortgage brokers, were held to be intermediary services amounting to negotiations, not merely the provision of information electronically.

AFFINITY CARDS FOR CHARITIES

11.59   Payments to charities from issuers of credit cards are normally:

(a)   a fixed payment to the charity when each card is issued;

(b)   an agreed percentage of the purchases made with the card thereafter.

In Notice 701/1 *Charities* (May 2004), section 8, HMRC say that, if you have separate agreements for (a) and (b), only a part of (a)—at least 20%—is regarded as standard-rated. The other 80% and the whole of (b) are seen as non-business.

The basis for the 80% of (a) is not explained; presumably it is assumed that the payment for it will be primarily contributions in respect of the use of the charity's name and/or logo—which is what the agreement for (b) should be restricted to—rather than the marketing, publicity services and access to membership lists, which are seen as standard-rated.

However, if the charity *acts as an intermediary*, the entire fees are exempt. That is likely to be better still, assuming the card issuer will not add VAT to its payment. It requires the charity to undertake preparatory work, such as completing the application form or assisting in doing it, forwarding it to the card issuer, and passing communications either way. A mere clerical task of providing a list of names or access to a database is not seen by HMRC as an intermediary service.

Item 6: Securities and secondary securities

11.60   *Item 6* exempts the 'issue, transfer or receipt of, or any dealing with, any security or secondary security' as defined. See the text of *Item 6* in *Sch 9 Group 5* for the full definition. It includes:

- stocks and shares, bonds and debentures including allotment letters and warrants;
- certificates of deposit;
- Treasury bills;
- unit trust certificates.

If a business holds shares purely as investments, its sales of them may well be non-business rather than exempt. That may be an advantage or a disadvantage if the business has other activities amounting to a business.

In *Wellcome Trust* (C-155/94), the ECJ held that buying and selling securities in other businesses as passive investments is not by itself a business activity—any dividends on the holdings are merely the result of ownership, not payment for a supply. Since its sales of investments were held to be non-business, Wellcome could not improve its input tax recovery by bringing into its partial exemption calculation its sales to non-EU purchasers.

Of course, if a business is one of buying and selling securities, the transactions are business supplies and the sales are exempt—though, if the business sells to purchasers outside the EU, see Chapter 23, *Exports and Imports of Services* re how an exempt financial supply can become outside the scope with recovery of input tax.

In *Kretztechnik AG* (C-465/03), the ECJ held that the issue of securities by a company was not a supply. The ECJ had already held in *KapHag* (C-442/01) that a fee charged by a partnership to a new partner was not payment for a supply. It took the same view on the issue of shares for the purpose of raising capital. A company that issued new shares increased its assets by the new capital, and granted the subscribing shareholders part ownership of those assets. The aim was to raise capital, not to provide services.

That means that an industrial company, which makes a rights issue, does not have an exempt supply—so the related input tax may be fully recoverable. For more details, see **24.38**.

In Revenue & Customs Brief 44/14 HMRC set out its position following the decision of the ECJ in the Danish case *ATP Pension Services* (C-464/12) concerning VAT and pension fund management services. The ECJ found that a pension fund which pooled investments from a number of defined contribution occupational pension schemes qualified as a Special Investment Fund (SIF) for the purposes of the VAT exemption for fund management services.

Prior to the ECJ's judgment in *ATP*, HMRC did not consider pension funds of any kind to be SIFs and therefore treated services provided in connection with all types of pension fund as falling outside the VAT exemption for fund management services and therefore standard rated.

In light of the *ATP* judgment, HMRC now accepts that pension funds that have all of the following characteristics are SIFs for the purposes of the fund management exemption so that the services of managing and administering those funds should be, and always should have been, exempt from VAT:

- They are solely funded (whether directly or indirectly) by persons to whom the retirement benefit is to be paid (ie the pension customers).

- The pension customers bear the investment risk.

- The fund contains the pooled contributions of several pension customers.

- The risk borne by the pension customers is spread over a range of securities.

In addition to funds that contain the pooled assets of defined contribution occupational pension schemes, such as that at issue in *ATP*, HMRC accepts that funds that contain the pooled assets of personal pension schemes and that have all of the above characteristics will also fall within the VAT exemption for fund management services.

UK legislation will be amended in due course to implement the *ATP* judgment. In the meantime, taxpayers may rely directly on EU law to exempt pension fund management or administration services in accordance with the policy outlined in this Brief.

HMRC is still considering whether the *ATP* judgment could have wider application and guidance will be issued if there are to be any further changes.

In the meantime exemption should be applied in line with HMRC's current published policy.

STOCK LENDING

11.61 *Stock lending* is the inaccurate description adopted by the financial markets to describe the borrowing of stocks or shares by market makers. If a market maker is short of a stock, and is unable to buy enough in the open market to deliver what it has sold without moving the price against it, it may arrange to 'borrow' the holding held by another institution as an investment. It contracts to replace the holding in due course, and to pay interest meanwhile, equivalent to any dividends due plus interest on the value of the stock.

Although called lending, this involves:

(a)   a sale of the stock by the lender to the borrower;

(b)   in due course, a sale of the replacement stock by the borrower back to the lender;

(c)   interest to the lender on its loan, which is represented by the debt outstanding for the stock. To the extent that this substitutes for any dividend due, the lender's outputs (probably exempt) are increased.

HMRC used to regard (a) and (b) as outputs at open market value even though no money passed. However, in *Scottish Eastern Investment Trust plc* (EDN/99/211 No 16882), a Tribunal held that the value of the output was the fee charged to the borrower. It was unreal to regard the transfer of legal title as creating an output. HMRC have accepted this.

SHARE REGISTRATION SERVICES

11.62   HMRC announced in *VAT Information Sheet 15/03* that, from 1 January 2004, share registration services would be seen as standard-rated—changing what was previously agreed with the British Bankers Association.

GLOBAL CUSTODY AND SAFE CUSTODY

11.63   Global custody—a package of services, which includes the holding of stocks and securities, collecting dividends or interest on them, and dealing with scrip or rights issues—is seen by HMRC as exempt. Do not confuse this with the standard-rated service of safe custody, which is primarily the physical safekeeping of stocks and securities.

Item 7 has been deleted and replaced by Items 5 and 5A

Item 8: Bank charges re current, deposit or savings accounts

11.64   This covers bank charges on the account, as opposed to interest.

Item 9: Management of unit trusts

11.65   *Item 9* exempts fees for managing:

- an authorised unit trust; or

- a trust-based scheme.

A requirement for the management to be by the operator of the scheme was held to be invalid in *Prudential Assurance Co Ltd* (EDN/00/37 No 17030)— it having been outsourced. The rule was then deleted with effect from 1 August 2003.

Item 10: Managing an 'open-ended' investment company

11.66   *Item 10* exempts the management of the scheme property of an OEIC. A requirement for the management to be by an authorised corporate director was held to be invalid in *Abbey National plc* (LON/00/928 No 17506) and was then deleted from 1 August 2003.

In another *Abbey National* case referred by the Tribunal to the ECJ, on 4 May 2006, the latter held that administrative management services performed by a third party, as opposed to core investment management services, were exempt provided that, viewed broadly, they formed a distinct whole fulfilling in effect the specific essential functions of the management of special investment funds (as defined by Member States) (ECJ C-169/04). HMRC accepted this in *Business Brief 7/06*, in which they set out examples of the distinction between a bunch of services, possibly priced individually but which together amount to a fund administration service, and individual services which do not.

For example, the daily valuation of assets together with related accounting and reporting functions is exempt, but the mere feeding of prices of individual stocks is not. Nor is the mere maintenance of a shareholders register. However, it is exempt if combined with the issue and redemption of units or shares and collating the number of shares in issue in order to establish the daily price. See the *Business Brief* for further detail.

EDUCATION—SCH 9 GROUP 6

11.67

Focus

Item 1: *The main exemption* exempts the provision by an eligible body of:

- education;

- research if supplied to another eligible body;

- vocational training.

Note 1 says that 'Eligible body' means (paraphrasing):

- schools, colleges, UK universities including any college, institution, school or hall thereof;

- government departments, local authorities and health authorities;

- bodies, such as charities, which are precluded from distributing profits. The body must plough back any profit made from *Group 6* education into that activity.

A trading subsidiary is not an eligible body.

The scope of 'education' is wide

11.68   The law does not define *'education.'* Nor does it say where the education has to be provided—only that it must be by an eligible body. The range of courses provided by educational institutions is so wide that one can find an argument for most subjects being 'education'. HMRC acknowledge this in Notice 701/30 (January 2002) *Education and Vocational Training* para 5.1, where they say:

'Education' means a course, class or lesson of instruction or study in any subject:

- whether or not that subject is normally taught in schools, colleges or universities; and

- regardless of where and when it takes place.

Education includes:

- lectures;

- educational seminars;

- conferences and symposia;

- holiday, sporting and recreational courses;

- distance teaching and associated materials, providing the student is subject to assessment by the teaching institution.

But does not include plays, concerts, sports meetings or exhibitions.

There is no need for any examination or diploma. Courses such as embroidery or basket-making are now accepted as being education.

See also the possibility discussed later for the course being vocational training.

In *TK Phillips* (LON/90/862 No 7444), motorcycle training was held to be education.

In *Allied Dancing Association Ltd* (MAN/91/84 No 10777), the Tribunal held that teaching ballroom dancing to juniors for the purpose of a test was education for life!

In *British Organic Farmers* (LON/87/164 No 2700) and *Buxton Civic Association* (MAN/87/385 No 3380) it was suggested that the teaching must be more than the provision of an occasional seminar or a one-off visit, but HMRC continue to accept that a single lecture can be 'education'.

In *Harrogate Business Development Centre Ltd* (LON/98/569 No 15565), advice and information for people starting businesses was held to be training when provided as part of the package which included training seminars. The services did not cease to be training merely because they included on the job advice.

In *Christine Joy Hocking v Revenue & Customs* [2014] UKFTT 1034 (TC) it was held that the teaching of pilates was not a subject normally taught in schools and so was not subject to the exemption.

An e-learning software package can be education

11.69 *Creating Careers* (MAN/04/717 No 19509) licensed its online learning packages to Further Education Colleges (FECs). Although the FECs allocated a tutor to each student, the latter was only involved in 11 hours out of the 120-hour course. The supply by CC was held to be an exempt educational project, not the mere provision of electronic textbooks.

This case was in relation to *Item 5A* rather than *Item 1*. It was held to be provided directly to the student seemingly because CC worked in partnership with the FECs. It is an interesting point as to what '*directly*' means in relation to modern e-learning. There was no contact between the student and CC, the course being self-contained with its own questions and answers.

There must be some structure to the education

11.70   In *North of England Zoological Society* ([1999] STC 1027), admission to a zoo was held not to amount to education, despite the efforts made to educate visitors. The key distinction here is that the average family at the zoo is looking for entertainment rather than education. The basic offer is of an afternoon out, not 'come and listen to lectures about the animals'. Having got them inside the gates, a zoo may make great efforts to teach them and many no doubt respond. However, the extent of that response will vary from a willingness to read a few explanatory boards to avid attention on an escorted tour. If this was education, many stately homes, for instance, could claim that they were educating their visitors.

Sport—the difference between education and the mere provision of facilities

11.71   HMRC accept that a class which is *'led and directed rather than merely supervised'* counts as education. That includes instruction in the use of equipment and in warming-up techniques.

However, the mere presence of staff to supervise on health and safety or insurance grounds, such as in a swimming pool, is not sufficient.

Research

11.72   The VAT exemption for business research supplied between eligible bodies was withdrawn for all written contracts that were not entered into by 1 August 2013.

However, there are transitional arrangements for supplies of research made under a written contract entered into before 1 August 2013 (whether or not work under these contracts has commenced by that date), which will allow the exemption to continue to apply for supplies within the scope of the contract as at 31 July 2013. There are however, certain restrictions on the scope of the transitional arrangements.

Prior to 1 August 2013 research was standard-rated unless supplied by one eligible body to another such body.

In *Revenue & Customs Brief 10/13*, HMRC confirmed that collaborative research arrangements where one body (normally a university or other 'eligible body') receives the grant funding, all research services provided by each of the bodies involved in the project are outside the scope of VAT, even if the funding may be passed on by the lead research body to others, and that only the lead research body is party to the contract with the funding body.

Vocational training

11.73

Focus

'Vocational training' is defined by *Note (3)* as training or retraining for:

- any trade, profession or employment; or

- any voluntary work connected with:

   (i)   education, health, safety or welfare; or

   (ii)   the carrying out of activities of a charitable nature

and includes the provision of work experience under training schemes for the unemployed.

Consultancy via a limited company

11.74   Educational institutions often put their consultancy and other trading activities through a limited company to preserve their charitable status for corporation tax purposes. The profit is then covenanted to the institution. Any education or training done by such a company cannot be exempt because the company is not an eligible body.

Trading companies can be grouped for VAT purposes with their parent institutions as these are corporations. This means that any management fees or other charges between them are outside the scope.

'English as a foreign language' courses

11.75   Courses teaching English as a foreign language are exempt, whoever provides them. *Note (2)* restricts the exemption to the teaching, which means that part of the charges may be standard-rated. However, following *Pilgrims Language Courses Ltd* ([1999] STC 874), HMRC accept exemption for all elements integral to the course, together with closely related supplies of goods and services, provided they are for the direct use of the student and necessary for delivering the education. This includes sports, recreational or social activities.

Item 2: Private tuition

11.76   Private tuition is exempt under *Item 2*, if 'it is in a subject ordinarily taught in a school or university by an individual teacher acting independently of an employer'.

In *C Clarke and E Clarke, A Clarke and H Clarke* (LON/96/1446 No 15201), the partners in a dance teaching business were held to act independently as principals so their charges were exempt as private tuition.

However, in *John Page (t/a Upledger Institute)* (EDN/99/14 No 16650), training in CranioSacral Therapy was held to be standard-rated to the extent of the 40% of income derived from fees for teaching by employees of Mr Page. This was not *private tuition by an individual teacher acting independently of an employer.*

Similarly, in *Brian Graham (t/a Excel Tutoring)* (LON/98/213 No 16814), Mr Graham recruited teachers as needed to coach pupils. The teaching was done by them, not him. His services were therefore standard-rated.

However, Mr Page, having lost his argument about supplies using staff as explained two paragraphs earlier, then formed a limited company and won his second appeal *Empowerment Enterprises Ltd* (EDN/04/22 No 18963). The Tribunal held that the *EC 6th VAT Directive* had not been properly transposed into UK legislation; it was wrong to exempt teaching by an individual as a sole trader but not as a one-person company. The decision appeared to agree exemption for the services of other individuals hired when required as well as for those of Mr Page. HMRC appealed this decision to the Court of Session ([2006] CSIH 46 XA30/05), which found in favour of HMRC, and restored the existing position. In finding for HMRC, the court had closely examined the wording of *Art 13A(1)(j)* of the *EC 6th VAT Directive*, from which *Item 2* of *Group 6* is drawn.

It stated the following in support of its decision:

> '[36] We have therefore come to the conclusion that, of the two interpretations of sub-paragraph (j) put forward by the parties, the Commissioners' interpretation is to be preferred for the reasons we have given In particular, it is the only one which gives proper value to the concept of "privately" as that concept is expressed in the various language versions of the sub-paragraph that we have considered. The situation is not one in which two interpretations are possible and the principle of fiscal neutrality can be relied on as pointing to the one which makes the form or identity of the supplier irrelevant. Rather, sub-paragraph (j) is an example of an exemption expressed in language which, despite the principle of fiscal neutrality, makes the nature or identity of the provider of the tuition an essential element in the definition of the scope of the exemption. On a sound construction of sub-paragraph (j), it applies only where the tuition is provided by a teacher acting in an individual or personal capacity, and does not apply to tuition provided by a teacher as an employee of a company or other organisation.'

Item 3: Examination services

11.77 Examination services are exempt under *Item 3*. *Note (4)* defines them as including the setting and marking of examinations, and setting and maintaining of educational training standards. In Notice 701/30 (January 2002), para 7.1, HMRC say that course accreditation services, validation and certification are covered.

The exemption applies if the supply is by or to an eligible body, or to a person receiving vocational training which is itself exempt, such as at independent fee-paying schools, or non-business such as at local authority schools.

Item 4: Closely related goods or services

11.78   *Item 4* exempts the supply of any goods or services closely related to the education, research, or vocational training.

This is an important part of the exemption because it covers a multitude of supplies made by educational institutions to their students.

The supply must be:

- for the direct use of the student;
- by the eligible body which educates or trains them; or
- by a second educational eligible body to the one, which does.

An example is catering.

A *student* is anyone, who is being educated, whether through a full-time course or an individual conference or lecture. HMRC accept that this includes a candidate for admission to the institution.

Not covered are goods sold from campus shops. It would be difficult to know which purchasers were students, let alone whether the item in question was related to that student's course. This particular issue was examined in detail in *Commissioners of HM Customs & Excise v University of Leicester Students Union* [2001] EWCA, Civ 1972, where the Court of Appeal considered the liability of sales of soft drinks to students from a shop run by the Student Union body. The court found that the Student Body was not an 'eligible body' under *Item 1*, and because of this, the exemption under *Item 4* was also not available to it either.

In the case of *Revenue & Customs v Brockenhurst College* [2014] UKUT 46 (TCC) the Upper Tribunal considered what were closely related goods and services. The appellant provided education which included the teaching of courses in catering and hospitality, and the performing arts. To enable students enrolled in catering and hospitality courses to learn skills in a practical context, the College ran a restaurant and exempted the charges for catering.

The catering functions of the restaurant were all undertaken by students of the College, under the supervision of their tutors, and members of the public

227

attended the restaurant and paid for their meal, the charge being around 80% of the cost of the meal. Similarly, for the performing arts course the College staged concerts and performances for paying members of the public, which it also exempted.

The issue in this appeal was whether the supplies of restaurant and entertainment services were, as the appellant claimed, exempt from VAT or, as HMRC maintained, were standard rated.

The Upper Tribunal upheld the FTT decision, holding that the FTT was right to conclude, on the basis of its findings, that the restaurant and entertainment services are exempt as 'supplies of services and goods closely related to the provision of education'. HMRC have decided to appeal this decision to the Court of Appeal (Revenue & Customs Brief 39/14).

Items 5 and 5A: Vocational training

11.79   *Item 5* exempts vocational training and, if by the same person, the supply of any goods or services essential thereto, which is funded under the *Employment and Training Act 1973* and similar law in Northern Ireland and Scotland (eg government approved training schemes).

Focus

Item 5A exempts both vocational training and education, including, if by the same person, the supply of any goods or services essential thereto, which are ultimately funded by:

- the Learning and Skills Council;

- the National Council for Education and Training for Wales;

- a Local Enterprise Company; or

- the European Social Fund (under a scheme approved by the Department for Education and Skills).

See the law for the precise wording of these items, and section 13 of Notice 701/30 (January 2002) *Education and Vocational Training*.

The effect of *Items 5* and *5A* is to exempt supplies made for profit by a business to the extent that they are funded by government or EU monies. Pitfalls include the possibility that if:

- an event, such as a workshop, is organised by an entity such as a chamber of commerce, it is not obvious that the funding is from a qualifying source or

- workplace training paid for by a commercial organisation is partly-funded by a qualifying source, the supply is only exempt to that extent.

It follows that, if a business is a supplier with mostly taxable supplies, it must check whether the input tax related to the exempt ones exceeds the partial exemption de minimis limits (see Chapter 24, *Partial Exemption*) and is, therefore, not recoverable.

Item 6: Youth clubs

11.80 *Item 6* exempts the provision of facilities by a youth club to its members, or by an association of youth clubs to its member clubs or direct to their members.

Note (6) defines a youth club as a non-profit making body established to promote the social, physical, educational, or spiritual development of its members, who must be mainly under 21 years of age.

HEALTH—SCH 9 GROUP 7

Group 7, Items 1–3: Services of doctors, etc

11.81 *Items 1–3* of this Group cover the services of doctors, nurses, dentists, pharmaceutical chemists, and other medically qualified people including osteopaths and chiropractors. See the law for the various registers, such as that kept under the *Health Professions Order 2001*, membership of which is required.

This creates a pitfall because, although the range of expertise covered by the registers is expanding, it is not all embracing. Thus, *Lawrence Yusupoff* (MAN/01/899 No 18152), a clinical psychologist, found that his services were not exempt and had to register for VAT retrospectively. However, that decision may have been incorrect because the ECJ ruled in *Christoph-Dornier Stiftung* (C-45/01; [2004] 1 CMLR 91) that psychotherapeutic treatment by qualified psychologists amounted to the provision of medical care, which is exempt under *EC 6th VAT Directive, Art 13A(1)(c)* (now *Directive 2006/112/EC, Art 132(1)(c)*), even though not accepted as such under German law, the latter being too restrictive.

One would, therefore, suppose that psychotherapeutic treatment by a psychotherapist was automatically exempt; not necessarily! In April 2006, the ECJ said in *H A Solleveld* (C-443/04) that *Art 13A(1)(c)* gave Member States discretion to define the paramedical professions and the medical care coming within the scope of such professions. So, to exclude the profession of psychotherapists was only wrong if psychotherapeutic treatment by other medical or paramedical professions would be exempt. In other words, a treatment by a psychotherapist qualifies provided it can be seen as of equivalent quality on the basis of his or her professional qualifications.

Similarly, the decision in *J E van den Hout-van Eijnsbergen* (C-444/04), heard with *Solleveld*, was that to exclude specific medical care activities, such as a treatment using disturbance field diagnostics carried out by a physiotherapist, was wrong only if it was exempt when carried out by doctors or dentists and could be seen as of equivalent quality having regard to the professional qualifications of physiotherapists.

If those two paragraphs are a heavy read, it is because the ECJ decision requires a careful analysis! It appears to say that a Member State, in exercising its discretion to decide the limit of the exemption for paramedical services, must ensure that a service is not just exempt when supplied by specified medical or paramedical professionals. It must also be exempt when supplied by others if it is of equivalent quality, that quality being based on the professional qualifications of those other people.

The exemption is limited to services in the branch of medicine in question related to the health of patients. It would not cover, for example, royalties for writing a book on a medical subject.

In *D v W* (Case–384/98; [2002] STC 1200), the ECJ ruled that the services of a doctor in conducting a genetic test to establish parenthood did not amount to the *provision of medical care*. That phrase, in the *EC 6th VAT Directive Art 13A(1)(c)* (now *Directive 2006/112/EC, Art 132(1)(c)*), only covered medical interventions for the purpose of diagnosis and treatment of diseases or health disorders.

In *Dr Beynon and Partners* [2005] BVC 3, the House of Lords held that personally administered drugs and medicines such as vaccines and injections were part of a doctor's single supply of medical care. The appellant had contended that there was a multiple supply of exempt medical services and zero-rated drugs (see **12.19**). The partners in the practice, who were all dispensing GPs, argued that when personally administering medicines to a patient who was entitled to receive NHS dispensing services from them, the patient received separate supplies of exempt medical services and zero-rated dispensed goods. However, the HL concluded that, in reality, the patient's visit to the doctor for treatment was one transaction. They said it was essential, for practical reasons, to have a rule which applied across the board to transactions of a certain kind. Accordingly, HMRC now say that where items such as diagnostic reagents, contraceptive caps, diaphragms and intra-uterine devices, and pessaries are personally administered or fitted ('immediately administered' in Scotland) to the patient by the doctor at the time of treatment, exemption applies to those too.

In *Dr Peter L d'Ambrumenil & Dispute Resolution Services Ltd* (LON/97/951 15977: C-307/01: [2004] 3 WLR 174; [2004] 2 CMLR 396) the ECJ held that tests of blood and other bodily samples for viruses, etc done on behalf of an employer or an insurance company, were not exempt if the aim was not therapeutic but obtaining health-related information. Similarly, medical certificates and reports related to fitness to travel, entitlement to a pension or litigation, were not therapeutic, but the obtaining of an expert opinion.

As a result of the *Dr Peter D'Ambrumenil* case, HMRC published *Revenue and Customs Brief 06/07* that announced new rules on VAT exemption for medical services with effect from 1 May 2007. All care and treatment provided through the NHS continues to be exempt from VAT, but medical services that enable a third party to take a decision will become liable to VAT.

In *Revenue & Customs Brief 06/07*, HMRC say the affected services are:

- *witness testimony/reports for litigation, compensation or benefit purposes;*

- *reports/medicals for the purpose of providing certain fitness certificates;*

- *some occupational health services.*

As mentioned above, these services became liable to VAT from 1 May 2007.

'Medical services' are defined as those services intended principally to 'protect' (including 'maintain' or 'restore') the health of an individual. Medical services which are primarily for the purpose of enabling a third party to take a decision—many of which are currently exempt from VAT under UK law—are taxable. This means that VAT liability is dependent on the purpose for which the supply is made—referred to as the 'purpose test'.

In this context, cosmetic surgery which is not part of the treatment of a patient will become taxable.

A problem for general practitioners

11.82 Following a change in Department of Health funding, dispensing doctors have had to register for VAT from 1 April 2006, in order to recover VAT incurred on the drugs, medicines or appliances they dispense. Drugs dispensed under NHS prescriptions are zero-rated, but they are standard-rated under private prescriptions.

Once VAT registered, a medical practice must account for VAT on any other standard-rated income it may have, and which escaped in the past because the total was below the registration limit. See below for some examples.

In a practice of two or more doctors, the usual rules about registration apply, so that any income which belongs to an individual doctor, rather than the partnership, is not caught—but, as always, there needs to be a legal basis for it belonging to the individual rather than the partnership. See some comment at **3.33**.

HMRC comments on exemption versus standard-rating

11.83

Focus

HMRC say that the following are also standard-rated:

- services which do not require medical knowledge, skills or judgment;

- services not related to care, such as paternity testing and writing books or articles;

- services carried out for legal reasons such as:

    (i)   negotiation or advocacy;

    (ii) arbitration, mediation or conciliation;

    (iii) investigating the validity of an insurance or negligence claim;

    (iv) considering medical reports and other evidence to try to resolve disputes;

    (v)   work carried out for lawyers and insurers;

- analytical testing services for medical trials which involve little or no contact with patients;

- countersigning passport applications, providing character references or photocopying medical records.

Work by unqualified people which is supervised

11.84   The exemption includes situations in which the work is done by someone not medically qualified, provided that the service is *wholly performed or directly supervised* by someone who is. In *Anthony John Lane t/a Crown Optical Centre* (LON/97/162 No 15547) a Tribunal held that the supervision test was satisfied when a qualified optician did all the eye tests and was present five days a fortnight. Evidence showed there were a few problems for him to resolve and he was available by telephone when not present. Similarly, in *Personal Assistance (UK) Ltd* (MAN/00/974 No 17649), a case concerning nursing care at home for seriously ill patients, part-time support provided by a qualified nurse, working six hours a week but on call the rest of the time, was held to provide the necessary supervision; on the other hand, the Tribunal held in the same case that the engagement as a 'consultant' of a nurse, who had a full-time job with the local health authority, did not. There was no appraisal of each new patient or allocation of a care worker to each patient and only a limited review of the care workers, most of the support being by telephone.

However, in *A & S Services* (LON/97/812 No 16025), an unregistered optician was found to be not directly supervised by an ophthalmic medical practitioner when the latter referred people needing glasses to him, but did not attend himself and merely checked that glasses previously supplied met his prescription if customers came back for further tests a year or so later.

In *E Moss Ltd* (LON/03/1048 No 19510), the Tribunal held that the services of unregistered chiropodists in its branches were exempt so long as a registered chiropodist worked in the same branch, and that branch was visited by a registered senior clinician. 'Direct' meant not through a third party, and 'supervision' meant the appropriate level depending upon the circumstances of the case. Direct supervision did not have to be constant and unremitting; it was a question of degree and related to the level of risk.

Staff supplied by nursing agencies

11.85   There is also exemption for the supplies of an employment bureau where the bureau acts as principal and the supply relates to the provision of nurses and nursing auxiliaries supplying care.

In 1998, HMRC issued guidance to confirm that bureaux acting in an employment business capacity will be acting as principals for VAT purposes, and, therefore, met the requirement for the care exemption to apply.

To qualify for the exemption, the nursing staff must be supplied directly to a nursing home and that:

● the supply is of nursing staff;

● the employment bureau acts in the capacity as principal; and

● before 1 October 2010 the employment bureau had to be registered with the Care Quality Commission (formally CSCI). With effect from 1 October 2010 (as a result of changes announced in the Health and Social Care Act 2008), the legal requirement for nursing agencies to be registered under the Care Quality Commission ceased and responsibility for quality standards passed to those organisations that provide the regulated activity.

The term healthcare professional is defined by HMRC in their Notice 701/57 and includes nurses who are enrolled or registered on the appropriate statutory register.

The notice states that care services performed by unregistered staff may also be included when the person providing the nursing care is under the direct supervision of a health professional or the care is provided in a nursing home. I would expect nursing auxiliaries and care workers to fall into this category.

Mixed supplies by opticians

11.86   For cases concerning the value of the exempt supplies by opticians, see Chapter 12, *Is there one supply or two?*

Supplies of staff versus medical services

11.87   Normally, the supply of medically qualified staff from one organisation to another is likely to involve exempt medical services, not just a standard-rated supply of staff. However, in *University Court of the University of Glasgow* (EDN/03/109 No 19052), there were tripartite arrangements between the University, its professors, and NHS trusts, under which the latter appointed university staff as consultants, but paid all or part of their salaries to the University. The University was held to make a standard-rated supply of staff; it was not involved with medical services as such, and there were contracts direct between its staff and the NHS trusts.

Group 7, Item 4: Charges by hospitals and other institutions

11.88   The exemption for charges by hospitals to patients is in *Item 4*. It covers the provision of care or medical or surgical treatment and, in connection with it, the supply of any goods. The supply must be in a hospital or 'state-regulated' institution. The latter is defined in *Note (8),* and potentially covers such establishments as nursing homes. However, the more reliable source of exemption may be *Item 9*. This is because, in *Kingscrest Associates Ltd and Montecello Ltd* (LON/2000/875 No 17244; [2002] EWHC 410 (Ch)), the High Court upheld the Tribunal's earlier decision that the association of the word 'care' with medical or surgical treatment meant that the care must be medically or surgically related.

In *Business Brief 10/2001*, HMRC said that residential care homes could continue to treat their supplies as exempt, and the law was then changed from 21 March 2002 to expand the coverage of *Item 9*.

In *Gregg* (C-216/97: [1999] STC 934), the ECJ ruled that the exemption covered individuals and partnerships running such institutions, as well as corporate bodies.

How wide is 'care'?

11.89   HMRC interpret the word 'care' as covering:

- the protection, control or guidance of an individual to meet medical, physical, personal or domestic needs;

- usually involving personal contact with the individual (Notice 701/2 *Welfare* para 2.1).

That of course covers care under *Item 9* as well as *Item 4*. HMRC say it includes:

- accommodation and meals for relatives staying with a sick child in hospital—but no other supplies to visitors, relatives or carers;

- assistance with daily tasks for residents of a home for disabled, elderly or infirm people;

- meals and accommodation for inpatients, residents or other care beneficiaries;

- supervising children in a day nursery or an after-school club;

- entertainment, leisure and other organised activities where these are not separable from the main supply of care or treatment.

It does not include catering for staff.

Who has to provide the care?

11.90   The person providing 'care' need not be medically qualified. The exemption covers supplies made by, for instance, a charity, which caters to patients in an institution, or by an outside contractor which supplies nursing services.

In *Crothall & Co Ltd* ([1973] VATTR 20 No 6) a VAT Tribunal held that services supplied by the company in hospitals, which involved personal contact with the patients, were exempt. Thus services on the ward in meeting patients on admission, making refreshments and delivering messages for them, escorting them about the hospital and arranging their discharge were exempt, as were the services of the staff controlling and supervising such duties.

Only the services of people not in personal contact with patients, such as receptionists, telephonists and cleaners, were standard-rated.

Thus, there is a distinction between services supplied direct to patients and those supplied to a hospital to enable it to supply its own services.

HMRC quote renal dialysis services in hospitals as one of a few examples of supplies by an outside contractor, which do qualify for exemption.

Supplies not amounting to care

11.91   In *MJ Coleman* (LON/92/1274 No 10512), the provision of hearing aids in a hospital was held not to amount to 'care'. The Tribunal held that the care had to be such as would ordinarily be regarded as treatment in a hospital.

This makes sense—otherwise, the supply of goods like hearing aids would be exempt if made within a hospital but standard-rated if sold from other premises.

The company *In Healthcare group SA* (LON/03/325 No 19593) was held not to provide healthcare when, through its subsidiary, Lister in Health Ltd, it employed radiographers to use scanners to provide magnetic resonance imaging in the grounds of a hospital. That was merely data which would be used by the medical staff. The Tribunal thought that the scanner unit was probably not a part of the hospital, which sounds odd! However, as there was no relationship with each patient, the service was seen as not hospital care. That seems a fine distinction compared with *Crothall* explained at **11.90**.

If you want exemption, make sure the business is statutorily registered

11.92   Health care is only exempt under *Group 7, Item 4* or *Item 9* if the hospital or clinic is registered under the appropriate law. Until it is so registered, its charges are standard-rated. You do not obtain a retrospective exemption by gaining statutory registration.

Beauty salons can be hospitals!

11.93   Under the *Care Standards Act 2000*, the prescribed techniques and technologies regulated by the Healthcare Commission include the use of class 3B and 4 lasers and Intense Pulse Light machines. This means that beauty salons using that equipment are classified as independent hospitals for the purposes of the care standards legislation.

HMRC clarified the position in *Business Brief 03/06*, which said that where the procedure using the equipment is supplied as part of the treatment programme drawn up by a registered health professional following the diagnosis of a medical condition, it is exempt. However, treatment carried out merely for a cosmetic reason is standard-rated.

Beware the difference! To justify exemption, documentary evidence of the treatment programme will have to be kept.

Group 7, Items 5–8

11.94   These items are of limited application. *Item 5* exempts the services of a person deputising for a doctor. *Item 6* exempts human blood and *Item 7* products for therapeutic purposes derived therefrom. *Item 8* exempts human organs or tissue for diagnostic or therapeutic purposes or for medical research.

Group 7, Item 9: Welfare services by a charity, state-regulated private welfare institution or agency or public body

11.95   The scope of *Item 9* was expanded from 21 March 2002 for the reasons explained in the comment on *Item 4*. It was expanded again from 31 January 2003 to cover agencies providing care and domestic help to elderly, sick or disabled people, who cannot perform the task themselves, provided that the agency is registered or regulated as detailed in the law. In *Business Brief 1/03* HMRC also said that various other agencies, such as those providing fostering, adoption, or nursing could qualify. Such agencies must supply a welfare service, not just an introduction fee or a commission, so beware the self-employment pitfall! Strictly, supplies are not exempt until the agency has become regulated. If the customers of a business cannot recover VAT, it will want to use the extra-statutory concession in *Business Brief 1/03*, confirmed in BB 5/05, which allows businesses to treat their supplies as exempt during the period that their application to the regulatory body is being processed. A commission for supplying self-employed carers, as opposed to staff, is standard-rated. Notice 701/2 *Welfare* refers.

The ECJ confirmed in *Kingscrest Associates Ltd & Montecello Ltd* (LON/ 2002/691 No 18184 ; C-498/03), an attempt by KAL to limit HMRC's 2002 widening of the exemption following its High Court win (see para 10.85), that 'charitable' in *Art 13(A)(1)(g) and (h) EC 6th VAT Directive* can cover a profit-making entity, which is providing welfare services. The ECJ said that it is for the national court to decide the position in individual cases. The High Court had found that Kingscrest was making taxable supplies, and was not covered by the exemption. Kingscrest, whose residents were predominantly paid for by local authorities, was then able to register for VAT and recover the VAT on its costs. The local authorities could recover the VAT they were charged, so Kingscrest and similar institutions found themselves in an advantageous position. HMRC disagreed with the principle of care becoming subject to VAT, and changed the law with effect from 21 March 2002 to exempt any 'state-registered' care home.

HMRC have not universally applied the High Court decision, so there is no compulsory requirement to register for VAT for turnover prior to 21 March 2002. They will, however, accept voluntary registration applications, so care homes have an opportunity for a VAT refund if they can identify a period of trading ending on 21 March 2002, in which capital expenditure is sufficiently high to create an overall repayment position. *Note (6)* defines *welfare services* as those directly connected with the provision of:

- care, treatment or instruction designed to promote the physical or mental welfare of elderly, sick, distressed or disabled persons;

- care or protection of children and young persons;

- spiritual welfare by a religious institution as part of a course of instruction or a retreat, not being a course or retreat designed primarily to provide recreation or a holiday.

11.96 *So what is exempt?*

A state-regulated private welfare institution can only exempt those services in respect of which it is regulated.

Note (8) defines *state-regulated*. See the law for the precise wording. For an agency, see the start of the comment on *Item 9* and the heading below *State regulation might exist without you having formal recognition*. An institution is one which is either:

- approved, licensed or registered under the relevant social legislation; or

- exempted from obtaining such an approval or registration.

HMRC quote as examples of such institutions:

- children's homes;

- residential homes for disabled, elderly or infirm residents;

- residential homes for people with a past or present dependence on alcohol or drugs, or a past or present mental disorder;

- nurseries, crèches or playgroups;

- after-school clubs or similar providers of non-residential care for children.

The latter two only need to be state-regulated if they exceed a certain number of hours of care to children under eight.

If you also provide care to children over eight, HMRC say you can treat it as exempt too if:

- you are a commercial institution providing care to children both under and over eight;

- your hours of opening are the same for all age groups; and

- you provide activities which are comparable for both age groups.

The item covers, for instance, religious retreats—provided that they are not primarily designed to provide recreation or a holiday! See *Notes (6) and (7)* for the full definition of *welfare services*.

In *Trustees for the Macmillan Cancer Trust* (LON/97/614 No 15603), charges to cancer patients and carers to stay for up to two weeks in an establishment run like a hotel with trained nurses in 24-hour attendance but without 'hands-on' nursing care were held to qualify as welfare.

State regulation might exist without an institution having formal recognition!

11.96 *In K & L Childcare Services Ltd* (MAN/04/129 No 19041;[2005] EWHC 2414 (Ch)), the High Court overturned the earlier Tribunal decision, and held that the company did not provide, as an agency, exempt supplies of child carers to kindergartens because it was not itself regulated.

Based on the ECJ decision in *Gregg*, mentioned earlier concerning *Item 4*, the Tribunal held that *Item 9(b)*, in referring to a state regulated private welfare institution or agency, had a meaning beyond what might be literally apparent concerning an agency.

Group 7, Item 10: Supplies by religious communities

11.97   This Item exempts supplies of goods and services incidental to spiritual welfare by a residential community to its residents in return for membership subscriptions. Again, it must be otherwise than for profit.

Group 7, Item 11: Transport for the sick

11.98   This Item exempts the transport of sick or injured people in vehicles specially designed for that purpose.

BURIAL AND CREMATION—SCH 9 GROUP 8

11.99   This group covers:

- the disposal of the remains of the dead;

- the making of arrangements for or in connection with the disposal of the remains of the dead.

This covers those charges which are strictly related to burial or cremation. 'Extras', such as flowers and headstones, are standard-rated.

For many years, this Group caused little or no trouble. However, there have been the following three cases in the last few years, which show that, even in undertaking, there is scope for argument on VAT!

Network Insurance Brokers Ltd ([1998] STC 742) concerned a commission on annual subscriptions paid at a rate per member by affinity groups, whose members were thereby entitled to a standard funeral service (retail value £1,000) provided by the Co-operative Wholesale Society. The commission was held to be standard-rated because it was earned in arranging payment for the disposal of the remains of the dead, not for the disposal itself.

In *Co-operative Wholesale Society Ltd* ([1999] STC 1096), a fee of £150 per member for 'facilitating and administering' a general benefit scheme on behalf of the Leeds Hospital Fund, was held not to be for the making of arrangements for or in connection with the disposal of the remains of the dead.

However, in *CJ Williams' Funeral Service of Telford* (MAN/98/654 No 16261), the storage of bodies and the provision of a chapel of rest to other undertakers were held to be part and parcel of the making of arrangements for or in connection with the disposal of the remains of the dead, not one stage removed from it.

TRADE UNIONS, PROFESSIONAL AND OTHER PUBLIC INTEREST BODIES—SCH 9 GROUP 9

11.100 This exempts the membership subscriptions of:

- trade unions and similar bodies;

- professional associations whose membership is restricted to those qualified or studying for the appropriate exams;

- associations concerned with advancing a particular branch of knowledge or fostering the professional expertise connected with its members' work;

- associations whose primary purpose is to lobby the government on legislation and other matters affecting the business or professional interests of its members; ie primarily trade associations;

- bodies with objects of a political, religious, patriotic, philosophical, philanthropic or civic nature.

Charges to non-members

11.101 *Note (1)* excludes admission charges to premises or events, which non-members have to pay. Other Notes contain various details or limitations to the different headings above. As always, check the law for the precise wording.

Goods covered by subscriptions

11.102 The exemption covers any goods which are covered by the subscriptions, and which are referable to the aims of the organisation. In practice, this is most often a journal or magazine for which one wants zero-rating under *Sch 8, Group 3* in order to recover the related input tax.

Although not strictly a planning point as such, the apportionment of part of the subscription as zero-rated is sometimes overlooked by associations and their advisers. It can be valuable. Sometimes, the cover prices of the journal or journals supplied to members come close to the entire annual subscription. However, the sales at these prices to non-members are often minimal. Clearly, the other benefits of membership are worth something and it is usually sensible not to be too greedy when negotiating an appropriate apportionment with HMRC.

Moreover, HMRC see an apportionment as a concession: Para 3.35 of Notice 48 *Extra statutory concessions* says:

'Bodies, that are non-profit-making and supply a mixture of zero-rated, exempt and/or standard-rated benefits to their members in return for their subscriptions, may apportion such subscriptions to reflect the value and VAT liability of those individual benefits without regard to whether there is one principal benefit. This concession may not be used for the purposes of tax avoidance.'

However, the Tribunal held in *The Royal College of Anaesthetists* (LON/01/170 No 18632) that there was a multiple supply of magazine and other membership benefits, even though the annual subscription was the same figure as the magazine subscription. Nevertheless, the maintenance of professional standards was a benefit, and the subscriptions should be apportioned on the basis of the cost of the journals provided, not their price to non-members.

On the other hand, beware the pitfall that, if the subscription includes admission to any premises, event, or performance for which non-members have to pay, it must be apportioned as partly standard-rated.

Additionally, in *Revenue & Customs Brief 06/09*, HMRC say that where the club's original returns were correct in law, they will not accept claims for repayment of 'overpaid' VAT based on reworking the past returns to claim the benefit of the concession.

What is a trade union, professional or public interest body?

11.103 Numerous cases have concerned claims by organisations for exemption under *Group 9*. The only one concerning a trade union is *Institute of the Motor Industry* (LON/96/224 No 16586: [1998] STC 1219). After a reference to the ECJ for guidance, the Tribunal decided that the Institute did not qualify as a trade union. The defence of the members' collective interests and representation of those interests in disputes was not a main aim. The Institute avoided taking sides in disputes between members and their employers.

Professional associations

11.104   *Allied Dancing Association Ltd* (MAN/91/84 No 10777) was a borderline case in which the Tribunal held that the teaching of dance by its members was a profession. The decision was based on the fact that the Association conducted its own examinations, and had a code of conduct. However, whether an association qualifies as professional is usually obvious. The requirement for a membership restricted to people qualified in the profession or students limits the possibilities.

Meaning of fostering of professional expertise

11.105   The majority of the arguments have, therefore, been about whether the body in question was an *'association concerned with advancing a particular branch of knowledge* or *the fostering of professional expertise connected with its members' work.'* HMRC have won the majority of the cases. This is partly because Tribunals have interpreted professional expertise in the traditional sense of that of a doctor, a lawyer, or an accountant, rather than someone doing a job to a professional standard. Thus, in *Institute of the Motor Industry* mentioned above, the Tribunal concluded that the expertise in question was that *of the sort carried on in any profession, whether its members be self-employed professionals or professionals employed in, for example, industry, commerce or public bodies.* The Institute did not qualify because its primary purpose was *the improvement of the standard of work by the individual members in their various employments, the improvement of career structures within the different sectors of the industry and the consequent enhancement of the public perception of the industry and the people working within it.*

However, *EMIS National User Group* (MAN/05/594 No 19645), a charitable company limited by guarantee, was held to qualify. It was set up to improve patient care through the better use of health information and information technology. It assisted users of EMIS software to get the best possible use from their computer systems, and it provided training and educational materials. Its primary purpose was held to be to assist and encourage its members to acquire and utilise the knowledge, skills and tools which enabled information to be collected, managed, used and shared to support the delivery of health care and promote health. Although a practical and pragmatic purpose, that was the fostering of medical professional expertise connected with the professions of its members, not just the provision of an IT support service. I can see further arguments about the distinction between learning to use an IT system, and the fostering of professional expertise in exploiting that system!

Advancement of a branch of knowledge

11.106 HMRC have seen the advancement of a branch of knowledge as referring to knowledge of an academic nature, despite *British Organic Farmers* (LON/87/164 No 2700), in which the Tribunal held organic farming to be a branch of knowledge—a branch of the science of agriculture. It was influenced by the fact that it was the subject matter of a course at two colleges. Similarly, counselling was found to be a branch of knowledge in *British Association for Counselling* (LON/93/1494 No 11855)—based on evidence of academic courses and the level of articles in the Association's journal.

However, *Permanent Way Institution* (LON/01/585 No 17746) has undermined the academic argument. The Tribunal was persuaded that the PWI's activities in furthering knowledge about the design, construction, inspection and maintenance of the permanent way of the railway amongst those who work on it, amounted to the advancement of a branch of knowledge. PWI publishes a journal and a leading textbook, *British Railway Track,* and runs conferences. PWI's role as a forum enables ideas not just to be put forward but to be discussed and refined. People from all levels of seniority within the industry meet on equal terms and, although there is some science and considerable engineering expertise involved, much of the knowledge being advanced is practical rather than academic.

Meaning of 'philanthropic'

11.107 In *Rotary International in Great Britain and Ireland (RIBI)* ([1991] VATTR 177 No 5946), HMRC argued that RIBI's functions were merely administrative and organisational. The Tribunal rejected that, commenting that what mattered was not what it did, but why. It did not perform its administrative services in a vacuum. Its purpose was to promote the purposes of Rotary International. That was philanthropic, being redolent of a desire to promote the well-being of mankind.

Meaning of civic nature

11.108 In the *Expert Witness Institute* (LON/99/1173 No 16842; [2001] STC 679; [2002] STC 42), the High Court held that EWI had aims of a civic nature. EWI had argued that a meaning of *civic* was *citizenship,* and that that included activities concerning the relations between the citizen and the state. The Court agreed. EWI's aims were fairly described as for the promotion and support of the proper administration of justice, and that was not subverted or undermined by other objectives, which benefited its members. This was confirmed by the Court of Appeal.

SPORT, SPORTS COMPETITIONS AND PHYSICAL EDUCATION—SCH 9 GROUP 10

11.109

Focus

This exempts:

- entry fees for competitions in sport or physical recreation where all the fees go towards prizes;

- entry fees in such competitions charged by non-profit-making bodies;

- fees for playing sport or for physical education charged by non-profit-making bodies to individuals. If there is a membership scheme HMRC took the view that charges to non-members were standard-rated, however, following the decision in the *Bridport and West Dorset Golf Club Ltd v Revenue & Customs Commissioners* [2011] UKFTT 354 (TC) green fees for non-members were viewed as covered by the exemption but HMRC appealed the decision to the Upper Tribunal which has referred it to the ECJ. The exemption is for services essential to sport or physical education in which the individual takes part so sales in the bar, for instance, are standard-rated.

Membership subscriptions

11.110 The key exemption is the third one for subscriptions charged by members' clubs for taking part in sport. It is very useful to local sports clubs of all kinds.

One planning point which arises is the need for careful negotiations with HMRC on how much VAT is recoverable when a new clubhouse or other expensive facilities are constructed. The club's income will be a mixture of standard-rated bar sales, etc and exempt subscriptions. The appropriate attribution of VAT incurred on capital expenditure is often open to argument. Following the ECJ decision in *Bridport & West Dorset Golf Club* (C495/12) the payment of green fees at golf courses is considered to be exempt from VAT. This will also apply to any temporary playing memberships of non-profit making sports clubs of less than three months which HMRC had previously ruled to be standard-rated.

Unfortunately, owners of commercial businesses providing sporting facilities started to try to take advantage of the exemption by forming members' clubs, which charged the subscriptions and ran the activities, the profit being extracted by the owner of the business as, for example, rent. Anti-avoidance rules were brought in and, as a result, this Group has lengthy notes attached to it aimed at restricting the exemption to genuine members' clubs.

What is a non-profit making body?

11.111 In *Kennemer Golf and Country Club* (Case C-174/00: [2002] STC 502), a Dutch case, the ECJ confirmed the UK's view that a non-profit making body can make surpluses provided that its constitution prevents it from distributing them to its members. 'Profits' in this context means financial advantages for those members, not merely surpluses which remain within the body to finance its future activities.

Subscriptions to a governing body may be exempt

11.112 HMRC took the view that subscriptions charged by the governing bodies of individual sports to their affiliated clubs are standard-rated. However, in *Canterbury Hockey Club & Canterbury Ladies Hockey Club* (LON/04/823 No 19146), the Tribunal found the national organisation, England Hockey, to be making the supplies to the members of its affiliated clubs, because the latter were unincorporated associations with no legal existence apart from the members of which they were composed. Those members had clubbed together to obtain, pay for, and use England Hockey's services.

The Tribunal conceded that the situation might be different if a club was a legal person in its own right. On appeal, the High Court ([2006] EWHC 581 (Ch)) partially overturned the decision, and referred the matter to the ECJ. The ECJ found in favour of the club (C-253/07: [2008] BVC 824), and ruled that the exemption was too narrowly construed in the UK and should include affiliation fees.

WORKS OF ART ETC—SCH 9 GROUP 11

11.113 This exempts the handing over to the Treasury of works of art in lieu of payment of tax under the 'douceur' arrangements. This is not an option open to most people and appears never to have caused any trouble, possibly because it is not often used.

FUND-RAISING EVENTS BY CHARITIES AND OTHER QUALIFYING BODIES—SCH 9 GROUP 12

11.114

Focus

Group 12 exempts the supply at a fund-raising event:

- of goods and services including advertising to sponsors;

> - by a charity, or charities, a qualifying body or a combination thereof;
> - in connection with an event whose primary purpose is fund-raising and which is promoted as such.
>
> There are various conditions including a limit of 15 events during the charity's financial year:
>
> - at the same location;
> - of the same kind,
>
> but you can ignore an event if the gross takings from that kind of event in that location do not exceed £1,000.

'Charity' includes a company which the charity wholly owns and whose profits are payable to it, whether or not under covenant (*Note (2)*).

'Qualifying body' means one which is:

- non-profit making and is covered by the exemption in *Sch 9 Group 9* already explained (for political, religious, patriotic etc bodies);
- a non-profit making body supplying facilities for sports or physical education, which meets the definition of 'eligible body' in *Sch 9 Group 10*;
- an eligible body as defined in *Sch 9 Group 13, Item 2* re cultural services.

What kind of event?

11.115   The exemption covers any activity recognisable as an individual event—as opposed to the regular opening of a shop or a bar. Thus, events such as horticultural shows, marathons and sports competitions are eligible.

Excluded are:

- fund-raising holidays or day trips covered by the Tour Operators' Margin Scheme; or
- any event including more than two nights' accommodation (*Note (9)*);
- any supply, the exemption of which would be likely to so distort competition as to disadvantage commercial enterprises (*Note (11)*);
- social events which happen to make a profit (HMRC's comment).

CULTURAL SERVICES ETC—SCH 9 GROUP 13

11.116   *Group 13* exempts charges by public bodies and eligible bodies for admission to:

- a Museum, Gallery, art exhibition or zoo; or

- a theatrical, musical or choreographic performance of a cultural nature. That does not include admission to a cinema (*Chichester Cinema at New Park Ltd* (LON/04/266 No 19344)).

In the case of a public body, exempting the supply must not so distort competition as to disadvantage a commercial competitor.

'Public body' means primarily a local authority but includes government departments and certain other non-departmental public bodies.

'Eligible body' means one which:

- is not allowed to distribute any profit it makes and does not do so;

- uses any profit from the exempted supply to continuing or improving the facility in question; and

- is managed and administered on a voluntary basis by people with no financial interest in its activities.

Although that typically means a charity, the requirement for voluntary management must be taken seriously.

HMRC announced a change of policy in *Business Brief 28/03*, and issued a revised version of Notice 701/47 (Dec 2003) *Culture*, following the ECJ judgment in *The Zoological Society of London* (LON/96/1766 No 15607: 2002 STC 521). This upheld the Tribunal's view that the Society was managed on an 'essentially voluntary basis' by its unpaid Officers and Council. The Tribunal distinguished between the management and administration of a body, and the activities it carried out. The existence of paid officials did not preclude voluntary management—so to hold would risk distortion between small and large bodies. If persons having a financial interest in the body do direct it under its constitution as, for example, members of the Council, it is for HMRC to consider whether the essentially voluntary character of the management or administration can be accepted.

So, an important planning point is to consider how to organise the control and management of a voluntary society. In *The Bournemouth Symphony Orchestra* (LON/03/479 No 18799; [2005] EWHC 1566 (Ch); [2006] EWCA Civ 1281), the Court of Appeal upheld the earlier Tribunal and High Court decisions that the taxpayer did not qualify as voluntarily managed because of its salaried managing director, a significant influence. Was that necessary? The decision could have been different if he had merely reported to the Board as the chief executive, rather than being himself a member of the Board. Contrast this with the decision in *Longborough Festival Opera*, where, despite an initial loss at Tribunal, the High Court, and Court of Appeal (where it was heard jointly with *Bournemouth*

Symphony Orchestra) agreed that exemption applied, even though issues of the case were similar to those in Bournemouth. See para **11.118** below for further details of the case.

In *The Dean and Canons of Windsor* (LON/97/552 No 15703), St George's Chapel was held not to be run on a voluntary basis because the Dean and Canons received stipends and part of their duties was to manage the Chapel and other buildings.

However, HMRC's argument that the Chapel was not a museum because it was the site of a living institution, was rejected. On the other hand, a restored garden open to the public was held not to be a museum in *Trebah Garden Trust* (LON/98/1372 No 16598).

Cultural charities need very careful legal planning

11.117   If a charity is set up using its own property, or is funded by an individual or institution which intends to generate exempt income under *Group 13*, it will need to be very careful! The law requires not just voluntary management and no distribution of profit; there must also be no possibility of any financial benefit. A genuine desire to produce a public benefit is not enough. The legal basis requires much more careful and sophisticated planning than might be supposed!

Martin Graham set up *Longborough Festival Opera* (LFO) (LON/04/115 No 19096; [2006] EWHC 40 (Ch); [2006] EWCA Civ 1281), a company limited by guarantee and registered as a charity, to organise performances of opera using a theatre which he had created on his property. LFO was allowed to use the theatre free of charge.

Under the memorandum of LFO, it could pay interest on any loan to it, and pay rent on premises let to it by a director. It was not doing either. There was a guarantee by Mr Graham, admittedly not legally enforceable, that he would fund any deficit. The Tribunal held that he had a financial interest in it.

The High Court disagreed. Mr Graham and his wife were disqualified in the company's articles from voting on any contract in which they were directly or indirectly interested. That met the requirement that, if an individual has an interest in the results of the activities of such an organisation, he or she must not be in a position to influence those results.

The decision makers would be the other two directors. Moreover, commercial contracts with directors were acceptable if they provided essential requirements on the best terms available, and without conferring any interest in the body's results or profits. Finally, a director did not have a financial interest merely because of giving the body a guarantee or an interest-free loan.

HMRC were refused an appeal to the CA, so a *Longborough* type situation is, in theory, okay. In practice, it will still be wise to separate as far as possible the management of the organisation from the directing of it. It is the directors who control what happens to any profits generated.

For instance, he could organise a payment of rent to himself, and he had an interest in ensuring that there was no deficit—a curious legal point but there you are! Importantly, of the four directors (trustees), two were himself and his wife; the articles of association made two directors a quorum, and gave him, as chairman, a casting vote if views were split evenly.

Thus, he could benefit from LFO, however unlikely that might be in practice, and he had the necessary management control. Therein lies a lesson; if an individual has an interest in the results of the activities of such an organisation, he or she must not be in a position to influence those results.

To achieve that needs careful thought where the landowner, no doubt financially well-off, has created at some considerable expense, a cultural activity much enjoyed by the public and with some support to other local institutions such as schools. No doubt, much of what is achieved in such situations results from the energy and commitment of the landowner. However, for the performance takings not to carry VAT, he or she must not be a director/trustee. Those, who are, must be able to demonstrate that they are in charge, not the landowner—even though the latter is likely to remain as chief executive.

SUPPLIES OF GOODS WHERE INPUT TAX CANNOT BE RECOVERED—SCH 9 GROUP 14

11.118 The heading of this Group is a little misleading. It was added in 2000 following the ECJ decision in *Commission of the European Communities v Italy* (C-45/95), and exempts the onwards sale of goods on which input tax was disallowed when they were bought under the rules for:

- business entertainment;
- non-building materials incorporated in a building;
- motor cars.

As there would normally be no VAT on such second-hand goods, the practical effect is to disallow tax on any sale costs, such as auctioneers' commissions.

INVESTMENT GOLD—SCH 9 GROUP 15

11.119 This group exempts the sale of gold and certain gold coins where the transaction does not involve a member of the London Bullion Market Association.

Notices 701/21 *Gold* and 701/21A *Investment Gold Coins* gives more detail.

COST SHARE GROUP EXEMPTION—SCH 9 GROUP 16

11.120 In 2010 HMRC confirmed that it intended to implement the EU cost-sharing exemption in the UK and announced a consultation process starting in summer 2011. The measure took effect on 17 July 2012 the date of Royal Assent to the *Finance Act 2012*. The legislation introduced a new *Group 16* to the *VATA 1994, Sch 9—Supplies of services by groups involving cost sharing*.

The exemption is provided for in EU law, *(Art 132(1)(f)* of the *Principal VAT Directive*) and applies where shared costs are recharged between partnered entities. The exemption removes the irrecoverable VAT cost that otherwise arises on recharges of costs when organisations such as charities and housing associations share back-office expenses. Typical examples of these shared expenses would be costs relating to staff, HR, and IT expenses.

Under the terms of the exemption, interested parties must come together to form a cost-sharing group ('CSG') which is able to meet the following conditions:

- an independent group must be formed;

- the group members must carry out exempt or non-business activities;

- the value of group charges for services must equal their cost;

- the services must be 'directly necessary' to the members' exempt or non-business activity;

- the services supplied by the group must not cause a distortion of competition.

The exemption applies when two or more organisations (whether businesses or otherwise) with exempt and/or non-business activities join together on a co-operative basis to form a separate, independent entity, a cost sharing group (CSG), to supply themselves with certain services at cost and exempt from VAT.

The exemption applies to supplies of certain qualifying services that are made by the representative member of the CSG to other members of the CSG.

The CSG is a separate taxable person from that of its members. It is therefore able to make supplies for VAT purposes to its members. These supplies will be exempt if the relevant conditions are met. This type of arrangement enables the creation of the same economies of scale for smaller businesses and organisations as larger businesses and organisations naturally enjoy. Thus, the more members of a CSG there are the greater the potential savings and lower the costs per member of operating the relevant CSG.

The cost sharing exemption should help exempt, partly exempt and non-business organisations by allowing them to pool together to form associations which could buy in or provide from their own resources VAT exempt services.

Although the exemption has strict restrictions including that the association must pass on costs without making any profit and must not be at a competitive advantage, this exemption is undoubtedly beneficial to charities who suffer VAT recovery restriction both on their exempt and non-business activities, as well as many other traditionally exempt and partly exempt businesses. These include businesses in the finance sector, schools, medical and welfare providers, property investment businesses and more. In practice, it is the small- and medium-sized sector which is likely to benefit as they do not have in-house resources to meet all of their needs and so have to buy in services on which VAT is charged and irrecoverable.

In one of the first Tribunal cases concerning the cost saving exemption, *West of Scotland Colleges Partnership v Revenue & Customs* [2014] UKFTT 622 (TC), there was an appeal against the refusal of a repayment claim for VAT of £102,216.77. The appellant claimed that this was incorrectly charged in respect of services rendered by it to the colleges of further and higher education which formed it.

The appellant claimed that its service became exempt under *VATA 1994 Sch 9, Gp 16* but HMRC argued that the criteria for 'exact reimbursement of its share of the joint expenses' was not met because all 22 colleges paid exactly the same despite being of different sizes and using the services in different amounts. The appellant argued that HMRC were enforcing the rules too rigidly. Members had been satisfied that they were paying only their own shares of costs incurred.

In reply HMRC submitted that one issue emerged from the evidence: were all services made equally to all members? While certain services were for individual members, these were charged separately and were not the subject of the assessment under appeal. Exact reimbursement was crucial. The colleges were of different sizes and provided different courses yet they each paid the same proportion of the appellant's costs.

The tribunal considered that the test which the appellant is required to meet is a high one. *Exact reimbursement* denoted a measure of precision. The word *exact* obviously has to be given its meaning. The tribunal considered that the appellant had fallen short of satisfying the test of *exact reimbursement*. For this reason the appeal was dismissed.

There is nothing in the legislation that would prevent individual members providing a service or services to other group members, for example one charity in the 'association' could provide all the IT services, another the HR function, etc, achieving greater economies of scale.

Other advantages, apart from not having to charge VAT on supplies from the association to the members could also be increased buying power which could apply to such services as IT, administration, accountancy and legal services.

Details of the exemption can be found in *Revenue & Customs Brief 23/12*.

Following an ECJ ruling on the application of the cost sharing exemption, HMRC has had to review its policy.

11.120 *So what is exempt?*

The following changes are effective from 22 March 2018.

(a)   The CSE is restricted to CSGs whose members engage in the exempt activities listed below. The activities are those which are covered by *Art 132(1)* of the *Principal VAT Directive* – the corresponding exemptions are in *Sch 9* to *VATA 1994*:

- postal services (Group 3);

- education (Group 6);

- health and welfare (Group 7);

- subscriptions to trade unions and professional bodies (Group 9);

- sport (Group 10);

- fund raising by charities (Group 12); and

- cultural services (Group 13).

(b)   The CSE is restricted to members and CSGs located in the UK.

(c)   The CSE isn't allowed where an uplift has been charged on transactions for any purpose.

The judgment did not cover non-business activities and therefore members engaged in these activities are unaffected by these changes.

Chapter 12

Is there one supply or two?

SIGNPOSTS

- You can have a multiple supply where different goods or services are supplied as a bundle, where each supply has a different rate of VAT or a composite supply, and where different goods or services are elements of a single supply at a single VAT rate (see **12.1–12.8**).

- This difference between a multiple and composite supply can affect the VAT liability of a supply with detailed examples (see **12.9–12.13**).

- Goods and services of different liabilities are sometime sold together with a low valuation placed on the zero-rated items in an attempt to obtain a tax advantage. When can it work and when does it fail? (see **12.14–12.34**).

- When supplies of different liabilities are made together an apportionment may be needed (see **12.35**).

12.1   This chapter discusses the possibility of making two or more supplies at different rates of VAT within a single price. This can have a big impact on consumer pricing.

For many years, the matter was relatively straightforward. The answer with goods was usually obvious. For instance, it was accepted that an audio cassette and a book sold together were respectively standard-rated and zero-rated. Equally, if goods with a separate identity were included in a price for a service, they were often treated as a separate supply. An example would be a journal as one of the benefits for a subscription to a professional body.

For services, being intangible, it was trickier to separate a supply consisting entirely of services. For instance, an airline ticket was held to cover a single supply of transport. A meal provided during the flight was not a separate supply.

The position is now much more complicated because the cases discussed in this chapter have overturned or challenged previous ideas.

THE PROBLEM

12.2

> **Focus**
>
> Is there:
>
> - a multiple supply at different rates of VAT; or
>
> - a composite supply consisting of two or more elements amounting to a single supply with the dominant element deciding the rate of tax?

SOME POSSIBLE EXAMPLES

12.3   Here are some examples of where there might be supplies at different rates of VAT. 'Might' because, as explained below, one cannot be sure in the present state of understanding of this subject:

- a home study course consisting of a manual and a cassette;

- a home study course consisting of books or booklets but the price of which also includes the right to submit work for a number of tutorials or critiques (although see *RSH Associates v Com of HMRC* No 19912 (MAN/05/0852) which showed the supplies to be a single standard-rated supply of distance learning);

- a container which is clearly designed for use independently of the product it contains, such as marmalade in a porcelain pot;

- a subscription to a professional body which includes a magazine.

Business Brief 2/2001, along with a number of Tribunal decisions, now requires the above and numerous other situations to be reconsidered. I believe that the answer often depends on the precise facts of the case.

HMRC has published guidance (Spotlight 38) on supply splitting tax avoidance schemes where businesses attempt to avoid VAT by splitting a single supply of goods or services into separate supplies.

This results in a lower rate of VAT on each separate supply than there would otherwise have been on the single supply, and is classed as supply splitting.

HMRC view all VAT supply splitting arrangements that have been designed to reduce the amount of VAT owed as tax avoidance.

HMRC consider that such arrangements should be taxed as a single supply:

- Where multiple suppliers are used where the same elements could be provided by one supplier; and

- Where the customer has no opportunity to decline to take one of the individual elements

HMRC say they will challenge any such arrangements.

THE LINKED SUPPLIES CONCESSION

12.4   In Notice 700/7 (March 2002) *Business Promotion Schemes*, HMRC make what they call the 'linked supplies' concession. If a minor item:

- is included with the main supply at a single price;

- costs no more than 20% of the total cost of the two items; and

- costs no more than £1, excluding VAT, if the goods are intended for retail sale or £5, excluding VAT, in other cases,

the minor item may be ignored. A typical example is the standard-rated CD-ROM on the cover of a zero-rated computer magazine.

KEY QUESTIONS

12.5   The ECJ in *Card Protection Plan* (*CPP*) identified the following key points. These had all been discussed in previous decisions, and thus were not new, but *CPP* is one of the trickiest cases so far, and is currently the most often quoted. See **11.27** for the details of *CPP*.

We have paraphrased the wording of the ECJ decision to make it easier to understand. If in doubt when applying them to a difficult situation, go back to the original wording and explanations in the judgment.

Focus

In order to determine whether a typical customer is being provided with several distinct principal supplies or with a single supply, consider the following:

- identify the key features of the transaction. Normally, each supply is regarded as distinct and independent but, if a supply is a single one from an economic point of view, one must not artificially split it so as to distort the VAT system;

- if a supply includes different features and actions, consider all the circumstances in which the transaction occurs;

255

- if one or more elements make up the principal supply and the others are ancillary to it, that is a single supply;

- a supply must be regarded as ancillary if it is just a means of better using and enjoying the principal one, rather than being an aim in itself for the customer;

- an all-in price is merely suggestive of a single supply, not a decisive factor. If the circumstances of the transaction indicate the customer intends to purchase two distinct supplies with different tax liabilities, the single price must be apportioned;

- any such apportionment should be done using the simplest possible method.

The above tests must all be considered in each situation. None is by itself decisive.

Further points from various judicial commentaries

12.6

- What is the legal effect of the transaction considered in relation to the words of the law?

- To decide that, one must ask what the business has supplied for the payment made. Motive and intention are irrelevant; the test is objective.

- Having identified and defined that, there is, in substance and reality, more than one supply, could the alleged separate supply realistically be omitted from the overall supply? Is it 'economically dissociable' or is it an integral part or component of the whole?

- Supplies by different suppliers cannot be fused together to make a single supply.

- One should treat a zero-rated or exempt supply as separate from a standard-rated one, if it is practicable and realistic to do so and the general scheme of the legislation can be followed.

CHARACTERISTICS OF A MULTIPLE SUPPLY

12.7   In *FDR Ltd* (CA [2000] STC 672), Laws LJ propounded the idea that a composite supply might be either:

- a single dominant supply forming an apex, other elements being merely ancillary to it; or

- several supplies, integral to each other but none predominant and forming a 'table top'.

In a table-top case, one must ask what is the 'true and substantial nature' of the supply. If the tax treatment is not then evident, one must look again at those core supplies and decide, possibly on a numerical basis, whether the taxable or exempt elements predominate!

SUMMARY OF THE ABOVE POINTS

12.8 Probably the key point of all those listed above, is whether the element of the supply, which one wishes to separate, can be seen as a key aim for the customer rather than merely enabling that customer to benefit from the main supply.

These are complex concepts, and it may take some time to fully understand the implications. Even experienced VAT specialists have difficulty in understanding some of the cases on which I have commented below, all of which took the above tests into account at least to some extent. If VAT specialists have problems in applying these tests, so will businesses and local HMRC officers, so they will continue to produce extensive litigation for some time to come!

SO WHY DOES ALL THIS MATTER?

12.9 It matters because some well-established situations have changed— or, at any rate, HMRC think they have! In *Business Brief 2/2001*, HMRC said that they required everyone to reconsider their position based on the tests laid down by the ECJ as to whether there was a single or a multiple supply situation.

The *Brief* said that supplies previously accepted as zero-rated or exempt might become standard-rated. Alternatively, the entire supply could be exempt instead of partly zero- or standard-rated, or even zero-rated instead of partly exempt or standard-rated.

SUBSCRIPTIONS, WHICH INCLUDE A MAGAZINE

12.10 For instance, HMRC questioned whether a journal supplied to members of an organisation as one of the benefits of a subscription was a separate zero-rated supply. They said in the *Brief*:

'Where a membership body supplies, in return for its membership subscription, a principal benefit together with one or more ancillary benefits, it will normally have to treat the subscription as being in return for that principal benefit. This means that the body will have to ignore the liability to VAT of the ancillary benefits and account for VAT on the whole subscription based on the liability to VAT of that principal benefit.'

The clumsy phrasing aside, that seems to be far too broad an assumption. There are undoubtedly cases where there are two or more principal benefits, each of which was an aim in itself. Subsequent cases support this view.

Presumably, HMRC no longer accept the validity of *Automobile Association* ([1974] STC 192), an early case in which the subscription to the AA was held to be part zero-rated on account of its year book was seen for many years as an important guide. It was referred to in detail in *Tumble Tots (UK) Ltd* (LON/05/28 No 19530; [2007] EWHC 103 (Ch)) together with numerous other cases.

The Tribunal's decision in *Tumble Tots* was that a subscription of £19 was primarily the supply of the right to attend the weekly classes for children run by franchisees—to whom separate fees were paid for each session—with a small proportion attributable to a zero-rated membership t-shirt for the child. The Tribunal did not believe that the supply of the *Right Start* magazines, the DVD, the CD, the gym bag, the handbook, or the insurance are for the typical consumer the reason for wanting to join. No zero-rating was thus attributable to the magazines or exemption for the insurance. Tumble Tots appealed the decision to the High Court, maintaining that a proper categorisation of the consideration for the membership fee would include at least the following benefits:

- registration as a member;
- insurance; and
- the membership pack (in particular, the t-shirt and the Right Start magazine).

HMRC cross-appealed, maintaining that the Tribunal should simply have confirmed the Commissioners' original ruling that the consideration consisted of a single rather than mixed supply. The High Court dismissed Tumble Tots' appeal, but allowed HMRC's.

Since the decision in *Tumble Tots* was based on what the court saw as the main objectives of the customer to obtain for the subscription, evidence on the marketing to customers seems likely to be important in this sort of case—plus copies of the magazines; seemingly, neither were produced as evidence!

Tumble Tots is only one of numerous decisions concerning whether magazines, books or training material are separate supplies—or even the main supply. So, look through the rest of this chapter for more on this aspect of whether there is a single or multiple supplies.

Weight Watchers (UK) Ltd concerned weekly meetings for slimmers, including weigh-ins, and literature provided on initial registration and at those meetings.

HMRC had previously allowed output tax to be declared on a proportion of income, but then issued a revised ruling stating that there was a single standard-rated supply of a weight loss programme.

At the Tribunal, the Chairman, through an analysis of case law, took the view that for cases involving a mix of goods and services, the *Levob* ECJ case (C-41/04) was the leading precedent, it having built on the earlier principles established in *the Card Protection Plan* case (C-349/96). He took particular note of the comment in Levob:

'where two or more elements or acts supplied by the taxable person to the customer, being a typical customer, are so closely linked that they form, objectively, a single, indivisible economic supply, which it would be artificial to split'.

The Chairman concluded that there was no single indivisible supply at the first or subsequent meetings, and that there was nothing artificial about splitting the printed matter and attendance at the meetings. A contributory factor to this conclusion seemed to be the fact that there were a certain number of slimmers, described as 'at home members', who receive the printed matter without attending any meetings. The appeal was thus allowed by the Tribunal with a comment that the zero-rated split on initial registration, where a 170-page handbook was supplied, would be higher than that on subsequent meetings where only leaflets were supplied.

In the High Court, counsel for HMRC put forward four challenges to the reasoning applied by the Tribunal in reaching its conclusion. The judge concluded that HMRC had not succeeded in demonstrating that any one of them represented an error of approach by the Tribunal. However, whilst the correct tests had been distilled (ie to the extent that the tests were a matter of law rather than fact), the judge considered that he had the right to reconsider the correct legal characterisation of the transactions, albeit that interfering with the Tribunal decision could only be done with circumspection.

Applying the 'ancillary' test as per the *College of Estate Management* case, the judge concluded that, as far as the subsequent regular meetings were concerned, the printed material was ancillary, and a differentiation between the printed material and the services provided would be artificial. The judge thus concluded that the subsequent meetings should be properly classified as a single supply of weight loss services. The judge then asked himself if any practical difficulties arose out of a conclusion that the charges for the initial meeting should be apportioned, but the charges for subsequent meetings should not. He decided not, noting that the Tribunal decision had already recognised different apportionments for the two types of meeting. The appeal was partly allowed to the extent of the treatment of subsequent meetings.

HMRC appealed to the Court of Appeal (CA) ([2008] EWCA Civ 715; [2009] BVC 91), which agreed with HMRC's original ruling that the Appellant makes a composite standard-rated supply of meetings and literature. The complexity of this area of the tax has been borne out by the fact that the Tribunal, High Court, and CA each reached wildly different conclusions on the same facts!

12.11   *Is there one supply or two?*

In the case of *Harley Davidson Europe Ltd v HMRC* [2017] UKFTT 873 (TC), the appeal related to the VAT treatment of supplies made by the appellant to members of HOG in consideration for membership subscriptions. HMRC's position was that the appellant made a single standard-rated supply of membership, and that the range of benefits provided were the means by which the members better enjoy that membership. The appellant's position was that it made a number of distinct supplies to each member, the tax treatment of each of which must be determined separately.

Under HMRC's approach VAT was chargeable on all membership subscriptions. The appellant contended that no VAT was chargeable on subscriptions by non-EU members, on the basis that those supplies should be treated as zero rated supplies of goods and/or supplies of services that are outside the scope of VAT. For EU members, the appellant claimed that a substantial proportion of the fee should be regarded as being paid for zero rated supplies, in the form of printed matter.

The Tribunal concluded from the evidence that the 'typical' member of HOG was someone who places real value on tangible items. Overall the Tribunal decided that the individual benefits provided were simply too significant in qualitative terms to allow the supply to be characterised as a single supply of membership, rather than as a number of independent supplies, so it found for the appellant.

For an Extra-Statutory Concession for subscriptions to non-profit making bodies, see **11.99**.

ENTRANCE FEES INCLUDING PROGRAMMES OR CATALOGUES

12.11   Certainly, HMRC are likely to challenge the zero-rating of a programme or catalogue when included with the entrance fee to an event such as a race meeting or an exhibition. In *Town and Country Factors Ltd* (LON/02/322 No 18569) the fee was held to be for a single supply. Although a racegoer could refuse to buy the programme and pay £3.50 instead of £5, very few did that.

Logically, one would think that if a programme or catalogue is sold on its own inside the event as well as with the entrance fee, all the sales should qualify as separate supplies. However, this was not a view shared by the Tribunal in *Manchester United plc* (No 17234), where the inclusion of a match-day programme in a hospitality package was found not to be an aim in its own right (per the *CPP* case), but a means of better enjoying the experience of watching a sporting event. As such, the full price of the package was consideration for a single supply of standard-rated hospitality.

COMPUTER SOFTWARE SOLD AND THEN CUSTOMISED—TWO SUPPLIES?

12.12   In *Levob Verzekeringen* (ECJ C-41/04), it was held that there was a single supply despite a charge for a computer licence for software handed over to the customer in the US, and a separate one for the subsequent installation and modification of it on Levob's computer system in the Netherlands. The ECJ said that there is a single supply if two or more elements or acts are so closely linked that they form objectively, from an economic point of view, a whole transaction, which it would be artificial to split. The ECJ then held that, under *Art 6(1)* of the *EU 6th VAT Directive*, the supply was of services where it was apparent that the customisation was of decisive importance in enabling the customer to use the software. See **23.16** for the basis of the supply being taxed as a reverse charge.

SO DOES AN OPTICIAN MAKE MULTIPLE SUPPLIES?

12.13   HMRC now again accept that, in addition to the eye test, which is exempt, the charge for spectacles can be apportioned between the exempt dispensing of the lenses and the standard-rated supply of the frames.

Years ago, the High Court upheld the apportionment in *Leightons Ltd/Eye-Tech Opticians* ([1995] STC 458). HMRC wrote to the Federation of Ophthalmic and Dispensing Opticians requiring opticians to standard-rate dispensing services from 1 June 2001. The resulting appeal by the same two companies was upheld (LON/2001/0302 & 03 No 17498). HMRC acknowledged defeat in *Business Brief 3/2002*.

The normal basis of apportionment between the exempt dispensing and the standard-rated supply of frames is a full apportionment of the costs. However, where a sole practitioner or a partnership of practitioners carry out the dispensing, the value of their time has to be calculated on the basis of their trading profit. In *FP Whiffen Opticians* (LON/01/1351 No 18951), the Tribunal assumed that 20% of the sole trader's time was spent on overhead matters such as management and administration—so 80% of the trading profit was the cost of his time related to the exempt supplies. By concession, opticians can also use the separately disclosed charges method, as detailed in Information Sheet 8/99. However, businesses should be wary of using this method, as HMRC have imposed the full cost apportionment method if they do not like the result, and assessed for tax they consider due. The only recourse in this situation is to complain to the Adjudicator, as the separately disclosed charges method is a concession, and not an appealable matter.

See **24.19** for comment on the *Optika Ltd* case, in which differing values of the floor area were rejected as the basis for a partial exemption calculation.

In *O-Pro Ltd* (LON/99/971 No 16780), the Tribunal held that mouthguards were a separate supply from that of the dental services of producing them. The selling price should therefore be apportioned.

Note, however, that the Tribunal found that the professional input involved in examining the child's mouth, taking an impression, and making inferences concerning the way in which the mouth would develop, required considerable skill and experience, as did the work of the technician in making up the mouthguard. This meant that the price of O-Pro's mouthguards was considerably higher than the lower quality ones available from sports shops. The Tribunal saw the professional input as by far the most important thing from the parent's point of view, and thus, very much an aim in itself. Does the average customer for glasses on prescription similarly see the dispensing skill as a key aim in itself?

GOODS—ONE SUPPLY OR TWO?

12.14

Focus

If goods at different rates of VAT are sold together, it is usually obvious. Attempts to reduce the output tax due on standard-rated goods by including zero-rated ones in the price are unlikely to work.

Many years ago, a petrol filling station offered carrots at a high price together with petrol at a nominal one. This did not work because HMRC pointed out that, if you could only have the petrol at the low price because you bought the carrots at a high one, that was non-monetary consideration for the petrol. The market value of petrol would therefore be substituted for the artificially low price charged.

However, an attractive biscuit tin was held to be simply packaging required for a presentation box of biscuits; the possibility of subsequent use did not make it a standard-rated container (*United Biscuits (UK) Ltd* ([1992] STC 325)). There is a distinction between packaging primarily intended for the product in question, and that clearly intended for further use, such as marmalade in an expensive porcelain pot. The fact that a pot can be bought separately without the contents is a strong indicator it is a separate product, not just packaging.

Kimberly-Clark Ltd (LON/01/1273 No 17861; [2004] STC 473) concerned a 'free toy box' containing 124 nappies, sold at the same price as a cardboard container of the same quantity. The Tribunal said it was a multiple supply of zero-rated nappies and standard-rated box. The High Court reversed that, holding the dominant supply to be that of the nappies to which the box was ancillary. The key transaction was the sale by the manufacturer to the retailer, not the subsequent one to the retail customer. To the retailer, the box was merely packaging with a promotional function. The judge accepted that the status of goods purchased wholesale by a retailer could change when sold individually, though he thought it would not have in this case.

In *MD Foods plc* (LON/2000/899 No 17080), a cardboard package containing a pottery butter dish and cover plus two 250g packs of butter, was held to be a multiple supply consisting of a standard-rated butter dish and zero-rated butter.

In the case of *W M Morrison Supermarkets Ltd v Revenue & Customs* [2012] UKFTT 366 (TC) Morrisons sold what are known as 'disposable barbecues'. This appeal concerns the VAT liability of the sale of these barbecues. The appellant contended that a reduced rate of VAT was payable on the sale of the charcoal element of the supply with the remainder of the supply being subject to the standard rate. HMRC contended that the whole supply was subject to the standard rate.

The appellant had accounted for output tax at the standard rate on sales of the barbecues. In a letter dated 5 November 2010 the appellant claimed a refund of VAT of £192,934.51. This reflected the difference between VAT at the standard rate and VAT at the reduced rate on the charcoal element of the supply over a period of some four years. The respondents refused to make the refund on the basis that the whole supply was properly treated as standard rated.

HMRC submitted that if there was a single supply it was artificial to split it. All elements of the supply had come together to make a new item, namely a disposable barbecue. That is a simple product and the simpler the product the harder it is to identify concrete and specific aspects of the product.

The Tribunal did not regard it as open to the appellant to treat the supply of barbecues as anything other than a single supply at a single rate. The appellant did not suggest that if the supply was to be treated as a single supply at a single rate it should be treated as a supply of charcoal at a reduced rate.

Schedule 7A of the *VAT Act 1994* applies to supplies of charcoal. Supplies of disposable barbecues are not supplies of charcoal and as such they do not fall within the scope of *Sch 7A*. In the circumstances the Tribunal found that the supply of disposable barbecues was standard-rated and the appeal was dismissed.

BOOKS AND TAPES OR CDS SOLD TOGETHER

12.15 Although HMRC see books and magazines packaged with other items as likely multiple supplies, they said in *Business Brief 20/03* that a book and a tape or a CD can be a single zero-rated supply. They quoted as examples:

- children's books where there is audible interaction between the book and the tape/CD;

- educational books where the tape/CD is subservient to the book, of negligible use without it and not separately available.

On the other hand, a tape/CD with a manual, which merely explains how to use it, is a single, standard-rated supply.

A SINGLE SUPPLY OF ZERO-RATED GOODS MAY BE PARTLY STANDARD-RATED!

12.16   Naturally, a single supply is normally taxed at a single rate. However, part of the price may be standard-rated if the relevant part of the zero-rating law so provides.

As noted in **10.31**, *Sch 8 Group 9* requires the removable contents supplied with residential caravans to be standard-rated. In *Talacre Beach Caravan Sales Ltd* ([2004] STC 817: C-251/05), the High Court agreed that there was only one supply. Nevertheless, since Note (a) to *Group 9* standard-rated removable contents, that element of the single price was subject to VAT.

The basis for this decision was:

- in contrast to exempt supplies for which the rules are the same throughout the EU, the zero-rating in the UK is under a derogation;

- the use of that derogation was challenged in certain respects by the EU Commission in the 1980s but not in relation to residential caravans;

- that appeared to approve the exception in UK law, as determined by Parliament, which standard-rated removable fittings;

- moreover, if the VAT status of a single supply must always depend on the principal element, making a standard-rated item ancillary to a zero-rated supply could avoid VAT;

- standard-rating the removable contents puts the buyer of a residential caravan in the same position as the buyer of a new house.

The *Talacre* case may seem to contradict the principle that ancillary supplies have the same VAT status as the main one. However, it concerns a specific exception in the law to the zero-rating and one designed to prevent a distortion in the rules concerning houses and caravans. *Talacre* appealed to the Court of Appeal, which decided to make a reference to the European Court for a decisive ruling. The ECJ subsequently confirmed that goods included with the caravan could be excluded from zero-rating (C-251/05 [2006] EWCA Civ 1571).

SERVICES—ONE SUPPLY OR TWO?

12.17   If either or both of the supplies for an all-in price are services, it is often more difficult to determine whether there is a multiple supply at different rates of VAT, or a compound supply consisting of two or more elements taxable at the rate applicable to the dominant element.

Examples of decided cases are:

- providing grazing, water and general care for an animal is a single standard-rated supply of the care and supervision of it, not one partly zero-rated for the animal feed element (*Scott* ([1978] STC 191));

- providing a meal on an air flight is incidental to the air transport and not a separately identifiable supply (*British Airways* ([1990] STC 643));

- but catering on a luxury train, on a trip sold partly on the basis of the quality of the catering, was a separate supply (*Sea Containers Services Ltd* ([2000] STC 82)).

SOME MORE RECENT CASES

12.18   The old Tribunal cases on services quoted above make practical sense, and so far, remain valid. In contrast, some more recent decisions, including those in the higher courts, seem distinctly odd! Practicality is often not a feature of the way the legal profession interprets a multiple or composite supply situation; worse still, some of the decisions lack clarity!

MEDICAL CARE AND DRUGS

12.19   The House of Lords held in *Dr Beynon & Partners* ([2002] STC 669; 2003 STC 169; 2005 STC 55) that there is a single exempt supply of medical care by an NHS general practitioner when drugs and other medical items are administered by the doctor—for example by injection. That overturned the decision by the CA that there was a separate zero-rated supply of the drugs.

The case of *Healthcare at Home Ltd (VTD 20,379)* considered the VAT liability of the appellant's supplies, which comprised the administration by nurses of drugs prescribed for patients, to those patients in their own home. The appellant said it made zero-rated supplies of goods, and as such, could reclaim all of its input tax. HMRC, however, argued that it actually made exempt supplies of care.

The Tribunal differentiated the case from that of *Dr Beynon & Partners* in so much as the principal supply was that of the drugs, with the administration by a nurse being incidental, (in the *Dr Beynon* case the reverse was true).

The Tribunal concluded that in all those cases in which a nurse attends a patient's home to administer a drug supplied by the company, the supply is of zero-rated goods. Although the patient cannot receive the drug without the nurse, it is more important to note that if the drug had not been prescribed for that patient, the company would make no supply at all. Therefore, it is the patient's need for the prescribed drug which determines the essential characteristics of the supply. What is supplied in these circumstances is not so much medical care, but the demonstration to the patient of the correct method of using the goods which have been supplied to him. The appeal was duly allowed.

INSURANCE SOLD WITH A CAR

12.20   *Peugeot Motor Co plc* ([2003] STC 1438) lost its argument that, when it sold cars with insurance included, part of the price of the car was exempt. However, in *Lindsay Cars Ltd* (LON/02/434 No 18970), it was held that part of the price of the car was for a separate supply of insurance because the customer got a two-year cover for which a premium for the second year was identified. The dealer arranged that with the customer and the latter could subsequently cancel and claim a refund for that second year's premium.

A TELEVISION SUBSCRIPTION, WHICH INCLUDES A MAGAZINE

12.21   It is unlikely that a subscription to a television service could be partly zero-rated merely because of the monthly magazine detailing the programmes—the supply is primarily the television service; the magazine is probably only ancillary to it.

However, suppose the magazine is supplied by a different company: *Telewest Communications plc* (LON/01/0679 No 17986; [2004] STC 517; [2005] STC 481) changed its contracts with customers so as to have it provided by a separate company, with the magazine subscription being collected on its behalf by the operating companies supplying the TV service. The Tribunal and the High Court held the scheme to be ineffective, and there to be no separate contract for the supply of the magazine. The Court of Appeal overturned that— seeing the limited paperwork and lack of positive acknowledgement by the customers as overridden by their lack of concern as to who made the supply and by the ongoing payment of subscriptions. The House of Lords refused to accept an appeal by HMRC. HMRC have subsequently blocked the scheme by amending the law (see **10.26**).

NEGOTIATING EXTENDED CREDIT AND SUBSEQUENT DEBT COLLECTION

12.22   In *Debt Management Associates Ltd* (MAN/01/0631 No 17880), it was held that the negotiation of extended payment terms for client debtors and the subsequent collection and distribution to creditors of payments, separate fees being charged, were separate supplies.

Following the ECJ judgment in *AXA UK plc* (C-175/09) HMRC published *Revenue & Customs Brief 54/10*. This stated that all payment-related services falling within the definition of 'debt collection' as outlined by the ECJ in the *AXA* judgment are now liable to VAT at the standard rate. This even applies to businesses that have previously received a ruling from HMRC that their services fall within the VAT exemption (or it has previously been treating its services as exempt in line with HMRC's published policy in this area) so VAT must be applied to these services from January 2011.

Following the *AXA* judgment 'debt collection' cannot be seen as applying solely to the service of chasing and recovering overdue payments on behalf of the creditor and all services principally concerned with collecting payments from the person owing them for the benefit of the entity to which those payments are owed fall within the exclusion to the exemption and are consequently liable to VAT at the standard rate.

PROCESSING INSURANCE CLAIMS NOT ANCILLARY TO TRAINING

12.23 In *Equitable Life Assurance Society* (LON/01/372 No 18072), a contract to handle insurance claims, whilst at the same time training the client's staff who were to take over the work at a different location, was held to be a multiple supply. It was illogical to regard the claims handling, which took two-thirds of the resources, as ancillary to the training.

A DEBENTURE, WITH TICKET PURCHASE RIGHTS, WAS A SINGLE SUPPLY

12.24 On the other hand, the issue of 75-year debentures, interest-free but giving the right to buy tickets, was held to be a single exempt supply of a security (*Rugby Football Union* (LON/02/443 No 18075)). HMRCs' argument that it involved an exempt supply of the right to repayment and a standard-rated supply of the benefits was rejected.

CORRESPONDENCE COURSES OR DISTANCE LEARNING

12.25 What was once a correspondence course is now often called 'distance learning', much of it being based on electronic rather than paper communication. However, many courses are still supplied as manuals, and the question is whether they are a supply of:

- zero-rated books or booklets; or

- exempt education; or

- a multiple supply of both.

12.25 *Is there one supply or two?*

The following cases illustrate how the scope for argument depends upon the precise facts. *International News Syndicate Ltd* (LON/96/130 No 14425) sold courses in journalism, media studies, and for cartoonists/illustrators. It offered the manuals at 15% discount if the customer did not want any tuition.

The Tribunal thought it important that:

- INS were publishers, not authors or teachers;

- one course was compiled by a related company and another was derived from a variety of sources, not written by INS;

- students did not receive tuition by submitting work after receiving each weekly 'tutorial'. Indeed, one course involved home assessment for almost its entirety and work was only seen at the end.

It held that the predominant supply was that of the manuals. Whilst undoubtedly anyone following a course could learn much from it, so would anyone who bought a teach-yourself book, but there was no question of standard-rating that.

The Tribunal then held that there was a single zero-rated supply of manuals to which the tuition was incidental because of:

- the small element of external tuition;

- 10% of customers chose not to pay for it.

In *International Correspondence Schools Ltd* (EDN/01/180 No 17662) courses consisting of a self-contained manual were also held to be a zero-rated composite supply. A key point was that only about 15% of the students took up the offer of support.

However, the *decision in College of Estate Management* (LON/02/145 No 18029; [2004] STC 235; [2004] STC 1471; [2005] STC 195) seems generally applicable. The College was a leading provider of distance learning courses for the property and construction professions. It had 2,300 students, mostly studying part-time whilst working and of whom 35% were in over 70 other countries.

The CA held that there were two supplies because, although getting a degree was the ultimate goal, obtaining the written material was an objective, which the students sought for its own sake to save their time. The HL reversed the decision of the CA, and confirmed the decisions of the Tribunal and the HC that there was a single supply of exempt education, the printed materials being a means of better enjoying that education.

Our interpretation of the HL's reasoning is that the overview of what the customer gets is more significant than the make up of the physical goods and the services provided. The printed materials were not even an ancillary supply; they were merely a key element in the single supply—just as drugs are when used in the course of medical treatment.

In the case of HMRC v Metropolitan International Schools Limited [2017] UKUT 431 (TCC) the Upper Tribunal held that distance learning services to customers should be treated as a single standard rated supply of educational services rather than a zero-rated supply of books.

SUBSCRIPTIONS, WHICH INCLUDE A MAGAZINE

12.26   HMRC regard a subscription, which includes a magazine or journal, as a single supply. However, for a case challenging that, and for details of a concession for non-profit-making bodies which allows them to zero-rate part of their subscriptions, see **11.102**.

COMPANY FORMATION SERVICES AND CONFERENCE/ FUNCTION ROOMS

12.27   In *Business Brief 1/06*, HMRC claimed that a company formation package is standard-rated, despite including printed copies of the *Memorandum* and *Articles of Association*. This was then confirmed in *Company Registrations Online Ltd* (MAN/05/232 No 19461).

On the other hand, HMRC accepted that the charge for a conference or function room is exempt even if the service is part of a package including meals and/or accommodation. See the comment concerning *Group 1* land at **11.3**.

THE GOLF COURSE AND THE GREENMOWER

12.28   In this case, a business rents a golf course and clubhouse to the club, which uses it together with various equipment such as mowers:

- is this the single supply of a fully equipped golf club?
- or is it an exempt licence to occupy; and
- the standard-rated hire of the equipment?

Here are the conclusions of the Tribunal in *Tall Pines Golf & Leisure Co Ltd* (LON/99/0266 No 16538):

- the supplies were made simultaneously;
- they were made by the same supplier, the owner of the course;
- the right to use the name 'Tall Pines Golf Club' was ancillary to the principal supply of the licence to use the course;
- the kit could not be used anywhere else, so the supply of it could not have been an aim in itself, but just a means of better enjoying the use of the course;

- the owner had the right to refuse permission to bring further equipment on to the premises;

- that separate sums were charged for the use of the equipment and for the licence to use the course was unimportant, given the essential features of the transaction as a whole;

- the commercial reality of the transaction was the supply of a fully-equipped golf club and course. The supply of the trading name and of the equipment was so dominated by the supply of the course itself, that they lost all separate identity for fiscal purposes;

- the true and substantial nature of the supply was the exempt licence to occupy a golf course.

This decision could offer planning opportunities where VAT on equipment has previously been recovered against taxable supplies—but exercise caution!

THE HELICOPTER COMPLETE WITH PILOT

12.29   Is the provision of an air ambulance (helicopter) and pilot two supplies—of aircraft and of pilot or is it a transport service?

This mattered because, if there was a hire of goods, the helicopter could be zero-rated under *Sch 8 Group 15, Item 5* via *Notes (3)(b)* and *(9)* to the two Air Ambulance Trusts. Key points were:

- the Trusts got control of and use of the helicopter as they desired, subject only to the pilot's right to refuse to fly on safety grounds;

- one of the two agreements did include the pilot in the price, consisting of a standing charge and a flying charge per hour. However, there was provision for extra charges for additional pilots. Moreover, that agreement provided for the fuel to be invoiced directly to the Ambulance Trust.

The Tribunal, therefore, found it clear in both cases that there were multiple supplies of the helicopter and its repair and maintenance, and of the provision of the pilot to fly it. It also commented that this was not a transport service just because a pilot was supplied. The machines and pilots were available on standby five days in a week. The Trusts supplied the transport to the NHS, not the helicopter company *Medical Aviation Services Ltd* (LON/97/016 No 15308).

A BOOK WITH A GAME

12.30   In *Games Workshop Ltd* (MAN/98/1073 No 16975), supplies of Warhammer games in boxed sets, which included a 288-page book together with miniature plastic figures and various items used to play the game including some cards and dice, were held to be a single supply.

This is a worrying case if you zero-rate a book as part of a supply with other items. Besides the rules, the book contained extensive explanations and stories about the fantasy world of Warhammer. One had to read much of the book in order to understand what fantasy war games were about, and how to play. Games Workshop had created a complete fantasy world, which amounted to a gaming cult for boys of 12 to 16. Despite the book being sold separately at £25, the Tribunal saw it as primarily a means of better enjoying the game.

A COURSE, WHICH INCLUDES A BOOK

12.31   Where a course fee has included a published book available separately, the latter has in the past been accepted as a zero-rated supply. Indeed, in *Force One Training Ltd* (LON/95/1594 No 13619), a Tribunal held that the manuals supplied to course students were zero-rated because they were physically and economically dissociable from the tuition, despite the fact that they were not sold separately.

What is the difference between the *Games Workshop* and the *Force One Training* situations? You tell us! See also the discussion of *The College of Estate Management* at **12.25** above.

SAILING DOWN THE RIVER

12.32   A client hires out a river boat for functions. The boat travels along the river whilst the hire business provides catering and, if required, entertainment.

The customer chooses the date, length of the trip and the route.

There is no argument about the catering and entertainment:

- however, the hire business says it is providing zero-rated transport;

- HMRC say they are hiring functions suites on the water.

Surely, that was a single supply? Not according to the Tribunal in *Virgin Atlantic Airways Ltd* (LON/94/1530 No 13840). It held that the supply was of transport, albeit in comfortable conditions. Only the separate charges for catering and entertainment were standard-rated.

IS STABLING FOR A HORSE SEPARATE FROM THE CARE OF THAT HORSE?

12.33   In *John Window* (LON/00/0011 No 17186), the provision of a stable for a horse and the care of that horse were held to be a composite supply, which was an exempt licence to occupy the stable. HMRC had agreed that charges merely for the use of a stable to those customers who looked after their own horses, were exempt. The dispute, therefore, concerned the full 'livery' charges, which included the care of the horse. The Tribunal held that the livery services, such as feeding and watering, cleaning out the stable, turning the horse out in a field, or exercising it, were ancillary to the principle service of an exempt licence to occupy the stable. The level of livery service provided varied from owner to owner.

It distinguished *Scott,* one of the cases mentioned earlier under the heading *Services—one supply or two?* because the main purpose of the supply in that case had been for the mares to be served by stallions. The accommodation and care were incidental to that purpose. The mares only went to the farm to be served; in contrast, the horses did not go to Mr Window's premises to be looked after, but to occupy the stables rented by their owners. Such livery services as were supplied were consequent upon that, and also incidental to it.

This decision is difficult to understand: it is feasible that the provision of a stable can be an exempt part of a charge for full livery in an establishment which offers the option to an owner of looking after his or her horse, but it is hard to see how the substantial additional service of care can be ancillary to that part. Indeed, in many cases, it would be a principal aim of an owner, who had a full-time job, to obtain that care. Only the provision of it would make it possible to own the horse.

It also seems that the reasoning in *Window* does not sit well with that of the House of Lords in *Sinclair Collis,* and in the hairdressing salon cases, discussed in **11.7**.

DOES MAIL ORDER INCLUDE DELIVERY?

12.34 A separate charge for delivery made by a shop is standard-rated even if the goods are zero-rated. You cannot isolate the postage element in order to make this an exempt supply by you—the exemption for postage is only for a supply by the Post Office. For the position of a mailing house see **6.17**.

However, if the contract includes delivery, there is a single supply. For milk or newspapers, it is zero-rated.

In mail-order situations, the price of the goods normally includes delivery taxable at the rate applicable to those goods. In *Book Club Associates* ([1983] VATTR 34), it was held that the contract to supply a zero-rated book by mail order included delivery to the customer's home.

The word 'normally' above has been qualified by the decision in *Plantiflor Ltd* ([2000] STC 137; [2002] UKHL 33; [2002] STC 1132).

Plantiflor said in its catalogue:

'Collection and Delivery:

Orders collected incur no handling charges. If you require delivery by carrier then a nominal charge is made to cover mail order packing and handling.

We will happily arrange delivery on your behalf via Royal Mail Parcelforce if requested, in which case please include the Postage and Handling charge on your order. We will then advance all postal charges to Royal Mail on your behalf.'

Plantiflor's argument that it disbursed the postal charges on behalf of its customer was rejected by the Tribunal and by the High Court, accepted by the Court of Appeal, and finally rejected by the House of Lords. The House of Lords decision that there was a single supply of delivered bulbs such that the delivery charge was part of the standard-rated supply, was by a majority of 3:2. Thus, as the three Court of Appeal judges upheld the appeal, the five supporting *Plantiflor* were more senior than the five for HMRC, even though the latter won.

The doubts which this provokes are reinforced by the lack of clarity in both the Court of Appeal and the House of Lords decisions. Whilst I believe the result was the right answer, there may well be a further challenge based on a more thoroughly drafted contract than that in *Plantiflor*. Further information can be gained by reading the Court of Appeal and House of Lords decisions!

SO HOW SHOULD A BUSINESS APPORTION THE PRICE BETWEEN EACH SUPPLY?

12.35

Focus

An apportionment of a price between two supplies at different rates of tax must be fair. It can be based either on a proportion of the cost of each item to total cost, or on an assessment of the market value of each supply.

Often, however, there is no obvious way of arriving at the market value because one or more of the supplies does not have a separate stated price.

In *Jarmain* ([1979] VATTR 41 No 723) the market value of a catalogue included with the entrance fee for an exhibition was calculated on the basis of the direct printing cost plus a percentage for overheads and a profit margin.

In the case of a subscription to a society, the cover price of the journal or journals included in the subscription sometimes covers all the latter or even exceeds it! However, these cover prices are often artificial—comparatively few copies are sold to non-members. In any case, one would expect the price

273

to the members to be substantially discounted because of the bulk order they represent. Obviously, there is a value attached to the other benefits of membership. Even if the cover price of the several journals or magazines received by members exceeds the membership subscription, 75% might be a fair apportionment for the zero-rated element of the subscription, although, of course, circumstances vary.

If a business claims a very high percentage for the zero-rated or exempt element of a multiple supply, it may have to argue the matter at a Tribunal. If so, the Tribunal is unlikely to support an artificial calculation. Moreover, there is always the possibility that it decides that there is, in reality, no separate supply at all.

In *Public and Commercial Services Union* (LON/01/717 No 18102), admittedly a case in which the accounting evidence was poorly presented, the Tribunal upheld HMRCs' argument that the apportionment should be based on cost, and even rejected the idea of a markup.

Chapter 13

What can a business recover input tax on?

SIGNPOSTS

- A business is not automatically entitled to recover all of the VAT it incurs on its purchases and must hold the required evidence before it can recover any input VAT (see **13.2**).

- If a business does not pay its supplier within specified time limits it must repay the VAT that it has claimed but it is also allowed to make late claims for input tax not claimed (see **13.3–13.4**).

- Make sure the invoice is addressed to the correct legal entity, although in some cases input tax can be deducted without a proper tax invoice (see **13.4–13.8**).

- Just because a business pays for a supply does not mean it is entitled to recover the input tax (see **13.9–13.11**).

- VAT on employees' expenses can be reclaimed in most cases but VAT cannot normally be reclaimed on business entertainment (see **13.15–13.25**).

- There are special rules relating to the VAT recovery on motor cars and motoring expenses (see **13.26–13.32**).

- Recovering VAT on business promotions using yachts, racehorses powerboats, etc (see **13.34–13.37**).

- There are special rules relating to the VAT recovery on goods with both business and private use (see **13.38–13.40**).

- There are special rules on VAT recovery on domestic accommodation used partly for business use and staff removals expenses (see **13.41–13.42** and **13.53**).

- There are special rules relating to VAT recovery on legal costs incurred on behalf of staff and directors and the business (see **13.46–13.51**).

13.1   This is a long chapter because the subject of when input tax is or is not recoverable is a big one. However, you may find that some of the later detail, such as owning a racehorse or a powerboat as a means of publicising the business, is unlikely to affect you directly, and will be of limited interest.

The rules dealt with here are those affecting every business. For those related to partly exempt businesses, see Chapter 24, *Partial Exemption.*

INPUT TAX RECOVERY IS NOT AUTOMATIC!
13.2

Focus

A VAT registration does not give a business an automatic right to recover VAT:

- the expenditure must be for the purpose of the business, not for private purposes, nor for the purpose of another business;

- the business must hold a valid tax invoice, which must be in its name. See Chapter 14, *What is a Valid Tax Invoice?* for more about this;

- the supply shown on the tax invoice must actually occur, and be made to the business reclaiming the tax;

- the VAT in question must not be caught by the rules specifically disallowing tax on:

  (i)   entertainment *(Value Added Tax (Input Tax) Order, SI 1992/3222, art 5)*;

  (ii)   cars *(Input Tax Order, art 7)*;

  (iii) directors' accommodation *(VATA 1994 s 24(3))*;

  (iv)   goods not ordinarily installed by builders as fixtures in new houses *(Input Tax Order, art 6)*;

  (v)   goods sold under a second-hand scheme *(Input Tax Order, art 4)*;

  (vi)   costs of a tour operator covered by the *Tour Operators Order (Value Added Tax (Tour Operators) Order, SI 1987/1806)*;

- if a business has exempt sales, it cannot recover the related VAT (subject to the 'de minimis limits'—see Chapter 24, *Partial Exemption)*, only that attributable to its taxable sales;

- if the business uses the Flat Rate Scheme for small businesses, it cannot recover input tax except on large capital expenditure of over £2,000 (including VAT). See Chapter 35.

The mere holding of a tax invoice is insufficient. There must also be a supply to the business. A tax invoice received in advance of a supply provides only a provisional right to recover. An invoice in the name of the business includes one in the name of a company within the same VAT group, because input tax of all companies within the VAT group is treated as that of the representative member.

IF A BUSINESS DOES NOT PAY ITS SUPPLIER, IT MUST REPAY HMRC THE INPUT TAX CLAIMED

13.3

Focus

A business can only keep the input tax it has recovered on a supplier's invoice if it pays the bill within six months of the date of the invoice, or if later the date on which payment became due. If you do not pay your supplier within that time limit, you must refund the input tax on the outstanding invoice to HMRC (*s 26A* and *regs 172F–J*).

The business makes the refund to HMRC by adding an appropriate negative amount of input tax to box 4 of the VAT return for the period in which the repayment came due. If the business has made a part payment, the refund required is based on the outstanding proportion of the invoice.

If and when the business does pay in whole or in part, it can then reclaim the input tax, or such proportion of it as relates to the part payment. In practice, this of course means that a business has a period of grace between the date on which the time limit runs out, and the end of the VAT period in which it happens, during which, it can pay the supplier and thereby avoid having to make the refund and subsequent reclaim.

Although this rule is designed to prevent the recovery of input tax on invoices which were never intended to be paid, it will also catch those cases where, for genuine business reasons, invoices remain outstanding for long periods. A basic planning point is, therefore, for the accounting system of a business to include a monthly review of all invoices still unpaid after six months.

LATE RECLAIMS OF INPUT TAX

13.4 HMRC accept in para 10.5.1 of Notice 700 *The VAT Guide* that a business can reclaim input tax late at any time up to four years after the date of invoice. The Notice only refers to claiming VAT late because the business did not have the necessary evidence at the right time. Presumably, on the grounds of practicality, HMRC would not usually object to claiming on a return within the four-year limit if the invoice had been held, but was overlooked or, perhaps, if the VAT had been incorrectly thought to be not recoverable on an individual invoice (although, technically, if the VAT amount was over £10,000 or 1% of turnover as declared on the VAT return for the period in which the errors are found, subject to an upper limit of £50,000, a separate voluntary disclosure may be necessary).

Where a claim to recover sums, which have previously been disallowed by agreement with or on the instructions of HMRC a voluntary disclosure is always required (if the VAT is over £10,000 or 1% of turnover as declared on the VAT return for the period in which the errors are found, subject to an upper limit of £50,000 it has to be notified separately in order to give HMRC the opportunity of objecting and to avoid any question of a penalty. Moreover, such a disclosure establishes the sums on which interest is to be calculated, assuming that the original non-recovery was due to an error by HMRC.

VAT LAUNDERING

13.5   A VAT registration must not be used to launder VAT on behalf of someone else, who cannot recover the tax. Examples of this include:

- expenditure incurred by an unregistered or partially exempt associate;

- expenses of a self-employed salesman;

- UK travel costs of executives from overseas who come to the UK on the business of affiliates abroad;

- goods bought for directors or staff and billed to their current accounts.

WHAT IF A BILL IS PAID ON BEHALF OF ANOTHER BUSINESS?

13.6   See **6.15** and **6.18** for more detailed comment.

If the invoice is in the business's name, either the input tax must not be recovered, or the net expenditure must be recharged plus output tax. If the invoice is addressed to the person to whom the supply was made, the business cannot recover the tax and must pass on the invoice to the named business so it can recover the VAT, subject to the normal rules, plus a request for payment of the costs the business has incurred on its behalf as a disbursement.

BEWARE OF THE PROBLEMS CAUSED BY A CHANGE OF INTENTION

13.7   Suppose a business plans a project and pays a deposit upfront to a supplier. Then, it decides that the project should be handled by an associate company—for reasons of tax liability, industrial practicalities, or whatever. In consequence, the entire supply is to the associate, not to the original named business.

Since the original business has not received a supply, it cannot charge on the deposit to the associate plus VAT. Nor can it retain the input tax already recovered. It must be refunded to HMRC on its next VAT return.

The correct way is to get the supplier to issue a credit note for the deposit including VAT, and issue a new invoice for the deposit to the associated company. No doubt, the supplier would retain the existing payment and would expect the businesses to make accounting adjustment to collect it from the associate company; however that would just be a refund of what was now seen as paid on its behalf; ie the gross sum including the VAT being refunded to HMRC, and which can now be recovered by the associate.

If the correct treatment is obvious, good! Other people get it wrong—as evidenced by a recent Tribunal decision. Do not confuse the position with the more common one, in which supplies are obtained as an agent for another business explained above.

CASES WHERE RECOVERY HAS BEEN ALLOWED WITHOUT A TAX INVOICE

13.8   Normally, you must hold a tax invoice in your name, subject to the minor concessions explained in **14.9** and **14.14**. The other exception is where the supply was by someone who was not registered but should have been, or issued a false invoice showing a sum purporting to be VAT. For reasons of equity, HMRC have published an Extra-Statutory Concession (ESC 3.9) which states:

'VAT: Recoveries under the VAT Act 1994 Schedule 11 paragraph 5

Where an amount is shown or represented as VAT on an invoice issued by a person who is neither registered nor required to be registered for VAT at the time when the invoice is issued, the provisions of Schedule 11 paragraph 5 of the VAT Act 1994 (formerly Schedule 7 paragraph 6 of the VAT Act 1983) enable the Commissioners to require that person to pay an equivalent amount to them. The Act does not provide any relief in respect of related VAT incurred by such a person. On the grounds of equity, a person making such a payment may be permitted to deduct from it the amount of VAT incurred on supplies to him of goods and services that were directly attributable to any invoiced supply in respect of which such payment is required.

Where such a person has made a supply to a taxable person and, on the invoice, showed or represented an amount as VAT, the recipient of the supply has no logical entitlement to treat that amount as his input tax. If it is clear that the taxable person who received the supply has treated such an amount as input tax in good faith, action to recover the amount so deducted may be remitted on grounds of equity.'

That said, the key to recovering input tax is to show that a business has received a supply. If it can demonstrate this, but lack a tax invoice, it can ask HMRC if they will allow recovery on the basis of whatever other evidence it has. HMRC have power to do so under *reg 29(2)*. Note, however, that the power of the Tribunal to intervene has been held to be supervisory rather than appellate. A supervisory power means that the Tribunal can only overturn HMRC's refusal to allow recovery if it decides that, in the circumstances of the case, that refusal was unreasonable. In other words, the Tribunal cannot send the matter back to HMRC for review merely because it would have come to a different conclusion—as it would be able to do if it had an appellate power. See *Richmond Resources Ltd* (LON/94/1496 No 13435).

Tribunals have occasionally upheld appeals outright when satisfied that a supply was made to the claimant. The following cases are examples but they were decided long before *Richmond*.

In *J E Morgan (t/a Wishmore Morgan Investments)* (LON/86/165 No 2150), the Tribunal overruled a refusal by HMRC to allow input tax on an invoice addressed to an associate company. It was satisfied that the supply was made to the claimant.

Similarly, in *Bird Semple & Crawford Herron* (EDN/85/35 No 2172), tax on agents' fees regarding a lease held by a nominee company, which did not trade, was held to be recoverable by a firm of solicitors. The sole purpose of the trustee company was to act as the nominee of the firm and simplify the administration of the leases of a property partly occupied by it.

In April 2007, HMRC issued *Revenue & Customs Brief 36/07* entitled '*VAT input tax deduction without a valid VAT invoice: Revised statement of practice*'.

The statement of practice is an update of an earlier July 2003 version, and is very much aimed towards the anti-MTIC fraud effort because of its specific address to supplies of computers, telephones and other related equipment, and also alcohol and oils. Although the new version is phrased in helpful tones, indicating a willingness on the part of HMRC to exercise their discretion to allow deduction if appropriate checks on the supplier have been made, it is more likely to be a reiteration of HMRC's position that, where involvement in a chain of supplies to facilitate MTIC fraud is suspected, they will look to challenge input tax deduction on the grounds that the documentation is invalid (to run alongside the 'should have known' test for disallowance based on the *Kittel* case).

The timing of the issue of this Brief suggests that the reason for its issue may have been a recent VAT Tribunal decision in *Pexum Limited* (VTD 20,083). In the *Pexum* case, HMRC disallowed over £1.5 million of input tax on 12 invoices for the purchase of goods described on them as 'CPUs'. This was on the grounds that the invoices were 'invalid' because the goods were not as described. As such, HMRC considered that an essential ingredient of the ability to 'exercise the right to deduct', namely the holding of a valid tax invoice or other document, was not satisfied under *SI 1995/2518, VAT reg 14(1) (g)*. Although the decision states that HMRC did not allege that Pexum or its suppliers were knowingly a party to any fraudulent activity, it was strongly implied that there may never have been any goods involved in the transaction, and certainly not those described on the invoices.

The Tribunal's written decision runs to 47 pages and covers various aspects, including the question of whether the appellant satisfied the HMRC statement of practice on deduction without a valid tax invoice. The three basic arguments made on behalf of Pexum were that the July 2003 statement of practice published by HMRC had been satisfied, that the operation of the VAT system relies on the tax authorities being satisfied that balancing output tax and input tax are being accounted for, and that HMRC's introduction of the concept of a 'right to exercise a right to deduct' (in this case infringed by the description of the goods on the invoices) is an unjustifiable restriction on the right to deduct.

The Tribunal Chairman found against Pexum, concluding:

> 'In our judgment, the invoices held by Pexum in support of its claim for input tax deduction, were not valid VAT invoices for the purposes of VATA or the VAT Regulations since they did not give a "description sufficient to identify the goods ... supplied", as required by Regulation 14(l)(g). Likewise those invoices did not contain details of "the ... nature of the goods supplied" as required by Article 22(3)(b) of the Sixth Directive.

If any goods were supplied to Pexum at all:

- the goods that were in fact supplied were not capable of being described as "CPUs", having regard to their physical characteristics and their lack of functionality; and/or

- the goods that were in fact supplied were not in any event genuine Intel P4 2.8GHz 800 CPUs or capable of being described as such.

> We therefore hold that Pexum had no right to deduct the input tax claimed because its purchase invoices described the goods purportedly bought by it as "Intel P4 2.8GHz 800" CPUs, manufactured by Intel.'

In conjunction with the revised statement of practice, HMRC have amended *reg 29(2)* so that they can now accept any alternative evidence for the deduction of input tax, not just documentary evidence.

In the case of *London Wiper Company Ltd v Revenue & Customs Commissioners* ([2011] UKFTT 445 (TC)) the appeal was against two decisions by HMRC disallowing an input tax claim. Both decisions were based on HMRC's conclusion that the invoices in relation to all the supplies were invalid, and that London Wiper did not hold sufficient alternative evidence for them to satisfy HMRC that the supplies underlying the disputed invoices took place. London Wiper said that the supplies did exist and that HMRC had acted unreasonably in not accepting alternative evidence as to the validity of all the invoices.

As a result of the evidence produced by London Wiper, the Tribunal was satisfied that all the invoices, when combined with the weighbridge certificates, provided all the necessary information to validate the invoices and that HMRC acted unreasonably in refusing to accept that there was sufficient alternative evidence. The Tribunals jurisdiction in this regard is supervisory, so they directed that HMRC arrange for the invoices to be reviewed again by different officers.

THE EXPENSE MAY BELONG TO THE BUSINESS, BUT DOES THE INPUT VAT?

13.9 The mere fact that a business pays an expense does not of itself mean that it is incurred for the purpose of its business. The business may be legally liable to pay, but there may not have been a supply to them.

Examples of expenses which are not supplies to a business

13.10 A credit card company is merely financing purchases of goods. The ECJ held in a Dutch case, *Auto Lease Holland BV* (C-1 85/01) that, when lessees of its cars paid monthly estimated amounts for the petrol they bought using a special card, and settled the balance at the end of the year, the supply of the petrol was to the lessees, not to Auto Lease.

When the loser of a legal dispute pays the costs of the other side, it is for supplies to that opponent, and is therefore not recoverable—as confirmed in *Turner t/a Turner Agricultural* (1992 STC 621). No doubt, it is salt in the wound for the loser that the input tax cannot be recovered—but a business does not pay that input tax until they have written confirmation that the winner cannot recover it either. If it concerns a business dispute, a VAT-registered winner should be able to recover the input VAT as a business expense, subject to any partial exemption disallowance.

The general scenario behind the *Telent plc v Revenue and Customs Comrs* [2008] STC (SCD) 202 case is that of a bank which, in providing a financial service to its client, incurs legal costs which, under the terms of the transaction, the client is responsible for paying. As the bank is unlikely to be in a position to deduct any input VAT on the legal services, the usual expectation is that the client pays the full VAT-inclusive cost of the legal services. The frustration for the client is that it knows it is paying a sum including VAT and, particularly if it is fully taxable, would normally have an expectation of an input tax deduction. However, the technical position is that the client cannot make an input tax deduction as the supply of the legal service is to the bank, albeit that he pays the invoice. The further practical issue is that the solicitors will consider they must address the VAT invoice to the bank as their client, albeit that the invoice may be annotated to the effect that it is payable by the bank's client. Any request for the solicitors to address their VAT invoice to the bank's client is likely to be refused.

The facts in this particular case are broadly as described, involving a major corporate restructuring, with the relevant parties being a firm of solicitors, two coordinating banks acting on behalf of the creditor banks, and the appellant.

Counsel for the appellant sought to construct an argument that, looking at the wider events, the appellant was either a joint recipient of the legal services (albeit not directly contractually so), or at least received a sufficient interest in the legal services to justify its right in principle to take an input tax deduction by reference to case law, in particular *Redrow Group plc* (see below).

Alas, the Chairman refused to accept the argument, finding that, in VAT supply terms, the supply of legal services was made wholly and exclusively to the coordinating banks. The status quo on this matter was thus preserved.

Example 13.1—Legal Costs

A similar situation arises if a business rents premises that it no longer needs, and wishes to get out of responsibility for the rent by assigning the lease to another business. It cannot do this without permission of the landlord.

Under the terms of the lease, the landlord is entitled to demand that, as a condition of granting permission to assign, the business pays the legal costs generated by the request; ie the expense of checking the credentials of the proposed tenant, and preparing the assignment.

The solicitor's invoice may well be addressed to the business, and it will include VAT if the landlord cannot recover this because the rent is exempt. However, that VAT is not recoverable by the tenant because the service was supplied to the landlord, not to the tenant, even though it is required to pay it.

It can be worse! Many leases entitle the landlord to claim rent from a previous tenant which the current tenant has failed to pay. Thus, a business could be faced with a demand for rent plus VAT under a lease, which it assigned some years previously. The VAT on that lease would not be recoverable by it because it would merely be compensating the landlord, not receiving any supply of use of the premises.

Example 13.2—Estate agents fees

The developer of an estate of new houses offers to pay the fees of the estate agent for prospective buyers for selling their existing house if they buy one of the new ones.

HMRC argue that the services of the estate agent are to the owner of the house, not to the developer, and that the developer, therefore, has no right to recover the VAT on the agent's fees.

On the basis of what has been said so far on this subject, the reader might think HMRC were right. However, in *Redrow Group plc* ([1999] STC 161), the House of Lords held that the company *could* recover VAT on the grounds that a supply was made to it. The details of these grounds are set out below.

THE SUPPLY MUST BE TO THE BUSINESS

13.11   In the *Redrow* case, the company was able to recover VAT on the following grounds:

- one must first identify the payment, which included the VAT to be reclaimed. If the goods or services were paid for by someone else, the trader had no claim to the deduction. Redrow had paid for the supply. *Note: This is how the judgment was worded. It does not necessarily mean you cannot recover the VAT if another VAT registered person pays on your behalf and re-invoices to you;*

- the Tribunal had found that the fees paid to the estate agents were incurred for the purpose of its business;

- the question was then whether Redrow obtained anything—anything at all—used or to be used for the purpose of its business in return for the payment to the estate agent for which it was liable;

- the Court of Appeal had been wrong in requiring there to be a 'direct and immediate link' between the agent's services and the sale of Redrow's houses. That was only relevant where, having incurred an expense for the purposes of its business, a trader had to make an attribution of that expense to either taxable or exempt supplies;

- Redrow:

(i)   chose and instructed the agent;

(ii)   agreed the asking price for the house on the basis of the agent's valuation and the house owner's expectations;

(iii)   kept in touch with the agent to ensure that maximum effort was being made to sell the house;

(iv)   paid the agent's fees once the house owner had bought a Redrow house; and

(v)   advised the agent to have a separate agreement with the house owner in case the latter did not do so. Under the agreement, the house owner could not unilaterally instruct a second agent because this would increase the fees payable.

Thus, Redrow obtained the right to have the householder's home valued and marketed in accordance with its instructions and under its control. That was different to the ordinary service of an estate agent, which was what was received by the householder if the latter became liable to pay the fees.

The circumstances in which *Redrow* is important are those where the person who pays the bill is not the most obvious recipient of the supply. However, it is not authority for VAT being recoverable just because of a payment.

Compare the example of the landlord's legal costs above with *Redrow*. Redrow did not just pay the bill and get a tax invoice addressed to it; at the outset, it had instructed the estate agent and had said that it would be responsible for the agent's fees if, in due course, the house owner bought a Redrow house. Thus, there was a clear basis for deciding that there was a supply made to it.

In contrast, a tenant cannot instruct a landlord's solicitor; only the landlord can do that and it would not be acceptable for the solicitor to have a duty of care to the tenant, let alone be supplying services to the latter.

In a further case, *Airtours Holiday Transport Ltd (formerly My Travel Group)* [2009] UKFTT 256 (TC) TC 0020 had input tax disallowed on professional advisory services necessary for a group of banks, providing a refinancing package to the appellant, where they were one of the parties who engaged the professional adviser and where they paid for the services.

HMRC argued that the supplies were only to the financial institutions notwithstanding that the appellant paid for the services.

The appellant argued that the supplies were to both the appellant and the financial institution, with the appellant able to take full input tax deduction on the grounds that the services are used in the course of its fully taxable business.

The background here is a financial crisis faced by the appellant in 2002 which necessitated the agreement of a rescue package involving the banks, bondholders and other creditors of the appellant (the 'institutions').

13.11 *What can a business recover input tax on?*

PricewaterhouseCooper (PwC) were appointed to provide a range of services consisting, in summary, of liaising with and making representations to banks and other creditors or bondholders of the appellant, carrying out a strategic review of the business and restructuring proposals, liaising with the Civil Aviation Authority and creating what was termed an entity priority model.

Key to the dispute was the manner in which PwC were engaged to provide the services. The decision records that the arrangements entered into are considered to reflect the existence of a tripartite contract between PwC, the appellant and the engaging institutions. The HMRC argument was that the critical question is what PwC were doing for the appellant and the HMRC argument was that the appellant received nothing from PwC by way of a supply.

The Judge concluded that the appellant did receive supplies from PwC which it used for the purposes of its business and so was entitled to deduct the input tax. HMRC appealed to the Upper Tribunal (FTC/46/2009 NCN [2010] UKUT 404 (TCC)) which overturned the First-tier decision and upheld HMRC's appeal stating that the First-tier Tribunal was wrong in law in its construction of the agreement.

In the case of *BAA Plc v Revenue & Customs Commissioners* (FTC/44/2010, FTC/73/2010 [2011] UKUT 258 (TCC)), BAA had been successful in the First-tier tribunal when it sought to recover VAT incurred following its acquisition by Airport Development Investments Limited (ADIL). However, the Upper Tribunal accepted HMRC's appeal which was then appealed to the Court of Appeal (*BAA Ltd v Revenue & Customs Commissioners* [2013] EWCA Civ 112) which again found for HMRC and so HMRC policy on input tax recovery in such circumstances remains unchanged.

The case centred on negotiations between ADIL and third parties to secure financing, which began before the takeover and continued after it. ADIL joined the BAA VAT group, the group claiming the VAT incurred on various costs associated with the takeover.

VAT charged by lawyers, accountants and financiers can usually be claimed back later by companies. However, HMRC argued that ADIL—which is owned by Ferrovial—was never really in business. It said the recovery of the VAT related to investment costs incurred by ADIL in raising finance to acquire BAA and that there was no immediate link between the supplies on which the VAT was incurred and any supplies that could qualify for VAT made by the BAA VAT group.

In the case of *Cloud Electronics Holdings Ltd v Revenue & Customs Commissioners* [2012] UKFTT 699 (TC) the appellant claimed input tax relating to professional fees for services of due diligence and other services rendered prior to the appellant's incorporation. It was incorporated on 28 February 2008 as the vehicle for a management buyout of Cloud Electronics Limited and was registered for VAT with effect from 1 March 2008.

HMRC decided that the input tax claimed related to advice commissioned by the management buyout team and was disallowed on the grounds that the supply had not been made to the appellant and that the services had been consumed within the acquisition process rather than for the ongoing business of the appellant.

The appellant's case, in summary, was that the benefit of the services was received by them, they paid for them and therefore should be able to recover the input VAT on the basis that they received the services.

Some of the professional advisers undertook a due diligence exercise. This was carried out not only on the initial instructions of the management buyout team but also at the request of the bank which was providing funding to assist with the acquisition.

The Tribunal concluded that services were indeed supplied to the appellant which was carrying out economic activity at the material times. The appeal was therefore allowed in full.

This is an important decision for those involved in management buyouts using a holding company as the vehicle for the acquisition as it acknowledges that costs incurred during and relating to, the acquisition process are recoverable.

In the case of *U-Drive Limited v HMRC* [2017] UKUT 112 (TCC) the appellant carried on a vehicle hire business. When one of its hire vehicles was involved in an accident that caused damage to a vehicle belonging to a third party, the appellant would sometimes agree with the car owner that, as an alternative to an insurance claim, the appellant would pay for the car to be repaired. The appellant contracted with a car repair business to carry out the repairs to the car owner's vehicle. There was no contract between the car owner and the repairer. The repairer invoiced the appellant for the repairs and the appellant paid the invoice, which included VAT.

The Tribunal considered that the appellant had no interest in the repairs other than as a means by which to meet (at reduced cost) a liability that would otherwise be incurred through the insurer. The fact that the appellant contracted to pay the repairers direct did not, given all the circumstances, make the appellant the recipient of any supply by the repairers and so the appeal was dismissed.

In the case of *Tesco Freetime Limited and Tesco PLC v HMRC* TC/2015/04342 the Tribunal looked at the proper treatment of one feature of the well-known loyalty scheme operated by the Tesco group of companies, the Tesco Clubcard programme. The scheme had expanded over the years and, in particular, points may be accumulated by a customer who makes purchases from Tesco online, and the vouchers may likewise be redeemed online. In addition, points may be collected on purchases from other retailers and service suppliers, known as Clubcard Partners. The Clubcard scheme was introduced in 1995 with the aim, like other similar schemes, of increasing customer loyalty and sales.

In 1999 the feature of the scheme to which this appeal relates was introduced. The option of using the vouchers to make a purchase from a Tesco store or online continued, but a Clubcard Member could instead have the vouchers converted to Reward Tokens which he or she could then use to make a purchase from a third party, known as a Deal Partner. Because the Reward Tokens have a greater face value than the vouchers for which they are exchanged this feature of the scheme is known as Partner Boost. The question in this appeal was whether the company which contracts with the Deal Partners and paid them the agreed charges for the provision of goods or services in exchange for Reward Tokens is entitled to recover, as input tax, the VAT included in those charges.

Having considered the facts the Tribunal found that there was a supply by the Deal Partners to Freetime and that they were entitled to deduct the input tax. This decision was appealed by HMRC and subsequently upheld by the Upper Tribunal ([2019] UKUT 18 (TCC)).

MEALS FOR PASSENGERS ON DELAYED FLIGHTS

13.12   An example of a *Redrow* situation is when an airline pays for food and drink supplied to passengers when a flight is delayed. In earlier cases, the supply had been held to be to the passengers, who consumed the food. Part of the reasoning for this was that the airline handed out vouchers for stated values rather than amounts of food. The passenger chose the food and had to pay any excess whilst not being given a refund if the items chosen did not reach the value of the voucher. The airline was, therefore, seen as merely handing out to passengers the equivalent of cash and not itself receiving the supply.

However, on the basis of *Redrow,* a Tribunal held in *British Airways plc* (LON/99/520 No 16446), that the airline could recover the VAT. By prior agreement with the food outlets, it obtained the right to have its passengers fed at its expense.

BEWARE OF THE UNREGISTERED BUSINESS SUCH AS A SELF-EMPLOYED PERSON

13.13   A business that is not registered for VAT cannot pass on VAT.

In *R Wiseman & Sons* (EDN/84/11 No 1691), Wiseman paid the maintenance and fuel costs for the vans used by self-employed milk roundsmen. It nominated garages where the roundsmen bought the fuel and obtained receipts for it. Envelopes containing sufficient cash for the fuel for each round were given weekly to each driver. The Tribunal rejected an argument that the fuel was bought by Wiseman through the agency of the drivers, in favour of

HMRCs' contention that the supply was to the roundsmen as independent contractors, who used the fuel for the purpose of the business subcontracted to them.

A KEY TEST IS INTENTION AT THE TIME OF INCURRING THE EXPENSE

13.14 The intention of a business at the time it incurs an expense is of fundamental importance. If it had genuine business reasons for doing so, the fact that they are subsequently frustrated does not affect the right to recover the input tax. Things go wrong in business. Whilst subsequent events may tend to support or undermine the assertions as to the intention when the business incurred the cost, they do not change it.

In a number of important cases concerning expensive projects to start businesses, it has been held that input tax is recoverable even if the project fails and no income is ever generated. Thus, an inventor can register for VAT and recover input tax on the costs of developing the invention from the prototype stage. HMRC cannot subsequently reclaim that VAT, even if the idea is eventually found not to work. Of course, there must be evidence of a serious business intent. Part of the logic is that, if HMRC could collect the VAT back from the inventor, individuals would be disadvantaged compared with companies, whose research and development expenditure is lost within departmental budgets.

Evidence of intention becomes particularly important when the expenditure is on something like a racehorse, which is normally owned for pleasure. See later concerning various cases in which it has been shown that a racehorse, powerboat or whatever, can be used to advertise a business.

EMPLOYEES' TRAVEL EXPENSES

13.15 Another example of a situation affected by *Redrow* is employees' travel expenses. HMRC have always accepted that input tax is recoverable on bills for hotel accommodation and meals, even if they are in the employees' names rather than that of the company. However, this was queried many years ago by a Tribunal Chairman, who suggested that the supply of the accommodation or meal had to be to the person who used or ate it.

Given that a business acts through its employees, it never made sense to argue that the supply to them of business travel was not to their employer. However, on 8 November 2001 in Case C-338/98, the ECJ said that the Netherlands was wrong to allow input tax recovery on a fixed percentage of allowances for motor expenses to staff, who used their own cars. The ECJ said:

'... under Article 5 of the 6th Directive, the supply of goods means the transfer of the right to dispose of them as owner. It is clear that use by an employee of his own vehicle in connection with his employer's business cannot constitute a supply, in that sense, to his employer. Accordingly, neither the vehicle belonging to the employee nor the fuel consumed by that vehicle can be regarded as "supplied" to the taxable employer, within the meaning of article 17(2)(a) of the Sixth Directive, simply because depreciation of the vehicle and fuel costs linked to such use give rise to partial reimbursement by the employer.'

In 2005, the European Commission argued successfully in the ECJ that the UK was wrong to allow recovery of input tax on the petrol element of mileage allowances. After negotiations with the European Commission, HMRC came to an agreement with them, and issued *Business Brief 22/05*. However, as with a lot of things published by HMRC to clarify the situation, it merely served to cause confusion and uncertainty. HMRC then addressed these matters in VAT Information Sheet 08/2005.

The changes have not had much impact on the recovery of VAT on road fuel. The only practical change to the previous system is that an invoice must be retained in support of a claim for VAT recovery—in the vast majority of cases, this will be a 'less detailed tax invoice'.

The change came in from 1 January 2006, regardless of the VAT return period end date. From that date, employers should retain VAT invoices, including less detailed VAT invoices, which their employees obtain from the fuel supplier as proof of purchase.

As with the old system, input tax may only be claimed on the cost of fuel for business use. As such, invoices only need to cover this amount, not the total amount of fuel purchased. HMRC accept that the amount of the invoice in many cases will not match the input tax claim in respect of business fuel in any one claim period, and invoices may cover more than one period, particularly where fuel is purchased towards the end of a period. Clearly, a claim cannot be supported by a VAT invoice which is dated after the dates covered by the claim. This means, in practice, that it may be advisable for employers to arrange for their employees who use, or may use, their cars for business purposes to retain all fuel invoices. This will ensure that, at the end of the claim period, the value of business fuel is covered by an invoice.

This will mean that employers will have to 'remind' staff to retain their petrol invoices.

In fairness to HMRC, they fought tooth and nail against the European Commission to avoid this extra compliance burden. That they implemented the change in such a loose manner is further evidence of their intention to minimise its impact. If you think about it, who is to say that the fuel receipts held even relate to the car shown on the claims? They could be receipts from other vehicles!

ENTERTAINMENT IS A DIRTY WORD

13.16

Focus

A business cannot normally recover VAT on the cost of entertaining someone who is not an employee.

'Entertainment' is a dirty word in the sense that this is an aspect of VAT which a business should expect a VAT officer to know about, and which is sure to be looked at sooner or later. If it sounds like entertainment, it probably is!

Moreover, it is not easy for a business with a large marketing budget to identify entertainment. Although it probably takes some care to vet employees' travel expenses for various reasons, it is all too easy for a large invoice covering a marketing event to slip through without the entertainment element being noticed. Even if an event is primarily to promote products or services, such as at a trade exhibition, there is likely to be some entertainment involved. Typically, such invoices do not give full details of the event, but merely refer to the quotation setting out the original proposals of the agency which organised it. Therefore, unless the marketing director, or whoever approves the invoice for payment, is aware of the problem, and codes the invoice as entertainment either in part or in full or provides to the accounts department the information needed to do so, how will the clerk processing the invoice spot the entertainment?

The wording of the law in *Input Tax Order (SI 1992/3222), art 5* is 'entertainment including hospitality of any kind'. This is strictly interpreted by HMRC.

Examples of situations caught are:

- travel expenses of anyone, who although working for the company, is not an employee, such as auditors, self-employed salesmen and consultants. Such people should pay their own way and invoice on the cost as part of their fees. Naturally this does not help if the person is not registered for VAT;

- it would be worse still if the business paid the expenses because the adviser was not VAT registered. HMRC might then argue that, in reality, it had paid for a part of the adviser's services. Although it could recover the input tax, it would have to recharge the expenses plus output tax, and the adviser would have to invoice back to them as an additional part of the services supplied—thus possibly pushing the adviser's sales over the VAT registration limit—thus generating a late registration penalty!

- hospitality element of trade shows, training courses for self- employed salesmen, and public relations events such as a reception to launch a product or open a factory. Although their staff are present, they are there to entertain the guests, so none of the input tax is recoverable—in contrast

291

to the staff party. Often in such cases, only part of the expense relates to the hospitality and entertainment. VAT on a cost, which can be shown to be of an advertising nature, such as the cost of visual aids supporting a presentation about the product being launched, is recoverable;

- the disallowance extends to any asset used to provide entertainment. If a business owns a racehorse or a yacht, it must demonstrate at least some business use extending beyond mere entertainment of customers, in order to recover any VAT on it;

- the annual staff party. Input tax is disallowed in the ratio of guests to staff. If each employee brings a partner, 50% is disallowed. If a small charge is made to guests then all of the VAT can be recovered (*Ernst & Young* (LON/96/1377) No 15100).

Other cases, such as a day at the races and similar corporate entertainment events, are obvious.

In *Frank Warren t/a Sports Network Europe* (LON/04/1250 No 19213), the use of a box at a football ground, in which guests received a meal and saw a match, was held to be entertainment despite important business deals being negotiated on those occasions. However, HMRC did allow recovery of 25% of the VAT on the fee representing the advertising at the ground, which was included.

In December 2008, the ECJ gave its ruling in the *Danfoss and AstraZeneca* joined cases (C-371/07), which provided an opportunity to reclaim certain VAT costs that were previously always considered business entertainment by HMRC. The ruling confirmed that, where meals are provided to business contacts during the course of meetings, as long as such catering is strictly for the purpose of the business, these costs should not be blocked from input VAT recovery. For example, many professional firms will have client meetings, seminars and other events where catering is provided internally.

HMRC have taken the view that this only affects input tax on the entertainment of overseas clients, and state that it does not affect the status of VAT recovery on UK entertainment.

If there is some marketing, get a detailed invoice

13.17 Where an event, like the ones described above, includes both marketing and entertainment, a business should make sure that the invoices from the suppliers give the necessary detail.

That the entertainment is ancillary is no help

13.18 In *Shaklee International Ltd* ([1980] STC 708) the Court held that it is irrelevant whether entertainment is ancillary to some other business purpose.

Shaklee had to put on training courses in product knowledge and selling skills for self-employed salesmen in order to run its business, but the VAT on meals and accommodation provided was not recoverable despite it being ancillary to the training. Note that the cost of hiring a room in which to do the training is recoverable. It is the hospitality which is disallowed.

If a business holds a reception to launch a new product, the input tax on the sustenance for the employees is disallowed as well as that of the guests because *Input Tax Order (SI 1992/3222), art 5(3)* disallows VAT on the entertainment of employees if it is *incidental to its provision for others.*

WHO COUNTS AS AN EMPLOYEE?

13.19   'Employees' include the staff of all companies within the same VAT group. Thus, there is no disallowance when a company pays for lunch or for a hotel bill for people visiting it from another company in its VAT group.

In most cases, someone will only count as an employee if they are on the payroll, or are a director, partner or, in the case of a sole trader, he or she owns the business. Thus, pensioners, former staff, and job applicants do not qualify because they are not on the payroll; nor does a shareholder, unless also an employee, nor an auditor.

However, in Notice 700/65 (May 2002) *Business entertainment,* HMRC say in para 2.3 that *employee* includes *self-employed persons (subsistence expenses only)—treated by you in the same way for subsistence purposes as an employee.* Firstly, HMRC do not define *subsistence,* but they obviously mean to restrict the concession to accommodation and meals used by the self-employed person and paid for by the client whilst travelling on its business. The phrase *treated by you in the same way for subsistence purposes as an employee* seems to restrict the recovery of input tax to those cases in which the consultant travels away from the base office. In most cases if the sub-contractor claims the expenses on the company expenses form that input tax recovery will allowed, other costs incurred by the sub-contractor will normally form part of the base cost of his supply and be invoiced on to the business.

The sporting events concessions

13.20   Notice 700/65 also says that *helpers, stewards and other people essential to the running of sporting or similar events* can be regarded as employees. In para 2.7, HMRC extend that concession to a *recognised sporting body which provides through necessity free accommodation and meals to amateur sports persons and officials who attend an event.* They say *a concession allows full recovery of the input tax occurred*—see Notice 48

Extra Statutory Concessions. Unfortunately, that statement as it stands is inaccurate—para 3.10 of Notice 48 says that the concession does not allow recovery on alcohol or tobacco, cigarettes or cigars.

It also explains that the concession is not normally needed for ordinary members of amateur sports clubs, since subsistence expenditure they receive can be regarded as paid for through their subscriptions. The concession is therefore intended to cover team members chosen from affiliated clubs by national bodies, together with committee members of those bodies. Presumably, the restriction on alcohol or tobacco is intended to cover drinking in the bar or, perhaps, champagne celebrations of success but, typically of this Notice, it ignores an obvious problem—drinks on invoices for meals. No doubt, in practice, input tax on such drinks is claimed as part of the meal, and reasonable amounts would probably not be challenged by HMRC.

A concession if a business entertains whilst travelling

13.21

Focus

Tax incurred on subsistence expenses of directors or partners and staff travelling on bona fide business trips is recoverable.

In Notice 700/65, *Business entertainment* (May 2002), HMRC said that para 3 covered tax on meals with guests provided that any entertainment was secondary to the main purpose of the trip. That comment was not repeated in the May 2002 version, but I understand that the policy remains the same. So, if whilst travelling away from the office, a customer is invited out to lunch, the entertainment element is the customer's meal. The VAT on staff meals is recoverable because it is viewed as subsistence.

In contrast, no VAT on either meal is recoverable when staff leave their office for a prearranged lunch. This concession is of limited value for head office staff because of the difficulty of persuading executives to keep reliable records concerning the circumstances of each meal. However, salesmen are usually out on subsistence.

Meals close to the office

13.22 If managers regularly lunch in a local hotel, where they can discuss problems free from interruptions, the business can reclaim the VAT. Notice 700 (April 2002) says in para 12.1.2, 'If your business pays for meals for employees you can treat any VAT incurred as your input tax'. Presumably, that covers breakfast or an evening meal when staff work out of normal hours, and working lunches out of the office.

That does not apply to sole proprietors, partners and directors. HMRC say that they 'cannot recover the VAT on meals which are not taken for business purposes'. Although the wording is far from clear, it seems that, in the context of para 12.1.2, they are likely to dispute recovery by the *owners or directors* of businesses on meals in the vicinity of the office because these individuals can decide on their own expenses. If a business thinks it has an argument of business purpose for, say, Board lunches, it should ask HMRC.

CANTEEN MEALS AND ACCOMMODATION FOR HOTEL STAFF

13.23   For the rules on canteen meals, and staff accommodation in hotels, etc for employees working there, see Chapter 8, *The Value of Supply Rules*. The related input tax is recoverable.

ENTERTAINMENT MUST BE FREE

13.24

Focus

If a business provides meals or accommodation as part of a contractual arrangement, it is not caught under the disallowance for entertainment and hospitality because the provision is not free. Thus, if staff contribute to the cost of entertaining their partners, the input tax is recoverable, and output tax is due on the sums paid. The possible planning point is obvious—but would your staff accept a ticket price of, say, £15 per guest? (see *Ernst & Young* (LON/96/1377) No 15100).

In *Celtic Football and Athletic Co Ltd* ([1983] STC 470), the Court of Session held that, because Celtic was obliged under the UEFA rules to pay for its visiting opponents' board and lodging, and would receive in return the same when visiting their country, the provision was not free. It was, therefore, not entertainment.

Similarly, in *Kilroy Television Co Ltd* (LON/96/677 No 14581), food provided to participants in a television programme was held to be in return for their participation. It was part of the deal that a train ticket would be sent to them, and a buffet meal provided on arrival at the studio.

However, such an argument may get a business nowhere if HMRC then say they have provided non-monetary consideration, the accommodation etc, in return for non-monetary consideration from the other party. Thus, arguably, *Kilroy* should have accounted for output tax on the supply to the participants, the value of the supply being the cost to it of the food. If the business cannot collect the output VAT, the end result is the same as if the input tax was disallowed.

That was the effect in *Peugeot-Citroen* (MAN/02/566 No 18681). A dinner dance and overnight accommodation for the best salesmen and their partners from Peugeot's customers, the retail dealers, was not entertainment because, in return for the promise of a double ticket, each had achieved the sales level; that was consideration. However, output tax was due.

That position could be worse if output tax was due on a cost, which included expenses not carrying input tax!

If the other party is VAT registered, it can of course recover the VAT charged. Since it is doing something in return, it is making a supply to the first business, and it too should charge tax to them on the value of the food, accommodation etc—in addition to any money charged to them.

A typical example is where a contractor stays overnight near the premises at which he is working, and his hotel bill is paid by the customer as part of the arrangements. Another is the conference organiser who pays for meals and hotel accommodation for lecturers. If the organiser agrees to pay for these as part of the arrangements under which the lecturer speaks, it is possible that the value is part of the supply by the lecturer to which VAT should be added. Frequently, both parties ignore the matter but, as a matter of VAT law, it is an addition to the value of the supply by the contractor or the lecturer.

That the amounts each party should charge to the other would offset each other might not prevent HMRC issuing an assessment, there being no guarantee, of course, that each side could recover the VAT charged to it.

The entertainment is by the company ultimately paying for it

13.25 If a business provides entertainment or hospitality to people as part of a marketing project being carried out on behalf of another business, it can recover all the VAT because it will recharge the costs to its client. It is the latter which suffers the disallowance for entertainment.

Thus, when a company provided food, sometimes sandwiches, sometimes a meal, to doctors to whom it was making presentations about drugs on behalf of a pharmaceutical company, the entertainment was by the latter because it agreed to pay for it—and the presentation was done in its name (*Quintiles (Scotland) Ltd* (LON/02/762 No 18790)).

MOTOR CARS

13.26

> **Focus**
>
> VAT on a motor car is recoverable if the car is used exclusively for business purposes. That eliminates most cars bought by businesses because the users travel to and from work in them. Getting to work and going home is a private activity, not a business one.

For the definition of a *motor car*, see **13.28**.

Numerous small businesses have argued that one vehicle is used only for business and that others are available to the owner and his or her family for private use. Unfortunately, most private cars are insured for private motoring as well as for use by the policyholder for his or her business. If the vehicle is normally kept at home too, it is available for private use.

That was confirmed in *C Upton (t/a Fagomatic)* ([2002] STC 640). The Tribunal's decision that a Lamborghini car was not intended for private use by a sole trader, who worked seven days a week, and claimed not to use the car for shopping or social occasions, despite having no other car, was overturned by the Divisional Court. The key was whether the vehicle was *available*, not the *intention* as to its use. The Court of Appeal confirmed this as the correct test, even though it was difficult for a sole trader to prevent himself using a car for private purposes.

DC Humphreys (LON/02/602 No 18390) illustrates the practical problems. He bought an Isuzu Trooper estate car in order to tow a very large trailer transporting high-value cars such as collectors' items and prototypes. He did 180,000 miles in two years, averaging 2,000 miles a week, mostly on weekdays for up to ten hours.

The car was normally kept at a farm eight miles away. So were the keys but he had another set at home. Moreover, he sometimes parked the car and trailer at home because of a late return or to facilitate departure early next day in a different direction to the farm. The Tribunal held that the Trooper was still available for private use despite:

- limited availability for private use, given the huge business mileage and that the trailer was normally attached to it; once off, it took two or three people to reconnect it;

- having another more comfortable estate car in which he did 15,000 miles a year, and a third car for his wife.

Insurance companies sometimes refuse to insure for business use only. Thus, a business might think from the *Humphreys* case that, for a small business to recover VAT on a car, it must be parked overnight at the business rather than at home and in circumstances making private use impractical. However, there has been a series of three recent cases which have moved the position forward, and effectively made it easier to recover the VAT on a motor car.

In *Elm Milk* [2006] EWCA Civ 164 ([2006] STC 792) the Tribunal held that a consultancy company, controlled by the family of the only employee, could recover VAT on a Mercedes E320. The employee had done over 50,000 miles in it. It was parked near the office and the keys kept there but it was within 50 yards of his home!

The key was a Board resolution saying that the company would buy the car for business use only, that it did not intend to make it available to anyone for private use and that such use would breach the employee's terms of employment. However, there was no formal job contract. Given that the employee claimed to use his wife's car for all his private motoring, you might think that Customs had a point in arguing that the Board resolution was not for real. The Tribunal found the employee to be a witness of truth. He had done what could be done to put a legal embargo on private use of the car, and he intended to stick to it. Any private use would be in defiance of the resolution, which contained the relevant terms of his employment. This was a decision by the President of the VAT and Duties Tribunals, so it has serious credibility, and has been subsequently confirmed in the High Court and Court of Appeal.

In *PJR Shaw* (MAN/05/334 No 19594), a farmer won recovery of input tax on a BMW X5 diesel station wagon for which he was the only insured driver. His intention was to use it only on his farm. The problem of availability for private use was met by him having bought at the same time a petrol version of the same vehicle. The Tribunal was satisfied that he had done enough to ensure for all practical purposes use exclusively for business purposes, even though it was insured for private as well as business use. He stated that this was because the insurance was cheaper, when HMRC challenged this at Tribunal he showed that is combined harvester was also insured for private use as it was cheaper. The Tribunal accepted his argument, as the realistic chance of private use was minimal. However, the decision was subsequently overturned by HMRC upon appeal to the High Court ([2006] EWHC 3699 (Ch) [2007] BVC 854), primarily because the farmer had done nothing to restrict the private use of the diesel vehicle.

In the larger business, the position is much the same with pool cars. If it can show that a pool car is only used during the day for specific business journeys, and that it is returned to the pool at night, it can recover input tax on it.

In one particular case, *Peter Jackson (Jewellers) Ltd* (MAN/05/615 No 19474), a Ford Ka was held to be intended for use as a pool car entirely for business. It was kept overnight in a leased space. Although taken home by one member of the staff when she needed to take stock the following day to a branch, and it saved time to start from home, that was arguably a necessary part of the business trip. Even if private, it was trivial. Moreover, despite merely verbal instructions to staff that only business use of the car was allowed, that particular trip was seen to be not as part of the intention at the time of purchase. The Tribunal saw the instruction as a legal restraint on private use by the staff under their employment terms.

However, one reason for having pool cars is usually so that, when a senior executive needs one, a pool car can be made available temporarily. Inevitably, such use will include journeys to and from work.

That may not apply where staff work from home and the cars are in constant use. In *MasterCard Security Services Ltd* (MAN/02/0169 No 18631), the Tribunal accepted that there was no intention to make available for private use the cars used by security guards. They worked 12-hour shifts. Guards living close together were paired so that No 1 coming off duty could collect No 2 from his home. They then drove to No 1's home where he got out and No 2 started the next shift. Private use was forbidden and was mostly impractical given a mileage of 150,000 miles in 18 months and usage logs maintained. Cars were, of course, sometimes parked at homes, presumably usually at weekends, but they had to be available for emergency call outs and they would in due course be collected. Disciplinary action had been taken in the few cases of private use discovered.

The only one authorised had allowed a guard, who had no car of his own, to drive to a hospital to which a family member had been admitted in an emergency. The car was then collected and the guard had to find his own way home. The Tribunal accepted that this one incident had not been foreseen and did not affect the intention at the time the cars were leased.

In *Squibb & Davies (Demolition) Ltd* (LON/01/653 No 17829), input tax recovery was allowed on a Range Rover and a Jaguar which were locked up at night in the company car park, and, for which, journey logs were kept. The Range Rover was used for emergency calls, often at night, and was equipped with fax and mobile phone points and carried tools, protective clothing etc. The Jaguar was used to transport clients. No director was allowed to use them privately and the Tribunal accepted that there was no intention to make them available for private use.

In practice therefore, VAT on a car is not usually recoverable except by:

- a motor dealer—because the dealer will charge VAT when the car is sold;

- a leasing company—because it does not even have possession of the vehicle. The corollary is that the lessee is only allowed to recover 50% of the VAT on the leasing charges;

- for use as a taxi; the actual wording is *to provide it on hire with the services of a driver for the purpose of carrying passengers*, which must therefore cover chauffeur driven cars, not just as ordinary taxis;

- for use for self-drive hire;

- for use by a driving instructor.

Although the use for business purposes in general must be exclusive, use as a taxi, self-drive hire or for driving instruction need only be primarily. Thus, a taxi driver can use his car for private purposes as well.

If a car, on which input tax has been recovered, is sold, VAT is due on that sale.

The detailed rules are in *Input Tax Order (SI 1992/3222), art 7.*

CAR LEASING AND HIRE CHARGES

13.27   As mentioned above, 50% of the VAT on the leasing charges for a motor car is normally disallowed to the lessee. That does not apply if the use is as a taxi, for self-drive hire or for driving instruction.

It does catch a hire whilst your normal car is off the road. However, HMRC accept that, in other cases, the 50% disallowance only applies after ten days (para 4.4 of Notice 700/64 (May 2006) *Motoring expenses*). Thus, a business can recover the VAT if, for instance, its staff travel on business by train or by air to another part of the UK and hire a car there for a few days.

The 50% leasing disallowance does not apply to the maintenance of the vehicle or road side assistance etc, if the charge for this is shown separately on the lessor's invoice.

If, after disallowing 50% on the leasing payments, a business receives a credit note from the lessor on early termination or at the end of the lease, they need only reduce the input tax by 50% of that credit.

THE DEFINITION OF A MOTOR CAR

13.28   Most of the time, it is obvious whether a vehicle is a motor car or not. However, people sometimes get it wrong because they have not studied the wording of the legislation. They think that, for example, a four-wheel-drive vehicle used on a farm or by a service engineer visiting customers is no longer a car because of what it is used for. This is not so! The key is the design of the vehicle as can be seen from the following.

Input Tax Order (SI 1992/3222), art 2 defines a car as a vehicle which:

- is constructed or adapted solely or mainly for the carriage of passengers; or

- has to the rear of the driver's seat roofed accommodation which is fitted with side windows or which is constructed or adapted for the fitting of side windows, but not if it is:

- capable of carrying ten or more passengers;

- or a payload of one tonne or more;

- or has an unladen weight of three tonnes or more.

Special purpose vehicles, such as hearses and street cleaning vehicles are also excluded from the definition.

A 'crew van' with folding seats, but no side or rear windows, was held to be a commercial vehicle, and not a car, in *Vauxhall Motors Ltd* (LON/04/1230 No 19425).

THE ONE-TONNE PAYLOAD

13.29 HMRC have an agreement with the *Society of Motor Manufacturers and Traders Ltd* under which manufacturers inform both dealers and HMRC of the ex-works payloads of their standard double cab pickup trucks. Accessories added by dealers can be ignored except for hard tops. HMRC accept a standard weight for a hard top of 45 kg. Since this reduces the payload, it could convert a pickup truck with a payload of just over one tonne into a car.

Maintenance of cars

13.30

> **Focus**
>
> A business can recover all the VAT incurred on *maintaining* a car. There is no restriction for private use, even if the business mileage is only a small proportion of the total.

This generous interpretation of the law by HMRC takes into account the fact that no VAT is recoverable on the car itself if there is any private use. Thus, the owners of businesses can reclaim VAT on car maintenance invoices as long as the business pays for the work, even though the car itself is not a business asset (para 5.1 of Notice 700/64 (May 2007) *Motoring expenses*).

In theory, an employer could agree to pay the maintenance costs of cars owned by staff and recover the VAT thereon. In practice, however, the direct tax consequences and the extra administration may make this not worth doing.

Fuel for cars—output tax on the fuel scale charge

13.31

Focus

If a business pays for *any* fuel used for private motoring by its owners, directors or employees, it has to pay VAT on the fuel scale charge based on CO_2 emissions as set by *s 57*.

When looking up the rates, which are based on CO_2 emissions from 1 May 2007, check that the figures are for the right year. They are altered annually, as explained below, and the latest figures can normally be found in an amendment to Notice 700/64 *Motoring Expenses*. They are published on HMRC's website and are on a schedule sent out with the next VAT return sent following the Budget. Prior to 1 May 2007, there were three rates for petrol engines determined by engine size, and two lower rates for diesels. Following the change to a CO_2-based method, there are now 21 rates at 5g/km intervals.

If a business has a car fleet, it will need to set up a spreadsheet on its computer and administer it carefully for all changes in the cars. Notice 700/64 *Motoring Expenses* explains the detailed rules in *s 56* concerning, for instance, what happens when a car is changed in the middle of a VAT period.

A possible pitfall is that the fuel scale charge changes each year for periods starting on or after 1 May. That means that, if the VAT return is quarterly and begins on 1 April, the business does not alter the VAT due until the return for July–September. It would be easy to overlook the change if the spreadsheet is based on monthly or quarterly sums of VAT per car. It was increased in 2006/07 and 2005/06 but *reduced* in 2004/05 and *increased* in 2003/04 so a business could have overpaid, if it had overlooked the change.

The scale charge assumes private motoring of 10–13,000 miles a year, which includes journeys from home to work.

If private motoring is low, consider the alternatives:

- not reclaiming input tax on fuel at all—although the gross cost of the fuel can be paid by the business. That means fuel for *any* vehicles including commercial, so it will not make sense if the business ran a commercial fleet;

- reclaiming VAT by calculating the proportion of business mileage to total mileage and reclaiming that proportion of the VAT on the total expenditure on fuel during the VAT period or for the year. To satisfy HMRC, a business will need to keep detailed records, recorded journey by journey, not estimates, together with the actual fuel bills;

- claiming the VAT back based on the fuel element of the mileage. Notice 700/64, does not say how to calculate the petrol element of the mileage allowance, but the figures quoted by the motoring organisations are likely to be acceptable, and normally range between 10p to 15p per mile.

In *Revenue & Customs Brief 11/12* HMRC announced that they would be amending the legislation on the fuel scale charges.

The changes have:

- brought into legislation the effect of two existing extra statutory concessions;

- simplified the legislation and the process for the annual revalorisation of the scale charges;

- withdrawn one extra statutory concession; and

- corrected a defect in the existing legislation.

Under the existing law, a business that has provided fuel to an employee for their private use and has made a charge for that fuel is required to account for VAT on the basis of the fuel scale charges, unless they have accounted for VAT on the basis of detailed records of private mileage or the charge made was at least for the cost of the fuel. HMRC now recognises that there is a defect in this aspect of current law and that, where the business does make a charge for the private use of the fuel, the business should be given the option of accounting for VAT on the basis of the amount charged to the employee.

Businesses making a charge for private use of fuel may, until the defect has been corrected, account for VAT on this basis in future returns. Any businesses who consider that they have overpaid VAT as a result of this defect may submit a claim for repayment of the difference between the amount already accounted for and the amount due on the basis of the charge to the employee. All claims which are submitted to HMRC must be supported by proper evidence and are subject to the normal rules for claims.

As an anti-avoidance measure where employers charge employees for road fuel used for private purposes at less than market value, those supplies will be valued at their market value, rather than at the amount paid. That will prevent tax avoidance whereby employers make an artificially low charge for the fuel used.

To prevent forestalling, any supplies made between the autumn announcement and the Finance Bill coming into force were valued by using the anti-avoidance rules, but only to the extent that the fuel is used after Royal Assent to the Act.

In *Revenue & Customs Brief 33/13* HMRC announced that the partial exemption concession on Road Fuel Scale Charges (RFSCs) had been withdrawn with effect from 1 January 2014. Taxpayers who used the concession will have needed to take action if they are to continue to achieve a fair result following withdrawal.

13.31 *What can a business recover input tax on?*

Where taxpayers are partly exempt and VAT on road fuel is treated as residual, declaring RFSCs can lead to unfair results. This is because output tax will be declared on the full value of private use fuel whereas input tax will only be claimable in part on that fuel according to the taxpayer's partial exemption recovery rate.

The concession corrected this unfairness by allowing the RFSCs to be reduced by applying the partial exemption recovery rate to them. This meant that the output tax declared on private use fuel was consistent with the actual input tax deduction on that fuel.This is no longer the case.

The current fuel scale charge rates in force from 1 May 2017 are:

Annual charges CO_2 band	VAT fuel scale charge, 12-month period (£)	VAT on 12-month charge (£)	VAT exclusive 12-month charge (£)
120 or less	563	93.83	469.17
125	842	140.33	701.67
130	901	150.17	750.83
135	955	159.17	795.83
140	1,013	168.83	844.17
145	1,068	178	890
150	1,126	187.67	938.33
155	1,180	196.67	983.33
160	1,239	206.50	1,032.50
165	1,293	215.50	1,077.50
170	1,351	225.17	1,125.83
175	1,405	234.17	1,170.83
180	1,464	244	1,220
185	1,518	253	1,265
190	1,577	262.83	1,314.17
195	1,631	271.83	1,359.17
200	1,689	281.50	1,407.50
205	1,743	290.50	1,452.50
210	1,802	300.33	1,501.67
215	1,856	309.33	1,546.67
220	1,914	319	1,595
225 or more	1,969	328.17	1,640.83

Quarterly charges CO_2 band	VAT fuel scale charge, 3-month period (£)	VAT on 3-month charge (£)	VAT exclusive 3-month charge (£)
120 or less	140	23.33	116.67
125	211	35.17	175.83
130	224	37.33	186.67
135	238	39.67	198.33
140	252	42	210
145	267	44.50	222.50
150	281	46.83	234.17
155	295	49.17	245.83
160	309	51.50	257.50
165	323	53.83	269.17
170	337	56.17	280.83
175	351	58.50	292.50
180	365	60.83	304.17
185	379	63.17	315.83
190	393	65.50	327.50
195	408	68.00	340
200	422	70.33	351.67
205	436	72.67	363.33
210	449	74.83	374.17
215	463	77.17	385.83
220	478	79.67	398.33
225 or more	492	82	410

Monthly charges CO_2 band	VAT fuel scale charge, 1-month period (£)	VAT on 1-month charge (£)	VAT exclusive 1-month charge (£)
120 or less	46	7.67	38.33
125	70	11.67	58.33
130	74	12.33	61.67
135	79	13.17	65.83

13.31   *What can a business recover input tax on?*

Monthly charges CO$_2$ band	VAT fuel scale charge, 1-month period (£)	VAT on 1-month charge (£)	VAT exclusive 1-month charge (£)
140	84	14.00	70.00
145	88	14.67	73.33
150	93	15.50	77.50
155	98	16.33	81.67
160	102	17	85
165	107	17.83	89.17
170	111	18.50	92.50
175	116	19.33	96.67
180	121	20.17	100.83
185	125	20.83	104.17
190	131	21.83	109.17
195	136	22.67	113.33
200	140	23.33	116.67
205	145	24.17	120.83
210	149	24.83	124.17
215	154	25.67	128.33
220	159	26.50	132.50
225 or more	163	27.17	135.83

Fuel scale charge rates in force from 1 May 2016

CO$_2$ band	VAT fuel scale charge, 12 month period (£)	VAT on 12 month charge (£)	VAT exclusive 12 month charge (£)
120 or less	467	77.83	389.17
125	699	116.50	582.50
130	747	124.50	622.50
135	792	132	660
140	841	140.17	700.83
145	886	147.67	738.33
150	934	155.67	778.33

CO$_2$ band	VAT fuel scale charge, 12 month period (£)	VAT on 12 month charge (£)	VAT exclusive 12 month charge (£)
155	979	163.17	815.83
160	1,028	171.33	856.67
165	1,073	178.83	894.17
170	1,121	186.83	934.17
175	1,166	194.33	971.67
180	1,214	202.33	1,011.67
185	1,259	209.83	1,049.17
190	1,308	218	1,090
195	1,353	225.50	1,127.50
200	1,401	233.50	1,167.50
205	1,446	241	1,205
210	1,495	249.17	1,245.83
215	1,540	256.67	1,283.33
220	1,588	264.67	1,323.33
225 or more	1,633	272.17	1,360.83

CO$_2$ band	VAT fuel scale charge, 3 month period (£)	VAT on 3 month charge (£)	VAT exclusive 3 month charge (£)
120 or less	116	19.33	96.67
125	175	29.17	145.83
130	186	31	155
135	197	32.83	164.17
140	209	34.83	174.17
145	221	36.83	184.17
150	233	38.83	194.17
155	245	40.83	204.17
160	256	42.67	213.33
165	268	44.67	223.33
170	279	46.50	232.50
175	291	48.50	242.50

13.31   *What can a business recover input tax on?*

CO$_2$ band	VAT fuel scale charge, 3 month period (£)	VAT on 3 month charge (£)	VAT exclusive 3 month charge (£)
180	303	50.50	252.50
185	314	52.33	261.67
190	326	54.33	271.67
195	338	56.33	281.67
200	350	58.33	291.67
205	362	60.33	301.67
210	373	62.17	310.83
215	384	64	320
220	396	66	330
225 or more	408	68	340

CO$_2$ band	VAT fuel scale charge, 1 month period (£)	VAT on 1 month charge (£)	VAT exclusive 1 month charge (£)
120 or less	38	6.33	31.67
125	58	9.67	48.33
130	61	10.17	50.83
135	65	10.83	54.17
140	69	11.50	57.50
145	73	12.17	60.83
150	77	12.83	64.17
155	81	13.50	67.50
160	85	14.17	70.83
165	89	14.83	74.17
170	92	15.33	76.67
175	96	16	80
180	101	16.83	84.17
185	104	17.33	86.67
190	108	18	90
195	112	18.67	93.33

CO$_2$ band	VAT fuel scale charge, 1 month period (£)	VAT on 1 month charge (£)	VAT exclusive 1 month charge (£)
200	116	19.33	96.67
205	120	20	100
210	123	20.50	102.50
215	128	21.33	106.67
220	132	22	110
225 or more	135	22.50	112.50

Annual charges CO$_2$ band	VAT fuel scale charge, 12-month period (£)	VAT on 12-month charge (£)	VAT exclusive 12-month charge (£)
120 or less	536.00	89.33	446.67
125	802.00	133.67	668.33
130	857.00	142.83	714.17
135	909.00	151.50	757.50
140	965.00	160.83	804.17
145	1,106.00	169.33	846.67
150	1,072.00	178.67	893.33
155	1,123.00	187.17	935.83
160	1,179.00	196.50	982.50
165	1,231.00	205.17	1,025.83
170	1,286.00	214.33	1,071.67
175	1,338.00	223.00	1,115.00
180	1,393.00	232.17	1,160.83
185	1,445.00	240.83	1,204.17
190	1,501.00	250.17	1,250.83
195	1,552.00	258.67	1,293.33
200	1,608.00	268.00	1,340.00
205	1,660.00	276.67	1,383.33
210	1,715.00	285.83	1,429.17
215	1,767.00	294.50	1,472.50

13.31   *What can a business recover input tax on?*

Annual charges CO$_2$ band	VAT fuel scale charge, 12-month period (£)	VAT on 12-month charge (£)	VAT exclusive 12-month charge (£)
220	1,822.00	303.67	1,518.33
225 or more	1,874.00	312.33	1,561.67

Quarterly charges CO$_2$ band	VAT fuel scale charge, 3-month period (£)	VAT on 3-month charge (£)	VAT exclusive 3-month charge (£)
120 or less	133.00	22.17	110.83
125	200.00	33.33	166.67
130	213.00	35.50	177.50
135	227.00	37.83	189.17
140	240.00	40.00	200.00
145	254.00	42.33	211.67
150	267.00	44.50	222.50
155	281.00	46.83	234.17
160	294.00	49.00	245.00
165	308.00	51.33	256.67
170	320.00	53.33	266.67
175	334.00	55.67	278.33
180	347.00	57.83	289.17
185	361.00	60.17	300.83
190	374.00	62.33	311.67
195	388.00	64.67	323.33
200	401.00	66.83	334.17
205	415.00	69.17	345.83
210	428.00	71.33	356.67
215	441.00	73.50	367.50
220	455.00	75.83	379.17
225 or more	468.00	78.00	390.00

Monthly charges CO_2 band	VAT fuel scale charge, 1-month period (£)	VAT on 1-month charge (£)	VAT exclusive 1-month charge (£)
120 or less	44.00	7.33	36.67
125	66.00	11.00	55.00
130	70.00	11.67	58.33
135	75.00	12.50	62.50
140	80.00	13.33	66.67
145	84.00	14.00	70.00
150	88.00	14.67	73.33
155	93.00	15.50	77.50
160	97.00	16.17	80.83
165	102.00	17.00	85.00
170	106.00	17.67	88.33
175	111.00	18.50	92.50
180	115.00	19.17	95.83
185	119.00	19.83	99.17
190	124.00	20.67	103.33
195	129.00	21.50	107.50
200	133.00	22.17	110.83
205	138.00	23.00	115.00
210	142.00	23.67	118.33
215	146.00	24.33	121.67
220	151.00	25.17	125.83
225 or more	155.00	25.83	129.17

Fuel scale charge rates in force from 1 May 2014:

Annual charges CO_2 band	VAT fuel scale charge, 12-month period (£)	VAT on 12-month charge (£)	VAT exclusive 12-month charge (£)
120 or less	627.00	104.50	522.50
125	939.00	156.50	782.50

13.31 *What can a business recover input tax on?*

Annual charges CO_2 band	VAT fuel scale charge, 12-month period (£)	VAT on 12-month charge (£)	VAT exclusive 12-month charge (£)
130	1,004.00	167.33	836.67
135	1,064.00	177.33	886.67
140	1,129.00	188.17	940.83
145	1,190.00	198.33	991.67
150	1,255.00	209.17	1,045.83
155	1,315.00	219.17	1,095.83
160	1,381.00	230.17	1,150.83
165	1,441.00	240.17	1,200.83
170	1,506.00	251.00	1,255.00
175	1,567.00	261.17	1,305.83
180	1,632.00	272.00	1,360.00
185	1,692.00	282.00	1,410.00
190	1,757.00	292.83	1,464.17
195	1,818.00	303.00	1,515.00
200	1,883.00	313.83	1,569.17
205	1,943.00	323.83	1,619.17
210	2,008.00	334.67	1,673.33
215	2,069.00	344.83	1,724.17
220	2,134.00	355.67	1,778.33
225 or more	2,194.00	365.67	1,828.33

Quarterly charges CO_2 band	VAT fuel scale charge, 3-month period (£)	VAT on 3-month charge (£)	VAT exclusive 3-month charge (£)
120 or less	156.00	26.00	130.00
125	234.00	39.00	195.00
130	251.00	41.83	209.17
135	266.00	44.33	221.67
140	282.00	47.00	235.00
145	297.00	49.50	247.50
150	313.00	52.17	260.83

Quarterly charges CO_2 band	VAT fuel scale charge, 3-month period (£)	VAT on 3-month charge (£)	VAT exclusive 3-month charge (£)
155	328.00	54.67	273.33
160	345.00	57.50	287.50
165	360.00	60.00	300.00
170	376.00	62.67	313.33
175	391.00	65.17	325.83
180	408.00	68.00	340.00
185	423.00	70.50	352.50
190	439.00	73.17	365.83
195	454.00	75.67	378.33
200	470.00	78.33	391.67
205	485.00	80.83	404.17
210	502.00	83.67	418.33
215	517.00	86.17	430.83
220	533.00	88.83	444.17
225 or more	548.00	91.33	456.67

Monthly charges CO_2 band	VAT fuel scale charge, 1-month period (£)	VAT on 1-month charge (£)	VAT exclusive 1-month charge (£)
120 or less	52.00	8.67	43.33
125	78.00	13.00	65.00
130	83.00	13.83	69.17
135	88.00	14.67	73.33
140	94.00	15.67	78.33
145	99.00	16.50	82.50
150	104.00	17.33	86.67
155	109.00	18.17	90.83
160	115.00	19.17	95.83
165	120.00	20.00	100.00
170	125.00	20.83	104.17

13.31 *What can a business recover input tax on?*

Monthly charges CO$_2$ band	VAT fuel scale charge, 1-month period (£)	VAT on 1-month charge (£)	VAT exclusive 1-month charge (£)
175	130.00	21.67	108.33
180	136.00	22.67	113.33
185	141.00	23.50	117.50
190	146.00	24.33	121.67
195	151.00	25.17	125.83
200	156.00	26.00	130.00
205	161.00	26.83	134.17
210	167.00	27.83	139.17
215	172.00	28.67	143.33
220	177.00	29.50	147.50
225 or more	182.00	30.33	151.67

The fuel scale charges from 1 May 2012 are:

VAT fuel scale charges

Businesses must use these new VAT fuel scale charges from the start of their next prescribed accounting period beginning on or after 1 May 2012.

CO$_2$ band	VAT fuel scale charge, 12-month period (£)	VAT on 12-month charge (£)	VAT exclusive 12-month charge (£)
120 or less	£665.00	£110.83	£554.17
125	£1,000.00	£166.67	£833.33
130	£1,065.00	£177.50	£887.50
135	£1,135.00	£189.17	£945.83
140	£1,200.00	£200.00	£1,000.00
145	£1,270.00	£211.67	£1,058.33
150	£1,335.00	£222.50	£1,112.50
155	£1,400.00	£233.33	£1,166.67
160	£1,470.00	£245.00	£1,225.00
165	£1,535.00	£255.83	£1,279.17
170	£1,600.00	£266.67	£1,333.33

CO_2 band	VAT fuel scale charge, 12-month period (£)	VAT on 12-month charge (£)	VAT exclusive 12-month charge (£)
175	£1,670.00	£278.33	£1,391.67
180	£1,735.00	£289.17	£1,445.83
185	£1,800.00	£300.00	£1,500.00
190	£1,870.00	£311.67	£1,558.33
195	£1,935.00	£322.50	£1,612.50
200	£2,000.00	£333.33	£1,666.67
205	£2,070.00	£345.00	£1,725.00
210	£2,135.00	£355.83	£1,779.17
215	£2,200.00	£366.67	£1,833.33
220	£2,270.00	£378.33	£1,891.67
225 or more	£2,335.00	£389.17	£1,945.83

VAT fuel scale charges

Businesses must use these new VAT fuel scale charges from the start of their next prescribed accounting period beginning on or after 1 May 2012.

CO_2 band	VAT fuel scale charge, three-month period (£)	VAT on three-month charge (£)	VAT exclusive three-month charge (£)
120 or less	166.00	27.67	138.33
125	250.00	41.67	208.33
130	266.00	44.33	221.67
135	283.00	47.17	235.83
140	300.00	50.00	250.00
145	316.00	52.67	263.33
150	333.00	55.50	277.50
155	350.00	58.33	291.67
160	366.00	61.00	305.00
165	383.00	63.83	319.17
170	400.00	66.67	333.33
175	416.00	69.33	346.67
180	433.00	72.17	360.83

13.31   *What can a business recover input tax on?*

CO$_2$ band	VAT fuel scale charge, three-month period (£)	VAT on three-month charge (£)	VAT exclusive three-month charge (£)
185	450.00	75.00	375.00
190	467.00	77.83	389.17
195	483.00	80.50	402.50
200	500.00	83.33	416.67
205	517.00	86.17	430.83
210	533.00	88.83	444.17
215	550.00	91.67	458.33
220	567.00	94.50	472.50
225 or more	583.00	97.17	485.83

VAT fuel scale charges

Businesses must use these new VAT fuel scale charges from the start of their next prescribed accounting period beginning on or after 1 May 2012.

CO$_2$ band	VAT fuel scale charge, one-month period (£)	VAT on one-month charge (£)	VAT exclusive one-month charge (£)
120 or less	55.00	9.17	45.83
125	83.00	13.83	69.17
130	88.00	14.67	73.33
135	94.00	15.67	78.33
140	100.00	16.67	83.33
145	105.00	17.50	87.50
150	111.00	18.50	92.50
155	116.00	19.33	96.67
160	122.00	20.33	101.67
165	127.00	21.17	105.83
170	133.00	22.17	110.83
175	138.00	23.00	115.00
180	144.00	24.00	120.00
185	150.00	25.00	125.00
190	155.00	25.83	129.17

CO$_2$ band	VAT fuel scale charge, one-month period (£)	VAT on one-month charge (£)	VAT exclusive one- month charge (£)
195	161.00	26.83	134.17
200	166.00	27.67	138.33
205	172.00	28.67	143.33
210	177.00	29.50	147.50
215	183.00	30.50	152.50
220	189.00	31.50	157.50
225 or more	194.00	32.33	161.67

Fuel for cars—invoices needed for input tax recovery

13.32   From 1 January 2006, a business must retain VAT invoices in order to recover VAT included in a sum paid as a mileage allowance. This is because of an ECJ decision that fuel bought by an employee is supplied to the employee, not to the employer (see **13.5** above).

We suggest that businesses take following measures:

- warn staff that expense claims can only be met for road fuel, whether on the basis of actual expenditure or as a rate per mile, if VAT invoices covering the amount of petrol are attached to the claim; and

- suggest that they always obtain invoices so as to have them when needed—but accept those obtained immediately after a trip.

THE DIFFERENCE BETWEEN PURPOSE AND BENEFIT

13.33   Expenditure is not for the purpose of a business merely because it benefits from it. The benefit may be incidental, for example, when a businessman makes a valuable business contact whilst on holiday, or it may be closely connected, as when a director is defended against a criminal charge arising out of the business activities. However, *benefit* is not enough. A business has to demonstrate a business *purpose*. See **13.46** *Legal costs* for more on this.

The business in question could be an existing one or a new one. For example, the ownership of racehorses may be justifiable:

- because the horse(s) help to promote another kind of business;

- because the breeding and/or dealing in horses itself amounts to a business.

In the case of *Folkestone Harbour (GP) Ltd v Revenue & Customs* [2015] UKFTT 101 (TC), HMRC argued that the input tax on a pavement fountain at the entrance to Folkestone's harbour redevelopment was not a genuine business expense as it was not directly related to the redevelopment project.

The Tribunal disagreed; the fountain and square were in fact the connection between the town and the seafront and had been part of the original development plan. The Tribunal considered it to be a marketing tool for the development project as it helped increase the footfall in the area. The brand awareness for the appellant was raised and a plaque near the fountain made it clear that it was part for the appellant's development.

Quite reasonably, the Tribunal found that that there was an obvious and clear association between the Appellant and the expenditure on the fountain and that no ordinary businessman would have incurred such expenditure unless it was for the purpose of the business and therefore upheld the appeal.

THE CARRYING OUT OR PROMOTION OF A BUSINESS WITH A RACEHORSE, POWER BOAT, YACHT, ETC

13.34   For obvious reasons, HMRC look carefully at the ownership of such desirable assets as racehorses and yachts. In the earlier years of VAT, numerous Tribunal cases established some ground rules. The one often quoted is *Ian Flockton Developments Ltd* (1987 STC 394) in which the High Court held that whether goods or services were used or to be used for the purposes of a business was a subjective test. The Tribunal must therefore consider what was in the trader's mind at the time the expenditure was incurred. So:

- a business must show a credible business purpose for incurring the expenditure, for example, that the horse will advertise the business to potential customers. Input tax is not disallowed merely because the decision was not a wise one. On the other hand, Tribunals have been inclined to support HMRC where the evidence showed that it was unlikely that the expenditure could have benefited the company;

- evidence of the intention at the time of purchase is important, such as minutes recording the background to the decision to incur the costs;

- a business should record the subsequent use of the asset, noting publicity received, sales leads obtained or other benefits.

If the expenditure is used for the purpose of entertainment, as opposed to advertising, the VAT will be disallowed. Thus, any advertising must be to racegoers generally. The cost of taking customers to the races is caught by the input tax block on entertainment.

In *Hillingdon Shirts Co* (MAN/78/26 No 678), a shirt manufacturer recovered tax on the cost of running a racehorse mainly because he produced a mock-up of a shirt to be launched bearing the name of the horse when the latter won a race. In other words, the quality of the business decision is not in question, merely whether or not the evidence supports the directors' assertion that they made a genuine business decision to acquire the asset for the purpose specified.

In *AJ Bingley Ltd* (LON/83/333 No 1597), a company making plastic bags used in supermarkets won its claim to recover input tax on the cost, which exceeded £250,000, of six racehorses. Six horses sounded rather a lot but the Appellant was able to produce evidence to the Tribunal that the senior management of the supermarkets tended to be interested in racing. Some of them owned horses. Bingley's ownership of horses provided talking points which enabled its salesmen to obtain interviews at which they could make sales pitches. As plastic bags were a low-value routine product, it was not easy to get in to see the buyer. Getting the interview was the crucial first stage, and the horse ownership facilitated this.

In *Demor Investments* (EDN/80/74 No 1091), a public house succeeded because its customers took an active interest in the horse. The pub was next to a betting shop, and most of its business came from people who came in to watch the racing, which they could not do in the betting shop. There was evidence that they came to regard the horse as their own, with consequent loyalty to the pub.

Think about the evidence to support a business promotion

13.35   Following the above cases and several others the stream of Tribunal decisions about promoting a business with racehorses, racing cars, yachts, etc greatly reduced. The next main case was *KPL Contracts Ltd* (LON/04/1605 No 19629). This illustrates how the correct handling of the bullet points under the main heading of this subject will maximise the chances of success on of VAT recovery.

The owner of KPL, a business which supplied and laid conducting media for the utilities industry, was worried about the adverse publicity when his business was raided by the then Inland Revenue and he was arrested. He decided to drive in motor-cross rallying as a method of promoting the company. KPL bought a second-hand car at £35k and a second the following year for £215k. Following success in 2003/04 evidenced by 80 newspaper clippings, KPL bought a new car for £355k plus VAT and, six months later, another for £300k.

The minutes produced to the Tribunal showed no real investigation into the likely cost of involvement in motor rallying; nor was there professional advice on the tax consequences. KPL did not use marketing consultants, despite having developed a marketing strategy with one on a previous occasion.

Although the Inland Revenue said verbally in spring 2003 that there would be no follow-up from the raid, that was not confirmed in writing until 2005.

The owner then decided to retire from the sport, the decision being motivated in part by the success in rehabilitating both himself and KPL. No personal advantage was to be secured by continuing in the sport, however successful.

The Tribunal noted the lack of the logical action required to maximise the potential benefit to the company but, on balance, decided in its favour. As KPL was dominated by its owner, the Tribunal did not distinguish between its advancement and that of the owner—thus turning down a point made by the Inland Revenue.

On balance KPL was a little lucky—not because of the owner, having arguably rehabilitated his reputation, as opposed to that of the company, but because there was seemingly no evidence of how the company benefited. There were only about 50 decision-makers with whom it needed to negotiate its contracts; yet it seems not to have used the rallying as a source of contact with them by, for instance, corporate hospitality at the events. KPL did establish a genuine business intent, but its case would have been stronger if it had handled the situation in a more business-like manner.

Now, many owners of small businesses would not expect to formalise in minutes the reasons for taking action; yet, when VAT recovery is involved it can be essential!

Racehorse owners' scheme

13.36   There is a special scheme for the VAT registration of racehorse owners which is covered in VAT Notice 706/67.

Following an agreement with the Thoroughbred Horseracing and Breeding Industry a scheme known as the VAT registration scheme for racehorse owners was introduced on 16 March 1993.

Owners can apply for VAT registration under the scheme if they are registered as an owner at Weatherbys and they:

(a)   own a horse or horses covered by a sponsorship agreement registered at Weatherbys; or

(b)   own a horse or horses covered by a trainer's sponsorship agreement registered at Weatherbys; or

(c)   can show they have received, and will continue to receive, business income for example from appearance money or sponsored number cloths (SNCs) from horseracing activities.

There are special arrangements for owners of point-to-point horses that qualify for racing in hunter chases.

Only the registered owner of a racehorse at Weatherbys may register for VAT under the scheme. The registered owner can be a sole proprietor, partnership or limited company. If you own a part share in a racehorse you can register for VAT if you own at least 50%, otherwise you can only register as a partnership with the other part share owners.

If, after registration, you lose your source of sponsorship, you will be able to retain your VAT registration if you can show you are actively seeking new sponsorship.

An owner registered under the scheme must account for output tax on the sponsorship income, prize money and appearance money received.

If an owner sells a horse or part share in a horse included as part of the business, they must normally charge and account for VAT on the full selling price.

PERSONAL NUMBER PLATES

13.37 HMRC are bound to see a personal number plate as being for the private satisfaction of the individual, rather than for the purposes of the business. To claim for input tax on the cost, a business must show that it is in some way promoting the business. In *Sunner and Sons* (MAN/91/1205 No. 8857), a Tribunal accepted that the number plate '7 SUN' was bought to promote the SUN name on own label goods sold in a supermarket called Sun.

In *Hooper* (VTD No 19276), a sole trader restaurant owner successfully argued that the VAT incurred on the purchase of the registration number 'HO 02 PER', for use on the appellant's car, was a deductible input. The restaurant was located in a small village away from a main road, and had been closed for two years prior to its acquisition. Mr Hooper said he had been forced to build up a local clientele, and that the personalised registration had been the most effective way of advertising the restaurant, as people associated seeing the car locally with the restaurant to such an extent that the restaurant had become known by local people as 'Hoopers', rather than by its actual name of the 'Windmill'. The Tribunal accepted that a car registration could form part of obtaining local publicity and concluded that, on the balance of probabilities, the purchase of the car registration was for business purposes, and allowed the appeal.

GOODS USED PARTLY FOR BUSINESS

13.38 If a business buys goods, other than land and property, which will also be used partly for either private or non-business purposes, it can either:

- apportion the input tax at the time of purchase; or

- recover it in full and account for output tax over the next few years based on the non-business use (the *Lennartz* principle—see below). Where use is not on a daily basis, the non-business element is calculated as a ratio of the total use in each VAT period, not of the length of that period. The cost of the goods is based on a maximum five-year life—at least 20% each year. Once the goods have been fully written off, no further output tax is due;

- however, the sale of an asset is fully taxable if the input tax on the purchase was recovered in full, even though part of it was then paid as output tax. In contrast, if it was apportioned, only the business proportion is taxable. In *Armbrecht* (1995 STC 997), the ECJ ruled that output tax was not due on a dwelling on which input tax had not been recovered, when it was sold as part of a business.

The right to choose to recover in full and then to tax non-business use is based on the ECJ decision in *H Lennartz* ([1995] STC 514). The ECJ held that:

'A taxable person who uses goods for the purpose of an economic activity has the right, at the time of the acquisition of those goods, to deduct the input tax in accordance with the rules laid down in Art 17, however small the proportion of use for business purposes'.

Typical assets, for which the choice is available, are computers, motor caravans, yachts and aircraft including the cost of a substantial refurbishment as opposed to ongoing maintenance. See **6.26** for further comment.

In 2009 the ECJ in the case of *Vereniging Noordelijke Land-en Tuinbouw Organisatie v Staatssecretaris van Financien* (C-515/07)—VNLTO—considered whether or not *Lennartz* accounting can be used by a taxpayer who engages in activities that are not within the scope of VAT. As a result of this judgment, it is now clear that EU VAT legislation does not give, and has never given, a right to use *Lennartz* accounting in circumstances such as those of the VNLTO case.

If goods are used for both business and private/non-business purposes, there is a choice about how to treat them for VAT purposes, which must be made at the time they are acquired, namely:

- as a wholly non-business or private asset, in which case the VAT is not deductible;

- as a part business, part non-business asset, in which case the VAT incurred is only deductible to the extent that it relates to the taxable business activities (*VATA 1994, s 24(5)*); or

- as a wholly business asset (the '*Lennartz*' approach) in which case the VAT incurred is treated as input tax and is deductible in full, subject to any partial exemption restriction; however, output tax must then be declared insofar as the goods are used for private/non-business purposes.

Lennartz accounting is not therefore available in cases where goods (including services used to create goods) are used wholly for business purposes.

From 22 January 2010, *Lennartz* accounting is only available where:

(a)   the goods are used in part for making supplies in the course of an economic activity that give a right to input VAT deduction (broadly, taxable supplies, supplies that would be taxable if made in the UK, or certain financial and insurance supplies to non-EC customers); and

(b)   they are also used in part for the private purposes of the trader or his staff, or, exceptionally, for other uses which are wholly outside the purposes of the taxpayer's enterprise or undertaking.

From that date, where *Lennartz* accounting is not available, and goods are used (or to be used) for both economic activities and non-economic business activities, the VAT incurred must be apportioned between these different activities on the basis of use (or intended use). The VAT attributed to the economic activities is input tax and is recoverable to the extent that the economic activities give rise to supplies with a right to input VAT deduction. The VAT attributed to the non-economic business activities is not input tax and cannot be recovered.

Under the above arrangements, VAT on land and property, boats and aircraft was recoverable upfront and in full on both the business and private use of the asset (subject to any partial exemption restriction). VAT was then payable over subsequent years in respect of the private use of the asset. The new legislation, introduced as a result of the new EU VAT law known as the Technical Directive, ensures that VAT recovery is restricted to the business use of the asset concerned, excluding any private use by the taxpayer or the taxpayer's staff. This VAT restriction does not affect owners of other types of asset.

The Technical Directive requires all Member States to introduce an adjustment mechanism to take account of changes in use of these assets when VAT recovery is restricted. The UK has adapted the existing CGS to provide for this adjustment mechanism.

Revenue protection legislation has also been introduced to ensure that existing *Lennartz* accounting users continue to pay the VAT due under the accounting mechanism.

The legislation relating to recovery of VAT on directors' accommodation will then be redundant, as the implementation of the Technical Directive and related European case law will ensure that there is no entitlement to any VAT recovery on the private use of directors' accommodation.

The changes to implement the Technical Directive and repeal the legislation relating to directors' accommodation came into effect on 1 January 2011. The revenue protection legislation is treated as having always had effect.

Expenditure on property and civil engineering works

13.39   HMRC initially sought to exclude property assets from the *Lennartz* mechanism by legal changes made in the 2003 budget. The ECJ case of *Charles* *and Charles-Tijmens* (C-434/03) made it clear that these legal changes were ultra vires, and thus ineffective. *Business Brief 15/05* therefore announced that Lennartz can again be used on property assets, and that retrospective adoptions back to the point the law changed can be made.

Following the subsequent ECJ case of *Seeling v FinanzamtStamberg* (C-269/00), HMRC also accepted that the *Lennartz* mechanism is available for the purchase of land, buildings, and civil engineering works with mixed business and non-business use, where those goods are allocated wholly to the business, even when the property asset is created or enhanced by the receipt of construction services, such as a major refurbishment or extension (see *Business Brief 15/05* and the earlier *Business Brief 22/03*).

HMRC initially considered an adjustment period of 20 years to be reasonable for property, but have since reviewed this and announced in Budget 2007 that from 1 September 2007, the adjustment period will be reduced to 10 years to bring it in line with the Capital Goods Scheme.

The basis of apportioning input tax

13.40   For both land and property and other goods, apportioning the initial purchase cost can only be done on the basis of intended future use.

Ongoing maintenance of all goods, including land and property, must then be made using the CGS.

RECOVERY WHERE ACCOMMODATION IS USED PARTLY FOR BUSINESS

13.41

Focus

When a business is run from home, input tax on part of the running costs of that home is recoverable. In practice, this is likely to be limited to a proportion of the VAT incurred on heat and light, and on the telephone where the business does not have a separate business line. Other costs, such as insurance and water tend not to carry VAT. The exception is when major maintenance or repair work is done on the property.

In *Sir Ian McDonald of Sleat* (MAN/81/150 No 1179), HMRC had accepted that one-third of the tax on the cost of repair work on a Queen Anne house could be recovered. Only the basement was mainly used for business as offices, storerooms, etc—one of three floors, ignoring the attics—though occasional meetings were held in the dining room and business guests stayed in the bedrooms. The gardens were open to the public from March to October but not the house. An agricultural estate of 2,000 acres with holiday cottages and caravans was attached, though not managed by Sir Ian himself. About two-thirds of the input tax in question of £6,376 was incurred on repairing the roof and on architect's fees. This related to the building as a whole and it is not clear from the decision why, on the above facts, the Tribunal increased the recoverable proportion to 60%.

In *Eccles* (EDN/85/71 No 2057), a cottage was renovated to make it suitable for a farm worker to live in, but the farmer's son then occupied it. A farm worker was needed on hand seven days a week, and to be available at short notice. The four farm workers lived from one to nine miles away. The Tribunal was satisfied that, without the son, an agricultural worker would have been installed in the cottage—and would be in a few years time when the son moved into the main farmhouse after Mr Eccles retired. The dominant purpose of the expenditure on the cottage was to provide, in the long term, suitable accommodation to enable seven days a week supervision of the farm activities. Though there was a useful subsidiary purpose in housing John Eccles and his wife, that was less important. Their occupation was unlikely to be indefinite, and 70% of the input tax was recoverable.

In *W A Patterson & Sons Ltd* (LON/84/377 No 1870), 50% was disallowed on the cost to a company of providing a flat above a newsagent in a property it owned. The Tribunal found there was duality of purpose, the director having to live above the shop under the terms of its service contract, but it being convenient for him to do so as he had to start selling newspapers at 5am. Moreover, he had needed to house himself in larger accommodation. Even though the property was owned by the company, the test of user was still appropriate. The occupation was partly for business and partly private.

A business cannot claim for accommodation merely because its staff live elsewhere

13.42   In *Bernheimer Fine Arts Ltd* (LON/86/182 No 2265), a company had two businesses, one in Germany, and one in the UK. The company claimed input tax on the provision of a small bedroom and ancillary shower room above an antique shop for use by its controlling director when visiting its UK premises (the main business being in Germany). The claim was disallowed. The expenditure was on the business premises, and for a pied à terre rather than a proper flat. It was held to be for domestic purposes, since it was the duty of the director to present himself for work.

There is now a specific disallowance in *s 24(3)* for VAT incurred on domestic accommodation for directors, but that does not affect the normal right to recover VAT where there is a mixed business and domestic use of the accommodation, or on hotel and other travel costs when away from the normal place of work, as explained earlier at **13.15**.

13.43 *What can a business recover input tax on?*

HMRC agree that where there is a mixed business and domestic use, a business may agree an apportionment using an objective test of the extent to which the room is put to business use.

INPUT TAX ON CLOTHING

13.43 VAT on work wear provided to staff such as overalls is recoverable, but not VAT on ordinary clothes. The normal rule is that input tax is not recoverable on clothing. One must turn up dressed appropriately for work.

A jazz musician's wig

13.44 See also *JM Collie* (LON/90/1382 No 6144) in which a jazz musician successfully argued that he could recover VAT on the cost of a wig used to promote his image as the 'wild man of jazz'.

An actor's health club membership

13.45 *Anthony Anholt* (LON/89/487 No 4215) recovered tax on a health club membership because he needed to stay fit in order to play a role in *Howard's Way*.

In *John Pearce* (LON/91/1638 No 7860), an actor recovered all the input tax on clothing bought for use in his profession. HMRC allowed full input tax recovery on items identified as stage clothes or uniforms. However, only 50% was allowed for clothing purchased from normal retailers suitable for ordinary use. The Tribunal overturned this. HMRC had accepted that it was bought partly for professional use. However, *Sch 4 para 5(4)* makes the loan of an asset for private use a supply of services by the business. *Sch 6 para 7(b)* makes the value of that supply the full cost of providing it. The rules are normally applied to such items as yachts and aeroplanes, but would also catch clothing. So Mr Pearce may have incurred greater administrative cost in accounting for output tax on his clothes than if he had accepted a disallowance on the purchase.

A key element of the calculation must be whether, when the actor goes to work dressed for the part, his journey to work is treated as business. If his office is at home and the locations are all different, he may have a good case for this. However, HMRC could then require him to keep adequate records of the date and reason for the use of each suit, including the calculations for the entries made in each return. Arguing the *Lennartz* principle is all very well, but HMRC have the means to get their own back!

LEGAL COSTS

13.46   VAT on legal costs is not recoverable if it is for the benefit of, say, a director rather than for the purpose of the business. The following cases illustrate the problem of establishing business purpose.

In *Wallman Foods Ltd* (MAN/83/41 No 1411), a Tribunal held that tax was not recoverable by the company on solicitor's fees for defending its managing director against a charge of handling stolen goods, which were sold in its supermarket. It was for the benefit of the company that expenditure be incurred in an attempt to prevent its managing director being imprisoned and thus unable to operate its business. However the Tribunal drew a distinction between expenditure for the benefit of a taxable person and that incurred for the purpose of a business actually carried on by him. The charge was against Mr Wallman personally, and there was no liability on the company. The invoice was addressed to him and it was clear that the services were supplied to him, not to the company. There was insufficient nexus between the payment of his costs and the company's business of retailing groceries.

In *Britwood Toys Ltd* (LON/86/280 No 2263), tax on the cost to the managing director of a successful defence against a charge of corruption in offering inducements to a civil servant was similarly held to be non-recoverable. Even though the company had been severely prejudiced by the cancellation by the Home Office of a contract, which the managing director hoped to have restored, and even though the judge had decided there was no case to answer, the Tribunal found that the expenditure was personal, not for the business of the company.

In *Rosner* ([1994] STC 228), the High Court held that there must be a clear nexus between the expenditure and the business. Although there was a connection between the school run by Mr Rosner and the criminal proceedings re immigration offences, in that the offences related to potential students, it did not relate to the carrying on of the business.

However, in *SR Brooks* (LON/94/412 No 12754), *Rosner* was distinguished. The trader succeeded in his claim for tax on the cost of defending himself against a charge of conspiracy (knowingly to acquire gold on which duty had not been paid). The nexus with the business existed here because every step in the alleged offence was one taken in the normal course of dealing in gold.

Libel actions

13.47   In *WG Stern* (LON/84/416 No 1970), the cost to a consultant of obtaining his *discharge from bankruptcy* was held to be mainly personal. The Tribunal accepted that it would also assist his business by re-establishing his integrity, but had no evidence on which to base an apportionment. Fees re *a libel action* were a business expense. The action arose out of Stern's appointment as a consultant to the administrator dealing with the disposal of Stern Group properties and, without the action, his activities as a consultant would have been prejudiced. The cost of attending a Parliamentary Committee of Enquiry was not for his business. Although he was vindicated, this was not for the purpose of his consultancy business, the reasoning being as in the *Wallman* case noted above.

Another libel action case was *Orrmac* (No 49) Ltd (EDN/90/185 No 6537). The legal costs were held to be 25% for the company's business, 75% to protect the personal reputations of two directors.

The defence of its staff by a company can be a business expense

13.48   In *P&O European Ferries (Dover) Ltd* (LON/91/2146 & 2532 No 7846), input tax on costs of about £3.5m spent defending seven individuals against charges of manslaughter after the *Herald of Free Enterprise* disaster was held to be recoverable. P&O instructed the solicitors acting for the individuals because:

- it was advised that it could face a charge of 'corporate manslaughter' if two or more of its employees were found guilty of gross negligence;

- if P&O itself had been prosecuted and convicted, the limitations of its insurance liability in relation to cargo claims might have been no longer available to it and it might therefore have borne the excess of loss liability;

- it was essential for P&O to defend a name under which many group businesses operated.

P&O's instructions to the seven firms of solicitors required them to work with P&O in planning the defence, and P&O approved both the choice of counsel and their remuneration. HMRC argued that the supplies of legal services had been to the individual defendants who had instructed them. However, the Tribunal found the evidence to show that P&O was the client of each solicitor:

- it had instructed that solicitor and agreed to pay him;

- the solicitor would have had no right to recover his fees from the employee, had the company refused to pay.

Of course, the employee was also a client of the solicitor, but that did not change the fact that the company was a client as principal in relation to each. The services were therefore provided to the company, notwithstanding that the individual employee also received the benefit of the services. The Tribunal also rejected HMRCs' argument that the expenditure was only for P&O's benefit, not for the purposes of its business. The size of the business and the serious consequences for it of conviction of those individuals were so great, that the financing of the costs of their defence could be seen as serving the purposes of the business, despite a substantial benefit being conferred on each of the seven men.

See **6.27** for comment on a possible output tax liability because of a subsequent change in the law.

VAT on defence of an employee under a motor insurance policy

13.49   In *Jeancharm Ltd t/a Beaver International* (MAN/2004/95 No 18835; [2005] STC 918), the High Court overturned the Tribunal's decision concerning the VAT on the legal costs of defending an employee against a dangerous driving charge. The supply was not to the company, even though it had paid the insurance premium covering both business and the private mileage under which the claim for legal support by the insurer was made. It did not instruct the lawyers and it did not pay them, let alone receive anything in return.

That resolved the matter but, in addition, the Tribunal had been wrong in stating that Jeancharm had claimed indemnity under the policy for its employee. The insurer was committed to indemnify the employee anyway.

Of course, it is unusual that an employee's personal liability is covered by a business insurance policy. The position was not the same as that in *P&O European Ferries*, or in any of the other legal action cases discussed above.

VAT on legal representation for pension fund beneficiaries

13.50   In a case similar in some ways to that of *P&O*, the *Plessey Co Ltd* (LON/94/254 No 12814) failed to recover VAT on the cost of legal representation for 14 representative pension fund beneficiaries. The company wanted to wind up three pension funds, but the trustees insisted on Court approval. This could not be had without the Court being advised as to the position of the beneficiaries who were not prepared to join the proceedings unless their costs were met. The input tax was disallowed because the advice was given to the beneficiaries, who were the clients, not to the trustees, let alone to the company, which sought the reclaim. The lawyers' invoices were addressed to the beneficiaries. Even though the Tribunal was satisfied that the trustees had to meet the cost and that the services were used for the purposes of the company's business, it found that they had not been supplied to the company, but to the beneficiaries. It distinguished *P&O* on the grounds that P&O had been the client of the solicitors whose services were supplied to both the employees and to P&O. The distinction may mean that the *Redrow* case, discussed near the start of this chapter, would not help in this kind of situation.

Legal action by a pension fund

13.51   However, *Ultimate Advisory Services Ltd* (MAN/95/2550 No 17610) was held to be entitled to recover VAT on the cost of defending a claim against the trustees of the company's pension scheme, despite the controlling director being the only member. The company had an obligation under the trust deed to pay the costs of the administration and management, and was, therefore, already liable for such fees before it instructed the solicitors. Although this was a one-person scheme, the provision by an employer of a pension scheme could properly be regarded as having been done in the course of the employer's business. The Tribunal saw the situation as similar to that in *Redrow*.

VAT ON INSURANCE CLAIMS

13.52   An insurer has to compensate the insured for the value of a loss. If the insured is a business, the loss does not include VAT to the extent that the business can recover it. For most business risks, the only question is whether the insured is partly exempt.

Unfortunately for the supplier of the goods or services, if the insured business fails to pay the VAT, a bad debt relief claim is only for the VAT fraction of the outstanding sum. See Chapter 16, *Bad Debt Relief.*

IS INPUT TAX RECOVERABLE ON EXPENSES OF STAFF?

13.53

Focus

For moves due to employment, tax is normally recoverable on the charges by the removal firm, and on fees of estate agents and solicitors for the sale and purchase of houses, even though supplied to the employee, not to the company.

It would be wise, however, to instruct them to invoice the business direct, for reasons explained above concerning travel expenses.

Similarly, a business could probably recover input tax on any costs incurred by the employee in looking after an empty house pending sale or on short-term hotel expenses in the new location. Again, it is best to have the invoices in the name of the business.

In *SSL Ltd* (LON/87/254 No 2478), HMRCs' argument that the supply was to the controlling directors personally, and that there was no contract committing the company to pay the cost, was rejected. The Tribunal did hesitate for lack of evidence, so issue written instructions to estate agents and lawyers, and get invoices in the name of the business.

VAT is not recoverable on any soft furnishings allowance—VAT was not recoverable when the furnishings for the previous house were bought by the employee.

In V1-13 5.24.2 of HMRC's *Internal Guidance*—published in the *Library* section on their website—under the heading *Relocation expenses* it states.

'If however the expenditure is not linked specifically to the relocation but forms part of the ongoing living expenses at the new property then it is not input tax. Thus the provision of new bespoke curtains or carpets for a new house is acceptable as it is a normal expense of moving house. Yet the provision of a new stereo system would not be acceptable as it is an expenditure unrelated to the relocation.'

Presumably, 'bespoke' means that the curtains or the carpet are measured to fit the room where they are installed, not just bought off-the-shelf. There are additional comments in V1-13 23.5.1 under the heading *Removal expenses*. That duplicates the comment about fees and furniture removal costs. It also says that services in plumbing in a washing machine or altering curtains can be accepted.

DISTINGUISH BETWEEN A BUSINESS AND THE OWNERSHIP OF IT

13.54   In *Shaw Lane Estates* (MAN/88/680 No 4420), tax was denied on the grounds that the legal action on which it was incurred, actually concerned the ownership of the business rather than that business itself.

A similar principle disallows input tax incurred by individuals on costs incurred in raising finance to put into a business. In *Rushgreen Builders Ltd* (LON/87/116 No 2470), a house was sold to raise money, not because of a move to another area. The fees were held not to have been incurred for the purpose of the business. The supply of the services was to the directors personally to enable them to invest money, even though the invoice was to the company.

In *Sally McLeod Associates* (LON/94/1080 No 12886), the VAT was incurred in defending an action by the bank to repossess the house, which was used partly as the appellant's home, and partly for her business. That 25% of VAT on repairs had been allowed for the business use element did not impress the Tribunal; nor did the claim that, for unspecified reasons, the business would not have been able to continue if the house had been lost.

MOBILE TELEPHONES

13.55 In *Business Brief 14/99* dated 2/7/99, HMRC said that, if a mobile phone is provided to an employee for business use, all input VAT on the purchase cost and on charges is recoverable *provided that they do not include any element for calls*:

- if a business has clear rules prohibiting private use, all input tax on calls is recoverable even if, in practice, the business tolerates a few private calls;

- output tax is due on any charges for private calls, all input tax being recoverable;

- if a business allows private calls, you must disallow the corresponding input tax on calls. HMRC say it is 'inappropriate' to account for output tax instead. A ratio based on a sample of bills taken over a reasonable period of time is acceptable;

- if the phone is bundled with some call time, the business must apportion the full charge.

The potential pitfall is growing

13.56 A specialist consultant said at a conference in June 2005 that his firm was finding 40-50% of the usage of mobiles provided to staff by its clients to be private—including 5% at premium rates! Some mobiles in use were held by former employees!

Since mobile phone companies are trying to expand the capability of their phones in order to generate more income, the risk of private use costing substantial sums is growing. It is not just downloading a fancy ringtone— for which one could possibly argue a business purpose as a means of identification—or music/video, which is unlikely to be for business use. One can pay for parking, CDs and cans of Cola with text messages, which also could be either business or private!

Given the temptation to staff, it seems sensible to impose an active control system to identify the private use. If that is not practical, the next best thing would seem to be a requirement for staff to identify the business calls on the invoices. Merely guessing the percentage, or relying on the staff to own up to the private ones, is likely to result eventually in a detailed investigation by HMRC with an assessment, a penalty and interest!

INPUT TAX RECOVERY AND FRAUDULENT TRANSACTION CHAINS

13.57 Two associated companies, *Calltell Telecom Ltd and Opto Telelinks (Europe) Ltd* (VTD 20,266) appealed against HMRC's refusal to repay two substantial input tax claims (totalling more than £18 million) on the grounds that the appellants were aware that VAT fraud was taking place elsewhere in the supply chain.

Following the ECJ cases of *Bond House* and *Optigen*, HMRC were forced to repay large quantities of input tax where it had previously refused repayments to innocent taxpayers because of a fraudulent link elsewhere in the supply chain.

The ECJ concluded that the right of a taxable person to deduct input tax cannot be affected by the existence of a prior or subsequent fraudulent transaction in the chain of supply, without that taxable person knowing or having any means of knowing that to be the case.

In order to establish both the existence of fraud and the taxpayer's knowledge of it, the Tribunal considered various transactions undertaken by the appellant in great detail. The detailed reasoning is specific to this case, so there is no need for a summary of the Tribunal's detailed conclusions here.

In this particular case, HMRC were ultimately successful in arguing that the appellants knew the goods were involved in fraud elsewhere in the supply chain. Therefore, the Tribunal supported HMRC's decision to withhold the business's repayment claims.

This case is significant in that it is the first time that the UK courts have accepted HMRC had proven that a taxpayer (who was not a direct participant in the fraud) had knowledge that fraud was occurring elsewhere in the supply chain. Although the case is fact-specific, the decision gives some useful hints as to what factors persuaded the Tribunal that the case for 'knowledge' had been proven.

In *Ross Pharmacy Ltd v Revenue and Customs Comrs* (VTD 20,634), the taxpayer appealed against HMRC's refusal to repay input tax on an inward supply of mobile phones to the appellant from a UK company. The appellant supplied the purchased mobile phones to a Dutch company (a zero-rated supply). This was an indirect dispatch, and the appellant did not inspect the goods. Instead they were collected from the UK company by a freight forwarder and shipped. HMRC initially denied the claim because the disputed supply formed part of a chain of supplies involving fraud, though the appellant was an innocent party. The phones sent to Holland were not the phones the appellant had bought and paid for, but were old and broken stock.

Following the ECJ *Optigen* decision, the input tax claim was still denied, but for an additional reason, which was that when the goods were inspected in Holland, the consignment consisted of old mobile phones which did not correspond with the description of the new mobile phones in the appellant's invoice to the Dutch company. Consequently, HMRC argued that it could not claim the input tax because it had not made an onward taxable supply of the phones.

The dispute involved two issues: one factual and one legal. The factual issue was whether the consignment of old phones had been sent in error, and that the correct consignment of new phones was actually subsequently delivered to Holland. HMRC contended that the appellant's claim for input tax principally depended on whether the onward supply to the Dutch company actually took place, relying on the wording of *s 26* of *VATA 1994*, which essentially restricts an input tax claim to so much of the input tax that was attributable to *'taxable supplies made or to be made by it in the course or the furtherance of its business'*.

The second issue was the appellant's legal entitlement to recover the input tax arising from the inward supply of new mobile phones from the UK company, irrespective of whether or not the outward supply to the Dutch company actually took place. The appellant and HMRC had opposing views on the legal requirements for recovering input tax. The appellant said its right to input tax derived from the fact that the purchase was for its taxable business. HMRC argued that as the appellant was not an intending trader, it could only claim the VAT if it made a taxable supply of the phones it had bought.

The Tribunal found that the appellant intended to make an onward supply but was prevented from doing so because of fraud committed by others. Therefore it found that the appellant satisfied *s 26* of *VATA 1994*.

HMRC argued the *Teleos* principle, which dealt with the requirements of *Art 28a* of the *Sixth Directive* for exempting intra-EC supplies from VAT, but could not apply it as they had not taken any formal steps to challenge the zero-rated status of the appellant's supply to the Dutch company. The Tribunal recognised that HMRC could have challenged the zero-rating as the phones appeared never to have left the UK, meaning conditions for zero-rating set out in *Teleos* were not met.

HMRC conceded that the appellant was an honest and an unwitting party to fraud. The appellant also had in place a standard procedure for conducting due diligence on prospective customers and suppliers. HMRC proposed that the appellant was required to take every reasonable measure to ensure that its onward supply of the mobile phones was actually made, based on the wording of para 65 in *Teleos*. However, the Tribunal did not agree with this interpretation, stating that the object of reasonable steps in para 65 of *Teleos* was the avoidance of participation in tax evasion, and not to ensure that the onward supply was actually made.

Ultimately, the Tribunal applied the principles in *Optigen,* satisfied that the input tax on the inward supply was attributable to a taxable supply. In *Optigen* the ECJ decided that

'the right to deduct input VAT…could not be affected by the fact that in the chain of supply of which those transactions formed part of another prior or subsequent transaction was vitiated by VAT fraud, without that taxable person knowing or having any means of knowing'.

The taxpayer's appeal was thus allowed.

In the joined cases of *Livewire Telecom Ltd* and *Olympia Technology Ltd* ([2009] EWHC 15 (Ch)), the High Court examined the application of the 'knowledge test'. Both Appellants were the ultimate exporters, and HMRC had refused to repay input tax on the exported goods on the basis that the taxpayers *'knew'*, or *'should have known'*, about fraud elsewhere in the supply chain. At the VAT Tribunal, where both cases were heard by the same Chairman, the taxpayers' appeals were allowed, prompting HMRC to appeal to the High Court.

The High Court found that the Tribunal had applied too high a legal test when considering whether the taxpayers 'knew' or 'should have known/ought to have known' about the fraud, by requiring HMRC to show that the taxable person must know or ought to have known of both the missing trader's fraud and the contra trader's involvement in that fraud. The court added that the misstatement had no impact on the case. With regard to the 'should have known' test, the Court reached a different conclusion in each case. In *Livewire*, the court concluded that HMRC had concentrated too narrowly on the missing traders in the fraudulent chain, and that HMRC were unable to suggest any other due diligence precautions that Livewire could have taken. Even perfect due diligence would not have indicated the fraud by the missing traders in the fraudulent chain. As a consequence of this, HMRC's appeal in respect of *Livewire* was dismissed. In *Olympia*, however, the court concluded that the Tribunal adopted a test requiring fewer precautions and a lower level of understanding than would have been required of a director of ordinary competence. Consequently, HMRC's appeal in *Olympia* was allowed in respect of the straight MTIC chains, and the case was remitted to the Tribunal to determine what Olympia should have known, applying the correct legal test. It found partly in favour of the appellant in that it should only have known in some, not all, of the cases.

INPUT TAX RECOVERY ON COMPANY PENSION FUNDS

13.58   HMRC issued *Revenue & Customs Brief 06/14* and *Revenue & Customs Brief 43/14* explaining their position following the decision of the ECJ in *Fiscale eenheid PPG Holdings BV* (C-26/12) and HMRC's revised guidance on the VAT recovery on company pension funds.

HMRC's old policy was to distinguish between costs incurred in relation to the setting up and day-to-day administration of occupational pension funds and the management of the investment activities of the fund.

HMRC allowed employers to reclaim the VAT on the general management of an occupational pension scheme on the basis that these costs are overheads of the employer and thus have a direct and immediate link to their business activities. However, they considered the management of the investment activities to be costs of the pension fund itself and not recoverable by the employer.

Where a single invoice was received, covering both the administration of the pension fund and the management of the investments in the fund, HMRC allowed the employer to claim 30% of the VAT as relating to the general management of the scheme and the pension fund (if VAT registered) to claim 70% as relating to the investment management activities.

As a result of the ECJ decision in *Fiscale eenheid,* HMRC have changed their policy on the recovery of input tax in relation to the management of pension funds so that employers may be able to claim more input tax in relation to pension funds based on the actual ratio of the general management of the scheme to the total charge.

However, HMRC will not allow VAT recovery where supplies were not made to the employer or where the supply is limited to investment management services only.

Where a business has applied the 70/30% split, a claim for a refund of input tax would entail a recalculation of the amounts of input tax proper to the employer and the fund respectively. Claims can be made for underclaimed input tax over the past four years. Any claim made must set out the basis of the error, the amount being claimed and show how that amount has been calculated.

INPUT TAX RECOVERY ON NON-BUSINESS ACTIVITIES

13.59   The 2015 Budget extended the rights of certain organisations to recover VAT on non-business activities by adding new *ss 33C and 33D* to the *Value Added Tax Act 1994.*

These changes allow input tax recovery on costs relating to non-business activities to the following organisations:

- palliative care charities (hospices);

- air ambulance charities

- search and rescue charities; and

- medical courier charities.

A new *VATA 1994, s 33E* will provide refunds to named non-departmental public bodies, and similar public bodies, of the VAT incurred as a part of shared services arrangements used to support their non-business activities.

The London Legacy Development Corporation was added to the specified organisation to which *VATA 1994, s 33* applies

Strategic highway companies appointed under *s 1 of the Infrastructure Act 2015* were added to the list in *VATA 1994, s 41(7)*, allowing VAT recovery by government departments and executive agencies.

The provision of care by these charities is generally not a business activity for VAT purposes where the cost is met from voluntary donations and public funding, rather than from fees charged. There is therefore no provision under normal VAT rules for these charities and specified bodies to recover the VAT paid on purchases made to support their non-business activities. The VAT charged on purchases for the purpose of their non-business activities is a cost to them and reduces their ability to provide their services.Details for how the scheme will work are contained in a new VAT Notice 1001: VAT refund scheme for certain charities.

The refund scheme will have its biggest impact on the hospice sector and will take a similar form to that introduced in 2011 for academy schools and will allow charitable hospices to reclaim VAT which relates to their non-business provision of palliative care, putting them on the same footing as NHS Trusts. Hospices which are registered for VAT will be able to reclaim it through their VAT returns in the normal way, while non-VAT registered hospices will need to make separate claims using a Form VAT126.

Hospices will need to consider a number of things in order to ensure that they make the most of the changes and fully benefit from the increased VAT recovery.Areas that they will need to consider include:

- ensuring that accounting systems identify VAT incurred on costs relating to palliative care;

- considering whether a proportion of VAT on overhead costs can also be claimed;

- reviewing the effect on existing partial exemption or business/non business recovery methods; and

- reviewing the effect on VAT recovery for capital projects.

INPUT TAX RECOVERY BY HOLDING COMPANIES

13.60 HMRC have published updated guidance on recovery of VAT by holding companies. The update had been expected to take the form of a Brief which would be published on gov.uk but instead HMRC have updated the VAT manuals (also on gov.uk) instead.

Following the ECJ decision in the joint cases *Larentia + Minerva,* HMRC has been reviewing their policy in respect of holding companies and deduction of VAT incurred on acquisition costs.

The ECJ held that VAT incurred by a holding company on the costs of acquiring shareholdings in subsidiaries to which it also intended to provide taxable management services, must be regarded as part of a holding company's general overhead expenditure and thus as deductible (subject to any partial exemption restriction).

Prior to this case HMRC's previous policy had been that VAT incurred on the acquisition costs of shares by a holding company was only deductible where it was directly attributable to the provision of taxable services. They also considered that VAT on costs incurred by holding companies was only recoverable if the intention was to recoup the expenditure by providing taxable services to subsidiaries within a 'reasonable' period of time.

The guidance covers:

- when a shareholding is regarded as being used as part of an economic activity;

- whether a holding company is the recipient of a supply;

- whether a holding company is undertaking economic activity for VAT purposes;

- whether a shareholding is acquired as a direct, continuous and necessary extension of a taxable economic activity of the holding company;

- whether there is an intention to make taxable supplies;

- contingent consideration for management services;

- the effects of a holding company joining a VAT group;

- stewardship costs; and

- mixed economic and non-economic activities.

Chapter 14

What is a valid tax invoice?

SIGNPOSTS

- A business should hold a valid tax invoice in order to support its claim for input tax. A tax invoice must contain certain information. You can use a less detailed tax invoice for purchases under £250 (see **14.2–14.7** and **14.9**).

- Businesses can issue electronic invoices, self bill and issue authenticated receipts in lieu of a tax invoice (see **14.12–14.14**).

14.1   This chapter explains the information which must be shown on a tax invoice, together with various other points about them. In theory, tax invoices, which are mostly produced by computer nowadays, should all comply with the law, and should be easily recognisable. In practice, the infinite variety of layout on invoices complicates matters.

If a business receives a substantial volume of invoices, it is bound to be at risk for amounts big enough to lead to possible penalties. The sheer volume of transactions means there is a risk of documents slipping through, which are not proper tax invoices. To reduce the risk to a minimum, both managers approving invoices and clerks processing them through the accounting system, must understand the importance of a tax invoice, and the details which it must contain. That requires training, which is not easy to carry out systematically, especially if there is a turnover of staff.

DOES A BUSINESS HAVE TO WORRY ABOUT ITS PURCHASE INVOICES?

14.2   In short, yes! If staff are not trained in what information is required on a VAT invoice, and there is not a sufficiently robust system for checking for the key information, a business may be at risk; It is inevitable that VAT will be recovered on some documents which do not qualify.

Purchase records should be checked for:

- supplier statements which sometimes show VAT;

- delivery notes, which are sometimes carbon copies of the invoice and could easily therefore show the VAT number if not the actual sum of VAT;

- requests for payment which often contain either the VAT number or the amount of VAT;

- pro forma invoices which may look much the same as an ordinary invoice

HMRC will certainly disallow input tax claimed on the basis of such documents, even if they take a more relaxed view on those which fail to state, for example, the type of sale, ie whether it is a sale, a lease, on hire-purchase, or whatever.

This does not mean that a business has to check every input invoice for every detail. However, staff do need to confirm that:

- the document is a tax invoice; and

- the VAT is being recovered in the correct period.

A business cannot recover VAT on a VAT return for the period ended 30 April if the invoice is dated 1 May!

INCORRECT VAT SHOWN ON INVOICE

14.3   If the amount of VAT on a VAT invoice issued is higher than the amount properly due, the business must account for the higher amount in its records, unless it corrects the error with its customer by issuing a credit note.

If the amount of VAT on a VAT invoice issued is lower than the amount properly due, then it must account for the correct amount of VAT due whether or not it corrects the error with its customer (for example, by issuing a supplementary invoice for the amount undercharged). Where the amount of VAT on an invoice is too low, the purchaser can only recover the amount shown and not the actual amount due.

INFORMATION REQUIRED ON A VAT INVOICE

14.4

Focus

Prior to 1 October 2007, a VAT invoice was required by *reg 14* to show the information set out in the bullet points below. After that date, additional requirements were added by VAT Info Sheet 10/07 which are outlined at **14.5**.

- an identifying number;

- the time of the supply;

- the date of the issue of the document;

- name, address and registration number of the supplier;

- the name and address of the person to whom the goods or services are supplied;

- a description sufficient to identify the goods or services supplied;

- for each description, the quantity of the goods or the extent of the services, the unit price, the rate of VAT and amount payable, excluding VAT, expressed in any currency. The unit price for services can be an hourly rate or a standard price. If the supply cannot be analysed, the total price is the unit rate. HMRC accept that the unit price need not be shown at all if it is not normally stated in a particular business sector and it is not required by the customer (Notice 700, para 16.3.2 as updated February 2004);

- the gross total amount payable, excluding VAT, expressed in any currency;

- the rate of any cash discount offered;

- the total amount of VAT chargeable, expressed in sterling (as a note if the invoice is in a foreign currency).

In theory, the rules are strict. If an invoice does not contain one or more of the above pieces of information, it does not qualify as the basis for recovering input tax. This was demonstrated in *ABB Power Ltd* (MAN/91/201 No 9373), where the Tribunal held that a document was not a tax invoice because it did not show the:

- type of supply—sale, hire-purchase, rental, etc (no longer required);

- correct tax point;

- rate of tax applicable.

The *ABB* argument was, in fact, about HMRC's right to demand output tax on a document issued by ABB.

In practice, if a document is obviously intended to be a VAT invoice, HMRC are unlikely to use minor deficiencies in it as a reason for disallowing input tax unless they have been unable to collect the output tax. However, they do insist on the key details, such as the name, address, and VAT number of the supplier, enough information about the supply to identify it as something bought for the purposes of the business, and the amount of VAT.

HMRC issued *Revenue & Customs Brief 36/07* on 11 April 2007 entitled 'VAT input tax deduction without a valid VAT invoice: Revised statement of practice'.

The statement of practice is an update of an earlier July 2003 version and is very much aimed towards the anti-Missing Trader Intra-Community Fraud (MTIC) fraud effort, as it specifically addresses supplies of computers, telephones and other related equipment, as well as alcohol and oils. Although the new version is phrased in helpful tones, which indicates a willingness on the part of HMRC to exercise their discretion to allow deduction if appropriate checks on the supplier have been made, it is more likely to be a reiteration of HMRC's position that, where involvement in a chain of supplies to facilitate MTIC fraud is suspected, they will look to challenge input tax deductions on the grounds that the documentation is invalid (to run alongside 'should have known' disallowance based on the *Kittel v Belgium State* (ECJ Case C-439, June 2006).

The timing of the issue of this Brief suggests that the reason for its issue may have been a recent Tribunal decision in *Pexum Ltd v Comm of HMRC* (No 20083), for a discussion of this case see **13.8**.

ADDITIONAL INVOICING REQUIREMENTS FROM 1 OCTOBER 2007

14.5   In March 2007, HMRC issued a consultation paper (Technical Paper (01) 07) through the Joint VAT Consultative Committee (JVCC) concerning the need for the UK to introduce additional invoice requirements in order to properly implement the EC Invoicing Directive. These additional requirements came into force on 1 October 2007 by amendment of the *VAT Regulations 1995 (SI 1995/2518)*.

In summary, the European Commission has identified three areas of weakness in UK law (as revised by the Invoicing Directive). These are as follows:

- the way in which individual invoices are numbered;

- the way reference is made to the VAT margin schemes when the invoice involves a supply subject to the second-hand or tour operators schemes; and

- the need for cross-border invoices to refer to the reason for any VAT exemption or reverse charge.

The changes can be summarised as follows:

'1. The number on the invoice

Regulation 14(1)(a) has been amended to include a requirement for an invoice to bear a sequential number based on one or more series which uniquely identify the document.

2. Reference to the margin schemes

Regulation 14 has been changed to add a requirement that invoices under the special arrangements for second hand goods, works of art and collectors items must include a reference to the nature of the treatment, which accords with the Directive. A revised version of Notice 731 will suggest alternative legends which may be adopted.

3. Reference to the Tour Operators' Margin Scheme (TOMS)

Regulation 14 has been changed to add a requirement that invoices under TOMS must include a reference to the nature of the treatment, which accords with the Directive.

4. Reference to the reverse charge or exemption (including zero rate despatches to other member states)

Regulation 14 has been changed to add a requirement that zero rate despatches and exempt or reverse charge invoices require a reference to the grounds for the treatment when the supply is to a business customer based in another member state. Regulation 14(5) has been clarified to make it clear that the requirement also applies to UK supplies where the customer accounts for the VAT, such as the gold scheme (VATA94 S55) or any reverse charge requirement introduced under VATA S55A.

5. References required

The regulations have been changed to make it clear that an invoice under those procedures must conform with the requirements of Article 226(11) and that the choice of legend is a matter for individual businesses to decide.'

The following are some of the example statements included in VAT Info Sheet 10/07 that HMRC say will be acceptable invoice narratives:

'This is a second-hand margin scheme supply' (margin scheme)

'This is a tour operators' margin scheme supply' (TOMS)

'This is an exempt supply' (intra-EU services)

'This supply is subject to the reverse charge' (intra-EU services)

'Zero rated intra-EC supply' (intra-EU goods)

Although HMRC has said that during the first year of the new rules, penalties for non-compliance would only be issued in exceptional cases. Now that this period of grace has ended it would be unwise for businesses to rely on this statement. VAT registered businesses should now ensure they meet the 1 October 2007 requirements.

From 1 January 2013, Member States introduced further changes to the time limit for the issue of VAT invoices for EU cross-border supplies. The change being introduced will align the rules on the time limits for issuing a VAT invoice, requiring the invoice to be issued by the fifteenth day of the month following that in which the goods are removed or the services performed. The changes will, in some cases, reduce the timescale for UK businesses to issue a VAT invoice. This potentially reduces the invoicing timescale, but will only impact supplies made after the midpoint of the month.

INVOICING IN A FOREIGN CURRENCY

14.6 A business can invoice in any currency it wishes, but the document must also state the sterling equivalent for the VAT charged so as to ensure that a UK customer reclaims the same sum that you account for as output tax.

Foreign currency conversions

14.7 A business can convert foreign currency at either:

- the market selling rate in the UK at the time of the acquisition. The rates published in national newspapers are acceptable; or

- the period rate of exchange published by HMRC and available from the National Advisory Service (see *Contacting HMRC* at the start of the book, page lxvii); or

- at a rate agreed with your local VAT office. See para 5.5 of Notice 725 *The Single Market* for more details.

A business can use a mix of the first two options for different kinds of transactions, provided it notes in its records which ones are used. If a business then wishes to change this mix, it must ask HMRC.

CREDIT NOTES TO CUSTOMERS IN OTHER MEMBER STATES

14.8 Credit notes to customers in other Member States must show the same details as are required on a VAT invoice. However, HMRC have not changed the existing rules for credit notes issued to UK customers.

LESS DETAILED INVOICES

14.9 Retailers are allowed to issue less detailed invoices up to £250 (£100 up to 1/1/04) (*reg 16*). Although certain information such as the name of the customer and the amount of VAT is not required, these still have to show key details such as the name and address of the supplier, the nature of the goods supplied, and the rate of VAT applicable. From 1 January 2013, this was extended to all VAT-registered businesses not just retailers.

Petrol filling station receipts are the most common example of a less detailed invoice which is used for VAT recovery. Credit card slips do not usually contain the right details, although the slips produced by modern tills often do.

No invoice is required for (Notice 700 (April 2002), para 19.7.5):

- coin-operated telephone;

- coin-operated machines, for example, vending machines;

- car park charges—except on-street meters;

- toll charges;

- petrol element of mileage allowances to staff. Notice 700/64/96 (January 2002), para 8.7 says nothing about invoices but, presumably, the statement in the 1996 version remains valid.

For the first four, the value limit is £25, and the supplier must be VAT-registered.

These are concessions by HMRC. No excuses are accepted in other cases because of the problem of whether the supplier is registered. That apart, the rule is no tax invoice, no VAT recovery!

MUST THE TAX INVOICE BE IN THE BUSINESS'S NAME?

14.10 A tax invoice is supposed to show the person to whom the goods or services are supplied. So, if an invoice is not in the name of the business, it usually means that the supply was not made to it. In principle, therefore, it should not recover VAT on invoices in the name of third parties. HMRC will sometimes allow this in circumstances in which they are sure that there was a supply made to the person claiming the input VAT, and that the same input VAT has not already been claimed by the party to which the invoice was addressed.

However, it is far better to obtain an invoice in the right name in the first place. The one common exception to that requirement is expenses incurred by employees. Whilst it is always a good idea to obtain an invoice addressed to the employer if possible for, say, hotel accommodation, HMRC do not insist on this. Naturally, the travel must be on business.

When part of an expense, such as business calls on a private telephone bill, is paid by an employer, HMRC will allow recovery of the appropriate proportion of VAT, provided, of course, that it obtains a copy of the bill in question.

WHAT IF THE BUSINESS FAILS TO GET A TAX INVOICE?

14.11 HMRC are likely to disallow input tax for which a VAT invoice is missing. Usually, the solution is to ask the supplier for one (or for a copy if the original has been lost), and, for routine transactions, HMRC are likely to insist on this.

For further comment, see **13.8**.

The extent to which a business is at risk for failure to obtain tax invoices must depend upon how many suppliers it has, whether it deals with relatively few of them frequently or infrequently, or deals with a large number of different ones etc.

HMRC have power to allow electronic invoicing, which assists those suppliers whose systems are closely integrated with those of customers. The rules have been around since long before the Internet, although no doubt this is encouraging the transmission of documentation electronically. If a business just uses the Internet instead of the post, and prints the invoices from its suppliers off its computer, HMRC may, in theory, have little concern. However, it might be wise to discuss the matter with them if only because of the risk that two copies of the document might be printed, without this being apparent. See the comments below from the supplier's point of view.

ISSUING TAX INVOICES ELECTRONICALLY

14.12   HMRC allow unsigned fax or e-mail invoices.

For real electronic invoicing up to 31 December 2012, see the criteria required by HMRC in Notice 700/63 (June 2007) *Electronic invoicing*. If a business starts to invoice electronically, it must tell HMRC within 30 days.

Systems for invoicing with a computer range from merely producing the document, which is sent by post, to a full-blown electronic data interchange system, known as EDI. Prior to 31 December 2012 a business must get approval from HMRC before installing an EDI system. It is wise in any case to consult them when developing a new computer system of any kind, because they may have useful comments to make about its design, quite apart from the risk that a business may fail to correctly address a VAT issue.

One point to consider is the control on duplicate invoices. Cheap modern printers mean that it is possible to print off a copy of an invoice without there being any indication that it is a copy. When planning a computer specification, consider a requirement that the second or subsequent copies of a document are overprinted stating that they are a copy with the date of printing.

Existing EU rules for electronic invoicing allow Member States to impose additional conditions on taxpayers wanting to use electronic invoicing as above. This includes the requirement to use technologies such as electronic data signatures and electronic data interchange.

Under new simplified rules, Member States can no longer impose conditions on the use of electronic invoices. From 1 January 2013, it is up to an individual business to determine the method used. The only condition is that the customer agrees to the use of electronic invoicing.

As such paper and electronic invoices are now treated equally. It is hoped more businesses will use electronic invoices and benefit from reduced costs.

SELF-BILLING

14.13   Since 1 January 2004, there has been no requirement to seek the Commissioners' prior approval to operate self-billing. Any business can use self-billing provided the arrangements meet the legal conditions laid down in *VAT Reg 13(3)* of *SI 1995/2518,* and in Public Notice 700/62 (December 2003) *Self Billing.*

Self-Billing is an agreement between businesses. Where a business does not wish to use the provision, it should not be forced into it by a potential or actual trading partner. However, commercial pressures may influence this decision.

The advantages of self-billing are:

- accounting staff will be working with uniform purchase documentation; and

- it may make invoicing easier if the customer (rather than the supplier) determine the value of purchases after the goods have been delivered or the services supplied.

Before a business begins self-billing, it should consider the following points:

- It can only recover the VAT shown on self-billed invoices if it meets the conditions explained in Notice 700/62.

- It may find it difficult to set up self-billing arrangements with its suppliers, or burdensome to maintain them.

- It will be responsible for ensuring that the self-billed invoices it raises carry the correct VAT liability for the goods or services supplied to it.

- If it is raising electronic self-billed invoices to large numbers of suppliers, it will need to ensure that its accounting system is robust and accurate enough to handle the demands that will be placing on it. There is more information about this in section 8 of Notice 700/63 *Electronic Invoicing.*

A self-billing agreement will usually last for 12 months. At the end of that period, the business will need to review the agreement so that it can provide HMRC with evidence to show that its supplier has agreed to accept the invoices raised on its behalf.

However, if there is a business contract with the supplier, it may not need to make a separate self-billing agreement. In these circumstances, the self-billing agreement would last until the end date of the contract, and it would not need to review the self-billing agreement until the contract had expired.

If a business self-bills, it must:

- raise self-billed invoices for all transactions with the supplier named on the document for a period of up to 12 months; or, if it has a contract with its supplier, for the duration of that contract;

- complete self-billed documents showing the supplier's name, address and VAT registration number, together with all the other details that make up a full VAT invoice.;

- set up a new agreement if its supplier transfers its business as a going concern, and both the business and the individual who has bought the business want to continue operating self-billing;

- keep the names, addresses and VAT registration numbers of the suppliers who have agreed to be self-billed, and be able to produce them for inspection by HMRC if required. HMRC recommend that a business reviews these details regularly so that it can be sure that it is only claiming VAT on invoices it has issued to suppliers who have valid VAT registration numbers. The simplest way of doing this is to keep a list of the suppliers that are self-billed.

A business must not issue self-billed VAT invoices:

- on behalf of suppliers who are not registered, or who have deregistered;

- to a supplier which changes its VAT registration number, until a new self-billing agreement is drawn up.

In the case of *Gemini Riteway Scaffolding Ltd v Revenue & Customs Commissioners* [2012] UKFTT 369 (TC) the appellant accounted for output tax incorrectly based on the self-billed invoice issued by its customer. They argued that as the customer had incorrectly assessed the liability of the supply as zero-rated they should account for the under-declared output tax rather than the appellant. The Tribunal found for HMRC and pointed out that a self-billed invoice can, pursuant to *VAT Regulations 1995, reg 13(3)*, be treated as the VAT invoice required to be provided by the supplier, but there is nothing in that regulation—or in any other provision of which the Tribunal was aware—which transferred the normal liability for VAT on a supply from the supplier to the customer because a self-billed invoice has been issued. The supplier is relieved of his normal obligation to issue a tax invoice, but that is all.

AUTHENTICATED RECEIPTS

14.14 *Regulation 13(4)* permits an authenticated receipt to be issued by the customer when paying a person supplying construction services. It then substitutes for a tax invoice:

- the authenticated receipt must show all the details required of a tax invoice;

- reclaim the input tax when the business pays the supplier but ensure that it gets back the authenticated receipt duly signed;

- if the supplier fails to co-operate a business should contact its local VAT office.

CAN A BUSINESS RECOVER VAT SHOWN ON AN INVOICE FROM A SUPPLIER IN ANOTHER EU STATE?

14.15 HMRC does not allow a business to recover non-UK VAT charged to it by suppliers in other Member States of the EU.

There is a system under which, in limited circumstances, a business can reclaim VAT incurred in another Member State under the *EC 8th VAT Directive*. See Chapter 27, *Recovery of Foreign VAT: the 8th and 13th Directive*s.

Chapter 15

Credit notes

SIGNPOSTS

- Credit notes can only be issued to correct genuine errors and adjustments to value or cancel an invoice issued to the wrong person. They should not be used to cancel an output tax liability because a customer will not pay (see **15.1–15.2**).

- HMRC accept that businesses can issue VAT-only credit notes to adjust VAT incorrectly charged (see **15.4**).

15.1   Credit notes are mostly routine. However, this chapter explains one or two points a business should know. One of the most important is that a business cannot cancel output tax with a credit note simply because the customer will not pay!

Credit notes for genuine corrections must be backed by evidence such as correspondence, quality control reports, goods returned notes, etc. In practice, HMRC are unlikely to challenge a credit note provided that it is issued bona fide in the course of settling a complaint from a customer. However, if a business issues large numbers of credit notes, it should check the documentary back-up.

A credit note to a UK customer does not have to include VAT. This is a matter for agreement with the customer. However, a customer, who cannot recover all the input tax he incurs, will want the VAT adjusted.

A credit note to a customer in another EU State must show all the details, including any VAT charged and now credited, as required on a tax invoice. See Chapter 14, *What is a valid tax invoice?*

The rules on credit notes are in the *VAT Regulations (SI 1995/2518). Regulation 15* provides for credit notes when the rate of VAT changes. However, the rules affecting day-to-day trading are confusingly entitled 'Adjustments in the course of business' in *reg 38*. They apply where 'there is an increase in consideration for a supply or there is a decrease in consideration for a supply, which includes an amount of VAT and the increase or decrease occurs after the end of the prescribed accounting period in which the original supply took place'. Thus, they deal with price increases as well as decreases.

The supplier must adjust the VAT-payable side of his VAT account up or down and the customer must do the reverse. The rules do not say this is to be via a credit note, but this is, of course, the usual way. A business adjusts its VAT account for the period in which the credit note is issued. The exception is for an insolvent trader, where the period of supply must be adjusted.

WHAT IF A BUSINESS IS ASKED TO CANCEL AND REISSUE AN INVOICE?

15.2 The above rules do not cover the situation when the wrong person is invoiced, for example, when a consultant invoices a professional adviser, only to be asked to bill the client direct.

If an original invoice is returned within the same VAT period, send the original, together with a credit note cancelling it, back to the person originally invoiced. On that credit note, cross-refer to a new invoice. Issue this under a fresh reference number, even if it is within the same VAT return period.

IF A BUSINESS ACCEPTS GOODS BACK FROM CONSUMERS, IT SHOULD BE CAREFUL OF ITS TERMS!

15.3 If a business takes goods back from customers in exchange for other goods, there can be a potential problem. In *S J Phillips Ltd* (LON/01/36 No 17717), the Tribunal said that a credit note can only cancel a supply, and therein reduce the output VAT, if the customer has the right under the sale contract to return the goods as unfit for the purpose agreed. If the business has merely agreed a price which it will offset against the value of a second sale, it has repurchased the goods, not cancelled the original sale. The value at which it repurchases from the consumer does not, of course, include any input VAT that it can recover; nor does it reduce the value of the second sale on which output tax is due.

VAT-ONLY CREDIT NOTES

15.4 In *Robinson Group of Companies Ltd* (MAN/97/348 No 16081), it was held that VAT incorrectly charged is not 'VAT'. This means that, in law, a business cannot issue a VAT-only credit note under *reg 38*. It is supposed to make a voluntary disclosure—which HMRC will, of course, refuse unless the business agrees to refund the VAT to its customer under the unjust enrichment provisions. However, in practice, HMRC accept that errors in charging VAT can be corrected either by credit notes issued by the supplier, or by debit notes from the customer, provided that it is done within four years of the end of the VAT period in which the original mistake was made. From 1 April 2009 the limits were increased from three years to four.

Chapter 16

Bad debt relief

SIGNPOSTS

- If a customer has not paid his bill then six months after the due date for payment you can write off the debt in your 'bad debt relief account' and reclaim the VAT on your VAT return under the bad debt relief provisions (see **16.1–16.3**).

- If you receive payments or part payments after claiming back bad debt relief you have to adjust the claim and repay HMRC (see **16.4–16.6**).

- There are special rules for assigned debt and debt factoring (see **16.7**).

16.1   A business can claim bad debt relief for VAT charged to its customers which has not been paid within six months of due date for payment. The law is in *s 36* and *VAT Regulations (SI 1995/2518), regs 165–172J*.

For sales after 1/1/03, a business need no longer inform its customer that it is claiming bad debt relief. However, see also **13.3** for the rule, which requires the customer to repay input tax on any invoice it has not paid to a supplier after six months from the date of issue.

Focus

Relief for bad debts can be claimed provided that:

- the debt is six months old from the date on which payment was due or, if later, that of the supply; and

- it has been written off in your accounts; and

- if the supply was of goods, ownership has passed to the customer.

TIME LIMIT FOR THE CLAIM

16.2   The claim must be made within 4½ years of the date on which payment was due or, if later, that of the supply. From 1 April 2009 the limits were increased from 3½ years to 4½.

WRITING OFF THE BAD DEBT

16.3   A business must create a *refunds for bad debts account*. The description of this both in the *VAT Regulations* and in Notice 700/18 (December 2002) is confused. To comply with the law, as written, may be impractical because of the descriptive information to be kept in the account—beyond the capability of most computer systems. You need the dates and reference numbers of the original tax invoices, the sums of VAT charged, any payments on account received and details of the claim. The Bad Debt Relief Account is not part of the statutory accounts and does not mean that the bad debt has been written off; it simply records debts that are overdue for payment by six months or more and is for VAT purposes only. The Bad Debt Relief Account is often kept as a separate manual record supplementary to the main VAT records. In *Alpha Leisure (Scotland) Ltd* (EDN/03/14 No 18199), a claim was held to be valid despite it having been discharged as valueless as part of an agreement when two businesses were separated. HMRC had claimed that the agreement extinguished the debt.

SUBSEQUENT RECEIPT OF PAYMENTS

16.4   Any money which comes in subsequently is considered to include VAT. A business needs a system for picking this up, since it normally accounts for output tax when the invoice is issued.

Businesses should, therefore:

●   either transfer the outstanding customer account to a bad debts section of the sales ledger; or

●   mark the account in some way so that the computer triggers a query when a payment is credited to the account?

As dividends in a bankruptcy or liquidation can arrive years afterwards, it would be all too easy to forget that bad debt relief had been claimed, and thus fail to pay output tax at the appropriate VAT fraction on the net sum received.

HOW TO MAKE THE CLAIM

16.5   Add the refund to the input tax being reclaimed for the period in which the claim is made. It is not a reduction of the output tax.

THE AMOUNT OF THE CLAIM

16.6   A business can claim for the output tax originally charged. It is irrelevant whether the rate of VAT has subsequently changed. Similarly, it pays

16.6   *Bad debt relief*

VAT on any sums subsequently received at that rate, not at the one applicable when the payment is received.

If the customer has paid sums on account, the business can only claim for the VAT included on the outstanding balance. A typical example of this is where a garage does accident repair work for a registered trader under an insurance claim. The customer is that trader, but the net amount of the invoice is often paid direct to the garage by the insurance company.

If the customer never pays the VAT, the garage naturally thinks that the outstanding sum is all VAT. Sadly, that is not so! The insurance company's cheque is a payment on account, which includes VAT. Bad debt relief can only be claimed on the outstanding sum at the VAT fraction.

Several Tribunal cases confirm the point!

Enderby Transport Ltd (MAN/83/304 No 1607) sold goods for £10,200 plus VAT of £816. The customer only paid £10,200, and the company claimed bad debt relief of £816. The Tribunal held that the outstanding debt of £816 should be treated as a gross debt inclusive of VAT, of which, only the VAT element could be recovered.

In *AW Mawer & Co* ([1986] VATTR 87 No 2100) a firm of solicitors acted for a company in an action to recover damages following a fire at its premises. The company was awarded costs of £7,127 plus VAT of £709. The defendants' insurers only paid £7,127. The company did not pay the bill, and went into liquidation. HMRC only allowed relief at the VAT fraction of the outstanding debt. The Tribunal agreed. The £709 was a debt owed to the solicitors by the client, and relief could only be given on the VAT element of it.

In *Times Right Marketing (in Liquidation)v Revenue and Customs Comrs* (VTD 20,611), the appellant claimant had rendered its VAT returns showing the output tax due on all its supplies, including the unpaid invoices that were the subject of the bad debt relief (BDR) claim. However, as it had gone into liquidation, it had not settled the liability shown as payable to HMRC on those returns. HMRC, therefore, refused the claim, on the grounds that the VAT due on the supplies forming the claim had not been paid in full, and so the conditions for a valid claim were not met.

At the hearing, the Tribunal held that the input tax credit shown on the returns in question amounted to part-payment of the output tax due for the periods. As a result, a partial claim could be made. The calculation of the claim was done as follows; the output tax due on the non-bad debts was calculated. This was all deemed to have been paid by virtue of the input tax credit. The excess input tax credit was then regarded as part-payment of the VAT due on the bad debt invoices, and this was the amount of the claim. The fact that not all of the VAT on the unpaid invoices could be shown to have been paid to HMRC did not prevent the BDR claim being made for the part that had been paid, by input tax credit, as EU law was less prescriptive than HMRC's interpretation. HMRC's interpretation made exercising the right to a BDR claim excessively difficult or impossible. The taxpayer's appeal was thus allowed.

As a result of the *Times Right Marketing* case, HMRC later issued *Revenue & Customs Brief 18/09*. It said HMRC now accepted the principle that input tax offset against output tax was a form of payment for BDR purposes. The Brief gives two examples of BDR claims under the revised treatment—the first where none of the net tax due has been paid, and the second where only a part-payment has been made. In example 1, there is output tax of £200K, input tax of £110K, and eligible bad debts in the period of £120K. Example 2 is the same, except that £20K of the £90K net tax due has been paid. The examples assume all of the other BDR conditions have been met, and show how BDR would now be available on the **excess of input tax over output tax due on non-bad debt supplies** (ie £110K minus £80K = £30K in Example 1, and £110K minus (£80K–£20K) = £50K in Example 2). The Brief invites retrospective claims for repayment of underclaimed BDR, but points out that the normal BDR time limits apply. Claims must be made within four years and six months of either the date on which the consideration that was written off as BDR was due and payable, or the date of the supply.

16.7   If a business sells its debts without provision in the contract for reassignment of them back to it, bad debt relief is not available. If the contract does allow it, only once the debts have been reassigned can bad debt relief be claimed.

Moreover, when a claim is made, the outstanding amount is net of any sums received by the assignee.

The payment from the factor for the debts is exempt, and is, therefore, ignored for the purposes of bad debt relief.

If a business has already claimed bad debt relief before it assigns a debt, *reg 171(5)* says it does not have to repay the VAT if the assignee subsequently receives a payment, unless the assignee is a connected person as defined under *Corporation Tax Act 2010, s 1122*.

Since the law provides that it is only the claimant, the issuer of the original VAT invoice, who has the right to make a bad debt relief claim and has the liability to account for VAT included in sums subsequently received, the assignee is not liable for VAT on any sum collected. The possible advantage is limited, given that the sum assigned, after bad debt relief has been claimed, will usually only be recovered in part. Of course, the assignee may gain, but that will only happen if the total sum collected exceeds what was paid when the debt was taken over. A business would have difficulty in exploiting that by assigning debt over six months old but which it expected to be paid; as already noted, it would be liable to pay VAT on sums collected by a connected person. Someone unconnected would only accept the debt at a discount.

THE PAYMENT OFFSET PROBLEM

16.8   *Regulation 172(3)* says that where the claimant owes an amount of money to the purchaser which can be set-off, the consideration written-off in the accounts shall be reduced by the amount so owed.

In other words, putting it in English, a business cannot claim bad debt relief on the gross value of its invoices if it also owes a debt to that customer. It can only claim on the net figure after taking account of what is owed in the other direction. There is usually no restriction in the commercial arrangements of the right to offset, and the bad debt relief claim must reflect the legal liability for the net sum.

Perhaps a loan for a stated period could not immediately be offset; however, there would then be a liability to pay the output tax again when the loan became repayable and the outstanding invoices were deducted from it—just when a payment is received after bad debt relief has been claimed.

REPAYMENT UNDER A GUARANTEE DOES NOT COUNT

16.9   *Interlude Houses Ltd* (EDN/94/65 No 12877) sold timeshare licences which the purchasers assigned to a bank as security for loans to them. Interlude bought back a licence from the bank if the purchaser defaulted on the loan. Unsurprisingly, its claim for bad debt relief was rejected because its repurchase of the licence from the bank was not a cancellation of its original sale.

THE POSITION IF THE BUSINESS OWNERSHIP HAS CHANGED

16.10   The new owner of an unincorporated business is not entitled to make a bad debt relief claim for previous debts, unless that owner has taken over the existing VAT number.

The same applies if a purchaser acquires a business from a limited company rather than purchasing its share capital.

DEPARTURE FROM A VAT GROUP

16.11   A company, which made a sale whilst it was within a VAT group, can claim bad debt relief after it has left the group. It does not matter that the supply was originally accounted for by the representative member.

In *Proto Glazing Ltd* (LON/95/573 No 13410) the Tribunal said it would be unfair to apply the VAT group returns system to the claim for bad debt relief. Output tax was paid on behalf of the company which had made the sale, and which had then suffered the economic loss.

GOODS SUPPLIED ON HIRE PURCHASE OR CONDITIONAL SALE

16.12   Supplies made by hire purchase or conditional sale have two components: a supply of goods and the exempt interest charges. When claiming bad debt relief, *reg 170A* allows the allocation of payments from defaulting customers to goods and to finance in the same ratio as the total sums due—thus increasing the VAT reclaim. This was originally a concession announced in *Business Brief 19/2001* from 6 December 2001.

HMRC also allow a business not to deduct the sum received from selling any repossessed goods from the outstanding debt *if the sale of the goods themselves was standard-rated*; that would be because the customer had acquired them for a business purpose, or had changed their condition prior to selling them. If the sale was not subject to VAT, the proceeds must still be deducted from the debt.

Chapter 17

What records are required?

SIGNPOSTS

- It is important to keep accurate records in order to avoid errors and the possibility of interest and penalties if you get into trouble with HMRC when they come to visit (see **17.1–17.2**).

- If you want to recover VAT you will need to have detailed records to support your claim in particular circumstances (see **17.3**).

- Businesses dealing with new suppliers and customers should check the validity of their VAT number and if in doubt inform HMRC in case of any possible fraud (see **17.10–17.13**).

- Businesses dealing in mobile phones and computer chips need to maintain special records and complete Reverse Charge Sales Lists (see **17.14–17.20**).

TAKING RECORDS SERIOUSLY

17.1 The key point in this chapter is that, by taking record-keeping seriously, a business will keep out of most trouble concerning the evidence required to satisfy HMRC.

HMRC do not specify exactly what records a business is required to keep, with the exception of a 'VAT account', ie a record of what goes on the VAT return, but they do require an audit trail that allows them to verify the business transactions, and can direct a business to keep specific records if they consider the existing records to be inadequate. HMRC's powers are contained in *VATA 1994, Sch 11, para 6(1)*. The main rules applicable to everyone are in *reg 31*, and in Notice 700 (April 2002) *The VAT Guide*, Chapter 19. However, many of the Notices on detailed aspects of the tax also contain rules on record-keeping. Examples are those concerning the various Schemes such as those for retailers, cash accounting, annual accounting, second-hand goods and tour operators.

The rules on evidence to support the zero-rating of an export of goods is a common problem area. See Chapter 20, *Exports and Removals of Goods* for details. An invoice addressed overseas is not enough. Evidence is also required as to the physical removal of the goods from the UK.

See **10.29** for another example of why it can be important to pay attention to records which are not part of ordinary accounting requirements.

Another example is in **13.34** where it is pointed out that many owners of small businesses would not expect to formalise the reasons for taking action in minutes, even though, when VAT recovery is involved it, can be essential—especially when a business buys a desirable asset like one of those!

HMRC HAVE POWER TO DEMAND TO SEE RECORDS

17.2   In addition to their power to say what records must be kept, HMRC can, and occasionally do, demand to see additional items using their power under *Sch 7(2)*.

In *Lloyd's TSB Group plc* (LON/04/232 No 19330), the Tribunal upheld the demand to see the management accounts. This was because HMRC saw the special method in use as distortive, and the Tribunal saw it as reasonable for them to wish to see those management accounts in order to understand the position.

WITHOUT ADEQUATE RECORDS, A BUSINESS CANNOT RECOVER VAT

17.3   Most record-keeping problems stem from simple points like the VAT audit trail not linking prime records, such as invoices to the VAT account, or a lack of evidence needed to justify the VAT treatment adopted.

Focus

Examples of situations in which particular records are required are:

- exports of goods;
- imports of goods;
- zero-rating for services under the International Services rules;
- claims for bad debt relief;
- input tax recovery;
- issue of credit notes;
- partial exemption;
- self-billing.

Consider too, the evidence as to the volume of the business's activity. Records attesting to this are often not of an accounting nature; yet they can be vital in supporting the accuracy of the recorded outputs, especially in cash businesses.

Examples are:

- an appointments book for a hairdresser;

- customer call records, or mileage figures for taxi firms.

RECORDS MUST BE RETAINED FOR SIX YEARS

17.4   VAT records have to be kept for six years—despite the fact that, in the absence of fraud, HMRC can only currently assess retrospectively for four. From 1 April 2009 the limits were increased from three years to four with certain transitional provisions meaning that no adjustment can be made for periods ending before 31 March 2006 (see **Chapter 39**, *Assessment and VAT Penalties* for details).

Moreover, certain rules generate a need for records beyond three years. For example a business recovers VAT now on the cost of a project which it expects to produce taxable income from in several years time. If, *within six years* of recovering the VAT, the income from the project achieved turns out to be exempt or only partly taxable, all or some of the input tax must be repaid. An example is an intended commercial property development project, the rent from which was intended to be taxable after deciding to opt to tax, but in the event, the land was sold to a housing association for a housing development, and the option to tax was disapplied. Similarly, if expected exempt income turns out to be taxable, a business can then reclaim the input tax previously disallowed. In both cases, the records of the project would be needed. Of course, it is relatively unusual for a project to take more than three years, let alone six, before generating income. However, the *Capital Goods Scheme*, described in Chapter 25, runs for up to ten years. Since it requires the repayment of input tax recovered, or allows the reclaiming of that previously disallowed for expenditure on computers and buildings, records of the cost and the taxable use over the years have to be kept; indeed, successive projects for work on a building can generate a succession of *Capital Goods Scheme* ten-year adjustment periods.

Once a business is aware of the *Capital Goods Scheme*, it should recognise the need to keep those records. That is not necessarily so for the *waiver of exemption or option to tax*, which lasts for at least 20 years. See the explanation at **26.98** as to why this creates the most dangerous records situation.

IS THE ACCOUNTING SYSTEM SELF-CHECKING?

17.5 Many common mistakes, even simple ones, could be avoided if accounting systems included common-sense checks to ensure, for example, that:

- the output tax is the correct percentage of the outputs;

- the input tax is the correct percentage of the inputs. If a supplier offers a cash discount, the overall percentage will be slightly less than the standard rate because the tax is calculated on the amount net of cash discount, regardless of whether or not it is taken as explained in Chapter 8, *The Value of Supply Rules.*

It is not sufficient for the accounting system of a business to check the VAT on individual invoices. It should prove the total for each day or batch of postings. Ideally, the figures for both input and output tax should be checked for the full month or quarter. See **18.15** for a case where the VAT cheque got posted as if it were input tax.

A BUSINESS SHOULD NOT TAKE ITS COMPUTER SYSTEM FOR GRANTED!

17.6 Since few computer programmers have much idea about VAT, it follows that computer systems can easily be deficient. For example, does the system incorporate a 'default' calculation of the input tax on an invoice? This means that when the net amount is entered, the computer automatically calculates the tax. The computer then has to say if the figure is not correct. This is bad programming. The system ought to require entering both the net and the tax, and for the machine then to query the latter if it does not match. Otherwise, it is all too easy to accept the default figure instead of entering the correct one.

One restaurant bought a computerised sales system, which summarised the daily sales by menu item. Unfortunately, it:

- produced only a customer copy of the individual bill—so no detail of sales customer by customer was available in the records;

- calculated the VAT line by line of each bill instead of on the invoice total. It then rounded down the VAT calculated up to 0.59p.

The result was to understate the output tax over a fairly short period by several thousand pounds.

HOW DURABLE ARE THE BUSINESS RECORDS?

17.7 Nowadays, most records in all but the smallest businesses are computer-based. Computer-based systems tend to be upgraded or changed every few years. So what about that six-year requirement for VAT records?

A business can download and store the data, but it needs to make sure that the storage medium chosen is durable. For example, data stored on magnetic tape used to become unstable if it was not rerun every 10–12 months. Moreover, will the business be able to read that data, if it needed to, in five years' time? Not many years ago, 5.25-inch floppy disks were standard, but how many computers these days have a drive capable of accepting and reading anything stored on one? Not only does a business need a means of storing the data, it has to conserve the equipment and operating systems needed to access it.

MAKING TAX DIGITAL ('MTD')

17.8   HMRC have published a new draft VAT Notice 700/21 giving guidance on what records must be kept digitally within functional compatible software in order to comply with the requirements of MTD. Any records not listed in the new notice do not have to be kept in any specific way.

By mandating digital record-keeping and filing, the government expects to reduce the amount of tax lost through error and failure to take reasonable care. MTD will affect businesses with a turnover of more than £85,000 per annum from 1 April 2019. Businesses that are VAT registered but have a turnover of less than £85,000 per annum in the 12 months prior to the introduction of MTD will not be required to participate but can do so voluntarily.

There are certain limited exemptions from MTD if HMRC is satisfied that:

- the business is run entirely by practicing members of a religious society whose beliefs are incompatible with the requirements of the regulations (for example, those religious beliefs prevent them from using computers);

- it is not reasonably practicable to use digital tools to keep the business records or submit returns, for reasons of age, disability, remoteness of location or for any other reason; or

- the business is subject to an insolvency procedure.

Under MTD for VAT, functionally compatible software will be used to maintain the mandatory digital records, calculate the return and submit it to HMRC via an Application Programme Interface or 'API' for short. HMRC has a list of software that can be used to submit VAT returns.

The complete set of digital records to meet MTD requirements do not all have to be in one piece of software. If there is a digital link between the pieces of software, records can be kept in a range of compatible digital formats.

For the first year of mandation (VAT periods commencing between 1 April 2019 and 31 March 2020) businesses will not be required to have digital links between software programs. The one exception to this is where data is transferred, following preparation of the information required for the VAT Return, to another product (for example, a bridging product) that is API-enabled solely for the purpose of submitting the 9-Box VAT Return data to HMRC. The transfer of data to this product must be digital.

Functional compatible software is a software program or set of compatible software programs that must be able to:

- record and preserve electronic records in an electronic form;

- provide to HMRC information and returns from the electronic records in an electronic form and by using the API platform; and

- receive information from HMRC.

Business must keep the following information digitally:

- business name;

- the address of the principal place of business;

- VAT registration number; and

- a record of any VAT accounting schemes used.

For each supply made the business must record:

- the time of supply;

- the value of the supply; and

- the rate of VAT charged.

For each purchase received the business must record:

- the time of supply;

- the value of the supply including any VAT that is not claimable; and

- the amount of input tax claimed.

The transfer of data from the mandatory digital records through to receipt of information by HMRC must be digital. Information can only be submitted to HMRC via APIs, this can be from software, bridging software or API enabled spreadsheets.

To show the link between the output tax in business records and the output tax on the return, the business must have a record of:

- the output tax owed on sales;

- the output tax owed on acquisitions from other EU Member States;

- the tax due under the reverse charge procedure;

- the tax that needs to be paid following a correction or error adjustment; and

- any other adjustment required by VAT rules.

To show the link between the input tax in the business records and the input tax on the return, the business must have a record of:

- the input tax claimable on business purchases;

- the input tax allowable on acquisitions from other EU member states;

- the tax reclaimable following a correction or error adjustment; and

- any other necessary adjustment.

Adjustments, such as partial exemption, can be calculated separately outside the digital records of the organisation and transferred in digitally or manually.

HMRC anticipates that there will be a soft-landing period (without application of record-keeping penalties) in the first year to allow businesses, in certain circumstances, extra time to update legacy systems to be fully compliant.

For most businesses the soft-landing period will run from 1 April 2019 to 31 March 2020. However, if the business has a deferred start date for MTD filing to the first VAT period beginning on or after 1 October 2019, the soft-landing for that business will run from 1 October 2019 to 30 September 2020.

Note the soft landing only applies to waiving the conditions for digital links between software products within the accounting system. It does not apply to penalties which may be applied for not complying with the requirement to file the VAT return using MTD-compatible software.

Information can only be submitted to HMRC via APIs, this can be from software, bridging software or API-enabled spreadsheets. Part of this process will include the VAT legal declaration by the customer. This maybe done through either the software (including bridging software), or API-enabled spreadsheet, or through a prompt presented to the customer by HMRC systems.

HMRC give a number of examples of sets of software with digital links that meet the requirements of MTD, including the following:

Example 1

A business uses one piece of accounting software to record all sales and purchases and transfers the totals into a spreadsheet that it uses to calculate the return. The information is then sent to a piece of bridging software which submits the return to HMRC.

Altogether the three pieces of software maintain the mandatory digital records, calculate the return and submit it to HMRC. The links between the three pieces of software must be digital for the set of software to be functional compatible software.

Example 2

A business uses one piece of accounting software to record all sales and purchases, this software then calculates the return and submits it to HMRC. As well as the records in the accounting software the business uses a spreadsheet to keep track of fleets of cars and work out its road fuel scale charges.

As the records in the spreadsheet are not listed by HMRC, the business can type the adjustment into its accounting software. However, a digital link will reduce the chance of errors.

Example 3

A VAT group uses three different software packages to record the mandatory records for different parts of the group. Each piece of software calculates the amounts needed for the return from each part of the group. A spreadsheet is used to compile the totals and create the return for the whole of the group. The information is then sent to a piece of bridging software, which submits the return to HMRC.

Altogether the five pieces of software maintain the mandatory digital records, calculate the return and submit it to HMRC. The links between the five pieces of software must be digital for the set of software to be functional compatible software.

Businesses may authorise their agent to submit their VAT return for them under MTD. To do this the agent must have access to the functional compatible software that holds the businesses' mandatory records.

Businesses can also make voluntary updates of information ahead of submitting their VAT returns. The businesses' software will also allow it to submit supplementary data to HMRC. Businesses can only do this when they send a VAT return or a voluntary update. If the business decides to send supplementary data its software will send additional information to HMRC.

Submission of this supplementary data is entirely voluntary. Businesses can send this each time they submit VAT information to HMRC or they can do this on an occasional basis. If a business is selected for a tax compliance check, HMRC will look at this information before contacting them. If this information is enough to give HMRC assurance that the return is correct they may not contact the business and inspection could be avoided. If an error is made in submitting supplementary data it can be corrected and submitted again. Businesses cannot receive a penalty for submitting an error in supplementary information.

HMRC has announced a deferment until 1 October 2019 of the obligation to file via the new API-platform for the following types of business:

- VAT groups;
- VAT divisions;
- non-resident traders;
- trusts;

- businesses on annual accounting ;

- unincorporated charities; and

- businesses on payments on account.

The six-month deferral will also apply to public sector entities required to provide additional information on their VAT return, such as government departments and NHS Trusts, local authorities and public corporations

THE ANTI-CAROUSEL FRAUD MEASURES

17.9   *Carousel fraud,* referred to by HMRC as *'Missing Trader Intra-Community fraud' (MTIC),* involves acquiring goods zero-rated as an acquisition from another EU Member State, selling them on plus VAT in the UK, and then disappearing without paying that VAT to HMRC. Sometimes, the fraudsters have operated through two or more VAT-registered companies in the UK, and the goods have been sold on zero-rated to a customer outside the UK. In some cases, the same goods have been bought and resold repeatedly.

Section 77A and *Sch 11, para 4* give HMRC draconian powers to stop this. They apply to computer equipment and mobile phones, the goods most commonly used by the fraudsters. They enable HMRC to attack such frauds by collecting the unpaid tax from any traders still around, who dealt in the goods, without HMRC having to prove that those traders were themselves fraudsters. This is known as 'joint and several liability'. Traders must check the credentials of those with whom they are trading because of the risk of having HMRC pin responsibility for the unpaid VAT on them.

HMRC can:

- demand a security:

    (i)   in respect of any repayment claim by a business concerning a *past* purchase of *any* goods or services; or

    (ii)   against the risk that VAT charged on a *future* transaction in *any* goods or services is not paid by another trader in the chain, whether that transaction was before the business bought those goods or services, or after it sold them on;

- claim VAT not paid by another trader in a past chain of transactions in, specifically, computer equipment or components and telephones, which occurred either before or after it bought the goods or services and sold them on. This applies to any or all traders in the chain, *'if they knew, or had reasonable grounds to suspect that, some or all of the VAT payable in respect of (their own) supply, or on any previous or subsequent supply of those goods or services, would go unpaid'.*

The law provides that the term '*goods*' also includes '*services*'. Of course, services cannot be passed around in the way that goods can. However, in para 17 of *VAT Notes* 1/2005, HMRC referred to checking 'your labour suppliers' and to the risk that other businesses in the supply chain might evade VAT. They threatened the possibility of a demand for security just as in goods situations. This often happens in the area of employment agencies supplying crop pickers and other similar activities.

A business will be presumed to have had *reasonable grounds* for suspicion if the price it paid for the goods was below market value or less than the figure paid previously for those goods, unless it can show it reflected excess stock or obsolescence.

OBVIOUS SUSPICIOUS CIRCUMSTANCES

17.10 Sometimes, it is obvious that a deal being offered is suspicious. Circumstances quoted in several Tribunal decisions include that the person offering the goods quoted only a first name and a mobile telephone number. Either no address was given, or the one that was given was just a postal accommodation address from which mail was collected. The customer was instructed to pay a third party.

HMRC quote a business paying £50,000 for computer chips, which it has not seen, to a supplier it does not know, who turns up at the door. It is, of course, hard to understand how a genuine business would operate like that, but that is not the point. The law could allow HMRC to demand VAT from businesses involved in genuine transactions, if fraud has occurred either before or after in the chain. Historically, where a business deals in computer equipment, components, or mobile telephones etc, it should maintain detailed supplier and customer files, including records of:

- their credentials—not just credit references, but trade reputation, how long established and who owned/run by etc—information of the latter kind can be obtained from the records publicly available at Companies House. If the name of a company is obviously one of those 'made up' ones like *Rangepace*, which are purchased from an off-the-shelf agency rather than a name related to the trade in which it engages, that is a possible clue to its background;

- the circumstances of individual deals including all correspondence, e-mails etc and details of each product specification. Depending on the nature of the business, it may need evidence that it bought specific products for an identified market—together with a note of how the price of each transaction was arrived at. Deals which involve the purchase and immediate resale of goods at a substantial profit are, by their nature, often suspect, given that the more normal kind of business requires one to buy for and sell from stock;

- records of the receipt and inspection of each consignment including IMEI numbers. Be especially careful if the goods are held in a third party warehouse. How can a business verify that they are new items, not old ones in battered containers being sold and resold but never used?

- check of the VAT numbers quoted; see below for further comment.

Those files will usually be kept in the purchasing or sales departments, but no such file should be destroyed without the agreement of the head of finance. Each should be kept for at least three years after the last transaction with the supplier or customer.

The significance of such records will depend on:

- the proportion of the business which is related to computer equipment and mobile telephones;

- whether a significant proportion of the purchases are from one or two suppliers or a significant proportion of the sales are to one or two customers.

A case, which illustrates the problem, is *Bond House Systems Ltd* (MAN/02/ 534 No 18100). A business, which had been established for ten years, was denied over £5m input tax incurred on 26 transactions in the following circumstances.

There was no evidence that Bond House was involved in the fraud or even aware of it:

- Bond House had files showing that it made the research referred to above into the credentials of the traders with which it did business, and it did co-operate in providing market information to HMRC;

- in May 2002, the month for which its repayment claim was refused by HMRC, 99.1% of its £95m sales were in 51 transactions and 32.5% of its sales by number were to customers in other EU States, almost always in Ireland;

- the bulk of its purchases were from two companies, both of which had only been in business for a year or so. One of them was owned and run by a 21-year-old woman, who a director of Bond House had met when they were both employed by another company and to whom he had made a personal loan to finance the start of her business;

- Bond House, an experienced trader, was buying monthly £30–£40m worth of computer chips from each of them—the bulk of its purchases. The Tribunal commented that it did not appear to have wondered how those newly-established companies could immediately have identified a source of supply from which they could buy in such quantities, and earn a profit on the resale;

- Bond House's own turnover increased from £258m in 2001 to a projected £1.5bn in 2002. It was not apparent how it had achieved that increase in a static or declining market;

- whereas its two little suppliers made margins of 25p and 50p per chip, Bond House made exactly £4 on purchases from the one and £3 per chip on those from the other. Combined with evidence which showed that, on the balance of probabilities, the chips were being circulated within the 'ring fence' of the carousel and that all the deals, both purchases and sales, were prearranged, these fixed margins suggested artificial transactions;

- that was reinforced by the fact that purchases from each supplier were always sold to the same two customers in Ireland; ie goods from A were always sold to C and those from B always to D—obviously unlikely in an ordinary commercial situation.

The above points are a summary of just some of the evidence in this case. In essence, the Tribunal felt that Bond House should have recognised the artificiality of the business being offered to it and that fraud was probably involved. It held that, despite Bond House's innocence of any wrongdoing and its ignorance of the fraudulent objective, the transactions were devoid of economic substance and the VAT paid out on them was therefore not recoverable.

Bond House appealed the decision of the Tribunal, and it was referred to the ECJ. The ECJ found in favour of Bond House. The Court has found that companies such as Bond House, unwittingly caught up in a carousel fraud orchestrated by others, are fully entitled under European VAT law to receive repayments of input VAT, and to deprive them of those repayments breaches European law.

Furthermore, it is not permitted in European law to view a series of transactions as a whole. Instead, each individual transaction must be examined on its merits and as a separate economic activity. In short, an innocent company cannot be held liable for the fraudulent activity of others.

Following this decision, HMRC has introduced three new pieces of legislation to combat fraud in this area. The most important measure will be the derogation from the former *EC 6th VAT Directive* that passes the liability for accounting for output tax from the supplier to the customer in transactions concerning 'specified goods'. This effectively introduces a 'reverse charge' similar to that successfully brought in to combat fraud in the gold sector. This measure will remove VAT from the transaction chain, so there will be no VAT charged, and paid for, that a missing trader can then run off with. This came into force on 1 June 2007, and affects all business to business transactions over £5,000.

A second measures clarifies HMRC powers to mark goods. This will mainly affect freight forwarders, and should allow HMRC to track goods within a fraudulent transaction chain. A third measure gives HMRC increased powers to make businesses maintain and retain records. This will allow HMRC to better track the movement of goods within a chain of transactions, and identify business trading within those chains. There will be a limited right of appeal in this area, but this has caused some disquiet in professional circles, as it seems the right of appeal granted shifts the balance in favour of HMRC, to the detriment of the business.

With the 2007 introduction of the reverse charge on mobile phones and computer chips, carousel fraud in this area has substantially reduced. However, it has not gone completely, and has moved into other related areas, for example, other electronics equipment such as digital and video cameras, scrap metal, etc. It has also moved into the lower end of staff employment bureaus, so businesses in these areas should be wary of new suppliers, and undertake checks into the background of the company.

CHECKING A VAT NUMBER

17.11 When a business sets up a new purchase ledger account, it is good practice to check the supplier's VAT number because, if it is invalid, so is the tax invoice. No doubt the majority of such cases are innocent errors, such as printing mistakes. However, the fraudulent use of another trader's number is prevalent in certain sectors of business, so checking is potentially a valuable precaution.

To confirm both that the number is valid *and* that it belongs to the trader quoting it, ring the NAS. See page lxvii at the start of the book under *Contacting HMRC*.

Unfortunately, the NAS will only tell an enquirer whether that number belongs to the trader whose name and address have been quoted. The *Data Protection Act* stops them giving information about another trader. Another drawback is that the information is often up to two months out of date, so a newly VAT registered business may not appear on the database and a deregistered business may still show up as being valid. When HMRC check the records on a visit this will not appear obvious so businesses should keep a printout of any checks made to confirm the information available at that time.

SHOULD A BUSINESS TELL HMRC ABOUT A POSSIBLE FRAUD?

17.12 That HMRC cannot give information about another trader does not stop them from asking for further information—for example about an invoice which quotes an incorrect VAT number. Logically, they should do that since the value of the invoice and the nature of the supply would usually indicate whether this was an innocent error, say a printing mistake, or a possible fraud.

If the latter, it would also be logical to suggest that the business faxes a copy of the invoice, together with any other information readily available about any other parties involved, the grounds for suspicion etc to one of the specialist offices dealing with fraud. One might hope that, if such information were provided promptly and confirmed in writing, and the business agreed not to alert the potential fraudster, HMRC might not disallow the input tax on the invalid invoice, although this probably a vain hope.

Since a business is unlikely to get anything more than a bare acknowledgment, if that, provide the information in writing, and keep copies of the letter and all attachments. If any discussions do result, whether by telephone or face to face, make a careful note of exactly what was said on each occasion, sign and date it, and send HMRC a copy.

THE POTENTIAL BENEFIT OF TELLING HMRC

17.13   Evidence that a business did contact HMRC could be crucial in defending against any subsequent notification of joint and several liability for VAT unpaid, if the business had done a deal in a chain of transactions which included a carousel fraud. It would have only 21 days from the issue of such a notice within which to show that it had no reasonable grounds for suspecting that fraud.

As the notice could be issued years after the transaction occurred, a file of information which had been offered to HMRC at the time of the fraud might well be the only protection a business has. Hence, our advice to be alert to unusual transactions, and that, if you do spot something like a false VAT registration, tell HMRC in writing.

Much the same applies to the risk of HMRC using their power to demand security from a business in respect of any future transactions. HMRC have said they will do that if a business ignores a warning to stop dealing with other parties they suspect of fraud. It is doubtful how this procedure will work in practice. A system of checking on business partners and of notifying HMRC of any doubts could be useful, should any mistake by the Department lead to a questionable warning.

REVERSE CHARGE ON SPECIFIED GOODS AND SERVICES

17.14

Focus

From 1 June 2007, a reverse charge was introduced on specified goods and has been extended to certain services. The specified goods to which the reverse charge applies are:

- mobile phones;
- computer chips;
- wholesale telecommunications services;
- emissions trading;
- wholesale gas and electricity; and
- standard rated supplies of gold.

Mobile phones

17.15   For the purpose of the reverse charge, the definition of a mobile phone takes its everyday meaning in the UK and includes:

- any handsets which have a mobile phone function (ie the transmitting and receiving of spoken messages), whether or not they have any other functions—it therefore includes other communication devices, such as Blackberrys;
- mobile phones supplied with accessories (such as a charger, battery, cover or hands-free kit) as a single package;
- pre-pay (or 'pay as you go') mobile phones, whether or not the selling price includes an element attributable to the cost of future use of the phones; and
- mobile phones locked to a network but not supplied with a contract for airtime.

However, the reverse charge does not apply to the following:

- mobile phones which are supplied with a contract for airtime;
- mobile phone accessories which are supplied separately from a mobile phone;
- walkie-talkies;
- WiFi phones, unless also intended for use with mobile phone networks; and
- 3G data cards and WiFi cards.

The reverse charge applies only to supplies of specified goods within the UK made by one VAT-registered business to another. The rules and procedures for sales to non-business customers, dispatches of goods to persons in another Member State and for exports outside the EU are unaffected by the introduction of the reverse charge.

The reverse charge does not apply to supplies with a VAT-exclusive value below £5,000. This figure is calculated on an invoice basis, ie the reverse charge applies if the total value of all the specified goods shown on an invoice is £5,000 or more. In that event, the reverse charge applies to the total value of the specified goods on that invoice.

Many businesses issue several separate invoices in relation to a single order, eg a separate invoice for each delivery. Where the order value is larger than the invoice value, it will be acceptable to apply the reverse charge to all invoices relating to the order, as long as the order value exceeds the £5,000 threshold, if both parties agree.

Where VAT is due on a value reduced by an unconditional discount then the discounted value is to be used to establish the value for the purpose of applying the de minimis rules. However, where there are contingent discounts or a delayed reduction in price, the full value shown on an invoice is to be used.

REVERSE CHARGE SALES LISTS

17.16   If a business make supplies to which the reverse charge on specified goods (mobile phones and computer chips) has applied, it must notify HMRC and submit regular statements (Reverse Charge Sales Lists⬚RCSLs) using the RCSL system. A business's accounts software may have the facility to export the required data, in the required format. Alternatively, the business has the option to key the required information into a web page.

The RCSL system, including notifications, is web-based and accessed through the HMRC website: www.hmrc.gov.uk. If a business does not already use an HMRC online service, it will first need to register for the Government Gateway. Guidance on how to register is available at www.gateway.gov.uk.

How does the RCSL system work?

17.17   The RCSL system is menu-driven and provides help for each option. All aspects require completion electronically.

Notification

17.18   A business must tell HMRC of the date on which it first makes a reverse charge sale. It must also give HMRC the name and telephone number of a contact. If a business then ceases to make such supplies, it must tell HMRC of the date on which it ceased to do so. However, if it subsequently again makes reverse charge sales, it must notify HMRC of the date it recommenced, and again provide contact details.

In each case you must tell HMRC within 30 days of the event.

RCSL

17.19   A business will have to submit an RCSL for each of its VAT return periods. The due date for submission of RCSLs is the same as that of the VAT return.

What information must I submit?

17.20   For each customer to which a business makes a reverse charge sale, it must tell HMRC:

- the UK VAT registration number of the customer; and

- for each calendar month in the period, the total net value of reverse charge sales to that customer.

Wholesales telecoms services

17.21   New anti-evasion rules were introduced by HMRC on 1 February 2016, which will affect how businesses account for VAT on wholesale telecommunications services in the UK. Businesses affected need to take steps to ensure that they account for VAT correctly.

The new measures introduce a mandatory reverse charge for wholesale supplies of telecommunications services within the UK. Under the reverse charge mechanism, the customer receiving the wholesale supply of telecom services must account for the VAT due rather than the supplier. As such it will only apply to B2B supplies where the intention is to sell on the supply with negligible consumption of the supply by the recipient business.

By shifting the onus of who accounts for the VAT on such sales from the supplier to the customer, HMRC hopes that this will remove the scope to evade any VAT owing to HMRC and is intended to counter missing trader intra-community fraud in the industry.

Businesses potentially affected by these changes are those which buy or sell wholesale telecommunications services in the UK, including:

- airtime carriers;

- network operators;

- message hubbing providers;

- short messaging services (SMS); and

- voice aggregators.

Businesses affected by the rules need to take appropriate steps to ensure that they comply. These will include:

- determining whether the supplies of telecommunications services are in fact one of the affected services;

- applying the domestic reverse charge where appropriate;

- ensuring the special invoicing procedures are in place for affected supplies; and

- updating VAT accounting procedures.

Reverse charge on labour in the construction industry

17.22 HMRC has finalised draft legislation for an anti-fraud measure designed to tackle organised tax fraud on labour supplies in the construction sector to prevent VAT and CIS losses estimated at £100m per annum by introducing a domestic reverse charge.

This means that the customer in the transaction becomes responsible for accounting for the VAT to prevent a fraudulent supplier collecting the tax and not paying it over to HMRC. The measure will not come into force until October 2019 in order to allow businesses in the construction sector to amend their accounting and IT systems to take account of the new rules. The measure will be similar to anti-avoidance measures introduced in the mobile phones, computer chips, wholesale gas and electricity, and emissions allowances sectors.

It has been confirmed that there will be no threshold so all businesses in the construction sector will be affected, this is to avoid creating considerable complexity for businesses and offering fraudsters a means to avoid the measure. It is anticipated that the measure will affect approximately 250,000 businesses, mainly small and micro-businesses.

It is understood that the reverse charge will not apply to zero-rated services or supplies of house-building services to the final consumer. HMRC are still considering whether the measure will apply to supplies of repairs and maintenance to existing buildings as well as the construction of new buildings.

The customer will be required to report these transactions in Boxes 1, 4 and 7 of their VAT return. There are no plans for a reverse charge sales list at present, which will mitigate the administrative burden of the measure. Some smaller businesses use the VAT they collect to ease their cashflow and provide working capital so they may be adversely effected by the measure.

The reverse charge will not apply to the final customer who will still be charged VAT at the appropriate rate of either 5% or 20%.

Chapter 18

VAT housekeeping for finance directors

SIGNPOSTS

- The finance director should take a keen interest in the preparation of the VAT return and ensure that the staff are properly trained, as poor housekeeping is the reason for most errors on the VAT return which can lead to interest and penalties (see **18.1–18.4**).

- Businesses should maintain a permanent VAT file that consolidates all pertinent VAT information including the build-up to the VAT return and any correspondence with HMRC (see **18.5**).

- Businesses should ensure that their VAT processes are reviewed regularly and that any communication with HMRC is channelled through a nominated individual (see **18.7–18.8**).

- If a business underclaims or overpays VAT, HMRC will only pay interest if they have made an error. If in doubt about the advice received from HMRC ask a second opinion (see **18.10–18.11**).

- Businesses should check that their VAT systems are producing the right figures, if you are designing a bespoke computer system, you should get HMRC to review the system to ensure it gives the right information (**18.13–18.18**).

- Be careful of getting involved in VAT avoidance plans as HMRC take a careful look at schemes and most common schemes have to be notified to HMRC (see **18.23–18.25**).

18.1 The head of finance may see VAT as a routine responsibility that can be delegated. This is probably an unwise view.

This chapter explains why a finance director needs to take an interest in the subject, and points out various aspects of it which may need attention because of the problems which could result from getting them wrong.

VAT problems are capable of seriously damaging the financial health of an organisation. Tribunal decisions concerning major businesses, involving well-known names, numbered about 30 in one 12-month period. These cases involved sums from a few hundred thousand pounds to many millions. Of course, some of the companies won their battles with HMRC, but they still had all the disruption of a major dispute and will not have recovered all their costs, never mind the management time.

Focus

Many VAT errors are caused by poor housekeeping. Tribunal decisions show that many careless mistakes are not spotted because:

- both management and staff are unaware of basic VAT rules;

- systems are inadequate;

- simple checks or common-sense points are ignored.

No head of finance can escape responsibility for such problems. They can delegate most of the work on VAT, but they still have responsibility for it! This chapter discusses what those responsibilities are, and suggests some practical precautions that might be taken to help keep the business out of trouble.

THE HEAD OF FINANCE

18.2 The head of finance should take some interest in VAT, because, in most organisations, he or she is the only representative of the accounts department who is in regular contact with the heads of other departments such as sales, marketing, research and development or production. Yet the heads of these other departments often take decisions on policy, sales or purchase contracts and so on, which have VAT consequences. If they do not ask for advice on the VAT aspects of what they propose doing, sooner or later it is inevitable that they will land the business with a VAT expense that could have been avoided. Examples of problems and planning points are highlighted throughout this book.

It is the responsibility of the head of finance to ensure that colleagues in other departments are aware of the need to think about VAT before they act! In fact, VAT is one of the best excuses a company accountant has for getting out of the accounts department to go visiting other parts of the organisation. If a business has a tax department, does the specialist responsible for VAT liaise with colleagues? In a large organisation, there is too much going on for the head of finance to be able to keep track of all of it. They will need other pairs of eyes and ears in support. The task is to make sure that other departments are aware of the VAT angles which might affect what they do in their respective responsibilities, and how getting it wrong could hit their budgets.

Here's a true story to illustrate the point. Whilst visiting one of their factories, the head of the tax department spotted a pack of a new product that was about to be trialled. It was the first he knew of this; yet the product was on the borderline between zero- and standard-rating, with the latter the more likely. Adding standard-rate VAT to a product can make a critical difference to the pricing and profit margin, yet the tax department had not been asked about it.

It was good that the head of tax went out visiting, good that he spotted the problem—but bad that it was possible for a new product to get that far in development without anyone checking its VAT status.

STAFF

18.3   Responsibility continues with the staff delegated to do the routine work. Have they had any training in those aspects of VAT which affect the business? Who completes the VAT return? Is it an experienced clerk with a knowledge of the organisation, or is this seen as a boring and unimportant job, which gets offloaded onto the latest arrival in the accounts department? That really does happen—and all too often.

For example, not just anyone can handle the VAT return of a banking or insurance business. The person doing so needs a reasonable working knowledge both of how the business earns its living, and of the partial exemption rules, which are one of the more complicated aspects of VAT.

When appointing someone to deal with the VAT returns, it is not enough to simply provide a file of calculations for past returns and send them off to a VAT seminar. The staff dealing with the detailed preparation of the return need to have some understanding of the business if the figures, with which they deal, are to mean anything to them. They need training and proper notes about the system before they are left to get on with the VAT return. Junior staff should be encouraged to visit other parts of the organisation to see how it works, and to meet the people who produce the information used to prepare the return.

BASIC TRAINING FOR STAFF

18.4

Focus

The training needed by staff will vary to some extent according to the nature of the organisation. However, it may include such points as:

- what the business does and how it earns its income;

- the status of that income, whether standard-rated, zero-rated, exempt, etc;

- where the figures for sales, etc, on which the VAT return is based, come from and who codes or otherwise determines the data, which goes into the computer system to produce those figures;

- the basis for using those figures to produce the information for the VAT return. For example, is the business using some special scheme, such as that for retailers, or is it partially exempt? In either case, there will be rules with which it must comply, which may be at least partly set out in a letter from HMRC received some years earlier;

- the tax point rules as they affect the organisation and the difference between tax invoices and requests for payment, pro formas, etc;

- the rules on credit notes and copy invoices;

- VAT grouping, if applicable—precise membership of the group and the consequences thereof.

The above points are just a few examples. The appropriate list varies from one organisation to another.

An instance of how poor training and/or systems got a business into trouble was *Uniroyal Englebert Tyres Ltd* (EDN/90/197 No 5637). A junior employee assumed that an associated company was in the VAT group, and failed to charge VAT on an invoice for services. Upholding the £39,899 penalty, the Tribunal criticised the lack of supervision of the clerk's work.

PERMANENT VAT FILE

18.5

Focus

A permanent VAT file is an important safety precaution. It should contain such information as:

- how the return is prepared for the organisation;

- where the figures for the return come from;

- rulings from HMRC on which the business relies, with emphasis on any conditions imposed by HMRC when granting the business permission to do something;

- if applicable, the legal basis for zero-rating or exempting outputs;

- any other VAT rules, which specifically affect the operations, such as the Special Schemes;

379

- advice from external advisers.

A prudent business would have three files for VAT:

- the VAT returns file containing copies of the returns, and details of the calculations and backup schedules from which the figures for each return were taken;

- a permanent file containing anything from HMRC of long-term importance, such as the VAT registration certificate, correspondence, rulings etc;

- an advice file for correspondence with external advisers.

The VAT returns file should be kept for six years, because that is the requirement for keeping VAT records. However, a business will not normally need to refer to copy returns and schedules more than a year or so old—although, if a dispute with HMRC arises, the old figures may be important.

The other two files contain the information which staff may need to refer to, or about which they need to know. Obviously, these documents must not be buried amongst the routine VAT calculations.

The reason for the separate advice file is that a business does not necessarily want HMRC to see the advice it receives. Whilst most of this will be straightforward, it may concern matters on which there is some room for argument as to the correct interpretation of the law. In such cases, a business is entitled to act according to its view of the matter, but it may not want to draw HMRC's attention to the point by including the advice on it in the permanent file, which officers are likely to see during visits.

Nor would a business necessarily wish HMRC to see, for instance, comment by advisers on possible weaknesses in systems. For instance, both internal and external audit reports may mention matters on which a judgment has to be taken. Officers have limited accountancy training, and sometimes misinterpret comment on such matters.

WHO SHOULD REVIEW AND SIGN THE RETURN?

18.6   The head of finance would normally delegate the detailed preparation of the return, but they should consider carefully who should sign it. See the comments at **5.25**.

This is one of the most important legal documents that the business submits to the tax authorities in the course of the year, and someone senior should sign it. When doing so, they should review the figures to make sure that they reflect any exceptional transactions which can create substantial amounts of output or input tax, such as:

- dealings in property;

- corporate activities such as 'rights' issues of shares and other ways of raising capital;

- takeovers or sales of businesses.

WHO IS RESPONSIBLE FOR VAT REVIEWS?

18.7   A business should ensure that its affairs are reviewed from time to time to see whether they are still being dealt with correctly. Depending upon the business, it might only be necessary to do this every two or three years but, if VAT is never considered, it will go wrong!

- Have there been any changes in circumstances which ought to be notified to HMRC, or which might affect how VAT law applies to the businesses operations?

- How does the business learn of any changes in VAT law affecting it, and how does it ensure that information about them is passed to those responsible for taking any action required? This is especially important in a VAT group. For instance, *VAT Notes*, which comes with the VAT return, will only be sent to the representative member of the group.

- Are any rulings from HMRC still valid? Have the law, the facts, or the circumstances so altered as to invalidate the agreed basis? HMRC frequently give 'rulings' which in reality are no more than agreement to a given basis for accounting on a point of detail. An example might be the basis for apportionment of a sale which includes supplies at different rates of tax.

A ruling can easily be invalidated by changes in circumstances. Moreover, if staff understand nothing of the basis, the local folklore soon becomes that the ruling is 'we charge x%', whereas this is merely the arithmetical result of the agreed calculation for one period. In the next, it may differ considerably.

RELATIONSHIPS WITH HMRC

18.8   The relationship with HMRC needs careful management. For instance, who asks questions on behalf of the business? Many VAT problems are caused by a junior member of staff asking a half-baked question, getting back an inaccurate or incomplete answer, and taking the wrong action in consequence.

Senior management should check all VAT queries to ensure the correct facts are identified, so that the right question can be asked. Junior clerks usually do not have enough understanding of the law or of the wider aspects of a problem to ensure that they ask the right question, let alone get a sensible answer.

Focus

So, if they are dealing with the VAT issues themselves, make sure they:

- write down the facts and the question;

- note the date and name of the person to whom they refer and the answer;

- agree the action to be taken.

HMRC had a generous policy on misdirection—although it was not necessarily generously applied! In Notice 48 (March 2002) *Extra-Statutory Concessions*, they say:

> 'If a Customs & Excise officer, with the full facts before him, has given a clear and unequivocal ruling on VAT in writing or, knowing the full facts, has misled a registered person to his detriment, any assessment of VAT due will be based on the correct ruling from the date the error was brought to the registered person's attention.'

However, HMRC announced in *Revenue & Customs Brief 15/09* that this concession was being withdrawn from 1 April 2009, a retrograde step in my opinion. The Brief says that a number of court cases in recent years have defined the circumstances in which HMRC can regard itself as bound by incorrect advice. In addition, HMRC now has a page on its website detailing the circumstances in which taxpayers can rely on advice received from HMRC and the previous Extra Statutory Concession is now incorporated into a Statement of Practice.

THE FOUR-YEAR TIME LIMIT ON CLAIMS FOR OVERPAID VAT

Unjust enrichment further limits the four-year time limit

18.9   If HMRC gives a ruling which a business thinks may be incorrect, it should dispute it in writing, and submit a claim for any VAT it believes has already been overpaid. The four-year rule in *s 80* limits the period for which a business can reclaim overpaid VAT. From 1 April 2009 the limits were increased from three years to four with certain transitional provisions meaning that no adjustment can be made for periods ending before 31 March 2006 (see Chapter 39, *Assessment and VAT Penalties* for details).

See **5.31** for more on this.

Even if the overpayment was within the last four years, HMRC can refuse to repay a business if to do so would *unjustly enrich* it. Broadly speaking, the latter means that, if a business has charged on the VAT to a customer, it can only get the money back from HMRC if it promises, in turn, to repay it to that customer under rules set out in the *VAT Regulations 43A–G*. This limit on repayment claims matches the four-year time limit for assessments by HMRC, which is explained at **39.3**.

Unfortunately, unjust enrichment applies regardless of whether the business made the mistake or HMRC did—even if the mistake was that they had not implemented EU law correctly.

Thus, there is a serious potential problem in accepting a ruling from HMRC which the business does not like. If a business has been overcharging VAT for four years already, time is now running against it. Moreover, it is all too often the case that traders who are shown to have overpaid are denied repayment under the unjust enrichment provisions, and, therefore, get no compensation for any commercial disadvantage they may have suffered in having to charge VAT.

HMRC have tended to win Tribunal appeals concerning whether allowing a repayment would unjustly enrich the claimant. However, in *Newcastle Theatre Royal Trust Ltd* (MAN/03/758 No 18952), it was held that it was not unjust enrichment to refund VAT to a non-profit-making trust which had fixed prices on the basis of what it could charge for each performance, and which would devote the refund to its ongoing promotion of live theatre.

THE INTEREST PROBLEM

Section 78 provides interest only on HMRC errors

18.10   Even if a business does get a repayment, HMRC may refuse to pay interest on it. The problem with interest is that *s 78* only makes HMRC liable to pay it on a mistake if it was they who made the error. If a business misunderstands the law, it is the one making the error. Do not confuse this situation with the one where a business wins an appeal against a decision or assessment by HMRC—see below re *s 84(8)*.

What a business may consider to be an HMRC mistake is not necessarily a justification for interest. For example, if an officer incorrectly refuses to allow input tax to be recovered on certain expenditure, this would be automatically seen as HMRC's mistake. Unfortunately, that is not necessarily an error subject to interest.

This story shows why a business should always pursue a point in detail.

In *Switzerland Tourism* (LON/99/0007 No 17068), the taxpayer failed to extract interest from HMRC on sums it had overpaid after HMRC had told ST to apportion its input tax between business and non-business activities.

In another case, *Netherlands Board of Tourism* (LON/94/607 No 12935) demonstrated that a tourist board could be wholly 'in business'. ST's adviser claimed that it could recover all its VAT on the basis of NBT. The officer replied:

'I do not agree that your client is entitled to full input tax recovery based upon the decision in the Netherlands case. The decision was based on the particular circumstances of the Netherlands Tourist Board. It is inappropriate to compare separate organisations when seeking to establish the amount of input tax recovery of a particular organisation.'

When the adviser replied:

'... in our opinion the circumstances are no different but we will decide in due course about the amount of input tax recovery.'

The officer said that the ruling in his previous letter must be followed on pain of financial penalties.

Several years later *Austrian National Tourist Office* (LON/96/0674 No 15561) won at Tribunal, and was then contacted by ST. On advice, they made a voluntary disclosure of the input tax disallowed over the previous three years. This was rejected, but the consequent appeal forced HMRC to consider ST's circumstances properly for the first time. After being provided with additional information, HMRC repaid the sum claimed.

The Tribunal rejected the contention that, when HMRC say 'no', they are to be presumed to have had all the knowledge required for them to make that decision, unless they can demonstrate otherwise. The Chairman did find it hard to resist the impression that the officer was doing his best to deter the Appellant's accountants from pursuing the matter. Normally, if a Tribunal has such an impression, HMRC are in trouble. However, the Chairman commented that the activities of tourist offices are not necessarily exclusively taxable as *Turespana* (Spanish Tourist Office No 14 568) had shown in 1996. It and the NBT and ANTO cases had shown that various matters must be considered.

Here, there was no clear evidence of reliance on a decision of HMRC made with the relevant facts before them. The Tribunal held that the true cause of the failure to claim input tax in full was the decision by ST and its adviser not to pursue the view that its activities were covered by the NBT case. The officer had said that each case depended upon its facts *which was in effect throwing down the gauntlet to the accountants to establish those facts in the light of the approach of the NBT Tribunal*. Note that the officer had not asked for any information, let alone specified what facts were needed. Thus the ST decision might be thought to provide an incentive to HMRC to make decisions upon the basis of the often limited information presented to them, rather than to ask further questions!

This story seems to be a warning to everyone! This was a harsh view and, possibly, a decision, which was wrong in law. However, assuming it to be correct, the inference is that a business should dispute decisions of HMRC which it does not like.

In a case in which HMRC are, in effect, refusing to discuss the matter, as the officer did in ST, a business can obtain a formal ruling by submitting an application for repayment of the VAT it believes to have been overpaid. This must show the sums in question by VAT return period for the last four years, assuming that the matter goes back that far. At the same time, the business should ask HMRC what further information they need in order to review their decision. Supposing that HMRC then reject the claim after being provided with whatever facts they may have asked for, the business should at least get interest from the date of that rejection, if not from the start of the period covered by the claim, if it eventually wins the argument.

ANOTHER TALE OF TROUBLE

A second story showing why a business should check what HMRC say

18.11   If a business thinks this may be overstating the problem, consider an import duty case, *Nor-cargo Ltd* (MAN/99/7038 No C133). The same Chairman as in ST upheld a refusal by HMRC to refund duty on peeled prawns in brine, which had been paid because HMRC thought that the import quota had been exhausted. The Customs office through which the goods were cleared, had said so on three occasions. The Chairman called them 'bad' errors, but it did not justify the claim for repayment of the duty because the importer could have found the right information on three databases, to which, there was electronic access.

If the money involved is significant, never take what an officer of HMRC says at face value. Always seek confirmation elsewhere.

IF A BUSINESS WINS AN APPEAL, INTEREST IS DUE UNDER SECTION 84(8)

18.12   *Section 84(8)* is the legal basis for interest to a trader who wins an appeal, including when HMRC give in prior to a hearing, not *s 78*. There are three main differences:

- If the dispute concerned a repayment return, and a repayment supplement is due, interest can be claimed as well—in contrast to the rules under *s 78* explained at **5.22**. Under *s 84(8)*, the repayment supplement is seen as a penalty payable by HMRC, not an alternative to the interest.

- The rate of interest can be decided by the Tribunal—although, in both *Olympia Technology Ltd* (LON/04/271 No 19145) and *RSPCA* (LON/02/161 No 19,440), the rate set was based on that due under *s 78*, which is set under *FA 1996 s 197* and *SI 1998/1461*. In contrast, in *Totel Ltd* (MAN/04/275 No 19578), it was set on the basis of a borrowing rate—3% above its bank's base rate—compounded, and therefore, to be calculated every six months.

- The Tribunal will decide the period for which the interest is payable based upon the facts of the case—started ten days after the receipt by HMRC of the repayment return in *Olympia Technology Ltd* (LON/04/271 No 19145) and 30 days, in order to allow HMRC time to investigate in a possible carousel fraud situation, in *Totel*.

The Tribunal in *Totel* noted that HMRC had appealed the RSPCA case and questioned whether it is right that, under *s 84(8)*, both a repayment supplement and interest can be claimed.

In the case of *F J Chalke Ltd & A C Barnes (Wokingham) Ltd,* High Court Chancery Division, 8 May 2009 the High Court decided that taxpayers were entitled to compound, rather than simple, interest. The case was appealed to the Court of Appeal [2010] EWCA Civ 313 which upheld the High Court decision. It is possible that there will be a referral to the ECJ.

In *Revenue & Customs Brief 20/14,* HMRC explained its position following the High Court judgment in Littlewoods Retail Ltd & Ors v HM Revenue & Customs [2014] EWHC 868. The High Court found against HMRC, deciding that Littlewoods' claim for compound interest succeeded in full.

HMRC said that this finding was based on the 'exceptional' circumstances specific to the Littlewoods claimant. HMRC does not consider that the decision provides a clear basis that could be applied to other claimants or a formula for doing so. They also disagreed with the decision and appealed the case to the Court of Appeal where they again lost and have now appealed to the Supreme Court.

The Court also held that the current statutory provisions relating to VAT did provide an appropriate amount of interest in many cases.

HMRC will not be making any payments to other claimants at this stage.

IS THE SYSTEM CAPABLE OF PRODUCING THE RIGHT VAT FIGURES?

18.13   Do not assume that a computer system is capable of producing the right figures just because the vendor said so, or that it has been approved by HMRC and/or has been sold to many other users. Ask exactly what the terms of any approval by HMRC are. In most cases, this will be no more than an agreement that, at a given date, the systems specification met HMRC's basic requirements. It may have been amended since then. In any case, it is unlikely that HMRC have done any testing of the final version.

Here are some points to consider, and some tests used by HMRC, which a business might like to try.

Avoid defaults in the computer programming

18.14 A 'default' is an action the computer takes unless it is specifically instructed otherwise.

Examples are:

- the system assumes that the entry is zero-rated unless the operator specifies standard rate;

- the system assumes that the input VAT for an invoice, which it calculates, is the correct figure unless the operator overrides it to input the amount actually on the invoice.

A default is often dangerous because, when processing large numbers of documents, it is all too easy to hit the return key to accept an incorrect entry.

Check the input and output tax figures

18.15 Do all purchase and sales invoice posting routines incorporate checks for each invoice or batch of invoices posted to prove that the VAT is 20% of the net? Cash discounts offered or received marginally affect the calculation, but do not invalidate this important credibility check.

In *Frank Galliers Ltd* ([1993] STC 284), a cheque to HMRC for a quarter's VAT was inadvertently coded by a clerk to the 'input tax to be claimed account', instead of the VAT Control account. A simple check to compare input tax with total inputs, and output tax with total outputs, would have shown up such an error.

Computer interrogation checks

18.16 Sophisticated checks, where it is possible to interrogate computer systems, include searching for:

- high value input tax—say greater than £1,000;

- input tax that is more than 21% or less than 19% of the net sum—to identify transposition errors;

- the date of purchase invoices—to prevent early claims of input tax;

- a check that invoice sequences are complete.

TALK TO HMRC WHEN DESIGNING A COMPUTER SYSTEM

18.17 When designing a computer system that involves financial transactions, it is wise to consult HMRC. They may have useful comments about potential VAT hazards. It is probably better to write rather than to ring the *National Advice Service,* since HMRC will need detailed information about the transactions with which the system will deal. See under *Contacting HMRC* on page lxvii.

See **14.12** for further comment.

The subversive spreadsheet

18.18   Spreadsheets are causing trouble in VAT! If a business works out figures on paper, it can check them by adding them up, visually testing them for credibility, and so on. It seems that is not being done when the figures are in the computer.

HMRC's experience suggests that people think spreadsheets can be taken for granted as straightforward substitutes for manual calculation. HMRC say that the price for cutting out all the sweat of calculation is a requirement to exercise intelligent control of the end result. In part, that is, of course, a matter of checking whether it makes sense both in absolute terms, and by comparison with previous numbers, just as it always has been. However, it also means controlling the mechanics of the spreadsheet. In an article in the *De Voil Indirect Tax Service* (January 2001), under the heading *The Subversive Spreadsheet,* an official from HMRC's *Computer Audit Operational Policy Team* explained how HMRC were finding material errors in 70%–80% of spreadsheets used in calculating tax liabilities. The examples he quoted included:

- a line added to record the liability of a newly-acquired subsidiary, which was not included in the calculation of the subtotal;

- a retailer, whose spreadsheet slowed down as the number of branches grew. When in a hurry on one occasion, they set it to manual recalculation. The next time they used it, they forgot to recalculate the totals;

- mistakes in programming calculations into the spreadsheet.

The article showed how easy it is for any spreadsheet to go wrong if it is not properly managed. For instance, less than one spreadsheet in 75 looked at by HMRC had any documentation or instructions for use.

This is not just a VAT problem. Spreadsheets are used throughout business for calculating all kinds of figures. If those used to work out the legal liability for VAT are not being properly specified, designed, tested, and maintained in a disciplined fashion, there are likely to be problems with the ones which are used for such purposes as management reporting, marketing, and so on. That could mean that a business is being managed at least partly on the basis of false information.

HMRC's spreadsheet Audit tool *SpACE* is now marketed by LexisNexis. Whether a business needs *SpACE,* or could manage well enough with some common sense and a more disciplined approach to its spreadsheets, the message from HMRC is clear. Businesses in general need to approach the use of spreadsheets more carefully. That's not just because failure to do so may land it with a substantial VAT bill; errors in one used as a basis for managing the business could break it!

The possible impact of mistakes in handling spreadsheets goes far beyond your tax liabilities. How about requiring staff, as part of their training, to compile documentation for spreadsheets you use, and offering a bottle of champagne for the person who finds the biggest mistake!

ERRORS

18.19 Naturally, a business complies with the VAT rules to the best of its ability. However, compliance involves more than just good intentions! Here are some points, which staff must understand.

Errors exceeding £10,000 or 1% of turnover as declared on the VAT return for the period in which the errors are found, subject to an upper limit of £50,000 cannot, in law, be corrected on the VAT return. They have to be disclosed separately to the regional Error Correction Unit (previously called the Voluntary Disclosure Unit). Failure to disclose could earn a penalty of up to 30%, as explained in Chapters 39, *Assessment and VAT Penalties* and 40, *Taking an Appeal to the Tribunal.* Interest is also due.

Does the VAT accounting system identify errors for past periods so as to permit disclosure?

WHAT IF THE CORRECT TREATMENT IS IN DOUBT?

18.20 Suppose, for example, a business is unsure about the correct VAT treatment of a transaction, such as whether it is standard-rated or zero-rated. Does the business always ask HMRC, or does it sometimes wait to see whether they challenge it? This should be a decision taken at finance director level, so do the staff always raise the query?

Where there is doubt, it is legitimate not to query the point with HMRC. However, companies sometimes indulge in wishful thinking for which there is no technical basis, so they should take advice before deciding, and record the basis of their decision in writing.

If HMRC were to decide that an error was so crass that it might be deliberate, they might interview the finance director and whoever signs the VAT return under caution, with a view to possible prosecution!

DOES A BUSINESS TRADE IN EQUIPMENT, COMPONENTS OR TELEPHONES?

18.21   *Finance Act 2003* gave HMRC some draconian powers to attack the 'carousel frauds'. If a business trades in computer equipment, components, telephones, or in sectors such as the fashion industry in which fraudulent transactions are prevalent, it is potentially at very serious risk. See Chapter 17, *What Records are Required?* for more details, and for comments upon the records which a head of finance may need to arrange for other departments to keep.

BEWARE THE SLIPPERY SLOPE!

18.22   Sooner or later, a senior financial manager is likely to meet a situation in which care about ethics is required. In the stress of the moment, it can be all too easy to do something which is near the edge of legality, and, which, at a later date, the business may have difficulty in defending. In numerous cases, people running companies have been prosecuted or penalised by HMRC for actions which involved dishonesty.

Suppose the business is short of cash. Although the VAT return is ready, the business cannot pay the sum due, so it holds up the return. The HMRC computer then produces an estimated assessment, which is for a much lower sum, so the business pays it and continues to withhold the return. That goes on for another three returns before HMRC come round to check up. They then realise that the business knew the assessments were understated, so, in addition to assessing the business for the underpaid VAT, they claim a 100% penalty from the director personally.

This happened in *Frank Thornber* (MAN/98/65 No 16235), in which, the Tribunal agreed that paying an assessment which is known to understate the true liability, amounted to dishonesty. For more on the 100% penalty for conduct involving dishonesty, see **39.34**.

Thornber shows how easy it is to do what is expedient when one is under pressure in business. What may seem the practical thing to do at the time can amount to dishonesty. I call this the *slippery slope* because, often, the first step is merely unwise/incorrect in tax law; however, rather than admit the initial mistake, the temptation is to go on doing the same thing, or, perhaps, something nearer to being dishonest, thus getting oneself deeper into trouble.

I have seen more than one such situation in which it was necessary to stop, think, and say 'no'. That is not always easy if a staff member is under pressure from colleagues. HMRC tend to make examples of professionals if they catch them failing to live up to professional standards. HMRC have put several barristers, solicitors, and accountants in prison in recent years.

VAT AVOIDANCE

18.23   Most businesses of any size are now regularly approached by tax advisers with supposedly cunning plans for avoiding VAT. The result is a much-increased emphasis by HMRC on anti-avoidance, about which they show some signs of paranoia.

Broadly, there are three approaches to VAT avoidance:

- we will have a go at anything which is legal;

- we like to know about schemes, but are cautious about using them;

- we will not touch anything which does not smell right.

A business should have an agreed policy on how aggressive it is prepared to be.

If it's worth doing, there will have enough VAT at stake for it to make a dent in the budget of the business by the time HMRC find out.

NOTIFYING CUNNING PLANS TO HMRC

18.24   HMRC now have to be told about certain types of avoidance schemes when they are thought up. I do not cover the detailed rules here because artificial schemes designed to avoid VAT are normally put forward by advisers.

Initially, a business had to inform HMRC if they were using an avoidance scheme, but from 1 September 2017, the responsibility for disclosing VAT avoidance schemes to HMRC moves from scheme users to scheme promoters. It also widens the scope of the disclosure regime to include all indirect taxes.

The measure will require promoters of indirect tax avoidance schemes to provide details of schemes at the earliest of:

- the date the promoter first makes a firm approach to another person about the proposed scheme;

- the date the proposals are first made available for implementation by another; or

- the date the promoter first becomes aware of any transaction which forms part of the scheme.

A business making a disclosure should contact the VAT Avoidance Disclosures Unit, Anti-Avoidance Group (Intelligence), HM Revenue & Customs, 1st Floor, 22 Kingsway, London WC2B 6NR or by e-mail to vat.avoidance.disclosures. bst@hmrc.gsi.gov.uk.

SOME CONSIDERATIONS TO BEAR IN MIND

18.25   There is a difference between straightforward planning, ie using the law in the way in which it is intended to operate, and doing something to achieve a result which was obviously not that intended.

Aggression tends to breed aggression. If a business upsets HMRC by doing something which they regard as not legitimate planning, they will not trust it in future. Worse, they might decide to get their own back by applying the rules strictly on, for instance, the need to have tax invoices containing all the details required by law in order to justify the recovery of input VAT. They have it in their power to make a considerable nuisance of themselves should they decide to do so.

Bear in mind that advisers may put forward ideas which are theoretically sound, but which require careful implementation in practice. In many cases, this means that to apply them correctly over time will give a business significant administrative aggravation. The more cunning the plan, the more likely it is that it must be applied precisely, no matter how artificial and administratively expensive it may be to do so.

CONCLUSION

18.26   Under the pressures of responsibility for such key tasks as financial control, budgeting, reporting to management against budgets, and working with colleagues to achieve them, it is all too easy for a finance director to overlook VAT. It may seem a routine matter of no great financial significance, provided that the return is completed, and the tax paid on time.

Not so! Whilst the degree of risk varies from business to business, it is, in most cases, sufficient for a serious mistake to cost a significant percentage of net profit.

Just as the production director must assess the risk of the factory blowing up, so must the finance director review how VAT could damage the financial health of the business.

Chapter 19

How does a business keep up to date on changes in VAT?

SIGNPOSTS

- There are a number of ways that changes in the legislation and its interpretation can occur, it is important to know how the changes take place and to keep up to date with the important changes (see **19.1–19.2**).

- Businesses should be aware of important Tribunal decisions but it is not necessary to read every one (see **19.3–19.7**).

- Businesses can consult HMRC using a telephone and written enquiries service although the quality of the service is doubtful (see **19.8**).

- The most effective way of keeping up to date with changes is to look at the HMRC website (see **19.11–19.16**).

19.1   It is important to stay up to date on VAT—insofar as it affects the business or those of its clients. In this chapter, I set out how the changes occur, how HMRC issue information about them, and how a business can find out about them.

For most businesses, VAT is merely one of the technical subjects it has to cope with, whether it is in industry or in professional practice. However, I have set out the circumstances of how changes occur in detail because a business may need to understand them. Should a business need to understand the full details of the change because of important effects to its business or that of a client, this chapter will help.

The source of VAT law is set out in Chapter 2, *Where to Find the Law.* However, when I refer here to 'rules', I mean not just the law, but the interpretation of it by HMRC set out in the guidance that they issue. Whilst that guidance is mostly not law in itself—and, it can, of course, be wrong—it can be very expensive to ignore it!

The VAT rules change throughout the year—sometimes several times a month. If a business spots a change and does not wish to apply it, it can challenge that view. It is potentially much more expensive if a change happens without a business being aware of it, and it is then several years before the failure to apply it is discovered—usually by a visiting officer from HMRC. The business may still be able to challenge HMRC's view—either that it is wrong in principle, or that it does not apply in a particular case, but the risk will be an assessment going back up to four years (see Chapter 39, *Assessment and VAT Penalties* for details).

Of course, a change could be in favour of a business. If a business fails to notice the change, and under-recovers input tax, it will get no interest on a subsequent repayment claim. If it has overcharged VAT, it can even be difficult to get it back again. In many cases, HMRC argue that to repay it to the business would unjustly enrich it! For more about unjust enrichment, see **18.9**.

HOW CHANGES OCCUR

19.2

Focus

Changes result from:

- the *Finance Act* each year;

- statutory   instruments—either   *Treasury   Orders*   or *HMRC Regulations*—which can pass through Parliament at any time when it is in session and which take effect in a few weeks, sometimes overnight;

- changes in HMRC's policy;

- Tribunal and Court decisions—which do not change the law, but can alter everyone's understanding of how it should be interpreted.

Thus, the rules include points of interpretation to be found in statements of policy by HMRC, or in court decisions. That those points are not always right is from time to time a cause of changes, sometimes repeated changes. It is usually because the matter has been argued in court with different results on appeal, but it can be merely because HMRC have altered their view.

Staying up to date on these changes is a serious problem—even for a VAT specialist. Often, several occur in a month and, apart from anything announced in the Budget, they mostly result from the numerous Tribunal and Court decisions. Most of the changes in HMRC's policy originate with one of those decisions.

IS IT NECESSARY TO READ EVERY DECISION?

19.3   In short no! It is not practical for a non-specialist to read every case. An auditor or an accountant in a commercial job will not have the time for what is marginal to their main work. The Tribunal decisions are numerous; although many are trivial, it takes time even to glance through a collection of those ones. Many of the more serious cases merely confirm the views of HMRC on points, which both that trader and the rest of us should have understood, but a specialist still needs to skim through them in order to identify the ones which matter.

The ones which do matter can take from 20 minutes to an hour or more to read. They are important because, every now and then, a decision concerning one business alters everyone's grasp of what the law means to others. That change can put those other businesses at risk for substantial sums if they have also been getting it wrong on past transactions.

Thus, keeping an eye on Tribunal decisions as they come out is demanding even for VAT specialists. Apart from the big firms, where one person is often delegated to read the cases and to produce internal guidance, most people have to rely on comment in the professional or trade press.

An auditor, or an accountant in a commercial job, may have to rely on announcements by HMRC in *VAT Notes* and in their *Revenue & Customs Briefs*. See **19.10–19.13** about these.

HOW TO FIND A TRIBUNAL DECISION

19.4   The decisions of the Tax Chamber of the Tribunal service are published at http://www.financeandtaxtribunals.gov.uk/Aspx/default.aspx The *Decisions Database* contains the decisions on all the taxes and duties handled by the Tribunals, not just those on VAT. It contains a list of them starting with the latest ones published; sadly, they are in the order in which they were released, not in numerical order. However, there is a search facility which can be used to find an individual case by quoting its name and/or its number. When it finds a page for that case, click on the link to the decision itself, which appears in Word.

HOW A SPECIALIST CAN ACCESS ALL DECISIONS

19.5   An alternative is the British and Irish Legal Information Institute site www.bailii.org. When on the homepage, click on *United Kingdom,* which is on the left-hand side, then *First-tier Tribunals (Tax)*. For older decisions click on *United Kingdom VAT & Duties Tribunal Decisions.*

A business can request Tribunal decisions to be e-mailed to it, but reading all the published Tribunal decision can be time-consuming.

PROMPT ACTION MAY BE NEEDED

19.6   As Tribunal decisions are often appealed, it can be five or six years, sometimes up to ten or more, before the matter is finally resolved. Meanwhile, one may need to submit a voluntary disclosure to HMRC either claiming back overpaid VAT, or owning up to underpaid sums.

If HMRC lost the case, and the decision suggests that a business has overpaid, the four-year time limit means it will want to reclaim that VAT as soon as possible in order to maximise what can be recovered on past transactions. If the sum exceeds £10k, it must be done by a voluntary disclosure, not on the next VAT return. See **39.26** for further comment. If HMRC's victory suggests a business has underpaid VAT—either undercharged on sales, or over-recovered on costs—the potential damage is an assessment for the last four years. The temptation may be to wait until HMRC find out what has been done because, if it takes them say a year to do so, the first of the four years will no longer be assessable. However, if the transactions in question have continued, a business will have to change what it is doing in order to stop the damage. If a business did that without making a voluntary disclosure of the past mistakes, HMRC might accuse it of dishonesty; that the original error was innocent because of a misunderstanding of the law is not the point. Once a business is aware of a mistake, failure to make a voluntary disclosure of it can be seen as dishonest. In a dishonest situation, the time limit rises to 20 years, and the penalty to up to 100% of the tax due!

Naturally, that depends upon the circumstances. If an unfavourable decision has been appealed by the trader involved, a business could argue that the past is still in doubt, and that it has changed its treatment of future transactions as a precaution. If a business does decide not to disclose, I suggest that the business creates a memorandum stating why and sign and date it. It would be a valuable defence, should HMRC question the non-disclosure.

HAS A DECISION BEEN APPEALED?

19.7   A business cannot rely on a decision, whether by a Tax Tribunal, or the Court of Appeal, unless and until it is known that there has been no further appeal. Sometimes, a matter is in abeyance pending a response to a question put to the Court of Justice of the European Communities. It is only when the Supreme Court decides the matter that no further appeal is possible.

On the HMRC website, there is a list of cases under appeal in VAT appeal updates, which is amended at least monthly. See **19.13** for how to find it.

Unfortunately, HMRC does not appeal against some of the Tribunal decisions, usually in cases it loses but does not accept. Often, it waits until it can make the same decision on the same point in another case in order that, if the trader appeals, it can re-argue the matter! Thus, unless HMRC say they accept a Tribunal decision, a business cannot rely on not having to argue the matter again itself.

ENQUIRIES

19.8   A business can of course telephone the National Advisory Service on 0845 010 9000 to ask for information and guidance from HMRC. That is useful for simple matters such as checking a VAT number quoted (incidentally, always state the name and address of the other business as well as the number because the full details can then be confirmed).

However, requesting advice about a problem of any complexity is usually a waste of time. A business will be asked to write in because it will need to state the full facts. Any guidance given over the telephone on the basis of an outline query is of limited value. It will probably be based upon what is said in a public notice and it could easily mislead the taxpayer. A business cannot rely on guidance given to it, either by HMRC or by an adviser, unless it has produced a full statement of the facts.

To find the address for written enquiries—which can be by e-mail or by post— click *Contact us* at the top of a page on the website (www.hmrc.gov.uk). Then click *VAT* which takes you to various alternative methods of contacting HMRC. If a business chooses to send its enquiry by post, please note that all written enquires are now dealt with by a new centralised unit in Southend. The current policy on written enquiries is extremely unhelpful, as in most cases the business is just referred to the appropriate VAT Notice and told to work it out itself.

In April 2008, HMRC introduced a new system of non-statutory clearances for businesses. At the time of introduction, a new Notice 700/6 (April 2008) was produced to help businesses get used to the new system. It did not start well, as it stated the following:

> 'This notice is for non-business customers only. Guidance for business customers seeking non-statutory clearances is available here'.

The Notice began by contradicting itself in virtually its first paragraph— although I feel that this actually set the right tone for the new system!

The new system effectively set up a two-tier service. It is HMRC's policy to try to encourage a greater use of its Public Notices and website by traders and the public, and most of its written advice simply guides enquirers to the relevant Public Notice. In a lot of cases, this is quite sufficient. Most small businesses and individuals needing clarification of a VAT problem are either unaware of the published guidance, or else cannot find it on HMRC's user-unfriendly website. As such, a simple reply referring them to the relevant paragraph can be enough to resolve the matter. However, in many cases, a business or its advisers have already read the guidance, and either do not understand it, or cannot apply it to the exact circumstances of the business. Consequently, further clarification is required. To simply be referred back to the same guidance that they did not understand in the first place causes great irritation, and a number of accountancy contacts of ours cannot be bothered to use the service anymore as they can get no useful advice from it.

The higher-tier service is supposed to provide businesses with the service that they need, but is also far from the mark in many cases. According to HMRC, in order to obtain a non-statutory clearance, businesses should provide the following information and include a completed checklist that can be obtained from the HMRC website:

- 'a clear explanation of the precise point(s) about which you are unclear of the tax consequences

- where you have received professional advice in respect of the tax question on which you are seeking a ruling, you must tell us the reason for uncertainty

- if you or your professional advisers have considered alternative tax treatments, you should give a brief indication of the alternative interpretations considered

- if the point at issue concerns a transaction which has yet to take place, you should provide a copy of the final draft contract, where appropriate, and full details of the other parties involved to the extent that this is possible

- where a ruling is sought before contracts are finalised, a ruling may still be given, but will not be binding if a contract is produced later and the relevant facts vary significantly from those disclosed (paragraph 3.3 below). You should come back to us to review our ruling where the relevant terms of the contract have changed

- copies of all of the relevant documents, with what you consider to be the relevant areas clearly highlighted (or otherwise drawn attention to)

- (so that we can target our resources appropriately) an estimate of the money associated with the decision, for example, the annual value of sales of an item, in respect of which you want a ruling on the liability to tax and

- any transactions (proposed or actual) related to, consequent upon, or forming part of a series with the transaction in respect of which a ruling is sought, whether or not these transactions are certain to take place.'

Unfortunately, even though many businesses write in requesting a clearance, HMRC vet all the applications, resulting in most being rejected and returned to the lower-tier service. According to HMRC figures, by October 2008, 17,000 written enquiries had been dealt with by the normal services, and only about 150 dealt with as clearances, and in the majority of these, HMRC did not agree with the trader's interpretation of the correct tax treatment.

In fairness to HMRC, when they have responded to a clearance request with a full reply, it has been comprehensive and well written, but it is the large majority of written responses to queries that have caused the most concern. Simply referring enquirers to a Notice they have already read and failed to understand, is not providing the trading public with the service that they require.

Taxpayers need certainty in their businesses, particularly in their tax affairs at this difficult time for the economy. HMRC do not consider that a non-statutory clearance provides a binding ruling or an appealable matter. So, if you are one of the lucky few that do receive a clearance, and you disagree with HMRC's analysis, you cannot appeal the matter (according to HMRC). However, as HMRC say it's not binding, you can simply ignore it, although HMRC will apply their interpretation at the next visit, and then you may get an appealable matter—an assessment. This clearly cannot be helpful to businesses.

HMRC also will not supply a 'rubber stamping' service. I do have some sympathy with them here, but not much. With large value transactions, businesses often want some handholding, as the VAT amounts can be huge. For example, a business is selling a property, and although it appears to fulfil the criteria for a TOGC, it writes to HMRC to have this confirmed. HMRC will refuse to do so, and write back, sometimes at length, saying why it will not give a reply and, you have guessed it, referring the enquirer back to the appropriate HMRC guidance. Would it not be simpler (and quicker) to just answer the question?

THE SPECIALIST OFFICE FOR CHARITIES

19.9 HMRC have a specialist office providing advice on charity related taxation issues, both to charities and to businesses and individuals dealing with them. The Charities Helpline is available 8am–6pm, Monday–Friday, except public holidays, on 0845 302 0203.

The address is HMRC Charities, St John's House, Merton Road, Bootle, Merseyside L69 9BB.

The website includes a section on *Charities* at www.hmrc.gov.uk/charities.

A BUSINESS SHOULD RECORD WHEN IT GETS ITS COPY OF VAT NOTES

19.10 *VAT Notes*, which is published quarterly on the HMRC website, tells about any new versions of, or amendments to, the *Public Notices*, and of any *Revenue & Customs Briefs* or *Information Sheets* issued (note that *Revenue &*

19.11 *How does a business keep up to date on changes in VAT?*

Customs Briefs replaced *Business Briefs* from 1 July 2007). See **19.13** for how to find it.

One possible problem is that a change has been introduced at short notice, but is supposedly to be applied by visiting officers with a 'light touch'. In *Information Sheet 8/2005*, HMRC were not to enforce the change requiring VAT invoices for fuel refunded to staff *'until such time as businesses have had a reasonable period to adjust to the new requirement'*. Now that may sound very fair. In practice, I will be surprised if it is applied fairly at all!

In the past, perhaps six months has been allowed in such circumstances—but the key point is that many smaller businesses do not get visits for several years after a change. By the time of the visit, the officer will have usually forgotten about such a 'light touch' when checking back for four years.

HOW ARE CHANGES OF POLICY ANNOUNCED?

19.11 Changes of policy are usually announced either in a *Revenue & Customs Brief,* or in a *Public Notice*. However, businesses also need to check *VAT Information Sheets*; supposedly, these are additional detailed guidance expanding on either a *Revenue & Customs Brief* or a *Public Notice,* but they could easily include new points as well.

Policy changes are usually announced in *Revenue & Customs Briefs*, which are not distributed in paper form, but are available on the HMRC website.

Businesses can sign up on the website for free e-mails called *Alerts Summary*, which list changed documents and new additions, including *Revenue & Customs Briefs*. Unfortunately, they are not necessarily accurate or complete, and often list documents to which there is no apparent change!

VAT Notes does usually refer to each *Revenue & Customs Brief* that has been issued, but it is often difficult to understand what that *Brief* is about; frequently, it mentions the case which has resulted in the *Brief,* but without saying what it refers to. In other words, until you see the *Brief,* you cannot discover the nature of the business, or the kinds of transaction which it affects.

SO, HOW DO I SUGGEST A BUSINESS STAYS UP TO DATE?

19.12 A relatively simple way is to visit the HMRC website, say once a month, and to look at any new issues of *VAT Notes* and *Revenue & Customs Briefs*. *VAT Notes* is normally on the site in the second half of April (following the budget in March) and of June, September, and December.

For a non-specialist, the problem is how to identify any relevant change amongst the mass of information published, without having to spend many hours reading everything. I therefore suggest concentrating on the *VAT Notes* and the *Revenue Customs Briefs* as they are issued. For warnings about changes in prospect and the potential impact of court decisions about which nothing has yet been said by HMRC, a non-specialist is likely to have to rely on guidance from an adviser, although articles in the professional press can be helpful.

A big organisation may subscribe to one of the loose-leaf reference books published both electronically and on paper. These are updated regularly, and may also give a business the right to receive e-mails informing them of the latest developments.

WHERE TO LOOK ON THE HMRC WEBSITE

19.13   The latest HMRC publications, Business Briefs, updated public notices etc can be obtained from https://www.gov.uk/topic/business-tax/vat/latest.

OBTAINING A PUBLIC NOTICE

19.14   If a business needs to see the latest version of a notice quickly, the website can of course be very useful—especially as a PDF version is easy to search, as explained below. When looking at the electronic version of Notice 999 *Catalogue of Publications*, go to the actual notice even if the list says it is the old one. You may find that the latest copy is there after all. The problem, generally, is that many of the new versions of notices, or amendments to existing ones, are announced up to a month or more before they are available as printed copies.

HOW TO SEARCH A NOTICE IN PDF

19.15   HMRC originally published all the notices on its new website in PDF versions. The advantage of a PDF version of a document is that users can use the PDF search facility—in the toolbar. That increases the chance of finding whether a particular subject or point is covered in the document.

That is a far more efficient search facility than the one on the website as a whole. For example, if users search for 'entertainment', the site will give numerous sources. It looks good—until you choose, say, the 'sponsorship' headline, which goes to that notice. Sadly, on arrival there, you are at the front page with no indication of where to look within it!

PRINTING FROM A PDF VERSION OF A NOTICE

19.16   If users want to print just a part of a notice, such as a form, enter just the page number(s) in the instructions to the printer. It should then print a page exactly as in the Notice—whereas if you cut and paste it from the PDF version, the result is often poor.

Chapter 20

Exports and removals of goods

SIGNPOSTS

- Goods that are exported to a destination outside the EU or removed from the UK to a VAT-registered customer in another EU Member State can be zero-rated providing the supplier has the required evidence of removal (see **20.5–20.9**).

- The National Export System is an electronic system for managing export declarations introduced by HMRC in 2003 (see **20.10**).

- Evidence of export/removal from the UK has to be obtained within certain time limits, the evidence has to be retained for six years and has to be in the required format (see **20.11–20.15**).

- There are special rules for transfers of own goods, sale or return, consignment stock and call-off stock (see **20.20–20.21**).

- If you sell to private individuals in other Member States of the EU by mail order or over the internet—distance sales—then you may be required to register for VAT in another Member State (see **20.22–20.23**).

- If a business buys goods from a supplier in another EU Member State and has them shipped direct to a customer in a third State, it is known as triangulation and there are special rules that simplify the process (see **20.25–20.27**).

- If you install or assemble goods in other Member States there are special rules (see **20.28–20.29**).

20.1   This chapter is relevant to all those businesses which move goods from the UK to another country. Usually, that means selling goods to customers abroad, but it also includes taking them to another branch or office of the same company outside the UK.

THE DIFFERENCE BETWEEN GOODS AND SERVICES

20.2   The place of supply of goods which leave the UK is deemed to be the UK (where the goods are located at the time they are supplied). That supply is then zero-rated, subject to the conditions explained in this chapter. There are different place of supply rules for services. As explained in Chapter 23, *Exports and Imports of Services*, certain services are zero-rated or outside the scope of UK VAT. In contrast to goods, the reason for not having to charge VAT on services is, in most cases, because the place of supply is outside the UK.

PLACE OF SUPPLY OF GOODS

20.3   The basic rule is that the place of supply of goods is where the goods are located at the time the goods are allocated or supplied to the customer. So, if the goods are in the UK and the customer is in the UK the sale is subject to UK VAT.

If the goods are supplied to an overseas customer and leave the EU the supply can be zero-rated as can supplies to VAT registered businesses in other EU Member States. However, supplies to private customers and unregistered businesses in other EU Member States are subject to UK VAT.

The legislation on the place of supply of goods is contained in *VATA 1994, s 7* and *Value Added Tax (Place of Supply of Goods) Order (SI 1992/3283)*. It should be noted that *s 7* is a hierarchical structure; the place of supply of any goods may be determined by working through the rules in order, until the one applicable to the supply in question is reached. The basic place of supply for goods can be summarised as being where the goods are located at the time they are assigned to the customer.

THE PLACE OF SUPPLY OF GOODS SOLD DURING A CRUISE

20.4   An exception to the above is the place of supply of goods sold on ships, aircraft or trains, during the transport of passengers within the EU. The place of supply is where the journey begins. However, in *Kholer* (C-58/04), the ECJ held that, when a cruise ship took passengers from Germany to Italy with stops at ports outside the EU, the place of supply for any goods sold from a boutique whilst in those non-EU ports, was there, not in the EU.

THE ZERO-RATING OF EXPORTED GOODS IS NOT AUTOMATIC

20.5   Beware of thinking that, if a business exports goods, zero-rating is automatic. This is not so! A business only obtains zero-rating if it meets HMRC's requirements on evidence. Whilst that is often simple enough, provided that the business and its staff understand what is required, there are many situations which require care. If a business takes the zero-rating for granted, it will get caught out sooner or later.

See also Chapter 22, *EC Sales Lists and Intrastat Returns*, for details of forms and records that a business may need to complete concerning EU trade:

- EC Sales Lists;

- Intrastat Supplementary Declarations;

- Register of Temporary Movements of Goods.

THE LAW

20.6   *Section 30(6)–(9)* zero-rates the export or removal of goods in various circumstances, subject to HMRC being satisfied that they have left the UK. HMRC are given powers to make regulations about the evidence they require in order to satisfy these conditions. The law is contained in the *VAT Regulations (SI 1995/2518), regs 128–155*, which say that zero-rating in a variety of circumstances is subject to such conditions as HMRC may impose.

The main sources of information on those conditions are VAT Notice 703 *Export and removals of goods from the UK,* and Notice 725 *The Single Market.* However, there are subsidiary Notices such as 703/1 *Freight containers supplied for export or removal from the UK,* and 705 *Personal exports of new motor vehicles to destinations outside the European Community from 1 January 1993.*

MEMBERSHIP OF THE EU

20.7   For a list of the Member States of the EU, see page lxxv at the start of the book.

EXPORTS VERSUS REMOVALS

20.8   An *export* of goods means to a destination outside the EU. A *removal* of goods is to a destination within the EU. Do not confuse them! The distinction is not academic; nor is it just a matter of jargon. The two systems of zero-rating are fundamentally different. Many people in business do not understand either set of rules properly so, if they use the word 'export' to cover both situations, sooner or later there will be a misunderstanding that could prove expensive! This situation will remain the same until at least the start of 2019 which is the earliest possible date for the UK to leave the EU.

EVIDENCE IS CRITICAL

20.9 All too often, businesses assume that a sale is zero-rated just because they know that the goods have left the country. It does not occur to them to consider how they are going to prove that to a HMRC officer up to four years later! Zero-rating is not automatic. HMRC must be satisfied that the goods physically left the UK, and that the correct documentary evidence is available to support it.

Following a recent ECJ decision in *R (on the application of Teleos plc) v Revenue and Customs Comrs* (C-409/04), HMRC issued *Revenue and Customs Brief 61/07*. The ECJ found that the supplier should not be unduly penalised for relying on seemingly legitimate proof of UK removal evidence that later turned out to have been falsified.

HMRC have outlined their interpretation of the ECJ's findings as follows:

- goods must physically leave the territory of the Member State of supply to qualify for zero rating.

If a supplier:

- acts in good faith and submits evidence establishing a right to zero-rate an intra-Community transaction; and

- has no involvement in tax evasion and takes every reasonable measure in their power to ensure that the transaction did not lead to their participation in tax evasion,

then the Member State cannot hold the supplier to account for the VAT on those goods if the information relied on subsequently proves to be false.

HMRC say the case will limit their ability to assess suppliers for incorrect zero rating, but acknowledge that the Court had to balance the benefit of legal certainty for suppliers who act in good faith, with the need to have stringent conditions to prevent fraud and abuse. HMRC say that the good faith of the supplier, the steps they took, and whether they are established as not participating in fraud, will become critical factors in deciding whether they can be assessed for output tax after the event.

Whilst HMRC do not expect many businesses to be on all fours with the *Teleos* case, they say that those who are can now appeal their assessment, subject to the normal time limits.

LOST, STOLEN OR DESTROYED GOODS

20.9A When supplying goods to a VAT registered business in another EU Member State, the VAT treatment of lost, destroyed or stolen goods is as follows:

- before the goods have been supplied, for example they are awaiting collection, no VAT is due as no supply has been made;

- while the goods are in transit in the UK, either under instruction of the supplier or customer, VAT is due unless you hold evidence of loss, destruction or theft (eg an insurance claim or police crime number or evidence of investigation);

- while the goods are being transported outside the UK by either you or your customer the goods may continue to be zero-rated provided you have valid proof of removal of the goods from the UK and the VAT registration number of your customer. However, your customer may still be liable to account for acquisition tax in the Member State of acquisition. There may also be additional VAT liabilities if the loss, destruction or theft occurs en route through a Member State. In that event HMRC advise that you should check on the position with the VAT authority in the Member State concerned.

The VAT treatment of goods destined for export outside the EC which have been accidentally lost, destroyed or stolen in the UK as follows:

- before you supplied them, in other words before you issue an invoice or start to transport the goods, for example when they are still in the warehouse or storage – no VAT is due;

- you supplied them for direct export (you arrange the transport of the goods) – no VAT is due provided that evidence of loss, destruction or theft is held, for example an insurance claim, police investigation or similar evidence; or

- you supplied them for indirect export (the customer arranges the transport of the goods) – VAT is due at the appropriate rate if the goods have been delivered to or collected by the overseas person, or their agent, in the UK.

THE NATIONAL EXPORT SYSTEM

20.10   The *National Export System* (NES) is an electronic system of managing declarations to HMRC concerning exports of goods. It began to take effect in 2003, when it was known until March 2007 as the 'New Export System', and has been implemented in stages by HMRC. If a business exports goods, it will have a major impact on how it obtains evidence of the goods leaving the EU, because the official material will be electronic. Businesses therefore need to understand what that material looks like and how it is to be retained, to what extent it is currently in operation at the ports or airports used, and what is likely to happen in the near future.

A fundamental aspect of the system is that HMRC routinely accept electronic declarations, and only respond, other than by a mere electronic acknowledgement, in those cases in which they wish to examine the goods or review the situation in more detail.

Large businesses may deal with NES direct. It is possible to obtain approval from HMRC for the warehouse and goods handling system of a business to link into the NES and make the necessary electronic declarations direct. Small businesses are likely to use export agents to handle the links with HMRC.

Whichever is the case, a business should discuss the system with the people who handle it, and make sure that they understand what electronic records will be obtained, and what extra commercial evidence will be needed. The traditional paperwork system is on its way out!

Information on HMRC's website about the NES Notice 275 is limited, mostly highly technical, and assumes a basic understanding of CHIEF. There is no 'layman's guide'. Indeed, even people within HMRC have said that they did not understand the system, and would welcome such a guide. Most people from industry and VAT consultants have never even heard of it!

That means serious prospective danger, since the people who handle the export of goods, whether they are in the dispatch department of a business or in an export agency, are not accountants, and often have little understanding of VAT. As such, they are unlikely to even consider, let alone organise, the necessary export evidence if left to their own devices!

TIME LIMIT FOR EVIDENCE

20.11

Focus

A business has three months from the date of each export or removal in which to get the evidence appropriate to that transaction. This is extended to six months if the goods are delivered within the UK for processing or for incorporation into other goods before leaving the country.

A common pitfall is failure to collect the evidence systematically. Then, when a VAT officer on a visit asks for the records, they are incomplete. The officer is entitled to assess straightaway for VAT on all shipments for which the evidence is missing. Even if a business is allowed, for example, a month's grace, that is very little time when chasing up paperwork on transactions up to four years old: especially if the people from whom they are trying to obtain it are transport contractors or freight forwarding agents acting for the customers rather than the supplier, and who have no financial interest in assisting them.

EXPORTS ARE CHECKED BY HMRC

20.12   An export of goods outside the EU goes through Customs controls at the point of exit. There may no longer be official paperwork. See above concerning the *New Export System*. The precise nature of this proof of export differs according to the means of transport used. See Notice 703 (November 2013), which, in para 6.4, also demands supporting commercial documentation.

REMOVALS ARE NOT SUBJECT TO FRONTIER CONTROLS

20.13   Within the single market of the EU, there are no Customs barriers. No official evidence of removal is therefore possible, but a business still needs evidence that the goods have left the UK. This is not always easy to obtain. Suppose a haulier employed by the customer collects the goods; the supplier has no control over the haulier, and will have no evidence of removal unless they make sure that the customer provides them with it.

Every time there is a removal of goods from the UK, the business must, therefore, pause to consider what evidence will be available to justify zero-rating.

THE EVIDENCE REQUIRED

20.14   Often, several pieces of commercial evidence, such as the haulier's invoice, ferry documentation, and a goods received note signed by the customer, are needed to provide a complete audit trail for HMRC. In *VAT Information Sheet 2/00*, they ask for such details as the vehicle registration number, name and signature of driver, route used, and trailer or container number.

Focus

In Notice 725 *The Single Market*, HMRC say a business can use a combination of the following:

- the customer's order (including customer's name, VAT number and delivery address for the goods);

- inter-company correspondence;

- copy sales invoice (including a description of the goods, an invoice number and customer's EC VAT number etc);

- advice note;

- packing list;

- commercial transport document(s) from the carrier responsible for removing the goods from the UK, for example an International Consignment Note (CMR) fully completed by the consignor, the haulier and signed by receiving consignee;

- details of insurance or freight charges;

- bank statements as evidence of payment;

- receipted copy of the consignment note as evidence of receipt of goods abroad; or

- any other documents relevant to the removal of the goods in question which you would normally obtain in the course of your intra-EC business.

The documents you use as proof of removal must clearly identify the following:

- the supplier;

- the consignor (where different from the supplier);

- the customer;

- the goods;

- an accurate value;

- the mode of transport and route of movement of the goods; and

- the EC destination.

All of this is somewhat vague, but it is up to the business to establish what evidence is available in the circumstances in which the business removes the goods from the UK. This is a problem of record-keeping on which HMRC have wide powers, so when they refuse to accept that goods have left the UK, HMRC nearly always win! It would be possible to fill several pages of this book with stories of the numerous Tribunal appeals against assessments by HMRC resulting from inadequate evidence that goods have been removed or exported. Here is an example.

DW Munge (LON/84/166 No 1852) shipped wallpaper to Ireland in lorries, which were returning empty from the continent via Dover to Ireland. The lorry drivers were the agents of the purchasers. Despite a statutory declaration by the managing director of the shipping line that the lorries had indeed passed through Dover, and bank documentation showing payments received from the customer, there was no evidence of the quantities of wallpaper, nor that the payments concerned such quantities. The Tribunal was satisfied that, on the balance of probabilities, the wallpaper had been removed to Ireland but it had no power to substitute its judgment for that of HMRC. This case is typical of the problems which arise from a failure to think things through! A business may know its goods leave the UK, but how will it prove that in several years time?

INTERNATIONAL CONSIGNMENT NOTES

20.15   *International consignment notes* (ICN) are issued under the *Convention on the contract for the international carriage of goods* (CMR Convention). There is no standard form, but each note must contain details of the date and place at which it is created, the names and addresses of the sender, of the carrier and of the consignee, the place and date of the taking over of the goods and the delivery address.

If the value of the goods being supposedly taken out of the UK by the customer (or by a third party on behalf of the latter) is high, or if the business has any reason to wonder whether the goods will leave, check the details on the ICN. The following story is of a situation in which a supposedly sound customer, and an equally legitimate shipping agent, between them produced false ICNs!

In *Atlantic Electronics* (LON/02/1141 No 19,256), HMRC found that one carrier did not exist, the address of it supplied by the solicitors for the Spanish customer being false and that the other carrier denied doing the business! One of the delivery addresses—in Calais, not Spain—was fictitious; the other did exist but the carrier was not there! The UK registration numbers of the supposed vehicles were not known to DVLA. Thus, the ICNs were clearly false.

Yet, Atlantic Electronics had met the directors of the Spanish customer, had carried out due diligence tests on the company, and had obtained confirmation from one of its own trading companies in Spain that the customer was a reputable company. It had checked with HMRC the Spanish VAT number of the customer. It had also investigated the UK shipping agent, and had visited it to check its procedures including the documentation demonstrating the removal of goods from the UK. It had previously done business with one of the agent's directors, and found that the agent was used as a bonded warehouse subject to monthly inspections by HMRC. It had checked its bona fides with the *Professional Association for Warehousing* and with an office of HMRC.

Thus, Atlantic Electronics had every reason to suppose that it was dealing with honest organisations. Yet, the paperwork supposedly showing that the three sales it made had left the UK did not stand up to scrutiny! One of life's lessons; do not assume transactions are sound just because they ought to be! One cannot verify everything but, if there is big money at stake in situations in which a business is not itself shipping the goods, spot checks of the paperwork are essential.

IF GOODS ARE RESOLD WHILST BEING SHIPPED, THERE IS ONLY ONE REMOVAL

20.16   If goods bought in EU Member State A by a trader in Member State B are promptly sold to a second customer in Member State B whilst being shipped, there is only one removal. In other words, only one of the transactions can be zero-rated against the customer's VAT number in Member State B. Which of the transactions is zero-rated will depend upon whether the first buyer takes ownership of the goods and organises their transport. That is unlikely if the first buyer is not VAT registered in A; in order to avoid incurring VAT there, the first buyer will need to quote a VAT number from B. Then, that first buyer must charge VAT in B to the second buyer (*EMAG* (C-245/04)).

Do not confuse the above with triangulation, explained later in this chapter, in which trader in Member State A buys goods from Member State B and sells them on to a customer in Member State C.

ARE THE GOODS DELIVERED IN THE UK, BUT INVOICED TO AN OVERSEAS CUSTOMER?

20.17   Beware the problem of assuming that the business need not charge VAT to a non-UK customer. The normal rules apply as to the evidence required. The goods must leave the UK to justify zero-rating. However sure the business is of the ultimate destination of the goods, they must standard-rate a delivery in the UK unless a special concession applies. There are only a few of these concessions. One example is for components delivered to another UK business, which incorporates them into other goods, and are then exported. If a business believes it qualifies for zero-rating under such a concession, check its precise terms carefully. See, for example, earlier in this chapter about evidence and time limits.

THE CUSTOMER'S VAT NUMBER

20.18

Focus

In addition to obtaining the commercial evidence of removal, a business must show the customer's VAT number in the other Member State on its sales invoice, although this requirement has been questioned by the ECJ decision in *Josef Plöckl v Finanzamt Schrobenhausen (Case C-24/15),* where the court ruled that if other evidence was available and no fraud was suspected the absence of the customers VAT number was not crucial.

A sale of goods to another UK business is standard-rated even though the goods may have been sent to France! The same rules apply when a business ships its own goods to a branch of its business in another Member State. That branch will be registered in that Member State. The records need to include an internal 'invoice' or debit note showing the branch's VAT number together with the usual commercial evidence. If this sounds odd, consider the problem for HMRC if the business did not have the full paperwork. A fraudster could claim that the goods had been shipped to his branch abroad, when he had, in fact, sold them within the UK.

THE INTRASTAT JARGON

20.19   As explained later, the Intrastat return records the EU movements of goods both out of, and into, the UK. The Intrastat jargon is not 'removals' but 'dispatches', possibly because certain 'dispatches' have to be recorded on the Intrastat Supplementary Statistical Declaration, but are not 'removals' for the EC Sales List.

TRANSFER OF OWN GOODS

20.20   The transfer of goods within the same legal entity from one Member State to another is deemed to be a supply of goods for VAT purposes and is subject to VAT under the normal arrangements for intra-EU supplies. If a business does not register for VAT in the other Member State it will have to charge UK VAT to itself, which it will be unable to recover. Therefore, in most cases it will probably need to register for VAT in the other Member State in order to account for acquisition tax and to obtain zero-rating in the UK by quoting its overseas VAT number.

'CALL-OFF STOCK', AND 'SALE OR RETURN' OR 'CONSIGNMENT STOCK'

20.21   If the UK business creates a stock of its own goods with the intention to sell the stock on from that Member State ('consignment stocks') it will be making taxable supplies in that Member State and will be required to register for VAT subject to the registration thresholds in force at that time.

Call-off stock differs from consignment stock in that it is allocated to a named customer at the time of transfer. In many EU countries call-off stock is treated in the same way as consignment stock and VAT registration in that Member State will be required.

However, subject to certain rules, a number of Member States require the final customer to account for acquisition tax, therefore, the UK supplier is not required to register for VAT in that Member State. The following Member States do not require registration for call-off stock, (although, due to a lack of published information other Member States may be similar):

- Austria—but only for intra-community goods;

- Belgium;

- Finland;

- France—provided title passes within three months (stock must be held by the final customer not an agent);

- Ireland—title must pass within three months;

- Italy—title must pass within three months;

- Luxembourg;

- Netherlands;

- Poland; and

- UK.

On the other hand, in some Member States, stock supplied on sale or return or on consignment is regarded as supplied when ownership passes. A business may, therefore, be liable to register in the Member State of its customer. Businesses supplying goods on sale or return, or on consignment, should check with the local tax authorities to see if they are creating a liability to register for VAT in that Member State.

'DISTANCE SELLING' (MAIL ORDER) TO CUSTOMERS IN OTHER EU STATES

20.22

> **Focus**
>
> A business can sell goods to unregistered customers by mail order anywhere in the EU, but it must charge UK VAT until its sales in a calendar year in any Member State reaches the distance selling limit of that Member State. Then the business must register there.

In the UK the limit is £70k. It is much smaller in some of the other EU Member States, and can alter as well, so a business should check the current figure for any Member States it makes sales to. A list of the distance sales registration thresholds is shown below.

The turnover for VAT-registration purposes is measured from 1 January each year, rather than on a rolling turnover basis as in the UK.

There are no distance selling limits for *excise goods*—any sales at all to unregistered customers in another EU Member State make it liable to register in that Member State.

Distance sales registration thresholds

Austria	€35,000
Belgium	€35,000
Bulgaria	€35,000
Croatia	270,000 kuna
Czech Republic	1,140,000 CZK
Denmark	280,000 DKK
Estonia	€35,000
Finland	€35,000
France	€100,000
Germany	€100,000
Greece	€35,000
Hungary	HUF 8,800,000
Ireland	€35,000
Italy	€35,000
Latvia	24,000 LVL
Lithuania	125,000 LTL
Luxembourg	€100,000
Malta	€35,000
Netherlands	€100,000
Poland	160,000 PLN
Portugal	€35,000
Romania	RON 118,000
Slovak Republic	€35,000
Slovenia	€35,000
Spain	€35,000
Sweden	320,000 SEK
United Kingdom	£70,000

Under the mutual assistance rules the UK and other EU tax authorities monitor sales over the internet and exchange information on businesses that they think should be registered for VAT in another Member State as a result of the distance sales thresholds. Businesses should therefore proactively monitor their turnovers to ensure that they remain compliant.

REGISTRATION OF AN EU MAIL ORDER BUSINESS IN THE UK

20.23   The UK law requiring a business based elsewhere in the EU to register here is in *Sch 2*.

NEW MEANS OF TRANSPORT

20.24   There are special rules concerning the zero-rating of new means of transport (NMT) sold to buyers elsewhere in the EU. In addition to the normal rules, the NMT must be removed from the UK within two months of the time of supply. A means of transport is defined as:

- a ship, including hovercraft, more than 7.5 m long (about 24.6 ft);

- an aircraft with a take-off weight exceeding 1,550 kg;

- a motorised land vehicle which:

  (i)   has an engine of more than 48 cc; or

  (ii)   is constructed, or adapted, to be electrically propelled using more than 7.2 kw (about 9.65 hp).

However, the above are not affected by these rules if they are not intended for the transport of passengers or goods. A means of transport ceases to be new when:

- more than three months have elapsed since the date of its first entry into service; and

- it has, since its first entry into service, travelled under its own power more than:

  (i)   100 hours in the case of a ship;

  (ii)   40 hours in the case of an aircraft;

  (iii)   3,000 km (about 1,864 miles) in the case of a vehicle.

'TRIANGULATION'

20.25   If a business buys goods from a supplier in another EU Member State and has them shipped direct to a customer in a third State, it is known as triangulation.

Example 20.1—Triangulation simplification

UK Ltd buys goods from a German supplier (GmbH) for shipment direct
to its customer in France (FR SA). Common sense says that UK Ltd
should be able to obtain zero-rating from its German supplier against its
UK VAT number, and to zero-rate on to its French customer against the
latter's French VAT number. However, the normal rules do not allow this.
They would require UK Ltd to register either in Germany or in France.
Registration in Germany would mean that GmbH charged German
VAT to UK Ltd. UK Ltd would then zero-rate the removal of the goods
from Germany to France against the French customer's VAT number.
Alternatively, registration in France would enable UK Ltd to quote a
French registration number to GmbH and thus obtain zero-rating from
Germany. UK Ltd would then charge French VAT to FR SA.

A simplification procedure avoids the need for UK Ltd to register in either
country.

CONDITIONS FOR USING THE SIMPLIFICATION MEASURE

20.26   You can only use the simplification measure if:

- the business is VAT registered in an EU Member State—so a non-EU
  trader has first to register;

- the business has no obligation to register in the Member State to which
  the goods go;

- the customer is VAT registered in that Member State.

HOW THE SIMPLIFICATION MEASURE WORKS

20.27

- the business quotes its VAT registration number to allow zero-rating for
  the dispatch of the goods from the supplier's Member State;

- it issues a zero-rated invoice showing, as normal, the customer's VAT
  number *and* up to 1 October 2007 endorsed with the wording *VAT:
  EC Article 28 Simplification Invoice*. This endorsement is no longer
  required but should be shown on invoices issued prior to 1 October 2007.
  In the UK, the invoice must be issued within 15 days of the tax point that
  would have been applicable under a normal transaction;

- the supply is recorded on the EC Sales List—explained in Chapter 22, *EC Sales Lists and Intrastat Returns*—separately from any ordinary supplies to that customer, and identified by the figure 2 in the indicator box;

- triangular transactions are not recorded on the VAT return or Intrastat Supplementary Declaration of the trader **using** the simplification measure;

- but the customer receiving the goods must record the transaction under the Intrastat rules, and account for acquisition tax.

In the UK, in addition to the above, a trader from another Member State must:

- write to the VAT Business Advice Centre 050, Custom House, 28 Guild Street, Aberdeen AB9 2DY stating:

  (i)   name, address and the EU VAT registration number used to obtain zero-rating for the supply of the goods;

  (ii) name, address and VAT registration number of the UK customer;

  (iii) date of delivery to the UK customer, actual or intended;

- copy that notification to the UK customer, no later than the issue of the first invoice, saying that customer must therefore account for acquisition VAT on the supply.

That notification covers all subsequent supplies to that customer, but separate notifications are required for any other UK customers. In practice, these notifications are hardly ever made, and HMRC do question the use of the simplification.

INSTALLED OR ASSEMBLED GOODS

20.28   If a business installs or assembles goods on its customer's premises, the place of supply is the Member State in which the customer's premises are located. If that is in another EU Member State, the business may be liable to register there. That creates a potential problem for the unwary, because suppliers typically think that they can zero-rate the goods as a removal from the UK, including in the price, the installation charge, and that they can get the customer to pay for the accommodation and meals of the staff who do the work. In practice, this is no doubt what often happens and, for one-off transactions, it is difficult for the fiscal administration of the customer's Member State to catch the transaction.

Trouble can arise if the business tries to get back VAT incurred locally through an *8th Directive* claim, as explained in Chapter 27, *Recovery of Foreign VAT*. If the Member State from which it is making the claim realises the situation, the claim will be refused—unless that Member State applies the same reverse charge rule as the UK. See below.

The UK law is in *s 7(3)*, which makes the place of supply of goods outside the UK '*where their supply involves their installation or assembly at a place outside the UK to which they are removed*'.

'This reflects the former *Art 8(1)(a)* of the *EC 6th VAT Directive* (now *Art 36 of Directive 2006/112/EC*)' which says:

> 'Where the goods are installed or assembled, with or without a trial run, by or on behalf of the supplier, the place of supply shall be deemed to be the place where the goods are installed or assembled.'

However, to avoid unnecessary VAT registrations, a number of Member States permit the customer to account for VAT on the suppliers' behalf ('reverse charge') thus avoiding VAT registration by the overseas supplier.

The following Member States definitely permit the use of the reverse charge:

- Denmark—only pieces of equipment; assembly lines etc treated as a building and registration required;

- Finland—although registration is required if the installation takes more than nine months;

- Germany;

- Italy;

- Netherlands;

- Spain; and

- UK.

In addition Portugal has no penalties for non-registration, and in the absence of a registration, requires the customer to account for VAT under the reverse charge if it is a taxable person.

EU suppliers installing goods in the UK

20.29   Para 8.11 of Notice 725 *The single market* (January 2007) details a concession which is not necessarily replicated elsewhere in the EU. The EU supplier can require the UK customer to reverse charge the VAT by:

- endorsing the invoice, which must be issued within 15 days of each tax point, '*Section 14(2) VAT invoice*';

- notifying the addresses and VAT numbers of both supplier and customer, and the date the work begins, to HMRC at VAT Business Advice Centre 050, Custom House, 28 Guild Street, Aberdeen AB9 2DY;

- copying the notification to the customer.

Chapter 21

Imports and acquisitions of goods

SIGNPOSTS

● Import VAT and duty are due on the import of goods from outside the UK, payment can be deferred under the duty deferment system and the use of an import agent can reduce the administrative burden (see **21.3–21.8**).

● Goods from other Member States of the EU are subject to acquisition tax by the purchaser but this can be claimed back on the same return so it is only a paper transaction (see **21.9**).

● Some imports are free from import VAT when using a Customs warehouse or it can be due at a reduced rate (see **21.13–21.18**).

21.1 This chapter covers rules which are largely administrative routine for fully taxable businesses which bring goods into the UK. However, misunderstanding them could cause problems. Moreover, VAT on goods bought outside the UK by a partly exempt business may not be recoverable. Failure to account for it correctly could lead to an assessment with interest and a possible penalty. Just as there are important differences between an export and a removal of goods, an import is different from an acquisition. Goods are *imported* from outside the EU. They are *acquired* from within it, ie from suppliers in other Member States.

See also Chapter 22, *EC Sales Lists and Intrastat Returns*, for details of forms and records a business may need to complete concerning EU trade:

● Intrastat Supplementary Declarations;

● Register of Temporary Movements of Goods.

THE LAW

21.2 *Sections 36A, 37* and *38* and various statutory instruments contain the rules. Of the latter, the *VAT Regulations (SI 1995/2518), Pts XII, XVI, XVI(A) and XVIII*, and the *Imported Goods Relief Order (SI 1984/746)* contain the main rules.

Notices 702 (October 2006) *Imports*, 702/7 *Import VAT relief for goods supplied onward to another country in the EC*, 702/8 *Fiscal warehousing*, and 702/9 *VAT: Import Customs Procedures* refer.

IMPORTS FROM OUTSIDE THE EU

21.3

Focus

Import VAT and, if applicable, duty, are assessed on goods at the port or airport by HMRC. They have to be paid either:

● under the deferment approval system; or

● in cash or by bankers' draft.

Alternatively, the import agent of a business may be prepared to pay on its behalf.

THE CHANNEL ISLANDS AND THE ISLE OF MAN

21.4   The Channel Islands are not a part of the EU for fiscal purposes, and import VAT is, therefore, due on goods brought into the UK from there.

On the other hand, the Isle of Man is treated as part of the UK, although it has its own Customs authority.

USE OF AN IMPORT AGENT

21.5

Focus

Most importers use an import agent to clear the goods through HMRC. Obvious reasons for this include the time saved in not attending at the point of entry in order to make the import declaration oneself, and the specialist knowledge of import procedures which the agent is supposed to possess.

Do not assume that the agent possesses that knowledge! It is a complex subject, and complying with the rules properly often requires a precise understanding of the nature of the goods being imported. That requires efficient communication between the agent and the importer, and an understanding by the latter of the key rules affecting the goods in question, and, thus, of the information which the agent needs. The Tribunal decisions I see concerning appeals on duty matters regularly reveal serious losses suffered by importers who have relied entirely on the expertise of their import agents, only to find that the latter have made mistakes resulting in subsequent post-clearance demands for underpaid duty or import VAT. Admittedly, many of the problems concern import duty rather than import VAT, and duty is not a subject covered in this book. However, it seems appropriate to warn readers of the potential pitfalls. For a horrendous example of the latter, see **21.17**.

IMPORT AGENTS

21.6   The above remarks concerning mistakes made will be no great surprise to most import agents, given the complexity of the rules with which they have to cope. Most of those rules concern import duty rather than VAT, and are not covered by this book. However, the case referred to above illustrates the need for agents to put considerable ongoing effort into maintaining and expanding their specialist expertise.

A pitfall specific to VAT for import agents is the situation arising if you pay import VAT and then fail to recover it from the importer. Only that importer has the right to reclaim it as import VAT. You therefore need to take some care before you pay VAT on their behalf, perhaps by obtaining a bank guarantee or some other assurance of the financial stability of your clients.

Only in very limited circumstances will HMRC repay the VAT to an agent. These include a situation where the client is in liquidation or administration, the goods in question remained under the agents control, were not used, and were then re-exported in the same state as they were imported. Obviously, those circumstances are unusual. See para 2.5 of Notice 702 (April 2014) for the full conditions applicable.

GOODS SOLD INTO THE UK USING AN ONLINE PLATFORM

21.6A   UK small businesses have been increasingly disadvantaged by overseas business selling into the UK through online market places such as Amazon and eBay and not registering for UK VAT. This means that UK businesses are effectively being undercut by 20%. Overseas businesses that sell goods (located in the UK at the time of sale) to UK consumers, mainly via online marketplaces, are not always paying the correct VAT and duty to HMRC. HMRC have therefore introduced a measure aimed at tackling this loophole and forcing overseas business to register for UK VAT and create a level playing field for UK businesses.

There are two aspects to the measure. The first part makes changes to the existing rules which allow HMRC to direct an overseas business to appoint a VAT representative with joint and several liability. The changes make this a more effective power and also gives HMRC greater flexibility in respect of seeking a security. The second part is the introduction of a new provision which will enable HMRC to hold an online marketplace jointly and severally liable for the unpaid VAT of an overseas business that sells goods in the UK via that online marketplace. In effect Amazon or eBay could have to account for any VAT unpaid by an overseas vendor trading through their site. Neither of these changes will apply automatically to any businesses and HMRC will use them on the highest risk cases to tackle non-compliance.

The objective of this measure is to give HMRC strengthened operational powers to tackle the non-compliance from some overseas businesses that avoid paying UK VAT on sales of goods made to UK consumers via online marketplaces. It is directed at getting overseas businesses that are or should be VAT registered in the UK paying VAT due either directly or through a VAT representative.

THE DEFERMENT APPROVAL SYSTEM

21.7   Under the deferment approval system explained in Notice 101 *Deferring duty, VAT, and other charges*:

* the business provides security to HMRC—usually a bank guarantee—to cover the expected maximum monthly liability for import VAT and import duty. HMRC relaxed their requirements for security for VAT alone from 1/12/03, albeit for approved importers, who must apply individually;

* it is allocated a Deferment Approval Number (DAN) which the business or its import agent quotes in respect of each 'entry' of goods;

* the total of VAT and duty due on imports during the month is deducted by direct debit from your bank account on the 15th of the month following that in which the import occurs.

A monthly computer-produced C79 certificate (see illustration) is the evidence required to support the recovery of the sums paid as import VAT. That the money has been deducted from the bank account by direct debit under the deferment approval system is insufficient by itself. Nor is it safe to assume that the amount collected by direct debit is the same as the input tax shown on the certificate. The latter might include duty as well as VAT.

Moreover, the C79 certificate will show the VAT assessed on all the goods imported by the business during the month. This includes any amounts settled at the time of entry rather than under the deferment approval system—perhaps because the security provided to HMRC is insufficient this month.

Some traders have recovered the sum shown on the documentation covering the tax paid on entry and, later, the amount shown on the computer certificate, not realising the duplication.

The risk of something going wrong could be higher if the imports are only occasional rather than regular, as staff may not use the system enough to become familiar with it.

Applications for VAT and duty deferment are dealt with at ASD 8D, Central Deferment Office, 10th Floor South East, Alexander House, 21 Victoria Avenue, Southend-on-Sea, Essex SS99 1AA.

SIMPLIFIED IMPORT VAT ACCOUNTING (SIVA)

21.8   HMRC allow businesses meeting certain criteria to not have to provide any security for their liability for import VAT. They must still do so for import duty and excise duty. Thus, if the expected total liability per month, called the *Deferment Account Level* (DAL) is £100, of which duty accounts for £40, the *Deferment Guarantee Level* (DGL), the business only needs a bank guarantee for the DGL. However, the DAL still limits the total value for which payment can be deferred. If it is exceeded in any month, and the business has not applied in advance for an increase in the DAL, it must arrange for additional security, or else pay on the spot.

The criteria include being VAT registered for three years, and having a good compliance history for submission of returns and payment of VAT and duty.

Applications on a special form are made to the SIVA Approvals Team, 6th floor North, Portcullis House, 27 Victoria Avenue, Southend-on-Sea, Essex SS2 6AL.

Permission to use SIVA should only be withdrawn on the basis of the risks to HMRC, not just because of a default surcharge due because a payment or a return was late (*Martin Yaffe International Ltd* (MAN/04/7035 No C197—part of the duties series).

ACQUISITIONS OF GOODS FROM SUPPLIERS IN OTHER MEMBER STATES

21.9   Goods 'acquired' without VAT from suppliers in other EU Member States are not checked by HMRC, and no VAT is assessed by them. It has to be self-assessed by the trader. This may seem simple, but problems include:

- acquisition tax must be entered in box 2, which is thus part of the total output tax in box 3. The reason for this is that the supplier will not account for it to HMRC, so the purchaser must do so instead;

- the corresponding input tax must be entered in box 4 with the rest of the input tax *if, and to the extent that*, it is attributable to taxable activities. The business cannot recover any part of it which relates to exempt ones;

- identifying all the deliveries of goods received from EU suppliers, if the business trades from various locations;

- accounting for the input and output tax on the correct VAT return. This is the one covering the month *following* the date of dispatch, or, if earlier, the date of the supplier's invoice;

- assessing the VAT on the correct valuation for the goods—normally the invoiced price plus any freight and insurance if charged separately.

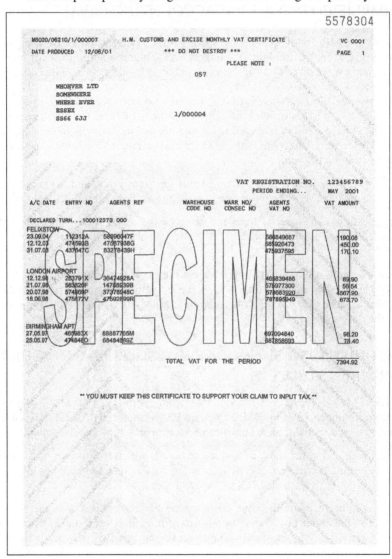

424

If a business acquires goods elsewhere in the EU, check whether these rules are understood, and are being complied with by the organisation.

The main problems are:

- failing to account in box 2 of the VAT return for acquisition VAT that is not recoverable as input tax in box 4 (ie because it relates to exempt outputs);

- worse still, claiming the input tax without accounting for the acquisition tax!

BUYING NATURAL GAS OR ELECTRICITY VIA A GRID FROM OUTSIDE THE UK

21.10   If a VAT registered business buys natural gas or electricity from outside the UK via a network or a grid, the place of supply is where the buyer belongs (*s 9A*). The buyer must account for VAT under a reverse charge for services covered by *Sch 5, para 5A* which reads:

'The provision of access to, and of transport or transmission through, natural gas and electricity distribution systems and the provision of other directly linked services.'

The rules only affect supplies of gas via a network, not liquid gas, or that bottled or delivered in a tanker. They also cover some specialist services such as providing data on network usage, storing gas within a distribution system, or injecting it into it.

Normally, the reverse charge will affect wholesalers, but a large business could buy direct. On the other hand, a non-UK supplier must register here if its supplies to unregistered customers exceed the VAT registration limit.

The reduced rate for domestic or non-business use can apply in a reverse charge situation, should a VAT registered customer use the fuel for such a purpose.

These rules were implemented from 1 January 2005 throughout the EU—so a UK supplier must know the VAT status of its EU customers, and may have to register in other EU Member States. These provisions were extended to supplies of heat and cooling in the June 2010 Budget with an effective date of 1 January 2011. It has no such problem for non-EU customers; as explained in Chapter 23, *Exports and Imports of Services* all such supplies are outside the scope.

Intermediate customers—landlords or VAT group members

21.11   If the customer is a landlord who sells on to tenants or a company, which, in turn, sell on to another in the same VAT group, the place of supply is that of consumption, not that of the customer. This maintains the same principle.

More detail

21.12   See Chapter 23, *Exports and Imports of Services*, for how the reverse charge system works.

Since these rules are only likely to cover large businesses in limited situations, I have not attempted to cover everything. See *VAT Information Sheet 10/04* for more detail. Further law is contained in the *Imported Gas and Electricity Relief Order (SI 2004/3147)*, the *Place of Supply of Goods Order (SI 2004/3148)*, *Sch 4, para 6(1)* and *reg 82A*.

SPECIAL RELIEFS FOR CERTAIN IMPORTS

21.13   The *Imported Goods Relief Order (SI 1984/746)* allows relief in the following situations:

- hologram, multimedia kits, and materials for programmed instruction produced by the United Nations or a UN organisation;

- capital goods and equipment imported when a business is shut down abroad and transferred into the UK—provided the business only makes taxable supplies;

- advertising materials, such as samples, catalogues, and goods imported solely for the purpose of demonstration at an event. See the law for the definition of *event*, which does not include a show at which the goods on display are sold;

- goods imported for examination, analysis, or testing in the course of industrial or commercial research;

- animals sent free of charge for laboratory use, human blood, certain goods imported for specified purposes, such as human organs, and reagents and pharmaceutical products for the use of persons or animals participating in an international sporting event;

- certain goods imported for charitable purposes, including fund-raising events;

- printed matter for use in a variety of situations;

- articles imported in situations such as copyright applications, evidence to a court or an official body, photographic material sent to the media, recorded media for the transmission of information, honorary decorations, cups, medals etc awarded to UK residents, gifts from one body to another and goods up to £18 in value reducing to £15 from 1 November 2011. From 1 April 2012 this relief has been withdrawn from imports from the Channel Islands;

- works of art and collectors' pieces imported by approved museums, galleries etc other than for sale and for non-business purposes. Fuel and lubricants for the use of the vehicle carrying them, litter, fodder and feed accompanying animals and disposable packaging;

- goods for war cemeteries, coffins, and urns containing human remains or ashes.

The above descriptions only cover the key points. If the relief appears relevant, check the precise wording of the law.

THE VALUE ON WHICH IMPORT VAT IS PAYABLE

21.14   Import VAT is due on the total of the invoiced price *plus* incidental expenses, which can be commission, packing, transport, and insurance up to the first destination of the goods in the UK (and on to a further destination in the EU if that is known at the time of import), plus any customs duty, levy, or excise duty payable.

5% FOR WORKS OF ART, ANTIQUES AND COLLECTORS' ITEMS

21.15   Works of art, antiques and collectors' items are subject to a reduced import VAT rate of 5%.

TEMPORARY IMPORTS AND RE-IMPORTS

21.16   If a business is importing goods temporarily for reasons such as:

- to have work done on them;

- works of art, antiques or collectors' items for exhibition in the hope of a sale;

- second-hand goods for sale at auction,

or it is re-importing goods that have previously been exported, it will need to understand in advance the relevant detailed rules. It may well be possible to avoid having to pay import VAT—and import duty—if the business complies with the rules set out in such Notices as 200 *Temporary importations*, 221 *Inward processing relief*, and 235 *Outward processing relief*.

VAT-FREE IMPORT OF GOODS SHIPPED ON AT ONCE TO ANOTHER EU STATE

21.17

Focus

An import agent or freight forwarder can clear goods through Customs free of import VAT if:

- the goods are removed to another EU Member State within a month; and

- the agent or freight forwarder invoices the goods—zero-rated under the usual rules for removals from the UK to another Member State— to his client's customer in that Member State; and

- records the 'sale' in the EU sales box of his VAT return and completes the EC Sales List, and, if required, the Intrastat return.

The big advantage is that no import VAT has to be paid anywhere since the customer in the other EU Member State merely treats the purchase as an acquisition. This therefore makes it much easier for an agent or freight forwarder to handle the transit of goods through the UK on behalf of a non-EU supplier. There are at least two potential problems.

In one case I know of, both the import agent who made the import entry, and the freight forwarder who shipped the goods on, failed to think it through! It did not occur to them that such an unusual procedure must have special conditions for record-keeping. Part of the problem was that the explanation given in the *Customs Tariff of Customs Procedure Code 42 00 00* said nothing about those conditions, nor the need to study Notice 702/7 *Import VAT relief for goods supplied onward to another country in the EC*, in which the rules in *reg 123*, made under *s 30(8)*, are (inadequately) explained.

That explanation is inadequate, because it does not say how a business could invoice goods which it does not own. In the course of the dispute, which involved post-clearance demands for £2.8m—enough to put them out of business— HMRC accepted the special wording that was subsequently proposed for the invoices, which stated that they were issued for VAT purposes only, and that payment should be made to the overseas supplier. Unfortunately, Notice 702/7, though at last revised, still does not cover the invoicing, and, therefore, remains a minefield for an unsuspecting trader.

VAT CAN BE DEFERRED OR AVOIDED BY USING A CUSTOMS WAREHOUSING REGIME

21.18   Customs warehousing is particularly useful if a business:

- wants to delay paying import duty and/or VAT on its stocks of imported goods;

- wants to delay having a customs treatment applied to imported goods;

- want to re-export non-Community goods (in which case import duty and/or VAT may not be payable at all);

- have difficulty at the time of import in meeting particular conditions (such as certain import licensing requirements);

- want to discharge another customs procedure (such as IPR) without physically exporting the goods; or

- want to use a customs warehouse for co-storage of goods subject to another customs procedure (such as free circulation, IPR, PCC).

Types of customs warehouses

21.19   EC legislation allows for six different types of customs warehouse, classified as A-F.

Types A, C, D and E are available in the UK.

Type	Description
A	A public warehouse
C	The basic private warehouse
D	An alternative private warehouse, appropriate to traders who primarily import goods for free circulation. Any removals to free circulation must be made using the local clearance procedure (see section 9) using the rules of assessment established when the goods are entered to the warehousing procedure. The rules of assessment cover the nature, value and quantity of the goods
E	Another form of private warehouse in which a company and its commercial accounting and stock control systems are authorised rather than a defined location. The rules of assessment arrangement applicable in a type D warehouse can also apply if requested

Goods that can be stored in a customs warehouse

21.20   The following goods can be stored in a Customs warehouse:

- non-Community goods liable to Customs duties and/or VAT (whether or not eligible for preference);

- non-Community goods for which necessary supporting documents (such as DoTI licence) are not available at the time of import;

- non-Community goods imported to another suspensive regime (such as IPR or TI) warehoused for export from the Community;

- non-Community PCC products;

- non-Community goods that are not subject to a full rate of customs duty in the tariff, but are liable to import VAT;

- Community produced goods or non-Community goods released to free circulation, eligible for CAP refunds on export. These goods should be warehoused in a specially approved warehouse under the CAP pre-financing arrangements; and

- non-Community goods in free circulation that are subject to a claim under the Rejected Imports arrangements.

Goods that cannot be stored in a customs warehouse

21.21   The following goods may not be stored in a Customs warehouse:

- meat, meat products and other goods subject to the Veterinary Checks regime unless the required import licence and/or health certificate have been presented and veterinary checks have been completed at the frontier;

- most other non-Community goods subject to prohibitions or restrictions applicable at the EC frontier unless necessary supporting documents (such as import licences, permits or other supporting documents) have been presented; and

- goods liable to excise duties unless the warehouse is additionally authorised as an excise warehouse or the excise duty is paid before the entry is made for customs warehousing (see *Notice 197 Excise Goods: Holding and Movement*).

Definition of a customs warehouse

21.22   A Customs warehouse can either be a defined location (such as premises or place) or an

inventory system authorised by HMRC for storing non-Community goods, that are:

- chargeable with import duty and/or VAT; or

- otherwise not in free circulation.

Depending on the circumstances, a defined location can be the whole of a building, a small compartment in a building, an open site, a silo or a storage tank.

Chapter 22

EC Sales Lists and Intrastat returns

SIGNPOSTS

- If your business trades with customers in other EU Member States you will need to complete special boxes on the VAT return and may also need to complete EC Sales Lists and Intrastat returns (See **22.1**).

- EC Sales Lists have to be completed for sales of goods and services to VAT registered businesses in other Member States (see **22.2–22.6**).

- If your sales (Dispatches) or purchases (Arrivals) of goods to other Member States exceed certain limits you will need to complete monthly Intrastat Supplementary Statistical Declarations (see **22.7–22.15**).

- If a business dispatches or receives goods to or from another EU Member State, and they are to be returned within two years, they have to keep a 'register of temporary movement of goods to and from other Member States' (see **22.16–22.18**).

22.1   This chapter briefly describes the special returns which must be completed by those who remove goods to, or acquire them from, other Member States of the EU. These forms will continue to be required until the UK leaves the EU. Following the UK's exit from the EU these forms will no longer be required. As explained in Chapter 5, *The VAT Return* there are special boxes on the VAT return in which the value of the goods sold to customers elsewhere in the EU, and of purchases from suppliers in other EU Member States, is shown and will again continue to be required until the UK leaves the EU. However, that is not the end of it!

Focus

Businesses may also have to complete:

- an EC Sales List. This shows their sales to customers in other EU States;

> • an Intrastat Supplementary Declaration, which shows movements of goods both sent out to, or brought into the UK from, other EU States. This is only required once the value of the goods exceeds a de minimis limit.

Section 14 of Notice 725 (January 2007) *The single market,* provides a detailed explanation of EC Sales Lists. Notice 60 *Intrastat—General Guide* covers Intrastat returns.

THE EC SALES LIST

22.2   From 1 January 2010, the EC Sales List (ESL) covers both the sales of goods to EU customers and services supplied to a business in other EU countries where the customer is required to account for VAT under the 'reverse charge' procedure. If businesses have 'non-standard' monthly or quarterly accounting periods for its VAT returns—such as to match 12- or 13-week accounting periods—a business can also apply for monthly or quarterly ESLs to cover the same periods.

The new requirement is one of five measures in a package of changes adopted by EU Finance Ministers in February 2008. The package of changes will be phased in between 1 January 2010 and 1 January 2015, and can be summarised as follows:

- changes to the rules on the place of supply of services for Business-to-Business (B2B) and Business-to-Consumer (B2C) transactions;

- requirement to complete EC Sales Lists for supplies of taxable services to which the reverse charge applies;

- introduction of an optional One Stop Scheme for B2C supplies of telecoms, broadcasting and electronically supplied services;

- introduction of an electronic VAT refund scheme;

- enhanced Administrative Co-operation between Member States to support these changes.

Brief 53/08 relates only to the second item above, and points out that EC Sales Lists will **not** be required for the following:

- supplies which are exempt from VAT according to the rules in the Member State where the supply takes place;

- B2B supplies where the recipient is not VAT registered;

- B2C supplies.

Focus

At present, HMRC uses the existing VAT101 form, which will require the following data:

- country code;

- customer's VAT Registration Number;

- total value of supplies in sterling;

- the indicator '3' will also be required to identify services.

In principle, the Directive provides that ESLs should normally be submitted monthly, but it allows Member States to offer their businesses certain options.

The UK has implemented the Directive as follows:

- ESLs relating to services may be submitted quarterly, on a calendar quarter basis.

- From 1 January 2010, ESLs relating to goods may be submitted quarterly, relating to calendar quarters, provided that the VAT-exclusive value of supplies of goods to other Member States has not exceeded £70,000 in any of the previous four quarters.

- A business entitled to submit quarterly ESLs for goods can continue to do so unless the VAT-exclusive value of supplies of goods to other Member States exceeds £70,000 per quarter from 1 January 2010 to 31 December 2011 or £35,000 per quarter from 1 January 2012 onwards.

- If a business exceeds the quarterly goods threshold by the end of the first or second month in a quarter, an ESL must be submitted at the end of that month, covering the month or months in that quarter. Lists must be submitted monthly from then on.

- Once a business is on a monthly cycle, because it has exceeded the threshold in any quarter, it must continue to submit monthly ESLs for goods until the value of its intra-Community trade in goods has been below the threshold for five consecutive quarter— it may then revert to quarterly submission if its trade remains below the threshold.

- A business required to submit monthly ESLs relating to goods, may still submit ESLs relating to services quarterly.

- Any business may submit ESLs for goods and/or services monthly, if it wishes.

- Online returns will have to be submitted within 21 days and paper returns in 14 days.

ELECTRONIC SUBMISSION FOR EC SALES LISTS

22.3   HMRC have not accepted paper schedules since 31 July 2006, but still accept the paper return. Businesses have to register for online submission even if they already have an ID and a password for another purpose, such as submitting VAT returns online; ie businesses must enrol for EC sales lists as an additional task for which they will use their ID and password.

Once a business has done that, it should be able to submit the information using bulk files from its system, assuming it is in CVS or XML formats.

PAPER SUBMISSION OF EC SALES LISTS

22.4   Businesses can choose any of the following methods:

- paper ESL, form issued automatically by HMRC each month/quarter;

- downloadable form VAT 101 EC Sales List and form VAT 101(A) EC Sales List Continuation Sheet available from the HMRC website; or

- paper form VAT 101 EC Sales List, available from the VAT Helpline.

If a business uses the downloadable forms, it must complete them onscreen before printing (single-sided) and posting to HMRC. A business must not download the forms and complete them by hand. If it wants to complete the form by hand, it must use one of the paper forms that HMRC send in the post.

SMALL TRADER CONCESSIONS

22.5   If a business uses the *Annual Accounting Scheme*, it can ask to submit an annual ESL if:

- its total taxable sales do not exceed £145,000 (*reg 22(1)(c)*); and

- its annual sales to other EU Member States do not exceed £11,000; and

- its sales do not include new boats, aircraft or motorised land vehicles.

A business can ask for permission to complete an *annual simplified* ESL, which just lists the VAT registration numbers of its EU customers, if:

- its total taxable sales do not exceed the current VAT registration limit plus £25,500 (*regs 21 and 22(1)(b)*); and

- its annual sales to other EU Member States do not exceed £11,000; and

- its sales do not include new boats, aircraft or motorised land vehicles.

INFORMATION REQUIRED

22.6   The information required includes the total value of sales to each EU customer—identified by registration number including the alpha prefix, not by name. See the sample form on pages 432–433.

[CHECK PAGE NUMBERS ON PROOF]

NOTES ON COMPLETION

These notes provide guidance on filling in this form. You will find more detailed information in VAT Information Sheet, VAT: Filling in your EC Sales List and in Notice 725, VAT: The Single Market and Notice 703 VAT: Exports and removals of goods from the United Kingdom.

If you have not been involved in any Intra-EC transactions during the period specified overleaf, DO NOT return this form. If no transactions have taken place you will not be liable to a financial penalty.

Do not write on or amend details in the green area of this form. If you think any of the pre-printed information is wrong, or if you need any help, contact your local office. The telephone number is shown overleaf.

Country Code

Enter your customer's country code, which can only be from the following list:

Austria	AT	Germany	DE	Malta	MT
Belgium	BE	Greece	EL	Netherlands	NL
Cyprus	CY	Hungary	HU	Poland	PL
Czech Republic	CZ	Ireland	IE	Portugal	PT
Denmark	DK	Italy	IT	Slovenia	SI
Estonia	EE	Latvia	LV	Slovak Republic	SK
Finland	FI	Lithuania	LT	Spain	ES
France	FR	Luxembourg	LU	Sweden	SE

Customer's VAT Registration Number

Enter your customer's VAT registration number in the spaces provided, starting from the extreme left hand side.

Do not repeat your customer's country code in this column or include any spaces, dashes or commas. Underline alphabetical characters.

Use one line only for each customer UNLESS you are an intermediate supplier in intra-EC triangular transactions. Show the total value of these supplies on a separate line and enter the figure '2' in the indicator column.

One of the conditions for zero-rating supplies of goods to other EC countries is that you must provide a valid VAT number for each of your customers. Once advised by HM Customs & Excise that a VAT registration number is invalid you must not continue to use it to zero-rate your supplies.

Notices 725 and 703 and VAT Information Sheet VAT: Filling in your EC Sales List all contain a table which details the only acceptable format of EC VAT numbers.

Total Value of Supplies

Only include the value of goods and related costs supplied to customers who are registered for VAT purposes in *other* EC countries where the goods are moved between EC countries. Related costs are services which form part of the price of the goods, such as freight and insurance charges.

Add up the value of goods and related services supplied to your customer, deduct credit notes, and enter the total, rounded to the nearest pound sterling in the space provided.

Do not include the pounds sterling symbol (£), decimal points (.) or commas (,). The figure must then be entered right aligned.

If the value of credit notes is greater than the total value of supplies enclose the figure in brackets. Do not use a minus sign.

Indicator

Leave this column blank, UNLESS:

you have made supplies as the intermediary in intra-EC triangular trade. Enter '2', with the details, on a separate line from your other supplies.

Lines Completed (this page only)

Enter the number of lines completed for this page only in the box provided.

Number of Pages Completed

Enter the number of pages completed in the box provided. Include all continuation sheets.

Common Errors

Before filling in this form, please take note of the list of common errors on page 5 of VAT Information Sheet VAT: Filling in your EC Sales List. This will help to ensure that we do not contact you unless absolutely necessary as every error you make has to be corrected. The Information Sheet is available from your local office.

Declaration

You or someone on your behalf must sign the form to declare that the information provided constitutes a true and complete statement.

VAT 101A (Continuation Sheet)

If you run out of lines on this form, contact your local office for a VAT 101A (Continuation Sheet). When you receive the VAT 101A complete the top of the form with the same information pre-printed on this form.

VAT 101B (Correction Sheet)

If you need to correct any data supplied in a previous period or supply any previously omitted data, contact your local office for a VAT 101B (Correction Sheet). When you receive the VAT 101B complete the form with the appropriate information.

Where to send this form

You must ensure that the completed form is received by the due date. Return it in the white pre-paid envelope provided, to:

The Controller, VAT Central Unit
H M Customs and Excise
21 Victoria Avenue
Southend-on-Sea X, SS99 1AN

Data Protection Act 1998

HM Customs and Excise collects information in order to administer the taxes for which it is responsible (such as VAT, insurance premium tax, excise duties, air passenger duty, landfill tax), and for detecting and preventing crime.

Where the law permits we may also get information about you from third parties, or give information to them, for example in order to check its accuracy, prevent or detect crime or protect public funds in other ways. These third parties may include the police, other government departments and agencies.

VAT 101 (Full)   **Page 1** PT1R (April 2004)

INTRASTAT SUPPLEMENTARY STATISTICAL DECLARATION

22.7 The Intrastat Supplementary Statistical Declaration (SSD) is a monthly return intended to provide trade statistics.

DE MINIMIS LIMIT FOR SSD

22.8 A business is not liable to submit the SSD unless its sales or purchases exceed the Intrastat thresholds. This was set by the *Statistics of Trade (Customs & Excise) Regulations (SI 1992/2790)*, as amended. From 1 January 2010 if a business's trade in goods to other EU Member States exceeds £600,000 for Arrivals or £250,000 for Dispatches in a calendar year then it is required to submit monthly Intrastat SSDs. From 1 January 2014 the Intrastat Arrivals Exemption threshold was increased from £600,000 to £1,200,000 and the Delivery Terms threshold has been increased from £16,000,000 to £24,000,000. The Dispatches threshold remained at £250,000.

The new Intrastat thresholds effective from 1 January 2015 for arrivals increased from £1,200,000 to £1,500,000.

The exemption threshold for dispatches (EU exports) remains unchanged at £250,000. The limit applies separately to goods dispatched and received, so a business may have to submit an SSD for its sales but not its purchases, and vice versa.

ELECTRONIC SUBMISSION OF THE SSD

22.9 From 1 April 2012, businesses can only submit their returns electronically. The website www.uktradeinfo.com offers a variety of information, together with the system under which a business can register to submit figures electronically—which it can do at intervals during each period when convenient. This could be helpful, because it avoids the need to provide a complete return in one go. Returns have to be made by the 21st day following the end of the reference period.

DISPATCHES AND ARRIVALS

22.10 *Dispatches* and *Arrivals* are the jargon used for SSD purposes, rather than *removals* and *acquisitions*, which are the terms used under the Single Market rules described in Chapter 20, *Exports and Removals of Goods*.

Focus

Separate returns are required for goods dispatched to, and received from, EU Member States. They cover movements of goods, not just sales and purchases. For instance, goods transferred to, or from, a branch elsewhere in the EU, and movements of goods for processing or repair are included.

The example of the form for *Dispatches* (see pages 431–432) shows what is required. The form for *Arrivals* is the same, bar its title, but the two sets of information must be reported separately.

'Acquisitions' of goods from the EU are delivered to various locations, even to such scattered points as construction sites. Consequently, the finance department of a business may need the cooperation of its shipping department, and of such people as site managers, who may not normally liaise closely with accounts. An *Acquisition* for VAT return purposes occurs when a business:

- buy goods from a supplier in another EU Member State;

- bring goods into the UK from a branch of its business in another EU Member State; or

- receive goods under a hire-purchase or a lease purchase agreement.

In addition, the following are also treated as *Arrivals* for SSD purposes:

- goods received for processing;

- goods in the possession of a business under an agreement by which ownership is intended to pass in due course. Thus a finance lease is an acquisition, but an operating one is not.

DUE DATE

22.11   The SSD is due with HMRC by the 21st day following the month to which it relates.

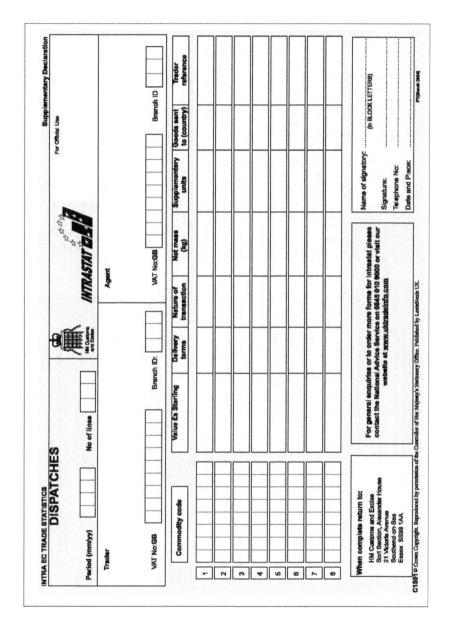

439

Notes on the compilation of INTRASTAT Supplementary Declaration (SD). Detailed advice on how to complete this form and an Intrastat generally can be found in The Intrastat General Guide, Notice 60.

Separate forms must be used for Arrivals (C1500) and Dispatches (C1501). Continuation sheets are available.

Period (mm/yy)	The period is the month and year to which the declaration refers, e.g. 11/01 for November 2001. For special periods see Notice 60 para 3.5f.
No of Lines	Show the number of lines of data entered on each declaration. If you are declaring more than 176 lines, please submit in batches containing no more than 14 continuation sheets to each header sheet (C1500 and C1501).
Sheet No.	Show the order of the sheets ie. 03 05 for continuation sheet three of a total of five.
Trader	Enter the name, address and post code of your business and quote your UK VAT number. The three digit Branch ID should be completed if you are providing data on a Branch basis and have already advised SATU Intrastat Operations.
Agent	This field should be completed only if an agent is completing the SD on behalf of a trader.
Commodity Code	You must classify goods using the appropriate code from the current Intrastat Classification Nomenclature (ICN), available on line at www.uktradeinfo.com. If you need advice, contact the Tariff Classification Helpline on 01702 366077.
Value £s Sterling	Show the value, as used for VAT purposes, in £s sterling rounded up to the nearest pound. Do not show the £ sign or pence.
Delivery Terms	See Notice 60 para 4.4 and Appendix E.
Nature of Transaction	See table opposite and Notice 60 para 4.4.
Net Mass	If required, should be shown in kilograms rounded up to the next whole kilogram. The current ICN gives details of those commodity codes where the provision of net mass is optional. Only show the figure, not the letters (kg).
Supplementary Units	Complete this box only when the current ICN indicates that supplementary units information is required.
Goods sent to/ Goods from (country)	You will find a complete list of Countries and Country Codes in the Notice 60 or on our website www.uktradeinfo.com.
Trader reference	The completion of this box, e.g. with an invoice number, may assist in resolving queries raised. Completion of this box is optional.

Useful e-mail addresses:

Tariff Classification helpdesk: classification.tso@hmce.gsi.gov.uk
Customer Services (Trade Statistics enquiries, Electronic Data Interchange [EDI],
Intrastat Policy queries, Complaints): uktradeinfo@hmce.gsi.gov.uk

C1501

CODES FOR USE IN COMPLETION OF INTRASTAT DECLARATION

Nature of Transaction	Code
a) All transactions involving actual or intended change of ownership for a consideration (except those appropriate to Nature of Transaction Code (NoTC) 2,7 or 8 (1st digit)). [This includes stock moved within this same legal entity (between Member Sites), and financial leasing].	10
b) Credit note value, where the goods are not returned, i.e. an amount used to reduce the overall value of the SD. The second digit "5" acts as a negative value.	15
c) Transactions which must be declared on SDs, but are not shown in boxes 8 or 9 of the VAT return, e.g. goods arriving in an excise or fiscal warehouse, or movements of goods involving stage payments (Second digit 7 can also be used with f), j), k), and L) below, e.g. 37, 77, 87 and 97).	17
d) Transactions which are declared in boxes 8 or 9 of the VAT return, but are only required on the SD for reconciliation purposes, e.g. goods leaving an excise or fiscal warehouse (to home use in the UK), stage payments made when no movement of goods occurs, or final stage payment.	18
e) Returned goods and replacement goods.	20
f) Free of charge (FOC) transactions involving permanent change of ownership.	30
g) Goods sent for processing or repair.	40
h) Goods returned following process or repair.	50
i) Movements of goods without transfer of ownership for hire operational leasing and other temporary use except process or repair, check Appendix D to see if a declaration is required.	60
j) Joint defence projects or other joint inter governmental production programmes (e.g. airbus).	70
k) Supply of building materials and equipment as part of a general construction or engineering contract. [The value of the goods actually moving goes in box 2 of the SD, not the total value of the contract].	80
L) Other transactions which do not fit any of the descriptions in a) to k) above.	90

*NoTC first digits 2,4,6, and 8 identify a transaction which should not be shown in box 8 or 9 of the VAT return.

Data Protection Act 1998

HM Customs and Excise collects information in order to administer the taxes for which it is responsible (such as VAT, insurance premium tax, excise duties, air passenger duty, landfill tax), and for detecting and preventing crime.

Where the law permits, we may also get information about you from third parties, or give information to them, for example in order to check its accuracy, prevent or detect crime or protect public funds in other ways. These third parties may include the police, other government departments and agencies.

NOTE: YOUR DECLARATION MUST REACH THE ADDRESS OVERLEAF BY THE END OF THE MONTH FOLLOWING THE PERIOD END.

Page 2 PT(S) (March 2004)

INFORMATION REQUIRED

22.12   The Intrastat requires information not by customer, but by international commodity code. Thus, if a dispatch is of goods covered by different commodity codes, the value, in sterling, must be split by code. The same applies to incoming goods.

Also to be shown are:

- delivery terms—if the value of dispatches in the previous calendar year exceeded £24m (£13.5m up to 31 December 2003, £14m up to 31/12/06, £14.5m up to 31 December 2008 and £16m up to 31 December 2013). The same applies for arrivals;

- nature of the transaction code (NOTC);

- net mass in kilograms—but not if a supplementary unit is required (optional for some commodity codes);

- the supplementary units (certain commodity codes only);

- the country the goods are dispatched to or came from.

A business can add its own reference if it wishes.

NATURE OF TRANSACTION CODE (NOTC)

22.13   The code has two functions:

- the first digit identifies the nature of the transaction for statistical purposes; and

- the first and second digits together identify reasons for differences between values declared in boxes 8 and 9 of your VAT returns, and the SSDs.

See the page of notes on completing the form for details.

COMMODITY CODES

22.14   Deciding the correct commodity code is often not a simple task. The International Standard Classification is a complex manual, even in the simplified version. For *Arrivals,* a business may want its supplier invoices to quote both the codes and such information as the net mass of the goods— needed even if the item is a single machine—as well as quoting them on the shipping documents. HMRC use it for a crude check on the value per kilo!

LOW VALUE TRANSACTIONS ON THE SSD

22.15 Invoices that include goods classifiable under two or more commodity codes with a total value not exceeding £180 (from January 2012) can be declared against a single low value code (99500000). This optional simplification applies regardless of the value of other goods on the invoice.

THE REGISTER OF TEMPORARY MOVEMENT OF GOODS

22.16 If a business dispatches or receives goods to or from another EU Member State, and they are to be returned within two years, they have to keep a 'Register of Temporary Movement of Goods to and from other Member States'.

Focus

Notice 725 says that this applies to goods:

Dispatches

- sent for processing, repair or alteration; or

- moved to another Member State for use in making supplies in that State;

- sent to other Member States under what would be Temporary Import Relief conditions if they were imported from outside the EU.

Receipts

- received for processing.

INFORMATION REQUIRED

22.17 The information required is:

- date of the initial dispatch or receipt of the goods;

- date of their subsequent return;

- description of the goods;

- the reason for the movement;

- the price charged for the processing or other work done on them, whether in the UK or elsewhere in the EU.

FORMAT OF REGISTER

22.18 The register can be in any convenient form which provides the information required.

Chapter 23

Exports and imports of services

SIGNPOSTS

- Before you can decide whether to charge VAT or not, you have to establish the place of supply. If the place of supply is outside the EU, the supply is outside the scope of EU VAT. If the customer is in business within the EU, the supply is also outside the scope of UK VAT; but if the customer is a private individual UK, VAT is due (see **23.1–23.6** and **23.27–23.31**).

- Even though the service may be outside the scope of VAT any associated input tax can be reclaimed (see **23.4**).

- There are special rules that help you establish if an EU customer is 'in business' (see **23.9–23.12**).

- Services purchased from suppliers outside the UK are subject to the reverse charge (see **23.14–23.16**).

- There are special rules to establish where a business belongs (see **23.17–23.26**).

- There is a new basic rule for the place of supply of services (see **23.27–23.31**).

- There are special rules relating to electronically supplied services and their use and enjoyment (see **23.32–23.35**).

23.1   Here, I discuss whether a business must charge VAT when it supplies services to a non-UK customer, or it does the work outside the UK. With services being intangible, the rules bear no relationship to those for goods. They are one of the most complex parts of VAT law. Various rules deal with different services in different ways.

If a business has any international operations, it will meet these rules sooner or later, even if it sells mainly goods rather than services. For instance, if it makes management charges between companies in different countries, it will need to understand enough to know how it can justify not charging VAT on them.

This chapter is called *Exports and imports of services* to distinguish it from that on *Exports and removals of goods*. However, the subject is often called 'International Services'. Either name will do as a general title for the subject, but neither is strictly correct. Although *Sch 8 Group 7* is called *International Services*, it zero-rates only certain supplies in somewhat specialist circumstances. The *Place of Supply of Services* rules are more important. If the place of supply of a service is outside the UK, it is outside the scope of UK VAT—not zero-rated. It may be outside the scope either with recovery of the associated input tax or without recovery. These two categories are equivalent to zero-rating and exemption within the UK.

Everyone finds these rules difficult at first. The best way to learn them is to understand the basic idea; then leave the detail until you have a real situation to which to apply the rules.

To add to the confusion, a number of changes took place to the place and time of supply rules for services from 1 January 2010.

THE LAW

23.2

Focus

In order not to charge VAT to a foreign customer, the supply must be:

- outside the scope of UK VAT because the place of supply is made outside the UK by the *Place of Supply of Services Order ('POSSO') (SI 1992/3121)*; or

- zero-rated under *Sch 8 Groups 7, 8* or *13* or the Terminal Markets rules in *s 50* re commodities; or

- covered by *concessions* made by HMRC; or

- exempt in the UK anyway—such as insurance or finance.

The EU law on the place of supply of services is contained in *Directive 2006/112/EC, Arts 43–59* (previously *EC 6th VAT Directive, Art 9*).

MEMBERSHIP OF THE EU

23.3   For a list of the Member States of the EU, see page lxix at the start of the book.

SO, CAN A BUSINESS RECOVER ITS INPUT TAX?

23.4   Not having to charge VAT to a foreign customer is only half the story. The other half is whether the business can recover the input tax it incurred in making the supply. A supply that would be taxable in the UK will be outside the scope with recovery of the associated input tax, if the place of supply is outside the UK.

A supply which is exempt in the UK will be outside the scope when the place of supply is outside the UK:

● with recovery if the customer belongs outside the EU;

● without recovery in most cases if the customer belongs within the EU.

See **24.8** for a fuller explanation.

THE STARTING POINT FOR THE PLACE OF SUPPLY

23.5   If the place of supply is the UK, a business must standard-rate a transaction unless it happens to be zero-rated under the rules noted above, or it is exempt.

Focus

The starting point for deciding on the place of supply depends on the nature of the customer. From 1 January 2010 there are two basic rules for the place of supply:

● if the customer is in business the basic rule is that the services are supplied where the customer belongs;

● if the customer is not in business the place of supply is where the supplier belongs.

These are the *starting points* because, in practice, the place of supply often changes under specific provisions.

Business-to-business supplies of services (B2B) are now taxed in the country where the customer is located. For cross-border transactions between two Member States, the recipient will be liable to account for VAT under the reverse charge mechanism. However, business-to-consumer supplies of services (B2C) will, in principle, continue to be taxed where the supplier is located until the UK leaves the EU.

Exception is made for certain services (such as restaurant services, services linked to cultural, sports, scientific and educational events, short-term hire of means of transport) which will, in all cases, be taxable in the country of consumption.

The introduction of the new place of supply rules took place on 1 January 2010, except for telecom, broadcasting and electronic services in a business-to-consumer environment, which will become effective only as from 1 January 2015. From this date, these services will be taxable in the Member State where the recipient is established. Further changes to the 'where performed' rule took place from 1 January 2011, although the effects seem basically the same, and for long-term hire of means of transport from 1 January 2013.

WHY DOES THE PLACE OF SUPPLY MATTER?

23.6   The place of supply matters because, if it is the UK, a business must charge UK VAT to the customer, even if the latter is in a country on the other side of the world.

If the place of supply is not the UK, the supply is not subject to UK VAT. In other words, it is 'outside the scope'.

Some supplies are always standard-rated. There is no automatic relief just because the customer is in another country, or the work is done outside the UK.

In practice, there often is a relief enabling the business not to charge UK VAT, but it is not automatic; a business must find a specific rule covering its particular supply.

Examples of standard-rated supplies

23.7

- *Travel costs* are always standard-rated, no matter who the customer is. People from overseas, even those here on business, have to pay VAT on hotel and restaurant meals, car hire and similar travel expenses here. Those who are in business overseas can then reclaim it under the *8th* or *13th Directive rules* described in Chapter 27, *Recovery of Foreign VAT*.

- *Running repairs to vehicles, light aircraft and the like.* There is a relief for work on goods which are either bought here or brought into the UK, in either case, for export once the work has been done. However, if a visitor's car breaks down on a motorway, that does not apply.

- *Services related to land* within the UK are standard-rated, no matter who owns it.

- *Training courses* held in the UK. A non-UK delegate has to pay UK VAT, but may then be able to make an *8th* or *13th Directive* claim to reclaim it.

TRANSACTIONS ON THE INTERNET

23.8   Taking orders via the Internet does not of itself change anything. If the business then delivers goods in physical form, the normal rules will apply.

It is when a business delivers services/goods in *electronic form* over the Internet that there are changes. For instance, computer software bought from a shop is a supply of goods but, downloaded from a website, it is a supply of services. Such a download might be from a supplier outside the EU or from one EU Member State to another. Treating the supply as one of services enables it to be taxed as a supply of copyright under licence to a business customer under the reverse charge rules explained later in this chapter.

If a UK business sells a product via a download to a private customer in another EU Member State, it must charge UK VAT.

If the seller is not VAT registered anywhere in the EU, the supply is dealt with under the V*AT E-commerce Directive 2002/38/EC* and the accompanying *Regulation 792/2002*. These were agreed on 7 May 2002 and came into effect on 1 July 2003, and require the non-EU business to register in one of the Member States.

For the rules on registration in those circumstances, see **3.11**. For details of the services in question, see **23.16** below.

If a customer is outside the EU, a business does not charge VAT.

IS THE EU CUSTOMER IN BUSINESS?

23.9   If the customer belongs in the EU, that customer must receive the supply for the purpose of a business carried on by him (*POSSO, art 16(b)*). Otherwise, the supply is standard-rated.

To check the VAT number, name and address of an EU trader, ring the NAS. See page lxviii. The electronic checking systems on the EU and HMRC websites are pointless, because they can only confirm the validity of the number, not that it belongs to the trader whose name and address you quote. The system is also 6–8 weeks out of date, so a newly registered business may not appear while a newly deregistered business may still appear registered.

Usually, it will be self-evident that the customer is in business. However, do not take that for granted. Here are some examples of possible pitfalls.

Government bodies, municipal authorities and similar bodies

23.10   In para 12.6 of Notice 741 (May 2008) *Place of supply of services*, HMRC say that government bodies, municipal authorities, and similar bodies, are not in business. Although they add the proviso 'unless the services are specifically received for the purposes of a business activity', we think that the statement is misleading. UK local authorities engage in numerous businesses, such as the running of car parks and leisure centres.

This may be less so in other Member States, and I understand that most of them do not register their local authorities. HMRC's view is presumably based on *Omnicom UK plc* (LON/93/2441 No 12605: [1996] STC 398), heard in the High Court as *Diversified Agency Supplies*. On the basis of the available evidence, which showed that the Spanish Tourist Office in Spain appeared not to be an independent body, but under the control of a Government Ministry, Omnicom's customer was held not to be in business. The High Court confirmed that a customer must not just be VAT registered, but must receive the supply in question for the purpose of a business.

Common sense suggests that, provided that the organisation can quote you a VAT number, the supply should be outside the scope of VAT: it should then be for the fiscal authority of the other country to determine whether the client was in business in the capacity in which it bought the services. Only that authority is in the position to gather all the necessary information. However, the High Court rejected that argument.

Is a tourist office in business?

23.11   There have been three UK Tribunal cases concerning whether tourist offices are in business. In *Turespana* (Spanish Tourist Office LON/96/002 No 14568), which followed on from the *Omnicom* case discussed above, the London office of the Spanish Tourist Office failed in an argument that it was in business in the UK, and therefore entitled to recover all its input tax.

The Chairman in *Turespana* questioned the decision in *Netherlands Board of Tourism* (LON/94/607 No 12935). However, *Austrian National Tourist Office* (LON/96/0674 No 15561) then won its case, thus confirming that it is possible for a tourist office to be in business.

HMRC have continued to question the status of tourist offices case-by-case. Although they have given in on two more cases, where the appeal did not reach a formal hearing, this has only been after a detailed examination of the facts of each case. It follows that HMRC might well dispute whether a tourist office in another Member State was in business.

International research establishments

23.12   A similar problem arises with research bodies that are largely funded by government. In the UK, these are legally independent in most, if not all, cases. Even where there is substantial business income, most of the input tax incurred relates to non-business fundamental research, rather than to the making of taxable supplies.

Suppose a business is supplying services to such a body in another Member State. How will it be able to persuade HMRC that its client is buying the services for the purpose of its business activities, rather than its non-business ones? The same comments apply as those made above concerning local authorities.

USE OF A CUSTOMER'S VAT NUMBER

23.13   For basic rule services a VAT number is not necessary in law, but getting the number is evidence that the customer is in business. However, a business does need the VAT number as a matter of law for those services covered by the rest of *POSSO*. Following the changes to the reporting requirements for EC Sales Lists from 1 January 2010, however, businesses will be required to obtain the customer's VAT number to quote on the ESL.

THE REVERSE CHARGE (VATA 1994, SECTION 8)

23.14   As explained above, a registered trader can buy a basic rule service from a supplier in another Member State without paying VAT in that Member State. Having done so, the reverse charge then applies: VAT is due in the trader's own Member State, and at the rate applicable in that Member State.

Focus

The reverse charge:

●   taxes basic rule services; but

●   bought from anywhere in the world, not just elsewhere in the EU.

This prevents unregistered or partially exempt traders from avoiding UK VAT by, for example, buying accountancy services from the Channel Islands. It makes no difference whether the business buys those accountancy services from within the UK, from another Member State or from outside the EU. The business has to account for VAT at the UK standard rate, and it can only recover this if it is attributable to taxable, rather than to exempt outputs.

THE WAY IT WORKS

23.15

●   The business self-assesses itself for *output tax* on the sum it pays for each reverse charge service—assuming, of course, that it is standard-rated in the UK;

- it includes the VAT in its output tax on its VAT return for the VAT period in which it pays for the supply;

- the corresponding input tax can only be included with the input tax on the return if it is attributable to taxable supplies made by the business. If it relates to exempt supplies, the business cannot recover it. That puts the business in the same position as if it had bought from a UK supplier.

Skandia America Corporation (USA), filial Sverige v Skatteverket (C-7/13), a reference to the ECJ from the Swedish courts, looked at the application of the 'reverse charge' to intercompany IT charges between the head office and the EU based subsidiary. Until then EU VAT law allowed countries to treat companies and their overseas branches as single entities for VAT purposes and therefore 'intercompany' charges were VAT free.

In its decision the ECJ found that these charges should be subject to VAT under the reverse charge. With fully taxable businesses this has no impact as the VAT they charge themselves is fully recoverable but exempt and partly exempt businesses, particularly in the financial services sector, will be unable to recover the VAT as it will relate to their exempt supplies.

HMRC's views on the impact of the ECJ judgment in the *Skandia* case and its implications for VAT grouping were published in Revenue & Customs Brief 02/15.

Under the UK's VAT grouping provisions, a body corporate such as a company must have an establishment in the UK to join a UK VAT group. However, unlike in Sweden, the whole body corporate is part of the VAT group, not just the establishment (branch or head office) in the UK. Therefore services provided between an overseas establishment and a UK establishment of the body are not normally supplies for UK VAT purposes, as they are transactions within the same taxable person.

The *Skandia* judgment did not consider the UK's different rules, which allow the whole body corporate into the UK group, and so did not rule this to be contrary to the VAT Directive. HMRC consequently does not consider that any changes to the UK grouping provisions are required.

However, in other circumstances there will be a change in the treatment applied to services performed on or after 1 January 2016. The implication of the *Skandia* judgment is that an overseas establishment of a UK-established entity is treated as part of a separate taxable person if the overseas establishment is VAT-grouped in a Member State that operates similar 'establishment only' grouping provisions to Sweden. This will be the case whether or not the entity in the UK is part of a UK VAT group. Businesses must treat intra-entity services provided to or by such establishments as supplies made to or by another taxable person and account for VAT accordingly:

- Services provided by the overseas VAT-grouped establishment to the UK establishment will normally be treated as supplies made in the UK under place of supply rules, and subject to the reverse charge if taxable.

- Services provided by the UK establishment to the overseas VAT-grouped establishment will normally be treated as supplies made outside the UK under place of supply rules. Therefore they will need to be taken into account in ascertaining input tax credit for the UK establishment. If the supplies are reverse charge services, they should be reported on the trader's European Sales Listing of such supplies.

If the UK entity is in a UK VAT group, the same applies to supplies between the overseas establishment and other UK VAT group members in the UK.

LIABILITY TO REGISTER FOR REVERSE CHARGE SERVICES

23.16 The value of reverse charge services received counts towards the registration limit. Therefore, an unregistered organisation might have to register for VAT purely in order to account for reverse charge services.

THE RULES ON BELONGING

23.17 Where a business or its customer *belongs* is often important. Although it is usually obvious, that is not always so.

Suppliers

23.18 *Directive 2006/112/EC, Art 43* (previously *Art 9(1)* of the *EC 6th VAT Directive*) says that the place where a service is supplied shall be deemed to be the place:

- where the supplier has established his business; or

- has a fixed establishment from which the service is supplied; or

- in the absence of such a place of business or fixed establishment, the place where he has his permanent address or usually resides.

Customers

23.19 *Directive 2006/112/EC, Art 56(1)* (previously *Art 9(2)(e)* of the *6th VAT Directive*) says that for *Sch 5* services the place of supply is:

- where the customer has established his business; or

- has a fixed establishment for which the service is supplied; or

- in the absence of such a place of business or fixed establishment, the place where he has his permanent address or usually resides.

UK law

23.20   *Section 9*, which puts that into UK law, says that, in both cases, a trader belongs in a country if:

- he has there a business establishment or some other fixed establishment, and that;

- if he has such establishments in more than one country, it is the establishment:

  (i)   which is most directly concerned with the supply in the case of a supplier;

  (ii) at which, or for the purposes of which, the services are most directly used or to be used in the case of a customer; and

- in the absence of such a place of business or fixed establishment, his usual place of residence is there.

Section 9(5) says that a person carrying on a business through a branch or agency in any country shall be treated as having a business establishment there.

The belonging rules may sound simple, but here are some of the arguments that they have caused.

SERVICES TO A JERSEY COMPANY OWNING A LONDON FLAT

23.21   *WH Payne & Co* ([1995] V & DR 490) concerned accountancy and tax advice in respect of letting a London flat, which Payne supplied to a company registered in the British Virgin Isles but managed from Jersey. Payne's client, Trafalgar, was held to have *established its business* in one of the latter places.

It did not belong in the UK at its flat. The flat was what it supplied, not a fixed establishment from which it made supplies.

In *Berkholz* ([1985] 3 CMLR 667), an ECJ case concerning gaming machines on a ferry, the Advocate General commented that a fixed establishment must be of a certain minimum size, and that the human and technical resources necessary for the provision of the services must be permanently present.

There were no such resources at Trafalgar's flat to enable it to receive Payne's services.

A SUBSIDIARY CAN CONSTITUTE A FIXED ESTABLISHMENT OF ITS PARENT

23.22   *DFDS A/S* was a Danish company supplying package tours. These were marketed in the UK through its subsidiary, *DFDS Ltd,* which acted as the

UK central booking office and provided administration services. The contracts were in the name of the Danish company. The UK subsidiary received 19% commission, and was reimbursed its UK marketing costs. It had premises and staff in the UK.

The European Court of Justice (Case C-260/95) held:

- DFDS Ltd was wholly owned. In the contractual circumstances, it was not independent, merely an auxiliary organ of A/S;

- it possessed the necessary human and technical resources to make the supplies in the UK;

- it was to be regarded as a fixed establishment of the parent, and as the establishment from which the supplies were made.

The Court commented that:

- where a business was established; and

- where it had some other fixed establishment,

were both primary criteria for deciding the place of supply. The first preference was normally the place where the business was established. However, if that did not lead to a rational result, or if it created a conflict with another Member State, the possibility of the supply being made at a fixed establishment must be considered.

DFDS is an important constraint on any cunning plan to escape charging UK VAT by setting up in another country, and using a UK agent to carry out whatever might need doing here.

DEFEAT OF A CUNNING PLAN ON PLACE OF SUPPLY OF GAMING MACHINES

23.23   *RAL (Channel Islands) Ltd* (LON/01/1979 No 17914; C-45 2/03) was set up in Guernsey by its parent company to manage gaming machines in the UK. It claimed that the place of supply was Guernsey, thus avoiding having to account for VAT on the takings.

The Tribunal held that the place of supply of gaming machines in UK amusement arcades was held to be the UK. The arcades were fixed establishments of a Channel Islands company formed for the purpose of renting the sites and the machines, and which arranged for their maintenance by companies in the same group as itself. The services company was acting as a mere auxiliary of the Channel Islands company, which was, therefore, making supplies from the arcades.

The ECJ held that the objective was to entertain the customers, for which, the place of supply was where the service, the entertainment, was physically carried out. Compare that with *Berkholz* (discussed at **23.21**), in which, the mere presence of machines on the ferry did not make that the place of supply.

A COMPANY CAN BELONG AT ITS REGISTERED OFFICE

23.24　In *Binder Hamlyn* ([1983] VATTR 171), Jamaica Sugar Estates Ltd (Jamaica) was held to belong at its registered office in Binder Hamlyn's offices for the purpose of receiving company registration services, including maintaining the UK share register. This was despite Jamaica having no trading activity in the UK, and it meant that Binder Hamlyn's services were standard-rated.

Similarly, in *Vincent Consultants* ([1988] VATTR 152), handling a company's statutory and tax returns was held to be standard-rated, because the establishment at which the services were used was its UK registered office.

USUAL PLACE OF RESIDENCE OF AN INDIVIDUAL

23.25　In *USAA Ltd* (LON/92/1950 No 10369), which sold motor insurance, the 'usual place of residence' of US officers on three-year tours of duty in the UK was held to be the UK, even if they still owned houses in the US. However, in *SA Razzak and M A Mishari* (LON/97/754 No 15240), it was held that:

- 'usual place of residence' in *s 9(3)* gives effect to the *EC 6th VAT Directive, Art 9(2)(e)* (now *Directive 2006/112/EC, Art 56(1)*) wording 'the place where he has his permanent address or usually resides';

- 'permanent' means the antithesis of purely temporary, and having a sufficient degree of permanence.

An Indian domestic servant had been brought to the UK under a domestic workers concession. After leaving her employers, she stayed in Asian women's refuges for four years with temporary visa extensions, until her action for damages for mistreatment was settled. She only remained in the UK in order to pursue the case, and for lack of money to return to India to look after her children. Her usual place of residence was held to be India.

USAA Ltd was distinguished because the officers were in the UK voluntarily on three-year tours of duty, which might be extended. The Tribunal was obviously sympathetic to the unfortunate circumstances of the case, and therefore stretched that logic to its limit.

HMRC guidance in *VAT Information Sheet 7/05* states that, if a person has no right to be here—such as an asylum seeker and anyone here without permission—he or she belongs in their country of origin—until they obtain a right or permission to remain in the UK.

BEWARE OF MULTIPLE BELONGING

23.26   A customer could belong in the UK as well as elsewhere in the EU. If it belongs here in the capacity in which it receives the services, the supply to it is standard-rated.

Where does an individual belong who owns homes in London and Bermuda, and spends six months of the year at each? The nature of the services provided may suggest one country or the other.

SECTION 7A AND SCH 4A

23.27   The most common reason for not having to charge VAT to a customer outside the UK is that the service is covered by *s 7A* and *Sch 4A* to the *VATA 1994*. This is, therefore, the logical place to begin studying the place of supply rules. Prior to 1 January 2010 there were other place of supply rules applying to services which are detailed in previous editions of this book.

The primary legislation is contained in *s 7A (1)–(7)* which makes the new basic rule for supplies of services to other businesses in the EU where the customer belongs, rather than the old basic rule which was where the supplier belonged. *Schedule 4A* replaced the old *Sch 5* of the *VATA 1994* from 1 January 2010. *Part 1* contains a list of general exemptions from *Sch 4A, Part 2* contains exemptions relating to supplies to business customers and *Part 3* covers supplies relating to non-business customers. A prime objective of the rules is to prevent people avoiding VAT by buying services from a supplier in another country rather than from one in their own.

Supplies from a head office to a branch

23.28   The UK does not see a charge for services from the head office of the company to one of its branches in another country or vice versa as being a supply; it is merely a transaction within the single legal entity. There is a supply for a transfer of own goods, however, as explained in **20.20**.

The lack of a supply of services from a head office in another country to a branch in the UK does not mean non-recoverable VAT can be avoided by having services billed to the head office and then recharged to the UK. See the end of this chapter for more about this, and about the anti-avoidance rule (**23.58**).

Supplies to business customers outside the UK

23.29

- *POSSO, art 16* makes the place of supply the country in which the customer 'belongs'. The invoice is thus outside the scope of UK VAT;

- if the place of supply is another EU Member State, tax is collected through the customer's VAT return in that Member State at the rate of tax applicable to the supply there. This is under the 'reverse charge' rules which are explained later.

Supplies to private EU customers outside the UK

23.30

Focus

- if a private customer belongs in another EU Member State, a business must charge UK standard-rated VAT on its supply— this is because the customer has no VAT return on which to pay the tax under the reverse charge mechanism;

- if a private customer belongs outside the EU, the supply is outside the scope of EU VAT and no VAT is charged.

In addition to this, following an ECJ decision in *Kollektivavtalsstiftelsen TRR Trygghetsrådet v Skatteverket,* a customer that has both business and non-business activities (for example a charity) will be treated as receiving the services under the reverse charge procedure even if the services are used for a non-business purpose. Therefore VAT will not be charged in the country of origin.

EXCEPTIONS FROM THE BASIC RULE FOR BUSINESS TO BUSINESS SUPPLIES OF SERVICES

23.31   *Services related to land*

The place of supply of land related services will remain unchanged, and will continue to be taxed where the land is situated (see **23.43**).

Hire of a means of transport

The place of supply of the hire of a means of transport depends upon whether it is a short-term or long-term hire. A short-term hire is where there is continuous possession of the vehicle for up to 30 days, or 90 days in the case of vessels.

The place of supply of a short-time hire will be the place where the vehicle is put at the disposal of the customer.

The long-term hire of a means of transport will fall under the general rule (ie supplier location for B2C supplies, customer location for B2B supplies). However, from 1 January 2013 for B2C supplies on long-term hire, the place of supply will be where the customer is established, except for pleasure boats where the place of supply will be where the vessel is put at the disposal of the customer if the supplier has an establishment there.

HMRC's view is that the term 'put at the disposal of' means the place where the vehicle is located at the time it is physically made available to the customer.

Evidence to prove that a hirer has made reasonable checks of where a customer belongs include a driving licence, utility bill or credit card billing address.

Cultural, artistic, sporting, scientific, educational, entertainment and similar services

From 1 January 2010 the place of supply of cultural, artistic, sporting, scientific, educational, entertainment and similar services has been where the activity took place. This is essentially the same as under the old rules, ie taxed where performed.

However, from 1 January 2011 supplies of cultural, artistic, sporting, scientific, educational, entertainment and similar services falls under the basic rule. Only supplies of admissions to an event and services ancillary to admissions will be taxed where the event takes place. Supplies to private consumers will remain unchanged.

The services of organisers are supplied where the person carries out their role. This is not necessarily in the same place as where the event is held. This treatment will remain unchanged on 1 January 2010. From 1 January 2011 B2B supplies of organisers' services fall under the new basic rule.

ELECTRONIC SUPPLIES OF SERVICES TO UNREGISTERED CUSTOMERS IN THE EU

23.32   The *E-commerce Directive 2002/38/EC* sets out the rules under which non-EU businesses are to register in a Member State of their choice, and charge VAT on services to private customers at the rate applicable in the Member State in which the customer belongs. See **3.11** for more details of the system.

A supplier of broadcasting services to UK consumers must register under the normal rules.

The rules only affect non-EU businesses. A trader in the EU charges VAT to customers in his own Member State, and to private customers in other Member States, under the rules explained in the rest of this chapter.

Communications by e-mail do not, of themselves, mean that a service comes within the provision of electronically supplied services. That means that a lawyer or an accountant could provide professional services by email without the fact of electronic transmission meaning that the supply is caught. Thus, a private customer can continue to buy legal or accountancy services from outside the EU without having to pay VAT on them. However, if the new system is effective in persuading the non-EU supplier to comply with it, a subscriber to an information service will have to do so. In theory, the larger suppliers will comply, if only because they will wish to maintain a good relationship with the EU because of other possible ramifications. That will give a competitive advantage to any smaller one, which believes that the EU will not be able to force it to register, and is prepared to risk any possible action against it. It remains to be seen what will happen. The system was originally introduced on a temporary basis for three years from 1 July 2003, but at the 28 November 2006 ECOFIN meeting (by which time, the original three-year timescale had already expired), the E-commerce Directive was extended to 31 December 2007.

Legislation was introduced in *Finance Ac 2014* to tax intra-EU business-to-consumer supplies of telecommunications, broadcasting and e-services in the Member State in which the consumer is located. These services are currently taxed in the Member State in which the business is established. The changes took effect from 1 January 2015 and implement already agreed EU legislation into UK legislation, ensuring that these services are taxed fairly in the Member State of consumption.

From 1 January 2015, new VAT rules were introduced which affect all businesses selling broadcasting, telecommunications and e-services to non-business customers (B2C) in other EU countries. It does *not* apply to business-to-business (B2B) transactions, which remain unaltered.

The rules only apply where a UK business meets all of the following conditions:

- you charge your customers for digital services (digital services given free of charge are not affected by the rules);

- you supply services from the UK to private consumers in another EU Member State;

- your EU customers are not VAT-registered businesses; and

- you do not sell your digital services through a third-party platform operator or marketplace (not your own website)

The platform operator or marketplace is supplying the customer if the platform operator identified you as the seller but, sets the general terms and conditions, authorises payment or handles delivery or download of the digital service. Then the platform operator would be responsible for accounting for the VAT payment that's charged to the consumer. E-Services are services that are heavily reliant on the internet for their execution and include the following services:

- video on demand;

- downloading of apps;

- music downloads;
- e-books;
- gaming; and
- anti-virus software.

B2C sales to customers located elsewhere in the EU are no longer subject to UK VAT but will be taxed in the country where the customer is based.

For example, if a business sells a new app for a smart phone or tablet to a private individual based in Italy, UK VAT of 20% will no longer be chargeable, and instead Italian VAT (which is currently 22%) will need to be charged.

To prevent the need for businesses having to register for VAT in every country where they supply e-services to non-business customers, a VAT Mini One Stop Shop (MOSS) has been introduced.

The MOSS is an online service from HMRC that gives businesses the option of registering in the UK to account for VAT on B2C sales of these services in all of the other EU Member States (at the appropriate rate for each country) by submitting a single return.

The good news is that this service will significantly reduce the administrative burden which would have existed if a requirement to register in multiple countries had arisen.

If a business is not registered for UK VAT as it is trading below the VAT registration threshold in the UK (currently £85,000), it may believe that these changes will not affect it. Unfortunately this is not the case. When a business makes supplies to another EU Member State there is a nil VAT registration threshold if it makes B2C sales so it will immediately have to register for VAT under a MOSS registration to account for VAT in the other EU Member State, but it does not need to account for VAT on sales to its UK customers. HMRC will not, however, force 'hobby businesses' to register under the MOSS scheme.

Businesses that are already VAT registered in the UK can register for the VAT MOSS scheme using HMRC online services. If the business is not already VAT registered (turnover below £85,000 per annum), then it will have to register for UK VAT before registering for the VAT MOSS, but it won't need to account for VAT on sales to its UK consumers.

From 1 January 2019, EU Member States introduced two VAT and invoicing simplifications to the B2C digital services MOSS regime. The two simplifications were:

(1) For small EU businesses selling less than €10,000 per annum to consumers in other EU States, they may continue to charge and report VAT under their national rates and rules. This includes following their domestic invoicing formats and obligations. Only once they pass this

threshold must they switch to the local VAT rates of their consumers' country of residence and report the VAT in the MOSS return.

(2)   For businesses selling less than €100,000 per annum in B2C e-services to other EU States, only one piece of evidence proving the country of residence of their customers need be obtained. For businesses above this limit, the current obligation of two pieces of evidence is still required.

Businesses must register for VAT MOSS by the tenth day of the month following their first B2C supply of digital services in another EU Member State.

The VAT MOSS returns are required each calendar quarter (end of March, June, September and December), so may well not coincide with a business's normal VAT returns. Provided that, when registered for VAT, the business selects 'supplies of digital services (below UK VAT threshold)' as its business activity, HMRC will ensure that the UK VAT return period is aligned with the VAT MOSS return period, so it can complete both the UK VAT Return and the VAT MOSS return at the same time. The return is due by the 20th of the month following the end of the VAT MOSS return period. Therefore, the return for the period ending 31 March would be due by 20 April.

It's still important to monitor the UK taxable turnover: once that exceeds £85,000 per annum, the business has to start accounting for VAT on your UK sales.

If a business wasn't previously registered for UK VAT but had to do so in order to register for VAT MOSS it doesn't have to charge its UK customers' VAT. Even though it is not charging UK VAT, it still has to complete a UK VAT return. It can complete a 'nil' return or, if it wishes, it can claim back the VAT it incurs in making B2C supplies of digital services to other Member States. It still won't be able to reclaim the VAT on the costs relating to its UK sales. For example, if a business buys a computer that it uses generally in its businesses, and 70% of its sales are to the UK and 30% to other EU Member States, it can claim back 30% of the VAT on its purchases. The same principle would apply to the VAT on its overheads.

A practical problem that arises is that when you make online sales you probably won't know where your customer is located. If a business intends to continue making B2C sales to customers in other EU Member States, they will need to know what country they are based in so that it can account for the correct amount of VAT. As all the Member States have different VAT rates, businesses could potentially have 27 different prices for the same downloads. Businesses with a turnover of less than the UK VAT registration threshold can now rely on any single piece of information, such as the address provided by the customer, to determine where their customer is located rather than the two that were previously required and is still required for businesses turning over more than £85,000 pa.

If a business charges customers a flat rate VAT inclusive price, then it will need to calculate what proportion of that price is VAT in order to be able to complete the VAT MOSS return.

For example, if you sell an e-book for £10 including VAT, regardless of where the customer is based. The amount of VAT in that £10 will vary, depending on the VAT rate applicable.

To calculate the VAT a business should use what is known as the 'VAT fraction' for the country. If you divide the total sales by the VAT fraction the result is the amount of VAT contained within the total sales. The VAT fraction is calculated as follows:

$$(100 + \text{VAT rate}) \div \text{VAT rate} = \text{VAT fraction}$$

Electronic services

23.33   If a business supplies electronic services covered by *Sch 5, para 7C*, it should take extra care if its sales to a customer exceed £500, either per transaction, or in total per quarter. HMRC expects a business to check with them the VAT number that is quoted.

HMRC also expects businesses to check if they have any reason for suspicion of a number quoted to them—including that the supply is of an item such as music, a computer game, a film, etc not normally sold to a business customer.

The use and enjoyment rules

23.34   The effective use and enjoyment rules in *arts 17* and *18* and *Sch 4A, Part 2* provide that:

- a non-EU provider of telecommunication, radio, or TV broadcasting services, is making a supply in the UK if the services are effectively used and enjoyed here, and is, therefore, liable to register here;

- where the services are effectively used and enjoyed outside the EU, the supply is outside the scope of UK VAT, even though the supplier or the customer may belong in the UK.

In the Spring Budget 2017 the government announced that it would remove the 'use and enjoyment' provision from B2C telecommunication services. This means that UK VAT will now be charged on such services used outside the EU by UK consumers.

That applies to electronically supplied services only if received by the customer for the purposes of a business. However, since HMRC recognise that a non-business customer will normally use the services where they belong, they say in *VAT Information Sheet 1/2003* that, if an existing accounting system is set up to tax supplies where they are effectively used and enjoyed, this can be applied to electronically supplied services, provided that it does not lead to abuse.

HMRC has proposed an anti-avoidance measure extending the use and enjoyment to advertising services following its extension to certain insurance products and repairs of vehicles in the 2015 Budget.

The use and enjoyment rules have been extended to certain supplies of insurance because a small number of insurers have structured their arrangements to avoid incurring irrecoverable VAT by undertaking to repair insured goods via an offshore insurance entity. Several other insurers complained that this practice challenges fair competition.

The measure ensures that repair services carried out in the UK for UK policyholders are subject to UK VAT irrespective of whether the insurer belongs outside of the EU. The measure came into force on 1 October 2016.

This measure counters VAT avoidance by those UK insurers who arrange their affairs so that the insurance to UK customers is in fact provided by a company based offshore, for example, in Gibraltar or the Channel Islands, where there's no VAT. Any insurance repairs are charged to the offshore company. As a result the insurer of the UK risk is not charged VAT which in normal circumstances it wouldn't be able to reclaim because insurance is VAT exempt.

HMRC has removed the VAT use and enjoyment provision for mobile phone services provided to consumers. The measure brings those services used outside the EU within the scope of the tax. It also ensures mobile phone companies can't use the inconsistency to avoid UK VAT. This brings UK VAT rules in line with the internationally agreed approach.

THE MEANING OF 'USE AND ENJOYMENT'

23.35   HMRC define *use and enjoyment* as occurring where the customer actually consumes the service irrespective of contract, payment, or beneficial interest. They say that it only changes the place of supply as between the UK and outside the EU. If the place of supply of a service is in the UK or elsewhere in the EU, that does not alter if it is used and enjoyed in a different Member State.

HMRC quote the example of a web hosting service supplied to a business in the US. Although the supply is received in the US, it is subject to UK VAT to the extent that it is used in the UK.

On the other hand, an electronic information service supplied by one UK business to another is used and enjoyed outside the EU to the extent that it is used in a non-EU country. In such situations I would recommend that a business keep a record of how it arrived at any apportionment it made.

SERVICES RELATING TO LAND

23.36   *POSSO, art 5* makes a service related to land taxable in the Member State in which the land is situated. It covers, for example:

- holiday property lettings;

- work on buildings and civil engineering work;

- services of estate agents, architects, surveyors and the like, including, for instance, seismic survey and associated data processing services.

Work on buildings can include installing or dismantling a machine.

If the land is in the UK, a supply relating to it is standard-rated to a foreign customer. In *McLean and Gibson (Engineers) Ltd* (EDN/01/119 No 17500), dismantling a massive paper-making machine 50-60 yards long and weighing 400-500 tons, a task which took three months, was held to be a supply relating to land. The charge to the foreign buyer for the work, including packing and delivering it to the port, was therefore standard-rated. Note: the possibility that the work could have been zero-rated under *Sch 8, Group 7, Item 1* as work on goods, which are then exported, does not appear to have been considered by the Tribunal. See **23.46**.

In *Mechanical Engineering Consultants Ltd* (MAN/93/1074 No 13287), a case I dealt with when an officer of the then HM Customs & Excise, the services of a consulting engineer concerning an incinerator complex were held to be services relating to land. Even though much of the plant was movable, the complex had to be looked at as a whole. In consequence, *para 3* did not apply, and the place of supply was where the land was.

A service is not caught by *art 5* just because it involves land. Administering a deceased's estate which includes land, or the advertising or insurance of overseas property, are not covered. Nor is general advice re the property market, as opposed to services concerning a specific property.

Legal services are often in relation to a contract term, rather than to the land to which the contract related, and are therefore covered by the basic rule not *art 5*. An example is legal advice to a mortgagee concerning a mortgagor's default. The hire of space at an exhibition is covered by *art 15*. See **23.42**.

TRANSPORT SERVICES AND SERVICES ANCILLARY THERETO

23.37   *Articles 6, 7, 8, 9* and *10* deal with the transport of passengers or goods in a variety of situations. Normally, the place of supply is where the transport takes place or the service is performed. However, the transport of goods within the EU is treated as made in the Member State in which it begins (*art 10*).

A pleasure cruise is treated as the transport of passengers, which includes any education or training during it (*arts 2* and *8*).

If the journey is between two points in the same country without visiting another, the entire supply is made there even if part of the journey is outside its territorial limits (*art 7*).

Examples of ancillary transport services are:

• loading, unloading, or reloading;

• stowing;

• opening for inspection;

• cargo security services;

• preparing or amending bills of lading, airway bills, and certificates of shipment;

• storage.

SERVICES SUPPLIED WHERE PERFORMED

Work on goods (prior to 1 January 2011 for B2B customers)

23.38 Physical work is required, not mere inspection. However, in *Banstead Manor Stud* (LON/78/412 No 816) the care and handling of a mare attending a stallion was held to be an essential adjunct to the services of the stallion.

Sporting services

23.39 In *John Village Automotive Ltd* (MAN/96/1384 No 15540), charges to sponsors of a racing team were held to be predominantly supplies of advertising rather than sporting services.

Ancillary services (prior to 1 January 2011 for B2B customers)

23.40 An example of an *ancillary service* is that of an organiser of an exhibition, who works on behalf of the exhibition owner. The place of supply of the organising service was where it was performed. This is not necessarily the location of the event.

In *J Dudda v Finanzamt Bergisch* (C-327/94), the ECJ ruled that an engineer who provided the sound amplification at a public event, performed an ancillary service because it was a prerequisite to the performance of the artists at the event. The place of supply was thus the country in which the event took place.

In *Sugar and Spice on Tour Catering* (MAN/99/1053 No 17698), a Tribunal adopted that purposive approach in holding that catering was also ancillary. Thus, the place of supply of catering at events to performers and the touring organisation, arranged by the tour manager but paid for by each promoter, was the Member State in which the event took place.

Veterinary services

23.41 By way of an example, suppose a Dutch vet supplies services to cattle farmers in Belgium. Where is the supply taxed? In *Maatschap MJM Linthorst, KG Pouwels en J Sheres* (C-167/95: [1997] STC 1287), the ECJ ruled that the place of supply of the services of a veterinary surgeon is the place where he has established his business, or has a fixed establishment from which the services are supplied.

The service was the scientific assessment of the health of animals, taking preventative medical action, and treating sick animals. Presumably this was not seen as a scientific service. Nor did it qualify as 'consultancy'.

Thus, UK VAT must be charged on veterinary services performed in another EU state for a non-UK client.

Conferences and exhibitions (old rules prior to 1 January 2011 for B2B customers)

23.42 These rules only apply to situation prior to 1 January 2011. From that date, B2B supplies are taxed where the customer belongs. For B2C customers these rules are still extant. The term *similar activities* has been interpreted as *services relating to exhibitions, conferences, or meetings.*

Conferences, meetings, etc come in all shapes and sizes, ranging from major international conferences and exhibitions to company meetings, training courses, and public relations events such as product launches and press conferences. Organising them requires a wide range of services by various types of business.

For a public conference at which places are sold, the place of supply *by the promoter/owner* must be where it is held. On the other hand, HMRC accept in para 5.7 of Notice 741 (March 2002) *Place of supply of services* that someone who organises an event on behalf of the promoter/owner, may be supplying those services from the office where the work is done, rather than at the event location. Similarly, HMRC say that a trade organisation, which provides a package of services such as exhibition space, consultancy, design of the stand, and so on, supplies those services *where they are physically carried out.*

That is insufficient comment, as is revealed by the next paragraph, which says that a comprehensive package of services is supplied at the exhibition in question. That does not make sense on the grounds that a package which includes stand space, must be essentially a supply of that space. Such a supply can only be at the event, even though other services, such as stand design, are supplied. However, HMRC then say that, if the event is in another Member State, but the UK supplier does not have to account for VAT there, and the services are otherwise physically carried out here, the supply is in the UK.

It is questionable whether this is correct. It is not practicable for the place of supply to depend upon whether an individual Member State enforces the rules correctly!

Then there is the problem of the public relations company that arranges an event on behalf of its client. An example of this might be the organisation of a conference in another Member State for distributors of the products of a non-EU company. The PR company merely did the organisation, including selecting the location, and most of this work took place in the UK. Places at the conference were sold by the non-EU company on whose behalf it was organised.

Representatives from the PR company did attend, but were there only in a supporting role, everything on the day being handled by the non-EU company. Arguably, therefore, the main supply took place in the UK, not at the event. The VAT authorities in the other Member State initially demanded VAT on the PR company's services, but then accepted that the place of supply was the UK.

However, in the light of the *Dudda* case on ancillary services, which is explained at **23.40** above, the position must be doubtful where there is any attendance in the other country. If a public relations company organises an event, it may be in charge of the organisation, with the executives of its client company merely responsible for the technical content of the presentation. Of course, organising a press conference might qualify as a supply of advertising, and therefore, be subject to the place of supply rules for *Sch 5* suppliers rather than that for a service relating to a meeting.

A further point is when a service becomes ancillary to an event, rather than merely a supply to the promoter or organiser in the latter's country. The answer is likely to depend on the precise facts—as is so often the case!

If a business sells a package of services for delegates attending an event, and this includes travel and hotel accommodation, the *Tour Operators' Margin Scheme* might apply. See Chapter 37.

Training (prior to 1 January 2011 for B2B customers)

23.43   *Article 15* made the place of supply of education where it was performed. This means that a commercial training course in the UK is standard-rated, no matter where the delegates come from. Those from outside the UK have to make *8th* or *13th Directive* claims to recover the VAT, as explained in Chapter 27.

Do not confuse standard-rated commercial training with that provided by universities and other eligible bodies, which is exempt under *Sch 9 Group 6* as explained in Chapter 11, *What is Exempt?*

Para 3.17 in Notice 48 (March 2002) *Extra-Statutory Concessions,* allows zero-rating where the charge is to a foreign government. The conditions are:

- the supply must be for the purpose of the sovereign activities of the foreign government;

- the supplier must obtain a written statement from the foreign government, or its accredited representative, that the trainees are employed in those activities.

The relief is intended to cover training in the UK of officials, public servants, armed forces, police, emergency services, and similar bodies that are answerable to the government concerned.

It does not apply to staff of state-owned businesses, or sponsored commercial organisations such as state airlines, where claims must be made under the *8th* or *13th Directives.*

THE ZERO-RATINGS IN SCH 8

23.44   As mentioned earlier, *Sch 8 Groups 7, 8* and *13* zero-rate specific services.

Group 7 'International Services'

23.45   *Item 1* zero-rates work on goods which are subsequently exported from the EU. The work must be prearranged, but the goods can be either imported into the EU or acquired within it with a view to doing the work.

Item 2 zero-rates agency services in arranging for:

- an export of goods outside the EU;

- work on goods where the work is zero-rated under *Item 1*;

- any supply of services made outside the EU, except those insurance and financial services, which would be exempt in the UK under *Sch 9 Groups 2* and *5*.

Thus, an agency commission to a UK manufacturer on a sale of goods dispatched to an EU customer is standard-rated, because the goods have not been exported. Of course, the UK manufacturer will recover VAT on the commission.

For details of why the goods were not exported, see **20.8** for the difference between an export and a removal.

Group 8 'Transport'

23.46   This Group covers a variety of services as noted in the chapter on zero-rating. They include services connected with movement of goods in or out of the EU.

Group 13 'Imports, Exports, etc'

23.47   This Group covers three miscellaneous cases which are concerned primarily with goods, although one does cover services connected with international defence projects. See **10.39** for more comment.

A SUPPLY DOES NOT 'DISAPPEAR' WHEN BILLED TO A HEAD OFFICE

23.48   Normally, where a supply by a UK business is made to a UK branch of an overseas company, but is invoiced to its head office in another country UK VAT applies to that supply. However, in certain circumstances, the reverse charge can apply. In *Zurich Insurance company* (LON/02/1080 No 19157: 2006 EWHC 593 (Ch)) the Tribunal held that the supply—of installing a new computer software system—was to the head office in Switzerland, and that the onward charge for the branch was not a supply.

The High Court overturned that, holding that the supply was to the business establishment in the UK, and that it was, therefore, taxable as a reverse charge when billed from Switzerland. The decision does not explain the difference between that and an ordinary internal charge, but we surmise that the payment by the head office was seen as merely on an agency basis—thus, passing on the supply.

The work was done primarily by a UK firm, which had billed to its own associate in Switzerland. The Tribunal had held that the supply was by the Swiss associate to the Zurich head office, because it had negotiated the contract and then procured that the work be done by the UK firm. The High Court saw the reality as a supply direct to the UK branch of Zurich—a key point being that this interpretation avoided the distortion of competition. The distortion would result from non-recoverable input tax being avoided if a branch could achieve a supply to its head office, based elsewhere, rather than direct to itself: for once, the law and commonsense match!

See also the anti-avoidance rule at **23.49**.

VAT GROUPS—ANTI-AVOIDANCE RULE

23.49   An anti-avoidance rule in *s 43(2A)* affects a business if:

- the UK branch of an overseas company is included in the VAT group; and

- that overseas affiliate supplies the UK companies in the VAT group, via its branch, with *Sch 4A* services it has bought in.

Such a situation is not caught by the reverse charge because there is no supply of services between branches of the same legal entity. HMRC were worried that international groups might arrange for services, such as telecommunications, to be billed to an overseas company rather than to the one actually using the services, and that the charge could then be passed back through the UK branch. As there would be no VAT on a charge between the branch and another company in the same VAT group, non-recoverable VAT could be avoided.

Some VAT advisers thought that such a scheme would not work because the supply was to the user company in the first place, and addressing the invoice overseas would not change that. However, HMRC decided to take no chances, so we have an anti-avoidance rule.

The rule is not confined to services sourced in the UK. It catches, for instance, legal services from a US lawyer bought by a US company, A Inc, and recharged to a UK subsidiary, B Ltd, via the UK branch of A Inc. This is a classic example of how aggressive tax planning can lead to anti-avoidance measures that have a wider impact than the original problem.

The rule taxes the *s 7A* service by creating a self-supply by the representative member of the group, the tax point being the date of payment for the supply. The output tax thereby created is only recoverable to the extent that it can be attributed to taxable supplies. A business can reduce the value of the supply if the service in question is made up partly from bought-in basic rule services and partly from in-house resources, such as the overseas company's legal department.

Remember that the problem only arises when the branch of the overseas affiliate, through which, the charge from the overseas company is passed, is a member of the UK VAT group. If the affiliate's UK branch is not VAT grouped, any onward charge by it to other UK companies will be standard-rated.

The rules affect all businesses, not just those which are partly exempt though, of course, there is no loss of VAT if the reverse charge tax can be attributed to a taxable supply.

That is just an outline of the rules intended to help businesses check whether they are affected. If a business is affected, it will need to study the law.

Finally, the amendments to the Directive make changes to the time of supply of services rules for services supplied to businesses in another Member State where the customer accounts for VAT under the 'reverse charge'. The changes are:

- the time of supply of such services will be the earlier of when the service is completed or when payment is made

- the time of supply of such services will be the earlier of when the service is completed or when payment is made;

- for continuous supplies of services, the time of supply will be linked to the end of each billing or payment period, but where no invoice or other accounting document is issued or payment made during the year, the time of supply will be the end of each calendar year.

HMRC say that these changes will determine not only when the customer has to account for VAT under the reverse charge when the service is received from a supplier in another Member State, but also when a supplier is required to include the transaction on an ESL.

Chapter 24

Partial exemption

SIGNPOSTS

- Partial exemption occurs when a business has both exempt and taxable outputs. Such a business calculates the amount of VAT it can recover by using a partial exemption method. If the amount of exempt input tax is below certain limits all the input tax can be recovered (see **24.1–24.6**).

- The partial exemption calculation has to be done each VAT period with an annual adjustment once a year—alternatively you can make one calculation a year and apply that percentage provisionally for the next 12 months. You can use either the standard method or agree a special method with HMRC (see **24.12–24.15**).

- The use of a special method has to be approved in advance by HMRC and providing it gives a fair and reasonable result any method can be used. Commonly used special methods are outlined for reference (see **24.16–24.22** and **24.60–24.62**)).

- There are special rules for dealing with outside the scope supplies (see **24.23–24.26**).

- Some supplies of capital items and incidental supplies are excluded from the calculations (see **24.30–24.31**).

- There are special rules relating to VAT recovery on share issues (see **24.37–24.41**).

- There needs to be a link between the input tax claimed and any output tax recovered (see **24.43–24.46**).

- Change of use of an asset can have tax consequences (see **24.55**).

- In cases where the standard method does not produce a fair result and the input tax involved is large there is a standard method override designed to produce a fair result (see **24.71–24.73**).

24.1

> **Focus**
>
> Partial exemption occurs when a business has both exempt and taxable outputs. Such a business calculates the amount of VAT it can recover by using a partial exemption method. Although they can be straightforward, partial exemption situations are often amongst the more complex aspects of VAT.

Do not confuse partial exemption with business/non-business situations. An example of the latter is a charity, which raises money through a business activity, such as retail shops. Its main charitable activity is non-business, and the VAT related to that is not even input tax, let alone recoverable input tax. However, the charity can recover the VAT related to the business side. Chapter 28, *What is a business?* deals with situations where at least a part of an activity does not amount to carrying on a business.

In practice, the method of arriving at the VAT related to the business side of an organisation is often the same as for partial exemption. Anyone involved in a business/non-business situation should, therefore, read this chapter.

Incidentally, partial exemption is one of those subjects where the main principles are relatively straightforward, but applying them in practice is much more complicated because of the infinite variety of situations in the numerous kinds of business affected. There is a limit to the amount of detail into which one can go in an explanation of partial exemption, without producing a detailed case study. Yet, such a case study would be of limited relevance to many readers. For example, even within banking and insurance, businesses vary greatly in the kinds of financial activity they undertake, the types of insurance they write, and so on.

THE LAW ON PARTIAL EXEMPTION

24.2 *Articles 17* and *19* of the *EC 6th VAT Directive* (now *Directive 2006/112/EC, Arts 167, 173–177*) are the basis for the rules, which each Member State must implement. However, they only state general principles. *Section 26* outlines those principles in UK law, and gives HMRC power to make the detailed rules. The latter are in the *VAT Regulations, Pt XIV (SI 1995/2518)*.

WHAT KINDS OF BUSINESS ARE PARTIALLY EXEMPT?

24.3

Focus

Examples of partially exempt businesses are:

- banks, finance houses, building societies, and finance brokers;

- insurance companies and insurance brokers;

- betting shops, bingo halls and casinos;

- hospitals, nursing homes, and care homes;

- opticians;

- pawnbrokers;

- professional associations;

- property investment companies—unless they have opted to tax all rental income;

- schools;

- undertakers.

Other businesses are at risk of partial exemption. Some only occasionally have exempt outputs. Others do so regularly, but the related input tax is below the 'de minimis limit' (see **24.5** and **24.6** below). In either case, they may become partially exempt because of irregular or exceptional exempt outputs. Builders and property developers are the most common examples.

WHAT IS 'EXEMPT INPUT TAX'?

24.4   'Exempt input tax' is the VAT which is attributable to the exempt activities of a business. This includes any VAT on overheads, which has to be apportioned, not just that which is directly attributable. The full definition in *reg 99(1)(a)* refers to VAT on supplies used, or to be used, in making exempt supplies.

THE DE MINIMIS LIMIT

24.5

Focus

A business is partially exempt if its exempt input tax exceeds the de minimis limit. At the time of writing, this is:

- £625 per month on average—which is £1,875 per quarter or £7,500 a year; and

- the exempt input tax must be no more than 50% of the total input tax.

HOW THE LIMIT WORKS

24.6 *Reg 106 says that where in any VAT return period, or 'longer period', the exempt input tax... does not amount to more than £625 per month on average.* The use of the word average means that, if a business first incurs exempt input tax on the last day of a monthly VAT return, the limit is £625 for the period. If it is on the last day of a quarterly one, the limit is £1,875 because the average is for the whole 'prescribed accounting period', meaning the period of the VAT return.

If a business has a case where regular subjective judgments concerning the amount of exempt input tax has to be made, and the figure is close to the limit, it would be wise to inform HMRC of the calculations and the basis for them. The coding of a single invoice might make the difference between being partly exempt, and being below the de minimis limit.

THE 'LONGER PERIOD' OR 'PARTIAL EXEMPTION YEAR'

24.7 The 'longer period', otherwise known as the partial exemption year, runs to 31/3, 30/4, or 31/5, depending upon the VAT return periods of the business, or to any other date to which HMRC agree. Thus, it can be aligned with the financial year end, provided that this coincides with the end of a VAT return, or with agreed non-standard accounting periods.

Both the de minimis calculations and the apportionment ones for ordinary returns are only provisional, and are reworked for the 'longer period'. This is normally a full partial exemption year.

There are special rules for applying the de minimis limit in the year in which the business first has exempt outputs. Whether it escapes under the limit in that first longer period depends upon these rules. They vary slightly depending upon whether it is newly registered, or is an established trader. See Notice 706 *Partial Exemption.*

If, in subsequent partial exemption years, the exempt input tax is below the de minimis limit for the full year, it can reclaim the input tax previously provisionally disallowed on the VAT returns during the year.

THE RIGHT TO RECOVER INPUT TAX

24.8   In order to understand partial exemption fully, a business needs to know the basis of its right to recover input tax. By this, we mean the rules dictating which outputs create recoverable input tax, and which do not. These rules are the basis of partial exemption calculations.

Focus

Section 26(2) lists the supplies in relation to which input tax can be recovered as:

- taxable supplies;

- supplies outside the UK which would be taxable if made here;

- such other supplies outside the UK, and such exempt supplies as are specified by Treasury Order.

The Treasury has duly made the *Input Tax (Specified Supplies) Order (SI 1999/3121)*, which details the supplies in question as the following.

Services

24.9

- supplied to a customer, who belongs outside the EU; or

- directly linked to the export of goods outside the EU; or

- agency services concerning either of the above,

provided that the supply is exempt, or would have been exempt under the rules for insurance (*Sch 9 Group 2*) or finance (*Sch 9 Group 5, Items 1–7*), if it had been made in the UK.

Goods

24.10

- sales of *investment gold* (*Sch 9 Group 15, Items 1* and *2*).

Thus, a business can recover input tax on insurance and financial services, or on commissions earned on them, provided that:

- the customer belongs outside the EU; or

- the services are directly related to the export of goods outside the EU.

HOW THE RIGHT TO RECOVER AFFECTS BANKING, FINANCE AND INSURANCE

24.11 The above rules tie in with those on the *Place of Supply of Services*, which are explained in Chapter 23, *Exports and Imports of Services*. Thus:

- banking and financial services are covered by *Sch 5 para 5*;

- *POSSO, Art 16* makes those supplies outside the scope of VAT to business customers within the EU, and all customers outside it;

- as set out above, the *Specified Supplies Order* makes the input tax recoverable on certain supplies, including some to non-EU customers, which are exempt in the UK.

If a business is not already familiar with *Sch 5* and *POSSO*, see Chapter 23, *Exports and Imports of Services*.

PARTIAL EXEMPTION METHODS

24.12

Focus

In order to calculate the exempt input tax, a business has to use a partial exemption method. It can use either:

- the 'standard method'; or

- a 'special method'—which means any method a business can persuade HMRC to agree to, provided it is fair and reasonable.

Whatever method is used, there are always two stages to it.

Stage 1: direct attribution

24.13   The first stage of a method is always to directly attribute the input tax as far as possible to either taxable or exempt supplies. Direct attribution means attributing input tax as far as possible to the outputs (past, present, or future) it relates to.

That means attributing to:

- existing outputs;
- a project, which will produce outputs at some future date;
- outputs which occurred in the previous year.

The words *'used or to be used'* in *reg 101* make it clear that the issue of whether or not any outputs have occurred is irrelevant; the question is one of whether the input tax in question has been incurred in respect of an activity likely to result in either exempt outputs, taxable outputs, or outputs that are outside the scope with recovery.

If the expenditure is being incurred some time in advance of any resulting income, it might seem more accurate to refer to *activities* rather than to *outputs*. However, as there must always be an output in prospect, however distant, that is the word we have used throughout this chapter.

In the case of *North of England Zoological Society v Revenue & Customs* [2015] UKFTT 287 (TC) the First-tier Tribunal looked at attribution in detail. The zoo made supplies of admission charges which are exempt for the purposes of VAT. It also made a variety of taxable supplies including catering and retail supplies.

HMRC contended that the animal related costs are a cost component of the exempt admission charges, but only some of the taxable supplies. In particular they contended that animal related costs are not a cost component of supplies of catering and merchandise. As such the standard method did not give a fair and reasonable apportionment and the standard method override ought to be applied. As a result of this HMRC issued an assessment for over £1m.

The appellant contended that the 'standard method' of input tax recovery represented a fair and reasonable apportionment of input tax to taxable supplies. The appellant contended that the animal related costs are a cost component of taxable supplies, including catering and retail supplies, as well as the exempt admission income.

The main issue in the appeal was essentially whether there was a sufficient link between the animal related costs and supplies of catering, merchandise and books to justify apportionment of input tax on the animal related costs to those taxable supplies as well as to other taxable supplies and the exempt supply of admission charges.

The parties quoted a number of authorities and the Tribunal considered that a number of principles emerged from these, amongst which were:

● Input tax will be recoverable where it has a direct and immediate link or is a cost component of taxable outputs of the business. The taxable outputs may be individual outputs or part of a class of taxable outputs.

● Cost components may be linked to a particular supply or supplies, or they may be linked to supplies generally, in which case they are overheads. Both can generate a sufficient link to lead to input tax being recoverable.

● Any given input may be a cost component of more than one category of supply. It may be more closely connected to one supply than another. The search is for a 'sufficient link', not the closest link. In other words the search is for a direct and immediate link, not the most direct and immediate link.

The Tribunal considered that there was a 'strong economic link' between the catering and retail functions and the animals although there was a stronger link to the educational aims of the appellant. Overall the Tribunal came to the conclusion that there was a sufficiently direct and immediate link between the catering and retail income and the costs of the animal feed for the standard method to provide a fair and reasonable result and so found in favour of the appellant.

In the case of *Bedale Golf Club Ltd v Revenue & Customs* [2015] UKFTT 446 (TC) the taxpayer appealed against an assessment for VAT claimed on the following items:

(1) maintenance and repair fees for the lift in Bedale's clubhouse;

(2) refurbishment of chairs in the bar and lounge area of the clubhouse; and

(3) new curtains in the bar and lounge area of the clubhouse.

The appellant was partially exempt as it made both taxable supplies of food and drink and exempt supplies as a non-profit making member's golf club. The appellant argued that the input tax on the costs were used or to be used exclusively in making taxable supplies of drinks and food and was therefore fully recoverable, whereas HMRC argued that the costs were residual as they were used for both taxable and exempt supplies and only a proportion was recoverable in line with the partial exemption standard method.

The essence of the appellant's case is that the costs were only used in relation to the taxable supplies of drinks and food. The lifts were barely used at all but allow people to get to the bar and lounge to buy drinks and food. People who bought drinks and food used the chairs and benefited from the curtains.

HMRC's case was that the costs were used for both taxable and exempt supplies. HMRC did not accept that the meetings and other uses were not supplies. HMRC argued that the use of the clubhouse by the members is an intrinsic part of their membership and is inseparable from the exempt supplies of sporting services. It cannot be said that either the physical use or the economic use are exclusively for the sales of food and drink.

The Tribunal considered that the lounge and bar were used for a wide range of other uses, which include those 'closely linked with and essential to sport'. The use of chairs and curtains is not of a type which inherently lends itself only to the consumption of food and drink. Similarly, the use of the lift is not restricted to taxable supplies as it can be used whatever the reason for going to the first floor. The fact that there might be a closer link between the costs and the taxable supplies does not mean that there is not a sufficient link between the costs and the exempt supplies.

The Tribunal considered that the costs were therefore residual and only partially recoverable and so the appeal was dismissed

Stage 2: apportionment

24.14   The VAT which is not directly attributable, called the '*residual input tax*' or '*the pot*' must be apportioned using either the standard method based on outputs, or a special method agreed in advance with HMRC.

The direct attribution stage always comes first. Apportionment under either the standard or a special method only affects the residual tax.

THE STANDARD METHOD

24.15   The standard method apportions residual tax to taxable outputs in the ratio of taxable outputs to total outputs for the period concerned. Thus, if a business has taxable outputs of £1m and total outputs of £3m, it can recover one-third of its residual input tax. The outputs method has the virtue of relative simplicity. Information on outputs is often more readily available than other data. However, if the output values vary significantly between kinds of output, or the ratio of taxable to exempt swings about, this may distort the recovery of input tax either for, or against, the business.

Focus

The calculation is based on the formula:

$$\frac{\text{total taxable supplies}}{\text{total taxable and exempt supplies}} \times 100 = \text{taxable}\%$$

This gives the percentage of non-attributable input VAT that can be recovered. The figure calculated is always rounded up to the nearest whole percentage, so, for example, 49.1% becomes 50%. This percentage is then applied to the non-attributable input VAT to determine the actual amount that can be recovered.

Any ratio is potentially dangerous if a business does not understand it properly. There is not necessarily a direct relationship between the output values and the input tax incurred in creating them. Output values for different transactions in the same business can vary considerably, but the underlying costs do not. For instance, a financial institution may have relatively small standard-rated fees for managing portfolios, and exempt outputs of securities in much larger values, but on tiny profit margins. In such a situation, a special method would have a better chance of providing a fair and reasonable apportionment than the standard method would.

In the admittedly specialist situation of a university, income values that included non-business grants were held to be distortive (*University Court of the University of Glasgow* (EDN/03/109 No 19052). Some of the costs of the non-business activities were either zero-rated or reduced rated, because of their use for charitable purposes; some of the funding financed expensive clinical research, primarily people-based and generating relatively little input tax—especially as it was often not even done on the University's premises. The purpose of the calculation was to identify the VAT related to the business activities—which would then, of course, mostly relate to the exempt education.

The Tribunal suggested that the input tax attributed to taxable activities as a percentage of the total input tax attributed to business and non-business ones, might be a fair apportionment of the residual VAT related to both—though the parties were left to discuss that. HMRC appealed to the Court of Session, but withdrew before the case was due to be heard in March 2006. Instead, a short narrative was placed on the 'VAT appeals Update' listing on the HMRC website, advising that the assessment had been *'amended down to reflect the findings of the Tribunal'*.

An example of a standard method calculation

		Taxable outputs	Exempt outputs
Total input tax for the period			£100,000
Stage 1:		£	£
Attribute as far as possible the input tax directly related		10,000	20,000
Stage 2:			
Apportion the residual tax of £70,000 in the ratio taxable outputs/total outputs	£1m	7,000	63,000
	£10m		
		£17,000	£83,000

Thus, on those figures, £17,000 is recoverable, and £83,000 is disallowed.

Note that there is not necessarily any correlation between the ratio of recoverable input tax at the direct attribution stage, and that calculated at the apportionment one. There is no law of accountancy or mathematics which entitles a business to expect that, merely because it recovers one third under direct attribution, it should get a similar proportion at the apportionment stage.

For instance, this business might be selling both standard-rated goods, on which it recovers directly attributable input tax, and a mix of standard-rated and exempt services for which there is relatively little directly attributable input tax, because most of the costs are overheads, which relate to both. Thus, there is nothing surprising in the ratios in this example of one-third and one-tenth.

Note also that the directly attributable proportion of the total input tax can vary widely, depending upon the kind of business. In many of those that sell financial services, most of the VAT is incurred on non-attributable overheads.

So far, only the standard method has been outlined. There are various detailed rules commented on later in this chapter.

See also **24.71** and **24.74** below for the anti-avoidance rules known as the *Standard Method Override* and the *Special Method Override*.

In January 2009, HMRC published the responses to a consultation exercise held in 2008 on proposed partial exemption and Capital Goods Scheme ('CGS') changes. The report recommended some partial exemption changes be included in Budget 2009 and other changes (specific to the de minimis test and a proposed joint partial exemption/non-business calculation) included in Budget 2010. The proposed changes to the CGS were included in the 2011 Budget.

Accordingly, HMRC issued *Revenue & Customs Brief 19/09*, which announced four changes to the partial exemption standard method effective from 1 April 2009 (with in-depth details provided in VAT Information Sheet 04/09). Three of the changes are optional, and can be adopted by businesses without approval from HMRC. The three optional changes are referred to as:

- in-year provisional recovery rate;

- early annual adjustment; and

- use-based option for new partly exempt businesses.

The final change, which is referred to as 'Widening the scope of the standard method' is compulsory, and affects businesses that make:

- supplies of services to customers outside the UK;

- certain financial supplies such as shares and bonds;

- supplies made from establishments located outside the UK.

In-year provisional recovery rate

This optional change enables a business to use its previous year's recovery percentage to determine the provisional recovery of residual input tax in each VAT return, which is then finalised as normal by way of an annual adjustment. The finalised annual recovery percentage is then used as the provisional recovery percentage for the next year and so on.

Example 24.1—In year provisional recovery rate

A business has a partial exemption tax year that runs from 1 April to 31 March. For the year ending 31 March 2009, its annual recovery percentage was 60 per cent. For its VAT returns in the tax year commencing 1 April 2009 it may now provisionally recover 60 per cent of its residual input tax, thereby saving the need to calculate separate recovery percentages for each return. At the end of the year it must perform an annual adjustment calculation in the normal way, using actual figures for the year, to account for any under or over-recovery of input tax.

Early annual adjustment

This optional change enables a business the option to bring forward its annual adjustment calculation to the last VAT return of its tax year.

Example 24.2—Annual adjustment

A business has a partial exemption tax year ending 30 June 2009 and would normally account for its annual adjustment in its return for the period ending 30 September 2009. Under the new rules the business may account for its annual adjustment calculation in its return for the period ending 30 June 2009.

Use-based option for new partly exempt businesses

This optional change enables a new partly exempt business to recover its input tax on the basis of use in the following situations:

(i)   *During its 'registration period'*. This is the period running from the date a business is first registered for VAT to the day before the start of its first tax year (normally, 31 March, 30 April or 31 May depending on the periods covered by the VAT returns).

(ii) *During its first tax year* (normally the first period of 12 months commencing on 1 April, 1 May or 1 June following the end of the registration period), provided it did not incur input tax relating to exempt supplies during its registration period.

(iii)   *During any tax year*, provided it did not incur input tax relating to exempt supplies in its previous tax year.

A recovery on the basis of use (or the principle of use) means that input tax is attributed in accordance with the use or intended use of input tax bearing costs in making taxable supplies. The principle of use comes from EU legislation and is supported by a wide body of European and domestic case law.

HMRC's published partial exemption guidance V1-15 provides an in-depth discussion on how the principle of use applies in practice. The guidance refers to the concepts of 'cost components' and 'direct and immediate link'. In simple terms, it requires a business to examine its main categories of expenditure and determine the extent to which they relate to taxable supplies. Most businesses that embark upon a new activity (exempt activity in this case) will have carefully considered how costs will be used, in accordance with cost accounting principles, when preparing its business plan. Provided this is logical, objective and transparent it will invariably form an ideal basis for a fair recovery of input tax.

Where a business adopts this change and calculates its recovery of input tax on the basis of use, it is also required to calculate its annual adjustment on the basis of use to ensure consistency. Also, where a business does not recover input tax on the basis of use but would nevertheless have been entitled to do so, it may still calculate a use-based annual adjustment. This gives new partly exempt businesses maximum flexibility to help ensure they recover a fair amount of input tax. There is no need to notify HMRC.

Widening the scope of the standard method

Under the old rules, the standard method only dealt with the recovery of input tax relating to taxable supplies made in the UK.

This compulsory change widens the scope of the standard method so that it now deals with input tax on all supplies unless it is dealt with separately under *reg 103A* (Investment Gold).

Supplies described in *items 1* and *6* of *Group 5* of *Sch 9* to the *VATA 1994* (mainly supplies of financial instruments such as shares and bonds) and supplies made from overseas establishments are catered for by the standard method but are excluded from the values-based calculation, irrespective of their place of supply. Instead, input tax relating to these supplies is ring-fenced and recovered on the basis of use.

All remaining input tax is recovered by reference to the values-based calculation (unless a new partly exempt business opts to recover on the basis of use).

From 1 April 2010 two simplified tests have been introduced for calculating the *de minimis* limit. The simplified tests save some businesses the need to carry out a full partial exemption calculation to confirm their *de minimis* status. If, in a VAT period, a business passes Test one or Test two (below) it may treat itself as *de minimis* and provisionally recover input tax relating to exempt supplies. The business is still required to review its *de minimis* status at year-end as before and account for any under/over recovery of input tax as part of its annual adjustment. The simplified tests are:

- total input tax incurred is no more than £625 per month on average and the value of exempt supplies is no more than 50% of the value of all supplies;

- total input tax incurred less input tax directly attributable to taxable supplies is no more than £625 per month on average and the value of exempt supplies is no more than 50% of the value of all supplies.

At the end of the partial exemption year, the business needs to apply the *de minimis* test to the year as a whole.

If the business passes Test one for the year, it can recover all of its input tax relating to exempt supplies and is not required to carry out any further partial exemption calculations.

When applying Test two, the business first needs to review how much of the input tax it has incurred over the year is directly attributable to taxable supplies. Then, if it passes Test two for the year, it can recover all of its input tax relating to exempt supplies and is not required to carry out any further partial exemption calculations.

If it fails Test one and Test two for the year, then it needs to carry out a full partial exemption calculation for the year to determine whether it passes the current *de minimis* test and accounts for any under/over recovery of input tax as part of its annual adjustment in the normal way.

Prior to 1 April 2010 the rules required a business to apply the *de minimis* test in each VAT period. If it passes the test it is *de minimis* and can provisionally recover input tax relating to exempt supplies in that period. This is subject to an end-of-year partial exemption calculation to review its *de minimis* status and any under/over recovery of input tax is accounted for in the annual adjustment.

The new annual test gives most businesses the option of applying the *de minimis* test once a year, instead of four or five times a year. It allows a business that was *de minimis* in its previous partial exemption year to treat itself as *de minimis* in its current partial exemption year. This means it can provisionally recover input tax relating to exempt supplies in each VAT period, saving the need for partial exemption calculations.

There are three conditions on using the annual test. The business must:

- pass the *de minimis* test for its previous partial exemption year;

- consistently apply the annual test throughout any given partial exemption year; and

- have reasonable grounds for not expecting to incur more than £1 million input tax in its current partial exemption year.

If any of these conditions are not met then the business is required to apply the *de minimis* test in each VAT period, which remains the default position.

The main risk of using the annual test is that a business provisionally recovers input tax relating to exempt supplies in-year, HMRC use the term] but then fails the test at year-end and is required to repay this input tax to HMRC.

SPECIAL METHODS

24.16

> **Focus**
>
> A business does not have to use the outputs ratio of the standard method. A business can use any special method of apportioning residual tax which HMRC accepts as being fair and reasonable.

Under *reg 102,* they have power to approve any method which is suggested, provided it produces a fair and reasonable result. HMRC can also direct a business to use one based on their own method where they think that the standard method is distortive, but cannot agree a special one with the business.

Examples of special methods of apportionment are:

- staff numbers engaged on different activities;

- transaction counts for each activity;

- floor areas occupied by activities;

- sectorisation of the different parts of a business.

Possible financial criteria are:

- the ratio of input tax directly attributable to taxable supplies, to total directly attributable input tax;

- the ratio of the cost of the supplies used exclusively in making taxable supplies, to the cost of those used exclusively in making taxable or exempt supplies.

The need to be fair and reasonable

24.17   Following a consultation process starting in June 2006, HMRC have implemented charges with effect from 1 April 2007. When applying to use a special method, a business is now required to declare that 'to the best of its knowledge and belief', the method fairly and reasonably represents the extent to which goods or services are used, or to be used, by him in making taxable supplies.

This change in the partial exemption rules enables HMRC to issue a notice requiring a retrospective recalculation if they later thought that the method did not produce a fair and reasonable result, and that the trader knew or should have known this when making the declaration.

Presumably, this proposal is based on the supposition within HMRC that traders propose special methods based on cunning plans which generate unfair recovery of input tax, and of which, the significance is difficult for HMRC to spot until they see the results. HMRC say that visiting officers will not impose these new rules on businesses, but will refer the matter to Head Quarters, who will decide if an assessment is appropriate. HMRC also expect that the addition of this new requirement will speed up the processing of special method applications, although in practice, this has not been the case.

In the case of *Lok'nstore Group plc v Revenue & Customs Commissioners* [2012] UKFTT 589 (TC) HMRC refused four different proposed special methods as they said that the standard method was fair and reasonable. The taxpayer appealed this decision. The Tribunal had to decide if the proposed special methods were fair and reasonable and, if so, whether they more fair and reasonable than the standard method. The Tribunal concluded that both the standard method and the proposed special method produced fair and reasonable results, but that the appellants produced an attribution which was fairer and more reasonable than the attribution that would result from the standard method and, therefore, the appeal was allowed.

Some comments on special methods

24.18   As noted above at **24.15**, sales values can be distortive. The Tribunal's suggestion of an input tax based method in the *University Court of the University of Glasgow* (EDN/03/109 No 19052) is explained there.

However, a special method basis, such as staff numbers, can be difficult to show it is any better. For instance, it is often difficult to identify with any precision, the people involved with different activities.

In *National Provident Institution* (LON/2000/879 & 1112 & 2001/381 No 18944), the Tribunal rejected a special method based on a headcount, which HMRC used to calculate the input tax related to transactions in securities. It was based on estimates without any supporting evidence. The expenses on which substantial input tax was incurred, did not seem to relate specifically to staff numbers. In the absence of anything evidently more valid, the sales value based attribution was as good as any, and had the merit of simplicity.

In *Business Brief 14/05*, HMRC said they had not appealed *NPI* because of the facts of that situation, but that they maintained their view that the values of sales of securities, when combined with those of different kinds of transaction, often did not reflect the input tax related to each kind. They may well be right in some cases; the facts need careful consideration.

Sales values can be distortive if they do not reflect the time or resources needed for the different transactions. However, any alternative idea that one produces will need supporting facts and logical argument; it may not succeed merely as an idea.

It should also be noted that a special method should not be so complicated that it is difficult to implement in real life!

Floor areas

24.19   In *Business Brief 34/04*, HMRC said they are likely to accept a special method based on the floor area when:

- most of the input tax is incurred on costs of the premises; *and*

- most of the floor space is used wholly for taxable or wholly for exempt activities—so just a minor area relates to both.

That seems an unusual situation. Even if VAT is paid on rent, how often would the tax on property costs exceed 50% of the total, except when the building is refurbished? As for the floor area, it is often difficult to identify even 50% as being used wholly one way or the other. Not only do sales departments tend to handle a mix of sales; much of the space is occupied by back office functions, marketing, accounts, etc which support the entire business.

HMRC's comments followed the Tribunal's decision in *Optika Ltd* (LON/00/1281 No 18627). The Tribunal rejected a special method based upon the floor areas of opticians. *Optika* argued that the front area of each shop was nearly all used to make taxable supplies, and that this area should be valued on the zoning principle used in fixing retail rents, ie that the front area attracted the customers, so the rent paid per square foot for it was much higher than for the back area.

Optika lost because all the customers used the front area, including to access the rear space used for eye tests, and often occupied it when arranging for exempt supplies as well as taxable ones. Moreover, the zoning of the space was merely a basis for calculating the rent; the latter then related to the space as a whole. Furthermore, input tax on overheads was incurred for the premises overall, rather than in proportion to the higher value front area.

A shop which offers insurance or an extended warranty when selling goods or services, is in a similar situation. Claiming that the exempt supplies are made only from a small desk area is unlikely to succeed (although we do have experience of it being accepted), as those supplies are tied to the sales of the goods or services made in the rest of the premises.

Those points were repeated in *Banbury Visionplus Ltd* (and three other companies in the Specsavers Optical Group) (LON/2004/0299 No 19266). HMRC's cancellation of the previously agreed special method was confirmed as reasonable. A key point was that, although the taxable outputs ratio used to apportion the input tax on the dispensed spectacles was 33%, the floor area calculation justified nearly 70% recovery of residual costs. Although the figures could differ, that extreme variance was telling.

COST CENTRE ACCOUNTING

24.20   Large organisations tend to use cost centre accounting to produce management accounts. That being the case, it is also the logical basis for splitting up the expenses amongst the different activities for VAT purposes. Such a method will involve:

- allocating costs to each department;

- re-analysing the support departments costs to those departments which generate income;

- attributing and apportioning the total VAT thus allocated, to each income generating department to the supplies which it makes.

Different methods may be suitable for the various activities. For example, one might use a transaction count for one department, and output values for another.

A business may find that a two-stage apportionment gives it a better result than a single ratio. For instance, the running expenses relating to a building used partly for taxable activity, and partly for exempt activity, might be apportioned on the basis of the respective floor areas. This would be desirable if it enabled more tax to be recovered than under the overall apportionment of residual tax.

HMRC will consider any combination of bases of calculation which are proposed. Although they have power to dictate the nature of a special method, it is rare for them to use it. A business knows its activities far better than HMRC do, and it is, therefore, best for the business to suggest the right method. An example of a cost centre-based method is on the next page.

A COST CENTRE ACCOUNTING PROBLEM

24.21   If a business is using cost centre accounting as the basis of its special method, how does it post the input tax? The options are:

- charge the invoice totals gross to the relevant expenses in each cost centre. The problem is then one of identifying the amount of VAT to be apportioned. Some businesses do this by estimating the VAT included within each expense heading. HMRC may accept this, but can the business identify any entries, which do not include VAT, and which find their way for one reason or another into expense listings that appear to be all standard-rated?

- have a VAT code for each cost centre. The VAT not recovered then appears as a cost, unless the business spreads it back to the underlying expenses;

- charge invoices gross and record the VAT as a memorandum total. Some computer software includes this facility. This then leaves a credit to the cost centre for the VAT recovered. Often, this is too small a figure for it to be worth bothering with spreading it back over the expense accounts.

THE 'OUTSIDE THE SCOPE' SUPPLY PROBLEM

24.22   In the cost centre example problem above, outside the scope supplies are included at stage three, in the apportionment for sales department number 3 which is based on turnover. HMRC may not allow the business to do this, because *reg 103(1)* requires use to be the basis.

In *Liverpool Institute of Performing Arts* ([2001] STC 891, HL), the House of Lords said:

- the standard method under *reg 101* calculates the VAT relating to supplies made within the UK;

- *reg 103(1)*, based on use of the inputs in question, decides the VAT relating to supplies made outside the UK.

This prevented LIPA obtaining full recovery of input tax on overheads at a time when it had *out of country supplies,* but had not yet made *exempt* ones, albeit that much of its activity was devoted towards preparing to.

AN EXAMPLE OF A SPECIAL METHOD BASED ON COST CENTRES

Stage 1—Code input tax by department

	Input tax split per sales CC	£
	split	VAT
Support depts		
Accounts	33.3% each	30,000
Overheads such as rent, telephone/audit fee (unless each invoice is to be multi-coded)	40%, 40%, 20%	40,000
Management & Administration (MD & non-exec directors, personnel, receptionists, cleaners etc)		
	33.3%	10,000
Back office (Such as policy admin or contract notes/ settlement depending on the business)	50%, 50%	20,000
Sales Dept		
Sales 1		40,000
Sales 2		50,000
Sales 3		20,000
		£210,000

Stage 2—Apportion the support departments

Sales 1 Directly incurred		40,000
Support Depts	10,000	
	16,000	
	3,333	
	10,000	
		39,333
Total		
Sales 1		79,333
Sales 2 Directly incurred		50,000
Support Depts	10,000	
	16,000	

		3,333	
		10,000	
			39,333
	Total		
	Sales 2		89,333
Sales 3 Directly incurred			20,000
Support Depts		10,000	
		8,000	
		3,334	
			21,334
	Total		
	Sales 3		41,334
TOTAL INPUT TAX NOW SPLIT BY SALES DEPARTMENT			£210,000

Stage 3—Apportion the sales departments

		Non-recoverable	Recoverable	
1.		£		
Sales 1	All outputs exempt		79,333	
Sales 2	Part taxable outputs:			
	Apportion using transaction count		40,021	49,312
	55.2% OS(R)			
	count 44.8% OS(NR)			

Sales 3	Part taxable outputs:				
	Apportion using sales value				
		£			
	Taxable	300,000			
	OS(R)	200,000			
		500,000	33.33%		
				27,557	13,777
	Exempt	1,000,000	66.67%		
	Total	£1,500,000			Recoverable
		Non-recoverable		£146,911	63,089
				Total	£210,000

WHAT DOES REGULATION 103(1) DO?

24.23 *Regulation 103(1)* covers two categories of outside the scope supplies:

- *out of country supplies*—those for which the place of supply is outside the UK, which would be taxable if they were made here;

- *specified supplies*—those which would be exempt if the place of supply was in the UK, and for which, the related input tax is recoverable because they are covered by the *Specified Supplies Order*—mainly finance and insurance supplies made from the UK to a customer who 'belongs' outside the EU.

Input tax is to be attributed to those supplies, and thus identified as recoverable, *to the extent that the goods or services are so used or to be used, expressed as a proportion of the whole use or intended use.*

HOW DOES A BUSINESS DEAL WITH 'NON-SPECIFIED' SUPPLIES?

24.24

Focus

'Non-specified' supplies are those:

- for which the place of supply is outside the UK;

- which would be exempt if made here; and

- which are not covered by the *Specified Supplies Order*.

That is, they are outside the scope without recovery. The main example is financial services to EU customers.

These supplies must be treated the same as exempt ones made in the UK:

- the VAT incurred in making them cannot be deducted;

- their value must be included in a standard method calculation.

WHAT IF A BUSINESS MAKES UK SUPPLIES AS WELL AS OUTSIDE THE SCOPE ONES?

24.25 If a business makes taxable and exempt supplies in the UK, as well as outside the scope ones:

Stage 1 Start by calculating the VAT that relates to *out of country* and specified outside the scope supplies, on the basis of use under *reg 103(1)*. A business can deduct this.

Stage 2 Deal with the VAT which relates to *taxable* and *exempt UK* supplies and *non-specified exempt* ones, under either a standard method or a special method.

At Stage 2, the standard method calculates the recoverable percentage as the value of *taxable* supplies divided by the total value of *taxable, exempt,* and *non-specified* outside the scope supplies. A business cannot include *out of country* and *specified* supplies. The input tax related to the latter has, of course, been dealt with at the first stage.

Following the decision of the CJEU in the *Credit Lyonnais* case (C-388/11) law has been aligned with EU law from 1 January 2016. The primary change is that the value of supplies made by overseas establishments will now be excluded from the standard method.

IS THE ABOVE PRACTICAL?

24.26 It is up to the business to decide how to attribute on the basis of use. HMRC will accept any method whose result seems fair and reasonable.

If all the supplies of the business are made from the same offices and, with the same people involved, it may not be practicable to attribute or separately apportion the VAT relating to different kinds of supply. If a business has a problem, it should discuss it with HMRC. They may agree that it can use a turnover calculation based on all its sales, including those covered by *reg 103(1)*, but it must ask. If they do agree, it will be a special method, not the standard one.

THE ANNUAL ADJUSTMENT

24.27 As explained above at **24.7**, the quarterly apportionments of residual tax are only provisional, whatever the method used. The figures must be reworked on an annual basis for the partial exemption year, in order to eliminate any distortions in individual quarters.

The annual adjustment is done on the return for the quarter following the end of the partial exemption year, thus giving the business a little extra time in which to do it. Naturally, the direct attributions do not change, just the apportionment of residual tax.

See also **24.71** et seq on the *Partial exemption override*, which requires larger businesses to consider whether the standard method has produced a fair result.

ROUNDING UP

24.28   Most businesses using the standard method can round up the percentage to the next whole number. Thus, 22.1% becomes 23%. However, a business cannot do this if the residual VAT under the standard method exceeds £400,000 per month on average; if it does, the business can only round up to two decimal places.

If a business uses a special method, it must always round up to two decimal places whatever the amount of tax being apportioned. The only possible exception is where the business is using a method which, although special, is based on a single calculation outputs ratio, and was agreed by HMRC prior to 1 April 2005. They used to allow rounding up in those cases, but will not do so in future if such a method is reviewed or updated.

In *The Royal Bank of Scotland Group plc* (EDN/05/21 No 19429), it was confirmed that, in a special method, HMRC can demand rounding up to two decimal places.

CORRECTION OF ERRORS

24.29   In Notice 706 (June 2011), para 12.6 HMRC say a business can only use the annual adjustment to correct its calculations to the extent that the annual adjustment would do this anyway, ie where the use of goods or services has changed during the year, and to apply the annual average for ratio calculations.

Errors must be corrected in the usual way by a separate voluntary disclosure, once the value in the period of discovery exceeds £10,000 or 1% of turnover, subject to an upper limit of £50,000.

CERTAIN OUTPUTS MUST BE EXCLUDED FROM THE STANDARD METHOD

24.30

> **Focus**
>
> When using the standard method, a business has to leave certain outputs out of the turnover figures (*reg 101(3)*). This is because they are likely to distort the calculations.

The list includes taxable transactions that would distort in its favour, not just exempt ones.

A business must exclude:

- *any sum receivable* by the business for a supply of capital goods used by it for the purposes of its business. There is no definition of *capital goods* but HMRC will only be concerned about sales large enough to distort. In *JDL Ltd* (MAN/98/297 No 17050: [2002] STC 1), demonstrator cars were held to be *capital goods* of a motor dealer. The sales of them, exempt under *Sch 9 Group 14*, therefore qualified for exclusion;

- the following *if they are incidental* to its business activities. That they be 'incidental' is the only requirement. *Incidental* is not defined in the law but see later:

  - (i) zero-rated interests in property (dwellings and those intended for relevant residential or charitable use) covered by *Sch 8 Group 5, Item 1* (new buildings) or *Group 6, Item 1* (reconstructed listed buildings);

  - (ii) Surrenders of interests in, rights over or licences to occupy land;

  - (iii) Rents or sales of land and property, exempt under *Sch 9 Group 1*;

  - (iv) Sales of 'new' buildings, or civil engineering works, which are standard-rated under the exception in *Sch 9 Group 1, Item 1(a)*;

  - (v) An interest in property, which is standard-rated as a result of a waiver of exemption under *Sch 10 para 2*;

  - (vi) Those financial transactions, such as interest, financial commissions, and sales of securities, which are exempt under *Sch 9 Group 5*;

- sales of goods on which input tax has previously been disallowed, such as cars. These are now exempt under *Sch 9 Group 14*;

- self supplies such as of stationery and of imported services (the reverse charged services) (*reg 104*). This prevents an artificial improvement in the ratio as a result of having these notional standard-rated outputs;

- on page 13 in para 4.4 of Notice 706 (October 2002), HMRC say that a business must also exclude the transfer of a business as a going concern.

MEANING OF 'INCIDENTAL'

24.31 The sub-headings (i)–(vi) above are only excluded if they are incidental to the business activities. Neither the *EC 6th VAT Directive*, *Directive 2006/112/EC* nor UK law define 'incidental'.

> **Focus**
>
> HMRC say that transactions cannot be incidental if they are carried out:
>
> - on such a scale, and with such regularity, as to constitute a business in their own right; or
>
> - in such a way as to constitute, in substance and reality, an integral part of the main business.

In *CH Beazer plc* ([1987] VATTR 164; *affd sub nom Customs and Excise Comrs v CH Beazer (Holdings) plc* [1989] STC 549) the President defined 'incidental' as *occurring or liable to occur in fortuitous or subordinate conjunction with*.

Much of the time, it is obvious whether or not transactions are incidental to the way the business earns its profit. However, do not take it for granted that the business can exclude, say, interest earned on client deposits.

In *Régie Dauphinoise—Cabinet A Forest Sàrl* (Case C-306/94 [1996] STC 1176), the ECJ ruled that interest earned on sums held by a property management company on behalf of the property owners was the *direct, permanent, and necessary* extension of its taxable activity. It was therefore to be included in total income for the purpose of the standard method of calculating deductible input tax.

However, the ECJ then held in *Empresa de Desenvolvimento Mineiro SGPS SA* (C-77/01), that the fact that the income generated by exempt financial transactions is greater than that produced by the main activity of the business, does not preclude their being incidental. Where the taxable turnover from the main activity is small, it would distort the calculation of recoverable input tax to include exempt transactions, which involve very limited use of assets or services subject to VAT, solely because of the extent of the income they produce.

AN OUTPUTS RATIO MUST NOT INCLUDE WORK IN PROGRESS

24.32   A business cannot include in its outputs ratio figures for work in progress not yet invoiced.

For example, consider a property owner/builder with exempt rents and a large construction project in progress. The business could attribute the input tax so far incurred on the project, to the future income expected from it. However, it could not improve its recovery of residual VAT on its overheads by bringing the value of work not yet billed into its outputs ratio. A tax point must have occurred (*Antonio Jorge Lda* (ECJ C-536/03). For construction projects, this will normally mean payment has been received, not just an architect's certificate and request for payment issued.

INTEREST CHARGED BY HOLDING COMPANIES TO SUBSIDIARIES

24.33   In contrast to the *Régie Dauphinoise* case noted at **24.31** above, the ECJ ruled in *Floridienne SA and Berginvest SA* ([2000] STC 1044) that, where loans to its subsidiaries did not amount to an economic activity, a holding company could ignore interest on those loans when using the standard method.

THINK CAREFULLY ABOUT THE ATTRIBUTIONS

24.34   A business might think that direct attribution of input tax is usually obvious. Indeed, much of the time it is apparent that a particular expense relates either entirely to taxable or exempt outputs. However, a flow of cases in recent years has shown that there is plenty of room for argument in the more borderline situations. The following comments demonstrate the problem.

Compare the wordings:

- tax on supplies which *'are used or to be used … exclusively in making taxable supplies (reg 101(2)(b))*;

- tax on supplies which are *'used or to be used by him in making both taxable and exempt supplies' (reg 101(2)(d))*.

Any element of use for taxable supplies, or for those outside the scope with recovery, means input tax incurred in making an exempt supply is part of the 'residual tax'. It is not directly attributable as non-recoverable. The reverse applies to tax mostly attributable to taxable supplies.

For instance, *Dial a Phone Ltd* (LON/01/14 No 17602: [2003] STC 192: [2004] STC 987) sold mobile phones and airtime contracts. Customers were given three months' free insurance, and Dial a Phone received exempt insurance commissions on those policies that were not cancelled. Its advertising and marketing costs were held to relate to both its standard-rated and its exempt income.

In *DFS Furniture Company Ltd* (TC00157) a further case which addressed the partial exemption implications of a retailer who, in addition to its main taxable business of selling furniture, generated a regular source of VAT exempt commission income from selling related insurance—anti-stain insurance for sofas and personal protection insurance (PPI) for customers who use credit terms.

The issues were:

- whether the receipt of the VAT exempt income necessitates a partial exemption restriction on general running costs;

- if so, on which costs in which areas of the operations; and

- what calculation should be used to give a fair and reasonable restriction of input tax deduction.

The case focused on VAT on advertising costs.

The conclusion of the case was that although the recoverability of VAT on advertising costs depended on the content and intention of the advertising concerned, in the case of store costs, head office costs and potentially even factory costs (on the facts in DFS some spraying of furniture linked to insurance was carried out in the factories) all related input VAT should be included in a standard partial exemption method calculation whenever exempt income is generated by activities in the stores.

This case is likely to encourage HMRC into looking very critically at the partial exemption positions of all retailers who generate any exempt income, however small or incidental, in their stores.

DOES THE SPECIAL METHOD FAIL TO COPE WITH CERTAIN INPUT TAX?

24.35   Special methods sometimes do not cover one or more aspects of the business—either because of a fault in the method, or because of a change in the business since the method was agreed. HMRC call that a *gap*.

From 1 April 2005, a business must now cope with the *gap* in the method by recovering the related input tax on the basis of the percentage of it *used* in making taxable supplies *(reg 102(6))*. HMRC expect the business to apply for a revised method covering the *gap,* and it is probably wise to do that in order to minimise the risk of future argument.

A RIGHTS ISSUE DOES NOT CREATE A SUPPLY

24.36

Focus

In May 2005, the ECJ confirmed in *Kretztechnik AG,* that the issue of new shares is not a supply, let alone an exempt one.

This is what had been argued in *CH Beazer plc* (1987 VATTR 164) but was rejected both then, and in various later cases. Following *Kretztechnik,* it is now recognised that issuing new shares in order to raise money for the business does not create a supply.

Do not confuse that with the sale of existing shares by one shareholder to another, which is a supply if the vendor trades actively rather than merely owning shares as a passive investment. See **11.59** for further notes on how sales of shares can be non-business.

In *Kretztechnik AG,* the ECJ said that *Art 5(1), EC 6th VAT Directive* (now *Directive 2006/112/EC, Art 14(1)*) means that a supply of goods involves transferring the right to dispose of tangible property as owner. Therefore, an issue of new shares, which are securities representing intangible property, is not a supply of goods. Just as a contribution required by a partnership from a new partner is not payment for a supply of services to that partner, nor is the issue of shares by a company to raise capital. The shareholder makes an investment, not a payment for a supply.

As a share issue increases the company's capital for the benefit of its economic activity in general, the costs associated with the share issue form part of its overheads, and the tax thereon is therefore part of the residual VAT. Any disallowance thus depends on whether the trading activities involve exempt outputs.

In *Business Brief 12/05,* HMRC initially accepted this. However, they had doubts about whether it covered the issue of shares as part of a merger or takeover, or a demerger, and were taking legal advice.

Meanwhile, companies which have made rights issues prior to November 2005, should have submitted claims to recover disallowed input tax immediately, because retrospective claims are limited by the four-year cap explained in Chapter 18, *VAT Housekeeping for Finance Directors.*

EXISTING RULES FOR INPUT TAX ON SHARE ISSUES

24.37   The following comments cover the UK law, which has been overruled by the ECJ decision mentioned above—at least in relation to rights issues. Whether all the following rules are now invalid will depend partly on the future interpretation of the decision by HMRC.

The services of advisers and other costs incurred on takeover deals, do not necessarily relate only to an exempt transaction. The position varies from case to case, and at least some of the expense often relates to the ongoing business rather than to the deal itself.

Until 3 December 2004, input tax incurred in relation to a deal that was not directly attributable to an exempt transaction in shares, was treated as residual just like ordinary overheads. If the business was fully taxable apart from the transaction in shares, that residual input tax could be recovered in full.

From 3 December 2004, *reg 103B* required the apportionment to be based on the ratio of: use for supplies in respect of which VAT is recoverable, to total use.

The use ratio applies to services from:

- accountants;

- advertising agencies;

- providers of listing and registration services;

- financial advisers;

- lawyers;

- marketing consultants;

- designers and preparers of documentation;

- businesses providing similar services.

This rule meant that if there was an exempt issue of shares, the VAT on an expense related both to it and to ongoing taxable supplies, had to be at least partly disallowed. Obviously, that does not now apply to a rights issue of new shares, and it will only affect any other transactions which HMRC successfully claim to involve supplies. A possible example is the issue of shares to the shareholders of a company being taken over—though, of course, that is still a new issue of shares; the difference is that what is received in exchange for them is existing share capital, not cash.

If the rule does apply, detailed fee notes may be needed. If the costs of an issue have to be identified for financial reporting purposes, the apportionment will normally be acceptable.

The following comments illustrate some typical situations as identified in a variety of cases.

Key questions

24.38

- does the deal involve an exempt output? The issue of financial securities, such as shares, does not; nor does the receipt of a fixed-term loan or an increased overdraft. Nor does buying the shares of another company—though swapping the shares of the company for new ones issued by the company taking it over, may be held to do so;

- are the costs incurred related entirely to the exempt output, or are there other aspects, such as the drafting of service agreements for directors, or minutes for meetings of the Board or the shareholders?

- do advisers' invoices fully identify the details of the work done? Unless they do, it will be difficult to justify apportioning the input tax to work not directly related to an exempt output;

- could the advisers exempt their services as intermediaries in arranging for the issue of the securities? That may be possible for a financial adviser, who is involved in negotiating a deal. It is not so in the case of those who provide audit-type reports or asset valuations. See the rules in *Group 5, Sch 9*, which are explained in Chapter 11, *So What is Exempt?*

In *RAP Group plc* (2000 STC 980) the input tax on an invoice from a firm of solicitors, which had advised over an issue of shares, was held to be residual. The detail on the invoice indicated that part of the advice had concerned:

- service contracts;

- a due diligence report on the company being acquired;

- investigating title to its properties;

- preparing papers for its AGM following the acquisition.

Thus, it was not all related to the issue of the shares, and was, therefore, residual. Invoices from other advisers gave no details, so the question could not be considered.

In *Easyjet plc* (LON/02/504 No 18230), it was held that input tax on fees related to a share issue, but including an audit, must be attributed (ie apportioned) under *reg 103(2)* on a use basis.

In *Southampton Leisure Holdings plc* (LON/99/0466 No 17716), it was held that, when a company issued shares in order to acquire another company, the costs were attributable as follows.

Partly to the business as a whole, and therefore residual

24.39

- merchant bank's services in advising and negotiating, making arrangements for due diligence investigations, and co-ordinating the work of other advisors;

- valuations of properties of company being acquired;

- investigating title to the properties, and drawing up service contracts for directors;

- advice on financing the offer, and due diligence investigation of the financial affairs of the company being acquired.

Wholly to the issue of shares

24.40

- printing the offer documents and press release;

- public relations services aimed at maintaining support for the offer.

Whether those three cases above, together with the new *reg 103B* mentioned earlier, have any ongoing significance, will depend on the precise interpretation of the ECJ ruling in *Kretztechnik AG,* explained above at **24.36**.

Holdings by UK nominees create UK supplies

24.41   In *Water Hall Group plc* (LON/00/1308 No 18007), it was held that where a nominee holds shares, the supply is to that nominee. Thus, if the nominee is in the UK, the place of supply is here, even if the beneficial owner belongs outside the EU.

INPUT TAX RELATES TO THE IMMEDIATE OUTPUT

24.42   Input tax must be attributed to any output directly resulting from it. Arguing that a business should be able to recover it because of a wider purpose will get it nowhere. Various cases have demonstrated aspects of this problem.

THE NEED FOR A 'DIRECT AND IMMEDIATE LINK'

24.43

Focus

Two decisions of the ECJ, *BLP Group plc* ([1995] STC 424) and *Midland Bank plc* ([2000] STC 501) have affirmed the need for a 'direct and immediate link' between the input on which a business reclaims input tax, and the output on which it based its claim to the deduction. That does not mean that input tax in general has to have a direct link to a taxable output—there is no such link for many overhead expenses. It means that, when, for partial exemption purposes, an input is attributed, there must be such a link, be it to a taxable or to an exempt output. Without such a link, the VAT must be apportioned as part of residual tax.

See **24.47** below for further comment on the concept of a direct and immediate link.

That is fundamentally important when the difference is between, on the one hand, full recovery or nil recovery and, on the other hand, recovery on the basis of the percentage calculated for residual tax.

In *BLP Group plc* ([1995] STC 424), the Tribunal rejected the wider purpose argument, and held that tax on the costs of a sale of shares must be attributed to that sale. When the point was referred to the ECJ, it stated the need for a direct and immediate link to a taxable transaction, and that the ultimate aim of the trader was irrelevant.

That principle was repeated by the ECJ in *Midland Bank plc* (LON/94/117 No 14144: Case C-98/98: [2000] STC 501). £315,000 input tax was incurred on legal costs in defending proceedings brought by British and Commonwealth Holdings plc against the bank's merchant banking subsidiary, Samuel Montagu & Co Ltd. The latter was accused of a negligent misrepresentation made when it had advised Quadrex Holdings Inc in a deal with British and Commonwealth. The Tribunal held the costs to be directly linked to the taxable supply of the fees charged by Samuel Montagu to Quadrex. By defending the proceedings, Samuel Montagu sought to reduce the claim for damages, and thereby quantify its exposure under its contract to supply services to Quadrex. The Tribunal accepted that there was a direct link with those services.

When, on appeal by HMRC, the High Court referred the matter to the ECJ, the latter again stated the need for a direct and immediate link. It said:

> '... the right to deduct the VAT charged on such goods or services presupposes that the expenditure incurred in obtaining them was part of the cost components of the taxable transactions. Such expenditure must therefore be part of the costs of the output transactions which utilise the goods and services acquired. That is why those cost components must generally have arisen before the taxable person carried out the taxable transactions to which they relate.

> It follows that, contrary to what the Midland claims, there is in general no direct and immediate link in the sense intended in the *BLP Group* judgment, cited above, between an input transaction and services used by a taxable person as a consequence of and following completion of the said transaction. Although the expenditure incurred in order to obtain the aforementioned services is the consequence of the output transaction, the fact remains that it is not generally part of the cost components of the output transaction ... Such services do not therefore have any direct and immediate link with the output transaction.'

The Court has, therefore, seen a distinction between expenditure incurred in the course of making a supply, and that which arises afterwards merely as a consequence of that supply. Further arguments appear likely on the seemingly fine dividing line between what is a cost component and what is merely a consequence.

Remember, none of this affects the right to recover VAT on the expense as a cost of the business; merely whether that recovery can be by direct attribution or must depend on the position concerning residual tax. It is therefore irrelevant for fully taxable businesses.

With regard to share issues, as outlined at **24.36** above, the decision of the ECJ in *Kretztechnik* confirmed that no [exempt] supply was made when a company issues new shares to raise capital (or issues other new securities such as bonds, debentures, and loan notes).The VAT incurred on the costs of a share issue, therefore, is residual in a partly exempt business (and wholly recoverable in a fully taxable business).

In *Deutsche Ruck UK Reinsurance Co Ltd* ([1995] STC 495), a Tribunal held that the VAT on legal fees incurred in disputing liability to pay claims under policies, for which the premiums were outside the scope with recovery, was held to be attributable to those premiums, not a part of the pot of overheads. Whilst this decision is now perhaps suspect, it seems arguable that disputing liability to claims is a cost component of providing the insurance in return for premiums. Obviously, dealing with, and negotiating, the value of claims is a cost component. Whether disputing liability altogether was a cost component, might perhaps depend on the extent to which the insurance company in question could show that this was typical of the way it conducted its business, as opposed to a one-off dispute!

Sheffield Co-operative Society Ltd ([1987] VATTR 216) is a more straightforward example of where the wider purpose argument fails. Tax on the refurbishment of a restaurant was held to be related to the exempt rents charged to the caterer, who had been granted a licence to occupy the area. It could not be attributed to the outputs of the store generally. That the cost was incurred to promote the store by having a smart restaurant was irrelevant.

Similarly, in *Brammer plc* (MAN/90/123 No 6420), VAT on 'reverse consideration' paid in order to assign a lease, was held to relate to the exempt sale of the land which was then made possible. The transaction was part of a complicated series aimed at freeing Brammer from its obligations under a potentially onerous lease. It enabled Brammer to procure a transfer of that lease to the company to which it paid the reverse consideration, and to which it also sold the freehold reversion. The VAT on the reverse consideration was thus attributable to the exempt freehold sale. The argument that it was incurred for the general benefit of the company was rejected.

Cheshire Racing Ltd (VTD 20,283) was an appeal by a bookmaker on the issue on input tax attribution, and whether there was a direct and immediate link in relation to input tax incurred on satellite information screen ('SIS') broadcasts in the shops.

The appellant argued that the input tax was partially deductible, as it related to the totality of operations in the shops, including the taxable activities of 'amusement with prizes' machines, and 'fixed odds betting terminals' ('FOBTs'). HMRC, on the other hand, argued that the input tax was irrecoverable, as it related directly and exclusively to exempt over-the-counter betting on horse and greyhound racing.

The case was similar to that of the June 2006 Tribunal case involving *Town and County Factors* (VTD 19,616), a Ladbrokes subsidiary, which found in favour of the appellant. However, HMRC later responded with a policy statement in

Business Brief 17/2006, which said they only accepted that SIS services could be treated as residual where (as with *T&CF*) the bookmaker added specific advertising items for its taxable services. This further case effectively questioned the validity of that further restriction imposed by HMRC. The appellant gave evidence of the way in which the 'betting shop experience' had evolved from the early days of austere premises providing only facilities to place bets, into a wider experience to which the screens provided a necessary background. The Tribunal accepted this, and also rejected the HMRC policy from *Business Brief 17/2006*, noting that, whilst T&CF, an organisation with 2,000 shops, might well choose to add its own specific advertising, it was unlikely to be realistic for an organisation with six shops to do the same. Consequently, the failure to add specific advertising did not mean that no direct and immediate link could exist between the SIS content and the taxable supplies. The Tribunal took from the *BLP* case an approach that one must take the wider view suggested by the appellant, and, on that basis, concluded that there was a direct and immediate link between the SIS services and both taxable and exempt supplies. The appeal was allowed, although HMRC took the opportunity to state that they reserved the right to question whether the partial exemption standard method provided a fair and reasonable attribution of the input tax.

SEEMINGLY OBVIOUS ATTRIBUTIONS CAN BE WRONG!

24.44   Sometimes, an attribution seems obvious—but the obvious can be wrong! In *The Mayflower Theatre Trust Ltd* ((LON/03/583) No 19254; [2006] EWHC 706 (Ch); [2006] EWCA Civ 116), the cost of a theatrical production paid to the production company was seen as directly related to the tickets sold—exempt as cultural services. The Tribunal saw no direct and immediate link between the cost of the production and the sales of programmes, confectionery, drinks, merchandise and corporate entertainment. This decision was overturned on appeal by the taxpayer to the High Court, where it was agreed that there was a direct and immediate link to the sponsorship package including a right to tickets. HMRC appealed to the Court of Appeal, but it upheld the High Court's decision, albeit on different grounds. The CA rejected the High Court's reasoning in favour of a view that the taxable supply to which the production costs have a direct and immediate link, is the supply of programmes. One of the judges, Chadwick LJ, expressed surprise that *reg 101(2)(d)* should operate in this manner.

Whether there is a direct and immediate link to individual supplies is important, but one must then ask oneself whether the use of the input is exclusive to generating those particular outputs. There may also be links to other ones. It is not just overheads which are residual.

On the other hand, in *Twycross Zoo East Midland Zoological Society* (MAN/04/62 No 19548) the Tribunal held that the input tax on looking after the animals was directly attributable to the exempt entrance charges. There was no direct and immediate link to the standard-rated sales from the cafes and the shops. However this case preceded the High Court and Court of Appeal decisions in *Mayflower*.

In *Town and County Factors Ltd* (LON/04/791 No 19616) [2006] BVC 4,095, the expense of obtaining racing and sporting information, which was broadcast on screens at licensed betting offices, was held to have a direct and immediate link with the taxable income from gaming machines and catering, as well as with the exempt over-the-counter betting. A key point in the case seemed to have been that the screens were thought to attract people into the betting office, thereby generating both standard and exempt income. A proportion of visitors did not place bets. The fact there was no evidence of how many did not bet, but did generate only standard-rated supplies from gaming machines or the catering, would not have mattered because with the income being significant, some of the betting customers must have generated it too. For the cost to be related entirely to the exempt betting, HMRC would have had to have shown that it was of no interest to anyone not placing a bet. Of course, the recovery of input tax based on the taxable turnover in the betting shops would be relatively small—though there were other relevant taxable supplies from other activities. HMRC announced in *Business Brief* 17/06 that they would not be appealing the decision, but said the partial exemption methods of bookmakers may no longer produce a fair and reasonable result, and may need to be amended.

THE FAILURE OF THE JOINT SUPPLY ARGUMENT

24.45 When calculating recoverable input tax, a business cannot ignore an exempt supply merely because it is closely linked to a taxable one.

Southern Primary Housing Ltd (LON/01/67 No 17770: [2003] STC 525: [2004] STC 209) agreed with a housing association to buy a plot of land, sell it on to the HA, and construct a block of flats on it. The contracts to sell the land and to construct the flats were signed at the same time, but were separate. The vendor of the land had opted to tax it, but Southern could not charge VAT on to the HA. As explained in Chapter 26, *Property*, a sale of bare land to a housing association is exempt because, even if an option to tax is made, it is 'disapplied'.

The Court of Appeal overturned decisions by the Tribunal and the High Court, that the input tax incurred on purchasing the land had been used for both the onward sale and the construction contract—and, in doing so, effectively also reversed the decision of the High Court in a similar case, *Wiggett Construction Ltd* (MAN/99/1047 No 16984: [2001] STC 933).

That the land purchase and onward sale was commercially necessary did not make it a cost component of the construction contract. The link was not direct and immediate. It is likely that the decision was correct, but on the wrong basis!

The decision was right because it is only possible to argue that a cost is related to different supplies, however closely the contracts for them are linked, if that cost is indirect rather than direct. The reasoning of the Tribunal and the High Court that there was a joint supply of both land and building services was questionable for two reasons. Firstly, with separate contracts, how can there be a 'joint supply'? Secondly, the apportionment of the input tax, which was left for the parties to discuss, logically must be based on the normal rules. Supposing one could attribute part of the input tax incurred on the land to the construction contract, so as to make it recoverable—what would be the basis for that calculation?

TWO CASES IN WHICH THERE WAS NO IMMEDIATE OUTPUT

24.46   Before jumping to conclusions on attribution, check the precise facts! If a person was asked about recovery on the cost of producing and screening a series of four TV commercials with a mortgage storyline, their first reaction would probably be that the VAT was attributable to the exempt mortgage interest resulting from the business obtained.

Well, in *Britannia Building Society* (MAN/96/174 No 14886), the evidence established that the commercials were designed to remind viewers of the existence of the Britannia Group, and that it provided a variety of financial services. They did not advertise individual financial products. They were designed to modernise the image of the Society, and were held to be part of general overheads, not directly attributable to the Society's exempt mortgages.

When a holding company buys a new subsidiary, HMRC say the input tax is residual. *UBAF Bank Ltd* (LON/91/2623 No 9813: [1996] STC 372, CA) was not a normal holding company, all its subsidiaries being dormant. UBAF itself conducted the business. The day after acquiring three companies, it itself took over their business, with the subsidiaries becoming dormant like the others. VAT on the acquisition costs was held to be directly attributable to the taxable supplies of leasing which UBAF acquired, and which it then made itself from then on.

The Tribunal said the question was the purpose for which the three leasing companies and their businesses were bought. What were the supplies used for? The transactions were intended to enable the bank to add substantially to its existing leasing business. There was no need to distinguish between tax related to the share purchases, and that on the subsequent transfers of the businesses. They were so closely linked that there was one purpose only, not a mixed or wider one.

A key point in both the *Britannia* and the *UBAF* cases was that there was no directly related exempt output—not the same situation as in *Sheffield Co-operative Society,* for instance.

INPUT TAX ON THE TRANSFER OF A GOING CONCERN

24.47   The sale of a business, or part of one, to a taxable person as a going concern, is outside the scope of VAT. This is explained in the chapter '*Buying or Selling a Business*'. In *Abbey National plc* (LON/94/2245 No 14951: [2001] STC 297), the ECJ agreed that the related input tax was residual, there being no directly related output.

> 'However, if the various services acquired by the transferor in order to effect the transfer have a direct and immediate link with a clearly defined part of his economic activities, so that the costs of those services form part of the overheads of that part of the business and all the transactions relating to that part of the business are subject to VAT, he may deduct all the VAT charged on his costs of acquiring those services.'

In *Business Brief 8/01* dated 2 July 2001, HMRC said they would see the input tax incurred on the sale of part of a business as an overhead of that part, and thus recoverable or not, according to the nature of the supplies made by it.

THE PROBLEM OF COSTS ON AN ABORTIVE PROPERTY PROJECT

24.48   Property developers often incur costs on a potential project before acquiring the site; examples are legal fees in negotiating with the owner, surveying the site, and applying for planning permission. In many cases such projects then have to be abandoned. In *Beaverbank Properties Ltd* (EDN/02/150 No 18099), it was held that the VAT on such speculative costs was attributable to the intended taxable supplies. The Tribunal accepted that it had been intended to opt to tax if the site had been acquired, as any ordinary and prudent businessman would. It rejected HMRCs' assertion that, in the absence of an option, the input tax had to be attributed to exempt supplies as the only possible ones.

This decision cannot be relied on in all abortive cost situations. Much may depend upon the precise circumstances. In *Business Brief 14/04*, HMRC say they require documentary evidence of a firm commitment to make taxable supplies. The longer the project continues, the more evidence will be needed that the developer intends to opt to tax. HMRC say that, if the opportunity to opt is merely kept open pending a deal, there is no specific intention to create a taxable supply—as was held in the *Royal and Sun Alliance Insurance Group* case. There, input VAT was being incurred on leased property prior to it being sublet (see **24.55** below).

As explained in Chapter 26, *Property*, a business can opt to tax a property before it owns it. If it does not opt, the owner or senior management should at least date and sign a memorandum of the intention to do so.

If costs are incurred at a stage in the project when it is not clear what type of project, if any, will occur, the VAT is not directly attributable to either exempt or taxable supplies. It is, therefore, treated as residual VAT relating to the business as a whole. If, in due course, an output occurs, that calculation can then be altered under the six-year rule explained at **24.55**.

EXAMPLES OF DIRECT ATTRIBUTION TO MINOR OUTPUTS

24.49   There are various minor taxable outputs to which the associated input tax can be directly attributed, and thus, recovered in full. This prevents a double charge when output VAT, which cannot be charged to anyone, must be accounted for. The input tax can be offset in full, instead of being partly disallowed in residual tax. Examples are:

Canteen

24.50   The input tax is attributable to that declared as output tax on any charges made. This applies even if the meals are free, because there is still a taxable supply even if the value of it is nil (*Sch 6, para 10*).

Petrol and gifts of goods

24.51   If staff are allowed to claim for petrol used privately, and the scale charge is applied, the input tax on petrol used privately is recoverable in full rather than being subject to apportionment. Fuel used for business purposes, however, must be apportioned.

The position is:

• output tax on scale charge is payable;

• input tax on fuel use for private purposes is recoverable in full—but must of course be identified;

• input tax used on business mileage is caught under your partial exemption calculations

• If the business cannot separately identify the fuel used privately, that too must be apportioned. However, to compensate for this, the scale charge may be reduced to equal the percentage of input tax recovered under the partial exemption method.

The same applies to goods given away on which output tax is accounted for under the gifts rules, or which are caught as promotional items handed out in return for consideration.

Staff magazines

24.52   In *Post Office* (MAN/95/1322 No 14075), three staff magazines were held to be gifts of zero-rated goods to staff, on which the input tax was recoverable, despite two being about management and technical matters.

Charges for use of company cars

24.53   The same principle applies where staff make contributions towards the running cost of the cars they drive. Some of the tax on maintenance costs is attributable to these contributions.

Payments for the use of cars are outside the scope of VAT, assuming that input tax was not recovered on the purchase, or, if the cars are leased, that the 50% disallowance applies.

BEWARE OF MANAGEMENT CHARGES

24.54   Making a management charge will not necessarily improve input tax recovery for a business in a partial exemption situation—especially if it is for the services of one or two individuals. Charges for the time of people do not justify much input tax recovery by direct attribution. Even accounting and other office services do not necessarily generate direct costs, as opposed to general office overheads.

The only tax attributable to a management charge might well be a share of the VAT on those overheads that could be argued to relate to the charge as well as to the exempt activities.

Thus, a property company with exempt outputs resulting from the redevelopment of property, will not recover input tax incurred on the redevelopment costs merely by making charges for the services of its managing director to other associated companies.

In *Neuvale Ltd and Frambeck Ltd* ([1989] STC 395), the Tribunal found there to be two activities; the renting of property, and the supply of the managing director's services. The input tax had to be attributed accordingly.

HMRC say that a company cannot supply the services of a director to another company, of which, he or she is also a director. This was disapproved as a categoric statement in *Withies Inn Ltd* (LON/95/1778 No 14257) but HMRC won on the facts. Those included that the charge was made to its subsidiary by a holding company that had no other income.

In *TS Harrison & Sons Ltd* (MAN/91/1178 No 11043), after a management charge had been invoiced and paid, a further invoice was raised for an additional charge in order not to have to pay back surplus pension fund contributions collected. The

Tribunal held this extra charge did not represent any supply made. The VAT on it was, therefore, not recoverable by the company to which the charge was made.

Though perhaps a 'one-off', this is a warning against having too glib an assumption that one can create a supply merely by raising a management charge at any time, and for any reason.

WHAT HAPPENS IF THE USE OF AN ASSET CHANGES?

24.55 If the initial attribution or apportionment of tax on an asset proves inaccurate, it must be corrected. Thus, if the asset is purchased for a project expected to produce taxable outputs, but intentions alter and, within six years, exempt or non-business outputs result instead, *reg 108* requires the attribution to be corrected. The correction must be made on the VAT return for the period in which the use occurs, or the intention changes.

Reg 109 provides for a similar correction if the use turns out to be taxable rather than exempt. An application for refund of the tax previously disallowed must be approved by HMRC before it is claimed on the VAT return.

In *Really Useful Group plc* (LON/91/136 No 6578), VAT was incurred on a building intended as the company's offices. It was then realised that it would be inadequate, and an exempt sale resulted. There had not been any use for taxable purposes by the company, so the provisional attribution of the refurbishment costs to its taxable outputs had to be corrected, and the VAT repaid.

In *Cooper and Chapman (Builders) Ltd* ([1993] STC 1), a house was converted into ten flats which were advertised as holiday accommodation. Holiday lettings were achieved for only four of them. All ten were then let for a year to a single tenant. *Reg 108* did not apply to those flats which had been let for holiday accommodation, because a taxable supply had occurred. However, it was held that an apportionment was required because the VAT attributable to the six that had remained empty before being let for an exempt rent, had to be paid back to HMRC.

Thus, a single week's standard-rated letting of a flat meant the input tax apportioned to that flat was recoverable. Without a standard-rated letting, none of it was. The *Curtis Henderson* situation described below did not apply, because there was no possibility of a zero-rated sale.

However, *Royal and Sun Alliance Insurance Group plc* (MAN/97/916 No 16148: [2000] STC 933:CA [2001] STC 1476: HL 22/5/03) held that *Reg 109* does not apply if a property has been vacant and available to let for some time. Opting to tax the lease eventually achieved, does not create a right under *Reg 109* to recover input tax incurred on rents and service charges paid to the superior landlord during the vacant quarters. Such input tax is, therefore, treated as an overhead cost—recoverable according to the partial exemption calculations for those quarters.

The House of Lords upheld the Tribunal's view that opting to tax a sub-lease did not allow reallocation to taxable supplies of input tax incurred on the superior lease in VAT periods long gone, even though there had been no exempt sub-lease. There was no direct and immediate link between the rent paid to the head landlord before the option to tax was exercised, and that charged to the sub-tenants in later periods.

To put it another way, just as the *failure to make a taxable supply* does not *prevent* the recovery of input tax related to the attempt, a *failure to make an exempt supply*—in this case by letting a property—does not *create* the right of recovery.

This was a 3:2 majority decision in favour of HMRC, but given that the High Court and the Court of Appeal, had supported *RSA* also by a majority, the judicial support for HMRC was actually five in favour, five against! See Chapter 25, *The Capital Goods Scheme* for the rules requiring an adjustment to be done once supplies have been made, because the level of taxable use of property and computers changes.

Revenue and Customs Brief 57/09 confirms HMRC policy on the VAT partial exemption 'payback' rules following the High Court decision in the case of *Community Housing Association (CHA) v Revenue and Customs Comrs* [2009] EWHC 455 (Ch).

CHA is a housing association providing mainly rental housing, which is exempt for VAT purposes. CHA incurred input tax related to the construction of new dwellings for use in its business. CHA subsequently changed its operation by inserting a new subsidiary between itself and its suppliers. Then, having raised invoices to the subsidiary for the value of work undertaken on uncompleted projects prior to this change, CHA lodged a 'payback' claim. They argued that input tax on costs for part completed projects incurred prior to the change were not used as originally intended and were now attributable to a taxable supply from CHA to the new subsidiary. HMRC rejected the claim on the grounds that there were no supplies of services between CHA and its subsidiary and, even if there were, the old costs did not become cost components of the supplies. The Tribunal agreed with HMRC.

The High Court overturned the Tribunal decision and allowed the payback claim. The High Court found as fact that CHA made supplies to its subsidiary and that the supplies transferred useful material and rights arising from the old supplies received by CHA. Based on these findings the High Court's decision was inevitable. HMRC have not appealed.

THE ZERO-RATED HOUSE/EXEMPT RENT PROBLEM

24.56 If a business cannot find a buyer for a house it has built, an obvious possibility is to let it for a year or two. Unfortunately, that then creates exempt outputs rather than taxable ones. In a number of cases, HMRC have argued that the original attribution must be corrected because the exempt output meant that VAT was not recoverable.

In *Link Housing Association* ([1992] STC 718) each house had first to be let for two years before the tenant could acquire the right to buy. Nevertheless, the sales to tenants by Link were held to be zero-rated, and the input tax on the costs of sale, presumably legal fees, was thus recoverable.

In *Briararch Ltd* ([1992] STC 732), a listed office building was renovated. Under the old rules, a zero-rated major interest lease was possible at the time, but a tenant could only be found for a four-year one. An apportionment to the exempt rent of 4/29ths of the input tax on the renovation cost was made by the Tribunal, on the basis that it was still hoped to grant a lease exceeding 21 years in due course. At the time, this would have been zero-rated, but Briararch would now have to opt to tax it.

Curtis Henderson Ltd ([1992] STC 732) acquired a building plot in 1988. HMRC granted registration in the usual terms, which required the repayment of input tax should taxable outputs not result in due course.

The house was completed in April 1989, just in time for the housing slump. The house was let for nine months. HMRC assessed for the entire £6,378 input tax incurred on its construction. The house was eventually sold in September 1990.

The Tribunal rejected HMRC's argument that the input tax was 'used' to grant the lease. It had been used to construct the building which then put the trader in a position to grant the lease and, later, to sell the freehold. In that sense, the goods and services were 'used' to make both supplies. The tax should be apportioned accordingly.

Both the latter cases seem to fit in with the principle of a direct and immediate link, which was explained earlier in the comment on the *BLP* and *Midland Bank* cases. The link of the original expenditure in such a case is more strongly to the intended taxable output, than to the short-term letting.

Similarly, the Tribunal found duality of purpose in *Scottish Homes* (EDN/99/126 No 16444), where houses were improved by major repairs or improvements, such as to kitchens or to central heating systems, for which there was no contractual obligation under the leases. The expenditure was partly for the purpose of the exempt rents, and partly to encourage tenants to exercise their right to buy.

HMRC have published Information Sheet 07/08 detailing how to calculate any adjustments—see Chapter 26, *Property*, para **26.8** for details.

IMPORTANCE OF A PROPER SYSTEMS FILE

24.57 Experience says that, all too often, junior staff are given responsibility for the VAT return in partially exempt businesses. Sometimes, it is the latest arrival in the accounts department!

The problem is that, to handle partial exemption properly, one needs firstly to understand what the organisation does and how, and, secondly, how some complex rules apply to the resulting transactions. Without that knowledge, mistakes are all too likely. Therefore, a business needs to make sure that:

- the system is set up by someone who thoroughly understands how the business works. That means how the profit is earned, not just how the accounts department records it;

- the staff who operate that system know both what they are supposed to do, and why;

- there is a systems file to which anyone with no knowledge of partial exemption could refer, to find out how and why it works in the organisation.

Detailed notes on how the partial exemption system works are vital. If a business lacks a proper file on it, mistakes are inevitable sooner or later when, due to staff changes, illness, or whatever, new or inexperienced staff have to cope with what is one of the more complex aspects of VAT.

Moreover, without such a file, how can a business review the system to see whether it is operating effectively, and that it has been recovering the maximum possible input tax?

MORE DETAIL ON SPECIAL METHODS

24.58   Under *reg 102*, HMRC can approve, or direct the use of, a special method of apportioning residual tax. A special method is any alternative to the standard method which HMRC will accept as fair.

See earlier in this chapter for some preliminary comment on possible methods. In the next few pages, some disputes are explained that have arisen on the detailed operation of special methods.

A BUSINESS MAY NEED A SPECIAL METHOD WITHOUT REALISING IT

24.59   The standard method is rigid. Any deviation from it is a special method, requiring HMRC's approval. A business cannot just do its own thing!

In *Credit Risk Management Ltd* (MAN/94/416 No 12971) the Tribunal upheld a refusal by HMRC to allow part of the input tax to be apportioned 50% to taxable activities as an intermediate stage, instead of in the residual ratio. This would have kept the exempt input VAT below the de minimis limit—but the company had not applied for a special method.

AGREEMENT BY HMRC IN WRITING

24.60

Focus

The agreement of HMRC to a special method must be in writing (*Reg 102(5)*). A business must obtain authorisation from HMRC before applying a special method. With effect from 1 April 2007, a business must declare that the special method provides a fair and reasonable attribution to the best of its knowledge and belief (sample declaration in HMRC Brief 23/07).

If HMRC consider that the business knew that the method was not fair and reasonable at the time of the declaration, they may issue a direction retrospectively, withdrawing use of the method. Usually, one writes to HMRC with a detailed explanation of the method requested. HMRC then reply in a letter, which is primarily made up of standard paragraphs, despite being several pages long. In essence, it says that one may operate the special method proposed, subject to the conditions that it sets out.

Be careful about the wording of the request. There have been several Tribunal cases concerning the interpretation of agreements on special methods. So far, the cases have tended to show HMRC's problem in setting out the terms of methods to cope with changes of circumstances or exceptional transactions. However, traders must also be vulnerable to suggestions that the method proposed was in some way inadequate, or has been incorrectly applied.

In *Kwik-Fit (GB) Ltd* ([1998] STC 159), the Court of Session found ambiguous the words:

> 'Where goods and services are procured by one member of the VAT group for use in whole or in part by another member of the VAT group, any input tax incurred is to be recovered in accordance with the recovery percentage of the group or company benefiting from the goods and services.'

In the context of the legislation, 'use' meant physical use by the other member. That excluded overhead expenses of the procuring member, such as telephone calls relating to the business of another member.

HMRC's interpretation of the wording that it covered such indirect costs, did not remove the ambiguity. A special method under *Reg 102* containing an ambiguous direction was not 'fair and reasonable', as required by *s 26(3)*.

In consequence, HMRC could not enforce use of the special method. Kwik-Fit was entitled to use the standard method until a new special one was agreed.

Labour Party (LON/2000/0337 No 17034) further emphasises how important the precise wording of a special method agreement can be. That method assumed that affiliation fees were non-business, and could, therefore, be left out of the partial exemption calculation. When it was realised that they were exempt, including them in the calculation increased the input tax recoverable! Of course, it ought to have made little or no difference, since VAT related to non-business or exempt transactions was not recoverable in either case, but the defective wording of the method had the opposite result.

The Tribunal rejected HMRC's argument that a partial exemption method could not cover the apportionment of input tax between business and non-business supplies. Thus, until a new method could be agreed or directed, the existing defective one remained valid.

In *Barclays Bank plc* (LON/89/787 No 5616) the assessment exceeded £4m. Barclays used a special method agreed by HMRC with the Committee of London Clearing Banks. The dispute concerned the assignment of third world loans under swap arrangements. Since the assignees belonged outside the EU, the related input tax was recoverable. The value over the three years exceeded £226m.

HMRC referred to the condition in the special method, which required that:

'any supplies whose output value is disproportionately greater than the related input tax or vice versa are excluded from the services/lending arrangement and the identification of any recoverable input tax related to them dealt with separately (e.g. sale of securities).'

'Any supplies whose output value is disproportionately greater than the related input tax or vice versa are excluded from the (calculations).'

In upholding the appeal, the Tribunal noted that the wording was part of the preamble which said that a clearing bank could adopt the method if three conditions, including the one quoted, were met. The way the document was drafted meant that the conditions in the preamble were matters of which HMRC had to be satisfied before a bank was allowed to use the method.

If that was wrong, and they were part of the detailed terms, para 7(IV) of those terms read:

'Supplies whose out value is disproportionately greater than the related input tax or vice versa. Such supplies, which will be kept under regular review as setout in the 'review' section on page 2, are set out in annex III.' Supplies whose output value is disproportionately greater than the related input tax or vice versa. Such supplies, which will be kept under regular review as set out in the 'review' section on page 2, are set out in annex III.'

'Supplies whose output value is disproportionately greater than the related input tax or vice versa. Such supplies, which will be kept under regular review as set out in the 'review' section on page 2, are set out in annex III.'

This was unambiguous. *Such supplies* could only refer to the previous sentence. Services not included in annex III did not have to be excluded, and there was no mention of assignments of debt in that annex. HMRC argued that the objective was to calculate the recoverable tax in a fair and reasonable manner. The Tribunal applied the principles of construing taxing acts under which intention is irrelevant. One must not read things in or imply terms; one must look fairly at the language used.

The agreement did not say how one decided whether the value of supplies affected the calculation 'disproportionately' to the related input tax. Therefore, this was not intended to be a substantive provision of the method. That the question was to be kept under regular review indicated that, if HMRC thought a particular supply was disproportionate, they could add it to the list in annex III, thus changing the method from then on.

BEWARE OF CHANGES IN CIRCUMSTANCES

24.61

Focus

An important condition imposed by HMRC is likely to be that the business has to notify it of any material changes in circumstances. This may require careful attention, especially as such a notification might be necessary several years later.

How will a business know if the circumstances of its organisation change?

In *Union Bank of Switzerland* (LON/86/713 No 2551), the change was favourable. HMRC had required UBS to inform them of 'a significant change' in its business. UBS started to do gold/currency swap deals without telling HMRC.

The Tribunal held that commencing these transactions was not a significant change. That had to be considered in relation to the business of the London branch, not to that of the bank as a whole, but evidence showed that they were only a small part of its activity anyway.

UBS thought HMRC had meant *any transactions which would significantly alter or affect the proportion of the input tax which the Bank can deduct.* That was not the same, and HMRC should have said so clearly. A trader should not be required to account for tax on a self-assessing system on the basis of vague general words, of which, varying views could honestly be taken!

CHANGING FROM ONE PARTIAL EXEMPTION METHOD TO ANOTHER

24.62

> **Focus**
>
> A business must obtain the agreement of HMRC to a change of method. Although it can use the standard method without their approval, any change to it, or from it, will involve a special method.

Reg 102(3) says that a trader using a special method must do so until HMRC approve or direct a change. Any such approval is often from the start of the next tax year, although they usually permit it from the beginning of the one in which they received the application. 'Tax year' is defined in *reg 99(1)*. Normally, it is the year ending 31/3, 30/4, or 31/5, depending upon the VAT quarters of the business.

HMRC have power to permit a change of method after less than two years. *Reg 109(2)* empowers HMRC to withdraw use of a special method, or of the outputs pro rata method, from such future date as they may specify.

HMRC also have power to permit a retrospective change (AJ Barrett as provisional liquidator for *Rafidain Bank* (LON/92/2732 No 11016) and *PL Schofield Ltd* (MAN/91/878 No 7736)). However, they can (and usually do) refuse to do so.

AUTHORITY OF THE TRIBUNALS

24.63 In *Chartered Society of Physiotherapy* (LON/97/185 No 15108), the Tribunal held that it had only a supervisory jurisdiction over a refusal by HMRC to allow a retrospective change. Broadly, this means that it will only interfere if it finds the refusal to have been unreasonable.

In *Banbury Visionplus Ltd* (2006 EWHC 1024), however, the High Court held that the right of appeal under *s 83(e)*, and the discretion to HMRC in their *reg 102*, did not limit the jurisdiction of the Tribunal. Thus, contrary to the views expressed in various previous cases that they only had a supervisory role, the Tribunals should consider the alternatives for attribution, and, where a method is to be terminated, whether the alternative is more fair and reasonable.

Note that the position was not the same as that for the issue of a notice demanding security, which HMRC can do *if it appears to the Commissioners requisite for the protection of the revenue*. Those words did confer discretion on HMRC alone.

ARGUMENTS ABOUT USE OF SPECIAL METHODS

24.64   In *Merchant Navy Officers Pension Fund Trustees Ltd* (LON/95/2944 No 14262) it was held that:

- the effect of a direction to stop using a special method is to impose the standard method, unless an alternative special method has been agreed;

- the taxpayer's appeal was upheld because the effect of the standard method was even more distorted than the special method, approval of which HMRC had withdrawn.

In *Glasgow Indoor Bowling Club* (EDN/96/75 No 14889), it was held that HMRC were entitled to withdraw the use of a special method that gave a 97% recovery rate following a change of subscriptions from standard-rated to exempt. The standard method, which became applicable, produced 47% recovery. If it seems too good to be true, it probably is!

Similarly, in *Aspinall's Club Ltd* (LON/99/540 No 17797), HMRC were held to be justified in withdrawing a floor area method which produced up to 55% recovery when taxable turnover was only 1%. One reason for the latter figure being so low was that the price of a meal was often not charged to a member who used the gaming facilities.

See also **24.19** for comments on cases in which HMRC have ceased the use of a special method.

CORRECTING THE APPLICATION OF A SPECIAL METHOD

24.65   In *Sovereign Finance plc* (MAN/97/778 No 16237) a Tribunal held that special method calculations could be corrected by voluntary disclosure. Hire-purchase transactions had been treated as wholly exempt.

DISTORTION IS THE KEY WORD

24.66   HMRC's main concern when considering a special method is to ensure that it arrives at a fair and reasonable result, and does not distort the position so as to recover more tax than is justified. For instance, they would be unlikely to permit a hire-purchase company to use an input tax ratio which included in the directly attributable tax, the VAT on the goods bought and resold. These large sums of tax are incidental to the way the business earns its profit by the charging of exempt interest.

SPECIAL METHODS AGREED BY TRADE ASSOCIATIONS

24.67   Notice 700/57 *Administrative agreements entered into with trade bodies* (August 2004) gives details of special arrangements agreed by trade associations with HMRC. Those concerning aspects of the partial exemption situations of their members are:

- ABI/Lloyd's of London/ILU/BIIA;

- Association of British Insurers;

- Association of Investment Trust Companies;

- Association of British Factors and Discounters;

- Brewers Society;

- MAT Insurance Underwriters.

THE EFFECT OF GROUPING ON PARTIAL EXEMPTION

24.68 Grouping a partly exempt company with a taxable one does not, in itself, increase the input tax recoverable. Normally, the advantage of grouping is in avoiding output tax on inter-company transactions that would not be recoverable as input tax by the company being charged.

Grouping, for VAT purposes, means that transactions between members of the group are ignored. All the third party inputs and outputs are treated as being those of the representative member of the group. However, for partial exemption purposes, input tax is normally attributed and apportioned, in the first instance, within the accounting records of each company. This is convenient, and usually reflects the use to which the expenditure is put.

If there are inter-company management charges, and some of the recipient companies are partially exempt, one must consider whether some of the input tax of the company making the charge should be disallowed as being related to the exempt outputs of the other company. One must 'look through' management charge, and consider the nature of the supplies by the other company the charge supports.

Each case depends upon its facts. The principle is that one cannot recover input tax merely by incurring it in another company in the same VAT group.

In Notice 706 (December 2006) para 12.1, HMRC say that a Group has only one partial exemption method. Presumably, they mean that a single method is supposed to include separate sections for each company.

TWO PLANNING POINTS FOR PARTIALLY EXEMPT BUSINESSES

24.69 The following are a couple of straightforward planning points for partially exempt businesses.

A company with exempt outputs should employ its own staff.

A partially exempt company should either employ its own staff, or be VAT grouped with the employer. Otherwise, non-recoverable VAT will be incurred when their salaries are charged to it by the employing company.

If staff work for several companies, and they cannot be grouped, have the one with the most exempt business employ them, and recharge part of the cost to the others. Even if the others are not fully taxable, this reduces the lost VAT. Alternatively, consider putting the staff on joint contracts of employment for the companies concerned. If the individual is jointly employed by all the companies, there cannot be any taxable supply of staff arising between them.

BUY FIXED ASSETS IN A SEPARATE COMPANY AND LEASE THEM

24.70   If a business is about to incur substantial input tax on computers or other equipment, consider buying them in a separate company outside the same VAT group. That company can then lease the goods to those which have exempt outputs. Although VAT on the leasing charges will be disallowed, at least in part, recovery of VAT on the original purchase cost can give a useful cash flow advantage. Do bear in mind, however, that HMRC have the power to add a company or remove a company from a VAT group if they feel there is a revenue risk. This idea no longer works at all for property, as there are now elaborate anti-avoidance rules in place for 'connected' parties.

Be reasonable about the rate of return to your in-house leasing company! HMRC have powers to direct the substitution of market value for an artificially low price, as described at **8.7**. They used them in *RBS Leasing & Services Ltd (No 1–4)* (LON/98/1005 No 16569), in which the Tribunal upheld a direction substituting market value for a sale by RBS to a subsidiary of leasing equipment it had bought and leased back at a 1% margin.

THE STANDARD METHOD OVERRIDE

24.71   The *Standard Method Override,* as HMRC have termed it, is an anti-avoidance measure introduced from 18 April 2002 *(regs 106A, 107A–E)*. It is intended to stop VAT being recovered under a standard method calculation, when the latter does not reflect the intended use of the costs in question; ie where:

• the costs relate to both taxable and exempt supplies, and are, therefore, part of residual VAT;

• but the standard method rate of recovery in the partial exemption year in which they are incurred, does not reflect the expected use in a later year.

Although the override is primarily an anti-avoidance measure, it may help a business if the situation is the other way round; ie where the standard method is unfavourable to the business because it does not reflect the expected future use of the inputs to support taxable supplies.

HOW THE OVERRIDE WORKS

24.72

Focus

The override only applies if the adjustment required to correct the distortion exceeds:

- £50K; or

- 50% of the residual input tax, and £25K.

Thus, an adjustment under £25,000 can be ignored. Between £25,000 and £50,000, it can also be ignored if it is less than 50% of its residual input tax.

Pro rata limits apply to part periods, starting from 18 April 2002 until the end of that partial exemption year.

A business should review the position in the quarter after the end of its partial exemption year, at the same time as it does the ordinary annual adjustment explained earlier in this chapter. A business has to consider whether, in addition, an override adjustment is required if:

- the residual tax exceeds £50,000 a year;

- or £25,000 if the business is a 'group undertaking' as defined in *Companies Act 1985, s 259*: in this context, that means a company which is required to be included in the consolidated accounts of the group, or which is exempt from that requirement, and which is not in the same VAT group as all its fellow undertakings.

How the business works out the adjustment will depend upon the facts of the case.

In *VAT Information Sheet 4/02*, HMRC quote the following examples:

- a business incurs costs in setting up a new activity, the outputs from which will significantly alter the percentage of exempt supplies in future tax years. A business calculates the adjustment by applying the expected percentage of taxable use to the VAT on those particular costs, instead of using that calculated under the standard method;

- exceptional high-value transactions, which do not generate proportionate input tax, distort the standard method recovery percentage. Remove the exceptional transactions from the standard method figures, and recalculate the percentage;

- the nature of the business is such that the ratio of the output values of taxable and exempt transactions does not reflect the use of the supporting inputs. HMRC say a business should *apply another suitable measure*. The legal basis for this seems doubtful. A trader is entitled to use the standard method unless a special one is imposed or agreed, and a special method is not normally retrospective. If normal output values create an overly favourable recovery on normal inputs, it is arguably up to HMRC to require use of a special method. Presumably, they will argue that they have done that by making it a general requirement for all traders to apply the override.

VAT Information Sheet 4/02 contains some more detailed points and a number of examples—though, in some of the latter, the input tax figures quoted are unrealistic in relation to the sales.

HMRC claim that, apart from businesses which have undertaken artificial planning schemes, the override will affect very few businesses. That may prove to be so in practice, but many companies that are not in a VAT group, but *are* part of a group for *Companies Act* purposes, will have more than £25,000 residual VAT, and will, therefore, have to consider their position each year. The representative member of a VAT group, though benefiting from the higher limit of £50,000, will have the added complication of having to review the position of each company within the VAT group.

LITIGATION INVOLVING THE STANDARD METHOD OVERRIDE

24.73   The first Tribunal case to examine the 'Standard Method Override' (SMO) was *Camden Motors Holdings Ltd (VTD 20,674),* one of two recent cases (the other being *Abbeyview Bowling Club (VTD 20,661)).* The Appellant had a mixture of taxable vehicle sales and exempt finance commission. Under the standard method, its exempt turnover of less than 1% and overhead VAT of less than £400,000 a month meant that it was within the '*de minimis* limits', so it enjoyed full input tax recovery. HMRC considered the standard method was not fair and reasonable. They were concerned that the method resulted in no VAT being allocated to what appeared to be the only part of the business generating any profit. (HMRC had allocated all salary costs to taxable sales).

The Tribunal first concluded that the SMO should not apply to a trader who is *de minimis* after the annual adjustment. It then went on to consider the substantive part of the appeal, and found the sale of the cars is the economic driver of the business. As such, it was wrong to focus on profit when attributing input tax and calculating recovery. The Tribunal also rejected HMRC's approach of allocating nearly all salary costs to the taxable side of the business to support a calculation that the exempt side made all the profit and the car sales were loss making. This was not factually correct, as the sale of finance involved higher paid employees. As salaries bear no VAT, they have little or no bearing on a use-based VAT recovery calculation.

In finding that the standard method did achieve a fair and reasonable result, the Chairman noted the far greater infrastructure and cost required to sell and service a car, and agreed with the Appellant's argument that if it stopped selling finance, the impact on its overheads would be minimal. He dismissed HMRC's emphasis on profit, confirming profitability is not a requirement for input tax deduction, and European legislation attributes inputs in accordance with how they are used. Any reliance on the relevant profitability of a sector to determine input tax recovery is contrary to the basic principles of VAT.

The decision is significant because it was the first on the Standard Method Override, and the Tribunal analysed the legislation carefully in reaching its conclusion. It has received wide publicity in the VAT world, and should help to rein in any over-zealous Officers on VAT visits going forward.

THE SPECIAL METHOD OVERRIDE

24.74   The *Special Method Override* rules in *regs 102A–102C*, which were introduced from 1 April 2004, permit either HMRC or a trader to serve a notice on the other:

- claiming that the special method in use does not fairly and reasonably represent the extent to which goods or services are to be used in making taxable supplies;

- requiring the attribution to be corrected from the next VAT return onwards.

In theory, this allows either side to correct the application of a special method that has turned out to be unfair, pending agreement on a new one.

Business Brief 27/03 set conditions under which HMRC would serve a notice. Of those, the need for HMRC to have tried to persuade the business to 'comply' was removed by *Business Brief 7/05* with effect from 1 April 2005. The practical significance of that may be to enable one to start a tribunal appeal. Without such a notice, one must wait until the often lengthy negotiations on a new special method finish, thus at last creating an appealable decision.

It does not enable an application to change from the standard method to a special one, to be dealt with this way. It only applies where a special method is already in use.

Chapter 25

The Capital Goods Scheme

SIGNPOSTS

- The *Capital Goods Scheme* (CGS) is designed to adjust the input tax recovered by partially exempt businesses on specified assets above a certain level over either a five- or ten-year adjustment period depending on the asset and has to be done annually (see **25.1–25.6**).

- Normally, fully taxable trading businesses can be caught by the scheme if they sell a commercial property on which they have recovered VAT within ten years without opting to tax (see **25.7**).

- The CGS does not cease to apply because the asset is sold in a transaction which is treated as a transfer of a going concern. The purchaser of the business must continue the annual adjustments for the balance of the adjustment period (see **25.11**).

25.1   The CGS applies if a business reclaims the VAT on a net spend of more than £250,000 on land or a building, or a net spend of £50,000 on a single piece of computer equipment. From 1 January 2011 this was extended to include ships and boats and aircraft costing more than £50,000. Although that means that many very small businesses do not have to worry about the CGS, the figure for property is not large at all.

PURPOSE OF THE SCHEME

25.2   The CGS requires the adjustment of input tax recovered by partially exempt traders and from 1 January 2011, businesses that have business/non-business use on property, computers, aircraft, ships and boats although I have never come across its use on computer equipment. The objective is to correct the recovery of VAT when, in subsequent years, the use in making taxable/business supplies varies from that in the year of purchase. That can be either good news or bad news; ie a business may be able to reclaim more VAT, or have to pay it back, depending on whether its taxable use has risen or fallen. The law is in *Pt XV* of the *VAT Regulations (SI 1995/2518)*. Notice 706/2 refers.

THE GOODS AFFECTED

25.3

Focus

The CGS affects (net of VAT):

- land and buildings costing £250,000 or more, whether the purchase of a freehold or of a lease at a premium, including the cost of standard-rated services 'for or in connection with' the construction of the building or work. This includes parts of buildings, enlargements, alterations, extensions, or annexes which increase the floor area by 10% or more, and refurbishments of existing buildings;

- civil engineering works such as roads, bridges, golf courses, sports grounds, and the installation of drainage;

- computers and items of computer equipment, aircraft and ships and boats costing £50,000 or more.

Note that the law refers to *capital items*, not just goods, so that it catches standard-rated construction services which are bought in, not just finished buildings.

Note also that 'for or in connection with' is interpreted widely by HMRC to include, for instance, professional services and landscaping (Para 4.4, Notice 706/2 (January 2002) but not legal or estate agency fees). Only capitalised expenditure counts as a *refurbishment*.

The capital expenditure in question includes everything which is part of the fabric of the building, but not items merely fixed to it such as furniture and machinery (para 4.11, Notice 706/2 (January 2002)).

'Computers' means individual machines or pieces of equipment, not the complete cost of an installation, and it means only hardware, not software. Equipment is not caught merely because it is controlled by a computer.

THE ADJUSTMENT PERIOD

25.4

Focus

This is:

- for land and buildings, approximately ten years (five years if the leasehold interest acquired is under ten years);

- for everything else five years.

The adjustment periods are not necessarily a full five or ten years. Strictly, the adjustment is for 'intervals' and the first such interval runs from the date of acquisition to the end of the current partial exemption tax year (*reg 114(4)*).

The initial adjustment starts in the period in which the tax point falls, not when you start the asset. Thus, if you occupy a building in March and your partial exemption year ends on 31 March, but the final invoice from the builder is received in April, the VAT on that invoice is subject to the partial exemption calculation for the coming year, not the one just ended (*Witney Golf Club* (LON/01/657 No 17706)).

THE ANNUAL CALCULATIONS

25.5   A calculation is done each year so as to reflect the usage of the asset in that year. Thus:

- in year 1, input tax is recovered in the usual way, subject to any partial exemption calculations applicable;

- in year 2 and later, the recovery is adjusted for any variance in the partial exemption percentage recovery.

Example 25.1— Capital Goods Scheme adjustment

	£
Computer bought in year to 31/3/03 for £100,000.	
Input tax	17,500
In year 1, partial exemption recovery percentage for 2003/4 = 50% recovery	8,750
In year 2, partial exemption recovery percentage is only 20% So recovery is adjusted thus:	
Input tax £17,500 over five-year adjustment period equals £3,500 per year.	
Recovery in year 1 at 50% of £3,500 was	1,750
Recovery entitlement in year 2: 20% of £3,500	700
Adjustment on VAT return to repay:	1,050

If, in year 3, the recovery percentage rose to 60%, there would be a clawback from HMRC of an additional 10% of £3,500 and so on.

CHANGES DURING THE YEAR

25.6   If the use changes during the year, the adjustment must reflect the number of days for each use. Thus, if, after 274 days, the use alters from 100% taxable to 80% taxable for the remaining 91 days, the calculation is:

$$\frac{(100\% \times 274) + (80\% \times 91)}{365} = \frac{274 + 72.8}{365} = 95\%$$

A POTENTIAL PROBLEM FOR INDUSTRIAL COMPANIES

25.7   Suppose a business buys or constructs an office or factory, on which, it recovers the VAT because it uses it for the purposes of its fully taxable manufacturing business.

If in year 2 or later, up to year 10, it lets surplus space in it without opting to tax the rent, the CGS kicks in. The letting might be to an associated company, and it might never occur to it that there was a problem with the recovery of VAT achieved several years earlier. Considerable sums of input tax might have to be repaid—plus interest and a penalty, when HMRC discover the position.

Even worse would be the situation where a business sells the property after five years without opting to tax, and then has to pay back half the VAT it has reclaimed to HMRC, plus, of course, interest and penalties. The way round the problem is to opt to tax the sale or renting of the property, so the future or deemed future supplies are taxable, and no adjustment is required.

A POTENTIAL PROBLEM RE RESIDENTIAL OR CHARITABLE USE

25.8   If a building was originally zero-rated because it was intended for relevant residential or charitable use, any change can create a self-supply on which output tax is due (see **26.29**).

WHEN THE ADJUSTMENT IS DUE

25.9   *Capital Goods Scheme* adjustments are due on the second return following the partial exemption year-end to which the adjustment relates, ie on the return ending either two months or six months after the end of the partial exemption year. This allows any partial exemption calculations to be made for the first return after the tax year, so that the percentage recovery is available for use in the capital goods adjustment, if required.

SALE OF A CAPITAL ASSET PITFALL

25.10　　During the 'interval' in which the asset is sold, the use until the date of sale determines the adjustment for the entire interval, even if the asset is sold only a few days after it begins. The remaining intervals are treated as either taxable or, in the case of property, exempt if the option to tax is not exercised.

If the sale is standard-rated, the input tax, recoverable for this period of notional taxable use, *cannot exceed the output tax charged on the sale (Reg 115(3))*. That is another problem with this draconian rule. HMRC will disapply it by concession if they are satisfied that the result is fair—but the business has to ask. If it failed to do so, and they subsequently refused to apply the concession, any right of appeal in law that could be found would be indirect, and would have, at best, a limited prospect of success.

SALE OF THE ITEM AS PART OF A GOING CONCERN

25.11　　The CGS does not cease to apply merely because the asset is sold in a transaction which is outside the scope of VAT because it is the transfer of a going concern. The purchaser of the business must continue the annual adjustments for the balance of the adjustment period (*reg 114(7)*).

This means that the purchaser must ensure that the records transferred include the necessary details of the date of acquisition, the input tax incurred at that time, and the percentage of that tax which was recovered by the vendor. It also means that the purchaser may be able to reclaim, or have to pay, some of that tax with a consequent reduction or increase in the effective cost to him of the asset.

Chapter 26

Property

> • Property owners have the option to charge VAT on supplies of commercial property (option to tax). There is anti-avoidance legislation that needs to be considered, particularly with connected parties where one makes exempt supplies (see **26.75–26.100**).

26.1   To cover all the rules on property, in detail, would take an entire book in itself. The purpose of this chapter, therefore, is to demonstrate, by outlining the rules and explaining the more straightforward traps for the unwary, and why property transactions are the quickest way of losing a really large sum of VAT.

Property is an important minefield. It is important because every business occupies property either as owner or as tenant. It is a minefield because there is a wide range of possible transactions; there are several sets of rules in different parts of the law; and those rules are very complex.

If a business does not know VAT law on property thoroughly, it should get advice from a professional adviser. In order to get good advice, a business will need to give a detailed explanation of the facts of a proposed transaction properly. A business cannot do that if it does not have any idea of the rules which might apply, and, therefore, the facts which might be relevant. Thus, anyone with senior accounting responsibilities needs to have some idea of the key rules on property, so that they can spot situations on which they need advice.

This chapter reviews complex rules, concentrating on the main points and highlighting the danger areas. It does not, for example, explain the anti-avoidance rules in any detail. Check the law before acting.

THE LAW

26.2   VAT law on property comes under six main headings:

- the zero-ratings in *Sch 8 Groups 5* and *6* for:

  (i)   the construction and sale or long lease of dwellings and certain other buildings;

  (ii)   the conversion of non-residential buildings into dwellings and certain other buildings;

  (iii)   alterations to listed dwellings and certain other buildings— withdrawn completely from 20 March 2013 with the exception of some transitional arrangements through to 2015;

- the reduced rate of 5% on certain conversion and renovation work;

- the exemption for sales and leases of existing property in *Sch 9 Group 1.* See Chapter 11, *So, What is Exempt?* Self storage is specifically excluded from the exemption from 1 October 2012 and is not standard-rated;

- the standard-rating for 'new' commercial buildings, ie those up to three years old, by exception from that exemption in *Group 1*;

- the waiver of exemption, aka 'option to tax', for sales or leases of land and commercial property in *Sch 10 paras 2* and *3*;

- the DIY builders and Charity self-build rules in *s 35*.

Although these main headings are in different parts of the law, and they could, in theory, be discussed separately, one often needs to consider two or more of them in relation to a situation.

Note: there are also several items of *Sch 8, Group 12* that zero-rate certain alterations work on buildings, such as the facilitating of access, when supplied to a handicapped person or a charity. See Chapter 10, *So, What is Zero-rated?*

OVERVIEW OF THE PROPERTY RULES

26.3   The rules listed above break down into the following main areas:

- constructing new buildings—standard-rated except for dwellings and certain others;

- working on existing buildings—standard-rated with limited exceptions, of which the most important are the zero-rating for altering a listed dwelling (up to 1 October 2012—with transitional provisions allowing some contracts to be zero-rated until 20 March 2013), and the 5% rate on certain conversion or renovation work;

- first grant of the freehold sale, or long lease for over 21 years (20 years or more in Scotland), of a dwelling or certain other buildings, by its developer—zero-rated;

- sale by subsequent owners of that dwelling, or the rental of it (including by the developer)—exempt;

- first grant of the freehold sale, or long lease for over 21 years (20 years or more in Scotland) of a dwelling, which has been converted from a non-residential building, such as a barn or a shop—zero-rated;

- sales of new commercial property—standard-rated if within three years of completion;

- sales of older commercial property, and rent of any commercial property—exempt unless opted to tax.

- recovery of VAT incurred by individuals and charities on non-business projects to construct or convert a dwelling and certain other buildings.

The very length of that list demonstrates the complexity of this subject. Moreover, each category is subject to detailed rules, which are explored in the following pages.

In an interesting case concerning what constituted a new build (*Hoylake Cottage Hospital Charitable Trusts v Revenue & Customs* [2011] UKFTT 48 (TC)), there was an appeal against a decision by HMRC in 2008 that the construction of a new kitchen and laundry block for the hospital complex did not qualify for zero-rating. The hospital contended that the construction of the kitchen and laundry block, albeit after the construction of the main body of the hospital, should be considered to be in the course of the construction of the hospital and therefore zero-rated. HMRC contended that the construction of the new kitchen and laundry did not qualify for zero-rating because it was an addition to a completed construction (that is the nursing home), and must therefore be standard-rated.

The hospital was constructed in two phases: the demolition of most of the original hospital followed by the construction of the 60-bed nursing home. The original kitchen and laundry were retained to service the new building while funds were raised for a new kitchen and laundry block to be constructed in the second phase. The original planning permission was for the full development of the site including the new kitchen and laundry. The regulatory body covering the hospital also required a new kitchen and laundry to be constructed for licensing purposes.

The Tribunal considered the facts and the law and decided that the construction of the kitchen and laundry block was a continuation of the original development and should be zero-rated. The Tribunal was satisfied that the kitchen and laundry are connected to the use of the building. When constructed they will form an integral part of the hospital's operation and will provide compliance for the requirements of the Commission for Social Care Inspection.

This shows that there can be a substantial delay between starting a construction project and completing it—several years in this case. Providing it can be shown to all be part of the same project then zero-rating can be secured for latter phases. This can be evidenced by the planning permission and other supporting evidence that shows that the original intention was to carry out one project even if construction was in several phases.

By contrast, the case of *York University Property Company Ltd v Revenue & Customs* [2015] UKFTT 225 (TC) involved a subsidiary company of the University of York. In 2003, the University obtained planning permission for the construction, in two phases, of a research building to be used by the University's Chemistry Department.

The phase 1 works were completed in August 2004, and the building was occupied and used by the Chemistry Department from September 2004. The wall on one side of this building was designed to be easily removable when the time came to undertake the phase 2 works.

In 2011, after additional funds had become available, the University commissioned the appellant to undertake the works for phase 2 of the construction. The wall was removed and phase 2 connected to phase 1 where the wall had previously been located. The phase 2 works, which were completed in 2013, essentially doubled the size of the building. The appellant contended that the supply should be zero-rated as a continuation of the phase 1.

HMRC ruled that Phase 1 had produced a complete building, which was used as a fully functioning stand-alone facility for some seven years before the phase 2 works were undertaken. Therefore, the phase 2 works were an extension to an existing building which was standard rated by virtue of *note 16* to *Group 5* of *Sch 8* to the *VAT Act 1994*.

HMRC did not challenge the general principle that 'phasing' provides a prima facie basis for treating each element of a phased development in the same way for VAT purposes. The concept of phasing implies that successive physical completion and occupation of elements must be allowable in principle.

Weighing the relevant factors in the present case, the Tribunal found that phase 2 of the building was an enlargement of or extension to phase 1, rather than a continuation of the original development of the building and the appeal was therefore dismissed.

THE CONSTRUCTION AND SALE OF ZERO-RATED BUILDINGS

26.4   *Sch 8 Group 5* zero-rates both the construction of, and the sale or long lease of, a zero-rated building. It also contains some of the rules on conversions, which, together with those on sales and long leases, are dealt with later in the chapter. This section starts with construction services.

CONSTRUCTION SERVICES

26.5

Focus

In general, *the construction of a building from scratch* is standard-rated, unless it is zero-rated under *Group 5 Item 2(a)*, for example, a residential property.

Demolishing a building, including a house, is standard-rated, but HMRC will allow zero-rating if the demolition is done as part of a contract for the construction of a new house.

In *Dart Major Works Ltd* (LON/03/1133 No 18781), the demolition of the remains of a building destroyed by fire was held to be a supply in the course of constructing the new house, because the delay of a year in putting out tenders was no more than the time needed. HMRC had not pointed out where the link to the construction project was broken.

In the case of *Abbeytrust Homes Ltd v Revenue & Customs* [2011] UKFTT 150 (TC), HMRC decided to assess the taxpayer for £34,000 of VAT on what they decided was standard-rated building work while the taxpayer argued that the supplies related to the zero-rated construction of a new house.

The Appellant undertook a project that involved the demolition of an existing house and the construction of a new residential property. He received sums of money from his client that he classified as loans used to buy materials rather than stage payments. During a VAT inspection HMRC examined the planning permission and it only showed an extension and loft conversion so HMRC ruled that the building work should be standard-rated. The Appellant pointed out that the local authority had made a mistake with the planning permission and would reissue with the correct details. An amended planning permission was issued showing a current date. HMRC said that any supplies after that date could be zero-rated but those before would still be standard-rated.

The Tribunal found that the receipt of monies from the client constituted payment and created a tax point. It also found that the new planning permission could not re-categorise the nature of the supplies already made and so found in favour of HMRC even though the end result was the construction of a new house.

This case shows how important it is for the builder to examine the planning permissions before they start work on a project and if there are any discrepancies to have them resolved before starting work.

The supply of scaffolding has always been seen as mixed—a zero-rated charge for constructing it, and a standard-rated charge for the hire of it by the builder. However, in *G T Scaffolding Ltd* (LON/02/1103 No 18226), it was held that the hire of it was part of the zero-rated construction service, because there had been no transfer of possession to the builder. The latter was not allowed to alter it, and was not responsible for any missing items.

HMRC do not accept that decision, and, in *R & M Scaffolding Ltd* (EDN/04/89 No 18954), the hire was held to be standard-rated. Admittedly, this was a less well-presented case because the customer contract was not produced, and a weaker one because it was admitted that the customers often did make unauthorised alterations. The Tribunal held that the customers had exclusive use, and de facto, control, which was consistent with the passing of possession.

Work on an existing building is also standard-rated, unless it is:

- an extension or enlargement which created an additional dwelling 'capable of separate use and disposal': see **26.10** below; or

- a conversion, for a housing association, of a non-residential building into a residential one; or

- reduced-rated (5%) as a conversion or renovation under *Sch 7A Groups 6* and *7*. See later in this chapter for the definition of a non-residential building.

The construction or demolition of a *civil engineering work* is standard-rated, unless it is:

- necessary to develop a permanent residential caravan park (*Group 5 Item 2(b)*);

- done in the course of constructing a zero-rated building (concession).

In *Virtue (t/a Lammermuir Game Services) v Revenue and Customs Comrs* [2007] BVC 2518, the appellants successfully argued that the supply of serviced plots to DIY housebuilders comprised a single exempt supply of land. See **11.5** for a detailed outline of the case.

In *Revenue & Customs Brief 40/12* HMRC announced a change in policy on first-time water connection charges supplied at the same time as the supply of water. Where a customer contracts with a water supplier to provide mains water and that necessitates a first-time connection to that water supply, the connection will be ancillary to the zero-rate supply of water providing the supplier of the water and connection are made by the same taxable person (or within the same VAT group) to the same customer.

However, if the customer is involved in a relevant industrial activity (eg manufacturing) the supply of the water and any connection will be standard-rated.

First-time connection of water pipe-work is standard-rated if at the time of connection, no water supplier had been identified. The zero-rating only applies if, in order to supply mains water for the first time, the supplier needs to carry out the connection (it is ancillary to the supply of water). However, where the connection is carried out for the first time without any reference to a water supplier, such work cannot be ancillary to the water supplier's supply. In such cases, the water connection will be a separate standard-rated supply.

Following two Tribunal decisions, HMRC announced a change in policy (Brief 13/16) relating to the treatment of dwellings that have been formed from either the construction of new buildings, or from the conversion of non-residential buildings into a dwelling. HMRC now accepts that single dwellings can be formed from more than one building. This follows the First Tier Tribunal cases of *Mark Catchpole* (TC 01995) and *Mr T Fox* (TC 01957) which decided that for the purpose of the *VAT Act 1994, Sch 8, Group 5* it was appropriate to interpret the law as allowing the construction of dwellings formed from more than one building, to be eligible for zero-rating. HMRC, having accepted this decision, considers that it can, in principle apply to some conversions.

HMRC said, to be eligible for the zero-rate, the buildings must meet all the following:

- The development must meet the conditions of a 'building designed as a dwelling' and to this end 'building' can mean more than one building

- All buildings must be constructed or converted under a single project and under a single consent, if a new dwelling that is made up of more than one building is constructed in stages, HMRC will view subsequent stages as annexes to the original building, which will not benefit from the zero-rate unless the buildings are on the same site and the stages are completed with no unreasonable delay between them and none of the buildings are occupied until all the stages are complete.

PROFESSIONAL SERVICES

26.6

Focus

The various zero-ratings only cover the work on the building. The services of architects, surveyors, site supervisors, and any similar providers, when supplied separately, are standard-rated.

If these services can be included within the supply of construction services, for example, a design and build contract, then they can benefit from the same VAT rate as the construction services when these are zero- or lower-rated.

ZERO-RATED BUILDINGS

26.7   The phrase 'zero-rated buildings' is used in this chapter to describe buildings for which the construction or sale is zero-rated under various parts of *Sch 8 Groups* 5 and 6. This avoids having to keep repeating the same descriptions. The phrase covers buildings:

- *designed* as a dwelling or number of dwellings; or

- *intended* for use solely for a relevant residential or a relevant charitable purpose.

Note the difference between design and intention.

See **26.10** and **26.22** below for more comment on houses.

WHAT HAPPENS WHEN YOU CANNOT SELL A DWELLING AND HAVE TO RENT IT OUT?

26.8   With the advent of the recession over the past couple of years the housing market has been hit particularly hard and has slowed almost to a standstill. As a result of this many house builders have had to consider renting out their unsold stock until such time as the market improves.

The freehold sale or grant of a long lease (21 years in England or 20 years in Scotland) in a new residential property is a zero-rated taxable supply and the house builder can recover all of its associated VAT. However, the renting of a residential property is an exempt supply and the associated VAT cannot be recovered.

So when the intention changes, from taxable to exempt, what adjustments to previously recovered input tax does the house builder have to make?

Obviously, HMRC have had so many queries on this subject that they have published a number of Information Sheets and Revenue and Customs Briefs on this subject to clarify the position for the beleaguered house builders.

The adjustments required to the recovery of input tax in these circumstances was covered by HMRC in *VAT Information Sheet 07/08*, which gives guidance (and worked examples—see below) on the VAT implications arising when house builders decide to temporarily let their new dwellings whilst trying to sell them.

The Information Sheet was issued in response to enquiries from the house building sector, and takes account of the High Court decision in the joined cases of *Curtis Henderson and Briararch* ([1992] STC 732), which took place in the early 1990s.

The key points to which the Information Sheet refers are summarised as follows:

- if you temporarily let a dwelling before selling it, you may affect the VAT you can recover on your costs;

- many house builders who temporarily let a dwelling will not be affected but you need to check this to avoid making VAT mistakes;

- there is an easy way to check if you are affected by applying what we describe here as a 'simple check for *de minimis*'.

If you fail this check, you may have to:

- adjust the VAT previously recovered on your submitted VAT returns;

- restrict the VAT to be recovered on your current and future VAT returns;

- both adjust your past VAT recovery and restrict your future VAT recovery.

The Information Sheet says that if a business needs to adjust VAT previously recovered, then exceptionally, and, if so preferred, it may do so without contacting HMRC.

A housebuilder is required to make a clawback adjustment as soon as the actual or intended use of a property differs from the original plans against which input tax was recovered. A clawback adjustment is a one-off event, and a housebuilder would only make a second adjustment if the building is never let. There is no need to amend the adjustment if the actual period of letting proves to be longer or shorter than anticipated.

Housebuilders that are not already partially exempt must first apply a simple '*de minimis* check'. If they do not fail this, there is no need to make an adjustment and no need to go on to the second stage. If the check is failed, however, it is then necessary to go on to the second stage to work out the actual clawback adjustment. Where a housebuilder already has a partial exemption method, it will need to apply his partial exemption method to check for *de minimis*.

The 'simple check for *de minimis*' is carried out by reference to the expected time period the housebuilder will let its building for as a proportion of the economic life of that building, which, for VAT purposes, is 10 years. Provided the total exempt input tax does not exceed £625 per month on average (up to £7,500 per year), and is not more than half of the total input tax, the input tax is *de minimis*, and the clawback is not required.

Example of a '*de minimis*' check taken from *Information Sheet 07/08*.

A fully taxable housebuilder recovered £20,000 input tax on a house that it expected to sell for £300,000. After the end of the tax year, it decides to defer the sale by letting for two years and so becomes partly exempt.

A simple check for *de minimis* is:

£20,000 input tax × two-year lease/10-year economic life = £4,000 exempt input tax.

The £4,000 exempt input tax is *de minimis* because, over the tax year, it does not exceed £7,500 or 50% of his total input tax. The builder has no need to adjust the VAT previously recovered on his VAT returns. An important point is to note if the input tax was incurred over more than one tax year, the *de minimis* test should be applied to the input tax incurred in each of the tax years separately.

If the *de minimis* test is failed, it will be necessary to make a clawback adjustment based on the housebuilder's realistic expectation, judged at the time the original plans were set aside. HMRC may ask for evidence to support this, such as:

• the business plan showing the price originally expected;

• reports of estate agents showing this price to be unobtainable, and maybe estimating when a sale will be achievable;

• board minutes from the time of the decision to grant short leases, or any other commercial documentation backing up the estimated use.

The housebuilder calculates its clawback adjustment by comparing the input tax deducted with the input tax it would have deducted had it held its changed intention all along. If the housebuilder is already partially exempt, it calculates the input tax it would have deducted by using its partial exemption method at the time the costs were incurred. If it was not already partially exempt, however, it must apply the standard method unless it obtains HMRC approval to apply a special method instead. If the housebuilder so prefers, it can exceptionally base its clawback adjustment on an alternative calculation (and without prior approval), provided that calculation is fair.

A calculation based on the values of supplies is normally fair and straightforward provided it is based on reasonable estimates and valuations.

Example of a 'value-based' fraction taken from *Information Sheet 07/08*:

$$\frac{\text{Estimated eventual sale value}}{\text{Estimated eventual sale value} + \text{estimated short let premiums and rents}}$$

Example 26.1—Input tax adjustment

A housebuilder expects to sell two houses for £500,000 each. The input tax recovered during the tax year was £50,000. After the end of the tax year, the decision is taken to rent them for a period of three years generating estimated rental income of £200,000. The housebuilder makes no other supplies.

$$\text{£50,000 input tax incurred} \times \frac{\text{£1,000,000}}{\text{£1,200,000}}$$

£50,000 input tax previously recovered, so £41,666 = £8,334 to be repaid to HMRC

No adjustment should be made for potential bad debts during the letting period. If it is not possible to fairly estimate the values, a different calculation may be needed. Apportionments based on the expected time period of the rental or short-term lease are not recommended, except where used as a quick *de minimis* check.

A housebuilder that decides to temporarily let before selling will need to apply a partial exemption method if it continues to incur exempt input tax in its current or future VAT periods. The exceptional treatment can only apply for the clawback adjustments. If the housebuilder is not already partially exempt, it must either apply the standard method, or else seek formal HMRC approval to apply a special method.

PLANNING POINT

26.9 HMRC have also issued *Revenue and Customs Brief 54/08* giving their view on what is acceptable and unacceptable VAT avoidance by housebuilders trying to avoid an adjustment to input tax recovery.

The Brief accepts that many housebuilders are finding that they are unable to sell newly built dwellings in the current economic climate, and are, instead, choosing to rent those properties in the short-term.

To avoid the problem of an adjustment to previously recovered input tax, some housebuilders have considered selling dwellings to a connected company to achieve a zero-rated sale. Any exempt supplies are then made by the new owner, thus minimising any VAT recovery restriction for the original builder. HMRC have been asked whether they will challenge such arrangements as avoidance (on the basis that VAT recovery rights cannot be obtained by sales which have no commercial purpose and are undertaken with the sole aim of obtaining a VAT benefit).

The Brief says HMRC do not consider that such a transaction would be unacceptable VAT avoidance in most cases, but goes on to outline the basic criteria in which a sale with the sole aim of preventing VAT costs would be considered abusive (eg where repair and maintenance costs are knowingly picked up by the original builder just before the transfer).

In addition, providing the property is sold to a connected company that is at least 75% owned by the vendor it will be considered to be part of stamp duty land tax (SDLT) group and no SDLT will be due on the purchase.This new guidance and the earlier HMRC Information Sheet on the consequences of a short let do not deal fully with all situations, and in particular do not deal with mixed developments. In addition they make no comment on direct tax consequences of selling a property to a connected company.

Finally, in the case of a speculative builder who constructs a house, is then unable to sell it, and then decides to live in it himself he has a number of options. If the builder operates through a limited company he can sell it to himself personally and would then have a zero-rated sale. He could rent it himself and the above adjustment would apply. In the event that the builder is a sole proprietor and he uses the house as his main residence, he will not have to make any adjustments to the input tax recovered. HMRC Internal Guidance, V1-8A, Section 22.8.2 states:

> 'When a sole proprietor is in the business of constructing property for sale and builds a house on his own land for his own occupation, or by a connected person, he can either:
>
> • recover the VAT through his VAT return in the normal way; or
>
> • claim the VAT through the Refund Scheme (DIY Housebuilders' Scheme).'

In these circumstances he would be entitled to recover the VAT through his own VAT return so there would be no need to make any adjustments.

WHAT IS A DWELLING?

26.10   Both the construction and the subsequent sale of a dwelling only qualify for zero-rating if that dwelling meets the relevant conditions in *Group 5, Notes (2)* and *(16)*.

Focus

Note (2) requires that:

- the dwelling consists of self-contained living accommodation;

- there is no provision for direct internal access from the dwelling to any other dwelling or part of a dwelling; an internal fire door, which can only be opened in an emergency, would not count;

- the separate use or disposal of the dwelling is not prohibited by the terms of any covenant, statutory planning consent, or similar provision; and

- statutory planning consent has been granted in respect of that dwelling, and its construction or conversion has been carried out in accordance with that consent.

Note that the points in *Note (2)* are conditions which a dwelling must meet, not the definition of it. Various Tribunals, such as the one in *Amicus Group Ltd* (LON/01/0309 No 17693), have held that they apply to the *completed building*. Thus, they are not relevant to:

- the status of an existing building, which must be non-residential if either the sale of it after conversion, or the conversion work itself when supplied to a housing association, are to qualify for zero-rating. In those cases, the building must have been neither designed nor adapted for use as a dwelling (*Sch 8 Group 5, Notes 7* and *7A*). See **26.70**.

- the definition of an existing dwelling in relation to the reduced rate for work in changing the number of dwellings in the building (*Sch 7A, Groups 6* and *7*).

Note also that, in *Hopewell-Smith*, a Tribunal held that, even though the planning permission contained a restriction on the use of the property, that did not prevent its separate *disposal*. See **26.41**.

Planning permission meeting the conditions of *Note (2)* must have been obtained before the work is done. Getting it later is no good—one reason being the need to determine the rate of tax due at the time the work is done (*Mr A E and Mrs J M Harris* (LON/2004/0185 No 18822)).

Note (16) says that the construction of a building does not include:

- the conversion, reconstruction, or alteration of an existing building; or

- any enlargement of, or extension to, an existing building, except to the extent the enlargement or extension creates an additional dwelling or dwellings; or

- adding an annexe to an existing building. See **26.18** for the meaning of 'annexe'.In *Amicus Group Ltd* (LON/01/0309 No 17693), bedsit-type accommodation was held to be dwellings, so conversion of the building into flats did not qualify for relief from standard rating.

In *Agudas Israel Housing Association Ltd* (LON/2003/0344 No 18798), which concerned the construction of a third floor to an existing care home, eight bedsitting rooms with shower rooms (presumably with toilets) and provision for fridges, kettles, and microwaves ovens, were held to be dwellings, despite not having kitchens. A key point was the access by lift or stairs direct to the square outside. They were found to be self-contained. Whether they could be separately used or disposed of, however, was not considered.

In the case of *Cameron Black Limited* [2012] UKFTT 257 (TC) the appellant carried out works on a dwelling on the top floor of a block of flats. The appellant application was '...to erect a one storey flat roof extension on the roof of the building to provide additional residential accommodation. This extension would be on top of the existing roof extension'. The planning permission stated that permission is granted for a 'sixth floor extension to existing apartment'.

The work consisted of the construction of a free-standing dwelling located on the roof of another building, part of which would be demolished and replaced by a new two storey building to be constructed in its place. The application also stated that the building below on which the existing dwelling was built would not be demolished.

Further planning permission was granted by the Council on 1 February 2011 for 'complete demolition of the existing fifth floor of the building and the addition of a sixth floor extension' (an amended scheme to previous planning permission to create a three bedroom dwelling) (retrospective).

The Tribunal found that in the 2007 planning application the description of the development was that it was to be an extension.

The Tribunal found that, at the time the demolition and construction took place, statutory planning permission had not been granted for the demolition and so the building did not qualify for zero rating at that time.

Whilst the correct planning permission was obtained on 1 February 2011 and was retrospective the Tribunal found that although the retrospection applies to the work carried out before 1 February 2011 it did not mean that the planning permission was effective before that date. It is therefore important to make sure that the correct planning permission is obtained at the time.

WHAT IS A 'RELEVANT RESIDENTIAL PURPOSE'?

26.11

Focus

Note (4) to Group 5 defines 'relevant residential purpose' as use for:

- a home or other institution providing residential accommodation for children;

- a home or other institution providing residential accommodation with personal care for persons in need of personal care by reason of old age, disablement, past or present dependence on alcohol or drugs, or past or present mental disorder;

- a hospice;

- residential accommodation for students or school pupils;

- residential accommodation for members of any of the armed forces;

- a monastery, nunnery or similar establishment; or

- an institution which is the sole or main residence of at least 90% of its residents, but it specifically excludes use for:

  — a hospital, prison, or similar institution

  — a hotel, inn, or similar establishment

SOME CASES ON THE MEANING OF 'RELEVANT RESIDENTIAL'

26.12   A student accommodation block probably qualifies as dwellings following the *Amicus* case (see **26.10** above). The alternative of relevant residential accommodation for a university will not apply if it is let to third parties in the vacations (*University Court of the University of St Andrews* (EDN/96/182 No 15243)).

However, the length of stay of the students does not matter. In *URDD Gobaith Cymru* (LON/96/1528 No 14881), use for accommodation for students on short courses qualified as a relevant residential purpose. Similarly, in *Denman College* (LON/97/756 No 15513), two blocks, each containing eight study bedrooms, were 'residential accommodation' despite having no cooking facilities, and despite being for students on short courses of three to six days. The phrase meant 'residential' in contrast to, say, office accommodation. It was unnecessary for there to be a degree of permanence as the person's home.

In *St Dunstan's* (LON/01/1069 No 17896), a residential care centre was held not to qualify because the building was not used *solely* for a relevant residential or relevant charitable purpose. Some people only came during the day. Others were short-term visitors on holiday rather than receiving care, so the use was partly as an establishment similar to a hotel.

A building can be for use for a relevant residential purpose as a *home*, even if it does not include sleeping accommodation. In *Hill Ash Developments* (LON/99/537 No 16747), turning a building into an administration block was held to be part of the zero-rated conversion of several listed farm buildings into a nursing home.

In contrast to a *home or other institution*, HMRC may see *residential accommodation for students* as restricted. A dormitory block might not qualify if it has any other facilities—even just an office used solely for pastoral counselling.

BEWARE OF THE EXCLUSIONS FOR HOSPITALS, PRISONS OR SIMILAR INSTITUTIONS

26.13   In *General Healthcare Group Ltd* (LON/99/916 No 17129), a home for the care and rehabilitation of people with brain injuries, at which, the average stay was 700 days, was held not to have the characteristics of a 'hospital'. In contrast, the Tribunal found in *Wallis Ltd* (LON/98/1516 No 18012), that a building for use as a low security unit for mentally ill persons, who typically lived there for one to two years, qualified as a hospital under the *National Health Service Act 1977* and the *Mental Health Act 1983*. A proportion of the patients were detained there under hospital orders. There is, thus, a fine line between a residential care home and a clinic which qualifies as a hospital.

In *Fenwood Developments Ltd* (MAN/02/257 No 18975: [2006] STC 644), a nursing home for the mentally ill was held to be covered by *Note 4(b)* to *Group 5 Sch 8*. It was for people who could not be cured, and who needed to be looked after, some of whom were sectioned under the *Mental Health Act 1983*. It was neither a hospital nor a prison or similar institution, and was, therefore, a building for a relevant residential purpose.

So was a building to house elderly people suffering from dementia. The Tribunal held that, despite an involvement with the *Mental Health Trust*, whose consultant saw the residents once a fortnight, and the administration of drugs to the residents, the intended use of the centre was to care for the residents during long-term stays, not to treat them (*Hospital of St John and St Elizabeth* (LON/04/780 No 19141)).

WHAT IS A 'RELEVANT CHARITABLE PURPOSE'?

26.14

Focus

Relevant charitable purpose is defined by *Note (6) to Group 5* as use by a charity:

- otherwise than in the course or furtherance of a business; or

- as a village hall or similarly in providing social or recreational facilities for a local community.

See **26.19** for *Note (17),* which provides zero rating for an annexe for use for a relevant charitable purpose.

See also **26.30** and **26.31** below.

THE CONCESSION FOR LIMITED BUSINESS USE

26.15   Prior to June 2000, it was much more difficult for a building to qualify as used for a *relevant charitable purpose,* as often, any use at all for business would disqualify it in law. The alternative use as a village hall has also been interpreted narrowly in a number of cases.

In *Business Brief 8/2000* dated 31 May 2000, HMRC announced that they were introducing a 10% 'business use concession' (ESC 3.29). Providing the business use was less than 10%, the building would still qualify as 'solely' charitable use. The 10% would be calculated on the following basis:

- time the building is available for use

- the use of floor space

- the number of people using the building for business purposes

In Budget 2007 (followed up later by *Revenue & Customs Brief 29/07*), HMRC advised that from 21 March 2007, where the 10% limit for non-qualifying use is breached in the 10-year period following zero-rating, and the breach was not anticipated, there would no longer be any requirement for a self-supply charge to account for the change of use. Moreover, any charity that had accounted for such a self-supply in the previous three years was invited to submit a request for a refund, subject to the normal rules. On the downside, HMRC said that if it is found that a breach *was* anticipated by the charity, they will consider that zero-rating should not have been applied in the first place, and pursue the matter on that basis.

Having made the system more user friendly, in June 2009 HMRC issued HMRC Brief 39/09 and VAT Information Sheet 08/09, announcing that on 1 July 2009, they were withdrawing the 10% business use concession. However, from 1 July 2009, the term 'solely' will only be met where there is a maximum 5% business use. On the upside, the new limit does not need HMRC permission to be adopted, and charities will no longer need to use one of the three prescribed calculation methods above—any reasonable calculation will now be accepted. HMRC put in place a 12-month transitional period to 30 June 2010 whereby charities still had the option of using the outgoing concession instead of the new rules, but from 1 July 2010, everyone has had to comply with the 5% limit. Under the new regime, zero-rating will be by statute rather than concession. The old 'change of use rules' will again apply, so HMRC will expect charities to do an annual check to ensure the 5% limit for business use is still being met. If it is not then a self-supply charge will need to be accounted for in relation to the change of use.

According to a spokesman for HMRC, the concession was specifically reviewed by the Department in 2007, but he conceded no formal consultation was entered into with the charity sector. The spokesman also said that HMRC does not anticipate any tax to be generated from the removal of the concession, and expects most, if not all, charities who previously qualified for the zero-rate, to continue to benefit under the revised rules. Clearly then, there are no new charitable buildings out there that either have or will have 90-95% charitable use!

The methods of calculating the adjustments were amended and clarified by HMRC in *Revenue & Customs Brief 49/10* in December 2010.

SOME CASES ON 'RELEVANT CHARITABLE PURPOSES'

26.16   In *St Dunstan's* (LON/01/1069 No 17896), referred to above under the meaning of *relevant residential purpose*, use for a *relevant charitable purpose* did not apply either, because charges were made—albeit only 15–20% of the estimated cost of the accommodation and care, and there was also some use by outside organisations for meetings and conferences.

In *St Dunstan's Roman Catholic Church Southborough* (LON/97/1527 No 15472), a garage was found to be for relevant charitable use by a parish. It housed cars provided to the priests. That the cars were used partly for private purposes by the priests, was not relevant.

The two cases, *Jubilee Hall Recreation Centre* (LON/95/549 No 14209: *St Dunstan's Educational Foundation* (LON/96/838 No 14901); [1999] STC 945), which were heard together before the Court of Appeal, illustrate the village hall problem. Both Tribunal decisions were overturned. The area of Covent Garden was not a local community of the kind served by a village hall, and use *similarly* did not cover the wide variety of commercial activities run in the *Jubilee Hall*.

In *St Dunstan's*, a sports hall built by a charity was not used by it because it was leased to the local authority. Use by a fee-paying school was not use *similarly to a village hall in providing social or recreational facilities for a local community.*

However, in *Bennachie Leisure Centre Association* (EDN/96/60 No 14276), a leisure centre serving various parishes within a six-mile radius was held to be similar to a village hall, and to serve a local community.

Then, in *Ledbury Amateur Dramatic Society* (LON/99/634 No 16845), a Tribunal found that a hall, so constructed that it could be used as a theatre or as a single or several meeting rooms, which was run by LEDS not for profit, was similar to a village hall. It was used by a variety of local organisations.

In *Southwick Community Association* (LON/97/1703 No 17601—heard after remission of decision 16441 back to a new Tribunal), the construction of a self-contained annex to existing buildings forming a community centre was held to be zero-rated. It consisted of:

- two large workshops used primarily by three local amateur theatre groups;

- a large meeting room used by various organisations;

- a small room used as a committee room and rehearsal area for one of the theatrical groups;

- various storerooms on the ground floor;

- a smallish room above housing six computers and used by a local college for adult classes.

The Tribunal found that 95% of the membership of the affiliated groups, by far the largest users of the annexe, lived within six miles. The business use by the adult education college and a commercial disco did not exceed 10% of the overall use, and was, therefore, covered by the extra statutory concession on this point. The three theatre companies were charities, whose activities did not amount to a business. The charges made by them for performances and to them by the Association were set merely to cover costs. There was a diversity of use by other organisations, which was sufficient to meet the requirement in *Note 6(b)* for use *similarly in providing social or recreational facilities for a local community.* HMRC appealed, but settled the case out of court on terms not revealed.

Sport in Desford (MAN/99/0803 No 18914), an organisation set up by the parish council with three councillors on the committee, qualified as a charity under the *Recreational Charities Act 1958* in providing sports and social facilities for the community at very low membership fees. A key factor was the registration as a charity five years later by the Charity Commission, its objects and activities having remained essentially the same. The clubhouse was intended for use as a village hall or similar in providing social or recreational facilities for the local community. Much of its funding was obtained by grants, and much of the work developing its sports and social facilities was done by volunteers.

In *HMRC v Caithness Rugby Club* UT/2015/0155, a new rugby club clubhouse was found to be similar to a 'village hall' on the grounds that it was land owned by the council, was used extensively by local organisations and the rugby club did not have 'first use' of the property.

Riverside Housing Association Ltd (MAN/01/745 No 19341; [2006] EWHC 2383 (Ch)) was held to be in business despite much of its funding being government grants. It was charging rents and making a profit. That the profit was put back into the business did not alter the position. The Tribunal disagreed with the decision in *Cardiff Community Housing Association Ltd* (LON/99/343 No 16841). Riverside appealed to the High Court, but it upheld the Tribunal's decision

In contrast, the use by the *Sheiling Trust* (LON/04/89 No 19472) of a building containing classrooms used by its Ringwood Waldorf School was held to be for a non-business purpose. Fees were not charged; instead, the parents were asked to make contributions on the basis of an annual budget, which indicated the average sum needed. Parents were encouraged to pay more if they could do so, because a small number paid nothing. The school operated in accordance with the principles of Rudolf Steiner. All the children of the right age group in each family attended the school, and the parents were expected to be involved in the running of the school according to their individual skills.

The Tribunal drew the following guidance from previous cases as to whether an activity is a business for VAT purposes:

- The intrinsic nature of the activity must be discovered by looking at the features of it and the manner and context in which it is carried out, including the relationship between all the parties.

- To comprise a business, an activity must have economic content—its intrinsic nature must be economic, not, for example, social or charitable.

- That a supply is made for a consideration in carrying out the activity is not in itself sufficient to give that activity economic content.

- A lack of profit is not in itself sufficient; in particular, an activity may have economic content when supplies at no profit are of a kind made commercially.

- That a charity carries out the activity to achieve its charitable objects is not conclusive, although it is relevant to the intrinsic nature of the activity and thus whether it has economic content.

- The six tests identified in *Lord Fisher* ([1981] STC 238) (see Chapter 28, *What is a Business?*) are useful tools in analysing an activity but are not a comprehensive and rigid code.

The Tribunal held that Sheiling was not engaged in an economic activity.

CONFUSING CASES ON NON-BUSINESS NURSERIES

26.17 In *Yarburgh Children's Trust* (LON/98/1426 No 17209: 2002 STC 2007), a building constructed for a charity, and let by it at a low rent to another charity for use for a children's play group, was held to be built for non-business use.

The building also qualified as a village hall despite its use by other groups, restricted because of the Children Act, being only occasional. Although the High Court approved the decision, some of the reasoning seems questionable. Unfortunately, HMRC's comments in *Business Brief 4/03* are of little practical help.

South Aston Community Association and IB Construction Ltd (MAN/00/0797 No 17702) did seem to limit *Yarburgh*. A centre built to provide facilities in a deprived community was not used solely for non-business purposes because part of it was let to an educational charity providing free adult education. The latter was in the business of education—publicly funded and the letting to it was business.

However, *St Paul's Community Project Ltd* (MAN/02/637 No 18466; [2005] STC 95) followed *Yarburgh* on similar facts concerning a day nursery. A key feature in both cases was setting the fees at rates designed to ensure that the operation broke even—in *St Paul's* after allowing for substantial grants and donations.

Although *Yarburgh* was managed by a committee of parents with a constitution excluding employees whereas parents were a minority on St Paul's committee, the key point was the activity, not the management.

A charitable activity carried on by a co-operative did not become a business when managed by those who performed it. The financial constraints were identical, and the fees were dictated by the available income and the costs of supplying the service, factors which would not change if parents dominated the committee or were its only members.

We have difficulty in reconciling *Yarburgh* and *St Paul's* with *Morrison's Academy and Boarding Houses Association,* and *Yoga for Health Foundation,* cases mentioned in Chapter 28, *What is a Business?*

HMRC said in *Business Brief 2/05* that they would accept that such activities are non-business in cases, which are 'broadly in line'. The Business Brief says little about the practical consequences, and I suspect that HMRC will require the facts to be near identical for a nursery. We doubt if they will accept that other activities are non-business on the basis of *Yarburgh* and *St Paul's*.

WHAT IS AN ANNEXE?

26.18 *Note (16)* excludes from zero-rating the construction of an annexe—though, for charities, see **26.19** below re *Note (17)*. *Cantrell (t/a Foxearth Lodge*

Nursing Home) (LON/98/195 No 17804: [2003] EWHC 404 (Ch): [2003] STC 486) is the lead case on interpretation of *annexe*. The subject was a nursing home unit for 'Elderly severely mentally ill' patients, self contained with its own facilities and staffed separately from an adjoining 'Elderly Medical' unit. The only access to the Elderly Medical unit was an emergency fire door.

After its original decision was sent back to it by the High Court for reconsideration, the Tribunal found for HMRC a second time. This was then reversed by the High Court, which held that an annexe was an adjunct or accessory to something else. In relation to a building, that meant a supplementary structure, whether a room, a wing or a separate building. The Tribunal's view that any association sufficed was wrong. The unit was a new relevant residential building, not an annexe.

Similarly, in *Alan Water Developments Ltd* (EDN/04/160 No 19131), a new care home was held to be a relevant residential building, not an annexe, despite being next to an existing home and attached by a corridor—not used for ordinary access. It had an extra storey, and was independently staffed for elderly people suffering from dementia. The other was for the frail elderly—a different role. Although the kitchen of the existing home supplied the food, this was held to be equivalent to using an outside caterer; moreover, the new home did have facilities which could be converted into kitchens.

In *Chacombe Park Development Services Ltd* (LON/05/110 No 19414), a building providing bedsitting rooms and communal facilities for elderly people needing personal care, was held to be neither an extension nor an annexe to the one to which it was attached by a 6.5 ft link structure. The other building provided both personal and medical care to its residents but:

- the design of the new building was different to the existing one—no specialist bathing or rehabilitation facilities but more communal ones and three storeys compared with two;

- the use was different. Separating the buildings avoided confronting the elderly but active residents with the much greater care needed by those in the other one.

- staffing was separate.

No one factor was conclusive; the decision was based on all the facts and on the resulting impression.

In the case of *Rebba Construction Ltd* ([2009] UKFTT 296 (TC)TC00240) a newly constructed building adjacent to a residential home was intended for a solely residential purpose. The first issue was whether the supplies relate to the construction of a zero-rated building. In deciding whether the building was a standard-rated extension, the Tribunal found that it was similar in appearance to the existing building, was dependent on the main building, and was inextricably linked to it for access. As such, it found that the new building was an extension. The second issue was that if the building was found to be an extension, it was not caught by the restriction for extensions under *Sch 8 Group 5, Note (16)(b)*, because it created additional dwellings. The Tribunal dismissed this argument. First of all, the zero-rating provisions applied to the construction of buildings as dwellings or intended for use solely for a residential purpose. The judge pointed out that the new building was either a residential home or a dwelling, but could not be both. This contention 'flew in the face of its evidence' that the building was a residential home, and contradicted its principal assertion. However, even if this was the case, the judge pointed out that the individual rooms did not meet the definition of a dwelling in *Group 5, Note (2)*. The Tribunal found that the building was not an extension that created additional dwellings, and so dismissed the appeal.

In the case of *TL Smith Properties Ltd and Tregwilym Lodge Ltd v Revenue and Customs Commissioners* ([2011] UKFTT 528 (TC)) the appellants appealed against a decision by HMRC dated 2 February 2009 that VAT at the standard rate was chargeable on certain construction work performed by TL Smith Properties ('TLSP') for Tregwilym Lodge Ltd ('TLL') (together 'the appellants').

The appellants appealed on 3 March 2009 on the basis that the decision was incorrect and the construction supplies qualified for zero rating.

TLL owns and operates a residential care home for the elderly and also a nursing home catering for elderly people with mental infirmity or dementia and is not registered for VAT.

TLSP's representative sought clearance from HMRC that construction work which they had performed for TLL was zero-rated for the purposes of VAT. HMRC replied to TLSP informing it that HMRC did not consider that the work undertaken satisfied the statutory test for zero- rating and it was therefore liable for VAT at the standard rate.

The appellant confirmed that previously the care home had no nursing services. It provided board and lodging and the personal, social and healthcare needs of the residents were provided by the district nursing team and community psychiatric nurses via the general practitioner.

He stated that demand for residential care services had always been high in the Newport area. However as the residents became more frail it became clear that the district nursing team could not meet all their needs. As a result the residents had to be reassessed and transferred to homes with nursing services which was difficult for them. It was therefore decided that following the grant of planning permission a new nursing facility would be built alongside the existing residential care home.

The appellant described the new structure in accordance with the plan provided and explained that because all the residents had a primary diagnosis of dementia and were moderately to extremely confused they were very vulnerable. Security and safety were therefore of the essence and there were swipe cards for access to the various areas which were provided only to the staff.

The old kitchen was replaced with new equipment and was developed on the edge of the newly built nursing facility and serviced both the needs of the nursing home and the residential care home. Entry and exit from the kitchens is by swipe cards. The new laundry was between the nursing home and the residential home and also accessed by swipe card.

The appellant confirmed that although the original plan was to have just one main entrance through the new structure because this was what the regulator wanted, in the event the old entrance to the residential home was kept and is used as an entrance and exit by visitors to this facility.

In summary the appellants contended that the new structure was not substantially physically connected to the existing building; the new structure was considerably larger than the existing building; it was intended to be used as a separate nursing home distinct from the existing building which is a residential home; the new structure was self-contained and functioned independently from the existing residential home; the new structure employed its own more highly qualified staff and the new structure's distinct purpose as a separate nursing home was separately registered.

HMRC argued that the buildings were linked by a corridor on the ground floor which provided a permanent access from the existing building to the new structure intended for routine use by staff. By virtue of this neither structure could be disposed of separately. Both buildings shared a common kitchen, laundry and plumbing facilities.

The Tribunal found that the new structure was an extension or an enlargement of the existing building linked albeit by doors which could only be accessed by the swipe cards provided to the staff who had access to all parts of the buildings. This would include the kitchen staff who would need such access to serve meals. Presumably other domestic staff such as cleaners and those who operated the laundry would also need to go backwards and forwards.

The Tribunal found that although the new structure was built for the purpose of accommodating those residents who needed nursing care, it was a building joined to the original on both floors with internal access for staff throughout. In addition, key services, kitchen and laundry were shared. The Tribunal found this made it an extension or enlargement which was not self-contained and nor could it function independently so the appeal was dismissed.

Annexes for relevant charitable purposes

26.19

Focus

Note (17) restores to zero-rating, the construction of an annexe which:

- is intended for use solely for a relevant charitable purpose; and

- can function independently from the existing building; and

- the only or the main access to the annexe is not via the existing building (and vice versa).

From 1 June 2002, *Note (17)* was amended to allow zero-rating where only part of an annexe qualifies: *Note (10)* then applies to apportion the work.

Solely means up to 5% business use.

CASES ON ANNEXES FOR RELEVANT CHARITABLE PURPOSES

26.20   It tends to be difficult for a project to qualify as an annexe, but some have.

In *Grace Baptist Church* (MAN/98/798 No 16093), a community building attached to a church, which replaced a smaller one, was held to be zero-rated as an annexe. See this case for a useful review of *Note (17)* concerning self-contained annexes, as opposed to entire buildings.

In *Torfaen Voluntary Alliance* (LON/03/756 No 18797), offices with kitchen and toilet facilities that were attached to, and integrated structurally with, a church hall, but had a separate entrance, qualified as an annexe. An internal connecting double door was normally locked, and the annexe functioned independently.

SPECIFIC EXCEPTIONS TO ZERO-RATING

26.21

Focus

The following transactions are standard-rated (*Group 5, Note (13)*):

- sale of a timeshare—though a sale of the dwelling itself may be zero-rated;

- a sale or long lease of a dwelling, which cannot be occupied throughout the year. An example is a holiday chalet, the planning permission for which, limits the period of occupation to prevent it becoming a permanent home.

The reason for these exceptions is to prevent new holiday accommodation from benefiting from zero-rating. Since holiday accommodation is also excluded from the exemption for land in *Sch 9, Group 1*, it is therefore standard-rated.

In an interesting case about the supply of holiday homes (*Lower Mill Estate Ltd and Conservation Builders Ltd* (TC000016)) two connected, but separately VAT registered companies, enter into contracts with a customer. Company 1 supplied the land on which the holiday home is built ('Landco'), and is taxable as an excluded item under Sch 9 Group 1 (*Item 1(e)* and *Note (11)*). Construction services are supplied by company 2 ('Buildco'), which zero-rates its supplies on the basis that they were in the course of the construction of new dwellings under *Sch 8 Group 5, Item 2*.

Landco marketed the holiday homes, and, in most cases, sold vacant plots to customers plus VAT. Following payment of a reservation fee, Landco enters into a lease agreement, and once it had been signed, the customer entered into a separate agreement for the construction services with Buildco. In theory, customers did not have to use Buildco, but everyone had. All payments are made by the customer to Buildco apart from when construction work has already started on a plot before it is sold. In that case, Landco invoiced the customer for stage payments to that date, including VAT.

In February 2008, HMRC assessed the appellants for standard-rated construction services, and gave the court the following three arguments in support of this:

1. *Single supply*—when the essential features are considered (ignoring the two separate contracts) there is a single taxable supply of holiday home by Landco.

2. *Joint supply*—HMRC originally had an alternative argument that Buildco made a supply of a completed holiday home to the customer. This was amended to argue there was a joint supply by the two companies. Buildco's share of this taxable supply was the value of its construction services.

3. *Abusive arrangements*—if the technical arguments fail, HMRC say the arrangements are abusive on the basis they resulted in a tax advantage contrary to the purpose of the *Directive*, and that the essential aim was to create a tax advantage. Following *Halifax* (Case C-255/02) the arrangements should be redefined as a single taxable supply of a holiday home.

In reaching its decision, the Tribunal evaluated the three HMRC arguments as in the same order they had been presented.

On *single supply*, the Tribunal found *CPP* (Case C-349/96) could not apply in terms of the supplies, as there was no principal and ancillary service. It found the construction services were a substantial business in their own right. The economic linkage argument in *Levob* (Case C-41/04) was distinguished on the basis that this case concerned one supplier. The appellants said it was not possible to treat supplies by two different suppliers as a single supply, citing *Telewest* (CA [2005] STC 481). The Tribunal did not address this specific point, but did dismiss *Telewest* as being more concerned about one supply being split into two than two supplies being recast as one. The Tribunal dismissed HMRC's argument on the basis that it was not possible to classify the supplies as a single supply using case law.

For the issue of *joint supply,* the Tribunal unequivocally dismissed HMRC's argument. Landco supplies the land, and the time of supply is on payment or invoice, both of which are prior to Buildco's involvement. Buildco has no interest in land, and can only supply construction services. The issue is thus whether the services are supplied to Landco or the customer.

Regarding *abusive arrangements*, in looking at the *Halifax* test the Tribunal found a tax advantage was obtained. This was achieved simply by a reduction of the taxable amount. The fact that an element of consideration paid for a new holiday home is VAT free is contrary to the *Directive*. The Tribunal then looked at whether the essential aim was to create that tax advantage. On this point the Tribunal looked at how the contractual arrangements were constructed. The Tribunal concluded that the way in which the holiday home is provided is aimed to create a VAT advantage. This was supported by the documentation and the packaging of the supplies. The Tribunal referred to the ECJ *Part Service* case (C-425/06), which suggested looking at the economic viability of a business when considered in isolation, and the profit margin it obtained. As Buildco's profit margin was only 3–5%, there was a question over its viability as a standalone business.

In finding for HMRC, the Tribunal then turned to the issue of redefining the transactions. Whilst some abusive arrangements can be complex, this case was relatively straightforward. The Tribunal confirmed that redefinition would result in a single standard-rated supply of a completed new holiday home being made by Landco.

It is clear the Tribunal did not consider the contracts a sham. It is also clear the Tribunal did not think it could recast the supplies under those contracts using the approach adopted in *Eastbourne Town Radio Cars* ([2001] STC 606, HL). However, this did not stop it considering *Halifax*.

This case is interesting in that the arrangement was not only in place from the start of the business, and there were some valid commercial reasons (eg a requirement from the funding company to hold the land asset in a separate company). The taxpayer even got confirmation from HMRC that their VAT treatment was correct in 1999. The Tribunal placed emphasis on the 'standalone' factors when examining the essential aim test, including the low profit margin for Buildco. This suggests the taxpayer would have had a stronger case if it had 'shifted' more value to the zero-rated construction.

See **11.13** for cases about holiday accommodation.

PROBLEMS WITH EXISTING HOUSES AND GRANNY FLATS

26.22 Work on a house is normally standard rated; for an exception, see **26.41**. Another possibility for zero-rating is an enlargement or extension to a house that creates an additional dwelling. If the possibility of separate use or disposal, noted above at **26.10**, is prohibited under the planning permission, adding a granny flat to an unlisted house is standard-rated.

Thus, rebuilding an existing house is also standard-rated, no matter how comprehensive the work may be. With the exception of the planning permission condition detailed in Note 18 below, the only way to avoid the VAT is to demolish it and start from scratch. The 5% reduced rate could apply, however, if it was split into two or more flats, and this will be explained later.

Focus

Note (18) says that the building only ceases to exist when:

● it is demolished down to ground level; or

● the part remaining above ground level is just a single facade or, on a corner site, a double facade, the retention of which is a condition of planning consent.

The above comments relate to the zero-rating for constructing a new building. See **26.42** concerning the reduced rate on certain conversion work to existing houses.

Angus MacLugash (t/a Main & MacLugash) (EDN/97/146 No 15584) illustrates the problem of obtaining zero-rating if anything at all remains of the existing building. The modernisation of an uninhabitable croft was held to be the alteration and enlargement of an existing building. The floor space was increased from 50m2 to 120m2. The front and rear walls were retained, the others being demolished. This is only one of numerous cases over the years in which projects such as barn conversions have been held to be standard-rated (or subject to the 5% reduced rate from 2001).

In the case of *Nigel Williams v HMRC* [2017] UKFTT 846 (TC), the appellant intended to reconstruct his house but as the work commenced it became clear that the building needed to be demolished. He had the house demolished and started construction of a new one. He obtained backdated planning permission for the construction but the Tribunal found that invoices issued by the builder for work done before the planning permission had been authorised should be standard rated as at the time the invoices were issued planning permission for the new house construction had not been obtained and so could not be zero-rated.

In the case of *Andrew Reeves v HMRC* [2016] UKFTT 195 (TC) although only one wall of the property was left standing it was not considered to be a façade. The Tribunal defined a façade as being 'more than a wall that has remained standing on a construction site, it is a street facing frontage that has character or significance to the area that would lead to its retention'. As the gable end was not street facing and had no architectural significance it could not be considered a façade and work to the property could not be zero-rated as a new build.

Another extreme example was in *Catherine McCallion* (EDN/05/40 19,367), where the only part of an existing building that was retained, was an internal chimney stack. The Tribunal commented that it was obvious by any objective standard that a new house was built, the chimney stack being of no particular consequence. However the law was unambiguous, and neither HMRC nor the Tribunal had any discretion to look at the 'whole fact of the construction'.

The same rule applies if you include an existing building in, say, a new house. In *Co-work Camphill Ltd* (LON/99/1351 No 17636), a building was held not to qualify as 'new' because it incorporated a barn, the footprint of which was about a quarter of the total.

With the introduction of the reduced rate for conversion work, the financial problem is much reduced, though there is still a difference between zero and 5% on work which does not qualify as the construction of a new dwelling. Moreover, not every project will qualify for the 5% rate. Study the rules explained later to check whether a conversion or renovation project does.

CONVERSION WORK FOR HOUSING ASSOCIATIONS

26.23 The only zero-rating available for the work of converting a non-residential building, as opposed to the subsequent sale of it, is where the client is a registered housing association and the project is to produce (*Sch 8, Group 5, Item 3*):

- a building designed as one or more dwellings; or

- a building or part thereof intended for use solely for a relevant residential purpose.

Again, the zero-rating does not cover the services of architects, surveyors and the like.

For an explanation of non-residential, see **26.70**.

BE CAREFUL ABOUT BUILDING CONTRACTS

26.24 Builders prefer to standard rate work if they have any doubt about its status. If a business thinks that the work could be either zero-rated or reduced rated, tell the builder before the contract is signed. Even if the business can recover the VAT, it is still at risk if the builder wrongly charges it but then fails to pay it to HMRC—or perhaps asks for the repayment of it.

If the builder disagrees on the VAT status, insist on the facts being presented to HMRC and a ruling obtained. As the customer, you can do that, but in reality, HMRC will often not even discuss the status of work with the customer, even though their published guidance (Notice 700/6, para 2.2) only says that they will **'normally'** provide the ruling to the supplier. This seems to be a view taken at a lower level within HMRC, as senior management say the policy is flexible and that they are prepared to provide rulings to customers (as stated in the Minutes of the JVCC meeting held in April 2007).

A business or individual should never pay VAT to the builder if it believes it should not have been charged. The problem is that, once it has been paid, the builder has no interest in arguing the matter with HMRC; the customer will probably have considerable difficulty in getting the matter looked at properly, and might have to sue the builder—an action which could prove difficult, given that the Court would not know the VAT rules, and would likely require an expert opinion.

One legal difficulty is that *Note (9)* to *Sch 8, Group 6* says that, where part of the work is a zero-rated alteration to a listed building, an apportionment *may* be made. Thus it is optional, and it might be difficult afterwards to sue a builder who had taken a decision not to apportion!

A business or individual might be able to get zero-rating if it agreed to a clause in the contract indemnifying the builder for any VAT subsequently found to be due on a review by HMRC. However, it would be at risk of a penalty being charged, as well as default interest.

BE CAREFUL OF VARIATIONS IN THE CONTRACT

26.25   If, in the course of constructing a zero-rated building such as a house, it is decided to add an outbuilding or alter it internally, make sure that work starts before the building is completed. Once a certificate of practical completion is issued or the house is occupied, HMRC will probably say that it is finished, and that any additional work is, therefore, a standard-rated alteration. See below re garages and last-minute choices, for some examples of the trouble this has caused.

GARAGES AS PART OF ZERO-RATED PROJECTS

26.26

Focus

Note (3) says that the zero-rating for building a dwelling or converting a non-residential building into one (for a housing association) includes the construction of a garage if:

- the garage is constructed or converted at the same time as the dwelling; and

- it is intended to be occupied with it.

Normally, this causes no trouble. However, in *Chipping Sodbury Town Trust* (LON/97/943 No 16641), a Tribunal held that the construction of a pair of semi-detached garages was standard-rated because they were built under a separate planning permission, and construction had not started until shortly after the date on which the Tribunal found the two semi-detached houses to have been completed. It found that the fact that access paths and garden fencing were only done whilst the garages were being constructed was irrelevant. It referred to these as 'external works'.

THE PROBLEMS OF DECORATIONS AND OTHER LAST-MINUTE CHOICES

26.27   Beware of work done either just before, or just after, the house is occupied. When a house buyer chooses final finishes, kitchen units, etc the work is, of course, usually done by the builder. However, in *C McAllister* (LON/02/408 No 18011), the buyer ordered special flooring and a cooker hood, which were installed by the respective suppliers, not the builder and invoiced to him direct. The Tribunal confirmed HMRC's refusal to repay him the VAT under the DIY Housebuilder's scheme because neither work was part of the construction of the house.

Similarly, if a person is having a house built on his own land and, for one reason or another, he wants to move in before it is completed, make sure the contract includes provisional sums for all work such as decorating. Moving in is evidence that the house is completed. Whilst HMRC might not challenge zero-rating for work which continued under the original contract, they probably would for anything done as additional work. They would claim that work to be an alteration to a completed house, regardless of its state when the owner first moved in.

In *Mr & Mrs James* (VTD 20,246), the appellants built a house using the DIY Builders Scheme, and were able to zero-rate the construction. The plastering of the house was subcontracted to a builder, but was then found to be defective, and had to be repaired.

A Certificate of Completion had been issued prior to the reparatory work being started, but the appellants saw the supply as zero-rated. HMRC considered the work to be an alteration of an existing house, rather than construction of a new house, and assessed the appellants on the basis that it was standard rated. The Tribunal reviewed the evidence and concluded that the original plasterwork was inadequate and dangerous, and that the new plasterwork was supplied in the course of the construction of the building. It was, therefore, eligible for zero-rating, and so the appeal was allowed.

RESIDENTIAL CARAVAN PARKS

26.28 In Notice 708, HMRC say that the zero-rating for civil engineering work in constructing a permanent residential caravan park covers pitches, roads, drains, sewers, mains water, and electricity, but not such facilities as a swimming pool or a shop. Sites which cannot be occupied for the full 12 months of the year do not qualify as permanent (*Group 8, Note (11)*). This was later confirmed by the High Court in *Tallington Lakes Ltd* (LON/05/177 No 19972, [2007] EWHC 1955 (Ch)). Alterations, enlargements and repairs are standard-rated (*Group 8, Note (9)*).

CIVIL ENGINEERING WORK—ACCESS ROADS AND SITE PREPARATION

26.29 As noted earlier, HMRC accept that civil engineering work done in the course of constructing a house is zero-rated. However, most people would think work on access roads, mains drainage and the like, did not form part of the construction of the individual houses on a site, and that it is standard-rated. This seems likely to catch out small subcontractors.

In *RD Gazzard* (L0N/89/1391 No 6029), a Tribunal confirmed that work to clear building plots ready for inspection by prospective buyers, who would then choose the design of house, was not done in the course of constructing those houses.

CERTIFICATES

26.30

Focus

In those cases where zero-rating depends upon intention as to use, the purchaser must provide a certificate of that intention. *Note (12)* requires this to be in the form published in Notice 708 para 18.

To print that form, find the notice on the HMRC website, as explained in Chapter 19, *How does a business keep up to date on changes in VAT?*, then enter just that page particular number in the instructions to the printer. It should then print a page exactly as in the Notice.

Note (12) also requires the certificate to be held prior to the supply in question being made. Whilst HMRC might allow retrospective zero-rating once a certificate had been obtained, an officer would undoubtedly assess for tax and interest if you could not produce it at the time of the visit.

CHANGE OF USE

26.31   If the intended or actual use of a relevant residential or relevant charitable building changes, VAT has to be accounted for by the owner of the building to HMRC under *Sch 10, para 1*.

This applies where:

- the intended use does not materialise; or

- within ten years, the use changes from a relevant to a non-relevant use; or

- the person, who benefited from the zero-rating, sells, leases or grants a licence to occupy the building to someone else, who does not intend to use it for a relevant purpose.

A change of use need not necessarily be complete. From 1 June 2002, the VAT due is reduced by 10% for each complete year of use for the charitable or residential purpose intended. From 21 March 2007, the VAT due was waived completely in respect of a change of use for a relevant charitable building (see **26.15** above) provided the charity could not reasonably have foreseen the change of use. This qualification was an anti-avoidance measure. However, if a change of use was foreseen at the time that ESC 3.29 was applied, HMRC would take the view that the building was not entitled to be zero-rated in the first place.

From 1 July 2009 the old 'change of use rules' again apply, so HMRC will expect charities to do an annual check to ensure the 5% limit for business use is still being met. If it is not then a self-supply charge will need to be accounted for in relation to the change of use (see **26.15** above).

Where a change of use applies within a 10-year period, a repayment of some of the VAT to HMRC will be required based on time apportionment over that 10-year period. Even if it is not registered for VAT it will still have to pay HMRC.

What HMRC consider to be change of use can cause problems to businesses. Obviously, if a business obtains zero-rating for the construction of a building to be used as an old peoples' home and then convert it into offices, or lets it to a tenant that converts it into offices, then it would expect a change of use charge to be triggered and have to pay a proportion of the VAT claimed.

On the other hand, a 'change in use' charge would not apply where all or part of the building is let to someone who continues to use it solely for a qualifying purpose so if the original owner leased it to another company that ran it as an old peoples' home no adjustment would be required.

HMRC says that if there is a TOGC and the freehold of the building is sold as part of the TOGC the seller will then need to account for a 'change in use' charge no matter how it is used by the new owner. In one recent example a chain of care homes reorganised its structure and transferred one home to a new company in the group. As it had been built after 1 March 2011 they got a huge bill for change of use even though it was still a care home! If the transferor does not transfer their entire interest in the building, then they need only consider a 'change in use' charge based on how the building is being used (its occupied use).

Examples: After five years, in order to raise capital, the company sells a long leasehold interest (for a premium) to a finance company. The finance company leases the building at an open market value rent back to the company, who continues to use the building as a care home. No sale of the property has occurred and no change of use charges apply.

No 'change in use' charge is due if a zero-rated qualifying building is demolished to ground level within 10 years of completion.

After five years, a care home is converted into apartments. HMRC says that the operating company will have to account for a change of use charge.

The mechanism treats the value of the original supply that attracted the zero rate of VAT as standard-rated but adjusts that value according to:

- the proportion of the building that is affected by the change in use; and
- the number of complete months that the building had been used solely for a qualifying purpose prior to the change in use.

VAT is then accountable at the standard rate on the charge calculated. This tax charge is a self-supply. A self-supply is a deemed supply to and by the person concerned.

PLANNING POINT

26.32   If a business wants to transfer part of a care business into another legal entity and the property was built after 1 March 2011, then either grant a long lease in it rather than a sale or retain a small interest in the building – sell 99% of the freehold. As there is no sale and use would remain the same, the charge would not apply.

SUBCONTRACTORS

26.33   A subcontractor can only zero-rate work on a new dwelling or an approved alteration of a listed building converted into a dwelling prior to 1

October 2012 when the zero-rating for approved alterations was withdrawn. Work on other zero-rated buildings is standard-rated, because only the main contractor holds the certificate of intention needed to justify zero-rating. See also later for a similar problem with work in renovating a house at the 5% rate.

BUILDING MATERIALS INCLUDED IN THE ZERO-RATING

26.34   If the service of construction work is zero-rated, so are the materials and other goods via *Sch 8 Group 5, Item 4*, if they are supplied by the contractor who installs them, and are *building materials*.

Building materials are defined in *Note (22)* to *Group 5* as:

'... goods of a description ordinarily incorporated by builders in a building of that description, (or its site), but does not include—

    (a)   finished or prefabricated furniture, other than furniture designed to be fitted in kitchens;

    (b)   materials for the construction of fitted furniture, other than kitchen furniture;

    (c)   electrical or gas appliances, unless the appliance is an appliance which is—

        (i)   designed to heat space or water (or both) or to provide ventilation, air cooling, purification or dust extraction; or

        (ii)   intended for use in a building designed as a number of dwellings and is a door entry system, a waste disposal unit or a machine for compacting waste; or

        (iii)   a burglar alarm, a fire alarm, or fire safety equipment or designed solely for the purpose of enabling aid to be summoned in an emergency; or

        (iv)   a lift or hoist;

    (d)   carpets or carpeting material.'

Where the builder installs non-building materials, it is only VAT on the goods themselves which is standard-rated. That on the installation service is zero-rated.

DISALLOWANCE OF VAT FOR HOUSE BUILDERS

26.35   A similar rule achieves the same result for speculative house builders. VAT on goods which do not qualify as *building materials* is disallowed to developers constructing zero-rated buildings for sale (*art 6* of the *Input Tax*

Order (SI 1992/3222)). This affects any building, the sale of which is zero-rated under *Group 5* or *Group 6*. In practice, it is only houses which are constructed speculatively. Relevant residential or relevant charitable buildings are constructed for individual clients, because their status depends upon the intent as to their future use.

Although the house builder zero-rates the sale of the completed house, the disallowed input tax is part of his costs. The objective is to prevent the inclusion in zero-rated houses of luxury fittings such as music systems.

A builder, who installs goods in both new and existing houses that do not qualify as *building materials*, may have to keep special records to decide how much input tax he can reclaim if the goods are taken from a common stock, or their use is uncertain when bought. He will only be able to reclaim tax on those units on which he has charged output tax.

PLANNING POINTS FOR PRIVATE CLIENTS

26.36 Only the supply of excluded goods themselves is standard-rated. The service of installing cupboards, carpets, etc in the course of constructing a zero-rated building is zero-rated, provided that it is separately identified.

If a person is having a house built, they should think carefully before personally buying things like bathroom fittings or kitchen cupboards. They will incur VAT on them whereas, if the contractor bought them, they would be zero-rated together with the charge for installing them—so long as they meet the rules for *building materials* explained earlier.

Admittedly, there is the possibility of making a DIY builders claim if a person is building a new house, or converting a non-residential building into a dwelling, as explained elsewhere in this chapter. However, they will avoid paying the VAT in the first place, together with the administrative problem of having to make the DIY builders claim where they obtain the goods through the contractor.

MEANING OF 'ORDINARILY INCORPORATED' BUILDING MATERIALS

26.37 *F Booker Builders and Contractors Ltd* ([1977] VATTR 203 No 446), an early case on a previous version of the law, concerned heating. Although that point is no longer in issue, the principles remain relevant. The Tribunal said that the correct question was firstly whether some form of heating was ordinarily installed—the previous wording. Having decided that it was, the Tribunal then held that radiators and fires were within the genus of heating appliances. It was not necessary to consider whether a particular type of heating was commonly installed. This illustrates the reasoning required for other kinds of goods.

In any case concerning whether an item is ordinarily incorporated, evidence is vital. A Tribunal is likely to refuse to make suppositions based on its own experience, or on statements made by the appellant. It will require evidence on which it can make a finding of fact that the goods in question are widely incorporated by builders in that type of building. In *GE Joel* (LON/88/403 No 3295), a safe was held not to be ordinarily installed in a dwelling.

In the case of *Rainbow Pools London Limited* (VTD 20,800) they supplied (optional) retractable insulated covers and moveable floors for indoor swimming pools. The basic position is that the construction of an indoor pool in a new house can be zero rated under *Item 2, Group 5, Sch 8 of VATA 1994.*

The Appellant argued that the covers and floors were zero-rated under *Item 4 Group 5*, as they fell within the definition of 'building materials' in *Note (22) of Group 5*. HMRC said the covers were electrical appliances, which are excluded from zero-rating, and that the floors were not '*ordinarily incorporated*' into a building, and so were similarly excluded.

At hearing, the Tribunal saw the electrically-powered, fully-retractable insulated swimming pool covers as 'building materials' because the covers were built into the pool structure; and were 'ordinarily incorporated' within new indoor swimming pools (the Tribunal noted that in *Leisure Contracts Limited* (VTD 19,392), these covers are often required under building regulations). HMRC argued the point that electrical appliances are excluded from zero rating. However, the Tribunal concluded that 'it is purely incidental to their description that they are electrically powered', making the analogy that 'curtains are curtains even though some in offices and luxury houses may be drawn electrically'.

The moveable floors, a new and interesting invention designed to enable the level of the swimming pool floor to be altered to create varying depths, was regarded as an exceptional item not 'ordinarily incorporated' in buildings of any description. To that extent, the appeal was partly allowed.

BEDROOM CUPBOARDS

26.38   There have been numerous cases concerning bedroom cupboards. In Appendix D of Notice 708 *Buildings and construction*, HMRC provide detailed guidance on what they will accept as *building materials,* and what they regard as *furniture.* A cupboard made by fitting doors right across the end of a room or by enclosing two walls of the house and a 'nib', which forms the end of the cupboard, is acceptable. On opening the doors, the back and inside walls of the house should be visible. Rear panelling or any internal fittings beyond a shelf and a hanging rail, are said to turn the cupboard into *furniture.* See the Notice for full details.

HMRC also say that using a prefabricated panel for its end, instead of a nib projecting from the wall of the house, turns a cupboard into *furniture.* This was supported by the Tribunal in *Moores Furniture Group Ltd* (MAN/97/142 No 15044), which also agreed that the addition of a floor converted even a cupboard enclosing the entire end of a room into *furniture*.

Thus, as soon as a builder smartens it up, even the most basic kind of cupboard is likely to change from *building materials* into *furniture*.

In *Christ's Hospital* (LON/04/1041 No 19126), concerning fitted bedrooms for students, databases and wardrobes were held to be fitted furniture, but individual simple shelves and desktops without drawers were not.

IS IT GOODS OR AN APPLIANCE?

26.39   Electrical items are not necessarily *appliances*, in which case, they are *building materials,* provided they are goods of a description *ordinarily incorporated*.

In *Garndene Communication Systems Ltd* (MAN/86/373 No 2553), concerning sheltered housing, alarm switches were held to be merely electrical goods, not appliances, and so the VAT could not be recovered. In *FH Milan* (MAN/87/89 No 3857), special blinds installed as an integral part of the windows of a house, and which were controlled by a light sensor and thermostat as an energy saving system, were held to be an electrical appliance on the principle that the goods were fixed, and were operated by electricity. Again, the input tax could not be recovered.

HMRC accept in Notice 708 that fixed amplification equipment in churches— relevant charitable buildings—can be zero-rated.

Electric window blinds were held in *Tom Perry* (LON/05/369 No 19428) to be domestic electrical appliances—not designed to heat space or to provide air cooling. Their purpose was to control the temperature of an eco-friendly house of unusual modern design, and were not ordinarily installed.

CARPETS DO NOT QUALIFY FOR ZERO-RATING

26.40   Of all the various forms of flooring, carpeting is the one singled out for disallowance. In *McCarthy and Stone plc* (LON/91/382 No 704), Sonicord, a material bonded to the concrete floor in order to meet the requirements of building regulations for sound proofing corridors in sheltered housing, was held to be caught. There is no problem with a permanent flooring, such as wood block. By definition, a building must have a floor, but some finishes are neither permanent nor ordinarily installed. Linoleum and cork are not carpet, but they still have to meet the test of being ordinarily incorporated in the type of building in question.

In *KC Eftichiou* (MAN/86/337 No 2464), a dense material made of fibres bonded together with resin was held to be 'indistinguishable in principle from carpeting', and 'more akin to carpeting than to linoleum, vinyl, or cork'. The appeal failed for lack of evidence that it was ordinarily installed (now *incorporated*). That it had been specified by the architects for a number of similar halls was insufficient.

ALTERATIONS TO ZERO-RATED LISTED BUILDINGS

26.41   Changes announced in the 2012 Budget have removed the zero-rate for alterations to protected buildings, mostly listed residential dwellings but also listed buildings used for charitable and other residential purposes from 1 October 2012. It does not apply to supplies of repairs and maintenance, which were already taxable.

The change removes zero-rating from building materials and construction services supplied in the course of an approved alteration to a listed building.

The zero-rate for the first sale or long lease of a substantially reconstructed protected building will be restricted so that the current zero-rating for reconstructions where 60 per cent of the reconstruction costs are approved alterations is removed but zero-rating is retained for buildings reconstructed from a shell.

THE REDUCED RATE FOR CERTAIN WORK ON PROPERTY

26.42   The reduced rate for certain property conversions and renovation work took effect from 12 May 2001, and was extended to cover certain additional projects from 1 June 2002. These rules will inevitably cause trouble, especially for small builders. They are complex, and the relationship of them to the zero-ratings discussed elsewhere in this chapter is easily misunderstood. It is advisable to confirm any view of the VAT liability of each project with HMRC.

Do not confuse:

- the reduced rate for *work on converting various kinds of property*; with

- the zero-rating for the *sale or long lease* of a converted non-residential building.

The only zero-rating for the *work* of conversion is that on a non-residential building for a housing association. This is discussed at **26.23** above.

THE KEY RULES IN SCH 7A, GROUPS 6 AND 7

26.43

Focus

A reduced rate of 5% applies to conversion work which:

- changes the number of dwellings in a building, including creating one where none existed previously by converting a non-residential building;

- converts a house containing one or more dwellings into one or more multiple occupancy dwellings, or vice versa. *Multiple occupancy* means a self-contained dwelling designed for occupation by persons not forming a single household. See later for some comment on the guidance on this provided by HMRC;

- converts one or more buildings or parts thereof containing only dwellings, including multiple occupancy ones and any ancillary outbuildings, and, from 1 June 2002, any building, into a building intended solely for a relevant residential purpose;

- renovates or alters, including a dwelling currently a single household, which has been empty for at least two years (three years prior to 1 January 2008). It can remain a single household. *Empty* means not lived in, so past use for another purpose, such as storage, is okay. From 1 June 2002, this rule was extended to cover relevant residential buildings and multiple occupancy dwellings that had been empty for three years (two years from 1 January 2008);

- converts a relevant residential building into a dwelling or dwellings— and, from 1 June 2002, into a multiple occupancy one.

The work eligible for the reduced rate is more or less the same as that zero-rated under *Sch 8, Group 5* in constructing dwellings. However, the wording is different, and site works such as landscaping may not be covered (see also **26.59** below).

THE COMPLICATIONS OF THE TERM 'NON-RESIDENTIAL'

26.44 The term *non-residential* appears in various places in this chapter with different meanings, which it is all too easy to confuse.

In relation to the zero-rating under *Sch 8 Group 5 Item 1(b)* for the sale of a completed conversion project, it means a building not designed or adapted for living in, or not used as such in the last ten years. For the full definition in *Notes 7* and *7A* to *Group 5*, see later in this chapter under the comments on the zero-rating for a major interest in a converted building.

In relation to most of the rules for the reduced rate for work on property, there is no such definition. Since the reduced rate applies to a *Changed number of dwellings conversion*, it is not necessary for the building to be non-residential in the first place. The requirement is merely that the number of dwellings in the building alters, which would, of course, include creating a dwelling out of a building that was not designed as a dwelling.

The only definition of non-residential in *Sch 7A, Group 6* is in *Note 9(4)*, in relation to the conversion of such a building into a garage (see **26.58** below).

In cases where an existing dwelling is renovated or altered, but still remains a dwelling, *Sch 7A, Group 7* requires it to have been empty for two years (three years prior to 1 January 2008). This should not be confused with the ten years needed to justify zero-rating for an onward sale under *Sch 8 Group 5, Item 1(b)*.

ADDING AN EXTRA DWELLING

26.45   Adding a *single household dwelling* does not include making a 'granny' flat or annexe. The same requirements, such as self-contained living accommodation and no direct internal access to another dwelling, apply just as they do for the zero-rating of the construction of a new dwelling (*Sch 7A Group 6 Note 4(3)*).

CONVERTING PART OF A BUILDING

26.46   Where work is done to a building, but the number of dwellings changes in only a part of it, only the done work in that part qualifies for the reduced rate (*Sch 7A Group 6 Note 3(3)*).

In *Wellcome Trust* (LON/02/975 No 18417), it was held that the 'part' of the building must be big enough to contain a single household dwelling, and be identified by its physical boundaries, ie its walls, floors and ceilings. If the part meets that test, a dwelling redeveloped there counts as the same, even if it does not have precisely the same footprint as before.

In *Wellcome*, six or seven flats on six floors in two interconnected terraced houses were converted into four flats. The work to the flat on the second floor did not qualify for the reduced rate, because there had only been one flat in that part previously. The fact that about 5% of the space had been used in order to enable the conversion of the flats on the other floors made no difference; there was still only one flat in that 'part'.

HMRC quote the example of a four-storey block of flats with four flats on each floor. A lift is installed, which requires alterations to the layout of each flat on the first three floors. On the top floor, the four flats become three:

- only the work on the top floor qualifies for the reduced rate, because it is only in this part of the building that the number of dwellings has altered;

- if the four flats on a different floor were changed to make five smaller ones, the work on that floor would also qualify. It would not matter that there were still 16 flats in total, because each floor is treated as a separate part of the building.

This rule is intended to prevent the deliberate planning of renovation projects so as to obtain the lower rate for an entire block merely by changing the number of dwellings in one part of it. However, it seems a pitfall, especially where extensive modernisation work is being done in large buildings.

Always check the plans for the precise facts. Projects have to take into account practical realities. For instance a developer cannot necessarily just refurbish a flat when, on the same floor, they are altering the fabric of the building. In *Note 3(3)* to *Sch 7A, Group 6* the problem is the extent to which the word 'part' is to be interpreted as relating to floor space.

EXISTING RESIDENTIAL ACCOMMODATION

26.47   Various cases are slowly clarifying the extent to which projects produce dwellings, the sale of which is zero-rated under *Item 1 Group 5 Sch 8,* rather than exempt.

In *Calam Vale Ltd* (LON/99/977 No 16869), a Tribunal decided that *Note (7),* which defines non-residential as not designed or adapted for use as a dwelling, is not subject to *Note (2)*, which says that a dwelling consists of self-contained living accommodation. *Note (2)* only applies to the finished dwelling.

Without the self-contained rule, bedsitter type accommodation qualifies, as subsequently held in *Amicus Group Ltd* (LON/01/0309 No 17693). It is now established that a dwelling is where someone lives. Thus, in *Kingscastle Ltd* (LON/01/47 No 17777), the room used by the manager of a pub as a bedroom was held to be a dwelling despite the fact that the shower and toilet facilities were communal for seven bedrooms, the rest of which were used to accommodate travellers and the kitchen was that of the pub on the ground floor. The sale of a converted flat which included that room, was therefore exempt.

That self-contained rule also appears in the definitions of a single household dwelling and a multiple occupancy dwelling in the reduced-rate rules for conversion work explained later, and again applies to the finished result.

The difference between what amounts to a dwelling at the start of the conversion work, and what qualifies when it is finished thus creates a problem. In *Calam*

Vale, it was held that the sale of the two homes created by a vertical split of a public house did not qualify for zero- rating because each included part of the previous landlord's accommodation.

Several years later, *Ivor Jacobs* (MAN/01/275 No 18489) appears to show that was wrong, given that the conversion of non-residential space in the pub had produced two dwellings where there had only been one.

Ivor Jacobs involved the conversion of a boarding school, for which the use had been to educate children and to accommodate them, together with staff, during the school terms. The CoA construed *Note (9) Sch 8 Group 5* as requiring that the result of the conversion creates in the building one or more extra dwellings. The fact that one or more of those dwellings might use some of the previous residential space did not prevent there being some zero-rating—whether justifying a DIY refund under *s 35* to a private person, or for the sale of the finished result by a developer.

HMRC have not appealed the Court of Appeal decision, but it remains to be seen to what extent they accept it and whether the law is amended.

Meanwhile, the new complication is the need to apportion the sale price between the non-residential space converted into the dwelling—zero-rated, and the previously residential area—exempt.

Another potential problem is the disapplication of an option to tax by a landowner who sells the property to a developer for conversion, but the developer cannot certify that he will produce only zero-rated supplies from it. Landowners in such situations will not be able to recover any VAT on their sale costs, even though the developer will have some recovery on the conversion project.

DOES A HOUSE CONVERTED TO ANOTHER USE COUNT AS NON-RESIDENTIAL?

26.48   HMRC say that a dwelling which has been converted into, for example, a dental surgery, is a non-residential building, and that changing it back to a house qualifies for the reduced rate.

They mean that the use of the entire house has been non-residential. Here are two examples which would not qualify:

- an osteopath practises from the front room of his house. HMRC say that the entire house is still designed as a dwelling, even though a part is in non-residential use. Therefore, work to convert the front room back again would be standard-rated;

- the ground floor is a dental surgery. A self-contained flat is on the first floor. Conversion back to a single house would be standard-rated because, just as for a pub with a self-contained flat, the work would enlarge the existing dwelling, not create a new one.

In *Mr and Mrs Emberson* (LON/00/963 No 17604), a house which had been converted 60 years previously into a hotel, was held to have reverted to residential use when lived in for five years prior to conversion into two dwellings.

HOUSES IN MULTIPLE OCCUPANCY

26.49   The terms *house in multiple occupation,* and *multiple occupancy dwelling,* both appear in the law, and seem to be interchangeable.

From 1 June 2002, the reduced rate applies to the conversion of any building that does not already include a multiple occupancy dwelling, into a building containing only one or more such dwellings (*Item 5*). Up to that date, the work only qualified if it was the conversion of a single household dwelling.

A multiple occupancy dwelling means (*Item 4(2–4)*):

- a dwelling which was and remains designed, or has been adapted, for occupation by persons not forming a single household;

- that is not to any extent used for a relevant residential purpose;

- which consists of self-contained living accommodation, and with the same requirements of no direct internal access to another dwelling, and no planning restrictions as for the construction of a new dwelling.

Similarly, the conversion of a multiple occupancy dwelling into a single household dwelling qualifies for the reduced rate (*Note 3*).

Not covered are alterations to a multiple occupancy dwelling which is already in multiple occupation—such as the addition of extra bedrooms.

HMRC give as examples:

- bedsit accommodation, presumably with shared facilities such as bathrooms;

- shared houses or flats;

- bed-and-breakfast establishments with a mix of short and long-stay residents.

HMRC say the relief is meant to encourage the provision of private accommodation for people who cannot afford a mortgage, or cannot obtain one.

They say that the phrases do *not* cover:

- hotels;

- dwellings with attached granny annexes;

- accommodation for au pairs, guests or lodgers.

By *shared house* HMRC mean one occupied by several unrelated people, such as students. The scope for argument may be restricted by the need for the conversion work to have received any required planning permission or statutory building control approval (*Note (10)*). However, would it be needed if an ordinary house was being done up in order to let it to students, let alone for long-term occupation by, say, people living together as friends rather than as a family?

A bed-and-breakfast establishment is to be distinguished from a hotel in this context by the source of its funds. Usually, it will provide accommodation for homeless people on housing benefit. The exclusion in the guidance, not the law, of accommodation for *guests or lodgers* is intended to prevent someone claiming that a house in multiple occupation is being created by adding a room for such a purpose.

CONVERSIONS INTO RELEVANT RESIDENTIAL BUILDINGS

26.50   The law refers to a conversion for a *qualifying residential purpose*, which has a similar meaning to that of *relevant residential purpose* in connection with the zero-rating for the construction of new buildings; ie it means such communal buildings as homes for children, students and old people.

There is one difference in the reduced rate rules. The premises being converted must be intended to form the entirety of the institution in question, such as an old people's home, unless the use is to be as accommodation for students, school pupils, or members of the armed forces. In those latter cases, the accommodation would, of course, often be part of a university, school, or a military camp, and could not be the entirety of the institution.

The conversion can be of any building, provided that it is not already being used to any extent for a relevant residential purpose.

The use immediately prior to the conversion must not have been, even in part, for a relevant residential purpose (*Note 7(4)*).

The conversion of a qualifying residential building back into a dwelling is also eligible for the reduced rate, being the change of the number of dwellings in a building from none to one.

CERTIFICATES OF INTENTION TO USE FOR A RELEVANT RESIDENTIAL PURPOSE

26.51   The reduced rate only applies when the supply is to the intending user of the premises for a relevant residential purpose. The builder needs a certificate confirming the intention of use *solely* for that purpose, signed by a responsible person on behalf of the home or institution (*Group 6, Note 8; Group 7, Note 4A(1)*).

THE RENOVATION OF EMPTY RESIDENTIAL BUILDINGS

26.52   Group 7 reduced-rates renovating and altering the following buildings which have been empty for at least two years (three years prior to 1 January 2008) up to the start of the work (*Item 3*):

- a single household dwelling—but, if it is now occupied again, see below for conditions under which the reduced rate can still apply;

- a multiple occupation dwelling;

- a building or a part of a building which, when last lived in, was used for a relevant residential purpose.

The reduced rate does not apply to an empty building within an operating relevant residential unit, such as a care home, which was part of that unit when it was last lived in. In such a case:

- the rest of that unit must also have been empty for at least two years (three years prior to 1 January 2008) when the work starts (*Note 3(2)* as amended);

- you do not have to renovate or alter every building which formed the original unit, but those which you do must form a unit solely for use for a relevant residential purpose;

- *Note 4A(2)* provides that, where several buildings on the same site are renovated/altered at the same time, each of them shall be treated as intended for use solely for a relevant residential purpose to the extent that it otherwise would not be.

If a dwelling, which has been empty for two years (three years prior to 1 January 2008) is now occupied (*Note 3(3)*):

- the supply of the conversion work must be to the person, whose occupation ended the empty period;

- no renovation or alteration must have been done during the two years (three years prior to 1 January 2008) preceding that occupation;

- that person must have acquired, at the time of occupation, a major interest in it (*Note 3(5)*);

- the work must be done within 12 months of that major interest being acquired.

PLANNING PERMISSION

26.53   The requisite planning permission and, if required, statutory building control approval for the work, must have been obtained (*Group 7, Note 4*).

EVIDENCE OF THE UNOCCUPIED PERIOD

26.54   There is a pitfall for builders in the need to obtain evidence that the building was unoccupied for at least two years (three years prior to 1 January 2008). HMRC say that a letter from an *Empty Property Officer* confirming this will suffice (even though a lot of local authorities do not appear to have such an officer!). A best estimate of the empty period is required if the officer is unsure of it, and HMRC may then require other evidence such as electoral roll, council tax data or utility companies.

ONLY 'BUILDING MATERIALS' QUALIFY FOR THE REDUCED RATE

26.55   As with the zero-rating for constructing a new dwelling, materials are included in conversion or renovation work taxed at the reduced rate, provided that they qualify as *building materials (Group 6, Note 12; Group 7, Note 6)*. In other words, the same restrictions apply as for new work; thus, for instance, kitchen cupboards and very simple bedroom wardrobes qualify, but elaborate wardrobes, much electrical equipment, and carpets do not. See **26.34** above for the full definition. Goods purchased separately will be subject to VAT at the standard rate.

INSTALLING NON-BUILDING MATERIALS

26.56   The service of installing non-building materials is not reduced-rated, in contrast to the zero-rating available when a new house is being constructed—as explained above at **26.34** *(Note 11(3))*.

SUBCONTRACTORS

26.57

Focus

A subcontractor must standard-rate his services to the main contractor in the case of:

- conversion for a qualifying residential purpose—only supplies direct to the intending user of the building (ie the issuer of the certificate) are eligible for the reduced rate *(Group 6, Note 8)*;

- renovation of a dwelling which was empty for two years (three years prior to 1 January 2008), but is now occupied—only supplies direct to the occupier are eligible *(Group 7, Note 3(3)(d))*.

There are at least two pitfalls here. There has long been one for subcontractors working on projects for which a certificate of intention as to use is required. Main contractors have had to understand that they must accept standard-rated invoices from subcontractors. That is now extended to the conversion situation.

The second pitfall is that a subcontractor should charge at the reduced rate for renovating a dwelling which has been empty for at least two years (three years prior to 1 January 2008), and is still unoccupied, but must obtain the same evidence as the main contractor, as explained above. However, the subcontractor's work is standard-rated if the empty period has been terminated by occupation. The difference may not be apparent; the new owner may have moved in for a few months whilst planning permission was obtained and a building contract agreed, but has had to move out again because of the extensive nature of the work. How will a subcontractor, who is only brought in after the work has begun, spot that distinction? Of course, one who understands the law will check the facts, but that is not the point.

GARAGES AS PART OF A REDUCED RATE PROJECT

26.58   Conversion work includes the construction of a garage or the conversion of a non-residential building, or a part thereof, into a garage, if it is carried out at the same time as the main conversion work, and the resulting garage is intended to be occupied with the main building (*Group 6, Note 9*).

The *non-residential* building converted into a garage has to be a building neither designed nor adapted for use as a dwelling, nor for a qualifying residential purpose. Of course, that will be the usual situation, but beware creating a garage out of part of what was previously a dwelling, as opposed to an outbuilding!

That is not a problem with a renovation/alteration project under *Group 7* where the building has been empty for two years (three years prior to 1 January 2008). *Note 3A*, from 1/6/02, covers the construction of a garage, the conversion of a building or part of a building into one, or the renovation or alteration of an existing garage. Again, the work on the garage must be done at the same time as the rest of the project, and it must be intended to be occupied with the main building(s). The previous omission was not deliberate so, for work prior to that date, HMRC might accept the reduced rate.

LIMITATIONS ON THE WORK ELIGIBLE FOR THE REDUCED RATE

26.59   The reduced rate applies to a *supply of qualifying services* to convert or renovate, which is defined as (*Group 6, Note 11; Group 7, Note 5*):

●   work on the fabric of the building; or

- within the immediate site of the building in connection with providing for the building water, power, heat, access, drainage, security, or waste disposal.

LANDSCAPING AND OUTBUILDINGS

26.60   The eligibility for the reduced rate is narrower than that for zero-rated construction work, which includes simple landscaping.

This creates a pitfall for builders who are used to including the cost of cleaning up the site in their zero-rated invoices. Whilst finishing it off with such basic features as paths to the front and back doors is covered by their reference to *access*, HMRC say that the reduced rate does not cover landscaping, such as a simple lawn.

Similarly, they say that work to outbuildings that remain outbuildings is standard-rated. Suppose that a pub is converted into a house. There might be various outbuildings, such as a store used for empty barrels and bottles. HMRC say, in relation to the conversion of a dwelling for a relevant residential purpose, that stables and barns are not part of a dwelling. That seems likely to be so in many cases, given that the normal usage is not domestic in nature. On the other hand, a fuel store is surely a part of a dwelling since its purpose is essential to heating it.

Although the dividing line may usually be obvious, it seems likely that there will be cases where work is done on outbuildings to tidy them up or make their use more practical, and HMRC may argue that this does not convert them into a part of the dwelling. An example might be a barn which is converted into a workshop so that the house owner can practise a hobby, such as wood turning.

DIY BUILDERS AND CONVERTERS SCHEME

26.61   The DIY Scheme rules in *s 35* allow someone acting in a private capacity, who does certain building work themselves, to reclaim the VAT incurred on building materials that are incorporated into the building. The VAT has to be correctly charged; if a supply should have been zero- or reduced-rated and the supplier charges standard-rated VAT, HMRC will not make a repayment and you would have to obtain a refund from the supplier (*Price v Revenue & Customs* [2010] UKFTT 634 (TC)).

So can a charity which uses voluntary labour. The idea is to put the individual or the charity into the same position as if a contractor had zero-rated the work including the materials.

The work in question is:

- constructing a building designed as a dwelling or dwellings;

- constructing a building for use solely for relevant residential or relevant charitable purpose;

- a residential conversion.

The DIY Scheme cannot be used to recover VAT on work being done on a new house that has been bought. See **26.27** re decoration.

The work must create a new dwelling in which the claimant or a relative will live. It cannot be used where the building will be used for commercial purposes such as property rental. Renovating part of an existing house does not count; nor does converting a non-residential building in the grounds of an existing house as an additional facility.

Another no-go is building or converting a property which is then to be sold or let out. That project would count as a business activity. To recover any VAT, the builder would have to register and create one of the zero-rated supplies explained elsewhere in this chapter. A normal domestic rent would be exempt, and thus, of no help.

If the project is a *residential conversion*, VAT on services carried out by a contractor is also recoverable—but not the services of an architect, surveyor, consultant or someone acting in a supervisory capacity. A *residential conversion* means converting a non-residential building, or a part of one, into a building designed as a dwelling or number of dwellings, or intended for use solely for a relevant residential purpose. Conversion for a relevant charitable purpose is not included.

A DIY Scheme claim can thus be made only for certain conversion projects— those where a developer doing the same work would be able to zero-rate an onward sale of the finished result, and thus recover the input tax incurred. For instance, work to convert a house into flats does not qualify under *s 35* because, although work by a contractor would be eligible for the 5% rate, the onward sale would be exempt. It follows that a private individual working on such a project should consider whether the reduction to 5% on work involving expensive materials might make it worthwhile having it done by a contractor.

See **26.44** above for a case in which a house, converted 60 years previously into a hotel, was held to be residential because of subsequent use as a house.

Building materials are defined by *Note (22)* to *Sch 8 Group 5*, as explained earlier in this chapter. The other notes to *Group 5* also apply. Thus, the pitfall in *Note (18)* for projects such as barn conversions, applies to DIY projects too (see **26.22** above).

The work must be lawful, so the necessary planning permission must have been obtained. Only a single claim for repayment is allowed, and it must be in the form and with the supporting evidence required by HMRC. Lady Blom-Cooper (LON/00/1342 No 17481; CA [2003] STC 669) was held not to be entitled to a repayment of the VAT incurred in converting a pub into a house.

The Court of Appeal disagreed with the view of the Tribunal and High Court that *Note (9)* to *Sch 8, Group 5* did not apply to *s 35*. Since the building already included living accommodation, no additional dwelling was created. See **26.47** for more about this.

In *Gerrard Silver v Revenue & Customs Commissioners* ([2011] UKFTT 644 (TC)) the appellant made a claim to recover £17,773.34 of VAT incurred by him on the conversion of a barn into domestic living accommodation. HMRC refused the claim.

The appellant applied for planning permission to convert the barn. The application described the planned conversion as 'listed building conversion of existing barn to additional living accommodation for Home Farm' and as a 'granny annex'. In his covering letter Mr Silver explained he wished to convert the barn into a granny annex for his mother to occupy. He stated 'It is not required that the barn can be subsequently offered on the open market for sale, but shall be kept as part of Home Farm'.

The planning permission contained a restriction on the separate *use* of Ye Oll Barn (that it could not be used 'other than for the purposes of ancillary residential accommodation to the adjacent farmhouse known as "Home Farm"'): there was no express prohibition on the separate *disposal* of Ye Oll Barn.

In practical terms the restriction on separate *use* would make separate *disposal* of Ye Oll Barn difficult. The Tribunal agreed that (assuming that the planning restriction could be enforced) the restriction is likely to have a very significant impact on the value of the barn if disposed of separately but that was not the issue. Separate disposal was not prohibited.

The effect of the planning restriction is that condition in the *VATA 1994, Sch 8, Group 5, Note 2(c)* was not met when the building was completed, therefore the barn was not designed as a dwelling within the meaning of the VAT legislation and Mr Silver was not entitled to DIY builders relief so the appeal was dismissed.

Revenue & Customs Brief 9/16 clarified HMRC policy concerning the VAT treatment of works where an individual planning application is not necessary because statutory planning consent has been granted though PDRs

HMRC will continue to require evidence to be produced that the work is lawful in order for the zero or reduced rate of VAT to apply or for a claim to be eligible under the DIY House Builder Scheme. All DIY claims are dealt with at HM Revenue & Customs, 2 Broadway, Broad Street, Five Ways, Birmingham, West Midlands B15 1BG and should be submitted within three months of the issue of a completion certificate or occupation, whichever is first.

SALES AND LONG LEASES OF ZERO-RATED BUILDINGS

26.62

Focus

Sch 8 Group 5, Item 1 zero-rates the grant of a major interest, which is a sale or a lease exceeding 21 years (20 years or more in Scotland):

- of a zero-rated building;

- for the first time, which might be several years after construction was completed;

- by the 'person constructing' it,

or

by a converter of a building after its conversion from a non-residential one into:

- a building designed as a dwelling or a number of dwellings;

- a building intended for use solely for a relevant residential purpose.

Note that there is no relief for a building which has been converted for a relevant charitable purpose.

See **26.44** above for the definition of non-residential building, and, in particular, for dwellings not occupied for ten years. The sale of the latter, after renovation, became zero-rated from 1 August 2001.

HMRC clarified their view on how deposits paid on sales of land, particularly by developers to registered social landlords (RSLs), should be treated in HMRC Brief 36/09.

When development land is sold to RSLs, it is normal for a deposit to be paid at exchange of contracts where construction has not started, and the land is bare land. Often, this deposit will be held by a stakeholder and will not create a tax point for VAT purposes until it is released to the vendor (or vendor's agent), normally at completion of contracts. Completion usually occurs at a time when construction of the dwellings has progressed beyond what is commonly known as the 'golden brick', that is, beyond foundation level. This means the supply can be zero-rated.

However, it has become increasingly common for the deposit to be made available to the vendor at the time of exchange, when the land is still bare land. This has raised questions about the VAT treatment of the deposit, particularly on whether it can be treated as part-payment for the future zero-rated supply.

HMRC's view is that where the deposit is released to the vendor, and it is clear from the contract that what will be supplied at completion, or the time of the grant, will be partly completed dwellings (ie beyond 'golden brick'), the deposit is part-payment for the grant/supply that will occur at that time. As such, zero-rating will be appropriate if the conditions for zero-rating will be satisfied at the time of completion (eg there is a clear intention that the vendor will have started construction of the dwellings at that time and acquired 'person constructing' status.

It is possible that the state of the land at completion will differ from that anticipated, and where this is the case, the VAT treatment of the deposit will need to be reviewed.

For holiday accommodation in which occupancy is restricted, see **11.13**.

COMMONHOLD ASSOCIATIONS: RTE AND RTM COMPANIES

26.63 The *Commonhold and Leasehold Reform Act 2002* created the possibility for:

- Commonhold associations;

- Right to enfranchisement (RTE) companies;

- Right to manage (RTM) companies.

A *Commonhold association* is an alternative to a developer retaining ownership of the common parts of a property, such as the entrance and corridors in a block of flats, and charging ground rents under the traditional long leases. The buyers of the flats can become freeholders of their respective units, and owners, through the association, of those common parts.

A *right to enfranchisement* company is the means by which existing leaseholders in a multi-occupancy building can acquire the freehold interest in the property through collective enfranchisement.

A *right to manage* company enables leaseholders to take over the management of the common parts, and collect the service charges from the landlord or service provider.

There are no specific VAT rules concerning the above three arrangements. The VAT status of charges made by developers or landowners when handing over the freeholds, and of ongoing service charges made from then on by such an association or company, depends on the normal rules, ie for the freeholds, zero-rating can apply for residential property sold by its constructor; commercial property may be standard-rated either because it is less than three years old, or it has been opted to tax; exemption is likely in other circumstances, including for the ongoing service charges.

Update 2 (May 2005) to Notice 742 (March 2002) refers.

MEANING OF 'PERSON CONSTRUCTING'

26.64   Taken literally, the zero-rating for the sale of a building by the 'person constructing' would mean that, once it was completed, the zero-rating ceased. Presumably, the draftsman used the word 'constructing' instead of the phrase 'has constructed' so as to allow for the sale of a building not yet finished. The Courts have interpreted the phrase as covering the sale by the original constructor, no matter that this is years after completion.

In *Link Housing Association* ([1992] STC 718), it was held that the sale by a housing association of dwellings to tenants was zero-rated, even though a tenant had to occupy a property for two years in order to acquire the right to buy it.

MAJOR INTERESTS IN RENOVATED DWELLINGS

26.65   The revised zero-rating for the sale of a renovated house now requires the latter to have been empty for ten years. That means prior to the date on which the major interest in the finished property is granted, not the date on which work begins—so the work cannot be within the ten-year period.

The dwelling could be in a block of flats, some of which are occupied. It is the dwelling in question which must have been empty for ten years.

If the building is intended to be used for a relevant residential purpose, the developer will need a certificate of that intention.

GRANTS OF MAJOR INTERESTS IN RECONSTRUCTED LISTED BUILDINGS PRIOR TO 1 OCTOBER 2012

26.66   As with a new zero-rated building, a major interest in a 'substantially' reconstructed listed one is zero-rated for the initial grant, and exempt thereafter. *Note (4)* to *Sch 8 Group 6* contains the following test of substantial reconstruction which apply up to 1 October 2012:

- at least 60% of the cost of the work must qualify for zero-rating; or

- the finished result must incorporate no more of the original before the reconstruction began than the external walls, together with other external features of architectural or historic interest.

From 1 October 2012 zero-rating only applies where a listed building is reconstructed from a shell.

In deciding whether the work on a building has amounted to reconstruction, one must compare its state before and after the work. In *Southlong East Midlands Ltd* (LON/03/789 No 18943), considerable work on a historic building, long unoccupied, was held to be a minor enlargement and modernisation of the house, not reconstruction. This was despite it including demolition of one part and replacement with an extension, together with much internal reorganisation of the rooms.

See **26.7** above for what is a zero-rated building. See the legislation for the precise wording.

SHORT LEASES

26.67   Do not grant a short lease of a new zero-rated building, or one which has been substantially reconstructed. To recover the associated input tax, you need a major interest lease, ie one exceeding 21 years (20 years or more in Scotland).

The test of reconstruction noted above is not easy to meet, so the number of cases has been small.

SALES OF LAND

26.68

Focus

The sale of land is exempt unless:

● it includes a new civil engineering work—which could be below the surface;

● the vendor opts to tax—see below concerning the option to tax for restrictions regarding dwellings.

See **26.5** above for the decision in *Virtue (t/a Lammermuir Game Services) v Revenue and Customs Comrs,* which involved the supply of engineering services supplied with DIY building plots.

GRANTING A MAJOR INTEREST IN A BUILDING AFTER CONVERSION

26.69   *Group 5, Item 1(b)* zero-rates the first major interest in a building which has been converted from non-residential into:

● a building designed as a dwelling or number of dwellings; or

● a building intended for use solely for a relevant residential purpose.

The pitfall in this is that the zero-rating is for the sale of the finished dwelling or relevant residential building. With the exception noted above at **26.34** regarding conversion work for housing associations, the conversion work itself is not zero-rated. The work should be at the 5% reduced rate, and professional fees are standard-rated. In order to recover this VAT, the site owner must either:

- create a zero-rated output by granting a major interest in the finished project to another legal entity; or

- use the DIY Scheme rules in *s 35* to recover input tax incurred on the project—but such a claim cannot be made by anyone using the building for a commercial purpose, such as renting out accommodation in it.

The DIY Scheme rules are, in many cases, a second best alternative because:

- only a single claim is possible, and not until the project is completed;

- records must be kept as required by HMRC;

- although VAT on conversion services can be recovered as well as that on materials, the VAT on professional services and overhead expenses is specifically excluded, in direct contrast to the position where the project is handled as a business transaction and it is sold.

Thus, the planning point of whether to carry out the conversion as a business transaction should be considered before the project begins.

WHAT IS A NON-RESIDENTIAL BUILDING?

26.70   A *non-residential building*, or part thereof, means a building which:

- is neither designed nor adapted for use as a dwelling or dwellings, nor for a relevant residential purpose; or

- if so designed or adapted, no part of it has been used for such a purpose in the last ten years (*Sch 8 Group 5, Notes 7* and *7A*).

However, a non-residential building does not include a garage occupied together with a dwelling (*Group 5, Note (8)*). An agricultural barn is obviously a non-residential building. A public house may appear to be non-residential, but it normally includes living accommodation for the landlord. Thus, when a former public house was split vertically to create two dwellings, the sale of the latter did not qualify for zero-rating: *Calam Vale Ltd* (LON/99/977 No 16869). See also **26.10** and in the comment on conversion work at reduced rate at **26.47**.

Note (9) to *Group 5* says that the conversion of a non-residential part of a building which already contains a residential part, does not qualify unless the conversion:

- creates at least one additional dwelling; or

- is to a building designed for a relevant residential purpose.

APPORTIONMENT FOR MIXED USE BUILDINGS

26.71   If a building only partly qualifies as zero-rated, there will have to be an apportionment of the price for its construction between the zero-rated and standard-rated elements (*Group 5, Note (10)*).

Examples

26.72

- office block including a penthouse or a caretaker's flat;

- shop with living accommodation;

- farm buildings, which include a farmhouse.

SALES OF NEW COMMERCIAL BUILDINGS AND CIVIL ENGINEERING WORKS

26.73   The sale of a new building or civil engineering work is standard-rated because it is an exception to the exemption for interests in land in *Sch 9 Group 1*:

- up to three years from the date of completion (*Notes (2)* and *(4)*), no matter how many other sales there may have been; and

- unless it is a zero-rated building.

This is nothing to do with the option to tax.

Note that *sale* means a sale. Do not confuse the sale of the freehold with the assignment of a lease at a premium!

Once a building is over three years old, the sale is exempt, unless the option to tax has been exercised. A building is completed when the architect issues a certificate of practical completion of the building, or, if earlier, when it is first fully occupied.

A civil engineering work is complete when an engineer issues a certificate of completion, or, if earlier, when it is first fully used (*Sch 9, Group 1, Notes (2), (4)* and *(5)*).

CIVIL ENGINEERING WORK

26.74   There is no definition of *civil engineering work* in the law. One might think that it would cover any structure which is not a building. However, in *GKN Birwelco* (MAN/82/74 No 1430), a Tribunal suggested that the construction of an oil refinery was not a work of civil engineering. It thought that a key factor was whether a civil engineer would be able to design a particular project, and that something was not civil engineering merely because a civil engineer was amongst the designers working on the scheme. The point is potentially important, because a new civil engineering work is automatically standard-rated for three years after completion.

In *En-tout-cas Ltd* ([1973] VATTR 101), the construction of a running track and of a sports ground were held to be civil engineering works. Because of the degree of levelling, grading, and draining, the works were much more than landscaping. A similar conclusion was reached in *St Aubyn's School (Woodford Green) Trust Ltd* (LON/82/260 No 1361), which concerned the conversion of an orchard into a playing field.

In theory, anyone selling land on which such work had been done would have incurred substantial input tax, and would, therefore, opt to tax the sale if they did not realise that it was standard-rated anyway. However, one should take nothing for granted in VAT! Suppose a business owns some building land on which substantial work is needed to clean up the site and prepare it, such as drainage and flood control works. If the business does that work using its own employees and equipment, the input tax involved may be small. Suppose they then receive an offer for the land, which is too good to refuse. Given that much of the work is below the surface, or involves earthworks which have been re-seeded, will they realise that they are selling a site which includes a new civil engineering work? In *Scotia Homes Ltd* (EDN/90/211 No 6044), house plots which included civil engineering work, had been sold without charging any output tax. One cannot opt to tax a house plot to a private buyer, but the option to tax is irrelevant where the civil engineering work is new, so some output tax was due. Thus, there is a pitfall in the rules on new civil engineering works, just as there are everywhere else in VAT!

THE OPTION TO TAX OR ELECTION TO WAIVE EXEMPTION

26.75

Focus

The option to tax—strictly speaking the election to waive exemption—converts an exempt sale or rent of property into a standard-rated output. The advantage of this is that related input tax is then recoverable.

Given that this could include tax incurred on the purchase, construction, or renovation of a building, large sums can be involved. The rules are contained in

Sch 10, paras 2–3. Apart from buildings and bare land, the option also applies to the rental or sale of civil engineering works. Since large sums can be involved, check Notice 742A *Opting to tax land and buildings* for any guidance from HMRC which is additional to, or subsequent to, the comments here.

A business cannot opt to tax—or rather, if it does, the option has no effect (referred to as 'disapplied') on the following (*para 2(2) and (3)*):

- a building intended for use as dwelling;

- a building intended solely for relevant residential or charitable use as defined—except use by a charity as an office; see **26.14–26.16** re relevant use;

- a house plot sold to a private individual on which a dwelling is to be built for that person;

- land sold to a housing association or social landlord (in either case registered under the relevant legislation) for the construction of dwellings or of buildings for relevant residential use;

- a pitch for a permanent residential caravan; or

- a mooring for a residential houseboat—residence permitted throughout the year.

See also **26.101** below, for a problem that arises if the tenant is partially exempt and connected to the landlord.

Prior to 1 June 2008, a single VAT1614 option to tax form was used for notifying HMRC of an election, but from that date, a new expanded range of VAT1614 forms came into force, and are listed below:

VAT1614A—Notification of an option to tax

VAT1614B—Ceasing to be a relevant associate

VAT1614C—Revoking an option to tax within six months (the 'cooling off' period)

VAT1614D—Certificate to disapply the option: Buildings to be converted into dwellings, etc

VAT1614E—Notification of a real estate election

VAT1614F—Notification of the exclusion of a new building from the effect of an option to tax

VAT1614G—Certificate to disapply the option: Land sold to Housing associations

VAT1614H—Application for permission to opt

VAT1614J—Revoking an option after 20 years.

PREVIOUS EXEMPT SUPPLIES MEAN PERMISSION IS NEEDED

26.76   If, prior to opting to tax a property, a business has already made an exempt supply of it—normally rent—it cannot opt without permission from HMRC; although it may meet the terms for automatic permission under one of the four conditions below. To obtain permission, a business needs to complete a form VAT1614H. From 1 June 2008, there is no need to separately opt to tax once permission has been granted.

Automatic permission of an option to tax

26.77   HMRC grant 'automatic permission' (ie a formal request is not required) in the following four circumstances, with each of the automatic permission conditions being referred to as an 'APC'):

- (APC1) It is a mixed-use development and the only exempt supplies have been in relation to the dwellings.

- (APC2) You do not wish to recover any input tax in relation to the land or building incurred before your option to tax has effect; and

    - the consideration for your exempt supplies has, up to the date when your option to tax is to take effect, been solely by way of rents or service charges and excludes any premiums or payments in respect of occupation after the date on which the option takes effect. Regular rental and/or service charge payments can be ignored for the purposes of this condition. Payments are considered regular where the intervals between them are no more than a year and where each represents a commercial or genuine arm's-length value; and

    - the only input tax relating to the land or building that you expect to recover after the option to tax takes effect will be on overheads, such as regular rental payments, service charges, repairs and maintenance costs. If you expect to claim input tax in relation to refurbishment or redevelopment of the building you will not meet this condition.

    Notes: When deciding whether you meet this condition you should disregard:

    — VAT refundable to local authorities and other bodies under *s 33(2)(b)* of the *VATA 1994*;

    — any input tax you can otherwise recover by virtue of the partial exemption de minimis rules (*Reg 106, VAT Regulations 1995*); and

—   any input tax you are entitled to recover on general business overheads not specifically related to the land or building, such as audit fees.

- (APC4) The exempt supplies have been incidental to the main use of land or building. For example, where you have occupied a building for taxable purposes the following would be seen as incidental to the main use and the condition would be met:

    –   allowing an advertising hoarding to be displayed;

    –   granting space for the erection of a radio mast;

    –   receiving income from an electricity sub-station.

The letting of space to an occupying tenant, however minor, is not incidental.

HMRC announced in *VAT Information Sheet 06/09* that, with effect from 1 May 2009, a new APC3 would replace the previous APC3, and had the force of law. The other APCs (1, 2, and 4 above) remained unchanged.

In order to use this new APC3, there are two conditions that need to be met. The first requirement relates to outputs and looks at future supplies. The second requirement relates to inputs and looks at VAT you incur on your costs or purchases.

The first condition relates to the use of the property and must be satisfied in all cases. If the property is to be used for supplies to a connected party and that connected party can recover 80% or more of their input VAT, then this condition is met.

The second condition only needs to be considered in specified situations. These are where the taxpayer expects to recover extra input tax on capital expenditure on the property as a result of opting to tax; and intends or expects to use any part of the capital expenditure for making exempt supplies. Examples of when this condition will be met include where the exempt supplies are 'permissible' or where the irrecoverable input VAT is expected to be £5,000 or less providing there is only business use.

The guidance contains some useful flowcharts to determine when these conditions are met.

Information required by HMRC with a formal request for permission

26.78   If the rules for automatic permission do not apply, a business must ask HMRC for formal permission (with a VAT1614H) so that they can agree the input tax recoverable—and can prevent artificial schemes. The business must quote a date at least a month ahead for the option to take effect, so as to allow HMRC time to consider the request. Until the business gets permission to opt, which will be from a current date, not retrospective, they should not charge output tax.

HMRC require the following details:

- a brief description of the future plans for the property;

- how much input tax they wish to recover, which was incurred in the ten years ending on the date on which the option takes effect;

- how much input tax it expects to recover in the future and on what expenses;

- the value of the exempt supplies in the ten years before the request, together with any more up to the date when the option takes effect. That includes details of any grants made for a premium or prepayment of rent;

- the expected future taxable supplies including how long existing leases are expected to run. The business must also disclose any anticipated exempt supplies, such as those to which the option to tax does not apply—as listed earlier in this chapter;

- whether the business or person funding the property, or anyone connected to either of them, is occupying or intending to occupy any part of it. That is so that HMRC can consider whether the option is disapplied by the anti-avoidance rules explained later in this chapter.

When a business claims for the tax already incurred, that which relates to the past exempt outputs remains irrecoverable. See the *Royal and Sun Alliance* case in **24.51**, re situations in which a property has remained unoccupied pending finding a tenant.

If VAT was incurred more than six months prior to registration, a business would not normally be able to recover it, because of the time limit in the rules explained in Chapter 3, *Registering for VAT.* However, an extra-statutory concession, referred to in *para 7.6* of *Vol V1–13, Chapter 2, Section 7* of HMRC's Internal Guidance Manual, accepts that this creates an anomaly compared with the position of a business already registered, and says that each case will be considered on its merits.

WHO CAN OPT TO TAX?

26.79 Anyone can opt in respect of any property—but of course, the option has no effect until they have an interest in that property. Where the legal owner of a property is, say, a bare trustee, but the beneficiary receives the income, it is the latter who is treated as making the supply, and who should opt to tax in respect of it (*Sch 10 Group 8*).

If a property is in joint ownership, and the supply is, therefore, by the two owners together, they must jointly elect. They will be treated as a single taxable person, and must register as a partnership, even if there is no other joint income.

WHEN SHOULD ONE OPT TO TAX?

26.80   There is no need to opt to tax until a business has incurred input tax related to the property. If the business is occupying the property for its business, the right to recover input tax will depend upon the nature of that business. Opting makes no difference *at that stage,* if there is no rental income. It does make a difference, however, if the business sublets part all of the property, because the right to recover then depends on the rental income being standard-rated. Even then, this only becomes critical once significant input tax is incurred. Note, however, the problem of VAT already incurred on a building subject to the *Capital Goods Scheme*. See Chapter 25 for what happens if the use of the building changes from taxable to exempt, and why a business may have to opt to tax in order to prevent that happening.

See also **26.92** and **26.98** below for further potential problems.

CERTIFICATES FROM PURCHASERS WHICH PREVENT THE CHARGING OF VAT

26.81   A Housing Association which intends to use the property as a dwelling or dwellings for a relevant residential use, or intends to construct that sort of property on the land concerned, must issue the vendor a certificate in the form of a VAT 1614G in order to avoid VAT on the purchase. The certificate must be issued before the sale is completed. That is so even if the intention depends upon obtaining the necessary planning permission.

If part of the future use of the property will be for business, the sale price must be apportioned accordingly. The planning permission could be for mixed use by the Housing Association—say, one or more shop units at ground level, with flats above.

PLANNING POINT

26.82   If you have opted to tax land or commercial property and you are intending to sell it to a Housing Association you could be in for a nasty surprise. A Housing Association can disapply your option to tax by issuing you with either a VAT 1614D form, which disapplies the option to tax on a commercial property that they intend to convert into residential use, or a

VAT 1614G to disapply the option to tax on bare land or to a building that is to be demolished.

If this happens the sale becomes exempt from VAT which could cause a problem to the vendor relating to input tax already claimed on the property which may need to be repaid to HMRC.

Costs of over £250k

If the property cost more than £250K or there has been a renovation or enlargement costing more than £250k it comes within the Capital Goods Scheme and an exempt supply is made of it within 10 years then part of the input tax claimed will have to be repaid to HMRC.

Example

The property was bought five years ago and cost £350k plus VAT of £61,250 (VAT charged at £17.5%). They opt to tax and rent it out for four years plus VAT. The tenant goes bust and the property remains empty for one year before a Housing Association offers to buy the site and intends to demolish the property and build housing on it, they issue a VAT 1614G. The property owner has to repay half of the VAT originally reclaimed (£30,625 five years/by the 10-year adjustment period) as the property is sold as an exempt supply.

No supplies of the property

A similar situation occurs if you buy a property and hold it as stock or do not rent out or trade from it for a period of six years and make an exempt supply of it you have to pay back all the VAT you have reclaimed.

Possible ways out

One way to avoid a VAT clawback is to start any redevelopment of the site, either by starting the conversion of a commercial property into residential or start the construction of the residential property (lay the foundations and one row of bricks) so that you get a zero-rated taxable supply and no clawback of any VAT already reclaimed.

If you have a property rental business you could sell the property with a sitting tenant and, providing the housing association is willing to opt to tax it before the sale, it will be treated as a transfer of a going concern and be free of VAT without having to disapply the option to tax; therefore, there is no clawback of the VAT already reclaimed. The tenant can then leave before the building work starts.

BE CAREFUL OF OPTING TO TAX A POTENTIAL DWELLING

26.83　If a purchaser claims that the option to tax is disapplied because of an intention as to use, ask for evidence of that intention. A disapplication in respect of a building intended for use as a dwelling, will probably apply to a commercial building for which planning permission to convert to a dwelling has been obtained.

In *PJG Developments Ltd* (LON/04/998 No 19097), the appellant bought a closed public house that the vendor had shut down after getting planning permission for conversion back into the two houses it had originally been many years ago. The vendor claimed that the option applied because it had not been told what PJG intended to do with the property, and the public house could be reopened. However, the Tribunal pointed out that the vendor had advertised the place as a *delightful residential opportunity,* so it did know what the likely use was—in contrast to the *SEH Holdings* case (explained below), where the facts were different. The option to tax by PJG was, therefore, disapplied.

In *SEH Holdings Ltd* (LON/98/1362 No 16771), a public house was resold instead of being converted by the purchaser. In confirming that the first sale was standard-rated, the Tribunal commented that, for the option to tax to be disapplied because of an intention to use a building as a dwelling, a vendor must be aware of the purchaser's intention, which must be of use by that purchaser. The option was not disapplied where the purchaser was to sell on to another party that would use the property.

HMRC were clearly mindful of the *PJG* and *SEH* cases when they reviewed the option to tax provisions, as the expanded range of VAT1614 forms introduced on 1 June 2008 included a new VAT1614D form which deals with both scenarios (HMRC have termed interim owners 'relevant intermediaries'—see below). Prior to this, where a purchaser intended to convert to a dwelling *and* make a zero-rated first grant of a major interest (under *Sch 8 Group 5, Item 1*—see **26.62** above), the seller's option to tax was disapplied unless the two parties agreed in writing in advance that it could still be applied.

'RELEVANT INTERMEDIARIES'

26.84   A business is a 'relevant intermediary' if it is purchasing an interest in a building or part of a building and:

- it intends to dispose of the whole of the interest it is purchasing to another, and

- the prospective purchaser has given it a certificate certifying that it:

    — intends to convert the building (or part of it) with a view to it being used as a dwelling or solely for a relevant residential purpose, or

    — is itself a 'relevant intermediary'.

If a business is a 'relevant intermediary', the certificate it receives from its prospective purchaser serves two purposes.

(1)　it will enable it to issue a certificate to disapply its supplier's option to tax (so that the purchase of the building, or relevant part, is exempt);

(2)　it will disapply its own option to tax (if it made one) when it comes to supply the building on to its purchaser (so that the sale of the building, or relevant part, is exempt).

CHECK THE LEASE

26.85　*Section 89* allows VAT to be added to a rent if it is opted, unless the terms of the lease expressly preclude that. Where precluded, the rent is treated as VAT-inclusive, so a landlord should check before acting.

APPORTIONMENT OF THE VAT

26.86　If an opted property includes a residential part, usually a dwelling, the sale or rent must be apportioned to reflect the exempt element. Examples include a shop with a flat above, and an office block with a caretaker's flat.

THE SCOPE OF THE OPTION

26.87　The option applies to (*para 3(3)*):

- the entire building including land within its curtilage;

- complexes consisting of a number of units grouped around a fully enclosed concourse, or buildings linked internally or by a covered walkway.

An initial six-month cooling-off period (three months prior to 1 June 2008) is allowed, during which a business can withdraw the option, subject to the written consent of HMRC (*para 3(5)*) provided:

- The opter has not recovered any input tax as a result of opting to tax.

- The opter has deducted input tax as a result of making an option to tax but will repay it either as part of their partial exemption method calculation (*VAT Regulations 1995, reg 107*) or under the clawback rules (*VAT Regulations 1995, reg 100*).

- The opter has deducted input tax as a result of making an option to tax, and this input tax relates exclusively to one capital item and amounts to less than 20% of the total input tax incurred on the capital item. This means that if at least 80% or more of the input tax was attributable to supplies other than those which would have been taxable as a result of the option, the option can be revoked and the input tax adjusted under the capital goods scheme.

Of course, any taxpayer who does not meet one or more of the conditions can seek the prior approval of HMRC to revoke their option to tax. Applications will be considered on a case by case basis, so it is difficult to make general statements about how this discretion will be applied. However, HMRC will not grant permission whereby a taxpayer is able to avoid or remove a charge to VAT or where there is recovery of VAT up front that is then repaid over many years (eg via the capital goods scheme) unless the total amount to be repaid is minor (less than 20%) when compared to the total VAT incurred on one or more capital items in the same property which have a first interval ending on the same day.

After that, the option is irrevocable for 20 years. Do not, therefore, exercise the option lightly. It has long-term consequences.

An option to tax exercised by any person in relation to a property where no interest has been held for over six years, is treated as being automatically revoked from the end of the six-year period.

However, the six-year revocation does not apply where the opter has been a member of a VAT group during any time in the relevant six-year period and any relevant associate of the opter (including those who were relevant associates prior to the start of the relevant six-year period) has left the VAT group with a relevant interest in the property.

A 'relevant six-year period' means any period of six years commencing with when the opter, or any relevant associate of the opter, ceases to have any relevant interest in the building.

WHAT ABOUT A BUILDING STANDING IN A LARGE AREA OF LAND?

26.88   The curtilage of the building, and thus, the area affected by the option, depends on the circumstances. In Notice 742A (March 2002) *Opting to tax land and buildings*, HMRC say the key is how far the services of the building can be utilised. They quote the example of a racecourse grandstand, which may provide electricity and shelter for stalls or other facilities within its peripheral area. The option would cover all the land using those benefits.

IS THERE A LINK OR NOT?

26.89   An internal fire door between two properties, which can only be opened in an emergency, does not count.

Covered walkways come in many forms. If there is a situation in which it is questionable as to whether two buildings are linked, possibly because the walkway is long and not fully enclosed, opt to tax on both of them to be sure.

On the other hand, if a business does not want the other one to be covered by the option to tax, it should explain that it does not think it is, and send a site plan and description of the walkway, perhaps with photographs, to HMRC to opt on the first one. They take a case-by-case view.

If the question has arisen subsequent to the rent or sale of one of the buildings, discuss the facts with HMRC.

SUBSEQUENT ADDITIONS TO AN OPTED SITE

26.90   Changes to a site after a business has waived exemption can complicate matters. The following is what is understood to be HMRC's views on the matter.

If, having opted to tax building A, a business buys more land adjacent to it, and builds an extension B, the latter is automatically covered by the existing option. However, if the business then builds a separate building, C, on the adjacent land, it is not covered. If it then links C to B, C is still not covered by the option.

From 1 June 2008, if a business constructs a new building on opted land (and that building is not within the curtilage of an existing building) it may exclude the new building (and land within its curtilage) from the effect of the option to tax.

If it decides to do this, the new building will be permanently excluded from the effect of the existing option to tax. But a business may, if it wishes, make a fresh option to tax in the future, subject to obtaining permission from us if appropriate.

A business must notify the exclusion **before the earliest of the following times** (which is when the exclusion will take effect):

● when a grant of an interest in the building is first made;

● when the new building, or any part of it, is first used;

● when the new building is completed.

Under no circumstances will HMRC accept a late notification.

Of course, HMRC may in due course change their views, or, a Tribunal decision may alter everyone's understanding of such situations.

It follows that:

● it would be sensible in many cases to attach a site plan to the notification to HMRC;

● each time further development occurs, consider whether a fresh notification is required, or whether the existing one covers the new work.

Example 26.2— Opting to tax

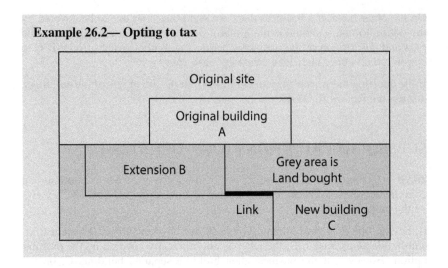

DEMOLISHING AN OPTED BUILDING

26.91 Prior to 1 June 2008, the option terminated if a building was demolished. That meant that a business had to opt to tax for a second time in respect of any new building it was about to construct.

From 1 June 2008, if a business specifies a building, the option to tax will continue to apply to the land on which the building stood if the building is demolished, and to any future buildings constructed on the land. If a business specifies land, the option will apply to any future buildings constructed on the land, but the business can specifically exclude new buildings from the effect of an option to tax if it so wishes.

TAKE CARE WITH NOTIFICATIONS TO HMRC

26.92 HMRC will accept notifications in respect of:

- individual buildings;
- all the buildings owned by a business—unwise; or
- all buildings with specific named exceptions—also unwise.

From 1 June 2008, a business may now make a real estate election which automatically applies the option to tax to all properties subsequently acquired by the business (and members of its VAT group).

Although the real estate election is itself irrevocable, the option over individual properties can later be revoked, provided the normal conditions for revocation are met. Businesses can also make sure that real estate elections do not apply to properties by using a company outside the VAT group as the acquisition vehicle.

Similar rules on revocation currently apply to individual properties acquired under a 'global option', but are set to be withdrawn from 31 July 2009. A business which has made a global option should, therefore, consider making a real estate election to preserve the ability to revoke options on a property-by-property basis where appropriate.

The real estate election will benefit businesses with substantial property portfolios by reducing the required levels of administration. Nonetheless, a real estate election is not beneficial to all. The election can be revoked in relation to each newly acquired property; however, it may be preferable, in order to make a property more marketable, to wait until a prospective purchaser/tenant and their VAT status has been identified. If the purchaser/tenant makes exempt supplies it will not be able to recover the VAT charged on the sale price/rent. If a real estate election has been made, it may be too late to revoke the election once the purchaser/tenant has been identified.

An option only takes effect from the date on which the decision is taken—although see later re input tax incurred prior to opting. For the option to be effective, a business must notify HMRC in writing within 30 days of making the decision, or, under the 'belated notification' provisions, any such longer period as the Commissioners may allow *(Sch 10 para 3(6)(b))*. HMRC will not, however, allow a retrospective notification.

To avoid VAT on property which you are buying as part of a business, the notification to HMRC must be before you complete the deal. See **38.14** and **26.101** below.

THE OPTION TO TAX OFFICE

26.93   Waivers of exemption must be notified to the Option To Tax National Unit, HM Revenue & Customs, Cotton House, 7 Cochrane Street, Glasgow, G1 1GY. They are also accepted by fax to 0141 285 4454, or by e-mail to optiontotaxnationalunit@hmrc.gsi.gov.uk.

However, if an application for a VAT registration is being made at the same time as opting to tax, submit the notification to the registration unit with the application to register.

NOTIFICATION

26.94   HMRC advise that the notification should be made using form VAT1614A or E, which can be downloaded from the HMRC website; see how to find it in the comments on using the website re forms in Chapter 19, *How does a business keep up to date on changes in VAT.* A business does not have to use the forms, and can write in with the notification instead. Where this is done, make sure all the necessary information is provided.

A notification can be in an e-mail; it need not even be as an attachment to the e-mail, so long as it contains all the information they require, and comes from an authorised signatory. However, we would advise against this in case the request is not received or actioned.

Of course, an e-mail can be printed, but writing a formal letter makes it more likely that the notification will be signed by someone who is authorised to take what is an important decision. Also, it can be important to make clear the extent of the property, just in case adjacent land is purchased later, and a plan of the site is often easier to enclose with a letter.

THE 20-YEAR TIME LIMIT

26.95   A paper record is further advisable because, once it has taken effect, the option cannot be cancelled for at least 20 years. How will the business have recorded the fact of having opted in a way which will alert the business and its advisers in, say, 15 years' time?

Suppose a business opted to tax the rent charged to an associated business occupying part of a new factory. It would do that to protect the right to recover the input tax incurred on it. If that business moved out after a few years and the factory was then fully used by the business, the people running it perhaps ten years later would probably know nothing about the letting, and could easily sell the factory without charging VAT on it.

Putting a copy of the letter in the property file is not necessarily effective; if, rather than title deeds, there is a land registry certificate, the latter will not be needed should the property be sold. For a small business, we therefore suggest that it might be useful to include a reminder in the annual accounts as of the option, and its effect on any future lease or sale. So:

- when opting a property, think what permanent record/warning can be created;

- before selling or renting out a property, check whether it could have been opted long ago. Probably, that means asking HMRC.

RECORD THE ELECTION AND AUTHORISE THE NOTIFICATION

26.96   In *Blythe Ltd Partnership* (LON/98/868 No 16011), it was held that:

- an election to waive exemption and its notification are separate matters;

- a notification is of no effect if an election has not been made, or if the person signing it has no authority to do so.

The case arose because the notification to HMRC covered more properties than Blythe had intended. Fortunately for the partners, the Tribunal held that the individual who signed the letter had not had authority to do so and, most importantly, that it had never been the intention of the partners to opt in respect of the additional properties.

Thus, whilst notification is normally evidence of the election, it can be important to make a formal note of the decision to elect, which specifies the properties covered.

WHAT IF A BUSINESS FORGETS TO TELL HMRC?

26.97

Focus

As explained in *Business Brief 13/05*, HMRC will normally accept a belated notification of a genuine decision to opt tax, provided the business can show that it has:

- given them all the relevant facts;

- charged and accounted for output tax from when you say you opted; and

- recovered the input tax related to the supposed taxable supply(s).

In contrast, they probably will not accept a retrospective date if:

- there have been letters or an investigation into the position since that date, and you have not mentioned the option to tax; or

- you have already put forward another reason for charging VAT, such as the supply was not of property or was of a sports facility; or

- a retrospective date would produce an unfair result, or is related to a tax avoidance scheme.

In *Marlow Gardner & Cooke Ltd Directors Pension Scheme* (LON/04/1147 No 19326), the Tribunal upheld the acceptance by HMRC of a notification of an option to tax nearly six years late, and after a building had been sold to Marlow! The challenge of that acceptance by Marlow was dismissed.

BUYING AND SELLING OPTED TENANTED PROPERTY

26.98   The date of notification is a potential pitfall when a business buys or sells tenanted commercial property. It is critical if the transaction is to qualify as outside the scope of VAT under the *Transfer of a Going Concern rules*. See Chapter 38, *Buying or Selling a Business* about these rules.

A deposit creates a tax point, if it is held by the receiving solicitor as agent for the vendor, rather than merely as stakeholder for both parties. In this case, a business must post its notification of the option to tax to HMRC no later than the same day as it pays the deposit. This is because *Special Provisions Order (SI 1995/1268), art 5(3)* makes the *'relevant date'* of the transfer the earliest tax point; ie that created by the deposit rather than when the balance is paid on completion. In *Higher Education Statistics Agency Ltd* ([2000] STC 332), a deposit creating a tax point had to be paid on the spot when the property was bought at auction. The subsequent notification was held to be too late.

Then, in *Chalegrove Properties Ltd* (LON/99/851 No 17151) concerning a negotiated sale rather than an auction, HMRC argued that the notification was late because, despite being posted first-class the day before the Friday on which the deposit was paid, it was not *given* to them no later than the *relevant date*, as required by *art 5(2)*. HMRC did not receive the letter until the following Tuesday.

The Tribunal saw it as unreal that letters of notification must be received before a deposit is paid on an agency rather than a stakeholder basis. To be safe, potential purchasers would have to confirm that receipt with HMRC. If HMRC were right, it also meant that transactions requiring a deposit were disadvantaged compared with those that did not. It held that notification was made in time if posted on the day on which the deposit was paid.

The rationale of the Tribunal's decision was as follows:

- *Section 98* says *that any notification to be served on any person for the purposes of this Act may be served by serving it by post in a letter addressed to that person*;

- *Interpretation Act 1978, s 7* says that service is deemed to have been effected by posting at a time at which the letter would be delivered ordinarily *unless the contrary is proved*. The exception is *unless the contrary intention appears* in the relevant legislation;

- the Tribunal said that *receipt* by HMRC of the notification was not required under the scheme of the TOGC code. A more balanced and workable interpretation was that *written notification* of the election was given when put in the post. In the circumstances of *art 5(2)*, the Tribunal was satisfied that a *contrary intention appeared*.

HMRC have accepted this decision and revised their policy. However, their nitpicking approach in the first place emphasises the need for care.

In *Dartford Borough Council* (VTD 20,246), the supply of opted development land was held to be a TOGC. The case concerned the appellant's sale of an opted freehold site near Dartford Bridge. A development agreement was in place with a third party, and agreements for lease to a supermarket (Sainsbury's) were in place but, at the time of sale, little actual development work had taken place on the plots beyond preparatory works. The sale agreement stated that the parties understood the transaction to be a TOGC, but HMRC sought to deny TOGC treatment with an argument that the *'same kind of business test'* was not satisfied.

HMRC contended that the appellant always intended to sell the plots and never intended to hold the plots and receive rent, whilst the purchaser intended to hold the plots and receive rent from them. The Tribunal rejected this contention, finding that the appellant did, prior to the sale, have an intention to hold the plots and receive rent. Thus, the same kind of business test was satisfied. This decided the case in the appellant's favour, but para 10 of the decision is also notable in that the Chairman suggested that, even if there had been a prior intention to sell the plots before completion of the buildings, TOGC treatment would still have applied.

On a wider point, the Chairman then went on to heavily criticise HMRC at paras 14 and 15, where, amongst other things, he accused the author of the HMRC Statement of Case of having *'no idea what an agreement for lease was'*. Ouch!

IF PAYING VAT ON AN OPTED PROPERTY, ALWAYS OBTAIN A VAT INVOICE

26.99   If asked to pay VAT on the purchase price of the property or on a rent because it is opted, request a copy of the notification to HMRC. Completion of the purchase of the property will involve paying a large sum of VAT, which it might be subsequently impossible to get back from the vendor should it transpire that the latter had not notified HMRC. Paying rent involves a longer-term relationship, and the possibility of being able to withhold the VAT from subsequent payments. All the same, it is wise is to make sure that the option is effective.

In *Russell Properties (Europe) Ltd* (EDN/95/330 No 14228), input tax on the purchase of a property was held to be irrecoverable because the vendor had failed to notify HMRC of its option to tax.

A tax invoice should be part of the documentation handed over between the lawyers at completion of any property transaction that includes VAT.

Possible traps include:

- a business is buying a building from a company it does not know, and which may not even be a UK one. How does it know the vendor is registered and, thus, in a position to issue a valid tax invoice?

- when a tax invoice is issued by the solicitor on the vendor's behalf—how will it be reflected promptly in each accounting system—for both input and output tax?

- suppose the solicitor issued the tax invoice prior to completion, on being asked by the other side 'so we can get it into our current return'?

- suppose the solicitor acting in a purchase completes without a tax invoice, either neglectfully, or possibly against a verbal assurance of one being forthcoming, and:

    (i)   the vendor is a company based in the Isle of Man, which is owned by a foreign national based overseas. It may not even be registered for VAT; or

    (ii)   the vendor is a Channel Islands company. Assuming the property is its only UK asset, it could not be registered—except as a consequence of opting and therefore making a taxable supply in the UK; or

    (iii) the vendor is a company in liquidation; or

    (iv)   the property is being sold by a mortgagor.

You might have much difficulty in obtaining a tax invoice!

SERVICE CHARGES AND THE OPTION TO TAX

26.100   Exercising the option to tax entails standard-rating service charges, since they follow the liability of the main supply of rent. It would be easy to overlook this, especially if the charges are collected by an agent separately from the rent.

ANTI-AVOIDANCE RULES

26.101

Focus

An anti-avoidance rule disapplies the option if:

- a business is selling or renting a property which is subject to the Capital Goods Scheme; and

- the use of the land will **not** be wholly or *substantially wholly* for making taxable supplies; **and**

- that use will be by the business, a person responsible for financing the development of the land, or a person connected either with the business or such a person.

HMRC say that *substantially wholly* means at least 80% taxable use (para 13.9.1 Notice 742A (June 2010)).The rule is complicated, as readers will discover if they try to follow it through the subparagraphs added to *Sch 10, paras 2* and *3*. However, a business will not need to worry about this anti-avoidance rule in most ordinary commercial projects to develop a property for sale or letting. It is aimed at preventing partly exempt businesses, such as banks and insurance companies, from reducing the non-recoverable input tax normally incurred when refurbishing existing offices or moving into new ones, by having an associated company incur the expenditure and renting the property to them. If the option to tax were effective in such a situation, it would enable the recovery of all the VAT on the capital expenditure, and the payment of much smaller amounts on the annual rent.

An example of the complexity of this anti-avoidance rule is *Sch 10, para 3A(7)* and *(13)*. These rules say that land is exempt, and that an option to tax is therefore disapplied if, despite granting a lease, the business still occupies the land either alone or together with others, even if they occupy only part of it.

In *Brambletye School Trust Ltd* (LON/2000/0456 No 17688), a school built a sports hall which it let to a company it controlled. Although the rent of £28,000 a year was paid, the company had no employees, and was managed by the school bursar. There were some bookings from outside organisations, but there were no outside members and the main use was by the school. The membership fees to pupils were charged as part of the school fees, and the pupils used the facilities under supervision by the staff. The Tribunal held that the school therefore occupied the sports hall itself. 'Occupation' was a less formal concept than 'possession'. Even if the pupils occupied the hall as members of the club, rather than as pupils of the school, the latter also occupied the hall at the same time through the presence of its staff.

From 18 March 2004, changes to prevent the sidetracking of the anti-avoidance rules were made by inserting *arts 5(2A)* and *(2B)* into the *Special Provisions Order (SI 1995/1268)* and by amending *Sch 10, paras 2* and *3A*. The rules now catch the sale of a building without VAT as the transfer of a going concern to an independent *Special Purpose Vehicle*, which then opts to tax a lease to the exempt user, or the sale of a company owning a building with a taxed lease. The option to tax by the purchaser is disapplied if it was, or would have been, by the vendor. The normal TOGC rules are explained in Chapter 38, *Buying or Selling a Business*.

The above comments are only a summary of complex rules. If a business thinks it might be affected by them, take professional advice.

In *Halifax plc v Customs and Excise Comrs* (C-255/02), the taxpayer undertook a planning arrangement in order to increase its VAT recovery on the construction of a new call centre. HMRC challenged this scheme, and the case proceeded to the ECJ together with two similar avoidance schemes (*University of Huddersfield Higher Education Corporation v Customs and Excise Comrs* (C-223/03) and *BUPA Hospitals Ltd v Customs and Excise Comrs* (C-419/02)). The ECJ addressed the question of whether transactions carried out for tax avoidance purposes could be supplies of goods or services and an economic activity. In the *Huddersfield* case the ECJ took it upon itself to additionally rule that the existence of a tax avoidance motive is irrelevant to the question of whether a transaction is a supply of goods or services.

The ECJ went further in the *Halifax* decision than the previous courts had done. It said that no right to input tax deduction existed where the claimant has engaged in an 'abusive practice', and that where an abusive practice exists, the transactions must be redefined so as to re-establish the situation that would have prevailed in the absence of the transactions constituting that abusive practice.

The Court added that an abusive practice can be found to exist only if, first, the transactions concerned result in the accrual of a tax advantage the grant of which would be contrary to the purpose of the Sixth VAT Directive, and, second, it must also be apparent from a number of objective factors that the essential aim of the transactions concerned is to obtain a tax advantage (as the Advocate-General observed in his Opinion, the prohibition of abuse is not relevant where the economic activity carried out may have some reason other than the mere attainment of tax advantages). The Court also noted that whilst Halifax appeared to have sought an advantage contrary to the purpose of the Sixth Directive, the problem in this case appeared to stem in part from UK law allowing the transactions in question to have the effect being sought after. Moreover, the Court also noted that:

> 'Where the taxable person chooses one of two transactions, the Sixth Directive does not require him to choose the one which involves paying the highest amount of VAT. On the contrary, as the Advocate-General observed in point 85 of his Opinion, taxpayers may choose to structure their business so as to limit their tax liability.'

Following the *Newham College* case ([2008] STC 1225) in the House of Lords HMRC have revised their interpretation of the law.

The change in interpretation concerns the correct test of 'occupation' for the purposes of anti-avoidance provisions in *VATA 1994, Sch 10, paras 12–17*. The revised interpretation acknowledges that physical presence on its own is not the correct test of 'occupation'. To be in occupation, there must also be the right to occupy as if that person is the owner and have the ability to exclude others. HMRC say '*this means a person must have actual possession of the land along with a degree of permanence and control*'.

With regard to the third bullet point above, the mechanistic nature of the anti-avoidance test has resulted in concerns about the effect of the measure on certain transactions. For example, an option to tax can be disapplied where a bank has provided finance to an unconnected developer for the construction of a shopping complex and, at the time the finance is agreed, intends to occupy one of the retail units. As a result of the disapplication, the developer's supplies are exempt from VAT and the VAT incurred on the construction work becomes an additional cost. The potential disapplication of the developer's option can also cause difficulties in relation to the raising of finance.

Under the amendments made with effect from 1 April 2010 an option will not be disapplied as long as the part of the building occupied by the financier is minor and the terms of the new '10% occupation rule' are met.

Occupation of any part of the land or building (even a very small proportion) normally counts as occupation for the purposes of the anti-avoidance test. However, from 1 April 2010 a person is not treated as being in occupation of a building for the purposes of the test where the conditions of the new 10% occupation rule are met. This new rule prevents disapplication of an option to tax where the occupation is by a development financier (see para 13.6 of Notice 742A) or a person connected to a development financier, and the part occupied is a small proportion of the total building.

Following the introduction of the 10% occupation rule a person who would otherwise be 'in occupation' for the purposes of the anti-avoidance test is treated as not occupying any part of a building if they satisfy the following conditions:

- the person(s) in occupation must not be the grantor or a person connected to the grantor;

- there must be no intention or expectation at the time of the grant that the person(s) will occupy more than 10% of any building (or part of a building) included in the grant at any time during the grantor's CGS adjustment period. Where the financier is in occupation together with persons connected to him, or alternatively, the occupation is by a number of persons connected to the financier, it is the combined occupation that counts towards the 10% threshold;

- the proportion of the building occupied is to be calculated in relation to the whole of the single building or where the grantor holds an interest in only part of the building, that part in which an interest is held immediately prior to the grant being made (this includes any part of the building in which an interest is held by a person(s) connected to the grantor);

- where a number of buildings are included in the same grant, the rule is applied to each building on an individual basis. Where the 10% threshold is exceeded in relation to any of the buildings, the conditions are not satisfied;

- for the purposes of the rule a single building takes its meaning from *VATA 1994, Sch 10, paras 18(4)–(7)* and includes some linked buildings and enclosed complexes; or

- the conditions are not satisfied where the person(s) occupies any land included in the grant which is not a building. However, the occupation of land that falls within the curtilage of the building or is used for parking vehicles can be disregarded as long as such occupation is ancillary to that of the building.

Chapter 27

Recovery of foreign VAT: the 8th and 13th Directives

SIGNPOSTS

- If you incur VAT in other Member States of the EU when you are on business you can recover that VAT from that national tax authority using an electronic-based recovery system until such time as the UK leaves the EU (see **27.1–27.4**).

- Some countries outside the EU have reciprocal agreements that allow VAT recovery from their national tax authority (see **27.5**).

27.1 This chapter describes the system which enables a VAT-registered business to reclaim from the fiscal administration of another EU Member State, the VAT it has incurred in that Member State. Similar rules apply to businesses established outside the EU. In some circumstances, it may even be possible to reclaim VAT from countries outside the EU.

THE LAW

27.2 The law is in *Pt XX* of the *VAT Regulations (SI 1995/2518)* for EU traders and *Pt XXI* for non-EU traders. Notice 723 covers both sets of rules.

VAT INCURRED IN OTHER EU MEMBER STATES (8TH DIRECTIVE REFUNDS)

27.3 The *8th Directive* enables traders registered in an EU Member State to recover input tax incurred in another EU Member State, provided that they are not liable to register there.

The rules apply primarily to services. Although a business may succeed with a claim for minor expenditure on goods used at, say, a trade exhibition, it cannot use the *8th Directive* to reclaim on goods bought for resale. Normally, these would be zero-rated by the supplier on removal to the UK anyway, under the

609

rules explained in Chapter 20, *Exports*. If they remain in the other Member State, the business will have to register there, and account for VAT when it disposes of them.

From 1 January 2010, the paper-based procedure for *8th Directive* refunds was replaced with a fully electronic system (NB the current *13th Directive* provisions are not affected).

Focus

Under the new electronic system:

- The claim will be sent to the Member State of Refund (MSR), via the business's own tax authority (the Member State of Establishment (MSE)) thus eliminating the need for a VAT 66 certificate of status.

- The format of the claim is to be simplified, introducing the use of standard fields for information and coding purposes. This more user-friendly approach will reduce the number of issues due to language problems.

From 1 January 2010, claimants have an extended period of nine months (rather than the previous six-month period) in which to submit claims for VAT incurred in the preceding calendar year. Once the MSR receives the claim, it must normally be processed within four months and, if approved, repaid within ten working days. If further information is requested by the MSR the processing period can be extended up to a maximum of eight months. If these time limits are exceeded then interest will be paid.

In the event that a claim is refused in whole or in part, the decision by the MSR can be appealed. The reconsideration and appeals process will be administered by the MSR in line with their existing procedures. Guidance on appeal procedures in each Member State will be made available by HMRC.

Businesses will be informed about the progress of their refund claims at certain key stages.

There are standard *de minimis* limits for claims that apply in all Member States. The following *de minimis* limits apply to claims:

- If the claim relates to a period of less than one year but not less than three months it must be for at least €400 or equivalent in national currency.

- If the claim relates to a whole year or the remainder of a year it must be for at least €50 or the equivalent in national currency.

A maximum of five claims can be submitted to each MSR per year—essentially one per quarter, plus a final 'sweep-up' claim to capture any invoices not previously claimed during that year. But businesses do not have to make quarterly claims; for example, it is possible to make two six-month claims or one 12-month claim. Claims may not, however, be made for a period of less than three months, unless they are for the remainder of a year.

A UK business that wishes to make claims for recovering VAT incurred in another EU Member State will have to register on the UK portal via the Government Gateway.

When submitting claims, a UK business will need to record some basic details (eg name, address, VAT number, bank account details) and declare that it does not account for VAT under a margin or flat-rate scheme nor make any supplies in the MSR. This information will be stored and automatically transposed onto the individual claim forms for each MSR as each claim is made.

The use of standard fields of information and standardised codes of information in the new electronic refund system will greatly reduce language problems. However, there are some limited free text fields and an MSR may also request further information. Applicants will have to follow the MSR language preferences for those fields. During the discussions on the development of the new system, many Member States indicated that as well as the language of that Member State, they intend allowing English to be used.

BAD NEWS ON TRAVEL COSTS

27.4   Unfortunately, many other Member States, including France and Italy, do not allow recovery of input tax by their own traders on such travel costs as hotel rooms and meals. That being so, they will not repay such VAT to a UK business either. The position does vary from State to State so, if the VAT is significant, it is worth checking.

However, all repay on exhibition stand costs, though with varying standards of efficiency. Italy, for example, has a poor reputation in this respect.

CLAIMS BY OVERSEAS TRADERS UNDER THE EC 13TH DIRECTIVE

27.5   The *13th Directive* permits traders from outside the EU to make claims from the VAT administrations of EU Member States. The rules are similar to those applicable to *8th Directive* claims, but the claim year runs to 30 June instead.

Claim form *VAT 65A* can be downloaded from HMRC's website. Alternatively, write to HMRC, VAT Overseas Repayments Unit, Foyle House, PO Box 34, Dungreggan Road, Londonderry, BT48 7AE, Northern Ireland (Tel: 02871 305100, Fax: 02871 305101, email: enq.oru.ni@hmrc.gsi.gov.uk).

BEWARE THE TIME LIMITS

27.6   Watch the time limits for claims. These are often enforced.

CLAIMS FROM NON-EU COUNTRIES

27.7   A business may be able to claim from non-EU countries. Some non-EU European States, such as Iceland and Liechtenstein, have a similar system. If a business is incurring significant non-EU VAT, ask if is possible to make a claim. If the claim is refused, the business can complain to HMRC, because they have power to withhold repayments under the *13th Directive* from traders in a country which does not reciprocate!

Chapter 28

What is a business?

SIGNPOSTS

- A business does not have to be carried out for profit so charities, trade unions, museums and similar organisations can be regarded as being in business and need to register for VAT (see **28.1–28.8** and **28.19**).

- Some organisations are partly business and partly non-business so not all input tax can be recovered (see **28.9–28.13**).

- Renting out an asset through an agent is not necessarily a business activity (see **28.14**).

- Some case studies in what constitutes a business (see **28.17–28.25**).

28.1   The question 'What is a business?' may seem unnecessary at first thought; the difference between a private individual and a business appears obvious. However, like so much in VAT, it is not as simple as that. Take a charity for the relief of distress, like Oxfam; its charitable activity is obviously not a business. However, its retail shops create substantial taxable supplies, and thus, a liability to be registered for VAT. Many other charities are in business through their fund-raising activities. This chapter explains the consequences, and illustrates the problem with stories from the large number of cases on the subject.

In the VAT case *CCE v Lord Fisher* [1981] STC 238 the judge laid down six tests for indicating that a business exists, they are:

- Is it 'a serious undertaking earnestly pursued' or 'a serious occupation, not necessarily confined to commercial or profit-making undertakings'?

- Is it 'an occupation or function actively pursued with reasonable or recognisable continuity'?

- Has it 'a certain measure of substance as measured by the quarterly or annual value of … supplies made'?

- Was it 'conducted in a regular manner and on sound and recognised business principles'?

- Is it 'predominantly concerned with the making of ... supplies to consumers with consideration'?

- Are those supplies 'of a kind which, subject to differences in detail, are commonly made by those who seek to profit by them'?

INTERNATIONAL ORGANISATIONS

28.2   See **23.38** for comments on whether an overseas customer is in business. That coverage also refers briefly to the status in the UK of tourist offices and international research establishments.

TRADE UNIONS, PROFESSIONAL AND OTHER PUBLIC INTEREST BODIES

28.3   Public bodies, such as professional associations, are usually in business because they supply services to their members. See **11.101** for the exemption for subscriptions—including notes on cases.

A quango-type public body might not be in business if all it did was to collect a statutory levy from all the organisations with which it was involved. In *Apple and Pear Development Council* (1986 STC 192), the levy paid by all growers to cover the administrative costs was held not to be for any supply because the individual growers did not receive specific benefits—just as one does not when paying council tax or business rates. However, a further voluntary contribution towards marketing the fruit was for a supply.

EXAMPLES OF ACTIVITIES WHICH ARE PARTLY BUSINESS

28.4   There are far more organisations whose activities are partly non-business than one might think. Examples are:

- relief of distress charities, which raise funds through trading;

- colleges and educational establishments, such as colleges and universities, which are engaged in the economic activity of education for fees, but which have some students under 19 who do not pay;

- museums that do not charge for entry to the main collections, but do charge for special exhibitions or have shops;

- public bodies, like the House of Commons, whose main activity is non-business, but which have income from sources such as restaurants and bars;

- churches that charge for entry to parts of the building or have shops.

SPECIAL RULE FOR FREE ENTRY TO MUSEUMS AND GALLERIES

28.5   *Section 33A* provides for a special refund to museums and galleries that do not charge for entry. This is claimed separately from the normal VAT system. Only bodies specified by the Treasury are eligible. The *Refund of Tax to Museums and Galleries Order (SI 2001/2879)* lists a wide range of such bodies of national importance, most, if not all of which, are publicly funded. The special refund is intended to encourage such institutions not to charge for entry.

A small museum owned by a charity could presumably apply to the Treasury to be added to the specified bodies, but it would only be worth doing so if the VAT reclaimed would exceed the possible income from admission charges.

FREE ENTRY DOES NOT NECESSARILY MEAN NON-BUSINESS

28.6

Focus

Input tax is not necessarily disallowed just because an activity includes doing something without charge.

In *Imperial War Museum* (LON/92/118 No 9097), the Tribunal held that there was only a single business activity even though admission charges were waived from 4.30–6 pm each day, and also for school parties and certain visitors. It rejected HMRC's argument that, although the business activity did not cease, the free admissions amounted to 'non-supplies'.

Taxable income was generated, even when entry was free, from:

- sponsorship—the proposition to sponsors was based on total visitor numbers;

- takings in the restaurant and the shop.

The strength of an argument that free entry does not necessarily mean loss of input VAT varies from case to case. For instance, a cathedral or large church will normally solicit donations from visitors, but may charge fees to enter a part of the building such as the crypt and/or have a shop. Thus, as taxable income is generated, there is a right to recovery of a proportion of the input tax incurred in maintaining the building as a whole. How to calculate that proportion must be negotiated.

CHARITIES

28.7   An organisation does not avoid being in business simply because it is a charity. Charities benefit from numerous reliefs from VAT. Examples are the zero-ratings in *Sch 8 Groups 12* and *15*, and the exemptions in *Sch 9 Group 7 Item 9,* and in *Groups 10, 12* and *13*. However, charities are subject to the same rules as everyone else. If they make taxable supplies in the course or furtherance of a business to a value exceeding the registration limit, they must register for VAT.

TO BE OR NOT TO BE IN BUSINESS

28.8   Sometimes, an organisation wants to be in business; sometimes, it does not. For instance, if the organisation is going to use a new building for a non-business charitable purpose, it can get the construction or purchase zero-rated. Thus, not being in business can save substantial VAT on a property project.

Of course, it is better still to have zero-rated *outputs*, since all related input tax is then recoverable including that on ongoing overheads; however, it is unusual for a charity to have all or most of its income zero-rated.

See **26.17** for comments about the non-business situations on *Yarburgh Children's Trust* and *St Paul's Community Project Ltd*. HMRC said in *Business Brief 2/05* that they would accept that the provision of nursery and crèche facilities by small charities was non-business in cases which are 'broadly in line'.

Further argument seems likely. For instance, if a charity is constructing a building for the provision of heavily subsidised education, and it could establish that it was not in business, it would avoid incurring input tax on the construction work that would otherwise be non-recoverable against its exempt supplies of education.

A scenario similar to this occurred in *Quarriers v Revenue and Customs Comrs* (VTD 20,660), where HMRC tried to argue that the provision of epilepsy support and care services by the appellant to the Scottish Health Boards was a business supply, the effect of this being that it would not be able to obtain zero rating for a new epilepsy centre building (the question of whether the building was 'relevant residential' was not explored by the Tribunal).

HMRC's argument was based solely on the fact that the appellant had a customer base, provided support services, and charged the Health Board for them. As such, there was an economic activity. The Tribunal was, however, swayed by the fact that the appellant was the sole supplier of the services in Scotland (there was no general marketplace or distortion of competition), and the charges to the Health Board simply covered part of the costs of the service.

As such, there was no profit motive, so the Tribunal used the principles set out in *Yarburgh* to allow the appellant's appeal.

Comment later in this chapter about the definition of 'business' and various cases, including *Yoga for Health Foundation*, illustrates the difficulty of establishing that income is non-business. For *Yarburgh* and *St Paul's* to have a much wider impact would require sidestepping, if not overturning, the principles of some of these older decisions!

HMRC has published updated guidance on the VAT treatment of grants and contracts to clarify which services are liable to VAT. This area has become increasing uncertain over the last few years and has caused some problems for the charity sector.

As part of the guidance, HMRC published a list of things that would indicate a service is 'business' and subject to VAT. These include:

- if the funder believes they are receiving something in return for a payment;

- if the contract between the supplier and funder is legally binding and connected to a business activity; and

- if the funder will attempt to control how the money is spent, maybe imposing specific targets in terms of quantity, quality, timeframes etc.

HMRC's guidance says in summary: 'The principal factor to consider is if a specific supply is made to the funder or a third party in return for a payment. If so then the payment is consideration for a supply, but if this direct link is not established then the payment can be treated as outside the scope of VAT.'

HMRC's guidance says that where the charity sets its own targets and the funder does not attempt to control how the money is spent beyond seeing that the funds are properly managed are likely to be a grant and outside the scope of VAT. Any monitoring is no more than simply ensuring the payments are appropriately spent.

THE CONSEQUENCES OF BEING PARTLY IN BUSINESS

28.9

Focus

Being VAT-registered because of a business activity does not mean that *all* the input tax incurred can be recovered. A business is only entitled to reclaim the tax which relates to a taxable activity *s 24(5)*.

Thus a charity can recover:

- all the VAT directly attributable to its taxable activities; and

- a proportion of the VAT incurred on the part of its overheads that are partly devoted to running the business side.

This is similar to the partial exemption calculations discussed in that chapter, although, in theory, the calculations are in two stages. That is to say:

- first, the organisation identifies the VAT attributable to the business activities. All that related to the non-business ones does not qualify as input tax, let alone input tax which might be recoverable;

- secondly, the organisation then identifies the business VAT related to the taxable activities. In other words, if there are any exempt supplies made by the business, it must carry out a partial exemption calculation.

In practice, the business/non-business and the taxable/exempt calculations are often done as a single combined stage, because it is difficult to separate the VAT related to the non-business side of an organisation that operates out of a single office, and, in which, everyone is involved in both the business and non-business activities. Of course, to do the calculation as a single stage, one needs to be able to value both activities on the same basis. Typically, this means using money values, those of the non-business side being represented by grants and donations, but each case depends upon its facts. However, this approach was rejected as inappropriate by the High Court in *Whitechapel Art Gallery* ([1986] STC 156).

HMRC subsequently announced that they regarded this as applying only to these circumstances—a gallery, many of whose exhibitions were free, but which charged entry fees for some events. They said nothing about the basis negotiated with *Whitechapel,* and they continue to use the method in other situations.

CHARITIES—INPUT TAX ON FUNDRAISING

28.10   Following *Church of England Children's Society* (VTD 18,633, [2005] EWHC 1692 (Ch))—appealed to the High Court and remitted back to the Tribunal—HMRC have accepted that input tax incurred on fund-raising is recoverable to the extent that the funds raised can be shown as related to the charity's business activities, as well as to its non-business ones (*Business Brief 19/05*). Of course, the proportion related to the business activities is only recoverable to the extent that they are taxable rather than exempt supplies.

Fundraising is done in many ways. A key point to understand is that input tax on fund-raising is an overhead, and is not disallowed just because it is being done in order to obtain donations which are themselves non-business. Given that most charities have some taxable supplies, a partial recovery is often possible.

ELABORATE SCHEMES CAN BE DIFFICULT TO MANAGE

28.11   Beware of advisers who seek to maximise the recovery in calculations, for which, they will charge fees. Of course, it is worth letting them get back whatever they can persuade HMRC to agree to, provided that their fees are merely a percentage of that recovery. However, be careful about the future accounting system. VAT specialists can produce sophisticated ideas, but they tend not to understand anything about the routine management of organisations. The danger is that the required procedures or calculations are so complicated, that the staff who must operate them are at risk of getting it wrong in future.

It is worse still for charities, because their administrators are unlikely to be knowledgeable about VAT; unsurprisingly, they often find it difficult to understand the principles of non-business/partial exemption recovery calculations and Capital Goods Schemes adjustments.

So, in any organisation, make sure that the way VAT recovery is worked out is carefully explained in a detailed document—which is held on the computer, and can be updated as new points arise.

PLANNING TO BE IN BUSINESS

28.12   Most of the time, one is 'in business' for VAT purposes whether one likes it or not. However, sometimes one wants to be in business in order to recover input tax being incurred on a project.

Suppose a local group has undertaken a project to restore a feature of historic interest, such as a derelict house or garden; the work takes many years, and substantial VAT is incurred on the cost. If the organisation can obtain VAT registration on the grounds that it either open it to the public, or intend to do so as soon as sufficient progress has been made, the VAT recovered will be substantial. Having to account for output tax on the entry charges and other income will be relatively unimportant, so this planning point could make an important contribution to the success of the project.

DEMONSTRATING THAT THERE IS A BUSINESS

28.13   The above example is relatively straightforward. Assuming that the group has got itself organised, there will be a plan with some financial projections of costs and possible income. As is discussed later in this chapter, it is now well established that one is entitled to register in advance of making any taxable supplies provided that input tax is being incurred for the purposes of a business.

It is not always clear that a business exists or, if it does, when it began. VAT is often incurred a long time, sometimes several years, before the taxable output, to which it is attributable, takes place. Property development projects are examples. In those cases, there is no doubt about there being a business since expenditure is being incurred in the hope of creating an asset, which can be sold at a profit. However, what about an engineer who spends several years working on a machine in his garage in his spare time, more as a hobby than with any expectation that a saleable product will result?

There is no simple answer. Each case depends upon its facts. In many instances, the VAT being incurred is relatively trivial anyway. However, if an engineer can show a credible intention to develop a machine into a saleable product, he is entitled to register for VAT. Having obtained that registration, the engineer is entitled to retain all the VAT claimed, even if the project fails.

Remember, VAT is not taxable on profits or losses but on transactions. Even if all the transactions are expenses, there can still be a business. Naturally, HMRC will look carefully at whether the expressed intention to develop a business is credible, and at whether each expense incurred is properly attributable to that intention.

In the case of *Gravel Road Records Ltd v HMRC* [2017] UKFTT 80 (TC), the appellant set up a sound recording studio but HMRC argued that there was never any intention to run a business and cancelled his registration. The appellant was not in a position to offer production and sound recording services immediately because it first had to construct the studio. The construction of the studio took much longer than expected and the two potential clients identified by the appellant dropped out of the project. Although efforts were made to secure other clients, none were identified as the recording industry was suffering difficult business conditions. The appellant evidenced its intentions to trade with various invoices for building works, equipment and advertising. The appellant estimated that the studio might generate fees of around £500 to £700 per day.

The Tribunal concluded that the appellant at all times intended to carry on a commercial business activity that was intending to make taxable supplies and was entitled to request that it be registered for VAT. The appeal was accordingly allowed.

RENTING OUT AN ASSET THROUGH AN AGENT IS NOT NECESSARILY BUSINESS

28.14

Focus

If an organisation wants to justify recovering input tax on an asset, such as a yacht, by hiring it out, it will need evidence of a serious effort to do,

---

> probably including advertising it. If it is handed over to an agent, make sure the agreement is for the agent to act on behalf of the owner, not to take full control and just share the proceeds.

In *Mark Berwick and Christine Berwick* (LON/00/1190 No 17686), a single charter to a yacht chartering organisation was held not to be an economic activity.

In contrast, *Trevor Brian Vaux Stockdale T/A Compass Charters* (LON/03/864 No 18757), who also handed over his yacht to an agency, was found to be in business. He insured it himself, and arranged for repairs. He only used it on individual days when it was not chartered out, not for weeks at a time, and he checked what repairs were recorded. Of the small differences from *Berwick*, an important one was his intention at the time to retain the yacht. He had engaged the agency on an ongoing basis, terminable annually, not on a four-year contract as in *Berwick*.

In *Heath House Charter Ltd* [2009] UKFTT 305 (TC) the appeal was against a decision by HMRC to refuse to register Heath House Charter Ltd ('HHC') for VAT on the grounds that it was not in business. HHC purchased a yacht in August 2006 which it said was for chartering through an agent to its directors and a variety of related companies and individuals.

HHC requested registration in July 2006, but was refused. According to HMRC, there was uncertainty around the financing of the purchase of the yacht, and the arrangement with the agent constituted a single charter for the yacht. The Tribunal found that the activities undertaken did actually constitute an economic activity for the purposes of *Art 9* of the *EC 6th VAT Directive*, and that they were carrying on a business in the course of which supplies were being made for a consideration. The appeal was therefore allowed.

WHAT ABOUT VAT INCURRED BEFORE AN ORGANISATION REALISED IT HAD A BUSINESS?

28.15   HMRC have no hesitation in demanding VAT from people who unexpectedly develop hobbies into full-scale businesses. Examples include:

- a professor, who wrote a specialist book on a medical subject which sold so well that the royalties exceeded the registration limit;

- a vintage car enthusiast, who restored vehicles as a hobby which he developed into a business, only to find HMRC refusing to allow him to offset the costs on the vehicles restored during the hobby period.

Of course, in such situations, the problem is often that there are no records of those costs, let alone VAT invoices.

Moreover, the ECJ held in *Watershap Zeeuws Vlaanderen* (C-378/02) that only a taxable person who was acting as such at the time of the purchase of goods, had a right to deduct VAT on those goods. It therefore rejected a claim from a public authority for the recovery of input tax on the cost of a sewage treatment plant, which it had built in its non-business capacity, but which it sold four years later to another body on which it opted to tax the sale.

Thus, though it may seem unfair that input tax incurred earlier in a non-business capacity cannot be recovered once a taxable sale is made, that is a feature of the VAT system. If an organisation was able to claim the input tax, and had the necessary records, there would then be a question of the extent to which the costs carrying the input tax had already been used up during the non-business period.

THE BASIS FOR CLAIMING REGISTRATION AT THE OUTSET

28.16   *Directive 2006/112/EC, Art 9(1)* (previously *Art 4* of the *EC 6th VAT Directive*) defines a 'taxable person' as *any person who, independently, carries out in any place any economic activity, whatever the purpose or results of that activity.*

It defines economic activities as any activities of producers, traders, and persons supplying services including mining, agriculture, and activities of the professions. It says that the exploitation of tangible or intangible property to obtain an income is included. In other words, both rents and royalties are caught.

The ECJ ruled in *Rompelman v Minister van Financien* ([1985] 3 CMLR 202) that one was entitled to VAT registration as soon as one started to incur VAT with the intention of creating taxable outputs. *Rompelman* was a Dutch case concerning the purchase of a flat with a view to making taxable supplies from it, presumably of holiday lettings.

Whilst it would no doubt be wrong to say that HMRC ignored *Rompelman* altogether, they continued to demand a close relationship between the expenditure being incurred and the prospect of taxable supplies, until they lost *Merseyside Cablevision* ([1987] VATTR 134). This involved a project to develop cable TV. Before any work on the cable system could start, a licence had to be obtained, and substantial costs were incurred in putting together the application for this. HMRC said there could be no business until Merseyside had the licence, which provided the legal authority for making taxable outputs in due course.

There may have been other issues but, on the face of it, HMRC never had a chance of winning this case. Whilst HMRC's policy-makers get it right most of the time, they do make mistakes so, if they say an organisation is not in business, do not necessarily assume that they are right!

THE NATIONAL TRUST—A BUSINESS/NON-BUSINESS SITUATION

28.17   *(Note: though detailed, the following comments are not based on any client relationship with the National Trust.)*

An organisation like the National Trust has income from entrance fees, whether paid at the gate or through membership subscriptions, and from shops at its properties. One might think that this would mean that all the input tax incurred on a property open to the public is recoverable. However, there is probably room for argument about this at the largest properties.

For example, some are lived in by members of the family that gave the property to the Trust, and all or part of their living quarters are usually closed to the public. Costs related to this part of a property are not incurred for business purposes, unless it can be argued that the family act as guardians. Any rent charged to them is an exempt supply against which input tax is disallowed.

In a big house, there are always areas not open for other reasons, such as that the access is unsuitable, they are of no interest, or whatever. The question then arises as to whether these areas count as business because they are merely adjuncts to the main parts on display, or whether they are not used for business. Often, it will be apparent that the areas not open are essential to the business consisting of those which are, not some separate activity. Alternatively, they may be used for the agricultural activities, which often take place on the surrounding estate. However, the point should not be taken for granted.

Then there are the properties not open to the public, or for which there are no entrance fees. There are various reasons for this such as:

- the property is currently being restored;

- the property is too small or of insufficient interest to be worth opening regularly, and is therefore let to a tenant; or

- the property is open space, such as seashore or downs, to which it is not feasible to restrict access.

VAT on restoration costs is recoverable, assuming that it is intended to open the property in due course. Properties without regular public access may still be viewable by Trust members that contact the tenant. Since the rent of a dwelling is exempt, this creates an interesting technical problem of deciding which VAT is attributable to the exempt rent, and which to maintaining the property for viewing by members. If one adds to that the possibility that the tenancy provides for the tenant to spend money on doing up the property in the first place, so that the VAT is not incurred by the Trust, there has to be a planning point here! If the property is open space, and charges are not made for access, HMRC are likely to argue that it is not a part of the business activity.

If so, the case of *British Field Sports Society* ([1998] STC 315) may be some help. The Society received several million pounds from members as donations towards a campaign on behalf of field sports. The Court held that the Society could recover the VAT incurred on the costs paid for by the donations, because the Society was carrying out activities on behalf of its members of the kind which they expected in return for their subscriptions. This was despite the donation income being much the larger sum. It suggests that the National Trust might be able to argue that property from which it does not derive an income is, nevertheless, held by it in the fulfilment of its general objectives for which its members pay subscriptions.

THE DEFINITION OF 'BUSINESS'

28.18   There is no definition in the law of what is a business activity. *Section 94* does say that 'business' includes any 'trade, profession, or vocation' and adds that 'deemed to be the carrying on of a business' are:

- club subscriptions;

- admission charges to premises.

Political, religious, patriotic, philosophical, philanthropic, and civic bodies are in business on account of their subscriptions, but the subscription income is exempt under *Sch 9 Group 9, Item 1(e)*. See **11.99**.

AN ORGANISATION CAN BE IN BUSINESS WITHOUT MAKING A PROFIT

28.19

Focus

There is no relief simply because an organisation is loss-making, or because it did not attempt to make a profit.

In *Morrison's Academy and Boarding Houses Association* ([1978] STC 1), the Court of Session pointed out that the meaning of business does not require the objective to be to make profit. This case concerned the provision at cost of accommodation to pupils of the Academy. This was not covered by the exemption for education in *Group 6 Sch 9*, because the Association was independent of the Academy. It was irrelevant that it was a charity and that any surplus income had to be applied towards scholarships at the school with which it was connected.

The Court pointed out that the supplies of accommodation were, with differences of detail, similar to those made commercially. The Association's activities were predominantly concerned with the making of taxable supplies to consumers for a consideration.

BEING IN BUSINESS DOES NOT JUSTIFY RECOVERING ALL INPUT TAX

28.20   The fact that a charity is in business making taxable supplies does not necessarily mean that all input tax is recoverable. In *Nottinghamshire Wildlife Trust* (MAN/03/130 No 19540), the Tribunal agreed that its farming activity of breeding sheep to produce wool and meat, and its management of woods to harvest coppice products and to produce timber, was entirely business. The Tribunal held that it was done in a businesslike manner, and rejected HMRC's argument that the business activity was only producing the outputs, not the management of the sheep and the woods throughout the year. However, that did not allow recovery of input tax on all the costs of managing the land. Although the maintenance of a public footpath could be an unavoidable burden for a commercial farmer, the obligation to repair it was a consequence of the Trust's principal conservation objectives, and should be considered in a different light.

This decision contained only limited facts, and left the parties to agree the matters of detail. However, it is an interesting example of the problem of how to distinguish between input tax related to the business activities, and that generated by the non-business ones. The Trust incurred many of its costs on land managed by volunteers to benefit wildlife, and land made accessible to the public which was also farmed as a business, albeit at a loss.

ASKING FOR MONEY DOES NOT OF ITSELF CREATE A BUSINESS

28.21   In *Lord Fisher* ([1981] STC 238), the judge commented that the Court in *Morrison's* had not intended to lay down principles which, if satisfied, would in all cases show that an activity was a business. They were *indicia*, some more useful than others. Lord Fisher had collected contributions towards the cost of running a shoot from relations and friends. It was held that this was not the making of taxable supplies in the course of a business. 'Business' excluded any activity which is no more than an activity for pleasure and social enjoyment.

Thus, there are no hard and fast rules as to what is or is not a business. One must look at all the facts, and come to a view in the light of the overall picture.

TO BE A BUSINESS, THERE MUST BE SOME CONSIDERATION

28.22 Before starting to incur VAT, stop to think what the output will be that the organisation intends to recover VAT against. There may be an important planning point to consider. In *Royal Exchange Theatre Trust* ([1979] STC 728), a charity raised the money to build a theatre, which it then handed over to the company intended operate it. The High Court held that the gift of the completed theatre was not a supply. A gift could be made in the course or furtherance of a business, but 'business' was not to be construed so widely as to cover a case in which there was no money paid. Moreover the majority of the sums raised had been by donations from the public.

Thus, the problem was the absence of any taxable supplies by the trustees, and without such supplies, they could not register for VAT and recover their input tax. The fact that their activities had been carried on in a businesslike manner was not sufficient. Looking at those activities as a whole, there was no commercial element that could be regarded as a business.

The *Trustees of the British European Breeders Fund* ([1985] VATTR 12 No 1808) did not want to have to charge VAT on the contributions which the fund collected from the owners of participating stallions based in the UK. It distributed those contributions, plus money added under an agreement with the equivalent bodies in other countries, as prize money for sponsored races. On the basis of *Royal Exchange Theatre Trust*, the Tribunal held that:

'... the activities of trustees, who receive money in circumstances in which they do not make taxable supplies in exchange and who then merely distribute such money in accordance with the relevant trusts in circumstances in which they do not receive any goods or services in return are not, in the absence of any other relevant factor, to be regarded as constituting a business.'

The Fund might have lost if it had itself published the lists of participating stallions. Entry in races sponsored by the Fund was restricted to their progeny, and publication might have been held to amount to something done in return, and thus, consideration for the contributions. However, the lists were published by the Thoroughbred Breeders Association, not by the trustees, and the latter had no contractual obligation to the owners of the participating stallions. The trustees, therefore, did nothing in return for the contributions paid to them.

However, consideration can be provided by a third party. See *Largs Golf Club* ([1985] STC 226), where loans to the trustees owning the course, which were made to finance its purchase, were held to be part of the consideration for the facilities of membership in addition to the subscriptions paid to the club.

CONTRIBUTIONS TOWARDS COSTS MAY NOT BE CONSIDERATION

28.23   In *Greater London Red Cross Blood Transfusion Service* ([1983] VATTR 241), 'capitation fees' or 'transfusion fees' negotiated with the DHSS were held not to be taxable supplies made in the course or furtherance of a business. They were intended to be a contribution towards the administration expenses of finding the volunteers. The latter donated their blood, and this was not a business activity. The fact that the blood was donated did not necessarily mean that the Service was itself in business—it merely illustrated the distinction between a voluntary service to the community and a business. The sole object of the Service was to provide a contact point between hospitals and those willing to provide blood, and this was not a business activity.

A PUBLIC FUNDED COLLEGE WAS NOT IN BUSINESS

28.24   *Donaldson's College* (EDN/05/12 No 19258), which educated only deaf children and others with communication disorders, was not in business when funded 60% by the Scottish Executive, 35% by the local authorities of each area from which a child came, and 5% from miscellaneous bequests and minor payments for the use of facilities. No supplies were made to the local authorities: the entire exercise was for practical purposes controlled by central government.

AN ACTIVITY MAY BE A BUSINESS DESPITE MUCH DONATED INCOME

28.25   In *Yoga for Health Foundation Ltd* ([1984] STC 630), a registered charity was held to be carrying on a business even though up to 43% of its income had come from donations. The Tribunal accepted that there was no commercial element or profit motive in the Foundation's activities. Nevertheless they 'bore the indicia of a business'. YFH demonstrates how difficult it can be to show that a charitable activity is not a business.

The *RSPCA* (LON/90/1111 No 6218) was held to be in business when it made charges for treating animals at its clinics. The clinics were running at a substantial loss. By agreement with the British Veterinary Association, local vets provided their services in rotation. Treatment at the clinics was only for emergencies, and where the owner was unable to pay normal veterinary fees. If an operation was done, a fee was agreed in advance, and in about 80% of cases, the whole fee was recovered, possibly in instalments. The Tribunal accepted that services in the clinics were akin to those in veterinary practices. There was a direct link between the payments made and the treatment provided. The fact that much of the RSPCA's income came from legacies was relevant only to the dividing line between its business and non-business activities. Having held that the income at the 37 clinics was received in the course of a business at those clinics, the Tribunal sent the parties away to consider an appropriate apportionment.

COURSES IN RELIGION CAN BE A BUSINESS ACTIVITY

28.26   Similarly, in *Holy Spirit Association for the Unification of World Christianity* (LON/84/179 No 1777), courses of a religious nature at a residential centre were held to be taxable supplies made in the course or furtherance of a business. The Association earned only a small part of its income from the courses. Substantial deficits were met by donations and a subsidy from the Moon Foundation. The Association argued that religious teaching by a religious charity was not a business, and that it had no overall business activity. The Tribunal held that the charges, even if only made to discourage those wanting a free weekend, were 'businesslike'. In *Church of Scientology of California* ([1979] STC 297), the High Court had held that, as a matter of law, there was no reason why a body which promoted a religion or a religious philosophy, could not do so as a business. The fact that the Association was subsidised did not prevent it carrying on a business.

In *Creflo Dollar Ministries* (MAN/01/64 No 17705), a religious convention that had free admission was held to be partly a business activity because its purpose, apart from promoting the Christian faith, was to publicise the videos produced both at it and at earlier events, together with books and audio tapes sold by the appellant. The Tribunal held that the input tax incurred in putting on the convention was recoverable in the proportion that CDM's business income bore to its total income.

RELIEF OF DISTRESS AT BELOW COST IS NON-BUSINESS

28.27   HMRC say on page 30(1) of the VAT Notice 701/1 *Charities* (May 2004) that:

- welfare services supplied by charities are non-business when supplied significantly below cost to distressed people for the relief of their distress;

- the subsidised price must be available to everyone—and the service must be to the individual, not to a local authority;

- 'significantly below cost' means the cost of providing the welfare is subsidised by at least 15% from the charity's own funds, ie that the recipient of the welfare supply pays no more than 85% of the cost of making the supply.

Chapter 29

Agency is special

SIGNPOSTS

- It is important to decide if you are acting as a disclosed or an undisclosed agent as the VAT consequences are different (see **29.4–29.9**).

- The withdrawal of the staff hire concession increased the costs of temporary staff to organisations that could not recover all of their VAT, but a recent Tribunal decision could get round the problem (see **29.12**).

29.1

Focus

A contract of agency involves arranging a supply of goods or services in return for a commission, rather than buying them and reselling at a profit margin.

Many businesses fail to recognise an agency situation when it arises, let alone work out the consequences and determine whether any action is needed to change them.

Although *s 47* contains some rules on agency, they only deal with certain situations. Agency crops up all over the place in VAT. Insurance and finance brokers earn commissions which are specialist subjects in their own right. See the comment on *Sch 9 Groups 2* and *5* in Chapter 11, *So, What is Exempt?* Then there are zero-ratings for several kinds of commission in *Sch 8 Group 7, International Services*. The *Place of Supply of Services Order* contains relief for various agency commissions in *art 14*, and in *art 16* via *Sch 5, para 8*. See Chapter 23, *Exports and Imports of Services*.

Thus, agency is, to a large extent, part of other subjects rather than one in its own right. However, there are points which need to be understood. This chapter explains them, and outlines why sometimes one wants to be an agent, and sometimes not.

WHY AGENCY IS SPECIAL

29.2   Agency is special because it involves a different kind of situation to the one normally met, one which can catch businesses out if they do not think carefully about it. Businesses are often casual in their use of language. They use the word 'agent' without understanding its legal significance. Thus, 'motor agents' are no such thing. They buy and resell vehicles.

Understanding the difference between acting as an agent and as a principal is important. An agent sells on behalf of a principal. Thus, for a sale for £100 on which the commission is 10%, the output is the £10 commission, not the £100. The latter is an output of the principal. This, of course, makes a big difference to their respective VAT responsibilities.

So, if a contract is of agency, there are two supplies: one of the goods or services by the principal, and one of the agency services by the agent. The VAT treatment can be different. For example, a commission is not zero-rated merely because the goods are. Thus, food and books are zero-rated, but a commission for selling them is standard-rated.

AGENCY VERSUS SUBCONTRACTOR

29.3   For a business which sells to retail customers, whether it does so as a principal or as an agent is often important. Examples are a hairdressing salon in which self-employed stylists work, and a taxi firm which uses self-employed drivers. If the salon or the taxi firm act as principals, they must account for VAT on the full retail price. If they are merely acting on behalf of the stylists or drivers in collecting their money, they need only charge VAT on the charges they make to those stylists or drivers.

See **3.32** for some comment on a case concerning a hairdressing salon in which the stylists were held to rent facilities from the salon owner and to sell to the customers. An important point was that there was a written agreement between the salon owner and the stylists, although this in itself is only a guide, and HMRC will take into account all of the circumstances before agreeing to the existence of an agency agreement.

In taxi firms, arrangements tend to be informal. As such, evidence tends to show that, although self-employed, the drivers are subcontractors, so the takings are usually seen as those of the taxi firm. In *Akhtar Hussain (t/a Crossleys Private Hire Cars)* (MAN/99/20 No 16194), the owner of a radio link was held to act as a principal in relation to account work because he bore any bad debts, occasionally gave discounts that were not passed on to the drivers, set the fares, and paid the drivers by deduction from their weekly charges for his services before billing the customer. The same was held in *Robert Snaith (t/a English Rose Collection)* (LON/00/0428 No 16997), where there was no plying for hire, so all work came through the firm; it supplied both account and cash customers, and there was no significant difference in the relationship with the two kinds of customer.

Selwyn Dorfman (MAN/2003/0578 No 18816) was held to be a band organiser who acted as a principal, not an agent on behalf of either the customer or the other musicians. All the fees obtained for gigs were, therefore, his; very expensive, since he paid out a large proportion to the other musicians! Those sub-contractors are unlikely to have been VAT registered, so there would be no input tax to offset against the output tax due.

THE UNDISCLOSED AGENT RULES FOR GOODS

29.4

Focus

An 'undisclosed' agent is a term meaning an agent who acts in his own name so that the supplier and the customer do not know each other's identity.

A commercial reason for this might be that, if the parties did know, they could deal direct and cut out the agent.

If the transaction is in goods, an agent acting in his own name is regarded for VAT purposes as buying and reselling them. That means that the agent is responsible for collecting and accounting to HMRC for the output tax on the full value of the sale. The position on the commission differs according to whether the supplier is another UK, business or is outside the UK.

Non-UK suppliers of goods

29.5 If the supplier is in another EU State, the supply is dealt with under what HMRC call the '*commissionaire*' arrangements. Despite the contract being one of agency, the agent is treated for VAT purposes as buying and reselling as a principal. The agent must obtain an invoice from the supplier for the value of the goods net of commission. Thus, if an agent sells on 20% commission:

- the agent invoices in his own name to the UK customer for £100 plus VAT;

- the non-UK supplier invoices for the goods at £80.

For goods from an EU source, the agent accounts for acquisition VAT, which he offsets in the usual way as input tax. However, the agent still has the output tax on the sale to pay to HMRC.

If the goods are imported, the agent will have import VAT to pay, which is reclaimed in the usual way as explained in Chapter 21, *Imports and Acquisitions of Goods*. The agent accounts for output tax when he collects this on the sale in due course.

HMRC accept that costs incurred in the UK, such as warehousing and handling, can be seen as supplies to the agent, who can therefore recover VAT on them. *Business Brief 9/2000*, which announced the change of policy on commissionaire arrangements, does not say how the charge to the principal to recover such costs shall be treated. Presumably, it will be treated as outside the scope of VAT, but the basis for this is unclear. If the supply is seen as being to the agent for VAT purposes, the refund from the principal can hardly be seen as repayment of a disbursement. Unfortunately, *VAT Information Sheet 3/00* does not deal either with this point or with how VAT on any retrospective volume rebate is to be dealt with.

These 'commissionaire' arrangements for goods brought into the UK avoid the UK agent having to charge VAT on commissions to non-UK principals that might be reluctant to pay it, even though they could reclaim it under the *8th* or *13th VAT Directives*. They were introduced from July 2000 because of the problem that, elsewhere in the EU, Roman law treats an agent acting in his own name in making the supply of goods. That meant that UK agents were at a competitive disadvantage in having to charge VAT on commissions to non-UK principals.

Remember that the commissionaire rules only apply to the VAT treatment of the supply. They do not affect the contractual arrangements between agent and principal.

WHY BUY AS AGENT?

29.6   To ensure that an agent need only charge VAT on the commission, make sure the customer is informed that the agent is selling as an agent in order to avoid the undisclosed agency or commissionaire rules in *s 47*. Notices in a shop and wording on any invoice issued should say so—quoting the supplier's name where that is practicable.

An alternative to acting as an agent is to have a contract under which the goods are bought at whatever sale price is achieved, less the agreed commission. That works for perishable items, such as vegetables, fruit or flowers, where the price varies according to market demand, and unsold goods have to be destroyed.

UK suppliers of goods

29.7   The normal position for supplies from UK suppliers is that the agent obtains a VAT invoice from the supplier for the same value as the sale. The input tax thus offsets the output tax. The agent's commission and VAT thereon is invoiced separately to the principal, whether this is the supplier or the customer. If the principal is the customer, the transaction can be shown on the same invoice as for the goods, in which case there are then two supplies and two sums of VAT on the document. If the principal is the supplier, the agent can, if they wish, use the commissionaire arrangements explained above.

Non-UK suppliers of services

29.8   Similarly, the commissionaire arrangements mean that UK undisclosed agents for supplies of services are treated as making the supplies. Where the place of supply for the service in question is the country of the supplier, this means that the onward supply is by the UK agent. If the service is covered by *Sch 5*, it will be subject to the reverse charge when imported by the agent. See Chapter 23, *Exports and Imports of Services*. In both cases, the onward supply by the agent is standard-rated to a UK principal unless, of course, it is exempt.

PLANNING POINTS ON AGENCY

29.9   Sometimes a business wants to be an agent, and sometimes it does not. Take second-hand goods, such as women's clothing. There is an active market in expensive dresses, suits, and accessories which are lightly worn. Typically, a shop will take these in, charging commission of 25% or so, on a basis such as this:

- initial price   £100
- if unsold after, say, two months, cut to   £50
- if unsold in a further two months, cut to   £25
- if unsold after, say, six months in shop, recycled or given away

What is a VAT-efficient structure for such an arrangement? Since the private owner of the clothes and any purchaser are unregistered, the shop should minimise the output tax on a sale. It could do this by using the *Second-hand Scheme,* under which, it would only have to account for VAT on the profit margin. See that chapter for details. However, using the *Second-hand Scheme* involves keeping special records. It might well be simpler for the contractual arrangement to be one of agency selling on commission, rather than buying and selling the clothes. The owner would not wish to buy the clothes before selling them anyway, in order to avoid unsold items.

If the shop was selling clothes for babies and young children, and it used the same arrangement, the commission would be standard-rated. Yet the clothes are zero-rated! The VAT-efficient arrangement this time is for the shop to take the clothes in on terms that, on selling an item, it buys it in for, say, 75% of the sale price.

Another case in which a business might want to sell as an agent is new goods such as craft items, produced by unregistered suppliers. If it handles the goods as an agent, it accounts for VAT only on the commission to the vendor. The sale of the goods themselves is outside the scope of VAT, being made by the owner (who is unregistered). The point does not apply to works of art bought from the artist, because a gallery is allowed to use the *Second-hand Scheme* for these.

AN EXAMPLE OF THE PROBLEMS OF AGENCY

29.10   One of the reasons agency causes problems is that its existence is not always obvious. For example, a music publisher had a contract with a newly-formed rock group, under which, he:

- hired recording studios and incurred various similar costs for which he paid; and

- was to recoup these in due course by deduction from the group's royalties.

The publisher was, thus, incurring the costs as the agent of the group, and, therefore, had no right to recover the VAT on them as input tax. The problem was that the input tax incurred on the costs was not input tax of the publisher, despite the fact that he had a legal responsibility to the various suppliers to pay for them. He was merely disbursing the money as the undisclosed agent of the rock group.

The contract ought to have provided for the publisher:

- to incur the various costs necessary to enable the group to make the recordings; and

- to make charges to the group, the amount of which would relate to stated expenses incurred in making the recordings, which would only become payable once there were royalties to meet them—when the rock group would either be liable to register, or could do so voluntarily and recover the VAT on the charges.

That would have ensured that the publisher incurred the costs in the first place, and subsequently made an onwards supply to recover the amount of them if the recordings were a success.

The law of agency has been the subject of numerous commercial law cases, let alone VAT ones. The relevant considerations as to what makes a contract of agency depend upon the circumstances, and it would be counter-productive and potentially misleading to attempt to summarise them here.

Allergycare (Testing) Ltd (LON/99/1338 No 18026) is another example of a misunderstanding of agency causing much financial damage. Allergycare charged a franchise fee to self-employed food allergy testers. It arranged with organisations such as health food shops, gymnasia, hotels, and pharmacies, for the testers to carry out tests on their premises. The fee paid by the customer was split between the tester, the venue, and Allergycare. The latter thought that it was supplying exempt medical tests to the public, the testers acting as its agents. The Tribunal found the tests were standard-rated but, luckily for Allergycare, it agreed with HMRC that the testers were not agents. VAT was therefore due on the sums received from the testers, not on the total charged to the customer. That was bad enough, of course, but if Allergycare really had achieved an agency agreement, it would have been far worse.

DOES AN AGENT COLLECT MONEY ON BEHALF OF THE PRINCIPAL?

29.11   There is a pitfall in any situation in which someone else collects money due to a third party. The liability for any output tax lies with the principal, not the agent. The principal, therefore, needs to make sure that it obtains statements promptly, showing the output tax for which it is liable, and any input tax it can reclaim on expenses disbursed on its behalf with, of course, the tax invoices related to the latter. Examples of possible situations are:

●   standard-rated rents collected, maintenance expenditure paid out on behalf of the landlord by a property agent;

●   takings collected by door-to-door salesmen;

●   VAT on the sale of a commercial property, which is held by the solicitor.

In theory, these sums should have arrived in the principal's bank account by the time that the VAT return is due at the end of the month following the end of the period to which it relates. However, that does not mean that they will have been accounted for as outputs of the period to which they relate, rather than of the one in which they are received. See Chapter 7, *The Time of Supply Rules*, for more comment.

EMPLOYMENT AGENCIES—STAFF HIRE CONCESSION

29.12   Under the staff hire concession, HMRC allowed employment agencies to charge VAT only on their commission where the client takes responsibility for paying the temporary employee. That includes when the salary is paid by a payroll company, even if it is owned by the employment business.

This concession was introduced in 1997. However. in the 2008 Budget, it was announced that the staff hire concession would be withdrawn from 1 April 2009. From that date, VAT has to be charged on the full salary, as well as any commission (NB the similar concession applying to secondments of staff for no profit continues to be available).

In profit-making terms, the only concession available now is where a nursing agency supplies nurses or nursing auxillaries to nursing homes and similar institutions, and the supply can be treated as exempt. To qualify, the supply by the agency must meet the following conditions:

- the supply is of nursing staff;

- the employment bureau acts in the capacity as principal; and

- the employment bureau is registered with the Care Quality Commission (CQC)

In the case of *Reed Employment Limited v HMRC* [2011] UKFTT 200 (TC) had accounted for VAT on the full value of its supplies of temporary workers to clients. In 1997 Reed applied for a repayment of overpaid VAT on the basis that it should only have charged VAT on the commission element of its fees.

Reed's argument was that it had acted as an intermediary in finding temps for its clients and had provided an introductory service on the grounds that the temps provided their services to the clients directly. HMRC argued that Reed had made supplies of staff to its clients as principal, the payment for which was the whole amount charged to the client.

In reaching its decision the Tribunal looked at the 'economic reality' of the supplies made by Reed to its clients. It found that Reed's activities did not amount to a supply of staff because Reed did not exercise control over the temps at any stage, meaning that no control of the worker could pass from Reed to the client. Consequently, Reed made a more limited form of supply—an introductory service combined with a number of ancillary services (eg evaluating the worker's skills, taking references and providing a payments service for the workers).

It followed that because Reed made supplies of introductory services, not of staff, VAT was only chargeable on the commission element of its fees, even though Reed invoiced its clients for a single, combined amount that included wages it paid to the temps and National Insurance.

However, it is clear from the Tribunal's decision that the facts and circumstances of each case will determine the VAT treatment of supplies of temps. Only where there is no control of the worker by the agency, and the arrangements effectively amount to an introduction of the worker, will an employment business potentially be able to rely on the decision. HMRC have not appealed the decision but have issued guidance. HMRC take the view that, as a judgment of the FTT, *Reed* is only binding on the parties to the appeal (they take this view when they do not like the decision!).

HMRC therefore do not regard *Reed* as having any wider impact, particularly in relation to the VAT treatment that should apply to employment bureaus operating in the current market conditions and regulatory regime.

CASES INVOLVING AGENCY

29.13 In *Spearmint Rhino Ventures Ltd v Revenue and Customs Comrs* [2007] EWHC 613 (Ch) (BVC 437), the appellant argued that self-employed dancers supplied their services directly to customers and that the supply was not made by the appellant themselves.

The Tribunal decision went into great detail on the arrangements behind the provision of entertainment at the six 'gentlemen's clubs' operated in the UK by the appellant.

The dancers were, by agreement of the parties, self-employed individuals, so the fundamental issue was one often litigated in businesses such as hairdressers and driving schools, ie whether, in the context of the clubs:

- the supply of entertainment services is made by the dancer to the customer in accordance with an individual contract negotiated by the dancer (as argued by the appellant); as such, the dancer makes the supply of entertainment services, and the appellant simply licenses the dancer to perform in its premises and provides specified services to the dancer;

- or (as argued by HMRC) the appellant provides entertainment to the customer through the dancers, whom the appellant has engaged.

The Tribunal had earlier reviewed the Dance Performance Licence ('DPL') between the appellant and the dancer, the local authority licensing conditions, and the manner in which dancers were recruited, retained and remunerated. The Tribunal Chairman had concluded that, whilst it was true that the dancer entered into a contract with the customer in relation to her services, that did not detract from the fact that there was an overall contractual framework within which the appellant provided the relevant services to the customer through the dancers as agents. The Tribunal accordingly dismissed the appellant's appeal.

Before the High Court, counsel for the appellant argued that he had no major disagreement with the Tribunal's analysis of the facts and the contractual relationships, but believed that the analysis could only point to a conclusion that the dancers contracted as principals to provide services to the customers in the appellant's clubs, and that there was no substantive evidence of the agency arrangement adduced by the Tribunal. Mr Justice Mann agreed with this, commenting as follows:

'35. It seems to me to be a very forced construction of events, if it is possible at all, to say that the dancers are contracting as agents for the club. The documents themselves have no particular badges of agency. The DPL is, in its terms, a licence permitting entry to the premises so that the dancer can apparently ply her trade. Background (2) expresses the desire of the club to give her a licence, and Background (3) expresses her desire to licence the premises for that purpose. It is not suggested that those expressions of desire are in any way a sham or are to be disregarded. The rest of the terms of the document (which, so far as relevant, are set out above) pursue that notion. Nothing in that document suggests that the dancer is vested with any authority to do anything on behalf of the club.'

The judge subsequently allowed the appellant's appeal.

In *Joppa Enterprises Ltd* (Scottish Court of Session [2009] CSIH 17), the appellant operated a sauna business in Edinburgh, and following a VAT assurance visit, had been assessed by HMRC for the full consideration paid at the door, as well money paid by the clients direct to the hostesses.

Previously, the VAT Tribunal had found for the Appellant on monies paid to hostesses, holding that they were self-employed, and the money received by them directly from customers was not the Appellant's income. However, regarding the money collected on entry, the Appellant kept a fixed £5 for itself, and also retained 50% of the remaining consideration, in respect of the supply of the room and facilities (the other 50% being passed onto the hostesses). HMRC had argued that the Appellant was required to account for VAT on the full value, not just the £5 and 50% share. The Tribunal found the facts of the case unique, but was of the view that the service provided was one of entry, and VAT was due on the full consideration received at the door. However, HMRC's assessment had included an estimate of the value of monies passing between the customers and hostesses, which had been calculated by scrutinising a website called 'Punternet'. The Tribunal found the assessment calculation to be flawed, and dismissed the appeal, directing HMRC to recalculate the assessment. The Appellant appealed against the Tribunal's finding that VAT was due on the full consideration paid at the door.

The Court of Session agreed with the Tribunal that the Appellant's business structure was different to that of previous self-employed hairstylist cases or the *Spearmint Rhino* case above. The Court also agreed that the entry fee was consideration for a supply by the Appellant to the customer of allowing entry and use of the facilities. The subdivision of money was irrelevant, and there was no suggestion that the collection of the entry fee was done as an agent.

In Newcastle United plc v Revenue and Customs Comrs ([2007] EWHC 612 (Ch)(BVC 449)), the taxpayer appealed against the VAT Tribunal's earlier decision which found, with limited exceptions, that the club was not entitled to deduct input tax on players' agent fees for player transfers and player contract renegotiations. The Tribunal said that, even though the club paid the fees, the supply of the agent's services was made exclusively to the player, and hence, the VAT thereon was not input tax of the club. The Tribunal also rejected a more detailed argument that, even if the supply was made primarily to the player, the club received sufficient benefit to give it a right of input tax deduction under the 'Redrow' principle.

This was the test case on the HMRC challenge to football clubs on such deductions (some may recall that the original test case involving Glasgow

Rangers got virtually to the steps of the Edinburgh VAT Tribunal, only to be pulled at the eleventh hour by HMRC—the view of the Edinburgh Tribunal was clearly that HMRC decided at the last minute that they were likely to get a more favourable ruling in a Tribunal South of the Border).

Mr Justice Mann allowed the club's appeal, remitting the case to the Tribunal for a rehearing, with a strong steer on how the second Tribunal should approach the issues raised. The judgment was fairly damning of the approach by Mr Demack in the Tribunal, broadly saying that the Tribunal formed a view at the start based on a number of misconceptions, in particular, the 'exclusivity' aspect of the players' agents operations, and then, in analysing the individual scenarios, fitted the facts around those misconceptions. The judge also took the view that the Tribunal was too easily influenced by what the documents stated, rather than what took place in reality. As such, the Tribunal's decision was flawed. The judge went on to list the misconceptions as follows:

'It is clear to me that the expressed rationale of the Decision cannot stand. In reaching its Decision the Tribunal was relying on several propositions or bases that are not correct.

First, it made a fundamental mistake about exclusivity. It misunderstood the express exclusivity provisions that it saw and assumed that there was a contractual obligation that the agent would not act for another. It got the exclusivity the wrong way round. The exclusivity operated (where it operated at all) so as to prevent the player from engaging another agent. As I have indicated, HMRC accept that the Tribunal did that.

It found that there was an implied exclusivity obligation of the kind that it relied on even where there was not an express one. That is a misplaced assumption, as I have already observed.

It seems to have considered that that sort of exclusivity obligation automatically prevented any contract existing between the Club and the agent. That is not correct. Even if such an obligation existed it would not necessarily prevent a contract arising. It would merely mean that the second contract was a breach of the first.

It may also have assumed that the conflict of interest that would arise if the agent acted for both Club and player would prevent there being a contract between Club and agent. If so that is wrong. It seems to me to be highly likely that a conflict would arise. As Mr Milne (Counsel for Newcastle United) observed, it might well expose the agent to claims from the player, because it is apparent from the Tribunal's findings that there was no disclosure of the terms on which the agent was acting for the Club. Its existence might even mean that on the facts it would not be right to find that a conflicting contract had come into existence. However, it does not automatically mean that the Club/agent contract did not or cannot exist. As is observed in *Bowstead & Reynolds on Agency*, 18th edn at para 2-013:

"Agent acting for both parties to a transaction. The agent of one party is not incompetent to act as agent of the other. Thus solicitors frequently act for both the buyer and the seller of a house, though there are many traditional warnings as to the dangers of this practice. It is perhaps more likely that an agent can unacceptably acquire the second capacity after the conclusion of the contract negotiated. Where there is no conflict of interest, the matter is straightforward. But an agent who does act in this way runs great risks of finding himself in a position in which his duty to one party is [in]consistent with his duty to the other, for example as regards information coming into his possession. In such a case he will be in breach of his duty to his first principal, and are liable accordingly, unless that principal has given his informed consent to the transaction with the other principal ..."

The Tribunal also apparently found that a Club/agent contract could not exist because it would breach FA and FIFA Regulations. Again, that is wrong. The Regulations do not regulate the technical capacity of the agent to enter into contracts. The Regulations are no more than a form of contract themselves, and they impose obligations, but an apparent breach of them does not necessarily mean that the breaching act did not in law happen (though the fact that a club/agent contract would be a breach might be a relevant factor in determining where in fact there was such a contract). So entering into a contract with the Club might be a breach of the Regulations, but it is a contract nonetheless'

Counsel for HMRC sought to argue that, notwithstanding the above misconceptions, there was still an absence of a necessary contractual arrangement between the agent and the club to substantiate a right to input tax deduction by the club. The judge rejected this, finding that the supply scenario was clearly similar to that addressed in the *Redrow* and *WHA* cases.

The judge then considered if he could make a final decision of his own, or whether he should remit the case back to the Tribunal, and decided on the latter.

In *Smith (t/a Qualified School of Motoring) v Revenue and Customs Comrs* [2008] ST 193 the Tribunal had to address two issues. On the first issue, the appellant argued that the driving tuition fees were exempt as 'private tuition' under *Sch 9, Group 6(2) VAT Act 1994*. On the second issue, the appellant argued that the individual driving instructors were acting as 'principals' for VAT purposes.

The appellant operated a school of motoring and had several instructors employed by him. The cars were generally supplied to the instructors and insured by the school. The school provided booking facilities, advertising for the services, and also provided the bulk of the students. For this, the instructors paid a fixed fee to the school. The instructors would sometimes be paid by cash/cheque, and other times, a cheque might be sent directly to the school, in which case, the amount would be deducted from the fixed fee.

Addressing the issue of VAT liability first, the Tribunal found that, although the school had provided some simple driving lessons and road safety to 15-year-olds after school, they were not lessons which were *'ordinarily taught in a school or university'*. Therefore, the conditions of the exemption were not satisfied, and the supplies were taxable.

On the second issue of who was actually making the supplies of driving tuition, the school contended that it provided administrative services only, and that the driving tuition was provided by the instructors as principal. However, after reviewing the evidence, the Tribunal concluded that there was a *'strong element of direction and control'* provided by the school to its drivers, and that the drivers were not free to run a business as they wished. Consequently, the Tribunal held that the drivers were supplying the services on the school's behalf, and dismissed the appeal.

Chapter 30

Joint ventures

SIGNPOSTS

- Joint ventures can be complex and cause confusion to businesses and HMRC alike. There are many different types of joint ventures that can have different VAT liabilities. Particular care has to be taken when properties are involved (see **30.1–30.2**).

30.1 'Joint venture' is a term used by people to describe a variety of situations. Few people understand the ramifications of these, and each case has to be looked at in the light of the facts. Everyone, including HMRC, finds this a difficult and complex subject, in which each situation differs from the next. This chapter, therefore, only attempts to provide some general guidance.

People use the term 'joint venture' loosely, and without really understanding what it means. This can create the dangerous situation that legally incorrect 'facts' are given to advisers. That is a recipe for trouble!

People devise schemes for making money in combination with others on the basis that they will share in the resulting profit. To them, the arrangement is straightforward. The lawyers then get involved, and agreements are drawn up which become more and more complicated as negotiations proceed. I have often found with property deals, for example, that by the relatively late stage at which a VAT adviser is sought, the legal contracts are so complicated, that it takes several hours of reading to discover what is supposed to be happening!

It is all too easy for lawyers to lose track of points of detail in the course of protracted negotiations, during which, they have to amend agreements. Our advice would be to keep it simple, if at all possible, and make sure you read the finished result before you sign it!

Focus

Examples of joint venture arrangements are:

- simple agreements to co-operate together, each side bearing its own costs;

- partnerships, albeit limited to a single project—though many agreements claim that they are not intended to create a partnership;

- a limited company in which each party has shares;

- an agreement under which a property entrepreneur takes possession of a site on terms which provide for a building to be constructed for the site owner, the remuneration to the entrepreneur depending upon success in meeting an agreed price, and with a bonus or a penalty if the cost comes in either lower or higher than budget.

Sometimes, it is practicable for the VAT accounting to be through the existing VAT returns of each party. This is most likely to be possible when the project is to produce a product or service which can readily be sold by one or both the parties. It is unlikely to be feasible where a single asset, such as a property or a ship, is involved—unless it is owned by only one of the parties.

PLANNING POINTS

30.2 Where a property is concerned, each party probably requires some security for the expenditure it incurs, especially if it is paying for renovation or construction costs. That usually means some form of joint ownership, with the proceeds being paid into a joint venture bank account before being distributed. Since it is not practicable to split a property sale into two or more parts so as to account for them through separate VAT returns, it follows that the joint venture is likely to have to register as such.

If the parties each make sales and incur costs, and simply combine the figures from these to arrive at a notional income and expenditure account for the venture, the resulting balance payable from one to the other could be a taxable supply or merely an outside the scope division of the profit or loss thereon, depending upon the precise facts. Thus, in *Thorstone Developments Ltd* (LON/01/0007 No 17821), a 'share of profit' was held to be standard-rated because there was no partnership. It was, therefore, a charge between the parties to a joint venture.

If a partner in a separately registered joint venture incurs costs related to it, they must be recharged with VAT to that joint venture. An example might be staff time. The division of the profit or loss resulting, is then an outside the scope distribution to each of the joint venturers.

In *Latchmere Properties Ltd* (LON/01/165 No 18533), a developer occupied a site to renovate/convert buildings into dwellings. The agreement provided for it to share proceeds with the owners if sales were achieved within a year of completing the work; alternatively it would buy the land if it failed to achieve a sale.

The position was arguable both ways. On balance, the Tribunal held that Latchmere did acquire an interest in the land, so the money it received was not payment for construction services. The contract terms were weak. They included that, when sales were achieved, the price was divided between the owner and Latchmere, rather than received by Latchmere and then split.

Since few people understand the VAT aspects of joint ventures, it follows that, as with agency, this is an aspect of commercial life which has VAT issues that need careful checking in each case.

Chapter 31

The Second-hand Goods Scheme

SIGNPOSTS

- There are a number of margin schemes available for businesses that sell second-hand goods, the advantage of these schemes being that VAT is only due on the profit margin, not the full selling price (see **31.1–31.7**).

- The Global Accounting Scheme applies to goods costing less than £500 and gives relief from VAT for any losses made on individual sales (see **31.8–31.15** and **31.17–31.18**).

- There are special rules for part exchange, stolen or lost goods, and sale and purchase to overseas customers (see **31.16** and **31.19–31.25**).

- There is a special scheme for auctioneers (see **31.30–31.36**).

31.1   The *Second-hand Goods Scheme*, often called the *Margin Scheme*, helps anyone who deals in goods bought from people not registered for VAT. It also covers second-hand cars on which the input tax was recovered when purchased.

THE LAW

31.2   The *EC 7th VAT Directive* sets out the rules for a scheme for second-hand goods throughout the EU. In UK law, the *Special Provisions Order (SI 1995/1268)* contains the main principles. Notice 718 sets out detailed rules on, for instance, record-keeping requirements, and contains regulations made by HMRC under powers given to them in the Order. Thus, the Notice itself has legal effect.

This chapter covers the main principles of the Scheme. For more details, including comment specific to vehicles, horses and ponies, see the relevant Notice.

KEY POINTS

31.3 The *Second-hand Goods Scheme* covers most second-hand goods, works of art, collector's items and antiques. The key points are:

- the business pays VAT on its profit margin, not on the selling price—though the latter remains the value of the supply. It is therefore sales, not the profit margin, which decides the liability to register;

- the business must have bought the goods either from an unregistered person, usually a private individual, or from another dealer under the Scheme, who could be in another EU Member State;

- the business can have bought a work of art from the creator or his heirs, either in the UK or from another EU Member State, whether or not VAT was charged;

- for items costing more than £500, a stock book and purchase and sale invoices are needed;

- *Global Accounting* allows purchases of all items costing less than £500 to be lumped together and offset against the total sales of such items. VAT is only due on the difference between total sales and total purchases of them. If purchases exceed sales, no VAT is due, and the excess is carried forward to add to purchases in the following period;

- for sales under *Global Accounting*, a business must have purchase invoices, although full supplier details are not required. Sales invoices are not compulsory unless the sale is to another dealer;

- goods, which a business has created itself, are not second-hand. That includes a horse or pony bred by the owner.

DEFINITION OF SECOND-HAND GOODS, ANTIQUES ETC

31.4 *Second-hand goods* are those usable now or after repair. It does not cover items of scrap, precious metals priced at the open market value of the metal, investment gold, or precious stones which are not mounted, set, or strung, ie diamonds, rubies, sapphires and emeralds.

Antiques are goods over 100 years old.

Works of art means pictures, paintings, collages, and drawings produced by hand by the artist. See Notice 718 for the law, which contains a detailed definition of, for instance, sculpture, tapestry, and photographs. It includes limited editions in tiny quantities but excludes technical drawings, maps or plans, hand-decorated manufactured items, and scenery including a backcloth.

Collectors' items covers pieces of zoological, botanical, mineralogical, anatomical, historical, archaeological, paleontological, ethnographic, numismatic or philatelic interest. Again, see Notice 718 for more detail.

THE SECOND-HAND GOODS SCHEME IS OPTIONAL

31.5 A business does not have to use the Scheme either generally, or for individual transactions, but it is likely to wish to do so unless it is selling to a VAT-registered buyer, who is not a dealer.

GOODS ELIGIBLE FOR THE SCHEME

31.6 Whilst most second-hand items are eligible, not everything is. The rules are:

- the goods must be moveable tangible property, so buildings are not eligible (*Special Provisions Order (SI 1995/1268), art 2*);

- the item must be 'suitable for further use as it is, or after repair';

- the business must not buy on a tax invoice—if it does, it can offset the input tax against the output tax on the full price outside the Scheme;

- whilst an item purchased from a vendor in another EU Member State under the Scheme is eligible, one bought from outside the EU or as an acquisition, is not.

A business trading in parts, such as components from scrapped cars, can use the Scheme subject to allocating a cost to any item costing more than £500.

The requirement that the goods be not bought on a tax invoice means that, within the UK, goods are not eligible until they have passed through the hands of someone not registered for VAT. Exceptions are:

- second-hand cars on which the input tax was blocked;

- works of art bought from the creator or the creator's heirs.

If an item is bought from a private individual or a dealer in another EU Member State, the former will not issue a tax invoice, and the latter will probably use the Margin Scheme. No acquisition VAT is then due and the goods are eligible. See **31.22** below.

VAT ON REPAIR AND RESTORATION COSTS

31.7 VAT on the cost of restoration or repair is recoverable outside the *Second-hand Goods Scheme*. That means that such costs cannot be added to the purchase price of the goods for Scheme purposes, and is a common error.

GLOBAL ACCOUNTING

31.8   *Global Accounting* calculates output tax liability on the excess, if any, of sales over purchases in each VAT period so:

- output VAT is due on the total margin using the VAT fraction 1/6th;

- any losses on individual items are allowed against profits on others within the overall total of sales;

- the offset of total purchases against total sales means that, when large purchases are made, the strain on cash flow is mitigated by the reduction in the output VAT payable. Of course, a business must understand this delaying of its output tax liability. Otherwise, in a corresponding period of high sales and low purchases, the VAT due will be a nasty surprise;

- any excess of purchases over sales is carried forward to add to purchases in the next period.

THE £500 LIMIT

31.9   *Global Accounting* cannot be used for items which individually cost more than £500. If a number are bought as a lot, *Global Accounting* can still be used provided that, on the basis of a fair apportionment of the cost, no item exceeds £500. If one or more do, their cost values must be removed from the *Global Accounting* records, and they must be sold under the ordinary *Second-hand Goods Scheme*.

OTHER GOODS NOT ELIGIBLE

31.10   The following goods are also not eligible for *Global Accounting*:

- motor vehicles;
- aircraft;
- boats and outboard motors;
- caravans and motor caravans;
- motorcycles;
- horses and ponies.

This is because dealers in these goods have no difficulty in keeping records item by item and in using the normal *Second-hand Goods Scheme*. In any case, the majority of items cost more than £500 each.

INITIAL STOCKS WHEN STARTING TO USE GLOBAL ACCOUNTING

31.11 When starting to use Global Accounting, existing stock on hand can be counted as purchases for the first period. This, of course, requires a stock valuation.

There is no set basis for valuing stock. If a business does not have records of the purchase cost of items held, selling prices less estimated profit margins might be an acceptable basis. The requirement to 'identify separately any eligible stock on hand' suggests that HMRC will require a detailed listing of stock quantities, even if an overall value is used.

It would be wise to discuss the facts of each case with HMRC, and to agree the valuation used.

RECORDS AND INVOICES FOR THE SECOND-HAND GOODS SCHEME

31.12

Focus

The records required for goods sold under the full Scheme are a stock book, and purchase and sale invoices containing the information specified below. The records for *Global Accounting* transactions are simpler. A stock book is not required for goods sold under *Global Accounting*.

There had been a long-standing requirement for Scheme sales invoices (and purchase invoices from other dealers) to include the declaration *'Input tax has not been and will not be claimed by me in respect of the goods sold on this invoice'* (as set out in para 3.7 of Notice 718). However, following the introduction of new VAT invoicing requirements on 1 October 2007, which were announced in *HMRC Brief 51/07* and *VAT Information Sheet 10/07*, this declaration was deemed no longer acceptable under EU law. From 1 October 2007, invoices must instead include one of three kinds of reference: a reference to the relevant article in the EC Directive, a reference to the relevant UK legislation, or any other reference indicating that a second-hand margin scheme has been applied.

As a transitional measure, HMRC allowed businesses to continue using the old declaration until they migrated to a new form of acceptable reference when reprinting invoices or upgrading software. A revised version of Notice 718 was later issued which included suggested alternative legends which may be adopted. Examples of alternative legends include:

- 'This is a second-hand margin scheme supply.'
- 'This invoice is for a second-hand margin scheme supply.'

In Budget 2009, HMRC announced the withdrawal of Extra-Statutory Concession 3.08 with effect from 1 April 2010. The concession, which allows second-hand car dealers to account for VAT on either the purchase price, or half the selling price, of a vehicle for which they do not hold all the necessary margin scheme records, was one of 10 ESCs that HMRC decided to withdraw following the House of Lords decision in *CIR v ex parte Wilkinson* [2005] UKHL 30, a direct tax case.

HMRC said the concession did not ensure that VAT was charged on the actual profit margin obtained by the dealer. Furthermore, it provided an advantage to the motor trade sector which is not available for any other types of second-hand goods. The concession has no basis in UK or EU VAT law, and as such, had to be withdrawn.

Accordingly, where dealers in second-hand motor vehicles fail to retain evidence of both the purchase *and* selling price of a particular vehicle in future, VAT will be due on the full selling price of that vehicle. This is the legal requirement when margin scheme records have not been kept.

HMRC said they will write to the representative trade bodies by the end of April 2009 to ensure that they are aware of the formal date for withdrawal. The withdrawal will also be included in an issue of VAT Notes sent out with paper VAT returns.

PURCHASE AND SALES INVOICES

31.13   Purchase invoices for *Global Accounting* are made out:

- if buying from a private vendor—by the dealer buying;
- if buying from another dealer—by the dealer selling.

Purchase invoices must show:

- the buying dealer's name and address;
- the seller's name and address;
- invoice number;
- date of transaction;
- description of goods stating their nature and number. 'Assorted goods' will not do;
- total price;
- endorsement as a *Global Accounting Invoice*.

Sales invoices for *Global Accounting* must show the selling dealer's name and address and similar details to those for purchases—though the buyer's name and address are only required if the buyer is another dealer, who needs a purchase invoice. On a sales invoice, the business can avoid mentioning *Global Accounting* by making the declaration quoted in **31.12**.

For invoices to customers in other EU Member States, see **31.23** below.

PURCHASE RECORDS

31.14   Purchase records must show invoice numbers, date of purchase, description of the goods, and total price. Even if HMRC are satisfied with a note of the nature of the goods, and the total number of items rather than a full description of them, such a purchase record is more detailed than many dealers would otherwise keep, especially when buying for cash.

SALES RECORDS

31.15   The records needed are:

- normal cash sale records, such as till rolls; and

- a list of sales to other dealers for which the business has issued invoices.

Credit sales must be accounted for at the time of sale, not when the cash comes in.

HOW DOES A BUSINESS TREAT PART-EXCHANGE GOODS?

31.16

Focus

If a business takes goods in part-exchange, the selling price for Scheme purposes must include the value of the part-exchanged goods.

Suppose a business sells a car for £2,500, and takes one in part-exchange for which it allows £500. The selling price in the stock book must be £2,500. The purchase price of the part-exchange car in the stock book would be £500 regardless of its trade value, since this is the amount, the business has allowed to the customer.

For various cases on this subject, see **8.21**.

If a business is buying from a private person or unregistered dealer, it can show the part-exchange items on its sales invoice, provided it includes the information needed for a purchase invoice.

LOSSES DUE TO BREAKAGES, THEFT, ETC

31.17   The *Global Accounting* purchases total must be reduced by the cost of losses due to breakage, theft, etc. This is because the global margin subject to VAT would otherwise be reduced by the full cost of losses. Under the normal *Second-hand Goods Scheme*, VAT is only due on those goods sold, but the margin earned on them is not reduced by the cost of losses.

The theory of this is understandable; how it is to be applied in practice is not, given the difficulty of identifying such losses. In practice, HMRC may only be able to enforce it where evidence of individual losses exists, such as an insurance claim.

STOCK ADJUSTMENT ON CEASING TO USE GLOBAL ACCOUNTING

31.18   If a business ceases to use *Global Accounting*, when, for instance, it deregisters or sells its business, it must make a closing adjustment by adding its *Global Accounting* stock at cost to the value of its sales. The business then deducts, as usual, its purchases during the period in arriving at the VAT due under the *Global Accounting* calculation. This collects VAT on the unsold stock, which has previously been allowed as a deduction from sales.

GOODS SOLD TO FOREIGN CUSTOMERS

31.19   Second-hand goods taken out of the UK remain eligible for zero-rating under the rules applicable to all goods. In practice, sales to customers within the EU are likely to be dealt with under the Scheme.

Do not confuse an export outside the EU with a removal within the EU. Second-hand goods sold under the *Second-hand Goods Scheme* are taxed in the country where they are sold. There is no zero-rating merely because they are removed to another EU Member State but a VAT-registered buyer in that Member State does not incur acquisition VAT.

SELLING TO FOREIGN CUSTOMERS UNDER THE NORMAL RULES

31.20   A business can account for an export to a customer outside the EU under the ordinary rules, but it must issue an invoice in the usual way. Although this will show the sale as zero-rated, proof of the physical export of the goods must be obtained. See Chapter 20, *Exports and Removals of Goods*.

If the customer takes the goods abroad, Notice 704 *VAT Retail Exports* applies. See in particular the comments re second-hand goods.

If the business sells for export, it must arrange its scheme records so as to be able to separate the zero-rated margins from those which are standard-rated.

For sales within the EU, both proof of removal and the customer's VAT number are required. As the EU purchaser will have to account for acquisition VAT, and will not then be able to sell the goods under the Margin Scheme in his own country, he is unlikely to wish to give a VAT number. Thus, in practice, a business is likely to account for VAT on its profit margin on sales to dealers elsewhere in the EU, rather than claim the zero-rating.

ADJUSTING GLOBAL ACCOUNTING PURCHASES FOR FOREIGN SALES

31.21

Focus

If a business zero-rates an export or a removal of goods included in *Global Accounting* stocks, it must reduce its purchases for *Global Accounting* purposes by the cost of the item zero-rated.

BUYING FROM ANOTHER EU MEMBER STATE

31.22 Correspondingly, a business should be aware of this pitfall if it buys from a dealer elsewhere in the EU. It should not give its VAT number. If it does, it may be able to negotiate a lower price for the purchase to reflect the VAT saving to the vendor, but it will then have to account for UK acquisition VAT and charge output VAT on the full price.

If a business buys from a registered trader in another EU Member State, which has recovered input tax on its purchase, that trader must charge tax on its resale. The business will zero rate it as a removal to the UK. Acquisition VAT is then payable by the UK business, and the item is not eligible for the *Second-hand Goods Scheme*.

SCHEME SALES TO, AND PURCHASES FROM, OTHER EU MEMBER STATES

31.23   Further to the 1 October 2007 invoicing requirements outlined in detail at **31.12**, invoices to customers in other EU Member States must include one of three kinds of reference: a reference to the relevant article in the EC Directive, a reference to the relevant UK legislation, or any other reference indicating that a second-hand margin scheme has been applied.

Purchase invoices from other EU Member States will either refer to *Art 26* or *26a* of the *EC 6th VAT Directive,* or will make the declaration used in that Member State.

Such an invoice might also show the VAT registration number of the business. If it is unclear whether the supplier has zero-rated the sale under the acquisition tax rules, or has made the supply under the margin scheme, it must check with the supplier.

VAT ON IMPORTS FROM OUTSIDE THE EU

31.24

Focus

The importer of goods purchased from outside the EU must pay import VAT. These goods are not eligible for the Margin Scheme, except for collector's cars and works of art, antiques, and collector's pieces.

A car bought under the Scheme from a dealer in another Member State who has imported it, can be sold in the UK under the Scheme. It cannot if the car is bought from the other dealer zero-rated as an acquisition—explained in Chapter 21, *Imports and Acquisitions of Goods.* Various Tribunal cases have shown that this pitfall has caught numerous UK dealers—in particular when buying cars from Ireland which were imported second hand from Japan.

Works of art, antiques and collector's pieces are taxed on import at 5%, but remain eligible for the *Second-hand Goods Scheme.*

Temporary import arrangements are available for goods brought in for auction, under which, no VAT is due if the goods are exported again—but not if removed. See **20.7** for the difference between an export and a removal.

AUCTIONEER'S COMMISSION ON IMPORTED GOODS

31.25   *Section 21* was amended by *Finance Act 2006,* following the European Commission's infringement proceedings against the UK (C-305/03).

From 1 September 2006, the value of imported works of art, antiques, and collector's pieces is no longer allowed to include the auctioneer's commission. The commission has, thus, become standard-rated.

AGENTS WHO SELL SECOND-HAND GOODS IN THEIR OWN NAME

31.26   An agent, who acts in his own name in the sale of goods, is regarded as buying and selling those goods, as explained in Chapter 29, *Agency is Special*. The agent must account for output tax on the sale of the goods, but can use the *Second-hand Goods Scheme*, subject to meeting its rules. The net effect is the same, provided that the *Second-hand Goods Scheme* is used.

ACTING FOR THE BUYER

31.27   If the agent acts for the buyer under the *Second-hand Goods Scheme*, the selling price of the goods for VAT purposes will be the buying price plus the commission. Thus, the VAT due will be on that commission, but under the Scheme.

If the goods are ineligible for the Scheme because the seller charges VAT on them to the agent, VAT is due on the full selling price including the commission to the buyer. However, the input tax is recoverable, so the net VAT due from the agent is the same.

ACTING FOR THE SELLER

31.28   If the agent acts for the seller, the purchase and selling prices will be the same. If the *Second-hand Goods Scheme* applies, no output VAT is due under the Scheme. It is due on the commission via an ordinary tax invoice issued independently of the Scheme.

If the seller is VAT-registered and charges VAT on the goods to the agent, the input tax incurred on the purchase will equal the output tax charged to the buyer. Both entries must, of course, be included on the agent's VAT return. The agent separately invoices his commission plus VAT to the seller.

NEED FOR VAT INVOICES IN THE CORRECT NAME

31.29   Agents, who act in their own names for sales not under the *Second-hand Goods Scheme*, should be careful to obtain purchase invoices from sellers that are addressed to them, not to the buyers. Theoretically, this should be automatic, since the seller will usually not know who the buyer is, but it would be wise not to take it for granted. HMRC may not take the point if invoices are incorrectly addressed, but this cannot be relied upon.

THE AUCTIONEERS' SCHEME

31.30   The *Auctioneers' Scheme* is a method of accounting similar to the *Second-hand Goods Scheme*. It covers the same goods as the *Second-hand Goods Scheme*. Thus, if the vendor charges VAT on the goods, they are not eligible for the Scheme. However, the auctioneer is still treated as buying and reselling the goods, and the normal rules for agents apply as explained earlier.

The auctioneer will normally wish to use it in order not to have to charge VAT on the full selling price to the buyer. The normal rules also apply if the auctioneer chooses not to use the Scheme.

An auctioneer might not wish to use the Scheme when selling to a dealer who intends to export the goods. If the auctioneer sells on a tax invoice, the dealer will then recover the VAT on any buyer's premium, in the form of a profit margin included in the selling price, against the zero-rated export sale.

Under the Auctioneers' Scheme, the accounting is not the same as for sales by an agent, despite the similarities.

HOW THE AUCTIONEERS' SCHEME WORKS

31.31   The auctioneer is liable for output tax at 1/6 of the margin between the purchase price and the selling price of the goods.

The purchase price is the hammer price less his commission.

If an exempt charge is made for insurance, this is also not a part of the margin calculations.

The selling price is the hammer price plus any buyer's premium and any other charges made to the buyer such as packing, transport and insurance, unless these services are a separate supply in their own right.

Example 31.1— Auctioneer's Scheme calculation

This example is based on a selling commission of 11.75% and a buyer's premium of 17.625%.

	£
Hammer price	1,000.00
Less commission 11.75%	.117.50
Purchase price	£882.50
Selling price £1,000 plus buyer's premium	1,176.25

Margin—selling price less purchase price   293.75
Output VAT 3 1/6ths   £48.96

If the goods are to be exported from the EU, the margin is zero-rated—subject to getting proof of export—as detailed in Chapter 20, *Exports and Removals of Goods*.

INVOICES TO VENDORS

31.32   The auctioneer issues an invoice showing:

- auctioneer's name and address;
- vendor's name and address;
- invoice number;
- date of sale;
- hammer price of goods (and, presumably, catalogue number if any, though HMRC do not state so);
- commission due from vendor;
- net sum due to vendor;
- when the vendor is registered, a declaration signed by the auctioneer to the effect that the supply is a second-hand margin scheme supply (see **31.12** for some examples of suggested wording from HMRC).

INVOICES TO BUYERS

31.33   The invoice issued to the buyer must show:

- the auctioneer's name, address and VAT number;
- buyer's name and address;
- invoice number;
- date of sale;
- catalogue number;
- hammer price;
- buyer's premium and any other charges which are part of the margin;
- amount due from buyer;
- a declaration to the effect that the supply is a second-hand margin scheme supply (see **31.12** for some examples of suggested wording from HMRC).

REFERENCE TO VAT ON INVOICES

31.34   The auctioneer must not show the amount of VAT on either purchase or selling invoices. HMRC accept references such as VAT-inclusive commission at 11.75%, or commission at 10% plus VAT at 20%. However, if such a reference to VAT is made, they require the addition of a statement on the invoice that this amount includes VAT which must not be shown separately, or reclaimed as input tax.

ZERO-RATED GOODS SOLD AT AUCTION

31.35   If the goods are zero-rated, such as books, so is the margin. VAT is only due on any charges made outside the Scheme.

CORRECT IDENTIFICATION OF GOODS IS IMPORTANT

31.36   Although most of the goods sold by auction will be eligible for the *Second-hand Goods Scheme,* and, therefore, for the *Auctioneers' Scheme,* not all will be. The following appear to be examples of where the auctioneer will have to collect VAT on the full selling price, because the sale to him by the vendor will carry VAT on the purchase price:

- industrial equipment, such as the contents of a factory;

- farm sales—though some items might be non-business assets of the farmer;

- retail stocks.

Auctioneers should be wary of handing over the proceeds including VAT of the sale of such goods, without first obtaining a tax invoice to support recovery of the input tax offsetting the output tax.

Example 31.2— Auctioneer's Scheme subject to VAT at 20%

The arithmetic works thus:

	£
Hammer price	1,000.00
VAT thereon at 20%	200.00
Total purchase price to auctioneer	£1,200.00

Hammer price	1,000.00
Buying premium @ 15%	150.00
	1,150.00
VAT thereon at 20%	230.00
Total selling price by auctioneer	£1,380.00

Thus, the auctioneer has output tax to account for of £230, against which, he offsets the £200.00 input tax from the vendor.

As this is not a *Second-hand Goods Scheme* sale, the auctioneer invoices separately to the vendor his selling commission plus VAT, just as any other agent would.

Chapter 32

The Retail Schemes

SIGNPOSTS

- Retail Schemes are designed to simplify VAT accounting for retailers who deal mainly in cash and credit card payments and avoids the need to issue and record invoices for each sale (see **32.1–32.2**).

- The are five basic retail schemes for different types of business and ones making supplies at different VAT rates, so it is important to choose the correct retail scheme. Businesses turning over more than £130m p.a. can have a bespoke retail scheme (see **32.3–32.12**).

32.1   The *Retail Schemes* are needed because retailers sell mostly for cash or against credit cards. It would be much too cumbersome for them to issue tax invoices for each transaction. Even though modern tills increasingly provide most of the detail needed, many small shops do not have such systems.

The Retail Schemes are a means of estimating the amount of VAT due on retail sales. It is 'estimating' because, if the retailer can accurately calculate the tax due, it would not need to use a Retail Scheme! Users often do not realise this. They see the Retail Schemes as a substitute for issuing tax invoices. In reality, the accuracy of a Retail Scheme depends on the circumstances in which it is used, and the retailer needs to think carefully about which is the best for them.

The Retail Schemes use such methods as calculating the estimated selling prices of only a proportion of the purchases of goods for resale, or using a ratio of goods bought at one rate as a proportion of total goods. Whilst this may have the merit of simplicity, it is all too easy for errors in the calculations, or distorting factors, to produce a result which causes an overpayment compared with that produced by the most favourable available Retail Scheme.

THE LAW

32.2   The *VAT Regulations, regs 66-75* say little. Notice 727 *Retail Schemes,* and its various subsidiary notices and updates, contain all the detailed law. This has to be published in the form of a Notice, in order that the rules on the records to be kept and the calculations to be made, shall be enforceable in law.

PAST DISASTERS

32.3

Focus

Take care over the choice of Retail Scheme. Numerous Tribunal cases have concerned choosing the wrong Retail Scheme, and paying too much VAT in consequence. That reduces the profit margin, and might well provoke a direct tax inquiry.

Time and again, in cases where traders and their accountants have at last woken up to the problem, HMRC have refused to allow a retrospective change. Tribunals have supported that refusal.

So, before choosing which Retail Scheme to use, take professional advice!

DOES THE BUSINESS HAVE A MIX OF SALES?

32.4   If a business makes both retail and wholesale sales, the retail scheme can only be used for the retail sales. VAT on the non-retail sales must be accounted for in the normal way.

Sales to other VAT-registered businesses must not normally be included in a *Retail Scheme*. However, *occasional* cash sales, such as a garage supplying petrol to businesses, or a retail DIY store supplying building materials to builders, may be included within a *Retail Scheme.*

BESPOKE SCHEMES FOR SALES ABOVE £130M

32.5   From 1 April 2009, the turnover limit of £100m beyond which retailers are not allowed to use any of the five published retail schemes (ie the Point of Sale Scheme, two Apportionment Schemes, and two Direct Calculation Schemes), was raised to £130m. Businesses with turnovers above the limit must either agree a Bespoke Retail Scheme with HMRC, or use the normal VAT accounting rules. A business must agree a bespoke Retail Scheme with HMRC. It is usually based on a published Retail Scheme, and may be a combination of them. Notice 727/2 gives some outline guidance.

The figure was raised in April 2000 from £10m.

THE BASIC SCHEMES

32.6   There are five basic schemes as follows:

- *Point of Sale Scheme*—The business identifies the correct VAT liability of supplies at the time of sale, eg by using electronic tills;

- *Apportionment Scheme 1*—This is a relatively simple apportionment scheme, designed for smaller businesses with an annual VAT-exclusive turnover of less than £1m. Each VAT period, the business works out the value of purchases for resale at different rates of VAT, and applies the proportions of those purchase values to sales;

  For example, if 82% of the value of purchases are standard-rated, it is assumed that 82% of takings are from standard-rated sales. Once a year, a similar calculation is made based on purchases for the full year, and any overpayment or underpayment is adjusted accordingly;

- *Apportionment Scheme 2*—Under this scheme, the business calculates the expected selling prices (ESPs) of standard-rated and lower-rated goods received for retail sale. The business then works out the ratio of these to the expected selling prices of all goods for retail sale, and applies this ratio to the takings;

  For example, if 82% of the ESPs of goods received for retail sale are standard-rated and 18% are zero-rated, then 82% of takings are treated as standard-rated, and 18% as zero-rated;

- *Direct Calculation Scheme 1*—A business can use this scheme if its annual VAT-exclusive turnover does not exceed £1m. It works by calculating expected selling prices of goods for retail sale at one or more rates of VAT, so that the proportion of takings on which VAT is due can be calculated.

  The business calculates the ESPs for minority goods, ie those goods at the rate of VAT which forms the smallest proportion of retail supplies. So, if 82% of sales are standard-rated and 18% are zero-rated, the business has to calculate the expected sale of the latter.

  ESPs of the zero-rated goods received, made, or grown for retail sale, are deducted from takings to arrive at a figure for standard-rated takings;

- *Direct Calculation Scheme 2*—This works in exactly the same way as Direct Calculation Scheme 1, but requires an annual stock-take adjustment.

COMPARING THE SCHEMES

32.7   Here are some comments to help choose the right Scheme.

Point of Sale Scheme

32.8

- this is the only available Scheme if all supplies are at the same rate;

- it does not involve stocktaking or working out expected selling prices;

- no 'annual adjustment' is required;

- if the business sells at two or more rates, the Scheme is the simplest and the most accurate if the business can consistently record sales by rate of VAT accurately. However, many shops have been caught out over that accuracy. It is suitable primarily for businesses with tills that can recognise the VAT rates from product bar codes.

Apportionment Scheme 1

32.9

- it cannot be used for services, catering supplies, self-made or self-grown goods;

- there is a maximum turnover limit of £1m;

- it does not involve stocktaking or working out expected selling prices;

- an annual adjustment is required;

- the Scheme is relatively simple. However, if on average, a higher mark-up is achieved for zero-rated goods than for standard-rated or reduced rate goods, more VAT could be payable under this Scheme than under an alternative one.

Apportionment Scheme 2

32.10

- it cannot be used for services or catering supplies, but can be used for self-made or self-grown goods;

- stocktaking is required at the start of using the Scheme, but not thereafter;

- expected selling prices must be worked out;

- no annual adjustment is required, but a rolling calculation is used;

- the Scheme can be complex to operate but, if worked properly, it will provide a more accurate valuation of supplies over a period of time.

Direct Calculation Scheme 1

32.11

- services can only be included if they are liable at a different rate from the minority goods;

- it cannot be used for catering supplies, but can be used for self-made or self-grown goods;

- there is a maximum turnover limit of £1m;

- expected selling prices must be worked out. The Scheme can produce inaccuracies if these are not calculated accurately. In addition, where expected selling prices are set for standard-rated goods and the stock of these goods has a slow turnover, the Scheme may not be appropriate, as VAT is paid in the period in which the goods are received, and not necessarily when they are sold;

- stocktaking is not required;

- no 'annual adjustment' is required;

- the Scheme is relatively simple where goods are sold at two rates of VAT, and most of the supplies are at the same rate. However, it can be complex where goods are sold at three rates of VAT.

Direct Calculation Scheme 2

32.12

- services can only be included if they are liable at a different rate from the minority goods;

- it cannot be used for catering supplies, but can be used for self-made or self-grown goods;

- expected selling prices must be worked out. The Scheme can produce inaccuracies if these are not calculated accurately. In addition, where expected selling prices are set for standard-rated goods and the stock of these goods has a slow turnover, the Scheme may not be appropriate, as VAT is paid in the period in which the goods are received, and not necessarily when they are sold;

- stocktaking is required at the start of using the Scheme, and annually thereafter;

- an annual adjustment is required.

IS PERMISSION NEEDED FROM HMRC?

32.13 A business does not have to ask HMRC before starting a particular Scheme. HMRC have the power to instruct a business to stop using it in the following circumstances:

- if its use does not produce a fair and reasonable valuation during any period;

- if it is necessary to do so for the protection of the revenue;

- if the business could reasonably be expected to account for VAT in the normal way.

ANOTHER DISASTER STORY

32.14   *Alan and Pamela Renshall* (MAN/98/1092 No 16273) had a general store selling mainly food, but also confectionery and fancy goods. Their first six returns went in on time showing small sums due to HMRC. Then came six repayment returns. Repeated repayment claims for a retailer are self-evidently incorrect!

A one-off claim is possible due to exceptional input tax on, say, refitting the premises, but not six in a row. It is unusual for a retailer to convert goods bought at standard rate into zero-rated sales. Normally, zero-rated sales mean no input tax. The relatively small VAT on such costs as telephone, stationery and the audit fee is unlikely to exceed the margin between output tax and input tax on standard-rated sales, unless VAT is payable on the rent as well, and the standard-rated sales are a small proportion of the total.

The assessment for the six periods was £17,187. Mr Renshall said that, when doing each VAT return, he looked back to see what he had done last time. Having inexplicably used the wrong column, he simply went on doing so.

Would the staff of a business notice what was wrong? Theoretically, the gross profit margins had inexplicably gone up, thus creating an incorrect direct tax liability, though the extent of this might have been masked by losses due to other problems. Would a business have noticed the change from payments to repayments? Do the people who run the business even look at the VAT returns, let alone do the check on the underlying calculations, which would have immediately revealed the mistake?

Chapter 33

Annual Accounting Scheme

SIGNPOSTS

● Under the Annual Accounting Scheme businesses with a turnover of less than £1,350,000 pa need only make one VAT return per year. The business makes nine monthly payments equal to 10% of the previous year's liability and in month 10 makes a balancing payment (see **33.1–33.3**).

33.1   The purpose of the Annual Accounting Scheme is to help small businesses by allowing them to submit only one return annually. In the meantime, they pay fixed sums based on the previous year's liability.

Professional accountants tend not to like the Scheme much, because they think that the discipline of preparing a quarterly VAT return helps clients to keep their records up to date.

THE LAW

33.2   The law is in *Part VII* of the *VAT Regulations (SI 1995/2518)*. Notice 732 (April 2002) *Annual accounting* sets out the full details.

KEY POINTS OF THE SCHEME

33.3   The key points of the Scheme have been amended, and, for periods starting on or after 1 April 2006, are as follows:

● a business may join the Scheme when it registers for VAT based on an estimate of turnover, provided it has reason for believing its taxable supplies will be below £1,350,000 pa;

● to join, the taxable turnover limit must not exceed £1,350,000 pa. It must cease using the Scheme if its taxable turnover exceeded £1,600,000 pa in the previous accounting year of the Scheme;

- the business makes nine monthly payments of 10% of the total paid in the previous year or, if newly registered, the amount it is expecting to pay in the next 12 months. Alternatively, it can choose to pay 25% quarterly;

- if the interim payments have been set too high or too low because the trading pattern has altered, HMRC may agree to change them;

- a careful choice of the scheme year may help. If the busiest trading is in the summer, a scheme year ending, say, 31 January, spreads the payments, thus assisting cash flow. It is also convenient to produce both the annual VAT return and the annual accounts at a quieter time of the year;

- payments start on the last working day of the fourth month of the Scheme's accounting year. They must be by standing order, direct debit, or other electronic means, not by cheque;

- a business submits its annual VAT return, together with any balance due to HMRC, two months from the end of the Scheme's accounting year; ie a business gets an extra month over the time limit applicable to a normal return;

- the business is not allowed to start the Scheme if it owes a significant debt to HMRC, but they will not necessarily refuse the use of it if the business only owes a small amount.

Users of the *Annual Accounting Scheme* can also use the *Flat Rate Scheme for Small Businesses*. See **Chapter 35.**

Chapter 34

Cash Accounting Scheme

SIGNPOSTS

- The key points to the Cash Accounting Scheme are that it effectively moves the tax point from invoice date to payment date and it has built in bad debt relief (see **34.1–34.3** and **34.6**).

- Businesses with a turnover less than £1,350,000 pa can join the scheme and once the turnover exceeds £1,600,000 they will have to leave the scheme, but they can leave voluntarily at any time (see **34.4–34.5**).

- There are special accounting requirements when on the scheme to record the dates of receipt and payments and you have to be careful when joining or leaving the scheme not to account for too much or too little VAT (see **34.7–34.12**).

34.1

Focus

The *Cash Accounting Scheme* is a valuable concession for small businesses. If a businesses turnover does not exceed £1,350,000 a year, it can use the Scheme without reference to HMRC. The business issues tax invoices as normal, but only accounts for VAT when, and to the extent, that payment is received. Thus, the business gets a cash flow advantage, which can be considerable, depending on how long customers take to pay their bills, not to mention automatic bad debt relief!

This advantage is offset by the fact that the business cannot recover input tax until it pays its bills, so the Scheme is most useful to a business selling services rather than goods, and which, therefore has relatively low taxable inputs.

Retailers selling for cash do not use the Scheme because they already have the money at the point of sale.

As for the other schemes:

- a business can use the *Cash Accounting Scheme* together with the *Annual Accounting Scheme*;

- alternatively, with *Annual Accounting* (see Chapter 33), it can also use the *Flat Rate Scheme for Small Businesses* (see Chapter 35);

- a business cannot use the *Cash Accounting Scheme* with the *Flat Rate Scheme for Small Businesses*. However, that does not really matter, because the *Flat Rate Scheme* has its own version based on when payment is received.

THE LAW

34.2   The law is in *Part VIII* of the *VAT Regulations (SI 1995/2518)*. Notice 731 (April 2004) *Cash accounting* refers.

ADVANTAGES AND DISADVANTAGES OF THE SCHEME

34.3   The advantages are:

- output tax is not due until the business receives payment of its sales invoices. If the customers pay promptly, the advantage will be limited to the tax on invoices issued in the last few weeks of each VAT quarter for which payment is not received until into the following one. Even so, the gain may be material;

- no VAT on bad debts because, if no payment is received, no output tax is due. There is an exception to this if a business has to leave the Scheme— see later.

The disadvantages are:

- no input tax recovery until a business pays the suppliers' invoices;

- the accounting system must record the output tax when it is received from the customers, and the input tax when the suppliers are paid;

- a business just starting up, which has substantial initial expenditure on equipment, stocks, etc so that input tax exceeds the output tax, should delay starting to use the Scheme. That way, it recovers the initial input tax on the basis of input invoices, as opposed to payments.

Note that the normal rules apply concerning recovery of VAT incurred prior to registration (see **3.25**).

KEY RULES

34.4   A business can use the Scheme if it has reasonable grounds for believing that its taxable sales in the next 12 months will not exceed £1,350,000 provided that:

- it is up to date with its returns; or

- it has agreed a basis for settling any outstanding amount in instalments; and

- in the previous year, it has not been convicted of a VAT offence, compounded proceedings in respect of one, or been assessed to a penalty for conduct involving dishonesty.

Zero-rated supplies count towards the turnover limit, but exempt ones do not.

A business can start using the Scheme without informing HMRC.

A business can start to use the scheme at the beginning of a VAT period.

The Scheme does not cover:

- lease or hire-purchase agreements;

- credit sale or conditional sale agreements;

- supplies invoiced where full payment is not due within six months;

- supplies invoiced in advance of delivering the goods or performing the services.

LEAVING THE SCHEME

34.5   A business must withdraw if its taxable sales, including any sales of assets (as confirmed in *Evans (t/a Coney Leasing)* (LON/98/217 No 17510)), in the previous four VAT quarters have exceeded £1,600,000. For example, if the sales in the quarter to 31 May and the previous three VAT quarters were £1,625,000, the business must leave the scheme as at 1 June. If a sales increase is exceptional and it can be shown to HMRC that the sales in the next 12 months will be below £1,350,000 (not £1.6m), they may allow the business to stay in the Scheme.

Provided that sales in the last quarter were under the annual limit of £1,350,000, VAT is not due immediately on all outstanding debts at the date of leaving the Scheme. It need only do so at the end of the next six months—but then Bad Debt Relief is available, as explained in Chapter 16.

TAX POINTS UNDER THE SCHEME FOR SALES AND PURCHASES

34.6   The date on which a business becomes liable for VAT under the Scheme on a sale is that on which it receives payment in cash or by cheque, or, if the cheque is postdated, the date of the cheque.

The business must account for credit card and debit card vouchers on the date on which they are signed by the customer, not when they are paid by the card provider.

The tax point on which a business can recover input tax under the Scheme is the date on which it pays in cash or posts a cheque to the supplier—but if the cheque is postdated, it is the date of the cheque, not that of posting.

If a business pays by credit card or debit card, the tax point is the date of the payment voucher.

Imports of goods are not covered by the Scheme, so the business recovers any import VAT under the normal rules. See Chapter 21, *Imports and Acquisitions of Goods*.

BE CAREFUL WHEN JOINING THE SCHEME

34.7   On starting the Scheme, the business records must differentiate between:

- payments received against invoices—VAT already accounted for under the normal system; and

- those for invoices dealt with under the Scheme. Otherwise, the business will account for the VAT twice.

SPECIAL RECORDS REQUIRED

34.8   The normal requirements for records, including lists of sales and purchase invoices, still apply.

A business still issues tax invoices at the normal tax point. The customers will usually require these before they will pay, and need them as evidence to justify the recovery of input tax, whether or not they are themselves users of the Scheme. Similarly, a business still needs tax invoices showing the VAT which is being reclaimed.

In addition, the business must keep a cash book summarising payments received and made, with a separate column for VAT, or some other record from which payments in and out can readily be checked to the records of sales and purchases.

The business must also obtain dated receipts for any payments in cash to its suppliers. The usual six-year period applies for all records, which must be complete and up to date, and must cross-refer. Thus, it must be possible to check each sales invoice with the cash received later, and each purchase invoice with the payment for it, using, for instance, bank statements, cheque stubs, returned cheques, and paying-in slips. These comments from Notice 731 may be impractical if taken literally. For instance, many businesses do not have their cheques returned to them.

In practice, a paying-in book of a business may be an adequate detailed record, provided that it identifies the customers by name and sales invoice number.

Beware of calculating the output VAT by applying the VAT fraction to the total banked. Even if all the normal sales are standard-rated, an invoice could include an amount not subject to VAT, because it is either zero-rated or is a disbursement outside the scope.

BEWARE OF NET PAYMENTS

34.9   If payments from customers are received net of deductions, such as commission due by the business to a third party, it must account for output tax on the full sum, not the net amount received, so an adjustment will be needed in the records.

If the person to whom the commission is paid is registered, the VAT charged by him to the business will be recoverable as input tax.

WHAT ABOUT PART PAYMENTS OR BARTER TRANSACTIONS?

34.10   If the part payment is of an invoice, which includes both standard-rated and zero-rated or exempt supplies, it must be apportioned between the supplies. HMRC say that this must be 'fair and reasonable'. This will normally mean that the standard-rated part of the payment is calculated in the ratio that the standard-rated supplies bear to the total of the invoice.

If a business pays or is paid either entirely or partly in kind, ie bartered goods or services for other goods or services, output tax is payable and input tax recoverable on the normal values of the transactions, not upon any net sum received or paid.

THE FIGURES FOR THE VAT RETURN

34.11   Not only the output and input tax figures for the VAT return are derived from payments; so are the respective values of supplies. Notice 731 says nothing of how these are to be calculated from the tax accounted for, and zero-rated or exempt amounts added.

THE LIABILITY OF A BUSINESS IF IT LEAVES THE SCHEME

34.12　If a business leaves the Scheme of its own choice, or because its sales exceed the Scheme limit, *reg 61* provides that it must account for the VAT included in all its outstanding invoices to customers. The business can claim an immediate offset for any debts over six months old under the rules for bad debt relief, as described in that chapter, provided that HMRC are not compelling it to leave the Scheme.

The business can offset all the input tax on invoices from suppliers which it has not yet paid—though, not on any over six months old. See Chapter 16, *Bad Debt Relief.*

TRANSFERS OF A BUSINESS OR PART OF A BUSINESS AS A GOING CONCERN

34.13　If a business sells all or a part of its business as a going concern, the transaction is outside the scope of VAT under the *Special Provisions Order (SI 1995/1268), art 5*. See Chapter 38, *Buying or Selling a Business.*

VAT Regulations (1995/2518), reg 6(3) allows for the purchaser to retain the VAT registration number. This is intended for such circumstances as when a partnership becomes a limited company. If used, this rule means the transferee accounts for tax on supplies made and received prior to the date of transfer, just as the transferor would have done, and takes over any liability for past errors.

Unless *reg 6(3)* is used, the business has to account for output tax when it sells its business.

Chapter 35

The Flat Rate Scheme for Small Businesses

SIGNPOSTS

- The *Flat Rate Scheme for Small Businesses* is designed as an administrative simplification for businesses with a turnover of less than £150,000 pa, not as a scheme to reduce the VAT payable. Depending on the business sector, the business applies a fixed percentage to all of its turnover (see **35.1–35.5**).

- Although the scheme is designed as a simplification, it is quite complicated and can lead to errors and costly mistakes (see **35.6–35.7**).

- There are turnover limits for joining and leaving the scheme and you have to be careful what is included in the turnover when calculating the Flat Rate percentage (see **35.8–35.14**).

- Worked examples and how the scheme operates (see **35.15–35.16**).

- Zero-rated and exempt turnover is included in the turnover on which the flat rate percentage applies, so some businesses can end up paying considerably more tax (see **35.17–35.18**).

- Care has to be exercised when choosing your business category and the appropriate flat rate percentage and you have to be aware of any changes in the nature of the business that can affect the percentage applicable (see **35.19–35.20**).

- There are special tax point rules for the scheme and how to deal with stocks and assets at registration and on leaving the scheme (see **35.25–35.28**).

- There are special rules relating to the purchase of capital assets over £2,000 (see **35.29**).

- You can apply to join and leave the scheme retrospectively (see **35.30–35.32**).

35.1   Do not confuse the *Flat Rate Scheme for Small Businesses*, which is applicable to any small business, with the flat rate scheme used by farmers—described in the next chapter.

THE LAW

35.2   The *Small Business Scheme* started for periods ending on or after 25 April 2002. The law is in *s 26B* and *Part VIIA* of the *VAT Regulations (SI 1995/2518)*. Notice 733 *Flat rate scheme for small businesses* explains the rules and contains certain statements concerning records, which have the force of law.

There have been various changes announced at short notice since the Scheme began so, when using Notice 733, check that it is the latest version, together with any updates—which might also update the commentary in this chapter.

AN OUTLINE OF THE SCHEME

35.3

Focus

- Calculate the VAT due on the *Scheme Turnover* using a Flat Rate percentage instead of the standard rate. That percentage depends on the trade sector into which the business fits;

- the *Scheme Turnover* is gross of VAT, not net. Moreover, it includes any zero-rated and exempt sales, not just standard-rated and reduced-rated ones;

- the sum calculated with the Flat Rate percentage is what the business owes HMRC. A business cannot reclaim input VAT on costs, except for capital expenditure exceeding £2,000 including VAT. See **35.29** below.

See **35.8** for the turnover limits.

WILL I PAY LESS VAT UNDER THE SCHEME?

35.4   A business *could* pay less VAT using the Scheme—it does work for some businesses. However, the two examples I prepared for this chapter suggest that it is more likely to cost extra. Comments I have heard from professional accountants confirm that only a minority of clients benefit from the Scheme! Key points include:

- which trade sector applies—sometimes, as I explain in **35.19**, two sectors could apply, and it is possible to justify using the one with the lower Flat Rate. A business has to decide on the right one from a list shown in **35.20**;

- how close the overall profit margin and the positive-rated expenses are to the average used by HMRC when deciding on the Flat Rate percentage for that trade sector. As businesses with similar descriptions often sell different mixes of goods or services and their profit margins vary accordingly, the Flat Rate percentage decided on by HMRC can only be for what is supposedly a typical business of that description. Many will actually differ;

- I suggest a business does not adopt the Scheme unless it is sure that it will pay less under it. A business should compare the VAT that it would have paid under the Scheme during the last year, or better still, the last two years, with that it did pay, or would have paid, under the normal rules.

DOES THE SCHEME SIMPLIFY VAT ACCOUNTING FOR SMALL BUSINESSES?

35.5   I believe the Scheme's claim to simplify VAT accounting has no basis!

- HMRC claim quicker bookkeeping and easier VAT returns on the supposition that people will record their purchases and their sales as gross sums. In that case, the VAT payable is a deduction from sales—or could be shown as an expense;

- HMRC do not mind which way the figures are recorded; a gain is subject to income or corporation tax and a loss is an expense;

- however, I believe it is unsafe in many cases not to record the input and output VAT! Failure to calculate the actual input tax paid but not recoverable, means no check on whether less or more VAT is paid under the scheme;

- moreover, a fundamental business measure—the gross profit percentage— is distorted! In businesses where that figure matters, I believe that the net gain or loss in VAT should be shown;

- a business which sells to other VAT-registered businesses must still issue VAT invoices—showing VAT at standard rate, not the Flat Rate. Even private customers may expect to get VAT invoices if prices quoted to them are plus VAT;

- furthermore, if all dealings are with private customers for cash without sales invoices, it is easy under the normal system to apply the VAT fraction to the total sales for the quarter to calculate the output tax. A retailer selling at two or more rates of VAT might find the Flat Rate calculation marginally simpler than a retail scheme, but the Flat Rate is more of an output tax guestimate.

THE DANGERS OF THE SCHEME

35.6   The Scheme will get some people into trouble because they have not understood the key rules. I have seen professional advisers getting the calculation wrong! I have also found HMRC themselves making mistakes in publicity for the Scheme—such as saying that a business calculates the VAT due by applying the Flat Rate to its *taxable* sales. If the reader does not immediately pick up that error, re-read what I have said so far!

The Scheme is not simple. Writing this chapter originally took several days because of the need for careful study of both the law and Notice 733. In its current version, the Notice remains, in my view, poorly written and with various ambiguities.

THE IMPORTANCE OF READING NOTICE 733

35.7   Obviously, what I am trying to do here is provide clear guidance on the possible advantages and disadvantages of the Scheme. I have ignored various points in Notice 733 which seem irrelevant to most small businesses. Thus, if a business decides to use the Scheme, check the Notice for any further relevant detail.

I have deliberately written the following explanations as if addressed to a potential user, although, of course, a reader of this book is more likely to be a professional adviser. Any professional fees in advising such a small business are likely to be low, and it will help advisers to provide the right advice if they can merely copy the appropriate parts of what I say—which they can do provided that they acknowledge the source as being this book.

THE TURNOVER LIMITS

35.8

Focus

A business can use the Scheme if the expected taxable turnover in the next 12 months will not exceed £150,000 net of VAT.

Up to 1 April 2009 there was an additional requirement that the expected total turnover, including exempt sales, will not exceed £187,500 net of VAT. From 1 April 2009 this limit was removed, leaving the single limit above.

THE TURNOVER FOR THE SCHEME LIMIT

35.9   The £150,000 figure is for all taxable supplies, so it includes those at standard rate, reduced rate and zero rate, including the sale values of any dealings in second-hand goods or investment gold. Keep a record of the calculations of the expected turnover. If it exceeds the limit, the business must be able to show HMRC that its estimate had a reasonable basis.

THE TURNOVER TO WHICH YOU APPLY THE FLAT RATE

35.10   Do not confuse the two turnover tests for Scheme limit purposes with the *Scheme Turnover* to which the business applies the Flat Rate.

Focus

The *Scheme Turnover* to which the business applies the Flat Rate is:

- the sales values including VAT—gross sales invoices or total retail takings;

- plus any zero-rated and exempt sales including rental income from residential investment properties. That includes sales of goods to business customers in other EU States. See **35.17** below;

- plus any sales of capital assets, such as equipment, the purchase of which was dealt with under the Scheme. For more details, see **35.29** below.

Para 7.3 of Notice 733 (February 2004) says that a business does not include non-business income or *any supplies outside the scope of VAT*. That includes any services on which the business does not charge VAT to a customer outside the UK—in contrast to zero-rated sales of goods to foreign customers.

ACQUISITIONS AND IMPORTS OF GOODS

35.11   Beware the pitfall of buying goods zero-rated from a supplier in another EU Member State. Do not forget to account for the acquisition VAT in box 2 of the return as normal. For instance, a business must pay the VAT, in addition to the Flat Rate VAT, to HMRC because it has not paid it to the supplier. Just as with UK purchases, a business cannot then recover the import VAT.

In contrast, VAT on imported goods has to be paid at the time the goods enter the UK, so the position is the same as with ordinary input tax.

EXPORTS AND IMPORTS OF SERVICES

35.12   Paragraph 6.3 of Notice 733 (April 2014) states that the flat rate turnover does not include any supplies of goods or services, for which the place of supply is outside the UK.

Paragraph 6.4 states that the purchase of reverse charge services should be dealt with outside of the FRS. They should be excluded from the flat rate turnover but they should be recorded in boxes 1 and 4 of the VAT return, as they would under normal accounting. See Chapter 23, *Exports and Imports of Services*.

SALES TO OR PURCHASES FROM OTHER COUNTRIES

35.13   Included in the Scheme turnover are any sales of goods to customers outside the UK, whether in or outside the EU. Supplies of services to customers that are treated as outside the scope of UK VAT (business customers in the EU and any customers outside the EU) are not included in the turnover on which the flat rate percentage is applied.

As mentioned at **35.11**, a business has to account, as usual, for acquisition VAT in box 2 of its VAT return on any purchases of goods from suppliers in other Member States. This is then not recoverable in box 4 under the Scheme, just as any other input tax is not. That puts the business in the same position whether it buys from a UK supplier or one in another Member State.

Imports of goods from outside the EU will be subject to import VAT, which will not be recoverable.

RESTRICTIONS ON USE OF THE SCHEME

35.14   A business can use the Scheme in conjunction with the *Annual Accounting Scheme*—described in Chapter 33. For comment on *Cash Accounting Schemes* users, see **35.25** below.

But a business cannot use the Scheme if:

- it uses the *Second-hand Goods Scheme*, the *Auctioneers Scheme,* or the *Tour Operators Scheme*—described in Chapters 31 and 37;

- it has to operate the *Capital Goods Scheme* (see Chapter 25);

- the business is *associated with another person*. That means another business in a situation in which one business is under the dominant influence of the other, or they are closely bound to one another by financial, economic, and organisational links. HMRC say that the test here is of commercial reality rather than the legal form. If one business is associated with another business, HMRC will still consider an application from it to be allowed to use the Scheme. In para 3.9 of Notice 733 (April 2014), they say that a husband and wife are not seen as associated, even if they share premises, providing a market rent is paid;

- the business is a company which is eligible for registration in a VAT group, whether or not it has been, or which is registered separately as a division of a company, or, in either case, has been during the previous 24 months.

Or, in the previous 12 months:

- it has ceased using the *Flat Rate Scheme*;

- it has been convicted of any offence in connection with VAT or have made any payment to compound proceedings in respect of VAT under *CEMA 1979, s 152*;

- it has been assessed to a penalty under *s 60* for alleged conduct involving dishonesty.

AN EXAMPLE OF HOW THE SCHEME WORKS WITH VAT AT 20%

35.15   Suppose the business is an accountant or bookkeeper, a computer/ IT consultant or a lawyer. Those descriptions cover many people who start to work for themselves—often from home. The flat rate percentage applicable to them is 14.5%. The figures might look like this:

	Output tax @ 20% on *VAT inclusive* turnover	Flat Rate 14.5% on *VAT inclusive* turnover
	£94,000	£94,000
	£15,666	£13,630
Costs not subject to VAT such as secretarial help, insurance postage, rail and taxi fares and depreciation: say	£20,000	£20,000
Vatable costs such as stationery, telephone, computer software, advertising, some travel costs, heat and light and sundries: say	£20,000	£20,000
Input tax add back	£4,000	
Net profit	£42,334	£40,370
Payable to HMRC	£11,666	£13,630
Result of using Scheme		
Net result of Scheme: Deducts from net profit:		(£1,964)

ANOTHER EXAMPLE—A BUSINESS SELLING GOODS

The lowest flat rate is 4% for a retailer of food, confectionery, tobacco, newspapers, or children's clothing. There will not be many such retailers eligible to use the Scheme because, even if the profit margin is as high as 20% on sales of £150,000 net of VAT, that only leaves £30,000 out of which to pay the overheads, let alone provide a profit. The figures might look like this:

Turnover	£150,000	Output tax (assuming 25% sales zero-rated) @ 20%	Flat Rate 4% on *VAT inclusive* turnover £180,000
		£24,000	£7,200
Cost of goods sold	£120,000	Input tax on 75% £18,000	
Non Vatable expenses: say	£7,000		
Vatable expenses: say	£7,000	Input tax £1,400	
Net profit	£16,000		
Payable to HMRC		£4,600	£7,200
Result of using Scheme			
VAT payable under Scheme	£7,200		
VAT due under normal system	£4,600		
Net result of scheme: Deducts from net profit	(£2,600)		

THE SENSITIVITY OF THE ABOVE FIGURES

35.16   Obviously, the precise position will vary from business to business, but the figures in both examples demonstrate that the sum payable under the Scheme could easily be more than under the normal system.

If the Flat Rate percentage applicable to a trade sector is more favourable than in the above example, the closer the turnover gets to the limit, the bigger any potential saving is likely to be, assuming that, for a business supplying services, the standard-rated costs tend to rise more slowly.

On the other hand, it will often be a mistake for such a business to adopt the Scheme in the first year or so, when overheads are relatively high in relation to sales, and there is start-up expenditure such as that on equipment. Note that the loss of VAT on equipment, etc is reduced by the rule, explained later, which allows a business to separately recover VAT on capital expenditure exceeding £2,000 including VAT.

Now that the flat rate for the retailer is 4% rather than 5%, the loss under the Scheme is due to 25% of sales being zero-rated but still subject to the flat rate. If all the sales were standard-rated, there would be a gain under the Scheme. The difference would be the result of the extra VAT payable under the normal rules on the additional standard-rated profit margin, less the input tax on the additional standard-rated purchases, and less the 4% flat rate on the extra output tax.

These examples are, of course, only valid to the extent that the figures compare with those of an individual business. Nevertheless, they suggest that, before adopting the Scheme, a business should first review the likely result using figures based on its VAT returns for the last year or, in the case of a new business, its budgeted ones.

BEWARE EXEMPT AND ZERO OR REDUCED-RATE TURNOVER

35.17   The total turnover limit allows for some exempt sales on top of the taxable sales limit. The most likely examples of exempt ancillary income are, according to HMRC, lottery commissions, or property rents, since exempt insurance or finance commissions are primarily received by brokers.

In the case of *Fanfield Ltd & Thexton Training Ltd v Revenue & Customs Commissioners* [2011] UKFTT 42 (TC) the taxpayers challenged HMRC's view that bank interest should be included in the amount subject to the Flat Rate percentage. The legislation states that any income received 'in the course or furtherance of business' should be included in the amount subject to the Flat Rate Percentage. HMRC guidance specifically states that bank interest is included but this does not have the force of law.

The taxpayers did not include bank interest in their calculations as they did not consider it to have been received in the course or furtherance of business. HMRC disagreed and issued assessments which were the subject of this appeal.

The Tribunal found that for most users of the Flat Rate Scheme the interest they earn is outside the scope of VAT as it fails the 'in the course or furtherance of business' test. The main basis for this finding appears to be that the business in this case, and probably in the majority of cases, used the bank accounts for the business: there being no intention or need to earn interest on the amounts involved.

The comments by the Tribunal suggest that for sole traders it is unlikely that the interest they earn on bank account deposits will be within the scope of VAT. This is good news as many sole traders that make the effort use such accounts to put aside money to meet future outgoings such as VAT and tax payments will now be able to leave the interest earned, albeit only small amounts, out of their turnover for the VAT calculation in the Flat Rate Scheme. HMRC have now accepted this view. Any businesses that have accounted for tax on these amounts will also be eligible to make a claim.

If a business has any exempt sales, the Scheme will probably mean paying more VAT because the Flat Rate percentage applies to your total turnover. The extra VAT under the Scheme is money which the business will not be collecting on its exempt income. A business does avoid having to do any partial exemption calculation, no input tax being recoverable under the Scheme anyway—but then, under the normal system, it may be able to recover the input tax related to your exempt income if it does not exceed the de minimis limits for Partial Exemption. See Chapter 24.

Also, beware if a proportion of your sales are taxable either at zero-rate or the reduced rate. Applying the Flat Rate percentage to the total sales may create a larger sum due to HMRC.

THE INCOME NET OF DEDUCTIONS AND BARTER PITFALLS

35.18   If a business receives income net of deductions, such as a commission or expenses charged by an agent, or PAYE deductions by an employer/contractor, it must gross up the income for Scheme purposes.

That means adding back not just the net expense but any VAT charged on it in order to calculate the gross income including the businesses own output tax. This is a point which could easily be missed by a small business.

The same is true of barter transactions. If a business sells and accept something in part exchange, it must record the gross price as its turnover, not the net cash received.

CHOOSING YOUR FLAT RATE PERCENTAGE

35.19

Focus

To decide the Flat Rate percentage a business must use, it chooses the trade sector in the table below which most closely reflects its business. If it makes supplies in more than one sector, it may choose the one in which its sales are largest.

I considered whether to create an alphabetical list of the kinds of business covered by the different sectors. I decided not to because I thought there would be a danger of someone finding an alphabetical heading which appeared suitable, without realising that there was another either closer or equally applicable, and with a lower percentage! For instance, a farm secretary probably does more bookkeeping than secretarial work. The rate for bookkeeping is 14.5%; that for secretarial services is 13%.

So, before a business chooses, it should read the entire table of sectors, marking all the headings which have any relationship to its business. Then consider whether the business can justify the one with the lowest Flat Rate percentage as being that most closely reflecting its business, or the one in which it sells the most.

I also worry that the categories are far from clear. Suppose an individual is working as a 'consultant'. What are the differences between:

- management consultancy;

- accountancy and bookkeeping;

- lawyers and legal services;

- computer and IT consultancy or data processing;

- investigation or security;

- all other activity not elsewhere specified; and

- business services not elsewhere listed?

Each of these categories might arguably cover some forms of consultancy; yet the rates vary from 12% to 14.5%.

For instance, is it obvious where a tax consultancy fits in? Such work is not 'management consultancy' in the usual sense. It can involve tax 'investigations' and 'legal services' in handling Tribunal appeals. The consultant may well be a qualified accountant or lawyer, so the 'accountancy' or 'lawyer' category could apply. 'Business services' covers services provided to businesses, such as cleaning services or market research. 'Any other activity' covers, for instance, driving schools, funeral services and telecommunications.

If a business has any doubt at all, check the *ready reckoner* on the HMRC website, to which, there is a link on the *Rates, Codes & Tools* page of the *VAT* section.

Management consultancy is a good example of the sloppy wording of the sectors! The categories of business supposedly covered are business consultancy, financial consultancy, management consultancy, and public relations. Financial consultancy and public relations are certainly not management consultancy. Goodness knows what the difference between the latter and business consultancy is supposed to be.

These examples show why much care is needed before you can be sure of the right sector.

In the case of *The Chilly Wizard Ice Cream Co Ltd* (VTD 19,977), HMRC challenged the trade classification chosen by the trader. The appellant sold ice cream and milk shakes from a kiosk in Christchurch, with limited seating accommodation nearby. The appellant adopted the Flat Rate Scheme under the classification '*retailing food, confectionery, tobacco, newspapers or children's clothing*', which attracts a flat rate of 2%. HMRC reclassified the appellant under the classification '*catering services including restaurants and takeaways*', which, surprise, surprise, attracts a flat rate of 12%.

The appellant appealed to the Tribunal on the basis that it was merely making simple retail supplies liable to the 2% rate applied.

In his written summing-up of the case, the Tribunal Chairman came to the following conclusions:

'We have found that on the evidence before us:

(1)   there is no catering and no supply of "catering services" here;

(2)   there is no restaurant here;

(3)   there is no takeaway here;

(4)   retailing is an appropriate categorisation, and catering is not.

Accordingly, as catering is not the right categorisation, and retailing is, the appeal is allowed with costs.'

The only thing that needs to be said about this particular case is: 'Nice try, HMRC', but it does show the dangers associated with the scheme, and HMRC's willingness to try and extract more tax from a taxpayer.

In a similar case, *SLL Subsea Engineering Ltd v Revenue & Customs* [2015] UKFTT 43 (TC), the appellant chose the business category 'Any other activity not listed elsewhere,' whereas HMRC took the view that the correct category was 'Architect, civil and structural engineer or surveyor', which had a higher flat rate percentage and assessed them for £4,272 in underdeclared VAT.

The appellant's specialism was in the oil and gas industry and in particular pressure-containing components such as valves and pipe structures. He designed and supported the assembly and manufacture of pressure containing subsea equipment.

It was argued for the appellant that the category must be determined by reference to the law not the guidance. It was further submitted that the appellant did not fall specifically into any of the categories listed in *reg 55K* and that therefore the correct category is either 'business services that are not listed elsewhere' or 'any other activity not listed elsewhere'. Both carry the same FRS rate of 12%.

Even if HMRC were correct in stipulating that 'Architect, civil and structural engineer or surveyor' is the correct category, nevertheless the appellant's decision was reasonable and HMRC should have applied their own practice and not changed the choice of sector. The Tribunal found that the decision underpinning the assessment was unreasonable and found for the appellant.

35.19A In the Autumn Statement 2016, the Chancellor announced the introduction of a new 16.5% VAT flat rate for businesses with limited costs which will take effect on 1 April 2017.

This measure has been introduced because HMRC consider that a number of businesses with limited input tax costs have gained a significant cash advantage by joining the FRS, charging 20% VAT on their sales and only accounting for a much lower rate (normally 12%–14%) under the FRS and retaining the difference.

Currently businesses decide which flat rate percentage to use based on their trade sector. From 1 April 2017, businesses on the FRS will also have to work out if they meet the definition of a 'limited cost trader'.

A limited cost trader will be defined as one whose VAT inclusive expenditure on goods is either:

- less than 2% of their VAT inclusive turnover in a prescribed accounting period; or

- greater than 2% of their VAT inclusive turnover but less than £1000 per annum if the prescribed accounting period is one year (if it is not one year, the figure is the relevant proportion of £1000).

Goods are defined as used exclusively for the purpose of the business but exclude the following items:

- capital expenditure;

- food or drink for consumption by the flat rate business or its employees;

- vehicles, vehicle parts and fuel (except where the business is one that carries out transport services – for example a taxi business – and uses its own or a leased vehicle to carry out those services).

These exclusions are part of the test to prevent businesses buying either low value everyday items or one-off purchases in order to inflate their costs beyond 2%.

HMRC will also introduce 'anti-forestalling' legislation to prevent businesses from continuing to use a lower FRS percentage by manipulating tax points.

CHANGES IN THE NATURE OF THE BUSINESS
35.20

Focus

A business only needs to review the balance of its ongoing business between sectors at each anniversary of joining the Scheme. It uses the

---

> Flat Rate of the sector in which it expects to make the largest sales in the following year—applicable from the start of the VAT period in which falls the anniversary.

If a business stops making sales in a sector, or start doing so in a new one during the year, the percentage applicable from then on is that for the sector in which it expects to make the largest sales.

If a business changes the flat rate as a result of the above alterations to its business, write to HMRC about it.

Also, tell HMRC in writing of any change in the sector rate the business uses, whether resulting from the balance of its business or from a change in its activities.

*Sector rates from 1 January 2010

Category of business	Appropriate percentage
Accountancy or book-keeping	13
Advertising	10
Agricultural services	10
Any other activity not listed elsewhere	10.5
Architect, civil and structural engineer or surveyor	13
Boarding or care of animals	10.5
Business services that are not listed elsewhere	10.5
Catering services including restaurants and takeaways	11
Computer and IT consultancy or data processing	13
Computer repair services	9.5
Dealing in waste or scrap	9.5
Entertainment or journalism	11
Estate agency or property management services	10.5
Farming or agriculture that is not listed elsewhere	6
Film, radio, television or video production	11.5
Financial services	12
Forestry or fishing	9.5
General building or construction services*	8.5
Hairdressing or other beauty treatment services	11.5
Hiring or renting goods	8.5

Category of business	Appropriate percentage
Hotel or accommodation	9.5
Investigation or security	10.5
Labour-only building or construction services*	13
Laundry or dry-cleaning services	10.5
Lawyer or legal services	13
Library, archive, museum or other cultural activity	8.5
Management consultancy	12.5
Manufacturing fabricated metal products	9.5
Manufacturing food	8
Manufacturing that is not listed elsewhere	8.5
Manufacturing yarn, textiles or clothing	8
Membership organisation	7
Mining or quarrying	9
Packaging	8
Photography	10
Post offices	4.5
Printing	7.5
Publishing	10
Pubs	6
Real estate activity not listed elsewhere	12.5
Repairing personal or household goods	9
Repairing vehicles	7.5
Retailing food, confectionary, tobacco, newspapers or children's clothing	3.5
Retailing pharmaceuticals, medical goods, cosmetics or toiletries	7
Retailing that is not listed elsewhere	6.5

Sector rates from 4 January 2011

Category of business	Appropriate percentage
Accountancy or book-keeping	14.5
Advertising	11

Category of business	Appropriate percentage
Agricultural services	11
Any other activity not listed elsewhere	12
Architect, civil and structural engineer or surveyor	14.5
Boarding or care of animals	12
Business services that are not listed elsewhere	12
Catering services including restaurants and takeaways	12.5
Computer and IT consultancy or data processing	14.5
Computer repair services	10.5
Dealing in waste or scrap	10.5
Entertainment or journalism	12.5
Estate agency or property management services	12
Farming or agriculture that is not listed elsewhere	6.5
Film, radio, television or video production	13
Financial services	13.5
Forestry or fishing	10.5
General building or construction services*	9.5
Hairdressing or other beauty treatment services	13
Hiring or renting goods	9.5
Hotel or accommodation	10.5
Investigation or security	12
Labour-only building or construction services*	14.5
Laundry or dry-cleaning services	12
Lawyer or legal services	14.5
Library, archive, museum or other cultural activity	9.5
Management consultancy	14
Manufacturing fabricated metal products	10.5
Manufacturing food	9
Manufacturing that is not listed elsewhere	9.5
Manufacturing yarn, textiles or clothing	9
Membership organisation	8
Mining or quarrying	10
Packaging	9
Photography	11

Category of business	Appropriate percentage
Post offices	5
Printing	8.5
Publishing	11
Pubs	6.5
Real estate activity not listed elsewhere	14
Repairing personal or household goods	10
Repairing vehicles	8.5
Retailing food, confectionary, tobacco, newspapers or children's clothing	4
Retailing pharmaceuticals, medical goods, cosmetics or toiletries	8
Retailing that is not listed elsewhere	7.5
Retailing vehicles or fuel	6.5
Secretarial services	13
Social work	11
Sport or recreation	8.5
Transport or storage, including couriers, freight, removals and taxis	10
Travel agency	10.5
Veterinary medicine	11
Wholesaling agricultural products	8
Wholesaling food	7.5
Wholesaling that is not listed elsewhere	8.5

*   'Labour-only building or construction services' means building or construction services where the value of materials supplied is less than 10% of relevant turnover from such services; any other building or construction services are 'general building or construction services'.

The Scheme is now more attractive for some businesses due to the reductions in the rates from 0.5% up to 3%—though mostly by 1% to 1.5%. Some of the alterations in categories also generated a percentage change—except for dry-cleaning.

1% DISCOUNT FOR NEWLY REGISTERED BUSINESSES

35.21

> **Focus**
>
> A newly registered business gets a 1% discount on the normal percentage for its first year—though not the full year if it registers late. That does not apply to a business already VAT registered for a full year.

THE READY RECKONER

35.22   HMRC have provided a *ready reckoner* on their website. However, it only shows the tax payable under the Scheme compared with that under the normal rules. It neither highlights the benefit or the loss, nor shows how the figures are arrived at. I would, therefore, only use it in order to check calculations already done because, unless you understand those figures in detail, mistakes are certain!

PITFALLS FOR BUILDERS

35.23   The 10% materials requirement in order to use the 9.5% Flat Rate rather than the 14.5% one, creates a pitfall for anyone who often does not supply materials.

Equally, a builder could suffer severely under the Scheme if contracts obtained turned out to be for zero-rated new dwellings or alterations to listed ones, or for reduced rate conversion work rather than standard-rated projects.

THE PITFALL IN CHANGES TO THE FLAT RATE TRADE SECTORS

35.24   The Flat Rate trade sector table in *reg 55K(4)* was amended from 1 May 2003, and again from 1 January 2004, 1 December 2008, 1 January 2010 and 4 January 2011. Anyone using the Scheme must apply a change in the table from its start date, which may well mean splitting the calculations for the VAT return in which the change occurs. Someone using the *Annual Accounting Scheme* as well might have two or more changes during the 12-month period.

Given that many small users of the Scheme are supposed to be minimising their bookkeeping costs, and will not normally use a professional adviser to prepare their VAT returns, I do not see how HMRC suppose that users will discover relevant changes in time to apply them correctly.

A business does not have to tell them if the change is because they have altered the table.

TIME OF SUPPLY UNDER THE FLAT RATE SCHEME

35.25   There are three possible methods of arriving at the Scheme turnover.

The *Basic Turnover Method* under the Scheme follows the normal rules. That is to say, if a business issues tax invoices, they create tax points and are the basis of a businesses Scheme turnover. However, if the business issues requests for payment under the rule for continuous services, as described in Chapter 7, *The Time of Supply Rules—When VAT Must be Paid*, the tax point will be when payment is received.

Although a business using the scheme is not allowed to use the *Cash Accounting Scheme*, it can use what HMRC call the *Cash Based Turnover Method* of calculating the VAT due in each period. The business applies the Flat Rate percentage to the cash received, rather than the invoices issued. This does not alter the tax point itself, although that would only matter if, for instance, there is a change in the VAT rate applicable to a businesses sales.

If a business is already using the *Cash Accounting Scheme*, it can change to this one without having to calculate the tax still owed at the time of change. It simply accounts under the *Flat Rate Scheme* for VAT on payments received subsequently. The same applies if it leaves the *Flat Rate Scheme* and goes back to the *Cash Accounting Scheme*.

If a business ceases to use the *Cash Based Turnover Method* of calculating its turnover, it has to include it in its Scheme turnover, for the period in which it reverts to the invoice basis, the sales made whilst using the Scheme for which it has not yet been paid.

Under the *Retailer's Turnover Method*, the business applies the Flat Rate percentage to its retail takings as calculated under the usual rules for retailers. For instance, a business has to include credit card sales as they are made by creating the voucher, rather than when it receives the money from the card issuers.

STOCKS AND OTHER ASSETS HELD AT THE DATE OF REGISTRATION

35.26

Focus

If, on registering for VAT, a business immediately starts using the Scheme, it can recover VAT on stocks and assets at the date of registration under the usual rules. See Chapter 3, *When to Register and Deregister for VAT.*

A business already registered has, of course, already reclaimed VAT incurred on the stock and assets held. If there is a substantial stock of goods for resale, there may be a marginal gain under the Scheme. The Flat Rate percentage is reduced to take account of input tax which will not be recoverable on future purchases, but which has already been recovered on the stock. However, a small business would not usually have enough stock for this to be a significant advantage unless the Flat Rate percentage happens to be favourable too.

THE TURNOVER LIMIT ONCE IN THE SCHEME

35.27 With regard to leaving the scheme, there is a requirement that businesses check annually whether their income exceeds £225,000, this increased to £230,000 on 4 January 2011. Where this is the case, the business must leave the scheme. An amendment has been made to the scheme rules which will allow the test to be calculated on the same basis that the entry calculation was made. For example, if entry eligibility was based on cash received, the leaving test can be based on cash received also. Likewise, if entry was based on invoices issued, then exit can be based on invoices issued too.

A business can remain on the scheme if it can persuade HMRC that there are reasonable grounds for believing that its turnover in the next 12 months will not exceed £187,500 for all supplies—including zero-rated and exempt ones.

A business also ceases to be eligible if there are reasonable grounds for thinking that its turnover will exceed £225,000 (£230,000 from 4 January 2011) in the next 30 days alone. Notice 733 does not say so, but this is, of course, an anti-avoidance rule. Anyone signing a contract likely to create such a situation would be aware of the sales implications.

If a business becomes ineligible because of a rise in turnover, it leaves the Scheme at the end of the quarter following the anniversary of joining, at which, it checked the total.

If a business becomes ineligible for any other reason, it must cease to use it at once.

In both cases, a business must tell HMRC in writing.

However, if a business using the flat rate scheme exceeds the annual exit threshold as a result of a one-off transaction but, in the subsequent year, expects its tax inclusive annual flat rate turnover to be less than £187,500, it may remain in the scheme with the agreement of HMRC. As a consequence of the increase in the VAT standard rate to 20% this threshold was increased to £191,500 to maintain the same effect.

STOCK ADJUSTMENT ON LEAVING THE SCHEME

35.28 If, on leaving the Scheme but remaining VAT registered, the standard-rated stock exceeds the value when it joined the Scheme, it calculates the increase, work out the standard rate VAT on it, and claim this on the next VAT return.

CAPITAL ASSETS

35.29

> **Focus**
>
> VAT on capital equipment bought when using the Scheme is treated like other input tax, and ignored unless the VAT-inclusive value is £2,000 or more.

In the latter case, a business can recover the VAT on its VAT return as usual if the goods are not:

- for resale or for inclusion in goods for sale—but then they would not be capital goods anyway;

- for hiring, leasing, or letting—presumably because the input tax is then equivalent to VAT on goods bought for resale;

- covered by the *Capital Goods Scheme*—unlikely for a small business, but see Chapter 25.

A complication of the Scheme concerns assets on which a business recovered VAT either at the date of registration or under the Scheme because the VAT inclusive cost exceeded £2,000. If it sells such an asset whilst using the Scheme, it has to charge tax in the normal way, and at the standard rate, not at the Flat Rate percentage.

If, at the date on which a business leaves the Scheme, it still holds capital equipment on which it recovered VAT under the Scheme, it has to account for output tax, presumably on the value at that date, although Notice 733 does not say so. A business can offset a corresponding sum as input tax, assuming that it goes on using the equipment to make taxable supplies.

APPLICATIONS TO USE THE SCHEME

35.30 There is a simple application form in Notice 733, which can also be found on HMRC's website. A business sends it to the office which handles registrations for its area. Keep a copy of it—the business may need to check, for instance, the Flat Rate percentage which it stated as applicable to its business.

A business cannot start to use the Scheme until it has been notified by HMRC of the date from which it may do so. If a business wishes to use the *Annual Accounting Scheme* as well, use the joint application form in Notice 732 *VAT: Annual Accounting*.

RETROSPECTIVE USE

35.31

> **Focus**
>
> Although HMRC do not publicise the fact, it is worth noting that they do have discretion to allow applications for retrospective use of the scheme (often desirable in cases of belated registration).

HMRC will usually approve such applications, provided certain conditions are met, such as a good standard of past compliance, eligibility of previous turnover, etc.

In a recent Tribunal case, *C J Anderson* (VTD 20,255), the Appellant, a self-employed lorry driver, applied to join the flat rate scheme for small businesses, requesting that the authorisation be backdated to the inception of the scheme some four years earlier. HMRC authorised the Appellant to use the scheme, but refused backdating.

On the basis of the individual circumstances of the case, the Tribunal allowed the appeal finding that:

- HMRC applied its policy on retrospection without regard to the individual circumstances of the Appellant; and

- their decision would not inevitably have been the same had account been taken of the individual circumstances of the Appellant.

RETROSPECTIVELY LEAVING THE SCHEME

35.32

> **Focus**
>
> HMRC have agreed in principle that they will apply proportionality to cases where unexpected amounts of VAT become payable under the Scheme and will allow businesses to retrospectively leave the scheme.

For example, there could be an issue with the sale proceeds of a buy-to-let property owned by a VAT registered sole proprietor, which is normally exempt from VAT. Under the Scheme the flat rate percentage would have to be accounted for on the sale proceeds. However, the positive point is that HMRC have confirmed that they will consider the issue of proportionality in cases where the application of the flat rate scheme gives a result that was unintended by the legislation.

HMRC has confirmed that in these circumstances it would allow the sole proprietor to retrospectively withdraw from the flat-rate scheme to reflect the principle of proportionality, however a visiting officer may be unaware of this policy so do not forget to remind him. On the down side the sole proprietor would have to recalculate his VAT from the period he retrospectively withdrew from the Scheme to a current date.

In addition to this, HMRC have also confirmed (PBNR33) that following the 1 January 2010 flat-rate percentage rises:

> 'HMRC also has the power to agree a retrospective leaving date and intends to use this sympathetically where businesses decide after 1 January 2010 that these changes have affected the scheme's suitability for them'.

I am not sure how far into the future HMRC will maintain this sympathetic view.

In contrast to this in a recent Tribunal case (*Brian Reynolds v Revenue & Customs* [2010] UKFTT 40 (TC) (21 January 2010) a taxpayer lost his appeal after he tried to retrospectively leave the Flat Rate Scheme for Small Businesses when he found that he was paying more tax than he would have done if he used the normal method of VAT accounting.

HMRC's policy is generally not to allow retrospective application or withdrawal from the flat rate scheme—and that retrospective applications should only be allowed in exceptional circumstances. The mere fact that a taxpayer will pay more tax under the flat rate scheme is not considered exceptional for these purposes. In the Tribunal's opinion the flat rate scheme is intended to provide a measure of simplification for small businesses, and is intended to be revenue neutral. The objective of the scheme is not to provide a mechanism for small businesses to pay less VAT—and this is clear from the provisions of the *6th VAT Directive* which allow Member States to implement simplified VAT accounting arrangements for small businesses.

The flat rate scheme is based on average rates of input VAT recovery for business sectors—and as it is based on averages, it is inevitable that some taxpayers will pay more (or less) than the average. In the Tribunal's opinion if taxpayers were allowed to join or withdraw from the scheme retrospectively, then this would defeat the simplification objectives of the scheme. Taxpayers could 'game' the system—and join the scheme on a 'punt', and after three years review their input VAT and apply to withdraw from the scheme with retrospective effect if they found they would pay less VAT as a result.

The Tribunal found that HMRC had acted reasonably in refusing to allow a retrospective withdrawal from the scheme in this case.

BAD DEBT RELIEF UNDER THE SCHEME

35.33 The bad debt relief rules, as described in Chapter 16, apply in the normal way if a business calculates its Scheme turnover based on invoices under the *Basic Turnover Method* and the invoice remains unpaid after six months.

If a business uses the *Cash Based Turnover Method,* it gets a special additional relief if it has written off the debt. HMRC also say the business must not have accounted for the VAT on it, which, of course, it will not have done under this method. Presumably, they mean that the business must not have accounted for VAT under the normal rules prior to joining the Scheme.

A business deducts the sum it would have paid under the Scheme from the VAT at the normal rate if the customer had paid up. The balance is a special allowance, which it can reclaim as input tax on its next VAT return. Thus, on an invoice of £1,000, the VAT is £200. If the Flat Rate percentage is 10%, that is £120 on the total of £1,200. You can reclaim the difference of £80.

APPEALS AGAINST DECISIONS BY HMRC

35.34 A business can appeal to the Tax Chamber of the Tribunal Service if HMRC refuse to authorise use of the Scheme, demand a business ceases using it, or disagree as to the trade sector and, thus, the Flat Rate percentage which applies to a business—or against an assessment resulting from such a decision.

Unfortunately, the Tribunal can only allow the appeal if it considers that HMRC could not reasonably have been satisfied that there were grounds for their decision (*VATA 1994, s 84(4ZA)*). This will make such arguments difficult to win.

Chapter 36

The Flat Rate Farmers' Scheme

SIGNPOSTS

- The *Flat Rate Farmers' Scheme* applies to small agricultural businesses—not just farmers—that wish to deregister for VAT while reducing the input tax loss by being able to charge the flat rate percentage on sales (see **36.1–36.3**).

- Businesses on the scheme charge the flat rate percentage of 4% on sales to VAT-registered customers that would normally be zero-rated. The supplier retains the flat rate percentage and the customer claims it back in the same way as he would VAT (see **36.5–36.8**).

36.1 The objective of the *Flat Rate Farmers' Scheme* is to provide a means for small agricultural businesses to escape the responsibilities of having to submit a VAT return, whilst at the same time, reducing the input tax lost as a result of not being registered. This chapter explains how the Scheme achieves this. The Scheme is not confined to farmers. As can be seen from the list of activities below, various kinds of small enterprise can use it.

However, do not confuse it with the *Flat Rate Scheme for Small Businesses* described in Chapter 35.

The Scheme is an alternative to VAT registration. A business that qualifies has the choice of staying VAT-registered or deregistering and using the flat rate scheme. A business that is not registered because its turnover is below the registration limit can also use the Scheme.

A Scheme user charges a flat rate addition of 4% to his sales to *VAT registered customers only*. He has no VAT return to complete, and he keeps this sum as compensation for being unable to recover any input tax in the normal way. The registered customer can recover the flat rate addition as input tax.

Section 54 and *Part XXIV* of the *VAT Regulations (SI 1995/2518)* contain the rules, which are explained in Notice 700/46 *Agricultural flat rate scheme*. There has been a very low take up of the scheme, so it will only be encountered occasionally.

698

QUALIFYING ACTIVITIES

36.2   Agricultural production activities

- general agriculture including viticulture;

- growing fruit, including olives and vegetables, flowers, and ornamental plants, both in the open and under glass. Production of mushrooms, spices, seeds and propagating materials, nursery stock.

Stock farming together with cultivation

- general stock farming, poultry farming, rabbit farming, beekeeping, silk worm farming, snail farming.

Forestry

Fisheries

- fresh water fishing, fish farming, breeding of mussels, oysters, other molluscs and crustaceans, frog farming.

Processing

- where a farmer, using means normally employed in an agricultural, forestry or fisheries undertaking, processes products deriving essentially from his agricultural production, it is regarded as agricultural production.

Agricultural services

- field work, reaping and mowing, threshing, baling, collecting, harvesting, sowing and planting;

- packing and preparation for market, for example, drying, cleaning, grinding, disinfecting and ensilage of agricultural products;

- storage of agricultural products, technical assistance;

- stock minding, rearing and fattening;

- hiring out for agricultural purposes, of equipment normally used in agricultural, forestry or fisheries undertakings;

- technical assistance;

- destruction of weeds and pests, dusting and spraying of crops and land;

- operation of irrigation and drainage equipment;

- lopping, tree felling and other forestry services.

NON-QUALIFYING ACTIVITIES

36.3

- dealing in animals;

- training animals, such as horses, dogs or racing pigeons—although breeding horses, pigeons or sheepdogs do qualify;

- breeding pets such as cats, dogs other than sheepdogs, budgerigars or butterflies;

- activities once removed from farming, such as processing farm produce. Examples are dairy co-operatives producing dairy products and sawmills.

Apart from those non-qualifying activities, individual sales which are of goods or services not listed above do not qualify, even if the customer is a farmer. Examples are:

- sales of machinery;

- sales of milk quota;

- repair and maintenance of farm buildings;

- bed and breakfast or holiday accommodation;

- charges to visit the farm;

- livery for horses and riding lessons.

If the value of the non-qualifying taxable sales exceeds the registration limit, the business cannot use the *Flat Rate Farmers' Scheme,* and must register for VAT under the normal system for all its sales. A possible solution is to put the non-qualifying activities into a separate business, such as a partnership or a limited company. If a business decides to do this it should be careful not to recover input tax related to the Scheme activities through the VAT registration.

The ECJ held in *Stadt Sundern* (Case C-43/04) that the grant of hunting licences by a flat-rate farmer was not an agricultural service covered by the flat-rate scheme. It would be contrary to the nature and purpose of that scheme to interpret the concept of 'agricultural service' in *Art 25(2)* of *EC 6th VAT Directive* (now *Directive 2006/112/EC, Art 295(1)(5)*) as covering a licensing operation such as the grant of hunting licences, which was not intended for agricultural purposes, and which did not relate to equipment normally used in agricultural, forestry, or fisheries undertakings.

NO OUTPUT TAX DUE ON DEREGISTRATION

36.4   If the business deregisters in order to use the Scheme, it does not have to account for output tax on stocks and assets on hand, even where input tax on them has been recovered.

THE FLAT RATE ADDITION APPLIES TO ZERO-RATED AGRICULTURAL PRODUCE

36.5   A Scheme user will charge the flat rate addition to VAT registered customers on his zero-rated agricultural produce. It is not a VAT rate, just a compensating amount to reflect irrecoverable input tax. The VAT liability of the outputs is irrelevant as to whether the flat rate addition is added.

A business does not have to add the flat rate, but as the VAT registered customer can reclaim it as input tax and the supplier does not have to pay it to HMRC, it will want to do so.

FLAT RATE INVOICES

36.6   The business issues flat rate invoices for all supplies to which the flat rate addition applies. Self billing by customers is possible with permission from HMRC.

Focus

An invoice must show:

- invoice number;
- the Flat Rate certificate number;
- the name and address and that of the VAT registered customer;
- the date and description of goods or services;
- the price before adding the Flat Rate;
- the rate and amount of the Flat Rate addition, described as Flat Rate Addition or FRA.

RECORDS REQUIRED

36.7   A business should keep its normal business records. Nothing special is required for the Scheme.

AUCTIONING AGRICULTURAL PRODUCE

36.8   If the auctioneer acts as an agent, he does not take title to the goods, so the sale does not attract VAT. The business can charge the flat rate addition to a purchaser of the goods, who is registered for VAT.

If the auctioneer acts as a principal, the seller charges the addition to the auctioneer.

SALES AND PURCHASES WITHIN THE EU

36.9   If a business sells to a customer in another Member State under the *Flat Rate Farmers' Scheme*, they only charge the flat rate addition if that customer is VAT registered in its Member State. It can then recover the addition from HMRC in the UK. Similarly, a business only has to pay a flat rate addition to a farmer in another Member State, under the equivalent scheme in that Member State, if it is VAT registered in the UK. It can then reclaim it from the VAT authority in that Member State.

SALES OUTSIDE THE EU

36.10   If a business sells under the Scheme to a customer outside the EU, and that customer buys for the purpose of a business, it can also charge the Flat Rate. That customer will then reclaim it from HMRC.

THE £3,000 LIMIT

36.11   HMRC can refuse an application to join the Scheme if the Flat Rate to be charged and retained by the business is likely to be £3,000 or more than the input tax that would otherwise be claimable. This will always be satisfied where the estimated value of agricultural supplies shown on the application form (VAT98) is £75,000 or less.

LEAVING AND REJOINING THE SCHEME VOLUNTARILY

36.12   To leave voluntarily, a business must have used the Scheme for at least a year. It can then rejoin at any time unless it has registered for VAT. In the latter case, at least three years must pass—or one year if the VAT due on assets on hand is less than £1,000.

Chapter 37

The Tour Operators' Margin Scheme

SIGNPOSTS

- The *Tour Operators' Margin Scheme* (TOMS) applies to businesses that buy in and re-sell travel, accommodation and certain other services as principal or undisclosed agent. VAT is only due on the profit margin and the scheme can apply to businesses other than just Tour Operators (see **37.1–37.2** and **37.9**).

- VAT is due on the margin on supplies made within the EU; holidays outside the EU are zero-rated (see **37.3–37.4**).

- The calculation is done annually, not holiday by holiday (see **37.5**).

- TOMS also covers in-house costs as well as those that are bought in (see **37.6–37.7**).

37.1   The *Tour Operators' Margin Scheme* (TOMS) is mainly intended to deal with the problem of package holidays sold in one country by a tour operator, and taken in another.

Without the Scheme, a tour operator who provided package holidays in other EU Member States would have to account for VAT in each country where his customers received the services. The Scheme is a simplification measure under *Art 26* of the *EC 6th VAT Directive* (now *Directive 2006/112/EC, Arts 306–310*), although anybody using the scheme would have difficulty in believing it was a simplification of anything! It allows tour operators to account for VAT entirely within their home country.

THE LAW

37.2   The UK law is in *s 53* and in the *Value Added Tax (Tour Operators) Order 1987 (SI 1987/1806)*.

Focus

Under the Scheme:

- VAT cannot be reclaimed on *margin scheme* supplies bought in for resale;

- VAT is only accounted for on the difference between the VAT-inclusive purchase price and the selling price (the 'margin');

- there are special rules for determining the place, liability and time of *margin scheme* supplies;

- VAT invoices cannot be issued for margin scheme supplies;

- there are special rules for calculating the VAT due on the margin; and

- the value of turnover for VAT registration purposes is the margin.

Notice 709/5 *Tour operators' margin scheme* refers. In some respects concerning the calculations and records, it has the force of law.

Following the 1 October 2007 introduction of the additional invoicing requirements (outlined in detail at **14.5**), any invoices issued to business customers are required to include one of three references: a reference to the relevant article in the EC Directive, a reference to the relevant UK legislation, or any other reference indicating that TOMS has been applied.

HMRC say in *VAT Information Sheet 10/07* that although the regulation of TOMS referencing is new, businesses will have a wide range of choice in deciding the best way of referencing TOMS treatment. HMRC will allow affected businesses the widest possible discretion in adapting commercial or industry norms to meet the 'any other reference' requirement.

HMRC give the following as examples of acceptable invoice narratives:

- 'This is a Tour Operators' Margin Scheme supply'.

- 'This supply falls under the Value Added Tax (Tour Operators) Order 1987'.

Hopefully, the following outline of the key rules will help a business to understand a part of the VAT system which many people dislike and avoid at all costs! If a business has to get involved with using TOMS, see Notice 709/5, which contains some sample calculations.

HOW IT WORKS FOR EU HOLIDAYS

37.3   A business cannot recover VAT which it incurs either in the UK or in any other EU Member State on services directly related to your package holidays. The UK or foreign VAT on those services is, therefore, part of the costs of the business. The gross profit (or 'margin') is then treated as VAT inclusive, and the amount of output tax owed is calculated using the VAT fraction. Thus:

- the EU Member States where the services are enjoyed get the tax on the hotel accommodation, meals, etc;

- UK HMRC gets the tax on the gross profit margin;

- the tour operator recovers the VAT incurred in the UK on overheads and other costs not directly related to individual package holidays;

- the net VAT paid is similar to that which would be due if the tour operator charged output tax on the value of a holiday and recovered all the input tax, no matter where it was incurred.

HOLIDAYS OUTSIDE THE EU

37.4   If a tour operator sells holidays outside the EU, it must still use the TOMS, but the profit margin on them is zero-rated.

If the tour operator sells holidays both inside and outside the EU, the gross margin is apportioned in the ratio of direct costs for EU destinations to the total direct costs. Alternatively, the tour operator can separate the costs and sales values for EU tours. The tour operator includes any mixed tours, and the apportioned sales value is treated as zero-rated.

The choice of method should depend on whether the profit margins differ; lower non-EU margins mean that a worldwide calculation produces a lower VAT liability than one separating the EU costs and sales. If the tour operator changes from one method to another, it must tell HMRC in advance—and, of course, the change can only be done at the start of each VAT year, given that provisional figures are used during the year. In other words, the tour operator cannot choose after the event the calculation producing the lowest liability.

If a tour operator fails to notify HMRC at the start of the TOMS year which method it wishes to use, it will be presumed to have chosen the same method as it used for the previous year (*MyTravel Group plc* (MAN/02/426 No 18940)).

THE CALCULATION IS DONE ANNUALLY, NOT HOLIDAY BY HOLIDAY

37.5   During the year, the tour operator pays VAT at a provisional rate. This is based on the previous year's gross margin calculated as a percentage of the sales for that year. That percentage is then applied to the current sales.

At the end of the year, the figures are then adjusted to the actual percentage.

SO WHAT ARE THE DIRECTLY RELATED COSTS?

37.6   The costs which are part of the margin calculation are those directly related to a holiday, as opposed to overheads of the business. They include transporting the customers, accommodation, car hire, trips or excursions, special lounges at airports, tour guides and features included in the package such as catering, theatre tickets, and sports facilities.

IN-HOUSE COSTS

37.7   All costs used to calculate the VAT inclusive margin must have been bought in. That means that if the tour operator uses its own facilities, such as a hotel, to provide part of the package, the package price has to be split between 'bought in' and 'in-house' supplies. The reason is that the tour operator will usually have to register for VAT in the UK or wherever else the hotel is, and will then be able to recover the input tax on the costs of running it. The tour operator must, therefore, account for output tax on that part of the package price rather than on the margin. The tour operator must use the market value for its in-house supplies and the calculation for this is found in the revised version of Notice 709/5: *Tour Operators' Margin Scheme*.

In *Madgett and Baldwin* ([1998] STC 1189) the CJEC held that market values should be used for valuing in-house supplies, not a cost plus basis. This can make a big difference to the total VAT payable. In HMRC Brief 27/09, HMRC announced the requisite use of market values for in-house supplies from 1 January 2010. See para **37.8** below for further details on this change.

If the tour operator owns a coach, transport in it in the UK will be zero-rated. However, if it runs trips elsewhere in Europe, the coach travel is treated as supplied in the EU Member States where it takes place. Thus, the tour operator may have to register and charge VAT in those Member States.

INVOICES TO BUSINESS CUSTOMERS

37.8   Up to 1 January 2010 HMRC would allow tour operators that sold travel to business customers to issue tax invoices to them outside the scheme if it asks permission from HMRC. This way, the business customer could recover the VAT it is charged under the normal rules.

However, in HMRC Brief 27/09, HMRC announced three key changes were to be made to the Tour Operators' Margin Scheme ('TOMS') from 1 January 2010, two of which relate to invoices to business customers. The changes were required in order for the UK scheme to comply fully with EU law (following written concerns from the European Commission).

The three changes concern:

- supplies to business customers for subsequent resale;

- supplies to business customers for their own consumption and supplies of educational school trips; and

- use of market values in respect of in-house supplies.

1. Supplies to business customers for resale (known as 'the opt in')

By concession, HMRC had allowed tour operators that normally make holiday sales to the public, but occasionally sell to other travel businesses for onward resale, the option of accounting for tax on the latter within the TOMS. This was intended to ease the administrative difficulties that tour operators might otherwise incur in having to use the normal VAT rules.

HMRC then decided that the UK had to accept that the EC VAT Directive refers to supplies made to the 'traveller'. The 'traveller' is the person who consumes the travel, and so the scheme should not be used when the travel service is sold to a person other than the traveller, such as when supplies are made to business customers for resale. Therefore, from 1 January 2010, affected tour operators have had to account for the VAT due under the normal VAT rules, which, in some cases, may give rise to a requirement to register for VAT in other Member States.

However, in *Revenue & Customs Brief 05/14* HMRC has explained how UK tour operators and other businesses supplying travel services will be affected by a number of ECJ decisions relating to the operation of TOMS. HMRC has decided not to apply these changes at this time as it is awaiting a further review of TOMS by the EU Commission. Any changes will be implemented after the review has been completed. However, it is open for any business to apply direct effect of the ECJ decisions and operate TOMS in accordance with the ECJ's decisions. For example, it is possible that some tour operators may gain a benefit from including wholesale supplies within TOMS, in which case they may choose to do so if they wish going forward.

2. Supplies to businesses for their own consumption and the provision of school trips (known as 'the opt out')

The TOMS had always included travel services which were supplied to other businesses for their own consumption in the special scheme. However, tour operators have been allowed to opt out of the TOMS in respect of such supplies, meaning that business customers have been able to recover VAT charged on those supplies. HMRC had also treated the provision of school trips as a non-business activity, and allowed them to be excluded from TOMS as well, enabling local authorities to recover the VAT charged in relation to LEA schools.

HMRC says that the Commission has clarified that the term 'traveller' should not be restricted to the physical person who consumes a travel package, but also covers legal persons that consume the travel package, for example, businesses which pay for employee travel, and the supply of school trips to local authorities. Accordingly, from 1 January 2010, businesses receiving supplies of travel services from tour operators will no longer be able to recover VAT on such supplies. Those LEA schools that previously took advantage of the concession set out at para 3.4 of *Public Notice 709/5* will no longer be able to recover VAT on UK school trips purchased from tour operators. However, there will be no change for trips organised directly by a school, such as day trips on coaches to a zoo or museum.

However, in HMRC Brief 21/10 HMRC stated that a hotel booking agent is entirely open to act as a disclosed agent, with the hotels supplying accommodation direct to their business clients, rather than buy in and supply the accommodation themselves. Following separate approaches by the Hotel Booking Agents Association and the Guild of Travel Management Companies, HMRC have agreed the arrangements detailed below where agents operate in this way. These arrangements are available generally to all business travel agents that wish to adopt them.

The agreed arrangements are:

- Invoices from hotels will be addressed c/o the hotel booking agent for payment. (This is to indicate that the invoice has been issued to the hotel booking agent in its capacity as an agent.)

- The booking field on the hotel invoice will identify the hotel guest, their employer and will ideally carry a unique reference number. (Until hotels can address their invoices directly to their business customers, it may be necessary for hotel booking agents to enter an employer identification number on the invoice.)

- The hotel booking agent will arrange for payment of the invoice(s) but will not recover the input tax thereon.

- The hotel booking agent will send the customer a payment request/ statement of the expenditure incurred by the hotel booking agent on its behalf, separately identifying the value of its supplies, VAT, etc.

- The payment request/statement should say something along the lines of 'The VAT shown is your input tax which can be reclaimed subject to the normal rules'.

- The customer will use the payment request/statement as a basis for their input tax reclaim.

- The hotel booking agent will retain the original hotel invoices and these will be made available if evidence of entitlement is required by VAT staff.

- The hotel booking agent will send a VAT invoice for its own services, plus the VAT. This may be consolidated with the statement of hotel charges, or it can be a separate document.

- The hotel booking agent will charge its client the exact amount charged by the billback supplier, as a disbursement.

3. Market values for in-house supplies

The current UK TOMS calculation requires the margin to be apportioned with reference to the actual costs incurred in putting the package together. However, in *MyTravel* (C-291/03) the ECJ held that where it is possible to establish an appropriate market value for that part of the selling price which corresponds to the in-house supplies, this should be used to apportion the selling price between in-house and bought-in elements. The margin can then be calculated on each element, and the scheme calculation completed accordingly.

However, the ECJ also said the cost-based method could be used where this accurately reflected the structure of the package. HMRC considers that, as the cost-based method assumes a fixed percentage mark-up across all elements of the package, the package should also be on a fixed mark-up basis to meet the condition. If it is not possible to determine a market value, tour operators can continue using the current cost-based method.

Whilst the concept of market values is complex, based on the ECJ's findings, certain parameters should be used when deciding whether it is possible to establish such a value:

- The market value (selling price) must be within the context of the tour operator's business, eg a tour operator could not use the price of a scheduled airline flight in determining a market value of the flight forming part of a package holiday.

- The market value must be on a like-for-like basis, ie it should be determined on the basis of the price of similar services supplied by the taxable person, and not forming part of a package. If the taxable person does not provide similar services, it may be possible to use the price of comparable services provided by other taxable persons.

- Across-the-board averages may be used if correctly weighted and reviewed regularly.

HMRC says that it is clear that market values need to be considered on a case-by-case basis. Where such values are to be used, they will simply slot into the current calculation method at the appropriate point.

SCOPE OF THE SCHEME

37.9   The Scheme does not just apply to anyone calling themselves a tour operator. Anyone who buys in and resells travel facilities for the direct benefit of a traveller, regardless of whether the facilities are used for holiday or business purposes, is likely to be covered.

There is no statutory definition of when a taxable person is acting as a tour operator for the purposes of the scheme. The ECJ has held that the *TOMS* can apply to a trader who is not formally classified as a travel agent or tour operator. For example, many schools can come within the TOMS when organising school trips. See *Madgett and Baldwin* ([1998] STC 1189).

ZERO-RATED TRANSPORT IN THE EU—A PLANNING POINT HMRC ALLOW

37.10   Transport from the UK to EU destinations is treated as standard-rated under the TOMS. However, the tour operator can set up a separate company which buys in the airline flights, coach trips etc and sells them on to the tour company (Tourco)—still zero-rated—at a profit. This increases the costs of Tourco, and thus, reduces its margin subject to VAT. HMRC accept this, provided that the mark-up does not reduce the profit below what it would have been had the margin been split between zero-rated transport and standard-rated hotels, etc.

INSURANCE AND CANCELLATION FEES

37.11   The margin on any holiday insurance sold is exempt. Cancellation fees are outside the scope of VAT, because no supply is made to the customer.

VAT ON OVERHEADS

37.12   The tour operator also recovers VAT on all overheads, such as office expenses which do not come within the scheme.

The *Tour Operators' Margin Scheme* is a part of VAT which most people avoid if possible! This means that, if a business is involved, it will need to do its homework carefully. There have been various important cases over the years which may need to be studied

INTERMEDIARIES ACTING AS AGENT OR PRINCIPAL

37.13   In the case of *Secret Hotels 2 Limited (Formerly Med Hotels Limited v Revenue and Customs Commissioners* ([2011] UKUT 308 (TCC)) the Upper Tribunal overturned the decision of the First-tier Tribunal in a case involving TOMS. The Upper Tribunal determined that it is the contractual relationships between the relevant parties that establishes whether an intermediary in a supply chain acts as a disclosed agent or principal. This is in contrast to the HMRC argument that was successful in the initial hearing, which focused on the day-to-day interactions between the parties and the widespread use of net rates.

This case is very significant because UK-based travel businesses acting as a principal are obliged to account for UK VAT under TOMS. Agents have no such obligation. This difference in tax treatment means it is far more beneficial from a UK VAT perspective to trade as a disclosed agent, but has resulted in HMRC launching a series of challenges to businesses using this model. This case has caused uncertainty for travel businesses when price-setting. This decision is therefore a very significant win for the taxpayer and will impact all intermediaries in the travel sector.

The decision is focused on the UK position and does not address some of the potential tax difficulties that might arise for travel intermediaries or their suppliers in the country of destination. However, it could provide much needed clarity regarding the position in the UK. All travel agents and intermediaries (especially those facing a challenge from HMRC) should review their position urgently in light of this decision.

In the case of *Lowcost Holidays Ltd T/A Lowcost Beds v HMRC* [2017] UKFTT 463 (TC), HMRC argued that the appellant provided hotel accommodation in other EU Member States as principle, and was therefore within the Tour Operators Margin Scheme (TOMS), the appellant argued that they acted as agents. The appellant had made a claim for a refund of £2m following its liquidation in 2016 which had been rejected by HMRC

Article 45 of the PVD provides that 'the place of supply of services connected with immoveable property … shall be the place where the property is located'. If the appellant was only providing services in this connection then, since the immoveable property in question was located in EU Member States outside the UK, those services would fall outside the scope of UK VAT.

The appellant's group financial controller gave evidence that from the outset the appellant's founder and CEO had been determined that the group would not take any risk as a principal in any commercial arrangements. He said that the CEO had 25 years' experience within the industry and this experience had persuaded him that travel agents should not take any risk as a principal. This had been the governing principle in all the appellant's activities.

In their dealings with customers the appellant dealt via a website. The Tribunal were shown copies of the Terms and Conditions which a customer would have to agree to, on the website, before he could make a booking on the site. These Terms and Conditions state in a number of places that the appellant was acting as an agent for the hotels, villas and apartments featured on the website.

The appellant's contracts with supplier's Terms and Conditions consistently referred to principal and agent. The appellant was entitled to a commission from the principal for arranging the hire of accommodation.

The Tribunal concluded that the appellant acted as agent and was not subject to TOMS and therefore found for the appellant.

Chapter 38

Buying or selling a business

SIGNPOSTS

- A key point to consider if a company is being sold is whether you are buying shares or the trade and assets of a business. If the trade and assets of a business are being bought as the transfer of a going concern (TOGC), then no VAT is due on the sale providing certain criteria are met (see **38.1–38.4**).

- There are some common pitfalls when purchasing as a TOGC and certain requirements that are necessary (see **38.5–38.10**).

- When buying a business as a TOGC you have to consider if you want to acquire the books and records and, most importantly, if you want to inherit the existing VAT number or have a new VAT registration (see **38.12–38.13** and **38.20**).

- There are special rules regarding the transfer of a property and the TOGC of a property rental business (see **38.13–38.16**).

38.1   Buying or selling a business involves VAT just like any other business transaction. Yet, amidst all the stress and excitement, it is all too easy for it to be overlooked. This chapter deals with a number of the potential pitfalls.

IS A COMPANY OR ITS BUSINESS BEING SOLD?

38.2   If a business is owned by a limited company, it has a choice:

- it can sell the share capital of the company; or

- the company can sell its business, leaving the shareholders still owning the shares.

A sale of the shares is an exempt transaction in securities, unless the buyer belongs outside the EU. See Chapters 11, *Exemption*, 23, *Exports and Imports of Services,* and 24, *Partial Exemption* for further comment on the various rules and implications.

There is one important comment to make here concerning the problem of buying the share capital of the company which is a member of someone else's VAT group.

INSOLVENT VAT GROUPS—JOINT AND SEVERAL

38.3   A company which is grouped with others under *s 43* is 'jointly and severally' liable for any tax due from the representative member of the group (*s 43(1)(c)*), therefore, it is jointly liable for all the tax due from the rest of the group during the period it was a member of the VAT group.

If a company is bought out of an insolvent VAT group, it may be several years before the balance of tax unpaid by the rest of the members of the VAT group is determined, and the HMRC claim is made. See **4.7** for more comment.

Preferably, do not buy the share capital, just the assets.

IN PRINCIPLE, VAT IS CHARGEABLE ON ASSETS SOLD

38.4   If a business sells its assets, VAT is chargeable on them in principle. It makes no difference that they are a bundle of assets making up a business. VAT is even due on goodwill, because it represents the right to carry on the business in that location and under that name, etc.

However, a set of rules known as the *Transfer of a Going Concern* (TOGC) rules take the sale of a business outside the scope of VAT if certain conditions are met. These rules simplify the sales of many businesses because it is not necessary, for VAT purposes, to put values on individual assets, and the purchaser's cash flow situation is eased because the price does not include VAT. The rules are also there to protect HMRC. Without them:

- VAT charged would become part of the vendor's assets, and at risk of being used to pay creditors, or, in an insolvency situation, subject to the claims of other preferential creditors before it was payable to HMRC on the next VAT return; or

- a vendor selling a business for a substantial sum could collect the VAT and retire abroad without paying it to HMRC.

THE TRANSFER OF A BUSINESS AS A GOING CONCERN

38.5

Focus

If the assets transferred constitute:

- an entire business transferred as a going concern; or

> - a part of the business capable of separate operation; and
> - the purchaser uses the assets in the same kind of business; and
> - the purchaser registers for VAT, if not already registered,
>
> the transaction is outside the scope of VAT. No VAT must be charged on any of the assets (*Special Provisions Order (SI 1995/1268), art 5*).

Strictly, the last requirement is that the purchaser 'immediately becomes as a result of the transfer, a taxable person', which means becomes liable to register (*s 3*). However, it is safest to regard the rule as meaning that the vendor should obtain proof that the purchaser has applied to register immediately. Not only does this minimise the risk of any possible inquiries by HMRC; it deals with the pitfall of a very small business with sales below the registration limit, the purchaser of which would not therefore automatically become a taxable person, and so would have to register voluntarily in order to do so.

Although simple in concept, these rules have tripped up many clients and their advisors. The subtleties of what is or is not a business, as opposed to a collection of assets, have been explored in numerous Tribunal cases.

COMMON PITFALLS

38.6 No tax is charged on the main assets of the business. This is correct, but one common mistake is that when the stock is counted at completion, the vendor and purchaser often deal direct without professionals on hand. The vendor sometimes wrongly adds VAT to the stock valuation, saying the purchaser can recover this. Subsequently, HMRC disallow the VAT as input tax because the vendor has failed to account for it to them. HMRC would not normally disallow the input tax if they had had the output tax, although they have the power to do so. It is then irrelevant whether the 'VAT' went to pay creditors, or whether the vendor simply pulled a fast one. Since the tax was not chargeable in the first place, there is no defence against the assessment.

Worse still, VAT is sometimes charged on the entire assets because the vendor and/ or his professional advisors assume it ought to be, and do not check the rules. The purchaser and advisors do not challenge this, and again the vendor fails to account for the tax, possibly because he is insolvent; same story, just a bigger mess!

YOU DO NOT NEED MANY ASSETS FOR THERE TO BE A BUSINESS

38.7 In *R Cuthbert* (EDN/99/611 No 6518), there was a TOGC because contracts were taken over and the trading name retained, even though there was little stock, no other assets, and no employees.

Similarly, in *Associates Fleet Services Ltd* (MAN/00/419 No 17255), the purchase of a batch of vehicle leasing contracts was held to be a TOGC, despite there being no transfer of goodwill, trading name, other assets, premises or staff. The purchaser did not need these in order to carry on the business transferred. The vendor's financial position was so weak that the absence of a restriction of competition clause in the contract did not matter to the purchaser.

KEY CRITERIA ON WHETHER THERE IS A TOGC

38.8   In *E C Reese Agricultural Ltd* ([2004] SWTI 445), when dismissing an attempt to justify charging VAT on the sale of the assets of a business, the Tribunal listed the criteria as:

● all the circumstances of the case;

● the substance of the transaction, not its form;

● whether the transferee obtained a going concern capable of continuing;

● many factors relevant, but few, if any, conclusive in isolation;

● an intention to change the business in the future irrelevant;

● any delay in restarting the business relevant, but of little significance;

● that the transfer is effected by several transactions, not just one, irrelevant.

MUST IT BE THE SAME KIND OF BUSINESS?

38.9   In *Zita Modes Sàrl* (C-497/01), the ECJ held that the sale of a business qualifies as a TOGC if the purchaser intends to *operate the business or the part of the undertaking transferred and not simply to immediately liquidate the activity concerned and sell the stock, if any.*

The Court also said that the transferee need not already be in the same kind of business prior to the transfer. That is not the same as saying that it may not be valid for UK law to require the transferee to carry on the same kind of business for which the transferor used the assets. On the other hand, does the need to operate the business necessitate that it be the same kind?

Of course, the use for the same kind of business will normally be automatic. For the purchaser to make a fundamental change to its nature is unusual. Arguably, it makes no difference if a business, such as a restaurant, is closed in order to refurbish it in a different style. See below.

USUALLY, A SHORT PERIOD OF CLOSURE IS IRRELEVANT

38.10   Normally, a transaction is not changed from a TOGC merely because of a temporary shutdown on change of ownership. Usually, the same kind of business is reopened in the same location. Moreover, in *H Tahmassebi t/a Sale Pepe* (MAN/94/197 No 13177), in which an Indian restaurant was closed on the day prior to the transfer, and reopened after a complete refurbishment as a pasta house, the Tribunal saw the key point as being 'what had been transferred to the purchaser', not 'what he had subsequently done with it'. He had bought the rights to the existing restaurant including a substantial payment for goodwill, and a key condition was that the alcohol licence was transferred to him. He could have operated the existing restaurant without a break. The fact that he had instructed the vendors to close it the day before the transfer did not affect this.

The Tribunal did accept that the new business was as different to the old one as chalk to cheese. However, a restaurant is in the same kind of business regardless of the type of food it supplies.

In contrast, in *Sawadee Restaurant* (EDN/98/43 No 15933), there was no transfer of a going concern when a Japanese restaurant closed down, the staff were dismissed, stock returned to suppliers, and a partnership of three terminated, and, seven weeks later, a new partnership, including one of the previous partners who held the lease, opened a Thai restaurant. The only assets reused were a few chairs and the lease. However, the key point was that the previous business was not transferred. It had ceased.

Denise Harrold (LON/25/693 No 19604) took over a public house which had been run by a licensee no longer able to open it. She was given a new three-year lease, took over no stock or staff, and paid nothing to the previous licensee. The pub was in a poor and unhygienic state. She had to clean it throughout and refurbish the bar—an unusual situation, which the Tribunal saw as a new business starting from scratch. As there was no continuity, it could not be a TOGC.

MORE ON THE SAME KIND OF BUSINESS

38.11   In *Paula Holland* (MAN/98/1031 No 15996), the transfer of a pub from management by the owner to a tenant was held to be a TOGC. Although the owner was now renting out the premises, what had been transferred was the pub operation. This was continued under the same name and with the same staff in the same location.

In various other cases concerning public houses, there has been held to be a TOGC even though the existing business was almost non-existent, the premises being in poor condition and trade very low.

In *R N Banbury (t/a Creative Impressions)* (LON/96/1720 No 15047) the sale of an embroidery machine by a limited company to its director was held to be a TOGC, even though the work was then for wholesale customers, not retail and not on goods for sale in a shop. Those were points merely relevant to the manner of carrying on the business, not to the kind of business.

However, in *Delta Newsagents Ltd* (MAN/86/69 No 1220) a franchisee bought the goodwill and fixtures and fittings of a retail shop and the franchise agreement was terminated. The franchisee was already running the shop. Although he acquired the assets used in it, no business was sold. The franchise at that location ceased. Therefore, there was no TOGC.

TRANSFERRING A BUSINESS INTO A VAT GROUP

38.12   In the case of *Intelligent Managed Services Ltd v Revenue & Customs* [2015] UKUT 0341 (TCC) the taxpayer appealed against a decision of the First-tier Tribunal in favour of HMRC that the transfer of its business to Virgin Money Management Services Limited (VMMSL), a member of the Virgin Money Group (VMG) VAT group, was not a TOGC and was subject to VAT.

At the time of transfer to VMMSL, IMSL had developed a banking platform (or 'banking engine') for the provision of banking processing services for banks which did not have modern systems or which did not wish to build their own advanced payment processing services. Following the transfer of the business, VMMSL provided banking processing services to another member of the VMG VAT group, Virgin Money Bank Limited (VMBL), which provided retail banking services to retail customers.

HMRC argued that because VMMSL was not the representative member of the VMG VAT group and that its supplies to VMBL fell to be disregarded by virtue of *s 43*, the effect was that VMMSL's business had effectively ceased. It did not therefore operate the same kind of business as that undertaken by IMSL prior to the transfer – indeed it did not operate any business – and accordingly VMMSL's acquisition of the business from IMSL could not be a TOGC.

It is accepted that if VMMSL were a stand-alone company all the conditions for the sale of the business to be treated as a TOGC would be satisfied. The only question was whether, when the transaction is regarded as a sale by IMSL to the VMG VAT group, that group fails to satisfy the same kind of business test.

Leaving aside the effect of the VAT group rules, it was accepted that VMMSL is, as a matter of fact carrying on the same business as that formerly carried on by IMSL. The question was whether the fiction created by the group rules, that of the single taxable person carrying on that business, in combination with the other businesses of the group, means that the VMG VAT group is not to be treated as using the assets transferred in carrying on the same kind of business.

In the Tribunal's judgment, there was nothing in the group rules that could prevent the transfer of IMSL's business to VMMSL from being a TOGC. The transfer was of the whole undertaking of IMSL in relation to the banking engine services. VMMSL was accepted as having had the requisite intention to carry on that business, and not to liquidate the activity or do anything else that could lead to the conclusion that this was no more than a transfer of assets. VMMSL provided the banking engine services to VMBL, which incorporated the product of those services into its own retail banking services that it supplied to third party customers. The Tribunal, therefore, found in favour of the appellant that the transfer qualified as a TOGC.

IS THE OUTSOURCING OF AN OVERHEAD ACTIVITY OF A COMPANY A TOGC?

38.13 In *Royal Bank of Scotland Group plc* (EDN/01/105 No 17637), the transfer of cheque clearing services by RBS to an outsourcing company, EDS, was held to be a TOGC.

HMRC did argue that EDS was not carrying on the same kind of business because it did not provide banking services, but that point was not specifically referred to by the Tribunal. It found that a part of the business had been transferred which was capable of separate operation.

HMRC made the point more clearly in *FMCG Home Services Ltd* ([2004] SWTI 447). In FMCG, the sale of the assets and transfer of the staff involved in collecting premiums for the Prudential Corporation was held not to amount to a TOGC because:

- the activity was merely part of the Pru's overheads. It only became a business when operated by the Appellant;

- the assets were not used in the same kind of business because they had been used by the Pru to supply insurance, but were now used to collect cash.

The case was argued on the basis of the opinion of the Advocate General in *Zita Modes*, not the Court judgment. The Tribunal did not set out its reasoning; it merely accepted HMRC's views.

RECORDS REQUIRED ON TRANSFER

38.14 Prior to 1 September 2007, *s 49* required the vendor of a business as a TOGC to transfer the records to the purchaser (although the seller could apply to HMRC for permission to keep the records).

With small businesses, this did not always happen unless the parties realised the problem. In the case of more substantial businesses, records were normally part of what was passed on because the purchaser needed them to be able to carry on.

From 1 September 2007, the seller of a TOGC retains the records. However:

- the seller must make available to the buyer any information needed by him to comply with his duties under the *VAT Act*;

- where the buyer submits a VAT68 application to HMRC for permission to take on the seller's VAT number, the seller is still required to transfer the records to the buyer, unless the seller needs to retain the records (in which case he may apply to HMRC for permission to do so).

HMRC add that they may disclose to the buyer any information it holds on the business that is needed by him to comply with his duties under the *VAT Act*.

Examples of where HMRC may be asked for information are:

- retail and second-hand schemes because they are part of the basis for the VAT return;

- property subject to the *Capital Goods Scheme* either because scheme calculations already have to be made or because information about the cost might be needed on a future change of use;

- partial exemption calculations if the basis of these is a method agreed with HMRC.

In *East Anglia Motor Services Ltd* (LON/99/64 No 16398), the appellant purchased a garage and service station. Shortly afterwards, it also bought the vendor's stock of second-hand cars under a separate contract. The vendor had intended to retain the cars, but changed his mind. The transaction was held to be part of the TOGC. This was a disaster for the purchaser because he had not acquired the records of the vendor, and so had no details of the purchase prices of the cars. Consequently, he had no defence against an assessment from HMRC that was based on the assumption that his profit margin was 50% of the sale prices.

PASS THE PARCEL

38.15   There is a serious problem when a business is transferred, only to be passed on again immediately. Examples are:

- a professional partnership breaks up. Two of the partners take part of the business as a going concern and immediately join another partnership;

- part of the business of a company is sold as a going concern to another company, which immediately passes it to a new subsidiary;

- a property, let to tenants and counting as a business, is resold immediately.

In none of these cases does either stage of the transaction qualify as a TOGC because the business in the middle does not trade. It therefore does not use the assets in the same kind of business.

Kwik Save Group plc (MAN/93/11 No 12749) showed this point to be a real problem. Various food stores were bought by Kwik Save from Gateway Corporation and other vendors. Some were immediately transferred to a subsidiary, Tates Ltd. Although the £395,000 VAT assessed on the invoices from Gateway to Tates for these stores was recovered by Tates, there was a £32,000 interest cost for this error.

Similarly, in *Winterthur Swiss Insurance Co* (LON/03/827 No 19411), it was held that the sale of goodwill by the Prudential Assurance Co Ltd to Winterthur was standard-rated because Winterthur in Switzerland immediately sold it on to a subsidiary in Bermuda. The place of supply was the UK, and it did not qualify under the TOGC rules—though Winterthur was held to be eligible for a refund of the VAT under the *8th Directive* as explained in Chapter 27, *Recovery of Foreign VAT*.

THE PROBLEM IF THE ASSETS INCLUDE PROPERTY

38.16   If the assets include property which is:

- a 'new' building or civil engineering work (for the meaning of 'new', see **26.75**);

- land, a building, or a civil engineering work, for which, the option to tax has been exercised,

the sale of the business as a going concern would enable the purchaser of the business to avoid paying any VAT on it. HMRC accept that a single building let as an investment property can constitute a business for this purpose, so if there was no legislation to prevent this, the avoidance possibilities would be significant. To prevent such avoidance, the *Special Provisions Order (SI 1995/1268), art 5(2)* takes the value of such property outside the Order, and thus makes it standard-rated unless:

- the purchaser of the business opts to tax the property from the date of the transfer; and, by the date of the transfer;

- gives HMRC such written notification of the election, as may be required by *Sch 10, para 3(6)*;

- and notifies the vendor that the purchaser's option will not be disapplied (*art 5(2A)* from 18/3/04). See **26.77** for the circumstances in which an option is disapplied. Examples are when it is for use as a dwelling, for relevant residential or charitable purposes, or by a housing association for constructing such buildings. See also **26.102** for the problem if the tenant is partially exempt.

The rule requiring this notification prevents any attempt to avoid a non-recoverable VAT charge on a property by buying it as part of a TOGC. Of course, the rule assumes that the buyer knows what the future use will be. In *Business Brief 12/04*, HMRC accept that if the notification turns out to be incorrect, they will not demand output tax from the vendor—though they will 'investigate the circumstances'. Presumably, that means they could challenge the transferee.

See **26.99** for details of *Dartford Borough Council* (VTD 20,246), where a supply of opted development land was held to be a TOGC.

TRANSFER OF A PROPERTY RENTAL BUSINESS

38.17   Here are some examples from HMRC (as listed in Notice 700/9) of when a business can be transferred as a going concern

If a business:

- owns the freehold of a property which it lets to a tenant and sell the freehold with the benefit of the existing lease, a business of property rental is transferred to the purchaser. This is a business transferred as a going concern even if the property is only partly tenanted. Similarly, if the business owns the lease of a property (which is subject to a sub-lease) and it assigns the lease with the benefit of the sub-lease, this is a business transferred as a going concern;

- owns a building which is being let out where there is an initial rent free period, even if the building is sold during the rent free period, the business is carrying on a business of property rental;

- granted a lease in respect of a building but the tenants are not yet in occupation, the business is carrying on a property rental business;

- owns a property and have found a tenant but not actually entered into a lease agreement when it transfers the property to a third party (with the benefit of the prospective tenancy but before a lease has been signed), there is sufficient evidence of intended economic activity for there to be a property rental business capable of being transferred;

- is a property developer selling a site as a package (to a single buyer) which is a mixture of let and unlet, finished or unfinished properties, and the sale of the site would otherwise have been standard rated, then subject to the purchaser electing to waive exemption for the whole site, the whole site can be regarded as a business transferred as a going concern.

Examples where there is not a transfer of a going concern

If a business:

- is a property developer and have built a building and it allows someone to occupy temporarily (without any right to occupy after any proposed sale) or it is 'actively marketing' it in search of a tenant, there is no property rental business being carried on.

- sells a property where the lease that has been granted is surrendered immediately before the sale, the property rental business ceases and so cannot be transferred as a going concern—even if tenants under a sublease remain in occupation.

- sells a property to the existing tenant who leases the whole premises, this cannot be a transfer of a going concern because the tenant cannot carry on the same business of property rental.

- have granted a lease in respect of a building and the tenant is running a business from the premises. The tenant then sells the assets of his business as a going concern and surrenders his lease. The business grants the new owner of the business a lease in respect of the building. This is not a transfer by the business of a property rental business.

Following the Tribunal decision in *Robinson Family Ltd v Revenue & Customs Commissioners* [2012] UKFTT 360 (TC) HMRC now accept that the fact that the transferor of a property rental business retains a small reversionary interest in the property transferred does not prevent the transaction from being treated as a TOGC for VAT purposes. Provided the interest retained is small enough not to disturb the substance of the transaction (no more than 1% of the pre transfer value), the transaction will be a TOGC if the usual conditions are satisfied.

The second bullet point in paragraph 6.3 of Notice 700/9 should now be ignored, as HMRC accept that the creation of a new asset (a lease or sub-lease) and the retention of the original asset (the freehold or a superior lease) is not automatically incompatible with TOGC treatment.

In the case of *Revenue & Customs v Royal College Of Pediatrics and Child Health & Anor* [2015] UKUT 38 (TCC) the Upper Tribunal considered an appeal from the First-tier Tribunal by HMRC against a decision that the sale of a property qualified as a TOGC, that the assessment was in any case out of time and that an adjustment under the Capital Goods Scheme did not apply.

In this instance the interesting part of the decision related to the TOGC treatment of the sale of the property. The appellant was a registered charity whose activities were predominantly non-business or exempt. The appellant let space in its existing premises to two further organisations: the British Association of Perinatal Medicine (BAPM) and the British Association for Community Child Health (BACCH). The latter two organisations were registered charities, with aims similar to each other and related to those of the Royal College.

The vendor of the property, Coleridge Ltd, was a property development company. It purchased the property in 2005 and opted to tax it. When purchased, the property had sitting tenants.

In November 2006 Coleridge paid the then tenants of the property to surrender their tenancy and in early 2007 undertook major refurbishment. On completion of the building works, Coleridge placed the property on the market. In 2007 the Royal College wished to move to new premises and identified the property and approached Coleridge with a view to purchasing it. BAPM and BACCH wished to move with the Royal College and remain its tenants.

On 2 October 2007, the Royal College elected to waive exemption for VAT over the property and in November 2007 Coleridge and BAPM entered into an agreement for a lease for a single room in the property for a premium of £1,000. The terms include the following: Clause 2.1 makes the agreement conditional on Coleridge exchanging an unconditional contract for sale of the property with the Royal College by November 2007, and, moreover, clauses 3.1.1 to 3.1.4 together provide that the premium will be repaid if the condition is not met or if completion of the lease with the Royal College has not happened by 31 March 2008.

HMRC ruled that this did not fulfil the requirements for a TOGC and assessed Coleridge for VAT on the sale. The Tribunal considered that for a TOGC to occur two things had to be transferred – an asset and a business or economic activity. In this case the Tribunal found that an asset had been transferred (the property) but there was no business to be transferred as the tenancy by BAPM was conditional on the sale of the property to the appellants. Without the sale of the property to the appellant there was no property rental business being undertaken by Coleridge and as such there was no TOGC. However, the Tribunal found that although there was no TOGC the assessment was still out of time so the appeal was dismissed.

This is still an interesting decision as it is not uncommon for a TOGC to be 'created' by arranging for a tenant to be negotiating with the vendor at the time of the sale in order to fulfil HMRC guidance in VAT Notice 700/9, para 6.2, which states that a TOGC occurs where the vendor:

> 'owns a property and have found a tenant but not actually entered into a lease agreement when it transfers the property to a third party (with the benefit of the prospective tenancy but before a lease has been signed);'

The key point is that in this case the lease and the sale were inextricably linked in the contract with the lease being conditional on the completion of the sale. If that is not the case and the two transaction are not linked contractually then it is possible that it could still qualify for TOGC treatment.

BEWARE IF THE PURCHASER IS A NOMINEE

38.18   If a business is selling a tenanted property to a nominee acting for an undisclosed beneficial owner, the transaction cannot be a TOGC.

If the beneficial owner is named, that person, the nominee and yourself can agree to treat the sale as a TOGC; each must sign a written agreement saying so (Notice 700/9 (March 2002) *Transfer of a business as a going concern,* Part 9). This is because the beneficial owner is regarded as the transferee for TOGC purposes, and the person who must opt to tax the property, issue a certificate to oneself—and of course register for VAT.

It is for the parties to decide whether to use this concession by HMRC. Of course, if it is not done and VAT is therefore charged, it will only be recoverable as input tax if the beneficial owner immediately opts to tax the property anyway!

THE PURCHASE OF A BUSINESS BY PARTIALLY EXEMPT VAT GROUP

38.19   If a partially exempt VAT group buys a business as a TOGC, *s 44* requires it to account for output tax on the value of the assets, other than items covered by the *Capital Goods Scheme*, bought by the vendor during the previous four years, and on which, the vendor recovered VAT. From 1 April 2009 the limit limits were increased from three years to four with certain transitional provisions meaning that no adjustment can be made for periods ending before 31 March 2006 (see Chapter 39, *Assessment and VAT Penalties* for details).

Corresponding input tax can only be recovered by the group to the extent allowed by the partial exemption rules. This prevents such a group from acquiring assets free of VAT in the course of a TOGC, after they have been bought by an associate company, used for a taxable business, and input tax recovered on them.

THE LANDLORD AND TENANT ARE IN THE SAME VAT GROUP

38.20   A single tenanted building can count as a business for TOGC purposes. However, that is not so if it is sold to a company in the same VAT group as the tenant. This is because HMRC interpret the grouping roles as meaning that, as there is no supply within the VAT group, the business ceases to exist.

Similarly, if the landlord sells the property to a third party outside the VAT group, thus creating supplies, the position is not that of an ongoing business being transferred.

In Notice 700/9 (March 2002) *Transfer of a business as a going concern*, HMRC do accept that there is a TOGC if there are other tenants outside the VAT group.

ARTICLE 5(2) OF THE SPECIAL PROVISIONS ORDER

38.21   *First*, the above rules create a pitfall for all concerned because of the need for the vendor to ensure that the purchaser opts to tax in respect of any property affected by the rule, and the need for the purchaser to understand that something done, probably through the solicitors, in the course of the purchase of the property has long-term consequences. For more on the option to tax, see Chapter 26, *Property*.

Secondly, there is a particular pitfall if a business buys a property at auction. A tax point is created when the business pays a deposit immediately after the auction to the vendor's solicitors. This is because such a deposit is held by the solicitors as the agent of the vendor, not as stakeholders, ie the deposit is not returnable because the business is committed to the purchase on the terms set out in the auction documents. In the event of this HMRC, advise that a business attending an auction takes a blank VAT 1614 option to tax form with them, so that if they purchase a property, they can fax the completed form through to HMRC on the same day, and they will accept that it is a TOGC.

In *Higher Education Statistics Agency Ltd* (LON/98/296 No 15917: [2000] STC 332), confirmed in the High Court, the purchase of a rented property at auction was held not to be a TOGC because the purchaser only opted to tax after the auction date, and therefore after it had paid a 10% deposit. Thus, if a business is contemplating buying a property at auction, it must notify HMRC of its election to waive exemption before it becomes the owner of it!

DO NOT TAKE OVER THE VENDOR'S VAT NUMBER

38.22

Focus

VAT Regulations (SI 1995/2518), reg 6 allows the purchaser of a business to take over the vendor's VAT Number. This creates a potential problem because, in doing so, a business takes on all the VAT liabilities of the existing registration, and could be caught out by an assessment for mistakes made by the vendor. The procedure is, therefore, only suitable when the two parties are closely connected.

A right to reclaim overpaid VAT belongs only to the person who overpaid it (*s 80(1)*). In *Shendish Manor Ltd* (LON/97//929 No 18474), this was held to be so even if the VAT number had been transferred. The *Special Provisions Order, (SI 1995/1268), art 6(3)(b)*, only transfers the right to repayment of input tax.

However, in *Pets Place (UK) Ltd* (LON/95/2986 No 14642) the purchaser was held not to be liable for an assessment disallowing input tax to the vendor. Pets Place had taken over the VAT number and signed a VAT 68, but the latter referred only to paying VAT on supplies made by the vendor, ie to output tax, not to input tax.

Chapter 39

Assessment and VAT penalties

SIGNPOSTS

- HMRC has the power to issue assessments if they discover under or overpayments of VAT. These assessments have to be issued within specific time limits (see **39.1–39.4**).

- Assessments have to be notified in a specified format and must specify the periods being assessed (see **39.6–39.7**).

- If a business does not submit a return, HMRC has the power to issue an estimated assessment (see **39.8**).

- If HMRC issue an assessment the taxpayer can ask for a reconsideration or appeal to the independent Tax Chamber of the Tribunal service (see **39.9–39.12**).

- Assessments must be made to best judgment (see **39.13**).

- When an error is discovered it is subject to interest and penalties (see **39.14–39.16, 39.29–39.34**).

- In some circumstances a penalty can be avoided by disclosing the error voluntarily, having a reasonable excuse for the error, or the size of the penalty can be reduced if there are mitigating circumstances (see **39.25–39.28, 39.35–39.36**).

- A previous system of penalties still applies to errors made before 1 April 2009 while errors arising after 1 April 2009 are covered by the new penalty regime (see **39.17–39.24, 39.30, 39.37–39.38**).

39.1   A business never knows when it may be faced with an assessment based on assertions by HMRC that a business has made mistakes in its VAT returns, so it needs to have some idea of how to deal with such a situation.

Hopefully, a business will never need to study most of the penalty rules in any detail, but it is as well to be aware of their existence, if only because one might have to point them out to colleagues or clients that are found doing something which is believed to be incorrect. See **39.13** below.

726

HMRC'S POWER TO ASSESS

39.2

Focus

Section 73 gives HMRC power to assess if they think that a business has declared too little output tax or reclaimed too much input tax on its VAT returns.

Such an assessment is not in itself any suggestion of dishonesty, merely that the business has made a technical mistake. If the value of the mistake exceeds the limits for a misdeclaration penalty, HMRC can assess a penalty as well. Default interest can also usually be payable.

TIME LIMITS AND THE CAPPING PROVISIONS

39.3

Focus

From 1 April 2009, under *s 73(6),* an assessment must be made within:

●   two years of the end of the VAT period in question; or

●   one year after evidence of facts, sufficient in the opinion of HMRC to justify the assessment, comes to their knowledge,

but, in any case, not more than four years after the end of the VAT period.

As it is often the one-year limit on which HMRC rely (because the long gaps between their visits to smaller businesses tend to mean that they are outside the two-year one), where HMRC assess within a year of discovering the problem, *s 77* imposes an overarching four-year time limit for the returns for which they can assess. Thus, they have to assess within four years of the end of the VAT period in which the underpayment occurred—except in a case of dishonesty or late registration, in which case the time limit is 20 years, or three years after death. Prior to 1 April 2009 the overarching four-year limit was three years.

A penalty must be assessed within two years of finally deciding how much tax is owed.

Having made an assessment, HMRC can reduce it or issue a supplementary one, but, outside the two-year period, they cannot withdraw it and substitute another one on the same basis unless they have new facts.

In *DFS Furniture Co plc* (2004 STC 559), the Court of Appeal held that a court decision had a legal effect, not a factual one. Thus, the two-year time limit started when HMRC were originally aware of the facts, not when the ECJ held in their favour in another case.

THE CAP FOR ANNUAL ADJUSTMENTS

39.4   In *Dunwood Travel Ltd* (MAN/05/261 No 19580; [2007] EWHC 319 (Ch)), an assessment by HMRC was held to be out of time because it related to the annual adjustment due in period 6/01 in respect of the year to 3/01 (ie under the then three-year cap). The Tribunal said that the assessment was thus for the year to 3/01. In applying the annual adjustment, the Commissioners must, of necessity, carry out the calculation in the following quarter, and apply the result to the prescribed accounting period immediately preceding that calculation. The Tribunal's reasoning behind its decision does appear somewhat flawed, which is presumably why HMRC appealed the matter to the High Court. Not surprisingly, the High Court promptly overturned the decision in favour of HMRC, stating in its decision that the analysis of the Tribunal was incorrect.

HMRC CAN MAKE ALTERNATIVE ASSESSMENTS

39.5   In *University Court of the University of Glasgow* (EDN/01/28/76/91/12 No 17372; CA [2003] STC 495) it was held that alternative assessments based on different legal analyses of a situation can be made—just as for Direct Tax.

FORM AND NOTIFICATION OF AN ASSESSMENT

39.6   The law does not state the form in which an assessment should be made, or how it should be notified. Usually, HMRC use standard paperwork produced by their computer system. However, various decisions, such as *Piero's Restaurant and Pizzeria* (LON/2001/927 No 17711), have established that an assessment can be in the form of a letter, provided that it clearly expresses a decision to assess, and that it, or accompanying schedules, gives details of the amounts for each VAT period.

In *Courts plc* (LON/00/048 No 17915), a *protective assessment* was held to be valid, the amounts and periods having been notified in a letter, even though it had not been processed, and the debt was not recorded in the traders' account in HMRC's books.

Although the law merely requires an assessment to be *made* within the time limit, not *notified* as well, this has created problems in the past when there has been a delay between the making of the assessment, and the notification to the trader. HMRC have now decided, as a matter of policy, that they must also notify within the time limit.

HMRC also have the power to amend an existing assessment, which can be done at any time after the assessment has been issued.

AN ASSESSMENT MUST BE FOR THE CORRECT PERIOD

39.7   HMRC's power to assess under *s 73* relates to a return which a trader is required to make.

In *M Weston* (MAN/01/0914 No 18190), an assessment was held to be invalid because it was for a final five-month period, for which HMRC had not issued any direction requiring a return. They had ignored the normal return for the first three months, which the Tribunal held to be valid, even though it was on a photocopy of a previous return with the details altered. Thus, it is sometimes possible to win an appeal on the basis of a technicality. Always look carefully at such details of an assessment as the date of issue and the period covered.

AN ASSESSMENT IN THE ABSENCE OF A RETURN

39.8   No appeal can be made against an assessment for a period for which no return has been submitted. However, the submission of a return automatically cancels the assessment, and substitutes what is shown as due on the return as the correct liability. If HMRC do not accept that, they can make a further assessment.

In the case of an initial long period for which no return had been submitted due to a failure to register, HMRC was held able to assess for that period (*Barry Hopcraft* (LON/02/459 No 19220)). In the letter making the assessment, they had notified the trader that a single return for that period could be made instead of paying the assessment.

APPEALS

39.9   A business *appeals* to the Tax Chamber of the Tribunal Service. If a business writes to HMRC asking them to think again, that is a request for a *reconsideration*, not an appeal. There are important differences.

ASKING FOR A RECONSIDERATION

39.10   Following changes to the Tribunals system on 1 April 2009 the VAT & Duties Tribunal was abolished along with the Commissioners and Special Commissioners and amalgamated into the Tax Chamber of the Tribunal

Service. From that date costs are not generally available to the taxpayer if they are successful at Tribunal. Asking for a reconsideration, now called an internal review, is, therefore, the first step in challenging an assessment from HMRC even if the system is skewed to favour HMRC.

VAT under-declaration cases often start with claims by HMRC which are either overstated or unsound for one reason or another. To establish this, and negotiate a reasonable settlement or even withdrawal of the assessment, it often takes much work and many months.

Usually, an officer, who has issued, or is threatening to issue, an assessment based on allegations of undeclared takings, has already made up his or her mind that the returns are inaccurate. Although the degree of obduracy varies, it is often only the fact, not just the threat, of a Tribunal appeal, combined with detailed argument, schedules of figures, etc which induces a more reasonable approach, and/or a willingness to settle.

Sometimes, it does pay to negotiate on the basis of a review by HMRC, rather than a formal appeal. However, in my experience, this is only where the client is in the wrong, and there is little prospect of a successful defence in law. A reasonable officer might, with a bit of luck, be persuaded to agree a lower figure. Such cases are more likely to concern technical points of law than under-declaration or dishonesty cases.

This is not to suggest that all HMRC officers get the law wrong. Some are very good indeed. However, advisers tend to see the less satisfactory cases for obvious reasons, and the above remarks are based on long experience.

Once an appeal is lodged, HMRC appoint a different officer to review the position. If there has been a mistake, this may be accepted by the reviewing officer, although recent experience is that they mostly rubber stamp decisions.

ALTERNATIVE DISPUTE RESOLUTION

39.11   Alongside a business's rights to ask for a reconsideration or appeal to a Tribunal HMRC has introduced a new Alternative Dispute Resolution (ADR) procedure following extensive trialling. This service aims to help resolve disputes or to get agreement on which issues need to be taken forward to the Tribunal for a legal ruling. In order to retain their legal rights, businesses should ask for a statutory review or enter an appeal to the Tribunal as well as asking for ADR. If negotiations are going badly a business can also ask for ADR before HMRC has made a decision.

The Tribunals support the new ADR and will 'stand over' a case for three months to allow mediation to take place.

HMRC will arrange for someone who has not been involved in the case to work with the business and the officer dealing with its case. The person leading the ADR is specially trained to act as a neutral third-party mediator. However, they do not take over responsibility for the case. The decision on settling a case stays with the business and the officer handling it.

The person leading the ADR will work with both parties to explore ways of resolving the dispute through meetings and telephone conversations. They will help focus on the areas that need to be resolved and, if needed, help re-establish dialogue. In some cases the business might agree with HMRC to jointly pay for a professional independent mediator—but obviously this will cost the business money.

A business can ask HMRC to consider ADR or its accountant or tax adviser can ask on its behalf. If you want to ask for ADR there is an online form to send your details to HMRC.

ADR can be particularly useful in long-running disputes where positions on both sides have become entrenched, or progress for whatever reason has stalled. For example, ADR could:

- narrow down the areas of disagreement in one or more component parts of a dispute by clarifying technical issues;

- identify points of difference whilst maintaining or creating good working relationships between the parties;

- unlock provision of further information or assist parties to agree key facts;

- clarify the key questions which need to be answered in order to resolve the dispute (ie agreeing a decision tree); or

- even if settlement is not reached, the process usually results in narrowing the particular points in dispute in preparation for litigation.

ADR is not appropriate for disputes about:

- payments;

- fixed penalties on the grounds of reasonable excuse; or

- cases being dealt with by HMRC's Criminal Investigators.

TIME LIMIT FOR AN APPEAL

39.12   A business is supposed to appeal to the Tribunal within 30 days of the decision or assessment in question. However, the Tribunals routinely extend this time limit although under the new procedures they seem to be less inclined to do so than before. If a business is out of time, lodge the appeal quoting the reason for the delay. HMRC will probably not object unless the appeal is years rather than months late, or they think that the appeal is frivolous.

In the case of *Graham (t/a Xs and Os Amusements) v Revenue and Customs* [2014] UKUT 75 (TCC), the Upper Tribunal ruled that the appellant was out of time to enter an appeal.

The appellant made voluntary disclosures in 2006 and 2010 for overpaid output tax on gaming machine takings following a decision of the ECJ in *Edith Linneweber*. The claim was rejected by HMRC. However, the appellant did not enter an appeal at the time as it considered that having entered a protective claim it had already protected its position and that it would wait until the lead case in *Rank* had been decided. If *Rank* won they would then ask for payment of the claim.

This was not unreasonable, as HMRC had previously paid out on protective claims if the taxpayer subsequently won. However, HMRC changed this policy and would now only repay amounts if an appeal had been entered.

Following the success in the *Rank* case, the appellant requested repayment of the overpaid output tax but this was rejected on the grounds that they had not entered an appeal at the time. The appellant asked the First-tier Tribunal (FTT) for the appeal to be heard out of time but this was rejected; they subsequently appealed to the Upper Tribunal.

The Upper Tribunal did not consider that that FTT had been unreasonable in the exercise of its discretion and had taken into account all the relevant facts. The appeal was therefore dismissed.

It is important to note from this case that if a business enters a protective claim based on a disputed decision and HMRC rejects it, an appeal should be entered within 30 days of the decision, as leave to appeal out of time will be rejected and the claim will be lost.

BEST JUDGMENT

39.13   An assessment for output VAT must be to the *best judgment* of HMRC (*s 73(1)*).

One for input tax is made under *s 73(2)* for which there is no such requirement. It must merely be bona fide, and not based on a mere whim.

Frequently, HMRC officers jump too readily to conclusions when assessing for output tax on alleged under-declarations. Often, they do not marshal the evidence properly. If this is the case, and especially if evidence such as observations of the premises, test meals, etc covers only a short period, it may be possible to defeat the assessment in its entirety on the grounds that it was not made to the best judgment of the Commissioners. Possible reasons include such mistakes as an unsound basis for the assessment, numerous errors in the calculations, or a failure to take into account some important factor or information. It is fair to say, however, that the best judgment defence is now more difficult to maintain than it used to be.

In *Mohamed Hafiz Rahman (t/a Khayam Restaurant)* (MAN/96/133 No 14918; [1998] STC 826; No 17135; [2002] STC 73; [2002] EWCA Civ 1881; [2003] STC 150), the judge in the first High Court hearing commented:

'The Tribunal should not treat an assessment as invalid merely because it disagrees as to how the judgement should have been exercised. A much stronger finding is required; for example, that the assessment has been reached "Dishonestly or vindictively or capriciously"; or is a "spurious estimate or guess in which all elements of judgement are missing"; or is "wholly unreasonable."'

After a rehearing by a different Tribunal, the case was appealed again to the High Court and on to the Court of Appeal. The latter commented that, in the usual situation in which the Tribunal can see why HMRC made the assessment, it should concentrate on deciding the correct amount of tax due. If that is close to the sum assessed, it may be a sterile exercise to consider whether HMRC exercised best judgment. If it is not close, the assessment may not have been to best judgment. However, even then, a Tribunal could substitute its view of the correct tax due, it being the underlying purpose of the law to collect that sum.

Thus, when it is clear that a VAT return was wrong, provided the Tribunal is able to decide the correct sum due, it is now unlikely to overturn an assessment on the technical grounds that it was not to best judgment.

THE COST OF GETTING IT WRONG

39.14   If a business gets it wrong, it may have to pay:

- interest at a rate high enough to hurt, and which is not allowable for corporation tax; and

- a penalty of up to 30% for careless errors.

Those sanctions are for *innocent* errors. Interest is automatic, but the business may be able to reduce the penalty if it has a 'reasonable excuse'—difficult in the case of a substantial business employing qualified accountants and advisers—or it can show reasons why it should be mitigated.

A business *may* also escape a penalty if it makes a voluntary disclosure to HMRC.

The following pages discuss the detailed rules, including those on the *Default Surcharge* for late returns (see **39.20–39.21**).

INTEREST IS DUE ON MISTAKES

39.15

> **Focus**
>
> Default interest is due under *s 74* on errors made, no matter what their value.

Interest is based on the average of the base lending rates of the six largest clearing banks *plus* 2.5% (*Air Passenger Duty and Other Indirect Taxes Order (SI 1998/1461)*). At the time of writing, it is 3%. As this is not allowable for corporation tax, it is sensible to pay up once the business or HMRC discovers errors exceeding £10,000, so as to stop interest running—even if the assessment has not yet been issued.

HMRC do not have to assess for interest—the officer can 'inhibit' it. However, if it is assessed, there is no appeal against the liability. A business can appeal against the basis of calculation, but not against whether it ought to pay interest.

HMRC have said that they will not normally assess for interest if the error is merely one of timing, such as accounting for output tax late or recovering input tax early, which was then corrected on the next return. HMRC also say that they will only charge interest for 'commercial restitution', for example if the under-declared output tax of a business can be fully recovered by its customer, there is no actual loss of revenue to the exchequer, and interest will not be charged.

If a business has made a voluntary disclosure of VAT overpaid that offsets part of an assessment, check whether the interest calculation has taken account of this. HMRC's computer system may have failed to do so.

For comment on your right to interest if you overpay HMRC, see **18.10**.

PENALTIES

39.16   A new system of penalties came into force on 1 April 2009 (see **39.17** for further details). *Note that the old system will still apply to periods ending before that date.*

As both systems will operate in tandem, I will outline the new system and then deal with the old penalties available to HMRC for periods prior to 1 April 2009.

The penalties that have been replaced are:

- The misdeclaration penalty: *s 63*
- The persistent misdeclaration penalty: *s 64*
- Failure to register on time: *s 67*
- Dishonesty under *s 60* and *s 61*

THE NEW PENALTY SYSTEM

39.17   The new penalty regime came into force on 1 April 2009 across all taxes administered by HMRC.

Not every error will incur a penalty. If a person takes reasonable steps to complete a 'document' correctly, even if it later turns out to be wrong, then a penalty would not be due. A penalty will be chargeable where any person gives HMRC an inaccurate document that satisfies two conditions.

The **first** condition is that the inaccurate document either amounts or leads to:

- an understatement of the person's liability to tax; or

- a false or inflated statement of a loss by the person; or

- a false or inflated claim to repayment of tax.

The **second** condition is that the inaccuracy was careless or deliberate.

An inaccuracy made by a person in a document may be:

- a mistake made despite the person taking reasonable care (no penalty); or

- careless; or

- deliberate but not concealed; or

- deliberate and concealed.

HMRC say that error penalties are designed to address the behaviour that led to the inaccuracy. Penalties for deliberate inaccuracies are therefore higher than those for careless inaccuracies. Within the deliberate category there will be varying degrees of seriousness, and the law reflects this by providing for higher penalties in those cases where the person has taken steps to conceal the deliberate inaccuracy.

Reason for penalty	Type of inaccuracy	Maximum penalty payable
Giving an inaccurate document	Careless	30% of Potential Loss of Revenue (PLR)
Giving an inaccurate document	Deliberate not concealed	70% of PLR
Giving an inaccurate document	Deliberate and concealed	100% of PLR
Understated assessment not notified	N/A	30% of PLR
Inaccuracy discovered later but no reasonable steps taken to inform HMRC	Treated as careless	30% of PLR

Where a person makes a mistake despite taking reasonable care to get things right, HMRC will not charge a penalty. HMRC would expect a diligent trader to:

- make prompt, complete and correct returns as required by the law;

- keep whatever records are necessary to enable them to make complete and accurate returns;

- read carefully the notes supplied with the return, so far as they affect their own particular circumstances;

- seek help with matters, such as the preparation of accounts or unusual transactions, which they are unable to cope with satisfactorily themselves, for example from a professional adviser, voluntary bodies or HMRC Contact Centre or Enquiry Centre.

Examples of errors where reasonable care has been taken might include:

- a reasonable view of the law that proves to be wrong;

- an arithmetical or transposition error that is not so large (relative to overall liability) as to produce an odd result or be picked up by a quality check;

- following incorrect advice from HMRC having contacted them and provided all the relevant information; or

- advice from a competent professional is followed but proves to be wrong despite the fact that the adviser was given a full set of accurate facts.

If an inaccuracy in a document is due to carelessness, a deliberate act, or failure to act, the person will be liable to a penalty even if there was no intention.

HMRC acknowledges that people's ability and experience will vary and the steps that a person takes to ensure a document is correct will depend upon the nature, size and complexity of their transactions. When an error is found in a document the person should have the opportunity to put forward their explanation of how the error arose and the steps they took in completing the document. HMRC will consider whether it was reasonable for them to act as they did in light of their circumstances at the time they completed the document.

Although *Hanson v Revenue & Customs Commissioners* [2012] UKFTT 314 (TC) is a direct tax case it has a significant bearing on the VAT penalty regime as they are covered by the same legislation. The appeal concerned a penalty imposed on the appellant pursuant to *FA 2007, Sch 24*.

Hanson appealed against the penalty on the grounds that the statutory phrase 'reasonable care' could not entail checking that his accountants had given him sound professional advice. HMRC defended its position on the basis that an error by an adviser was still the responsibility of the taxpayer.

Schedule 24, para 18 deals with the liability of a taxpayer to penalties under the schedule where agents are acting on behalf of the taxpayer. The relevant sections state:

> '(1) P is liable under paragraph 1(1)(a) where a document which contains a careless inaccuracy (within the meaning of paragraph 3) is given to HMRC on P's behalf.
>
> (3) Despite sub-paragraphs (1) and (2), P is not liable to a penalty under paragraph 1 or 2 in respect of anything done or omitted by P's agent where P satisfies HMRC that P took reasonable care to avoid inaccuracy (in relation to paragraph 1) ....'

The Tribunal judge found for the taxpayer, who himself had taken reasonable care even though it was now clear there had been carelessness on the part of the accountancy firm.

As things stand there appears to be no provision for anyone to be charged penalties if an accountant makes a merely careless error which results in understatement of a client's tax liabilities.

Examples of 'carelessness':

- A shopkeeper decides to replace his old van with a new vehicle. He buys an estate car so that he can use it for business trips to his local cash and carry, and uses the vehicle for personal use in the evenings and at weekends. The shopkeeper is not sure about what input tax he can claim for his vehicle, but he does not bother to contact HMRC or his accountant for advice. He wrongly claims all the input tax he paid on the car. This indicates a lack of reasonable care.

- Gary, a window cleaner, accepted that he had sent HMRC an incorrect return but said this was because he had little understanding of official forms and poor literacy skills. Gary's limited ability does not mean that his actions were not careless. He should take reasonable steps to submit an accurate return. If he cannot be sure whether what he has done is right or wrong, Gary should take steps to check. If he has difficulty with forms, he could, for example, seek help from the Contact Centre or Enquiry Centre.

HMRC should look sympathetically at his circumstances, although, in determining whether Gary took reasonable care, HMRC should ask Gary how he manages with other aspects of his life such as domestic bills, insurance, banking or other official forms.

A 'deliberate inaccuracy' occurs when a person intentionally makes an error in a document sent to HMRC. It can also be a failure to act, where this is done deliberately to avoid paying what is due.

For behaviour to be seen as deliberate, HMRC must have grounds to believe that the person intended to submit a document that they know is inaccurate.

Examples of a 'deliberate inaccuracy' might include:

* not recording all sales, especially where there is a pattern to the under-recording in circumstances that appear to rule out genuine misunderstanding;

* describing transactions inaccurately or in a way likely to mislead; or

* a person repeatedly submitting a VAT return that includes a figure of net VAT due that is too low because he does not have the cash at that time to pay the full amount, and later telling HMRC the true figure when he has the funds.

This type of action could include a shopkeeper who takes £50 per week from the takings as 'pocket money'. This money goes unrecorded when the weekly takings are calculated and entered into the records. Those records form the basis of the turnover figures on the VAT return, which the shopkeeper knows to be incorrect.

The shopkeeper has deliberately recorded the wrong figure of sales in the business records. However, there is no evidence of additional artificial or false records being produced to support this deliberate inaccuracy.

Any error that is not apparent on the face of a document could be seen as hidden, but HMRC will only apply 'deliberate and concealed' to cases of the most serious conduct. In these cases, there will be more than an attempt to deliberately record an error in a document; there will be additional signs that active steps have been taken to cover it up, either before or after the document is submitted.

There are two steps to consider for a penalty to be based on a deliberate and concealed inaccuracy:

* the error or omission was deliberate; and

* steps were taken to conceal the inaccuracy.

Examples of 'deliberate inaccuracies with concealment' might include:

* creating false invoices to support inaccurate figures in the return;

* backdating or postdating contracts or invoices;

* creating false minutes of meetings or minutes of fictitious meetings;

* destroying books and records so that they should not be available;

* systematically diverting takings into undisclosed bank accounts and covering the traces;

* false description of expenditure in the business records as business-related when it is in fact private (possibly with the supplier agreeing to change the description on the relevant invoices); or

* alteration of genuine purchase invoices to inflate their value.

An example of this would include a self-employed hairdresser, where, during a VAT inspection, a bank account is discovered containing undeclared income. The hairdresser produces a letter supposedly from her aunt to support her explanation that the source of the funds in the bank account was a gift from her aunt.

In this case, the hairdresser has taken active steps to conceal the inaccuracy by creating an alternative explanation of the source of the funds in her undeclared bank account.

HMRC will also charge a penalty where:

- an assessment issued by HMRC understates a person's liability to VAT; and

- the person fails to take reasonable steps within 30 days of the date of the assessment to tell HMRC that it is an under-assessment.

In considering whether a penalty is appropriate in cases of under-assessment, HMRC must consider:

- whether the person knew or should have known, about the under-assessment; and

- what steps (if any) it would have been reasonable for him to take to tell HMRC about the under-assessment.

HMRC has launched a consultation, originally announced in the 2016 Budget, on a new penalty for VAT fraud, which includes introducing potential fines on companies that 'knew or should have known their transactions were connected with fraud'.

One of the main reasons for considering a new penalty is that the current regime imposes different levels of penalty for careless and deliberate 'errors' in cases where a business should have known of the fraud, and a business may fall between the two level of penalties. HMRC have got round this problem to date by waiting until any litigation is completed before imposing a penalty. The new penalty would allow HMRC to issue penalties sooner.

SPECIAL REDUCTIONS AND SUSPENDED PENALTIES

39.18   Special reductions are available when there are special circumstances that should be taken into account when setting the level of penalty. Special circumstances occur where there are either uncommon or exceptional facts that should be considered, or where the strict application of the penalty laws produce a result that is contrary to the clear compliance intention of the law.

There have been recent Tribunal cases on whether penalties should be subject to a special reduction and HMRC has been shown to be 'flawed' in their decision making process when assessing if there were special circumstances. One example was *White v Revenue & Customs Commissioners* [2012] UKFTT 364 in which the penalty was reduced to 6% by the Tribunal.

HMRC can suspend penalties in suitable cases involving careless error. However, this action does not normally apply where the error was a one-off. With a suspended penalty certain conditions are applied by HMRC which the taxpayer must adhere to for a specified time period—normally between three and 12 months. If the taxpayer complies with the conditions, and no further errors are identified when the period of suspension ends, the penalty is waived.

There is some fairly detailed guidance on penalties for errors and whether penalties should be suspended in HMRC's Compliance Handbook Manual. Of course, the guidance only provides HMRC's view on the subject, and does not carry the force of law. A useful point that is made in this guidance is that HMRC must consider suspension of the penalty for *every* penalty involving a careless error. So always ask if HMRC have considered suspending the penalty because if they have not the decision-making process is flawed and a Tribunal would probably throw out the penalty.

NEW PENALTY FOR LATE REGISTRATION

39.19   From 1 April 2010 a new penalty for late registration was introduced that effectively mirrored the penalty regime introduced on 1 April 2009 using the same four categories, namely:

- 'reasonable excuse';
- 'not deliberate';
- 'deliberate'; and
- 'deliberate and concealed'.

'Reasonable excuse'

There is no penalty due where a reasonable excuse exists. This is the same basic position as with the outgoing regime.

HMRC give the following as examples of a reasonable excuse:

- the death of a partner or close relative; or
- you, your partner, or a close relative had a serious illness.

'Not deliberate'

Where notification is unprompted and made within 12 months of the registration date, there is a minimum penalty of 0%, and a maximum penalty of 30%, depending on the level of mitigation. If the notification is unprompted but more than 12 months late, the minimum penalty is 10% and the maximum penalty is 30%, depending on mitigation. Prompted disclosures made within 12 months carry a minimum penalty of 10%, and maximum penalty of 30%, again depending on mitigation. Prompted disclosures after 12 months have a minimum 20% penalty and maximum 30% penalty.

'Deliberate'

There is no 12-month dividing line for deliberate penalties. Quite simply, where the notification is unprompted, there is a minimum penalty of 20%, and a maximum penalty of 70%. Where prompted, there is a minimum penalty of 35%, and a maximum penalty of 70%, depending on the level of mitigation.

'Deliberate and concealed'

Not surprisingly, there is no 12-month dividing line for deliberate and concealed penalties either. Where unprompted, there is a minimum penalty of 30%, and a maximum penalty of 100%. Where prompted, the minimum penalty is 50%, and the maximum penalty is 100%, once again depending on the level of mitigation.

Mitigation

The penalty amount can be reduced depending on the level of assistance given to HMRC in establishing the arrears. The following are quoted by HMRC as ways in which a mitigation reduction can be earned:

- telling HMRC everything about the failure and tax liability—up to 30%

- assisting HMRC in working out the net tax due—up to 40%

- giving HMRC access to your figures—up to 30%.

In the case of *Paula Thorne v Revenue & Customs Commissioners* [2012] UKFTT 529 the appellant appealed against a late registration penalty on the grounds of reasonable excuse.

Mrs Thorne took over The Turberville Hotel, Llanharan on 1 November 2010. She was obliged to register for VAT within 30 days. As this was a penalty case, the burden of proving the alleged default lay with HMRC.

On 20 May 2011 HMRC wrote to inform her that they proposed to charge a penalty for late registration. The appellant pointed out that she had sent the necessary registration documents to HMRC in good time and then asked HMRC to say on what date they contended that they had received the documents. Instead of receiving the courtesy of a proper reply to that query, the appellant then received an 'Amended Notice of Penalty Assessment' dated 9 December 2011 in the sum of £631.

The appellant's response was that she had sent the necessary registration forms to the respondent, by post, on 26 November 2010. HMRC upheld the penalty after undertaking a review that completely failed to address the real issue, that the appellant had in fact submitted her registration forms on time.

There were three possibilities. They were that the appellant did not post her registration form on 26 November 2010 and that she had lied; that delivery of the posted form was delayed by the Royal Mail; or that the form was posted and delivered but not properly logged and dealt with once it arrived with HMRC.

The Tribunal decided that HMRC had come nowhere near to proving that the appellant had lied. The registration form was dated 24 November 2010, only two days before the appellant says that she put it into the post. There was no purpose to be served by her delaying its submission to HMRC. Therefore the Tribunal found there was a reasonable excuse and no penalty was due.

It is up HMRC to prove that a penalty is due and in the absence of any credible evidence that the forms had been received late the penalty was not due.

In the case of *James Hillis v Revenue and Customs Commissioners* ([2013] UKFTT 196 (TC)) HMRC imposed late registration penalty on the taxpayer. In this case there were a number of unusual circumstances which had led to the taxpayer delaying notification for over a year, including advice received from his accountants not to approach HMRC until he had sufficient funds to pay his VAT liability. However, late registration penalties can normally only be reduced to nil if the failure is notified to HMRC within 12 months (in addition to being unprompted, unconcealed and a non-deliberate failure). As James Hillis notified HMRC more than 12 months after his failure to register, HMRC believed that his penalty could only be reduced to 10%.

The Tribunal decided to look beyond the letter of the law. In reducing the penalty to nil, the Tribunal examined Parliament's Public Bill Committee's minutes in order to establish what was in the minds of the legislators. It noted the following:

'The report on proceedings of the HC Committee stage of the Finance Bill 2008 emphasised taxpayers who have made genuine mistakes should not be deterred by fear of penalties from coming forward and regularising their affairs. Further the 12-month threshold for unprompted disclosures whilst introducing certainty was not set in stone. The HC Committee envisaged that there would be a margin of appreciation for those taxpayers outside the 12-month limit who have made an honest mistake, albeit in the form of a reasonable excuse.'

This leaves taxpayers with a new possible defence of 'legislative intention' in Belated Penalty Notice appeals.

THE DEFAULT SURCHARGE FOR LATE RETURNS: SECTION 59 (UP TO 31 MARCH 2010)

39.20 If a business is late with its VAT return and/or payment, HMRC can issue a surcharge liability notice (SLN). This lasts for 12 months from the date of the default. See Chapter 5, *The VAT Return,* re the due date.

Once an SLN has been served on a business, the surcharges are:

- for the next default in the next 12 months—2% of the unpaid tax (minimum £30);

- for a second default in the next 12 months—5% (minimum £30);

- from then on—by 5% a time, to a maximum of 15% (minimum £30).

If a surcharge at the 2% or 5% rate is under £400, HMRC do not assess it, but:

- a *Surcharge Liability Extension Notice* is issued extending the surcharge period; and

- the surcharge rate for the next default goes up.

THE DEFAULT SURCHARGE FOR LATE RETURNS: SECTION 59 (FROM 1 APRIL 2010)

39.21   For businesses with a turnover under £150,000 p.a., a late return and/or payment generate a SLN. The next late return generates a 'help' letter advising the business on how to manage its payment of VAT. Subsequent late returns generate penalties as in **39.17** above. For businesses with a turnover above £150,000 p.a., the penalty system remains the same as pre-31 March 2010 (**see 39.20 above**).

WHAT IF A BUSINESS DISASTER MAKES THE FIGURES LATE?

39.22   Ask HMRC for permission to estimate the missing information for the period the business has been unable to process the figures. HMRC can allow that for either input or output tax either in an emergency, or regularly if, in the exceptional circumstances of the business, it cannot have the figures ready on time.

A business must ask permission. Do not wait until the return is late: the business should ask as soon as it realises that sickness, a computer breakdown, or whatever, risks making the return late.

EXCUSES FOR LATE PAYMENT

39.23   A business has a defence to missing the time limit on any of the occasions for which a default is 'material to the surcharge' if:

- the return or tax was dispatched *at such a time and in such a manner that it was reasonable to expect* that HMRC would get it on time; or

- it has a reasonable excuse for that not having been done.

Lack of money is not such an excuse, but see above. Late delivery by someone who prepares the VAT return for a business is unlikely to be an excuse either. As the Minister commented in Parliament, that would be too easy. It would put a premium upon the services of dilatory advisers!

In a recent VAT Tribunal case, *PTE Plc t/a 'Physique'* (VTD 20,722), the Appellant appealed against the imposition of a default surcharge of nearly £20k for the submission of a late return for the period 11/07. The Appellant was successful in the appeal, and the penalty was removed on the grounds that the company had a 'reasonable excuse' for sending in the return late.

The background to the case was that in early 2007, PTE had a number of staff changes in its accounts department and reorganised its business. By early October, it became apparent that it would not be able to complete its 11/07 VAT return by the due date. The company sent a fax to HMRC on 11 October 2007 explaining the situation, and stressing that it wanted its current return period changed to a December end, and that all future returns would end December, March, etc as it was not able to complete the return on time due to the pressure of work.

On 2 November, HMRC replied saying 'This has now been approved and your VAT returns will now end on the last days of…'. Not unreasonably, the client considered this to be agreement to the change, particularly as it had made it clear that it needed the change in the current period in order to get the return in on time. The company did not take much notice of the rest of the letter, which said: 'Before this change becomes effective you may receive a VAT return under the old arrangements. If this happens you must complete the return and send it to …'. Doing this, of course, would have completely negated any benefit from changing the VAT return stagger.

The Appellant received the 11/07 return as usual, and a one-month return for December 2007. It naturally threw away the November return, and assumed that the December return was for four months. It filled it in, and sent it on time for what it thought was a four-month period. HMRC replied 'oh no, we want two returns and the November one was late so we will impose a penalty for a late return'.

Similarly ambiguous wording was responsible for two Tribunal appeals in 1995 and 2001, which HMRC also lost. The Tribunal Chairman expressed concern that, despite this, HMRC had still not changed the wording of these letters, and the meaning was still unclear.

The Chairman said:

> 'We do not see why it should be the duty of a taxpayer to make inquiries as to the meaning of a letter which the Commissioners have written, just in case there should be some hidden ambiguity in it. The Commissioners should be taken to mean what they say; it is, in our judgment, up to them to say what they mean.'

Not surprisingly, in this case, the client's appeal was successful.

There are two main points to take from this case. Firstly, if you do ask for a change of VAT stagger, you should always complete any outstanding returns, even if the authorisation letter seems to make it clear that the change is current rather than from a date in the future. Secondly, if HMRC continues to produce ambiguous letters with unclear meaning, you may have a reasonable excuse for your mistake and avoid a penalty.

It must be hoped that HMRC will now take the Tribunal's advice onboard and change the wording of these letters, so that their meaning is clear and these misunderstandings do not happen again in the future.

In the case of *Morrisroe UK Ltd v HM Revenue & Customs* [2015] UKFTT 400 (TC) the grounds for the appeal were that there were reasonable excuses for the defaults and that the surcharge was disproportionate.

The first late payment, for the period 01/14, was due to cash flow problems experienced by the appellant. This was in turn due to cash flow problems experienced by their customer, a group company, which was awaiting a large VAT refund from HMRC. The second late payment, for the period 10/14, was due to exceptional circumstances experienced by their accountant on the day the VAT payment was due to be made.

The accountant had family illnesses and other problems that he proved to the Tribunal's satisfaction. As a result of these problems he was called home and subsequently returned to work and submitted the VAT returns and authorised payment. However, the authorisation for payment was made after the cut-off point for electronic payments that day and was consequently received late by HMRC.

The Tribunal considered that although mere reliance on a third party cannot constitute a reasonable excuse, neither can it remove the possible defence of reasonable excuse if unforeseen events happen to that third party.

The Tribunal therefore considered the following questions:

(1)   Was it reasonable for the appellant to rely on its accountant?

(2)   If it was, was there a 'reasonable excuse' for the late payment?

The Tribunal considered it was reasonable for the appellant rely on its accountant, as he had performed the duty in question for the company for a considerable period of time without any problems. During the week and the day in question he was clearly doing the work required and this was observed by the company secretary.

The appellant stated there were back-up plans for the preparation of the return, and payment of VAT, but not for the sudden deterioration of circumstances on the day in question.

The Tribunal therefore found that the reasonable excuse relied on was not 'the fact of the reliance on the third party' nor 'the dilatoriness of the third party' but

'the third party, on whom it was reasonable to rely, had a reasonable excuse.'
The Tribunal found that there was a reasonable excuse in this instance.

See also earlier re excuses for innocent errors concerning sickness, etc.

HMRC have produced a new form (WT2) for businesses to claim a 'reasonable
excuse' against a surcharge for the late submission of online VAT returns. The
completed form should be sent to the HMRC Default Surcharge Review team
if a business wants to claim 'reasonable excuse' because it has received a
surcharge for submitting its online VAT Return late due to:

- an IT problem; or

- any other reason.

HMRC want all relevant information to support the claim to be submitted with
it as they will not normally contact the business for additional information
once they have received the form.

PROPORTIONALITY

39.24   The law says that Government activities, including taxation, must be
proportionate to the desired end and strike a fair balance between the public
interest in enforcing or collecting tax and the right of taxpayers not to be
unfairly penalised.

Therefore, the default surcharge penalty must be proportionate.

The leading case in this area is *Enersys Holdings UK Ltd* [2010] TC00335,
which was one day late in paying. A surcharge of £131,881 was imposed which
amounted to an annual interest rate of 1,825%. The Tribunal decided that
assessing a £131,881 default surcharge at the rate of 5% was disproportionate
to the conduct. Thus, the Tribunal completely discharged the assessment.

In the absence of any power to mitigate or otherwise reduce a penalty,
discharging the assessment completely is the only course open to a Tribunal
which concludes that a surcharge is disproportionate.

However, the Tribunal thought that generally the default surcharge is
proportionate, but on the facts in *Enersys* this was an exceptional case where
the law produced a result that was 'not merely harsh but plainly unfair' and the
surcharge was wholly disproportionate to the gravity of the offence.

This decision indicates that if the result is 'plainly unfair' an appeal may
succeed, but if the result is merely 'harsh' an appeal will fail.

Eastwell Manor Ltd v Revenue & Customs Comrs [2011] TC 01155 shows
the difficulty of using the decision in *Enersys* as a precedent for dismissing
a default surcharge for late payment of VAT. The First-tier Tribunal decided
that a surcharge for about £18,500 for a delay of one day is 'harsh', that the

punishment did not fit the crime and that the consequences were excessive. Nonetheless, the company was already in the default surcharge system, it knew that its cash flow needed managing, and the VAT liability for the relevant period was not exceptional. Thus, the company failed to pass the high test that must be satisfied that the penalty was wholly unreasonable.

Similarly, in *Eco-Hygiene Ltd v Revenue & Customs Comrs* [2012] TC01591, *Saint-Gobain Building Distribution Ltd v Revenue & Customs Comrs* [2011] TC01311 and *Luxottica (UK) Ltd v Revenue & Customs Comrs* [2011] TC01198, although the payment was late by only a few days, and although the surcharge might be regarded as harsh, the Tribunal decided that the taxpayer had failed to show that the surcharge was 'plainly unfair'.

However, in *Total Technology (Engineering) Ltd v Revenue & Customs Comrs* [2011] TC 01323, where the payment was late by only one day, the Tribunal decided that the surcharge of over £4,000 was disproportionate for a small company with annual profits of around £50,000. The surcharge was not only harsh, but plainly unfair and the taxpayer won. HMRC appealed to the Upper Tribunal which overturned this decision finding in favour of HMRC. The Upper Tribunal held that there is nothing in the VAT default surcharge which leads to the conclusion that its architecture is fatally flawed.

After detailed analysis of ECJ and human rights case law on proportionality, the Upper Tribunal concluded that it is open to tax tribunals to consider individual default surcharges without having first concluded that the default surcharge regime as a whole is disproportionate. The Upper Tribunal considered six features of the regime which might be said to result in unfairness. It concluded that there must be some upper limit on the penalty for a default which was proportionate, although it was not sensible for the Upper Tribunal, in this case, to suggest where that might be. The other features examined did not result in the regime failing to comply with the principle of proportionality at the level of the scheme as a whole. The absence of any power to mitigate the penalty was not such a flaw. On the facts of a particular case, a tribunal might be able to conclude that the penalty is disproportionate.

Generally, the *Enersys* defence only succeeds if the delay is of only one day and, in the light of all of the circumstances, the surcharge appears 'plainly unfair'. The default must not have been deliberate, eg paying the VAT must not have been delayed to keep within the overdraft limit and the amount of the surcharge must be high compared to the taxpayer's usual turnover and profit.

In the case of *Trinity Mirror PLC v Revenue & Customs* [2014] UKFTT 355 (TC), the appellant appealed against a default surcharge of £70,909.44 arising from a one-day delay in filing its VAT return and paying the VAT due. The appellant argued that the penalty was disproportionate.

The Tribunal considered that, as set out in the case of *Total Technology,* the default surcharge regime, being part of the UK implementation of the Sixth VAT Directive imposed obligations on traders to pay VAT and to make returns, but is also subject to compliance with the Community law principle of proportionality.

In the case of *Total Technology*, the Upper Tribunal stated that proportionality must be assessed at the level of the default surcharge regime as a whole and at the individual level by asking whether the penalty imposed on a particular taxpayer based on the facts of the case are proportionate.

The Tribunal decided that a surcharge of £70,909.44 imposed on an otherwise compliant trader to penalise a one-day default was plainly unfair. Taking into account the decision of the Upper Tribunal in *Total Technology,* which gave a benchmark figure that they thought would be disproportionate (a £50,000 penalty would be disproportionate in respect of a third default), the penalty imposed on the appellant was harsh. The Tribunal, therefore, found for the appellant.

MITIGATION

39.25   *Section 70* allows mitigation by either HMRC or the Tribunal of a penalty as far as zero, but excludes 'lack of funds', 'no loss of tax', and 'good faith as factors'.

WHEN CAN A BUSINESS VOLUNTARILY DISCLOSE?

39.26

Focus

In practice, HMRC accept voluntary disclosure up to the time when the officer starts investigating the matter in question. Often, disclosure is accepted during a control visit—though not if it is felt that it was only made because of the visit.

Once the officer has asked about a matter, he or she will not normally accept a disclosure as voluntary. If a business spots a problem in an aspect of its affairs, which is being looked at by HMRC at that moment, record the error and the intention to disclose it in a memorandum to the Board and/or the auditors, so as to preclude any suggestion of dishonesty.

However, in the case of *United European Gastroenterology Federation v Revenue & Customs* ([2013] UKFTT 292 (TC)) the taxpayer appealed against a penalty for a careless inaccuracy in their VAT returns for the periods 06/09, 09/09 and 12/09. The penalty totalled £104,973.

Where the taxpayer discloses the inaccuracies to HMRC the penalty can be reduced to nil. For careless errors a penalty range of 15–30% of the potential lost revenue for 'prompted' disclosures and a range of 0–30% for 'unprompted' disclosures.

In view of the quality of the appellant's disclosure HMRC accepted that it was entitled to the maximum mitigation that was permitted for prompted disclosure. They therefore imposed a penalty at a rate of 15%. The appellant maintained that its disclosure was unprompted and therefore qualified for 100% mitigation.

The question of whether the disclosure was prompted or unprompted was therefore the main issue between the parties.

Deloitte had been compiling the appellant's financial accounts for the calendar year 2009. It was only when doing so that they identified the mistake that had been made and contacted HMRC on 19 May 2010.

It was agreed that the 21 May visit previously arranged by HMRC should be deferred in order to enable Deloitte to investigate the position fully.

They submitted the disclosure was unprompted because:

- the evidence clearly showed that the disclosure would have been made irrespective of any planned visit by HMRC; and

- the facts were such that the appellant had no reason to believe, at the time it made the disclosure, that HMRC was about to discover the error.

The Tribunal found that the appellant's disclosure was prompted within the meaning of *Sch 24, para 9(2)(a)* and therefore the imposition of a minimum penalty of 15% was reasonable.

If you discover an error after HMRC has arranged a visit and disclose it you could still be liable to a penalty.

THE PERIOD OF GRACE

39.27   HMRC will not normally demand a penalty when they find an error on a return during a visit prior to the date on which the return is due for the following period. This lets off those cases where, had the officer not come in just after the return was sent, the trader might have found the error when preparing the next return.

COMPENSATING ERRORS

39.28   Nor will an error normally be penalised if it is 'corrected' by a compensating one in the following period. However, HMRC will do so if the error is a repetitive one—otherwise, they could never catch such mistakes.

DISCLOSING ERRORS

39.29

Focus

Errors cannot be corrected on the VAT return unless the net value of errors found in a period is under £10,000 or 1% of turnover as declared on the VAT return for the period in which the errors are found, subject to an upper limit of £50,000 (*VAT Regulations (SI 1995/2518), reg 34(3)*). Correcting on the current return means that the business escapes interest as well as any penalty but HMRC should still be notified of the error.

Errors totalling above £10,000 or 1% of turnover as declared on the VAT return for the period in which the errors are found, subject to an upper limit of £50,000 must be disclosed separately. HMRC provide Form 652, but a letter will suffice provided that the business gives details of the periods involved. A business pays interest but no penalty, provided disclosure counts as voluntary. See page lxvii at the start of the book for how to find where to write to.

In order to keep track of the value of errors on previous returns, period by period, a business needs to be able to identify the journal entries correcting them or, where the tax is on purchase or sales invoices recorded late, to identify those invoices.

Instant disclosure is not essential. If a business normally discloses at the end of each period, it will still be regarded as voluntary even if a visit has meanwhile uncovered the problem. However, a business should make a journal note of the correction as it finds each error as proof of an intention to disclose.

If the error was made three years ago or more prior to 31 March 2009, or more than four years ago from 1 April 2010, see **5.31**.

See also Chapter 5, *The VAT Return*, for the rules enabling a business to correct errors totalling up to £10,000 or 1% of turnover as declared on the VAT return for the period in which the errors are found, subject to an upper limit of £50,000 on its next VAT return, and the three-year time limit (four years from 1 April 2010) on both the right to reclaim overpaid VAT and the duty to disclose underpaid tax.

THE OLD PENALTY SYSTEM FROM PERIODS PRIOR TO 1 APRIL 2009

MISDECLARATION PENALTY: SECTION 63

39.30   If a business makes a mistake, the value of which exceeds the de minimis limits for a penalty, it is liable for a misdeclaration penalty of 15%. The taxpayer's innocence is irrelevant. Dishonesty, however, carries a maximum 100% penalty under *s 60* (see below).

Section 63 applies even if the error is merely a timing one, such as recovery or payment in the wrong return and regardless of whether the tax is recoverable by the customer. The reason why HMRC still apply a penalty when there is no tax loss (unlike default interest) is that, otherwise, businesses with unregistered customers, such as retailers, would be treated differently for making the same mistake.

MISDECLARATION PENALTY: SECTION 64

39.31   If a business makes a *material inaccuracy*:

- HMRC can serve a *penalty liability notice* (PLN) on a business before the end of its fourth subsequent VAT period;

- the next material inaccuracy during the following eight periods, starting with that in which the PLN was issued, escapes; but

- a second one earns a penalty of 15% of the error.

A material inaccuracy is one which exceeds:

- 30% of 'GAT' (see **39.34** below); or

- £500,000.

De minimis limits

39.32   If the net value of errors in a period is less than the following limits, a business will avoid the penalty:

Both penalty and interest

39.33

- from 1 July 2008 errors less than £10,000 or 1% of turnover as declared on the VAT return for the period in which the errors are found, subject to an upper limit of £50,000, can be corrected on the current VAT return, and no interest or penalty is charged.

Penalty only

39.34

- 30% of the *gross amount of tax* (GAT), meaning 30% of the combined value of the output tax and input tax figures that should have been stated on the return;

- but the business is caught automatically if the net value of the error(s) exceeds £1m.

Thus, from £10,000 or 1% of turnover as declared on the VAT return for the period in which the errors are found, subject to an upper limit of £50,000, an error escapes a penalty if it is below 30% of GAT. That is a generous limit for many businesses. However, it becomes much less generous if the outputs are either zero-rated or exempt, so that the business only has input tax on which to calculate it.

Overstating a repayment claim is caught as well as understating a sum due. However any offsetting errors in favour of HMRC are taken into account to reduce the sum of *tax lost*, which is measured against the above limits, and on which, any penalty is calculated.

POSSIBLE DEFENCES

39.35   A business will have a defence:

- if it can show a *reasonable excuse* for its conduct. Lack of money is not a reasonable excuse (*s 71* (see below)), nor is reliance on others;

- if a business voluntarily disclosed the error under the Errors Correction procedures at a time when it had no reason to think HMRC were investigating its VAT affairs (*s 63(10)* or *s 64(5)*).

REASONABLE EXCUSES FOR INNOCENT MISTAKES

39.36   Reliance on another person to perform any task is not an excuse (*s 71*).

Typical reasonable excuses are:

- sickness, departure of key staff, or computer faults, but only until the business could have been expected to cope by taking action to recruit staff, obtain backup, etc; or in circumstances where the problem caused extra stress, which could not have been anticipated, and which lead to the error;

- complexity of the legal point involved;

- that, in the light of the information available to the business and of its understanding of the situation, its actions were reasonable when judged by the standards of the ordinary businessman.

The Court of Appeal held in *Steptoe* (LON/89/745 No 4283: [1991] BVC 3; [1992] BVC 142) that a taxpayer's late VAT payment could be excused because the single customer, on whom he was reliant for 95% of his business, consistently paid its bills late. That case established the need to look beyond the immediate cause of the late payment (in *Steptoe* insufficiency of funds— an excuse disallowed by statute) to the underlying cause. In *Steptoe*, that underlying cause was the late payment by the single customer.

The Tribunal decision in *CH Clifton & Sons Ltd* (LON/92/156 No 9593) has shown that the same principle can work for the taxpayer where an important element of the underlying cause is late payment by a number of customers.

PENALTY FOR FAILURE TO REGISTER ON TIME: SECTION 67

39.37   The penalty for failure to register on time is a percentage of the net tax due from the correct date of registration to that on which the business tells HMRC, or on which they become *fully aware* of a liability to register. The percentages are:

- 5% up to nine months late;

- 10% up to 18 months late;

- 15% thereafter.

The percentage is a flat rate for the whole period, not a stepped one.

DISHONESTY CASES

39.38   HMRC have powers under *s 60* to assess a penalty of up to 100% of the tax evaded for conduct involving dishonesty.

They have power under *s 61* to assess part or all of that penalty on an individual director, if they think that the behaviour of the company was due to the dishonesty of that individual.

Alternatively, *s 72* provides a financial penalty of up to three times the amount of the VAT or seven years in prison, if HMRC choose to prosecute.

Only the most serious VAT frauds result in criminal prosecutions. For these, a solicitor is required to handle the legal aspects of the prosecution, even if an adviser provides the technical input on VAT.

However, most cases are dealt with under *s 60*. The 100% penalty is mitigable under *s 70* if the trader helps establish the amount of the dishonesty. In practice, the maximum likely mitigation for full co-operation is a reduction to 20%.

Whilst a business may need a solicitor's help with a *s 60* case, especially if it goes to a hearing, much of the groundwork is likely to be of an accounting nature.

GET THE FACTS AGREED

39.39   As soon as an adviser becomes aware of an investigation by HMRC he should establish the facts as best he can with the client, for instance:

- does the client admit any inaccuracy in the returns?

- if so, roughly how much, for how long, etc?

- get any admission confirmed in writing, with authority to disclose to HMRC. An adviser may or may not already have the right to disclose under the terms of the engagement letter and/or, to HMRC, by virtue of acting as the client's agent in relation to his direct tax affairs.

OWN UP AT ONCE

39.40   If any inaccuracy is admitted to, it should be disclosed as soon as possible to HMRC. If work still has to be done to clarify the extent of the problem, indicate its general nature and promise fuller information once available.

CONCLUSION

39.41   This chapter provides only a brief review of the various penalties. In my experience, each situation is different and, sometimes, it is only after a most careful review of the facts against the law that one can find the weakness in HMRC's case.

VAT law is complicated, as are the penalty rules which deal with infringements of it. HMRC officers, under pressure of work, tend to issue assessments plus penalties and wait to see what defence the trader can produce. They do make mistakes, and it is often possible for a VAT specialist to find something wrong with an assessment for tax, and/or the penalty based on it.

Unfortunately, the amount of money at stake for a small trader often does not justify spending the necessary time to do this. I believe that many assessments for tax, and some for penalties, are collected in cases in which the assessment is unsound. Of course, in some of these, the trader does owe some money and, it not being a fair world, there is an element of rough justice in the system!

So, if a business believes that HMRC is wrong, it should give careful consideration to the costs involved before it enters an appeal.

Chapter 40

Taking an appeal to the Tribunal

SIGNPOSTS

- If a taxpayer receives an assessment or a ruling that it does not agree with it has the right to appeal to the Tax Chamber of the Tribunal Service. In the first instance the appeal is to the First-tier Tribunal with the right of appeal to the Upper Tribunal (see **40.1–40.2**).

- Certain procedures have to be followed when making an appeal and it is essential that you prepare well before the hearing. In some circumstances a 'skeleton argument' will need to be prepared along with a list of documents, witness statements and an agreed bundle (see **40.5–40.12**).

- Even if you are successful in the appeal you are unlikely to have your costs paid (see **40.17**).

40.1 This chapter discusses appealing to the Tax Chamber of the Tribunal Services against an assessment for tax and penalties which HMRC can impose for innocent errors, and in a variety of other situations. As explained in the previous chapter, *Assessment and VAT Penalties*, an appeal is to an independent Tax Tribunal, not to HMRC. Taking a case to a Tax Tribunal is a subject in itself, and there is only space here for a few brief comments. Readers will find more detailed coverage in *Tax Investigations Service* (Bloomsbury Professional).

A trader can represent him or herself. Many do, and some win their cases. However, many more make a mess of presenting the case because they have no idea how to do it. Unfortunately, that is also true of many professional accountants and some solicitors when they take cases on behalf of clients. So this chapter is intended to ensure that businesses and advisers do understand the basics of handling an appeal.

The Tribunals Service has undergone a full review, with a new structure being implemented from 1 April 2009 (see **40.2** below for more details).

THE TRIBUNALS SERVICE

40.2 The Ministry of Justice reviewed the operation of the Tribunals Services across the board, and a new Tribunals system came into force on 1 April 2009. In light of the amalgamation of the former Inland Revenue and HM Customs & Excise, it made sense to bring together the appeals procedures so that there is a common system across the taxes.

This structure was put in place by the *Tribunals, Courts and Enforcement Act 2007 (TCEA 2007)*.

TCEA 2007 put in place a two-tier structure for most jurisdictions: a First-tier Tribunal, and an Upper Tribunal.

The independent Tax Chamber considers appeals against decisions made by HMRC in relation to direct and indirect taxation. This replaced four distinct Tribunals:

- the General Commissioners of Income Tax (General Commissioners);

- the Commissioners for the special purposes of the *Income Tax Act* (Special Commissioners);

- the VAT & Duties Tribunal; and

- the Tribunal constituted under *s 706* of the *Income and Corporation Taxes Act 1988*.

Most cases from the four tax appeal Tribunals go to the First-tier Tribunal.

For cases heard in the First-tier Tax Chamber, there is generally an onward right of appeal on a point of law and with permission to the Upper Tribunal. It is also possible for certain cases to be heard by the Upper Tribunal in the first instance.

The Upper Tribunal plays a central role in the Tribunal system, enjoying a position in the judicial hierarchy at least equivalent to that of the High Court in England and Wales. Appeals from the Upper Tribunal are to the Court of Appeal with permission and from there to the Supreme Court (up to 1 October 2009 this was called the House of Lords).

The Upper Tribunal is a superior court of record. Its decisions are to be binding on lower Tribunals and authoritative on the interpretation of the law (subject to onward appeals to the higher appeal courts).

Up to 1 April 2009, if a taxpayer appealed a VAT assessment or ruling and was successful at Tribunal, he was entitled to claim back his costs. Only fair and reasonable, you may think, as why should he be out of pocket when challenging an incorrect assessment by HMRC? Unfortunately, this was not the case in the direct tax world, so, yes, you've guessed it; the changes did away with the provision of costs in VAT Tribunals.

In my experience, small businesses often get inaccurate assessments for relatively small sums (under £10,000) and have appealed them on the understanding that they will get their costs back, if successful. This is no longer the case, and has resulted in many small businesses deciding that it is not cost effective to appeal, and simply paying the assessment. It will, of course, also mean that the advisers of business will not be asked to handle the appeal either, given the additional irrecoverable fees that this would inevitably involve. In light of the ineffectiveness of the current reconsideration process, some businesses might try to defend the assessments themselves, with much reduced chances of success. So, in this brave new world, and in the spirit of fairness and equality for all, only large, well-off businesses would actually have adequate recourse to the legal process!

This has been a far-reaching change that has significantly disadvantaged smaller businesses, and has effectively removed their ability to challenge smaller assessments, as it will not be cost effective.

HUMAN RIGHTS

40.3   The *Human Rights Act 1998 (HRA)* provides various rights to the citizen. Most are not strictly relevant to VAT, but they do include the right to a fair trial.

HRA, art 6(3) gives everyone charged with a *criminal* offence the following minimum rights:

- to be informed promptly, in a language which he understands and in detail, of the nature and cause of the accusation against him;

- to have adequate time and facilities for the preparation of his defence;

- to defend himself in person or through legal assistance of his own choosing or, if he has not sufficient means to pay for legal assistance, to be given it free when the interests of justice so require;

- to examine or have examined witnesses against him, and to obtain the attendance and examination of witnesses on his behalf under the same conditions as witnesses against him;

- to have the free assistance of an interpreter if he cannot understand or speak the language used in court.

On occasions, officers can be either careless or over-zealous in the way they deal with assessments and in their handling of relationships with traders. However, it is questionable whether the *HRA* will affect civil penalties other than the one of up to 100% under *s 60* for conduct involving dishonesty. In *GK Han & D Yau* ([2001] STC 1188) the Court of Appeal confirmed the view of a Tribunal that *s 60* penalties are similar to ones imposed under criminal prosecution, even though *s 60* is part of the civil code in *VATA 1994*. That does not mean that the *HRA* can be quoted in relation to the rest of the civil penalties, although, of course, HMRC have always had a duty to behave fairly and reasonably. This was then confirmed in *Ferrazzini v Italy* (Application No 44759/98) ([2001] STC 1314). The European Court of Human Rights (Note: *not* the ECJ) held (six out of 18 judges dissenting) that tax disputes fell outside the scope of civil rights and obligations, regardless of the financial cost to the taxpayer. *Article 6(1)* was therefore not applicable.

In *N Ali & S Begum (t/a Shapla Tandoori Restaurant) and five other appellants* (LON/95/355 No 17681), the Tribunal sided with the minority in *Ferrazzini* and held that the other civil penalties, such as that for misdirection in *s 63*, late registration in *s 67* and the default surcharge in *s 59*, together with the power in *Sch 11, para 4(2)* to demand security, were civil in nature, and within the scope of *HRA, Art 6(1)*. However, it then held that they were not criminal in nature but were regulatory, being designed to penalise a failure to meet the standard of compliance demanded by the VAT system. Reversing this burden of proof would not assist a trader when the misdirection penalty, for example, was an arithmetical exercise.

In my view, human rights as an appeal point may well be valuable in individual cases, but usually as part of a good defence which shows that HMRC have got it wrong in other ways too. It will be rare to win just because HMRC have not followed the procedures as fairly as they might have, given that we already have rules concerning time limits, etc and a requirement that HMRC assess to 'best judgment'. Indeed, in *Nene Packaging Ltd: KM Curtis Watkins: P Collins: A Ponte Sousa and MA Ponte Sousa: A M Rahman: D R M Spankie and B Spankie* (LON/00/355 No 17365), the *Tribunals Rules (SI 1986/590)*, which require from HMRC a statement of case and list of documents and give the trader the right to ask for additional material held by them, were said to be adequate protection. Issues, such as pre-trial disclosure, should be viewed in the light of the overall fairness of the proceedings.

Of course, the *HRA1998* emphasises the need for care by HMRC in ensuring that the trader has a fair hearing at every stage of their investigations, never mind before the Tribunals. For example, an interpreter may be needed if the trader does not speak good English.

Ajay Chandubhai Kumar Patel (LON/99/1144 No 17248) illustrates what seems likely to be the main problem in many cases. The decision contains the following points based on the right to a fair trial:

- Any admissions by the appellant must have been properly obtained.

- An appellant is presumed innocent until proved guilty. One cannot imply under *s 60(7)* any burden of proof on an appellant in respect of the amount of the sum evaded.

- An appellant is entitled to be informed in detail of the allegations against him. HMRC's statement of case must be in proper detail, and their list of documents complete. Presumably, a tribunal would allow subsequent additions if notified to the appellant in good time.

- An appellant is entitled to examine HMRC's witnesses. Matters which ought to be established by a witness should not be introduced in another way—such as by a copy of a visit report.

- An appellant has a right to silence and, once criminal proceedings, including (per *Han & Yau*) civil penalties for conduct involving dishonesty, are contemplated, the trader must be cautioned before further questions are put, even by letter. The Tribunal noted the view expressed in JL Murrell (LON/99/121 No 16878) that the inducement to speak in Notice 730, in order to obtain a reduction in the penalty for co-operation, was the opposite of telling the trader of his right of silence.

  However, in *Wong Li Ma and Pauline Ma t/a Paradise Garden* (MAN/02/0113 No 19150), the Tribunal held that, if no caution had been given, it had to decide whether or not to admit the evidence after considering whether the failure to administer a caution was due to bad faith, and whether an admission of the evidence would be unfair.

  Moreover, in contrast to the EU Directives, the *Convention on Human Rights* was not legislation which must be implemented. *Section 3* of *HRA* required interpretation of domestic legislation as far as possible in a way compatible with the *Convention* rights. That did not give the power to disregard the domestic provision. Moreover, *Art 6* of the *Convention* said nothing about the admissibility of evidence beyond the provision that a person charged with an offence is entitled to a fair hearing. That did not mean one artificially weighted in his favour; rather one objectively fair. If evidence had been unfairly obtained, it might be appropriate not to admit it at all or to do so only with safeguards. However, the mere failure to administer a caution could not of itself amount to unfairness.

- The requirement in *r 7(1)(b)* of the *Tribunals Rules (SI 1986/590)*, as amended, to serve a defence setting out the matters or facts on which an appellant relies, can only be reconciled with the right to silence if the appellant need not state any matters or facts which do not advance his case.

The Tribunal found that Customs had failed to adhere to several of these points. For example, their bundle of documents included a visit report typed and not signed, and without the officer's original notes. The officer had left the Department and was not called as a witness. This conflicted with the right to the appellant to examine the witness. The Tribunal disregarded the visit report, except in so far as facts in it were admitted by the appellant. A witness statement taken from an accountant, who had prepared the appellant's VAT returns during most of the period covered by the assessment, was brief and inadequate—and conflicted with the evidence given at the hearing by that accountant.

The interview with the appellant had not included any caution, and Notice 730 had been given to him. A joint typed note, produced by the two officers the next day, was misdescribed as a 'transcript' in HMRC's list of documents. It was, in fact, a reconstruction of an interview of which no proper note was taken, and included considerable material not in the notes and left out material which was in them. The Tribunal disregarded this evidence too.

Despite these flaws in HMRC's case and what the Tribunal called their 'casual approach to inquiries into serious matters', it upheld most of the penalty because Mr Patel could not explain the difference between the sales declared on his VAT returns, and those in the annual accounts. Thus, however clumsily HMRC may handle an investigation, and despite the burden of proof of dishonesty being on HMRC, a trader must still be able to explain seeming discrepancies. If there is an apparent case to answer, it must still be answered before the Tribunal even if earlier interviews etc can be disregarded.

Some people have suggested that advisers should take great care to argue any possible point under the *HRA,* because otherwise they run the risk of being sued for negligence. I suspect that, in practice, it will be found that any significant point would be raised by a good adviser anyway. Moreover, the objective is usually to settle a dispute with a tax authority quickly and at the lowest practicable cost. I question whether that responsibility will be met in the majority of cases by dragging out proceedings in raising technical issues, such as demanding formal interviews with interpreters, etc and thus raising costs, rather than dealing with the matter more informally. Of course, one must be alert to the possibility of HMRC putting pressure on the trader to admit something is wrong just to settle the matter, but that has always been a problem. In those cases, which involve an admission of some under disclosure and the possibility of settling for relatively small sums of money, we suspect that it may even be counter-productive to worry too much about the *HRA*.

Of course, in a case of alleged dishonesty, one should always mention its existence to the client, in case the latter feels aggrieved at some aspect of his or her treatment. However, I think that it is only in the large cases that it will be found to have any real significance.

WHO CAN APPEAL?

40.4

Focus

Normally, it is the supplier who appeals concerning the status of the supply—HMRC usually do not discuss it with customers. However, the latter can appeal once the supplier has received a decision from HMRC—as has been agreed by Tribunals many times over the years.

HMRC may try to get the appeal thrown out on the grounds that their decision was not to the appellant, but keep going!

An extreme example—and unusual situation—was HMRC's attempt to prevent *Canterbury Hockey Club and Canterbury Ladies Hockey Club* (LON/04/823 No 19086) from continuing to argue that the national body England Hockey's subscriptions to its affiliated clubs were exempt. England Hockey had abandoned its appeal. HMRC then tried to get the appeals of the two Canterbury clubs struck out.

The Tribunal held that they were entitled to go on arguing the matter because they had not been involved with the appeal by England Hockey. They duly did—and won as explained in **11.111**.

BASIC PROCEDURE

40.5   An appeal should be entered to the Tribunal Service within 30 days of the disputed decision. The Tribunal Service will allow late appeals in exceptional circumstances but they are becoming increasingly unwilling to do so, so it is best to make sure that the appeal is entered within the 30-day time limit. If a claim for overpaid VAT is entered on the back of a disputed decision while that case is still proceeding through the courts and HMRC reject the provisional claim, the taxpayer should enter an appeal within 30 days of the decision. If the taxpayer relies on HMRC paying out on the claim if the lead case is eventually won in the higher courts, they will be sadly disillusioned unless they have entered an appeal (*Graham (t/a Xs & Os Amusements) v Revenue and Customs Commissioners* [2014] UKUT 75 (TCC).

When making an appeal the taxpayer is normally required to pay any assessment before the appeal will be heard; however, they can avoid paying the assessment by claiming 'hardship'. If the taxpayer can show HMRC, or on appeal the Tribunal, that the payment of the assessment would cause them financial hardship they will be allowed to make the appeal without payment of the assessment.

The Tribunal Service will acknowledge an appeal and forward a copy to HMRC, who then have 30 days within which to submit a *Statement of Case* in response, which justifies the original assessment or decision. HMRC hardly ever meet that time limit because of their workload. Usually, they will submit several requests for an extension of time.

If the case is urgent, contact the Solicitor's Office a few weeks after receiving the acknowledgment from the Tribunal, and ask to speak to whoever is handling the appeal. This may be, at that stage, merely one of the administrative staff, rather than a solicitor. By explaining the need for urgency, it may be able to get the matter looked at by a lawyer and dealt with as a priority. Even then, it is unlikely that a hearing can take place within six months; 12 months is more typical, and a written decision by the Tribunal can then take anything from two weeks upwards, frequently two months and sometimes longer.

When HMRC submit their *Statement of Case*, the Tribunal Service will forward it to the appellant or their representative. A little later, they will ask for dates over the next few months during which the appellant is not available, which of various possible locations would be preferable for the hearing, how many days it will take, and how many witnesses will be called.

Careful consideration of the likely duration of the hearing is important. Whilst it is possible to get through a case in a single day, this becomes less likely if the appellant or HMRC have a witness, and unlikely if there are two or more because of the time taken up in the giving of evidence and cross-examination on it by the other side. If in doubt, discuss the point with the solicitor representing HMRC—whose name may be found at the end of the *Statement of Case*. It is better to ask for two or three days if there is doubt that the matter can be dealt with in a single one. Although this may delay the hearing, it is much better to complete it in one than to find that there is not enough time, and it has to be postponed to a further hearing two or three months later. Not only does that tend to increase costs because of the need to go through the file again; everyone involved forgets the issues, evidence given etc and has to refresh their memories.

PREPARATION, PREPARATION, PREPARATION!

40.6   A case is often won on the basis of evidence carefully prepared. Good preparation requires careful assessment well in advance of:

- facts upon which the case depends;

- evidence of those facts;

- relevant documentation, such as copies of contracts;

- possible witnesses.

One can still occasionally read reports of cases presented by Counsel, where a failure to identify the key facts and/or to bring evidence of those facts has undermined the trader's case.

PREPARE A SKELETON ARGUMENT

40.7   A *skeleton argument* is a set of notes prepared in advance, which is handed in at the start of the hearing. As with the bundle of documents, on which we comment later, they will need at least three copies—for the Tribunal Judge, for HMRC's representative and for the appellant. Check with the Tribunal Centre beforehand whether there will be one or two lay members sitting with the Judge, because they will want copies as well. In the skeleton argument, set out the key facts on which documentary evidence is being presented, cross-referring them to the documents in the bundle. Then set out the law which is being relied upon. Doing this in advance will help to organise the presentation of the case, and may speed things up by reducing the number of notes which the Tribunal members have to take.

Do not write the presentation word for word. That will tend to make it more difficult to add extra points, which are often thought of at the last minute. Moreover, it is boring for the Tribunal members to have to listen to someone reading a prepared text which is already in front of them.

LIST OF DOCUMENTS

40.8   In theory, a list of documents must be provided to the other side within 30 days of the Tribunal Centre acknowledging the appeal. Both sides often ignore this time limit, the problem being to identify all the documentation in question until much nearer the hearing. However, the appellant must make sure that they supply copies of documentary evidence, such as contracts, brochures and the like, to HMRC before the hearing. Otherwise they are entitled to ask for an adjournment, with the appellant paying the costs of the extra time.

It is advisable to study HMRC's list and obtain copies of anything which is missing. If HMRC's case depends upon the observations of the business, discussions during visits or whatever, obtain copies of all the calculations and notes made by the officers.

HMRC MIGHT DEMAND TO SEE ADVICE RECEIVED BY THE APPELLANT

40.9   In *Burghill Valley Golf Club (a Partnership), Burghill Valley Members Club Ltd & Burghill Visitors Club Ltd* (LON/03/1054 No 18876), HMRC were held to be entitled to see some confidential material. It included the advice letter from a consultant, the engagement letter, fee notes, and minutes of meetings—which indicated the basis of the reorganisation of the business—attempting to use the exemption for subscriptions from playing members. HMRC were also entitled to a list of documents for which legal professional privilege was sought.

Similarly, in *MM02 plc* (LON/04/2396 No 19514) the Tribunal accepted HMRC's application for the disclosure of external advice from tax and other advisers, plus internal documentation concerning the scheme to form O2 Communications supplying mobile telecommunications services from Ireland.

Admittedly, these were both cases of attempted VAT avoidance, but they show that sensitive material may have to be disclosed!

EVIDENCE

40.10   Letters from friends, suppliers, customers or competitors supporting the case are usually useless as evidence, because HMRC cannot cross-examine the writers. The Tribunal is unlikely to take any notice of them whatsoever unless the appellant has shown them to HMRC beforehand and has persuaded them to accept the statements they make without the writers attending to give evidence.

Documents, such as contracts or customer brochures, will usually be accepted by HMRC without formal proof.

WITNESS STATEMENTS

40.11   A formal witness statement can be lodged with the Tribunal, but HMRC usually object to it because they wish to cross-examine the witness. However, a written statement of evidence by a witness—in legal jargon, a *proof of evidence*—is well worth preparing in advance. Not only does this help to clarify precisely what evidence the witness can give; it can be produced at the hearing when witnesses are called.

Often, the Tribunal Judge agrees to read the statement, following which, supplementary questions can be asked, and HMRC can cross-examine the witness. This speeds up proceedings because it does not have to extract the evidence by question and answer, and the Tribunal Judge does not have to write everything down.

AGREED BUNDLE

40.12   Often, both sides produce a bundle of documents, many of which duplicate each other. Try to agree a bundle with HMRC before the hearing. Bundles should commence with the assessment or decision in dispute and immediate supporting papers, followed by the correspondence, etc in date order, earliest date first.

All pages of a bundle should be numbered sequentially 1, 2, 3, etc even if, within the bundle, individual documents already have their own page numbers. This is because, in the middle of a hearing, it wastes time if everybody cannot find their way quickly to the page to which is being referred to the Tribunal.

DELAY BY HMRC COULD WIN THE CASE FOR THE APPELLANT!

40.13   In just a few cases, failure by HMRC to handle a case promptly has caused an appeal to be upheld. As noted above under *Basic procedure*,

HMRC must submit a *Statement of Case*. In *Neways International (UK) Ltd* (LON/02/351 No 17888; [2003] STC 795), their repeated failure to do that, due to inefficiency in the Solicitor's Office, led to the appeal being upheld for that reason alone.

However, that is unusual. Of course, HMRC normally comply with the rules, any delays being relatively minor. In *Baines & Ernest Ltd* (MAN/03/661 No 18516), the position was reviewed in the light of several previous cases and, in particular, the comments of the High Court in *Neways* that the Tribunal should balance the consequences of the default of the 'innocent' party against those of any sanction against the other party. The possible action ranges from dismissing or upholding the appeal to granting an extension of time on no other terms than that the party in default pays the costs of the other in obtaining that extension. Intermediate possibilities include imposing terms.

In *Baines*, HMRC had been given a verbal 14-day extension of time at a directions hearing but the written confirmation was not sent to them until after the date set. When Baines queried the position on the day after that due date, HMRC faxed the Statement of Case that day. The Tribunal held that the prejudice to HMRC would be great if the appeal was upheld, and that of the delay to Baines was small. It therefore extended the time by the extra day, but it awarded Baines costs of the hearing about this point and said it would impose a penalty on HMRC of £500, subject to any representations they made!

However, in *UK Tradecorp Ltd* (LON/04/1206 No 18879 & 18992), the appeals were upheld because HMRC had not complied with the Tribunal's directions issued at a preliminary hearing. HMRC had not devoted proper resources to the appeal. Such action as awarding costs or interest would not compensate the appellant for its loss of business or its expensive borrowing.

In case 18879, although witness statements were only submitted four days late, that disrupted the timetable in arranging the hearing for the case; moreover, four of the 11 statements failed to include the exhibits to which they referred. Those exhibits had still not been provided. HMRC had also not copied the appellant the items in their list of documents despite repeated requests. Nor had they provided the Tribunal a list of dates to avoid for the hearing.

The appellant had had to borrow funds meanwhile, part of a repayment claim having been rejected by HMRC. It had clearly been prejudiced by the appeal being delayed by probably two months. Of course, for a delay to cause such serious damage to a trader is unusual.

In case 18992, HMRC had failed to provide a full list of documents and three witness statements were late—only two weeks before the hearing. Shortage of resources was no excuse—as HMRC regularly point out to traders!

Thus, if HMRC fail to do something they should, including providing copies of documents or details of evidence, it may be worth applying to the Tribunal for a direction that they do so, and for a further direction if they still do not comply.

PROCEDURE AT HEARING

40.14   A Tribunal hearing is relatively informal, but evidence is given on oath:

- normally the appellant, must present its case against the assessment or decision, and call witnesses;

- HMRC then reply and call their witnesses;

- the appellant has a right of reply.

In dishonesty cases, HMRC start first because they have to prove the dishonesty.

PRESENTING THE CASE

40.15

Focus

Do not assume the judge understands the case. He or she will have looked at the papers beforehand but, possibly, not until just prior to the hearing. Depending on how much detail is in the notice of appeal, etc he or she may know little of the case. In any event, do not assume the judge understands the nature of the business. Take care to clarify the background of business practices, etc as well as the nature of the law in dispute.

Having explained the nature of the dispute, the appellant sets out the facts either by reference to documents or by calling witnesses. They then demonstrate how the law relates to those facts.

One of the reasons for preparing a statement by the witness beforehand, and asking if the Tribunal will either read it or allow the witness to do so, is that a representative cannot 'lead' the witness. That is to say, the questions must not suggest the answer which is wanted. It can therefore sometimes be quite difficult to extract information from the witness under oath in the witness box, which the witness gave readily when the 'proofs of evidence' was taken beforehand!

REMAIN CALM AND COURTEOUS

40.16   Just occasionally, a trader representing him or herself in the Tribunal gets upset and accuses HMRC of malpractice of one kind or another. It is unusual for officers to misbehave. They get the wrong ideas and demand VAT which is not due, but that is not misbehaviour. If it is felt that an officer has done something wrong, say so quietly, understating rather than overstating the point. If there is a valid complaint, the Tribunal will take due notice without the appellant having to complain vociferously about it!

COSTS

40.17   In most cases, the decision is not given on the day, and it can be many weeks before it is issued.

Under the Tribunal structure introduced on 1 April 2009 (see **40.2** above), costs will only be available in very limited circumstances; in complex cases heard before the First-tier Tribunal, and for cases heard in the Upper Chamber. In the case of costs awarded in the First-tier Tribunal, this has to be agreed beforehand, and if the appellant loses, he will also have to pay HMRC's costs. Costs which can be claimed are primarily the time of a professional adviser, expert witness, or interpreter. A sole trader or partner cannot claim for his own time, although he can for travel and subsistence expenses associated with the appeal, together with those of any witnesses. A limited company may succeed with a claim for the time of an in-house lawyer.

A professional adviser should record their time in detail as the case develops. That means in lodging the appeal, consulting with the client, building up the evidence, asking witnesses about the evidence they will give, and so on. It is not sufficient merely to keep the usual professional time records, which tend to contain very little detail.

If HMRC do not pay the full costs claim the appellant can continue the appeal before the Tribunal on that point alone. In most cases, the threat of a further costs hearing will make HMRC pay up. In major cases, the costs may be referred to a Costs Judge of the High Court, in which case a costs draughtsman will probably have to be used. However, it is always worth asking HMRC for an offer in the hope of settling the matter informally.

In the case of *Reddrock Ltd v HMRC* [2014] UKUT 61 (TCC), they appealed against a decision of the FTT. In its decision, the FTT rejected Reddrock's appeal against HMRC for disallowing claims for input VAT in a total amount of about £273,000 and awarded costs to HMRC.

The onus of establishing its entitlement to recover input tax in respect of these supplies rested on Reddrock. It was therefore necessary for Reddrock to establish, on the balance of probabilities, that the relevant supplies had in fact been made.

While, in general, orders for costs are not made by the FTT, the law gives the Tribunal discretion to make an order in respect of costs in appropriate cases.

The ground on which the FTT made an order for costs in favour of HMRC was that Reddrock acted unreasonably in bringing the appeal in circumstances where it knew that the supplies had not in fact taken place. This appeared to be a compelling ground on which to exercise the discretion to order costs. As Reddrock had failed in its appeal on the substantive ground and the Upper Tribunal found that the supplies in fact never occurred, there was no basis for interfering with the exercise by the FTT of its discretion to make an order for costs against Reddrock.

The above is only a brief collection of points about making an appeal. If a business has a good case, it is well worth having a go at representing itself if it cannot afford professional fees. However, it might well pay to take advice beforehand on how to present it from someone experienced in the Tribunals.

Index

Index